Classics in Risk Management
Volume I

Wherever possible, the articles in these volumes have been reproduced as originally published using facsimile reproduction, inclusive of footnotes and pagination to facilitate ease of reference.

For a list of all Edward Elgar published titles visit our site on the World Wide Web at
www.e-elgar.com

Classics in Risk Management Volume I

Edited by

W. Kip Viscusi

John F. Cogan Jr. Professor of Law and Economics
Harvard University, USA

and

Ted Gayer

Assistant Professor of Public Policy
Georgetown University, USA

An Elgar Reference Collection
Cheltenham, UK • Northampton, MA, USA

Published by
Edward Elgar Publishing Limited
Glensanda House
Montpellier Parade
Cheltenham
Glos GL50 1UA
UK

Edward Elgar Publishing, Inc.
136 West Street
Suite 202
Northampton
Massachusetts 01060
USA

A catalogue record for this book is available from the British Library

Library of Congress Cataloguing in Publication Data

Classics in risk management / edited by W. Kip Viscusi and Ted Gayer.
        p. cm. – (Elgar mini series) (An Elgar reference collection)
    Includes index.
    1. Risk management. I. Viscusi, W. Kip. II. Gayer, Ted, 1970- III. Series. IV. Series:
An Elgar reference collection

    HD61.C594 2004
    368—dc22

                                                                    2004046043

Printed and bound by MPG Books Ltd, Bodmin, Cornwall

ISBN   1 84064 032 4 (2 volume set)

Contents

Acknowledgements

The editors and publishers wish to thank the authors and the following publishers who have kindly given permission for the use of copyright material.

American Economic Association for articles: W. Kip Viscusi (1993), 'The Value of Risks to Life and Health', *Journal of Economic Literature*, **XXXI** (4), December, 1912–46; Joni Hersch (1998), 'Compensating Differentials for Gender-Specific Job Injury Risks', *American Economic Review*, **88** (3), June, 598–607.

Blackwell Publishing Ltd for articles: M.W. Jones-Lee, M. Hammerton and P.R. Philips (1985), 'The Value of Safety: Results of a National Sample Survey', *Economic Journal*, **95**, March, 49–72; Gary H. McClelland, William D. Schulze and Brian Hurd (1990), 'The Effect of Risk Beliefs on Property Values: A Case Study of a Hazardous Waste Site', *Risk Analysis*, **10** (4), December, 485–97.

Brookings Institution for excerpt: T.C. Schelling (1968), 'The Life You Save May Be Your Own', in Samuel B. Chase, Jr. (ed.), *Problems in Public Expenditure Analysis*, 127–62.

Elsevier for articles: Paul R. Portney (1981), 'Housing Prices, Health Effects, and Valuing Reductions in Risk of Death', *Journal of Environmental Economics and Management*, **8**, 72–8; Pauline M. Ippolito and Richard A. Ippolito (1984), 'Measuring the Value of Life Saving from Consumer Reactions to New Information', *Journal of Public Economics*, **25**, 53–81; W. Kip Viscusi and Michael J. Moore (1989), 'Rates of Time Preference and Valuations of the Duration of Life', *Journal of Public Economics*, **38** (3), April, 297–317.

Industrial and Labor Relations Review for article: Robert S. Smith (1979), 'Compensating Wage Differentials and Public Policy: A Review', *Industrial and Labor Relations Review*, **32** (3), April, 339–52.

Kluwer Academic/Plenum Publishers for articles: Sherwin Rosen (1988), 'The Value of Changes in Life Expectancy', *Journal of Risk and Uncertainty*, **1** (3), September, 285–304; Maureen L. Cropper and Paul R. Portney (1990), 'Discounting and the Evaluation of Lifesaving Programs', *Journal of Risk and Uncertainty*, **3** (4), December, 369–79; John K. Horowitz and Richard T. Carson (1990), 'Discounting Statistical Lives', *Journal of Risk and Uncertainty*, **3** (4), December, 403–13; Thomas J. Kniesner and John D. Leeth (1991), 'Compensating Wage Differentials for Fatal Injury Risk in Australia, Japan, and the United States', *Journal of Risk and Uncertainty*, **4** (1), January, 75–90; M.W. Jones-Lee (1991), 'Altruism and the Value of Other People's Safety', *Journal of Risk and Uncertainty*, **4** (2), April, 213–19; Magnus Johannesson, Per-Olov Johansson and Richard M. O'Conor (1996), 'The Value of Private Safety Versus the Value of

Public Safety', *Journal of Risk and Uncertainty*, **13** (3), November, 263–75; Karen E. Jenni and George Loewenstein (1997), 'Explaining the "Identifiable Victim Effect"', *Journal of Risk and Uncertainty*, **14** (3), May/June, 235–57.

MIT Press and the President and Fellows of Harvard College for articles: W. Kip Viscusi (1978), 'Wealth Effects and Earnings Premiums for Job Hazards', *Review of Economics and Statistics*, **60** (3), 408–16; V. Kerry Smith and William H. Desvousges (1986), 'The Value of Avoiding a *LULU*: Hazardous Waste Disposal Sites', *Review of Economics and Statistics*, **68** (2), 293–9; W. Kip Viscusi and Michael J. Moore (1987), 'Workers' Compensation: Wage Effects, Benefit Inadequacies, and the Value of Health Losses', *Review of Economics and Statistics*, **69** (2), 249–61; Scott E. Atkinson and Robert Halvorsen (1990), 'The Valuation of Risks to Life: Evidence from the Market for Automobiles', *Review of Economics and Statistics*, **72** (1), 133–6.

MIT Press and the President and Fellows of Harvard College and the Massachusetts Institute of Technology for articles: Ted Gayer, James T. Hamilton and W. Kip Viscusi (2000), 'Private Values of Risk Tradeoffs at Superfund Sites: Housing Market Evidence on Learning about Risk', *Review of Economics and Statistics*, **82** (3), August, 439–51; W. Kip Viscusi and Joni Hersch (2001), 'Cigarette Smokers as Job Risk Takers', *Review of Economics and Statistics*, **83** (2), May, 269–80.

National Bureau of Economic Research, Inc. for excerpt: Richard Thaler and Sherwin Rosen (1976), 'The Value of Saving a Life: Evidence from the Labor Market', in Nestor E. Terleckyj (ed.), *Household Production and Consumption*, 265–98.

Oxford University Press for article: Michael J. Moore and W. Kip Viscusi (1988), 'The Quantity-Adjusted Value of Life', *Economic Inquiry*, **XXVI**, July, 369–88.

University of Chicago and *Journal of Law and Economics* for article: Mark K. Dreyfus and W. Kip Viscusi (1995), 'Rates of Time Preference and Consumer Valuations of Automobile Safety and Fuel Efficiency', *Journal of Law and Economics*, **XXXVIII** (1), April, 79–105.

University of Chicago Press for articles: E.J. Mishan (1971), 'Evaluation of Life and Limb: A Theoretical Approach', *Journal of Political Economy*, **79** (4), 687–705; Glenn Blomquist (1979), 'Value of Life Saving: Implications of Consumption Activity', *Journal of Political Economy*, **87** (3), 540–58; David S. Brookshire, Mark A. Thayer, John Tschirhart and William D. Schulze (1985), 'A Test of the Expected Utility Model: Evidence from Earthquake Risks', *Journal of Political Economy*, **93** (2), April, 369–89.

Richard J. Zeckhauser for his own article: (1975), 'Procedures for Valuing Lives', *Public Policy*, **23** (4), Fall, 419–64.

In addition the publishers wish to thank the Marshall Library of Economics, Cambridge University, the Library of the University of Warwick and the Library of Indiana University at Bloomington, USA for their assistance in obtaining these articles.

Introduction

W. Kip Viscusi and Ted Gayer

The management of health and safety risks became a salient policy concern in the 1970s. Since that time the importance of health, safety, and environmental regulations has become so great that they comprise the largest share of all regulatory costs in the United States as well as in many other countries. These regulatory ventures raised new questions for economists as well. If the government is going to intervene, when should it do so and to what extent? Determining the level of stringency has proven to be more problematic than the framers of regulatory policy envisioned in that they failed to recognize that achieving zero risk was not a feasible goal.

The considerable economic literature that has emerged over the era of societal risk management has been stimulated in part by these policy initiatives. Economics in turn has also provided valuable guidance for enhancing the design and performance of regulatory policy.

This set of collected papers brings together many of the most influential contributions that have shaped the subsequent economic literature and continue to provide guidance for policy management. Among the key concerns is how the benefits of risk reduction policies should be valued. Given that a zero-risk goal is not feasible, the regulatory process requires that we attach a value to the reduced risks to life and health in order to properly address the tradeoffs inherent in risk reduction decision making. However, the benefit value may also depend – among other things – on the extent of life at risk, raising sensitive issues pertaining to the role of age adjustments. Examination of such benefit assessment issues is the focus of Volume I.

In Volume II we turn to a wide range of issues linked to regulatory performance. Whether risk regulations on balance are in fact health enhancing can be assessed using the tools of risk-risk analysis and by undertaking studies of regulatory performance. The inability of command and control regulations to be effective in some contexts has led to the adoption of warnings policies as a regulatory tool. Informational regulations and the public's response to situations of risk ambiguity will continue to be critical regulatory concerns as they are closely linked to policy design issues with respect to newly emerging risks. We discuss these issues and how they are addressed within this collection in the sections that follow.

Volume I, Part I

Efficient regulation of health risks is achieved when the net benefits of the risk reduction are maximized. Thus, determining whether a regulation is efficient requires reliable estimates of the costs and benefits of the proposed regulation. Indeed, even policy processes that do not take efficiency as their objective often require that there be an assessment of the benefits and costs of the different policy options. Estimating regulatory costs is straightforward methodologically, though difficulties sometimes arise in projecting future compliance costs. Estimating benefits is generally believed to be a more difficult two-step process. The first step is to estimate the health effects that would result from the regulation. The second and perhaps more difficult step is to convert the estimated health benefits into dollar values so that they can be compared to the regulatory costs. For example, after estimating the human health effects of different arsenic levels in drinking water by using animal bioassay analysis, one must then calculate the dollar value of these risk reductions to see if the regulatory benefits are commensurate with the costs. Only then can one determine the efficient reduction of arsenic in drinking water.

The value of the benefit for any policy is society's willingness to pay for these benefits. In the case of risk management efforts this benefit is the value society attaches to the reduced probability of some adverse health outcomes. As a consequence, what is of interest is the value of reduced risks or the statistical lives that will be saved, where this value ideally should be in monetary terms to be commensurate with cost amounts.

Converting risk reductions into monetary values is often a controversial undertaking. However, even if policymakers and regulators were to avoid confronting this task explicitly, any regulation that does not make an unbounded commitment to safety implicitly places a finite value on the risk reduction. Explicitly monetizing the value of risk reduction allows for a reasoned and transparent approach to evaluating and setting risk regulations.

Historically the dominant approach to valuing fatalities for regulations was based on the procedure used to compensate victims in personal injury cases. In particular, the value of life was related to the present value of a person's earnings. This shortsighted approach may have a reasonable foundation from an insurance standpoint, but it is not linked to the risk-money tradeoff that people have for small risks.

The first analysis to put this line of research on sound footing was that by Schelling (Volume I, Chapter 1), who indicated that the value of risk reductions to the individual is the person's willingness to pay for decreases in risk. Subsequent researchers have generalized this individual value of risk reduction to values that should be applied in the policy realm. Unlike most consumer goods, risks are not traded explicitly in markets. Rather, these health risks are tied to implicit trades as health risks are bundled with other attributes of jobs or consumer products. This aspect of health and safety risks complicates the task of estimating individuals' willingness to pay for reductions in risk.

The articles in Part I track the initial debate and development of the welfare economic approach to valuing health risks. Schelling's early paper develops the willingness-to-pay approach in which he describes the difference between the value of preventing a certain individual death versus the value of preventing a statistical death. A statistical death occurs when there is an increase in the risk to a certain population, which leads to the death of one person who is unidentifiable a priori.

Mishan (Volume I, Chapter 2) formalizes the valuation of changes in risk within a welfare-economic framework. He shows that the criterion of achieving a potential Pareto improvement (i.e., a reallocation in which the net gains can be redistributed so that at least one person is made better off with no one being made worse off) would require that a death be valued by reference to the individual's compensating variation (i.e., the minimum sum the person is prepared to accept for the death). Given that policies deal with statistical risks (and not certain, identifiable deaths), he demonstrates how the pertinent value is the sum of each individual's compensating variation for avoiding a risk of fatality, which leads to the concept of the value of a statistical life.

Zeckhauser (Volume I, Chapter 3) questions Mishan's reliance on potential Pareto improvement as the guiding criterion. His concern is that this criterion presumes that compensation from the winners to the losers is feasible, thus resulting in an outcome in which no one is made worse off. While Zeckhauser does not specifically propose an alternative model, he does caution against trying to obtain unequivocal answers to the value of health risks; instead, the aim should be for benchmarks and guidelines to help the policy process.

One approach to ascertaining the willingness to pay values for greater safety is to simply ask people what these amounts are. While well-constructed surveys can serve a useful foundation, obtaining meaningful responses requires that the survey reconstruct a simulated market transaction. An alternative approach that has dominated the literature has been to estimate the implicit value of risk reduction that individuals reveal through their own risk-taking decisions. The studies in Part I provide an overview of this approach that is explored with greater specificity in later sections of this volume.

The dominant statistical approach has been to analyze the equilibrium set of tradeoffs observed in the market, where this relationship is known as the hedonic function. These analyses focus on choices made in labor, housing, or product market transactions. The articles in Part II focus on the hedonic wage model of labor markets, which will be extended to other markets in later sections. The articles in Part III rely on housing or product market transactions in order to estimate the benefits of risk reduction. These articles are discussed in more detail below. Other papers included in Part I explore some of the nuances with respect to establishing values of statistical lives. The article by Michael W. Jones-Lee (Volume I, Chapter 6) explores how altruistic concerns with other people's lives should be taken into account in a proper economic analysis. Similarly, the chapter by Johannesson et al. (Volume I, Chapter 8) examines the discrepancy between the private value of safety to the individual versus the value more generally to the public. In each case, the focus is on statistical lives. Why identifiable and statistical lives differ in terms of their valuation is the focus of the paper by Jenni and Lowenstein (Volume I, Chapter 9).

Estimates of the risk-money tradeoff from market decisions may have additional implications as well. In the paper by Viscusi and Moore (Volume I, Chapter 5), they show that the wage-risk tradeoff from the market can be used to determine whether the level of social insurance being provided through workers' compensation is at the optimal level. For example, very low rates of wage offset in response to higher workers' compensation benefits would imply that workers do not value such compensation amounts to the same extent as their actuarial cost, which in turn would imply that benefit levels are too high. Viscusi (Volume I, Chapter 7) offers an overview of the empirical issues surrounding value-of-life studies and reviews the literature of these empirical works.

Volume I, Part II

The hedonic wage model examines the set of equilibrium outcomes generated by labor supply and labor demand in order to estimate the average rate of tradeoff between wages and job risk, controlling for other aspects of the job. The hedonic wage function is the locus of tangencies formed by the optimizing behavior of both firms and employees. It is consequently incorrect to refer to this relationship as reflecting worker preferences alone. Figure 1 illustrates this

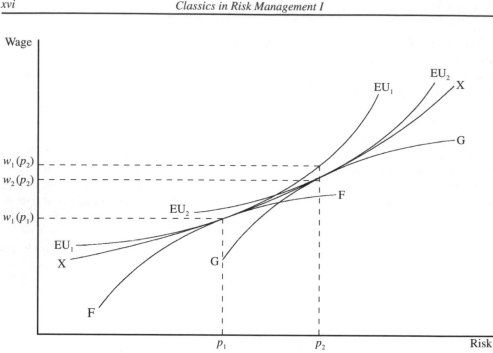

Figure 1   The Hedonic Wage Model

interaction. The curves FF and GG are isoprofit curves, or offer curves, for two different firms. They illustrate the various combinations of job risk and wages that have the same level of profits for the firm. These isoprofit curves rise at an increasing rate as risk levels are reduced. Since reducing risk is costly, wages must be lower at higher levels of safety to keep the firm at the same level of profits. The wage offer curves are consequently increasing functions of risk. Different firms have different production functions, which is why the isoprofit curves differ for the two firms illustrated in the figure. The outer envelope of these offer curves is the market opportunity locus facing workers.

The standard economic model of the supply side is that workers optimize in accordance with a von Neumann-Morgenstern expected utility model with state-dependent utilities. Suppose that utility depends on one's wages (w), and that utility in the unhealthy state $[V(w)]$ occurs with probability p, and utility in the healthy state $[U(w)]$ occurs with probability $1 - p$. If there is a workers' compensation program for the unhealthy state, these payments are typically functions of the wage rate. The functional form for $V(w)$ captures this influence. The curves EU_1 and EU_2 represent indifference curves for two different workers. They are derived by assuming a fixed level of expected utility, Z, and by then tracing out various combinations of p and w that keep utility constant at Z. This set of combinations satisfies the following equation:

$$Z = (1 - p)U(w) + pV(w). \tag{1}$$

The wage-risk tradeoff along this curve is given by the following equation:

$$\frac{\partial w}{\partial p} = \frac{U(w) - V(w)}{(1-p)U'(w) + pV'(w)}. \tag{2}$$

If we assume that individuals prefer being healthy to being unhealthy $[U(w) > V(w)]$ and that the marginal utility of income is positive $[U'(w) > 0, V'(w) > 0]$, then equation (2) is positive, indicating a positive slope of the expected utility functions diagramed in Figure 1. The two different expected utility curves in the figure differ due to different preferences of the two workers.

The hedonic wage function is formed by the tangencies of the firms' offer functions and the workers' constant expected utility loci. The workers each select the available risk-wage bundle that maximizes their expected utility. Firms, on the other hand, select the available risk-wage bundle that maximizes their profits. The firms' offer functions serve as a constraint on the workers' expected utility optimization decision, and the workers' bid functions serve as a constraint on the firms' profit optimization decision. Each hired employee therefore represents the tangency of a bid and an offer function, and the locus of these tangencies forms the hedonic wage function, depicted as XX in the figure. The points (p_1, w_1) and (p_2, w_2) represent two such points along the hedonic wage function.

In an empirical hedonic analysis, the economist only observes points on the hedonic wage function, not the points on the expected utility functions. Since the latter reflect individual preferences, one would ideally want to estimate the structural expected utility functions in order to obtain accurate welfare measures of changes in risk. For example, suppose that the risk to the first worker changes from p_1 to p_2. The wage increase the worker requires to accept this risk increase is $w_1(p_2) - w_1(p_1)$. However, applying the hedonic price function to this change in risk yields an estimate of $w_2(p_2) - w_1(p_1)$, which underestimates the worker's true willingness to accept. By fitting a curve through the wage and risk data, the economist estimates the hedonic wage function, which provides estimates of the local willingness to pay values for *marginal* changes in job risk (which will also equal the willingness to accept values for small changes in risk). These wage-risk tradeoffs serve as the basis for estimates of the value of statistical life, since such estimates are based on marginal changes in risk.

In the special case where all workers had the same preferences, then there would be only one expected utility curve in Figure 1, and the observable points on the hedonic wage function would be the same as the points on the expected utility curve. Such a situation would generate empirical estimates that would provide information on valuations of both marginal and infra-marginal changes in risk. Likewise, if each firm had the same production function, then the hedonic price function would be the same as each firm's offer curve, and one could easily estimate the costs to the firm of marginal and infra-marginal changes in risk. Unfortunately, the typical (yet more realistic) assumption is that workers and firms are heterogeneous. Therefore, in order to estimate *infra-marginal* changes, one would need to estimate the expected utility functions, which is a considerably more difficult task.

While some studies have attempted to estimate the structural expected utility equations, the more frequent approach is to estimate the first-stage hedonic wage function. Most policies aim to reduce health risks by small amounts so that the marginal willingness to pay derived from a hedonic price function serves a useful purpose of estimating welfare effects and deriving the value of a statistical life. The value of a statistical life is given by equation (2) and is the average willingness to pay for a reduction in risk divided by the risk reduction. Therefore, if a policy would reduce risk by 1 in a million, and the affected population is willing to pay on average $6 for this risk reduction, then the value of a statistical life is $6 million. By using actual labor market decisions to estimate the hedonic wage function, one can then use the estimated changes in wages due to a small change in risk in order to estimate the value of a statistical life.

Each of the articles in Part II uses labor market data to estimate the hedonic wage function. The paper by Thaler and Rosen (Volume I, Chapter 10) was one of the early empirical analyses to estimate the compensating differentials for risk using individual data. They use risk data from the 1967 Occupation Study of the Society of Actuaries. These data measure risks associated with very high-risk occupations. To the extent that people more willing to bear risk tend to select into such occupations, the empirical results will underestimate the population-wide wage-risk tradeoff. Their estimates suggest a value of a statistical life of $16 000 to $260 000 (1967 dollars).

Viscusi (Volume I, Chapter 11) uses a more representative sample taken from the 1969–1970 University of Michigan Survey of Working Conditions and couples it with different risk measures in order to estimate compensating differentials for risk. His analysis also uses a self-assessed measure of whether the worker believes the job to be dangerous. The advantage of this measure over an objective measure of job risk is that it reflects the subjective beliefs of the workers, which is the pertinent measure that motivates individual behavior. The analysis also estimates separate specifications in which the variable of interest is the number of disabling injuries per million hours worked in the worker's industry. The results suggest that workers who perceive their job as dangerous earn an annual premium of $375, and they receive an additional $26 each year for a one-point increase in the frequency of disabling injury per million hours worked. That paper also explores the negative relationship between worker wealth and risk levels, which is a relationship that comprises the key component of the risk-risk analyses discussed in Volume II, Part V.

Estimates of the value of statistical life may vary intentionally because of differences in worker wealth and preferences as well as different offer curves from the demand side of the market. If the hedonic function is nonlinear over income, then heterogeneity of income across countries would lead to different estimates of the marginal willingness to pay for risk reduction. Moreover, institutional labor market differences across countries, such as the level of unionization and government involvement in setting wages, could generate structural differences in the hedonic wage functions across these countries. The article by Kniesner and Leeth (Volume I, Chapter 12) examines whether compensating differentials vary across Australia, Japan, and the United States. They find that workers exposed to the average Japanese manufacturing fatality rate receive only 0 per cent to 1.4 per cent higher pay than they would in a perfectly safe Japanese manufacturing industry. However, their small sample limits the precision of the estimates. They find a rather robust compensating differential of 2.5 per cent for Australian workers. They have a considerably larger sample for their U.S. estimates, and they find a 1 per cent compensating differential for risks in the manufacturing industries.

The value of a statistical life is also likely to vary across different sub-populations. Thus, a benefit-cost analysis of a risk-reducing policy aimed at a certain sub-population would need a reliable estimate of the risk-dollar tradeoff for that group, assuming one wanted to assess population-specific benefit values. Disaggregating differences in risk valuations is difficult to accomplish, especially since most risk and wage data aggregate across sub-populations. For example, most wage hedonics studies rely on industry-level risk data; however, if women tend to select safer jobs within industries, then matching industry risk to female workers' wages will lead to misleading estimates of the risk-dollar tradeoff. Hersch (Volume I, Chapter 13) uses gender-specific estimates of injury and illness on an occupational level in order to estimate the compensating differentials for women. She finds that women are in fact exposed to substantial risks of injury and that the value of a statistical injury or illness for women ranges between $20000 and $30000.

The value of a statistical life will also differ across groups that value risk differently. That is, people who are relatively more risk loving will select different risk levels along the hedonic wage function, and they are likely to have differences in their wage-risk tradeoff. If different preferences for risk affect workers' behavior, then the nature of the labor market opportunities may differ as well. Viscusi and Hersch (Volume I, Chapter 14) test this hypothesis using smoking behavior as a proxy for risk preferences. They find that smokers choose jobs in higher risk industries as one might expect, but that they have a sufficiently lower wage-risk tradeoff so their total risk compensation is less than that of non-smokers in safer jobs. The set of results for smokers and non-smokers is inconsistent with the standard model of compensation differentials in which workers select different points off a common offer curve. What these findings suggest is that there are distinct labor market equilibria for smokers and non-smokers, as these two groups are selecting jobs from different opportunity loci. Thus, the standard theory of compensating differentials must be generalized to take into account that different segments of the population may be selecting jobs from quite different labor market offer curves.

Volume I, Part III

The value-of-statistical life estimates obtained from labor market studies are pertinent when considering health-reducing policies in the labor market. For example, a benefit-cost analysis of a job safety policy that reduces the on-the-job risk of asbestos exposure may rely on labor market studies in order to estimate the benefits of the policy. However, it is not always warranted to use labor market estimates of the value of a statistical life to estimate the benefits of non-labor market risk reductions, such as environmental protection or transportation safety. For any individual, the marginal value of a statistical life should be equalized across different domains of choice. However, the preferences of people bearing the risk may differ depending on differences in the exposed populations. The ideal approach is to use market transactions of the affected population in order to estimate the risk-dollar tradeoff. Some researchers also suggest that the character of the fatal events may differ, which in turn will affect risk valuations. Fatal job accidents may not be tantamount to environmentally induced cancers.

For reductions in environmental health risks, studies typically rely on hedonic property models, which are analogous to wage hedonic studies. The logic behind such models is that, all things equal, houses that have higher exposure to environmental risks will have lower equilibrium prices. Figure 2 is similar to Figure 1, except that it shows the market relationship between housing price, h, and household environmental risk exposure, p. In this case, the firms are the suppliers of the houses, whereas the residents are the demanders of the houses. If we

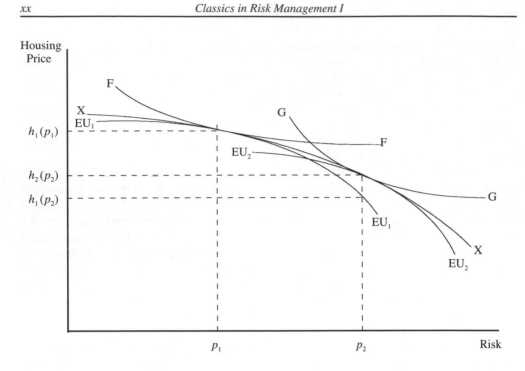

Figure 2   The Hedonic Property Model

assume that the representative consumer purchases one house, then the consumer maximizes
the following expected utility function:

$$\text{Max } Z = (1 - p) U(x, s) + p V(x, s),\tag{3}$$

where p is the health risk, U is utility in the healthy state, V is utility in the unhealthy state, s is
a vector of characteristics of the house, and x is a composite good. The consumer is constrained
by the following equation, in which y is the consumer's income and h is the price of the house:

$$y = x + h(p, s).\tag{4}$$

The price-risk tradeoff along the expected utility curves is given by the following equation:

$$\frac{\partial h}{\partial p} = \frac{V(x, s) - U(x, s)}{(1 - p) U'(x) + p V'(x)}.\tag{5}$$

Given the assumptions that for any given level of income people prefer being healthy $[U(w) >
V(w)]$ and that marginal utility of income is positive $[U'(w) > 0, V'(w) > 0]$, this equation
indicates that the price-risk tradeoff is negative, as illustrated in Figure 2.

   As with the labor market hedonic model, hedonic property model studies estimate the locus
of tangencies formed by the optimizing behavior of sellers and buyers of houses. For an
increase in risk from p_1 to p_2, the appropriate willingness to accept measure is $h_1(p_2) - h_1(p_1)$.

However, the hedonic price function underestimates this value by estimating $h_2(p_2) - h_1(p_1)$. Again, the hedonic property model does provide accurate welfare estimates for *marginal* changes in risk.

One of the primary difficulties of estimating hedonic property models is the problem with obtaining measures of the health risks to each of the pertinent households. In contrast, the Bureau of Labor Statistics, the Society of Actuaries, and the National Institute for Occupational Safety and Health regularly publish estimates of various job risks. No such data sets are readily available for household exposure to environmental risks. As a result, hedonic property models typically rely on distance to the environmental disamenity as a proxy for the health risk. The distance proxy is an imperfect measure for a number of reasons: it does not consider weather patterns and geographical contributors to risk exposure; it does not allow for a straightforward aggregation of risk from multiple sources; it conflates health risk with other disamenities associated with the environmental problem, such as aesthetic problems; and it does not consider variations in exposure pathways that are only weakly correlated with distance. What's more, an estimation of the price-distance relationship does not lend itself to estimates of the value of a statistical life. It therefore is more difficult to use such studies in a benefit-cost analysis of a proposed reduction of environmental risk.

Nonetheless, if the objective is to estimate the benefits of removing a neighborhood disamenity, such as a hazardous waste site, the use of the distance proxy can be very useful. Smith and Desvousges (Volume I, Chapter 20) estimate a partial equilibrium model of demand for distance from a landfill with hazardous wastes. Since they use a survey instrument, they are able to estimate the structural willingness to pay function, rather than the approximation of the hedonic price function. They find that the average household would gain a consumer surplus between $330 and $495 (1984 dollars) annually for each additional mile their house is from the landfill. McClelland, Schulze and Hurd (Volume I, Chapter 22) also survey residents near a landfill; however, they solicit opinions on the subjective neighborhood risk and residents' perceptions of such things as the odor of the site. They find that subjective risk differs from the expert assessments, and that the housing market decreased in value by about $40.2 million (1984 dollars) from the landfill.

Portney (Volume I, Chapter 16) devised a creative way of estimating the hedonic property function with respect to air pollution risk by coupling together estimates from previous studies. He starts by assuming a simple model in which housing price, h, is a function of (among other things) the risk of death from air pollution (R), which in turn is a function of air quality, Q. That is, $h = h[R(Q)]$. Differentiating and rearranging terms leads to the following hedonic price function: $\partial h/\partial R = (\partial h/\partial Q)/(\partial R/\partial Q)$. In other words, the price gradient with respect to risk is equal to the effect of air quality on price divided by the effect of air quality on health risk. He obtains estimates of each of these terms on the right-hand side of the equation from different studies and combines them to find that the implied value of a statistical life for people under 45 is between $377 000 and $567 000 (1978 dollars).

Gayer, Hamilton and Viscusi (Volume I, Chapter 24) were the first to incorporate explicit measures of household environmental risk within the hedonic property model. They examine the housing market in greater Grand Rapids, Michigan – a housing market that contains a number of hazardous waste sites. By calculating the excess cancer risk to each household and aggregating risks across hazardous waste sites, they estimate a hedonic property model that yields estimates of the price-risk tradeoff. They find that after being informed of the risks from the hazardous waste sites, the implicit value placed on avoiding a statistical cancer case was approximately $4 million. This finding is consistent with estimates of the value of a statistical life derived from labor market studies.

The study by Brookshire et al. (Volume I, Chapter 18) also analyzes a hedonic property model, although they focus on the price effects due to risks from earthquakes. The independent variable of interest in their hedonic model is whether the house is located in a Special Studies Zone (SSZ), which is an area designated by the state as having elevated relative earthquake risk determined by potentially and recently active earthquake fault traces. They find that housing prices increase by $4650 (1978 dollars) in Los Angeles County if a house is located outside of the SSZ, and housing prices increase by $2490 in the Bay Area if a house is located outside of the SSZ. They use these estimates to make a strong case that residents engage in self-insuring behavior that is consistent with the expected utility model.

The other papers presented in Part III of Volume I estimate hedonic models for a variety of product markets. The underlying model behind these studies is similar to the labor and housing hedonic models. Blomquist (Volume I, Chapter 15), Atkinson and Halvorsen (Volume I, Chapter 21), and Dreyfus and Viscusi (Volume I, Chapter 23) use measures linked to motor-vehicle safety decisions in order to estimate the value of a statistical life. They find estimated values consistent with those found in labor market studies. Ippolito and Ippolito (Volume I, Chapter 17) use changes in consumption of cigarettes over time as the risk information changes in order to estimate the price-risk tradeoff. They estimate a value of a statistical life of $300 000 to $600 000 (1980 dollars). This comparatively low value is consistent with smokers being more willing to bear risk.

All the articles we have considered thus far use market data in order to estimate the risk-dollar tradeoff. Another way to estimate these tradeoffs is by using a survey in which the respondents are asked their values for different changes in risk. The survey approach has the advantage of obtaining estimates for the structural willingness to pay for non-marginal changes in risk, as illustrated in Figure 1. However, the main shortcoming of surveys is that, unlike the market approach, they rely on hypothetical questions, which are subject to strategizing and biases. Nonetheless, we include in Volume I the article by Jones-Lee, Hammerton and Philips (Volume I, Chapter 19), which is an early survey approach to estimate the value of a statistical life. Interestingly, policy analyses in the United Kingdom have relied primarily on values of statistical life from surveys rather than market studies because the market estimates for the UK have often been quite high and unstable.

Volume I, Part IV

Individuals who are at risk differ in terms of the length of life that is being exposed to risk. There are also important lifecycle effects that may affect people's attitudes toward risk. Estimation of a single value of life for the population assumes that an elderly person values a risk reduction the same as a young person, even though the latter is likely to forego more life years should the risk materialize. The articles in Part IV seek to address this concern by computing the tradeoff between dollars and the discounted lost life years due to the health risk. That is, the appropriate independent variable in the hedonic model is the expected years of life lost, and this value must be discounted to reflect the greater utility placed on life lived now relative to life years later. The easiest way to account for years of life lost is to interact the risk variable with the age of the individual. Thaler and Rosen (Volume I, Chapter 10) and others have used this approach and found that the price-risk gradient decreases with age. However, this formulation doesn't account for the role of discounting.

The appropriate measure for the discounted loss of life expectancy should take the following form:

$$p(1 - e^{-rT})/r, \tag{6}$$

where p is the fatality risk, r is the rate of discount, and T is the remaining period of life. Moore and Viscusi (Volume I, Chapter 25) include this expected loss in life expectancy in the hedonic equation instead of the job risk variable and find an estimated rate of time preference of 10–12 per cent with respect to expected life years. They find an estimate of the implicit value per life year that ranges between \$171 000 and \$195 000 (1986 dollars).

Viscusi and Moore (Volume I, Chapter 27) develop a model of lifetime job choice and derive a functional form for the worker's decision to engage in potentially hazardous work. They use a Markov decision model of lifetime choice of job risks in order to estimate the discount rate people place on future life years and find that workers discount future life years by 11 per cent.

Part IV also includes other studies of the role of discounting with respect to years of life. These estimates often vary across studies, but they tend to be in a much more reasonable range than similar estimates of implicit rates of time preference, such as those that have been estimated for differences in energy efficiency of appliances. Using such differences in the quantity adjusted value of a statistical life for policy purposes remains much more controversial than the use of average values of statistical life. Moreover, the various studies included in Part IV address these discounting issues for adults, but do not examine the role of discounting for people at the tails of the population, such as young children and the elderly. These groups are often those most vulnerable to environmental risks.

Volume II, Part I

The articles in Volume I establish how economists would value risk reductions from regulatory policies. Using these values as a guide, one can set the stringency of regulations in a way that balances the competing effects. By comparing the benefits to the costs of the regulations, one can arrive at the efficient outcome in which net benefits are maximized.

By contrast, the articles in Volume II start out by assuming an imperfect world in which efficient regulation is not attainable. There are many impediments to efficient regulation; most notably, many environmental and health regulations in the United States are based on legislation that seemingly forbids the use of benefit-cost analysis in establishing standards. For example, the Clean Air Act states that ambient standards for common air pollutants cannot be set in a manner that considers compliance costs and should be set at levels that provide an 'adequate margin of safety'. Standards for hazardous air pollutants should be set at levels that provide an 'ample margin of safety'. The Federal Water Pollution Control Act of 1972 established that all of the nation's water bodies should be 'fishable and swimmable'. The Occupational Safety and Health Act (OSHA) of 1970 set a goal 'to assure so far as possible every man and woman in the Nation safe and healthful working conditions'. At face value, the legislative terminology gives very little leeway for agencies to use benefit-cost analysis in promulgating its standards. Indeed, the legislation also makes no mention of cost considerations.

Given the stringent nature of the legislative goals, the question of whether benefit-cost analysis is allowed has frequently been the object of judicial challenges. For example, the Supreme Court ruled in 1981 that the legislative mandate for OSHA is to achieve a regulatory goal that is 'capable of being done', rather than one that passes a benefit-cost test. In its 1999 ruling on the setting of national ambient air quality standards (NAAQS), the D.C. Court of Appeals ruled that the Environmental Protection Agency (EPA) 'is not permitted to consider the cost of implementing standards', thus forbidding the use of benefit-cost analysis.

In contrast to the legislation and judicial review that frequently precludes benefit-cost analysis, all presidential administrations since Ronald Reagan have required an analysis of regulatory costs within the decision-making process. President Reagan's Executive Order 12291, issued in 1981, required that agencies explicitly consider the costs involved in a 'major rule' (i.e., one with an annual effect on the economy of $100 million or more). The order stated, 'Regulatory action shall not be undertaken unless the potential benefits to society for the regulation outweigh the potential costs to society.' To oversee this process, the order transferred regulatory oversight to the U.S. Office of Management and Budget's Office of Information and Regulatory Affairs (OIRA). President Clinton's Executive Order 12866, issued in 1993, stated, 'Each agency shall ... propose or adopt a regulation only upon a reasoned determination that the benefits of the intended regulation justify its costs.' Thus, the current regulatory framework is inconsistent in that the executive branch requires the use of benefit-cost analyses in the promulgation of regulations, yet the legislation frequently prohibits it.

Even when legislation does not forbid the use of benefit-cost analysis, its use is sometimes restricted due to the distrust many regulatory officials have in the process. Also, while benefit-cost analysis leads to efficient regulation, it does not in itself address the equity concerns of different regulations. Thus, where compensation from the 'winners' to the 'losers' of a given regulation is impossible, the efficiency criterion may be a lesser concern in the regulatory framework, and the need for monetizing the health benefits is lessened.

Given that the regulatory policy cannot be subjected to a requirement that benefits exceed costs, is there some weaker test that might be applied to eliminate the most inefficient regulations? Surely regulations for risk and the environment should on balance be safety-enhancing for them to be considered warranted. Assessing these net risk effects has come to be known as risk-risk analysis.

Volume II, Part I, features this type of analysis. Whereas the efficiency criterion establishes the goal of maximizing net benefits, risk-risk analysis uses the less restrictive criterion that a health regulation should only be promulgated if it reduces the overall risks to society.

There are many ways in which a risk regulation could lead to a net increase in risk to society, and there are different levels of complexity involved in risk-risk analyses. A rudimentary risk-risk analysis would compare the risk reductions that would result from the regulation to the competing risk increases that result from the regulation. For example, a regulatory decision to ban the sale of the artificial sweetener saccharin might reduce cancer risk; however, if people then substitute sugar in place of saccharin, the resultant increases in obesity would pose an increase in health risk. The risk-risk regulatory criterion holds that the ban should only take place if the health improvements from reducing the cancer risk are greater than the diminishment in health due to the increased incidence of obesity. Another example of multiple, competing risks resulting from a regulation would be the increase in occupational risks resulting from the transportation and installation of control technologies to reduce risks from emissions. In the risk-risk framework, any regulatory decision on whether to institute these control technologies would need to consider these competing risk increases.

A slightly more complex risk-risk analysis considers the offsetting behavior that would result from a proposed regulation. Some researchers refer to these consequences as moral hazard effects. The classic example of such compensatory behavior is presented in Peltzman's (Volume II, Chapter 14) article on automobile safety. He found that the increased safety provided to drivers by vehicle regulations leads them to drive more recklessly, largely offsetting the risk reductions of the regulation and posing a net increase in risk to pedestrians. Thus, a risk-risk analysis of vehicle regulations would need to examine whether the net effect of the regulations is an increase or decrease in risk. These behavioral responses also influence the overall effect of the regulation on safety, which is the subject of Volume II, Part IV.

The most thorough and complex type of risk-risk analysis considers the health effects that result from the opportunity costs of a regulation. The promulgation of each regulation requires the allocation of scarce resources to the regulation, and diverting such resources results in a decrease in national wealth. Squandering resources on policies that have little beneficial effect has a real opportunity cost in that it takes funds that consumers otherwise could have spent in a more health-enhancing manner. Given the long-observed link between wealth and individual risk (see Viscusi, Volume I, Chapter 11), such a diversion of resources would result in an increase in health risks. That is, the empirical evidence suggests that risk reduction is a normal good; so as one's wealth increases, one will spend more on healthful practices such as better nutrition and preventive care. Any decrease in wealth resulting from a regulation would therefore result in an increase in health risks. Thus, a risk-risk analysis of a government regulation must compare the health improvement to the indirect increase in health risk due to decreases in economic resources and the resulting reduction in the disposable income of individuals.

The articles featured in Part I all explore the link between wealth and risk in order to assess whether risk reductions meet the risk-risk standard. Their goal is to estimate the risk increase per dollar reduction in national wealth due to a regulation. Keeney (Volume II, Chapter 1) was the first to estimate the negative effects of regulations on fatality risks due to the opportunity costs of the regulations. Using estimates from other studies of the relationship between mortality rates and income, he considers both the cost of a regulation and the distribution of the burden of the cost as a function of income. He finds that a $12.3 million loss of income (1992 dollars) results in one statistical death. Lutter and Morrall (Volume II, Chapter 3) use international data on gross domestic product and mortality to estimate the wealth-mortality relationship, and they find that a loss of income between $8.0 million and $9.6 million will result in an additional statistical death.

The correlation between wealth and health is commonly accepted. What is subject to more debate is the direction of the causality: does wealth lead people to invest in and improve their health, or do healthier people tend to make more money? Chapman and Hariharan (Volume II, Chapter 2) attempt to disentangle these effects by controlling for initial measures of health, thus isolating the effect from wealth to health. They find that a $12.2 million loss of income results in one statistical death.

Risk-risk analyses seek to identify the dollar regulatory expenditure that leads to the loss of one statistical life. In contrast, the literature that was the focus of Volume I addressed how much people were willing to pay to save a statistical life. These magnitudes must be related, as the risk-risk amount must be below the willingness to pay amount or else all lifesaving expenditures on balance will be counterproductive.

To address this issue and to avoid the problems associated with estimating wealth-health linkages, Viscusi (Volume II, Chapter 4) develops a theoretical model that links the value of a statistical life with the health-wealth relationship. He shows that the regulatory expenditure that leads to a loss of a statistical life is equal to the marginal value of life divided by the marginal propensity spent on health, which is always below 1.0. For example, given an estimate for the value of a statistical life of $5 million and an estimated marginal propensity to spend on health of 0.1, any regulation that results in an income loss of more than $50 million will lead to a net increase in risk.

Lutter, Morrall and Viscusi (Volume II, Chapter 5) generalize this model to include expenditures on harmful behavior, such as drinking and smoking, that result from income gains. Doing so reduces the estimate of the cost at which regulations become risk increasing to a level of approximately $20 million. Finally, Gerdtham and Johannesson (Volume II, Chapter 6) examine data from Sweden to estimate the cost at which regulations become risk increasing. They find that the income loss that induces an expected fatality is approximately $6.8 million when the costs are borne equally among all adults, $8.4 million when the costs are borne proportionally to income, and $9.8 million when the costs are borne progressively to income.

Volume II, Part II

The articles in Parts II–V examine the regulatory performance of health and safety regulations. To assess the overall benefits of a regulation, the analyst must couple the benefit of a risk reduction with the expected risk reduction that will result from the regulation. This yields a benefit estimate of the regulation that can then be compared to the regulatory costs, arriving at an efficient regulation in which net benefits are maximized. Typically, this assessment takes place before a regulation is promulgated. The case studies in Volume II address both such ex ante assessments as well as ex post assessments of performance.

Unfortunately, the regulatory record suggests that regulations seldom pass an efficiency test. As alluded to earlier, one reason for the regulatory shortcoming is that costs are often left out of the regulatory decision. Regulators often aim to eliminate lifetime fatality risks such as those that are as low as one in a million, no matter what the costs involved.

Morrall (Volume II, Chapter 7) attempts to quantify this misuse of regulatory resources based on information generated in regulatory impact analyses. The heart of Morrall's paper is his analysis of 44 proposed, final, or rejected federal rules that were aimed at reducing mortality risks. Using information on the anticipated risks, benefits, and costs of the regulations provided by the agencies, he calculates the cost per life saved of each of the regulations. What is startling about his finding is the wide variation in cost per life saved across regulations. These values range from $100 000 cost per life saved for the National Highway Traffic Safety Administration's (NHTSA) steering column protection regulation to $72 billion cost per life saved for the

Occupational Safety and Health Administration's (OSHA) formaldehyde regulation (costs in 1984 dollars). The exorbitant estimates of the cost per life saved for many regulations demonstrate the negative ramifications of failing to base regulatory standards on the efficiency criterion. Any reasonable benefit-cost analysis of the formaldehyde regulation would lead to the regulation not being adopted, since the cost per statistical life saved far exceeds the commonly accepted estimates of the benefit of a statistical life saved. Morrall's analysis makes clear the undesirable outcomes resulting from unsound regulatory policy. By shifting resources from the formaldehyde regulation to the steering column regulation, society can save many more lives for the same amount of money or, likewise, society can save the same number of lives for much less money.

There are a number of studies that question whether the risk assessment practices of regulatory agencies are misleading and lead to a misallocation of resources. For example, the multiplicative effect of using numerous conservative parameter assumptions significantly overstates the risk as discussed by Nichols and Zeckhauser (Volume II, Chapter 28). Another possible source of bias is the commonly used assumption that the relationship between the dose of the contaminant and the risk is linear. Also, some observers contend that regulatory agencies are more prone to regulate synthetic risks than natural risks, even though the former may pose a much smaller health threat.

In Part II, we offer the article by Ames, Magaw, and Gold (Volume II, Chapter 8) as representative of the considerable literature on cancer risks. They rank the risk from a variety of rodent carcinogens and find that many naturally occurring substances pose substantially greater risk than more frequently regulated pesticide residues and water pollution. For example, the main fumigant used for grain was banned even though the aflatoxin in the average peanut butter sandwich poses 75 times the risk of cancer. Such studies raise serious concerns about the performance of many health and safety regulations.

Volume II, Part III

According to economic theory, the government's role is not to aim to reduce all health risks to zero, but rather to regulate risks when a market failure leads to inefficient outcomes. Where health and safety risks are concerned, there are two prevalent market failures: (1) individuals are ill-informed about the risks they are exposed to, and (2) there exist externalities, in which economic activity is negatively affecting a third party not directly involved in any voluntary transaction involving the damage. In situations where people are fully informed of the risks and there are no externalities, then optimizing behavior will lead to an efficient outcome. Nonetheless, while efficiency implies that net benefits to society are maximized, it does not suggest the outcome is equitable. Distributional equity may be a legitimate component of a broadly defined efficiency test to the extent that society has a positive willingness to pay for such equity outcomes.

The early 1970s saw a wave of regulatory efforts aimed at addressing health and safety risks. The three biggest efforts by Congress to regulate risks were the establishment of the National Highway Traffic Safety Administration (NHTSA) in 1966, and the establishment of the Occupational Safety and Health Administration (OSHA) and the Environmental Protection Agency (EPA) in 1970. The underlying rationale for these regulations had little to do with any explicit recognition of market failure. Instead, the regulatory approach adopted during this time was to seek technological solutions, such as capital investments in the workplace or changes in the safety design of automobiles, in order to reduce risks as much as possible with no regard to costs. In other words, the general approach was that risks are undesirable, and with the right technology they can and should be eliminated. This naïve approach led to unrealistic expectations, such as the claim by a co-sponsor of the Occupational Safety and Health Act, Representative William Steiger (R-Wis.), that by 1980 workplace injuries would be reduced by 'fifty per cent or something like that'. Similarly, proponents of seatbelt standards promulgated by the National Highway Traffic Safety Administration (NHTSA) predicted that the occupant death rate due to car crashes would drop by 10 to 25 per cent within two years.

In the three decades since the creation of OSHA, NHTSA, and EPA, many researchers have examined the performance of these agencies. These analyses typically use three criteria to judge success: (1) whether the agencies' regulations have been effective in reducing risks, (2) whether the agencies reduced risks efficiently (rather than the costs not justifying the benefits of the health improvement), and (3) where efficiency has failed, have the regulations been adopted cost-effectively (i.e., whether the same gains could not have been achieved at lower cost to society). Parts III, IV, and V of Volume II examine the performance of these agencies in regulating job risks, product risks and environmental risks, respectively.

Much of the literature on regulatory performance has focused on the weak effects of these efforts on safety. Regulations will only have a potential for influence if they establish incentives for compliance. Thus, the cost of compliance must be below the expected cost of noncompliance, which is equal to the product of the probability of inspection, the number of violations per inspection, and the penalties per violation. These incentives are in fact quite small for job safety regulation, which accounts for the very small impact of such efforts.

Smith (Volume II, Chapter 10) conducted an early analysis of the effectiveness of OSHA at reducing workplace injury rates. He uses plant-level data on inspections and injuries, coupled with plant-specific information. In his research design, plants inspected later in the year are used as a control group, since forces at work prior to the inspection predominantly affect their injury rates. His treatment group consists of firms inspected early in the year. His results suggest that OSHA inspections in 1973 reduced injury rates by about 16 per cent, but that 1974 inspections had no statistically significant effect.

Viscusi (Volume II, Chapter 11) considers the behavioral response to safety regulations. In the case of OSHA, higher expected penalties would increase firms' investment in safety. However, a rational behavioral response by workers to increased safety equipment would be to decrease the level of care and precaution they take in their work actions. Thus, the effectiveness of OSHA regulations would depend on the net effect. Using a pooled time series (1972–1975) and cross section of industry health and safety investments, he finds that OSHA penalties did not have a significant impact on injury rates. More recent studies have shown some beneficial effect of OSHA on safety, but far less than the framers of these policies predicted.

Volume II, Part IV

The early performance of product safety regulation was also disappointing. Peltzman's (Volume II, Chapter 14) article evaluating efficiency of seatbelt regulations failed to find a risk reducing effect. Peltzman uses a time-series analysis of annual death rates, controlling for income, the price of an accident, alcoholic intoxication among the population, average driving speed, and the ratio of young drivers to older drivers. His findings suggest that any reduction in fatalities due to the vehicle regulations of the late 1960s and early 1970s is offset by an increase in pedestrian fatalities, which is consistent with there being a behavioral response to seatbelt regulations. A more recent analysis of highway safety by Keeler (Volume II, Chapter 17) uses county-level data from 1970 to 1980 in a first-difference model, which allows for a much richer analysis than using annual nationwide data. As with the Peltzman analysis, Keeler also finds very weak evidence of a regulatory effect on reducing traffic fatalities.

The behavioral response in the Peltzman model presupposed a rational moral hazard response to regulation. The consumer product safety analysis by Viscusi (Volume II, Chapter 16) takes a different approach in that it hypothesizes that consumers may be victims of a 'lulling effect'. Safety devices may give consumers a false sense of security and lead them to overestimate the efficacy of safety devices. Government officials, for example, routinely referred to safety caps as being 'childproof' not 'child resistant'. The result is that there is no observed beneficial effect of the regulation. In addition, there is an adverse spillover effect. Diminished parental responsibility regarding access to drugs by children that occurred after the advent of safety caps has led to increases in poisonings for acetaminophen products such as Tylenol.

There are two other articles in our collection that examine motor vehicle regulations. Arnould and Grabowski (Volume II, Chapter 15) conducted an early benefit-cost analysis of passive restraint systems. They find that automatic seat belts yield high benefits relative to costs, but that air bags were less advantageous due largely to their high costs. Finally, we include a recent article by Levitt and Porter (Volume II, Chapter 18) that analyzes the effectiveness of seat belts and air bags in reducing fatalities. Most of the previous analyses of this issue rely on data collected only for fatal crashes. Their innovation is recognizing that this can lead to sample selection bias, since the use of the safety device influences the likelihood of fatalities, which in turn determines whether the crash is included in the data set. In other words, if seatbelts reduce the likelihood of a fatality, then many crashes in which people were wearing their belts and thus did not die won't be included in the data set, and the effectiveness of the seat belts will be underestimated. They address this problem by limiting the sample to crashes in which someone in a different vehicle dies. They find that seat belts are more effective and air bags are less effective than previously found.

Volume II, Part V

We include two articles that examine environmental regulation. Cropper et al. (Volume II, Chapter 19) examine whether the Environmental Protection Agency (EPA) balances the risks of pesticide use against the costs of banning pesticides in their regulatory decision making under the Federal Insecticide, Fungicide, and Rodenticide Act. They find that the EPA does indeed balance benefits against costs even though the regulations may not pass a formal benefit-cost test; that is, the likelihood that a pesticide is banned is positively correlated to the risks to human health and the environment and negatively correlated with the benefits associated with the pesticide. They also find that political factors such as lobbying by special-interest groups affect the regulatory decision making.

Hamilton (Volume II, Chapter 20) also analyzes the role of political factors in the regulatory decision-making process in his examination of the existence of environmental racism. He offers and tests three hypotheses for the existence of differential environmental risks by geographical concentration of ethnic groups. These hypotheses are as follows: (1) pure discrimination in which firms and politicians actively locate polluting plants in nonwhite areas; (2) differences in the willingness to pay for environmental amenities, which is a function of income and education; and (3) variation by income and race in the propensity to engage in collective action to oppose environmental disamenities. By examining the decision to expand hazardous waste sites as a function of race, income, education, and propensity to engage in collective action, he finds that it is collective action that offers the best explanation for capacity expansions. This fits the Coasian model in which polluters seek out locations in which expected compensatory payments will be the least.

Volume II, Part VI

Part VI explores a range of issues pertaining to the role of risk beliefs and the use of warnings to convey risk information. From an efficiency standpoint, a market failure occurs if individuals are not informed of the risks involved in their consumption decisions. Lichtenstein et al. (Volume II, Chapter 21) do indeed find that people tend to misperceive risks, systematically overestimating low-probability events and underestimating high-probability events. Therefore, such things as warning labels can presumably alleviate this source of inefficiency. The study by Viscusi and O'Connor (Volume II, Chapter 22) assesses the efficiency of warnings for job risks, which will affect worker risk perceptions, quit intentions, and reservations wage rates.

Information efforts do not, however, guarantee accurate risk beliefs. Warnings for cigarettes, for example, imply that smoking is dangerous, but do not indicate the level of the risk. The result is that there is overestimation of the risk, which is consistent with the patterns observed for highly publicized hazards. The other chapters in this section all examine whether (and to what extent) individuals misperceive certain risks.

Volume II, Part VII

Few risks are known with precision. Instead, risks are often ambiguous, leading to well-established anomalies such as the Ellsberg Paradox (Volume II, Chapter 26). Aversion to ambiguous risks has profound ramifications, particularly in that similar biases are also reflected in government policy (as discussed in Nichols and Zeckhauser, Volume II, Chapter 28). And, as discussed in Kunreuther, Hogarth and Meszaros (Volume II, Chapter 30), ambiguity bias may also impede the effective functioning of insurance markets.

An interesting phenomenon occurs in situations in which there are competing risk experts whose statements give rise to the risk ambiguity. The results reported in Viscusi (Volume II, Chapter 31) indicate that people are most prone to alarmist responses when there are divergent sources of risk information. Thus, disputes between experts from industry and government are more likely to lead to higher risk beliefs than are two divergent views from government scientists. People place the greatest weight on worst-case scenarios in that instance.

Conclusion

Risk management policy has raised a wide variety of issues of interest to economists, whose work in turn has informed regulatory policy. While the state of economic research now appears to be far ahead of the development of sound policies, many salient research questions have yet to be resolved. For example, risk-risk analysis in principle has a sound economic foundation, but a consensus on the empirical bases for such an analysis has yet to emerge. Similarly, behavioral responses to regulations are widely believed to be important, but we are less able to predict the contexts in which such efforts will prove to be important. Indeed, in the case of reduced tar cigarettes, there continues to be substantial debate over the extent of the behavioral response. As research on these and other risk-related issues continues, it will serve to provide policy makers with the tools needed to be more protective of individual health while at the same time recognizing the tradeoffs associated with particular interventions.

Part I
The Value of Life: Overview and Surveys

[1]

T. C. SCHELLING*

The Life You Save
May Be Your Own

THIS IS a treacherous topic, and I must choose a nondescriptive title to avoid initial misunderstanding. It is not the worth of human life that I shall discuss, but of "life-saving," of preventing death. And it is not a particular death, but a statistical death. What is it worth to reduce the probability of death—the statistical frequency of death—within some identifiable group of people none of whom expects to die except eventually?

Worth to whom? Eventually I shall propose that it is to the people who may die, or who may lose somebody who matters to them. But the subject is surrounded by so much mystery, sentiment, moral consideration, husbandry, and paternalism, that some of the fringe issues need to be discussed first, if only to identify what the subject is not. Some of these issues are exciting, more exciting than the economics of life expectancy. They involve the special qualities that make an individual's life unique and his death an awesome event, that make hangmen's wages a special market phenomenon and murder the only crime worth solving in a detective story.

The first part of the paper examines society's interest in life and

* Professor of Economics, Harvard University.

death; the second part surveys the economic impact of untimely death, viewing it more as a loss of livelihood than as a loss of life, seeing how the losses and any possible gains are distributed among taxpayers, insured policyholders, and others who have no personal connection with the deceased. The third part deals with the consumer's interest in reduced mortality and how that interest can be identified, expressed, or allowed for in government programs that, at some cost, can raise life expectancy. It is here that we recognize that life as well as livelihood is at stake; so is anxiety, and the life at risk concerns the consumer personally.

Social Interest in Life and Death

"Pain, fear, and suffering," we are told, " . . . are considered of great importance in a society that values human life and human welfare."[1] They are important, too, to ordinary people who do not like pain and suffering. We have been told that the value of a human life ought to be considered, at least partially, without regard to whether the person who might die is a producer or not, that this value should result from a collective decision concerning the "expense that the nation is willing—as a moral judgment—to undertake, to save one of its members."[2] Why a moral judgment? Why not a practical judgment—a consumer choice—by the members of society about what it is worth to reduce the risk of death? Is death so awesome, so frightening, and so remote, that in discussing its economics we must always suppose it is someone *else* who dies?

What is moral about wanting to live? People who do not care at all for each other, or for society, or for the value of human life, will take care to avoid pain and death. Why should it require a moral judgment for me to hire a policeman to protect my life, along with the lives of my neighbors who pay their share of his salary, but a purely economic judgment to hire him to protect my shop window, my payroll, or my automobile?

"For a variety of reasons it is beyond the competence of the econ-

[1] D. J. Reynolds, "The Cost of Road Accidents," *Journal of the Royal Statistical Society,* Vol. 119 (1956), pp. 393-408.

[2] Selma J. Mushkin, "Health as an Investment," *Journal of Political Economy* (October 1962), Supplement, p. 156. She cites an unpublished paper by E. E. Pyatt and P. P. Rogers.

omist to assign objective values to the losses suffered under [pain, fear, and suffering]."[3] The same is true of cola and Novocain, one of which puts holes in children's teeth and the other takes the pain out of repairing them. If they were not for sale it would be beyond our competence, as economists, to put an objective value on them, at least until we took the trouble to ask people. Death is indeed different from most consumer events, and its avoidance different from most commodities. There is no sense in being insensitive about something that entails grief, anxiety, frustration, and mystery, as well as economic privation. But people have been dying for as long as they have been living; and where life and death are concerned we are all consumers. We nearly all want our lives extended and are probably willing to pay for it. It is worth while to remind ourselves that the people whose lives may be saved should have something to say about the value of the enterprise and that we analysts, however detached, are not immortal ourselves.

Individual Death and Statistical Death

There is a distinction between individual life and a statistical life. Let a 6-year-old girl with brown hair need thousands of dollars for an operation that will prolong her life until Christmas, and the post office will be swamped with nickels and dimes to save her. But let it be reported that without a sales tax the hospital facilities of Massachusetts will deteriorate and cause a barely perceptible increase in preventable deaths—not many will drop a tear or reach for their checkbooks. John Donne was partly right: the bell tolls for thee, usually, if thou didst send to know for whom it tolls, but most of us get used to the noise and go on about our business.

I am not going to talk about the worth of saving an identified individual's life. Amelia Earhart lost in the Pacific, a score of Illinois coal miners in a collapsed shaft, an astronaut on the tip of a rocket or the little boy with pneumonia awaiting serum sent by dogsled—even the heretofore anonymous victims of a Yugoslavian earthquake—are part of ourselves, not a priceless part but a private part that we value in a different way, not just quantitatively but qualitatively, from the way we measure the incidence of death among a mass of unknown human beings, whether that population includes ourselves or not. If

[3] Reynolds, *op. cit.*

we know the people, we care. Half the entertainment industry and most great literature is built on this principle. But our concern in this paper will be statistical lives.

We must recognize, too, that the success of organized society depends on traditions, attitudes, beliefs, and rules that may appear extravagant or sentimental to a confirmed materialist (if there is one). The sinking of the Titanic illustrates the point. There were enough lifeboats for first class; steerage was expected to go down with the ship. We do not tolerate that any more. Those who want to risk their lives at sea and cannot afford a safe ship should perhaps not be denied the opportunity to entrust themselves to a cheaper ship without lifeboats; but if some people cannot afford the price of passage with lifeboats, and some people can, they should not travel on the same ship.

The death of an individual is a unique event. Even an atheist can wish he had been nicer to someone who recently died, as though the "someone" exists, which the atheist believes he does not. If death indeed is final, it is only so for the person who dies. Whatever the source of the mystery, most of us have very special feelings about suicide and euthanasia, birth control and abortion, bloodsports and capital punishment, and there is no way to deny these feelings in the interest of "rationality" without denying most of what makes us human. We go to great lengths to recover dead bodies. We give a firing squad one blank cartridge so that every member can pretend he did not take a life.

Responsibility for death introduces special problems. A man can be sent on a mission or on repeated missions with small probability of survival, but sending a man to certain death is different. The "chance" makes the difference, apparently because people can hope —the people who go and the people who send them. Guilt is involved; one of the reasons for having a book of rules about when to run the risk and when not to—when to land the disabled aircraft and when to abandon it and take to parachute—is to relieve the man who gives the orders, the man in the control tower, of personal guilt for the instruction he gives.[4] Safety regulations must be partly oriented toward guilt and responsibility. A window washer may smoke on the job until he gets lung cancer, and it is no concern of his employer; but his safety belt must be in good condition.

[4] This important point was brought to my attention by Jack Carlson, whose Ph.D. thesis dealt with the subject. "Valuation of Life Saving" (Harvard University, 1963).

To evaluate an individual death requires attention to special feelings. Most of these feelings, though, involve some connection between the person who dies and the person who has the feelings; a marginal change in mortality statistics is unlikely to evoke these sentiments. Programs that affect death statistically—whether they are safety regulations, programs for health and safety, or systems that ration risk among classes of people—need not evoke these personal, mysterious, superstitious, emotional, or religious qualities of life and death. These programs can probably be evaluated somewhat as we evaluate the commodities we spend our money on.

What is the alternative to death? It depends. For the paralytic it is a life of paralysis; for someone who escapes a highway accident it is the same life as before, unless the near miss changes his behavior. The type of risk that might be reduced is likely to be correlated with age, sex, income level, number of dependents, and life expectancy. Any program that reduces the risk of death will be discriminatory. Infant mortality affects infants and those who have them; motor accidents affect people who use the roads; starvation kills the poor, and a regulation that surrounds swimming pools with fences will affect different age groups according to the height of the fence. Even lightning is not random in its choice of victims; and any analysis that initially ignores the specific group affected has to be adaptable to the specific deaths that would be averted by a given program.

Where does the problem arise? It arises in disease, road accidents, industrial safety, flood control, the armed services, safety regulations, personal protection, and all the things that people do that affect their life expectancy. In the marketplace it arises in the choice of hazardous occupations, in home safety, in residential location, and in risky everyday enterprises like diving and swimming. It is often hard to discern, though, or to separate, the things that people do to save their own lives or that governments do to save the lives of citizens, because mortality is so closely correlated with other things that concern people. We eat for satisfaction and avoid starvation, heat our homes to feel warm and avoid pneumonia; we buy fire and police protection to save economic loss, pain, embarrassment and disorder, and in the process reduce the risks of death. When we ride an airplane, death is about the only serious risk that we consider; but if we compare an advanced country with a backward one the difference in safety to life is correlated with so many comforts, amenities, and technological advances that it is hard to sort out life-saving and life-risking components. The impact on life expectancy of, say, the electric light, is so cumulative and indirect that it would hardly be worth sorting out if we could sort it out. The universal employment of snow blowers would spare us all those heart attacks that the newspapers so faithfully report after a blizzard; but what number of us would eventually die younger for lack of exercise is not so readily estimated.

Who loses if a death occurs (or has to be anticipated)? First, the person who dies. Exactly what he loses we do not know. But, before it happens, people do not want to die and will go to some expense to avoid death. Beyond the privation that death causes the person who dies, there is the fear of death. The anxieties are visible and are real. Few who are sentenced to die, or have received the announcement that their deaths are inevitable, seem to consider those last few days or months the best of their lives. We may be in the grip of an instinct that has value for the race and not for the individual; but if we ask, who is willing to make an economic sacrifice to prevent a death, in most societies there is at least one unequivocal answer: the person who is to die. By all the standards that economists take seriously, the prospective victim loses.

Second, death is an event—and the prevention of death a consumer good—that in our society inextricably involves the welfare of people close to the person who dies. Death is bereavement and disturbance of integral small societies—families—where people play roles that are often unique and always difficult for others to fill.

Finally, there is "society"—other people. They can lose money or save as a result of a death with which they have no personal connection. In a few dramatic cases—the inventor of a wonder drug, a poet, statesman, or a particularly predatory criminal—the impact of a death may be out of all proportion to the victim's personal economics—to his earnings, expenditures, taxes, contributions, and his exploitation of public programs and facilities. The rest of us, though, are known to the economy mainly by the money we earn and spend and the money that is spent upon us; and an accounting approach will uncover most of the impact.

Death is a comparatively private event. Society may be concerned but is not much affected. There is a social interest in schools and delinquency, discrimination and unrest, infection and pollution, noise and beauty, obscenity and corruption, justice and fair practices, and in the examples men set; but death is usually a very local event. The victim and his family have an intense interest; society may want to take that interest seriously, but it is hard to see that society has a further interest of its own unless, as in military service or public orphanages, there is an acknowledged public responsibility. Society's interest, moreover, may be more in whether reasonable efforts are made to conserve life than in whether those efforts succeed. A missing man has to be searched for, but whether or not he is found is usually of interest—intense interest, to be sure—to a very few.

But the taxes we pay and the school lunches we eat have their impersonal ramifications and can motivate someone else to take an economic interest in our longevity. The accounting for those ramifications is the subject of the next section.

Economic Interest in Lost Livelihoods

When we consider the costs of a death to society—the costs that might be decreased by a program that reduces deaths—it is as important to discover where the costs fall as to aggregate them. There is a convention that nations are the bases of aggregation, but costs can be local, regional, or national; they can fall on particular sectors of the economy, particular levels of income, particular groups of taxpayers or welfare recipients.

Especially if there is an opportunity to prevent the death—to reduce the incidence of death within some part of the population—there is as much interest in who would have borne the cost of the death as in what the total cost would be. First, interested parties may have to be identified, to persuade them that they should bear the cost of reducing some mortality rate. Moral judgments are fine, but in the end it may be airline passengers who want more air safety, parents who want children better protected, Oklahomans who want better tornado warning; it is worthwhile to identify the people who might care enough to do something about it. Second, if the losses are to be compensated, their location and size must be known. Third, if a sense of justice or social contract requires that the beneficiaries pay for the benefits, we want to know who benefits.

Someone may care about the effect of a death on the gross national product, though I doubt that anyone cares much. Still, the GNP is so often taken as the thing we care about that at least passing attention should be devoted to the aggregate effect of death and its postponement on the economy.

Population Economics

At the GNP level, death is mainly a matter of population economics. Population has both a territorial and a national significance. The GNP was raised when Hawaii and Alaska were assimilated; it could be raised more by bringing Canada into the United States. This is a purely "national" consideration, having to do with the virtues of being a big country.

There may be scale effects in efficiency or in the provision of public services, but it is hard to tell whether the United States is richer as it becomes more dense and more congested. Military considerations aside, it is not obvious that in a country like this the number of people makes much difference.

If it did, we would probably have a conscious policy of migration. We might also have a conscious policy of family incentives, subsidizing children or taxing their parents or designing social security programs to give incentives for larger or smaller families. It is hard to escape the conclusion that if people are what we want, programs to reduce mortality are a sluggish way to get them.

A question that has received some attention in efforts to put a wealth value on human life is how to calculate the worth of a child. There has been, it is often observed, some investment in the child and, with accrued interest, this investment is lost if the child dies. Alternatively, the child will produce income in the future; and though the investment is sunk, the future income is lost if the child dies and his discounted net contribution, positive or negative, goes with him. This is complicated: if he lives he will produce and he will procreate; if he dies he may leave dependents of his own.

I doubt whether this kind of population economics is worth all the arithmetic. At best, it is the way a family will deal with the loss of a cow, not the loss of a collie. Though children are not pets, in the United States they are more like pets than like livestock, and it is doubtful whether the interests of any consumers are represented in a calculation that treats a child like an unfinished building or some expensive goods in process. At best this would be relevant to a kind of replacement cost; but it tells little about the cost of replacement— whether a new-born baby is as good as a teenager if you cannot have the particular teenager whose death caused grief and loneliness.

No. Population economics is important, but if life-saving deserves our attention, it is probably in some other context.

Assessing the Costs of a Death

If a lonely, self-sufficient hermit dies—a man who pays no taxes, supports no church, is too old for military service and leaves no dependents, owning nothing but a burial plot and a prepaid funeral— there are no costs or benefits. Whatever he would have paid, to make his life safer and to increase his life expectancy, he is dead now and no one knows the difference.

If a Harvard professor dies—a taxpaying man with a family, who contributes to the United Fund and owns twice his salary in life insurance, is eligible for social security and has children who may go to college—the accounting of gains and losses is complicated.

The largest losses will fall on his family, and we should distinguish at once between his life and his livelihood. His family will miss him, and it will miss his earnings. We do not know which of the two in the end it will miss most, and if he died recently this is a disagreeable time to inquire. Let us for the moment leave aside the grief, the loneliness, the loss of direction or authority in the family, the emotional privation, and all the things the man represented except his income. The reason for leaving them out at this point is not that they are unmeasurable, or none of our business, but that they are nontransferable and nonmarketable, and there is no "accounting" way to estimate them. For the moment look at the material losses, and get the pure accounting out of the way.

How much of the loss of livelihood falls on the family depends on institutional and market arrangements. In an extremely communal society or an extremely individualist one, there may be a rule or tradition for sharing the loss: orphans may be supported by contributions, rotated among the neighbors, taken in by next of kin, absorbed in a communal orphanage, or otherwise supported at the expense of society at large or of a select responsible group. Alternatively, life insurance may accomplish somewhat the same thing. Whether a "protective benevolent society" is a genuinely fraternal institution or a modern insurance company with a quaint name, the effect is to share the costs.

It is somewhat arbitrary to say that the cost "really" falls on the family and the rest is redistribution, or the cost "really" falls on the committed members of the community, or on the policyholders whose premium payments will reflect the death. The family, the community, and the insurance market are all social institutions characterized by a system of enforceable or honored obligations; and it is a matter of social choice whether, in addition to identifying the child with its father, its consumption is identified with his earnings. The important question is who pays the costs or suffers the losses, not which losses are original and which are transferred.

Who pays the cost of the professor's insurance, and how much do they pay? Policyholders pay it, in proportions that reflect the size of their premiums and, if the man was in a preferred-risk or other special category, the actuarial correlation of his mortality class with theirs. The extent to which people share the burden of lost livelihoods in society is not altogether determined by social philosophy and legislation but can be determined by individual choices in an organized market where people can hedge against death somewhat the way they can hedge against crop failure, inflation, or fluctuating exchange rates.

As a matter of fact, policyholders all have quite a stake in each other. Through an impersonal market mechanism, they have placed bets—each in his own way—on their lives and collectively have arranged to share some of the burdens of an individual death. There is no logical limit to this process, at least until pecuniary suicide, or homicide, becomes a problem and a limit must be placed on the bets. Up to the point where death becomes financially attractive, life insurance offers a straightforward way of identifying a group of people who have a financial interest in each other's longevity, and to whom the cash value of improved mortality has an unmistakable meaning. (Insurance-company campaigns to keep us from getting fat reflect this interest.)

Insurance and National Policy

In the United States there is no national policy on life insurance, as there is for retirement, unemployment, and now for certain kinds of medical care. (There is life insurance in the social security program, but it appears to be more a by-product of retirement than an explicit survivors' program.) There is, in some states, mandatory liability insurance for people who drive cars; there is not, except under social security, mandatory life insurance for people who bring children into the world. If you are hit by a car, your right to collect damages is recognized in some states by a law obliging the driver to have made financial provision in advance; if you are merely born, and have the bad luck to lose your father, the law has not obliged him to make financial provision for you.

If there were a national policy on life insurance, it could be interpreted as a national policy on sharing the financial losses that result from a man's death. (In fact, if there were mandatory life insurance in an amount determined by a man's income, life insurance could almost be dispensed with by merely revising the tax schedules. This is what, to a large extent, is done with retirement insurance.) If that were done, the cost of a man's death to the nation at large would be substantially reflected in the survivor's benefits paid out under the program, plus the lost taxes.

If one thinks that everybody with dependents ought to be "fully" insured—that his death should not affect the standard of living of his dependents—then one presumably believes that the full loss of a man's livelihood to his family is a proper burden for the nation and ought to be an actual burden for the nation. It should then be worth at least as much to society to keep the man alive as to replace his family's share in the livelihood he earns. (One also then presumably believes that the actuarial cost to the nation of a man's having children should be an actual cost to the man, in the form of taxes or mandatory premiums, though one can probably adduce other considerations for redistributing the taxes or premiums.)

One who believes instead that insurance is a private matter, not one for national policy or government intrusion, should concern himself with whether the market for life insurance is well organized and consumers are properly knowledgeable, and with how policyholders—the people who pay the premiums that are geared to mortality rates—get their interests represented, or could get their interests represented, in government or private programs that reduce the risk of death.

Policyholders constitute an enormous potential lobby with an interest in saving lives. And like the beneficiaries of any government programs—programs to prevent property damage, to reduce congestion, to improve communication or to reduce transport costs, to raise agricultural productivity or to preserve the fisheries—they are a biased sample of the population and cannot claim, any more than other groups can, that what is good for policyholders is good for the country.

Noncontractual Claims

Less contractual, but somewhat like insurance, are a variety of claims on relatives, friends, and welfare agencies. The family may cease to be a net contributor to a church, possibly become a beneficiary. The children's eventual claims for college scholarships will be enhanced, unless they are obliged to give up college altogether. The United Fund, the Girl Scout Cookie Drive, time volunteered to civic programs, and all the other informal taxes and transfer payments that people participate in, will be affected. These are not trivial: there are crude data to suggest that the impact of voluntary "social security" and voluntary "taxes" are at least of the order of magnitude of, say, a fairly progressive state income tax.

It is interesting that some of the claims a man's dependents may make on others are themselves insurable, although brothers apparently do not insure each other's lives to protect themselves against having to care for each other's children at their own expense. Corporations insure the lives of employees, naming the survivors as beneficiaries, partly as a way—I have been told by a corporation executive who dealt with these matters—to minimize their vulnerability to the importunities of a man's dependents—to the claim of a widow, for example, that the corporation ought to give her a job. A large corporation can of course rely on self-insurance if these events occur with statistical regularity; but it may prefer the contractual formality of insurance, just as a person may want full collision coverage when he borrows a friend's car, to avoid the embarrassment of personal negotiation.

Taxes

Turn now to the real taxes that a man would have paid, had he lived, to the federal government, to the state he resided in or earned his living or spent his money in, and to the local community that his taxes helped to support. These taxes are a man's share in the overhead cost of government, in the provision of public goods and services that are not used up by the taxpayer himself. There are economies of scale in government; when a man dies he stops paying his share in the space program, and the rest have to make it up. Somebody loses transfer payments, or pays more taxes, when one of the net contributors disappears.

The man's taxes are positive or negative according to whether he is a net contributor or a net recipient, and according to how much cost his very presence in society imposes on government. Dead, he won't drive, steal, go to school, or leave unextinguished campfires; and various levels of government save an amount to offset against his taxes. (His death can be a gain to federal taxpayers and a loss to his city, or the other way around.)

These costs or losses, positive or negative, due to a man's death, could be approximately offset by replacing the man. In principle, selective immigration might compensate society for the man's death. There are societies in which immigration works in this fashion, or immigration policy reflects the loss of citizens through death. Without any policy, immigration works this way for local communities. Possibly with some conscious though indirect policy behind it, it works that way for the state of Alaska, and has worked for frontier societies and developing nations.

The main reason why immigration could not in principle handle the problem is that there is one obligation of citizenship that the immigrant is unlikely to assume. That is the family obligation of the man who dies. There have been frontier societies that imported wives, even husbands. But to achieve a genuine economic replacement for the taxpaying father who dies, one would have to find bachelors and widowers seeking ready-made families to marry into; this is undoubtedly asking more than either the free market or individually negotiated immigration could manage. Most income-taxpayers probably spend more to support families than to support their government, and that contribution is a hard one to replace.

What are the taxes to be accounted for, and how are they to be accounted for? The man's property taxes can be excluded; the taxes will go on being paid by whoever owns his property—his family or the person who buys his house or automobile. (There will be a slight change of interest to local governments, a tendency for property assessments to change with the turnover of real estate, or for values to be depressed by an increment in the supply of houses—a matter of elasticity estimates, not of accounting.) The issues mainly concern federal and state income taxes, employment taxes, excise and sales taxes, net of the costs of collecting them and net of transfer receipts; and the subject of inquiry is the difference between the taxes (net of transfers) that he and his family would have paid had he not died and the taxes they go on paying, and the man's (or the child's) utilization of government benefits, valued at marginal cost.

The difficult problems relate to the income tax, or to the income tax as well as to other taxes; if the income tax is examined, probably most of the interesting problems will have been discussed. One set of problems relates to how taxable incomes are; this depends on source of income, the jurisdiction a man lives in, and what constitutes taxable income. Another set relates to the distribution of taxable income in an economy like ours. What happens to taxable income when the Harvard professor dies? Is there merely a subtraction from the tax rolls of one income in a fairly high bracket? Or are there economic laws that impose a shape on the distribution of income independently of who dies? The professor will be replaced, by a man who in turn may be replaced by the institution he left to go to Harvard. Even if marginal productivity theory states that the GNP goes down by approximately what the man was being paid, it will not say that taxable income goes down accordingly. If there is a loss to the economy because the man is replaced by a marginally less competent man at the same salary, this would show up as quality depreciation of Harvard's product, and would be of interest to the Internal Revenue Service only as it influences future tax rates.

If one takes the extreme position that the distribution of taxable income is unaffected by the particular incidence of death by tax brackets, the reduction in income tax would be proportionate to the man's income, not to the taxes he paid. Thus, if the Harvard professor has twice the income of a high school teacher and pays four times the income tax, the impact on income tax revenues of his disappearance from the tax base is only twice that of the high school teacher, not four times. The alternative bench mark is the hypothesis that the remaining distribution of income is unchanged—there is just a little nick in the frequency distribution at the income of the man who died, and a little cusp at the new level of income for his family—and everybody else's tax return goes on being just what it would have been. I doubt whether the state of economic analysis permits us to identify which of these two hypotheses is the more plausible or what compromise is most valid.

Taxes and Fiscal Policy

The next interesting problem about the income tax is one of fiscal philosophy. To Massachusetts the man's taxes were spendable revenue, just as his contribution to the United Fund was spendable revenue to that organization. State governments cannot engage in functional finance, accommodating fiscal and monetary policies to the tempo of economic activity. National governments can.

It is saving that causes the problem here. If the man and his family always consumed exactly the amount of their income after taxes, the government could marginally adapt to the man's death by reducing expenditure (or raising other people's taxes) in an amount equal to the man's income tax. But if, before he died, the man saved part of his income, and with the loss of his income there is a reduction in saving, the difference between the decline in (full-employment) GNP and the decline in consumption is greater than the income taxes the man paid. The accommodation of government programs would have to equal the sum of his taxes and his saving.

The treatment of saving in the economic evaluation of a man's death ought to be easy. All that is needed is a reliable theory of the role of saving. A reduction of saving due to death need not have an impact different from the reduction in saving due to some economic casualty—loss of a car or loss of a business—or due to any other change in tastes, institutions, or the distribution of income. It may not be easy to identify just what the changes in saving are that result from a death; this will depend on some of the things that have been discussed, like the way the costs of maintaining dependents are shared, contractually or institutionally. But once the aggregate change in saving has been identified, it should be possible to handle it with any good theory of the role of saving, without much regard to the specific event or institutional change that caused it. That is a topic to be treated in full by someone else at another time.

Consumer Interest in Reduced Risk

The avoidance of a particular death—the death of a named individual—cannot be treated straightforwardly as a consumer choice. It involves anxiety and sentiment, guilt and awe, responsibility and religion. If the individuals are identified, there are many of us who cannot even answer whether one should die that two may live. And when half of the children in a hospital ward are to get the serum that may save their lives, half a placebo to help test the serum, the doctor who divides them at random and keeps their identities secret is not exclusively interested in experimental design. He does not want personally to select them or to know who has been selected. But most of this awesomeness disappears when we deal with statistical deaths, with small increments in a mortality rate in a large population.

Suppose a program to save lives has been identified and we want to know its worth. Suppose the population whose vulnerability is to be reduced is a large one, and approximately identifiable. The dimensions of the risk to be reduced are fairly well known, as is the reduction to be achieved. Suppose also that this risk is small to begin with, not a source of anxiety or guilt.

Surely it is sensible to ask the question: What is it worth to the people who stand to benefit from it? If a scheme can be devised for collecting the cost from them, perhaps in a manner reflecting their relative gains if their benefits are dissimilar, it surely should be their privilege to have the program if they are collectively willing to bear the cost. If they are not willing, perhaps it would be a mistake to ask anybody else to bear the cost for them; they, the beneficiaries, prefer to have the money or some alternative benefits that the money could buy. There are reasons why this argument has to be qualified, but there is no obvious reason why a program that reduces mortality cannot be handled by letting the beneficiaries decide whether it is worth the cost, if the cost falls on them.

There are two main ways of finding out whether some economic benefits are worth the costs. One is to use the price system as a test of what something is worth to the people who have to pay for it. It is possible to see what people are willing to pay for the privilege of sitting at tables rather than counters in a restaurant, what they are willing to pay to use library books or to save an elm tree in the front yard.

Sometimes the market is poor; sometimes analysis is confused by joint products; sometimes consumer behavior is subject to inertia and the information is needed before the market adjusts. But at least we can try to observe what people will pay for something.

Another way of discovering what the benefits are worth is to ask people. This can be done by election, interview, or question-naire; the more common way is to let people volunteer the informa-tion, through lobby organizations, letters to congressmen or to the newspapers, and rallies. There may be—some of C. E. Lindblom's work suggests this—something a little like a price system here if peo-ple are allowed to show the trouble they will go to, or the expense they will incur, to lobby for or against something.[5] Like the price sys-tem, these methods may be ambiguous.

It is sometimes argued that asking people is a poor way to find out, because they have no incentive to tell the truth. That is an im-portant point, but hardly decisive. It is also argued, and validly, that people are poor at answering hypothetical questions, especially about important events—that the mood and motive of actual choice are hard to simulate. While this argument casts suspicion on what one finds out by asking questions, it casts suspicion too on those mar-ket decisions that involve remote and improbable events. Unexpect-ed death has a hypothetical quality whether it is merely being talked about or money is being spent to prevent it. Asked whether he would buy trip insurance if it were available at the airport (or would de-cline to fly an aircraft that had a statistically higher accident rate than another if it would save an overnight stop), a man may not give ver-bally the same answer that his actions in the airport would reveal; he still might not feel that his actual decision was authoritative evidence of his values or that, had mood and circumstance been different— even had the amount of time for consultation and decision been different—his action might not have been different too. This problem of coping, as a consumer, with increments in the risk of unexpected death is very much the problem of coping with hypothetical ques-tions, whether in response to survey research or to the man who sells lightning-rod attachments for the TV antenna. If consumers regu-larly retained professional consultants in coping with such decisions, there might be a good source of information.

[5] Charles E. Lindblom, *The Intelligence of Democracy; Decision Making Through Mutual Adjustment* (Free Press, 1965).

In any case, relying exclusively on market valuations and denying the value of direct enquiry in the determination of government programs (or even the programs of nongovernmental organizations) would depend on there being, for every potential government service, a close substitute available in the market at a comparable price. It would be hard to deduce from first principles that this is bound to be the case. Voting behavior is probably to be classed somewhere between a purchase and a questionnaire: an individual's vote is indecisive, while the election as a whole is conclusive.

Small Probability of Large Events

A difficulty about death, especially a minor risk of death, is that people have to deal with a minute probability of an awesome event, and may be poor at finding a way—by intellect, imagination, or analogy—to explore what the saving is worth to them. This is true whether they are confronted by a questionnaire or a market decision, a survey researcher or a salesman. It may even matter whether the figures are presented to them in percentage terms or as odds, whether charts are drawn on arithmetic or logarithmic scales, and whether people are familiar with the simple arithmetic of probability.

The smallness of the probability is itself a hard thing to come to grips with, especially when the increment in question is even smaller than the original risk. At the same time, the death itself is a large event, and until a person has some way of comparing death with other losses it is difficult or impossible to do anything with it probabilistically, even if one is quite willing to manipulate probabilities.

What it would be like to grow old without a companion, to rear a family without a mother or father in the house, to endure bereavement, is something that most of us have no direct knowledge of; and those who have some knowledge may not yet know the full effects over time. Many of us think about it only when we make a will or buy life insurance, suffer a medical false alarm or witness the bereavement of a friend or neighbor.

As consumers we can investigate the subject. It may be no harder to cope with than choosing a career, nor more painful than some of the medical decisions we actually have to take. But most of us have not investigated; the cost of doing so is high, and there is not much fun in it. In a program of interrogation, even a sales effort, some people will just not cooperate. Others, if they have to make a decision, would rather make a hasty one that may be wrong than a more painful or embarrassing decision that is more nearly right. Some of the reluctance may be unconscious, with a resulting bias that is hard to identify.

Furthermore, this is, more than most decisions, a family one, not an individual one.[6] Nearly every death involves at least two major participants, typically the immediate family. It is not even clear who it is that has the greater stake in a person's not dying—himself, his spouse if he has one, his children if he is a parent, or his parents if he is a child—and the subject is undoubtedly a delicate one for the members of the consuming unit to discuss with each other. Whatever the motives of a respondent when being interviewed alone about a safety program or a hazardous occupation, his motives are surely complex when he talks to his wife about how much he would miss her or she would miss him, the likelihood of a happy remarriage, or which of them would suffer more if one of the children died.

Death versus Anxiety

The problem is even harder if the risk to be attenuated is large enough, or vivid enough, to cause anxiety. In fact, the pain associated with the awareness of risk—with the prospect of death—is probably often commensurate with the costs of death itself. A person who sooner or later must undergo an operation that carries a moderate risk of being fatal will apparently sometimes choose to have the operation now, raising the stakes against himself in the gamble, in order to avoid the suspense. Wives of men in hazardous duty suffer; and most of us have sat beside someone on an airplane who suffered more with anxiety than if he had been drilled by a dentist without Novocain, and who would have paid a fairly handsome price for the Novocain. Let me conjecture that if one among forty men had been mistakenly injected with a substance that would kill him at the end of five years, and the forty were known to the doctor who did not know which among them had the fatal injection, and if the men did not know it yet, the doctor would do more harm by telling them what he had done than he had already done with the injection.

---

[6] The family gets little attention in economics. It is an income-sharing unit, a consumption-sharing unit, and a welfare-sharing unit. That is, they live off the same income, share the same bathroom, and care about each other.

This anxiety is separate from the impact of death itself. It applies equally to those who do not die and to those who do, to people who exaggerate the risk of death as much as if their estimates were true. It counts, and is part of the consumer interest in reducing the risk of death. It is not, or usually not, any kind of double counting to bring it into the calculation. But it is—except where knowledge of risk permits people to make better economic decisions, or exaggerations of risk lead them to hedge excessively and uneconomically—almost entirely psychic or social. Relief from anxiety is a strange kind of consumer good. What the consumer buys is a state of mind, a picture in his imagination, a sensation. And he must decide to do so by using the same brain that is itself the source of his discomfort or pleasure. However much "rationality" we impute to our consumer, we must never forget that the one thing he cannot control is his own imagination. (He can try, though; this accounts for the business in tranquilizers, and for the readiness of airlines to serve their passengers alcoholic beverages.)

Consumer Choices and Policy Decisions

These, then, are some of the reasons why it is hard for our consumer to tell us intelligently what it is worth to him to reduce the risk of death, why it may even be hard to get him to make a proper try. These are also reasons why the consumer may be poor at making ordinary choices about death in the market place. He may not do much better in buying life insurance or seat belts, using or avoiding airplanes, flying separately or together with his wife when they leave the children behind, selecting cigarettes with or without filters, driving under the influence of liquor when he could have taken a taxi, or installing a fire alarm over the basement furnace.[7] Some of his market-

---

[7] Many parents try not to fly on the same plane (although they usually drive home together on New Year's Eve). I took for granted that this was sensible, though extravagant—a matter of the nuisance one would incur to reduce the risk of leaving the children without any parent at all—until Richard Zeckhauser suggested I think it over. Should one double the risk of losing one parent to eliminate the risk of losing two? I decided then that the answer was hard to be sure of, and probably sensitive to the number of children and their ages, even if only the welfare of the children is taken into account, and more so of course when the parents' welfare is too. (Evidently happily married childless couples should travel on the same plane.) The point is not that I am right, now, where I was wrong before, but that I hadn't thought about it. Also that, now that I come to think about it, I'm not sure; and I still do not intend to discuss it with my wife, especially in the presence of the children.

place decisions may be more casual (perhaps out of evading his responsibilities, not meeting them) but they may be no better evidence than the answers he would give to questions.

Consumers apparently do often evade these questions when they have a chance. In matters of life and death doctors are not merely operations analysts who formulate the choice for the executive; they are professional decision makers, who not only diagnose but decide for the consumer, because they decide with less pain, less regret, cooler nerves, and a mind less flooded with alternating hopes and fears.

Still, in dealing with death-reducing programs, these are the kinds of decisions that somebody has to make. We can do it democratically, by letting the consumers decide for themselves through any of the market-place or direct-inquiry techniques that we can think of. Or we can do it vicariously, paternalistically, perhaps professionally, by making some of these highly introspective and imaginative decisions for them, briefing ourselves on the facts as best we can, or perhaps hiring out the decisions to people who have professional knowledge about the consequences of death in the family.

If then it turns out that the safety device or health program is a public good and not everybody wants it at the price, or that the tax system will not distribute the costs where the benefits fall, so that we are collectively deciding on a program in which some of us have a strong interest, some a weak interest, and some a negative interest, that makes it rather like any other budgetary decision that the government takes.[8] We need not get all wound up about the "pricelessness" of human life nor think it strange that the rich will pay more for longevity than the poor, or that the rich prefer programs that help the rich and the poor those that help the poor. There may be good reasons why the poor should not be allowed to fly second-class aircraft that are more dangerous, or people in a hurry should not be allowed to pay a bonus to the pilot who will waive the safety regulations; but these reasons ought to be explicitly adduced as qualifications to a

---

[8] Divergent interests are almost bound to arise when the decision involves restricting the activities of some people for the safety of others. Some of the simple economics of taxes and insurance premiums, in relation to automobile safety, are in Stefan Valavanis, "Traffic Safety from an Economist's Point of View," *Quarterly Journal of Economics* (November 1958), pp. 477-84. For an enthusiastic defense of fast driving, see John D. Williams, "The Nonsense about Safe Driving," *Fortune*, Vol. 58 (September 1958), pp. 118 ff.

principle that makes economic sense, rather than as "first principles" that transcend economics.

Some Quantitative Determinants

What results should we anticipate if we engage in the kind of inquiry I have described, or if we survey the market evidence of what people will pay to avoid their own deaths or the deaths of the people who matter to them? Is there any *a priori* line of reasoning that will help us to establish an order of magnitude, an upper or lower limit, a bench mark, or some ideal accounting magnitude that ought to represent the worth, to a reflective and arithmetically sophisticated consumer, of a reduction in some mortality rate? Is there some good indicator—life insurance, lightning rods, hazardous duty pay—that will give us some basis for estimate? Is there some scale factor, like a person's income, to which the ideal figure should be proportionate or of which it should be some function? And to what extent should our estimate be expected to depend on social and economic institutions?

At the outset, we can conjecture that any estimate based on market evidence will at best let us know to within a factor of 2 or 3 (perhaps only 5 or 10) what the reflective individual would decide after thoughtful, intensive inquiry and good professional advice. This conjecture is based on the observation that most of the market decisions people make relate to contingencies for which the probabilities themselves are ill-known to the consumer, sometimes barely available to the person who seeks statistics, invariably applicable in only rough degree, and mixed with joint products that make the evidence ambiguous. What will somebody pay for a babysitter who, in case of fire, will probably save the children or some of them? With a little research one can find out the likelihood of fire or other catastrophe during the time that one is away from home, the likelihood that they would be saved if a babysitter were on guard, and the likelihood that they would save themselves or otherwise be saved if no one were home; an upper or lower limit of "worth" may be manifested in the price that one pays or refuses to pay to a babysitter. It would take a good deal more research to relate this to the age and type of furnace, the shape and composition of the house and the location of roofs and windows, the performance of babysitters of different ages and sexes, the ages and personalities of the children, the season of the year, the quality of the fire department, the alertness of neighbors, and the hour of day or night that one is going to be away. In addition, baby-sitters perform other services; they help get the children to bed, soothe the child that awakes from a bad dream, telephone parents or doctor in case of sickness, let the dog out, guard against burglary, and sometimes even clean the dishes.[9] What the family pays for the babysitter will depend, furthermore, on whether it is the husband or the wife who decides, on what the local custom is, and on what vivid experience some acquaintance had in recent years. The evidential value of this "market test" will barely give us an estimate to within a factor of 2 or 3.

WORTH AS A FUNCTION OF INCOME. Is there some expectable or rational relation between what a man earns and what he would spend, or willingly be taxed, to increase the likelihood of his own survival or the survival of one of his family? Specifically, is there any close accounting connection between what he might spend and what he can hope to earn in the future, or what he owns?

So many examinations of the worth of saving a life are concerned with the fraction of a man's income that he in some way contributes, that there may be a presumption that the outside limit of the worth of saving his life is the entirety of his expected future earnings. It does seem that if we ask ourselves the worth of saving somebody else's life, and he is somebody who personally makes no difference to us, his net contribution to total production may be the outside limit to what we can interest ourselves in. But when we ask the question, what is it worth to him to increase the likelihood of his own survival (or to us, our own survival), it is hard to see that his (our) future lifetime earnings provide either an upper or lower limit.

There is no reason to suppose that what a man would pay to eliminate some specific probability, P, of his own death is more than, less than, or equal to, P times his discounted expected earnings. In fact there is no reason to suppose that a man's future earnings, discounted in any pertinent fashion, bear any particular relation to what he would pay to reduce some likelihood of his own death.

I am not saying that a man's expected lifetime income is irrelevant to an estimate of what he would pay to reduce fatalities in his age group. But discounted lifetime earnings are relevant only in the

[9] Readers with small children will appreciate that this is a theoretical paper.

way that they are relevant to ordinary decisions about consumption, saving, quitting a job or buying a house. They are part of the income and wealth data that go into the decisions. Their connection is a functional one, not an accounting one. What a man would pay to avoid death, to avoid pain, or to modernize his kitchen, is a function of present and future income but need bear no particular adding-up relation.[10]

Let me guess. If we ask what it is worth to them to reduce by a certain number of percentage points, over some period, the likelihood that they will die, they will find it worth more than that percentage of the discounted value of their expected lifetime income. Arithmetically, if we tell a man that the likelihood of his accidental death over the next three years is 9 percent and we can reduce this to 6 percent by some measure we propose, and ask him what it is worth to reduce the probability of his death by 3 percent over this period (with no change in his mortality table after that period), my conjecture is it is worth to him a permanent reduction of perhaps 5 percent, possibly 10 percent, in his income.

This is conjecture. It is based on conversational inquiry among a score of respondents, and relates to fathers in professional income classes. The reader can add himself to my sample by examining what his own answer to the query would be.

DEATH ITSELF VERSUS ANXIETY. In conducting this inquiry it is important to make the distinction mentioned earlier between death itself and anxiety about death. If one asks, for example, what it is worth to eliminate the fatality of certain childhood diseases (or—taking for illustration a problem that is commensurate with the problem of death—to reduce the danger of congenital defects and foetal injuries that cause infant deformities), he may discover that he is as preoccupied with the anxiety that goes with the risk as with the low-

---

[10] People get hung up, sometimes, on the apparent anomaly that if a man would yield two percent of his income to eliminate a one percent risk of death, he'd have to give up twice his entire income to save his own life—which he cannot do if his creditors are on their toes. But he doesn't have to. I'd pay my dentist an hour's income to avoid a minute's intense pain—even to prevent somebody else's pain—without having to know what I'd do if confronted with a lifetime of intense pain. This is why the worth of saving a life is but a mathematical construct when applied to an individual's decision on the reduction of small risks; it has literal meaning only if we mean that a hundred men would give up the equivalent of two incomes to save one (unidentified) life among them.

probability event itself.

A special difficulty of evaluating the anxiety and the event together is that they probably do not occur in fixed proportions. That is, their quantitative connection with the reduction of risk may be quite dissimilar. To be specific, there are good reasons for considering the worth of risk-reduction to be proportionate to the absolute reduction of risk, for considering a reduction from 10 percent to 9 percent about equivalent to a reduction from 5 percent to 4 percent. There is no reason for the anxiety to follow any such rational rule. Even a cool-headed consumer who rationally examines his own or his family's anxiety will probably have to recognize that anxiety and obsession are psychological phenomena that cannot be brought under any such rational control. If they could be, through an act of judgment, an act of self-hypnosis, a ban on disquieting conversations, or the avoidance of factual and fictional stimuli, through surgery or through drugs, the anxiety could perhaps be wholly disposed of. A family that lives with a "high" low probability of death in the family, high enough to cause anxiety but low enough to make it unlikely, may benefit as much from relief as from longevity if the risk can be eliminated.

The anxiety may depend on the absolute level of risk and the frequency and vividness of stimuli. There may be thresholds below which the risk is ignored and above which it is a preoccupation. It may depend on whether the risk is routine and continuous or concentrated in episodes. It undoubtedly depends on what people believe about risks, and has no direct connection with what the risks truly are. The existence of one source of risk may affect the psychological reaction to another source of risk. Furthermore, the anxiety will be related to the duration of suspense and can even be inversely correlated with the risk of death itself.

In other words, decision theory, probability theory, and a rational calculus of risks and values will be pertinent—not compelling, but surely pertinent—to the avoidance of the event of death, but may have little or no relevance to choices involving fear, anxiety, and relief. People may, however, by engaging in enough sophisticated analysis of risk, change their sensitivity to the perception of risk, possibly but not surely bringing the discomfort into a more nearly proportionate relation to the risk itself.

There is a special reason why it is hard to separate the anxiety from the event itself. A person is unlikely to have pure or raw preferences involving small risks of serious events. He does not know what the elimination of a .0002 chance of death is worth to himself unless he can find some way of comparing it with the other terms of his choice, of making it commensurate with the other things that money can buy. One can hardly have a feeling about a .0002 chance of death quite the way he has a feeling about pain in the dental chair, the loss of an hour in a traffic jam, or even the loss of a favorite tree in his yard. It takes a little arithmetic even to remember that 1 chance in 5,000 is 1/50th of 1 chance in 100, 20 times 1 chance in 100,000. A person may have to explore until he finds a magnitude of risk about which he has, or can imagine his way into, a feeling of the kind we associate with preferences and tastes. The risk may have to be brought above some threshold where the size has some feel or familiarity, where the intensity of his feeling is too strong to escape his efforts to respond to it. If he can find a favorite level of risk, a familiar bench mark, a degree of risk that he can in some way perceive directly rather than through pencil and paper, there may then be a possibility of scaling the risk and its worth to find a proper or rational valuation of smaller or larger risks. The anxiety associated with the risk, though, may be quite unamenable to any such scaling.

Scaling of Risks

There is a good case, though not necessarily persuasive, for scaling risks. It is illustrated as follows.[11] A person is asked what risk of

[11] The "scaling" principle sketched here follows from modern decision (utility) theory as presented in R. Duncan Luce and Howard Raiffa, *Games and Decisions: Introduction and Critical Survey* (John Wiley, 1957), pp. 23-31, and especially reflects the authors' assumptions #4 (substitutability) and #2 (reduction of compound lotteries). It is consistent with the conclusions reached by Armen A. Alchian, "The Meaning of Utility Measurement," *American Economic Review* (March 1953), pp. 26-50, especially p. 43. It can be simply construed from the "sure-thing" principle of Leonard J. Savage, *The Foundations of Statistics* (John Wiley, 1954), pp. 21 ff. It is being used here, though, to cover an irreversibility in the "continuity" assumption (#3) of Luce and Raiffa. That continuity assumption implies that the certainty of any finite loss of income is equivalent to some probability of death; it does not say that the consumer can identify some finite loss of income, the certainty of which is equivalent to some specified probability of death. If, though, he can identify a loss of income the certainty of which is equivalent to some specified probability of some specified larger loss of income, it may be possible to fill in these gaps in the con-

death is equivalent to certain blindness—at what risk of death he would prefer certain blindness, at what risk of death he would rather run the risk than be surely blind—and his point of indifference between the two is found. Since this is a decision that can arise, it is presumed that a man can answer the question—not offhand, but after some study and advice. Suppose he says that certain blindness balances out at about a 1/10 chance of death; he would run the risk of death to avoid blindness if it were less than 1/10, not if it were more than 1/10. He is then informed that a 1/10 chance of blindness must be equivalent to 1 chance in 100 of death. If he denies this, insisting that what holds for large probabilities does not hold for small ones, or that certainty is different from risk, the first question is rephrased as follows: If he had to choose between sure blindness and some risk of death, what risk of death would be equivalent to certain blindness. He may say he does not know and cannot find out because a hypothetical question will not motivate a meaningful answer. To make it meaningful, he is told that it may be necessary to incur some fatal risk to avoid blindness; there is, for instance, a surgical operation that cures certain kinds of blindness but involves a certain risk of death; there is some likelihood that this person will prove upon further diagnosis to be faced with that choice and he must make his decision now in case the contingency arises. If he can answer this contingent question—if he can say for the event that he must choose between certain blindness and some risk of death, an event with a yet unspecified probability, what risk of death he is just willing to incur to avoid otherwise certain blindness—then he has in effect chosen between some (unspecified) probability of blindness and a probability of death equal to that same probability multiplied by the contingent risk he said he was just willing to incur. He is now told that there is a 50:50 chance, or that there is one chance in 20, that the diagnosis will make his contingent answer relevant; if he lets his answer stand, he has, in effect, stated his indifference between a 0.5 chance of blindness and a 0.05 chance of death, and also between a 0.05 chance of blindness and a 0.005 chance of death.

The argument may not be compelling, but it helps in establishing

sumers' utility map. Thus we have a technique for making roundabout comparisons when the individual is unable to make a direct comparison. It may or may not be helpful.

at least a presumption in favor of a scaling principle that, at first glance, might have appeared implausible.[12]

What has been said about anxiety, though, could interfere. It will probably not interfere much if the outcome is to be known soon; the discomfort of suspense probably depends on the duration, and ought to be negligible if the man will know the outcome the next day. It could be considerable if he will not know for a year or two and if he cannot keep his family from knowing the kind of risk he has accepted.

AN ILLUSTRATIVE APPLICATION. Imperfect as it is, this argument can be a tool for helping some people think about unfamiliar probabilities. A man who cannot come to grips with 1 chance in 1,000 of death may be able to come to grips with 1 chance in 10, or vice versa. He is asked, for example, what reduction in income after taxes he would incur in perpetuity to avoid a 10 percent chance of death (his own or somebody's he cares about). Suppose he says that he will give up one-third of his income to avoid an immediate 10 percent chance of dying. How can it be calculated from this what he might give up to avoid 1 chance in 1,000 of dying? Rather, how can he tell from the answer he has given what his answer ought to be to the question containing the 0.001 risk? Dividing both figures by 100, he would give 1/300 of his income. But if successive increments of income lost are of progressively larger concern to a man, a loss of 0.33 percent of income will not look one-hundredth as bad to him as the loss of 33 percent of his income. He might, however, be asked what fraction of his income he would give up to avoid a one-tenth chance of losing one-third of his income. This is an ordinary insurance decision, which he can presumably make (and he may be expected to give an answer that exceeds one-thirtieth of his income). The process could be repeated for a one-hundredth chance of losing a third of his income, but possibly it is not necessary when it is a question of dealing with increments on the order of a few percent. Suppose he says that he would give up 5 percent of his income to avoid a 1/10 chance of losing 33 percent. Is he willing to give up about 0.5 per-

[12] As a behavioral proposition, the "scaling" principle was not supported by answers, given perhaps in haste, on a brief questionnaire circulated among members of the Brookings Conference. I remain sanguine that many, perhaps most, of the respondents could be persuaded that "inconsistent" answers were inconclusive; still, giving consistent answers is much easier than giving right answers.

cent to avoid a 10 percent chance of losing 5 percent? Not exactly; he may say approximately, perhaps somewhat more—say 0.6 percent. There is now a series of statements about bets he would place, suggesting that he considers the loss of 0.6 percent of his income (after taxes) in perpetuity about equivalent to 1 chance in 1,000 of immediate death.[13]

Let it be assumed that the man is in his early forties, with expected lifetime earnings to accrue on a rising scale over twenty-five more years. Discounting this income at something like the mortgage rate of interest—lower than the rate on consumer credit, higher than the earnings on conservative retirement plans, say 7 percent—its capitalized value would be about ten times a year's income; 0.6 percent of that is about 6 percent of a year's income.

If similar answers were obtained from 1,000 men of similar incomes and ages, it could be concluded that they would together rather give up the equivalent of six discounted lifetime incomes than suffer one immediate accidental death. ("Accidental death" is used to keep the arithmetic simple; the idea is to leave the population unchanged in its life expectancy.) In the age group of our man, that turns out to be about sixty annual incomes. Does this look high? Does it look low? It is up to the reader what figure he finds plausible, either for himself or for a man interviewed at random at the airport. (It is up to the reader both as an analytical reader and as a consumer of life-saving programs.) It is also up to the reader, or to the man at the airport, whether it is of any help to break the decision into a series of comparisons like this.

Try now a comparison. Turn the choice around and ask the man what compensation he demands for running some additional risk. Should there be, for small increments, the same figure of worth? Would he run an additional chance in a thousand for a bonus equal to 6 percent of a year's income? Should the answer be symmetrical? Probably not for the anxiety, not for the superstitious element in gambling, not for any special sense of regret that might ensue if the death could actually be identified—in case it occurred—with his choice to incur it. Otherwise, although symmetry cannot be demand-

---

[13] This technique, whatever its strengths and weaknesses, does *not* treat the marginal utility of income as constant. It never "scales" income, or any other quantitative variable except pure probabilities.

ed, it should probably be expected, or at least be treated as one more test.

As a check—after the price has been set by examining small increments in a small risk—the sample of a thousand men could be asked whether they would in the end rather take the cash as compensation. Rather than pay six lifetime incomes in total to avert one death among the thousand, might they prefer to run the risk and put the proceeds into life insurance? That would compensate the bereaved family with a sixfold rise in its income.

Or they might want to split the difference: to pay half the price they originally decided on, leave the risk intact, and triple the income of the family of the man who dies. If so, their best buy is life insurance; they gave a wrong answer in haste, and the exercise should be repeated. (If they retort that they are already insured up to that level, the inference is that their original answer was a financial calculation of what it was worth to save the cost of insurance.)

This line of reasoning leads to a distasteful question—one, though, that may be worth asking along with all the others in the attempt to help a man identify his own preferences. Is there some level of adequate compensation for the family? It is distasteful to ask how much monetary compensation a family needs in order to suffer no long-term loss in welfare when a member of the family dies; and an answer that makes a person priceless cannot be rejected. Symmetry cannot be adduced to prove that an infinite "selling" price would mean an infinite "buying" price. That is, a family that would not give up all its income to save one member can nevertheless refuse to consider any economic compensation adequate for the loss of a member.

But a person can run a risk for cash. And he may prefer, if he runs the risk, to trade the cash for some still larger amount invested in life insurance, that is, for a greater "expected value" correlated with death itself. If so, compensation tends to be commensurable with life-saving at the margin of small risks, and provides a helpful check on the consistency of a series of choices.

At this point, reexamination of both the life-saving decision and the life-insurance decision may be needed; apparent inconsistency can mean that either decision was out of line with the other.[14]

[14] Both introspectively and in conversation I have been surprised, in writing this paper, at how far life insurance can go toward meeting the demand of middle-aged fathers, after some sustained reflection, for their own mortality reduction. I was sur-

Inquiry suggests that, to earners of income in college-professor brackets, saving one among their lives may be worth anywhere from 10 to 100 times a year's income. Or, to put it in absolute terms, professional people with earnings in the range from $20,000 to $30,000, which would include senior officials of government, professors at major universities, successful engineers, doctors, and lawyers, might value a life to be chosen at random among themselves at something like a million dollars. In crude numbers this could mean that a Boeing 707 full of professional business people might value their own lives in a way that would make prevention of the fatal crash of a (yet unidentified) full airplane worth about $100 million. This is but an order of magnitude; any figure between $30 million and $300 million would fit the crude data. The reader is invited to supply his own figure for his class of passengers.

DISCRIMINATING FOR WEALTH. A special matter of policy is bound to arise here. If a government is to initiate programs that may save the lives of the poor or the rich, is it worth more to save the rich than to save the poor? The answer is evidently yes if the question means, is it worth more to the rich to reduce the risk to their own lives than it is to the poor to reduce the risk to their own lives. Just as the rich will pay more to avoid wasting an hour in traffic or five hours on a train, it is worth more to them to reduce the risk of their own death or the death of somebody they care about. It is worth more because they are richer than the poor. A hospital that can save either of two lives, but not both, has no reason to save the richer of the two on these grounds; but an expensive athletic club can afford better safety equipment than a cheap gymnasium; the rich can afford safer stoves in their homes than the poor; and a rich country can spend more to save lives than a poor one.

OTHER MEMBERS OF THE FAMILY. Most of this discussion has been focused on the man who earns a living for his family. To deal comprehensively with the subject, the problem should be recalculated from his point of view, but putting wife or child at risk, and from his wife's point of view, putting her own life or one of the children's at risk. (To get a proper feel for the subject, the children might be given

---

prised, some years ago, at how helpful logic could be in turning up fallacies in my own thinking about insurance. See Robert Eisner and Robert H. Strotz, "Flight Insurance and the Theory of Choice," *Journal of Political Economy* (August 1961), pp. 355-68.

a chance to express their views; their immaturity should not offhand make what they say irrelevant.)

There is a qualification about families and children: the values placed on lives by members of the family, as well as the costs to society involved in somebody's death, are not additive within the family. If death takes a mother, a father, and two children, each from a different family, the consequences are different from the death of a family of four in a single accident. This is true both of the costs to society, because of the differential impact of dependents' care, and of the personal valuations within the family.[15]

Conclusion

We have looked now at several ways to approach the worth of saving a statistical life.We have had to distinguish between the life and the livelihood that goes with it. We have had to distinguish between the loss of that livelihood to the consuming unit—the family— and the loss of the share that went to other members of the economy —the taxpayers, insurance policyholders, and kin. We have considered some of the ways that reduction of the risk of death differs from other commodities and services that consumers buy.

To recapitulate: (1) Death is an awesome and indivisible event that goes but one to a customer in a single large size. (2) For many people it is a low-probability event except on special occasions when the momentary likelihood becomes serious. (3) Its effect on a family is something that many consumers have little direct acquaintance with. (4) In an already advanced economy many of the ways of reducing the risk of death are necessarily public programs, budgetary or regulatory. (5) Reduction of risk is often a by-product of other programs that lead to health, comfort, or the security of property, though there are some identifiable programs of which the saving of lives is the main result. (6) Death is an insurable event. (7) Death is more of a family event than most other casualties that one might like to avert; its analysis requires more than perfunctory recognition

---

[15] If a family of four *must* fly, and has a choice among four aircraft of which it is known that one is somewhat defective but not known which one it is, it should be possible to persuade them to fly together. "Society's" interest, in support of the family's interest, should be to see that they are permitted to. Society's economic interest in this case will usually coincide.

that the family is the consuming unit, the income-sharing unit, and the welfare-sharing unit.

Still, though these characteristics are important, they do not necessarily make the avoidance of death a wholly different kind of objective from others to promote the general welfare. While it is important to be aware of how the avoidance of death differs from other programs, it is equally important to keep in mind in what respects it is similar. Society may indeed sometimes express its profoundest moral values in the way it deals with life and death, but in a good many programs to reduce fatalities society merely expresses the amount of trouble people will go to, or the money people will spend, to reduce the risks they run. There is enough mystery already about death, not to exaggerate the mystery.

A good part of society's interest in the livelihood that may be lost is no different from its interest in saving a man's barn or his drugstore. What are the costs of a fire that burns property? Everything that was said about taxes, saving, insurance, and contributions to the United Fund is equally pertinent to this case. The fact that an appraiser can value the barn more readily than a vocational analyst can appraise a man's livelihood simplifies the problem in only one dimension: estimating the value of the barn is only a point of departure for tracing out society's interest. As a statistical aggregate, the national wealth goes down if I lose my home and furniture, but who cares except me? If my bank cares, or my insurance company, or the taxing authorities of my town, we are on the track of some interests that matter. But society has no direct interest in the national wealth. It is not owned collectively, not in the United States.

What makes the barn or shop easier to evaluate than a life (not livelihood) is that it is less difficult to guess what it is worth to the man who owns it. Its replacement cost sets an upper limit. Even that, though, does not directly tell the worth of a small increment in a small probability of material destruction; it is the insurability of the structure, with a policy that pays off in the same currency with which one buys replacement, that makes it possible to estimate the worth to a man of an incremental change in the risk of fire, collision, or windstorm.

The difficult part of the problem is not evaluating the worth of a man's livelihood to the different people who have an interest in it, but the worth of his life to himself or to whoever will pay to prolong it.

This is what is not insurable in terms that permit replacement. This is the consumer interest in a unique and irreplaceable good. His livelihood he can usually insure, not exactly but approximately, sharing the loss and making it a matter of diffuse economic interest; it is valuing his life that poses the problem.

And the difficulty is not just that, as with so many government budgetary and regulatory programs, the government has to weigh the divergent interests of various beneficiaries and taxpayers. Nor is it that, as with so many government programs, the government has to investigate how much the program is worth to people. The main problem is that people have difficulty knowing what it is worth to themselves, cannot easily answer questions about it, and may object to being asked. Market evidence is unlikely to reveal much.

Dealing with small changes in small risks makes the evaluation more casual and takes the pricelessness and the pretentiousness out of a potentially awesome choice. The question is whether the consumer, at this more casual level of straightforward risk reduction, has any sovereign tastes (or thinks he has) and can be induced to place his bets as calmly as he would fasten a seat belt or buy a lock for his door. If it appears upon inquiry—an inquiry that the man participates in—that he has been casually deceiving himself that his decisions are the right ones, it is necessary to decide whether that is his privilege and he wants it respected, or he should be goaded into an agonizing reappraisal or the reappraisal should be made for him. Scaring people is usually bad, and the airlines can hardly be expected to cooperate—or their passengers either—in a survey that quickens a man's appreciation of danger at the moment he settles into his seat.

In the end there may be a philosophical question whether government should try to adapt itself to what consumer tastes would be if the consumers could be induced to have those tastes and to articulate them. There may be a strong temptation to do the consumer's thinking for him and to come out with a different answer. Should one try to be guided by what the consumer would choose, when in fact the consumer may refuse to make the choice at all? If a doctor is asked to make a grave medical decision that a patient, or a patient's spouse, declines to make for himself, is the doctor supposed to guess what the patient, or the patient's spouse, would have decided if he'd had to decide for himself? Or is the doctor to decide as he thinks he would himself decide if he were in the patient's position? Or is he to make a welfare decision for the whole family or some other small society? Should the doctor ask the patient which among these criteria he wants the doctor to use, or does that merely upset the patient and lead to the doctor's having to decide how to decide on the criterion?

The gravity of decisions about life-saving can be dispelled by letting the consumer (taxpayer, lobbyist, questionnaire respondent) express himself on the comparatively unexciting subject of small increments in small risks, acting as though he has preferences even if in fact he does not. People do it for life insurance; they could do it for life-saving. The fact that they may not do it well, or may not quite know what they are doing as they make the decision, may not bother them and need not disfranchise them in the exercise of consumer-taxpayer sovereignty.

As an economist I have to keep reminding myself that consumer sovereignty is not just a metaphor and is not justified solely by reference to the unseen hand. It derives with even greater authority from another principle of about the same vintage, "no taxation without representation." Welfare economics establishes the convenience of consumer sovereignty and its compatibility with economic efficiency; the sovereignty itself is typically established by arms, martyrdom, boycott, or some principles held to be self-evident. And it includes the inalienable right of the consumer to make his own mistakes.

Still, if it is a government program, not a market competition between buses and airplanes or electric and gas furnaces, the decisions will be made vicariously, with perhaps some attention to evidence of consumer tastes, but only some.

Maybe a sample of civil servants or legislators, perhaps under the guidance of the Brookings Institution, can be induced to take the plunge, explore their values, and share their wisdom. But if they can, what is wanted is not their evaluation of other people's lives, nor an expression of their responsibility for the lives of their constituents. They must speak for themselves, or for themselves and others like them, when it is their own lives that are at risk. And they must not be in a mood to save lives but in a mood to change risks, usually small risks. We often know who died for lack of safety; we rarely know who lived because of it. What the government buys, it if buys health and safety, is a reduction in individual risks. The lives saved are usually a mathematical construct, a statistical equivalent to what, at the level of the individual, is expressible as a longevity estimate but not a finite extension of life.

[2]
Evaluation of Life and Limb: A Theoretical Approach

E. J. Mishan

London School of Economics and American University

None of the existing methods of evaluating loss or saving life, or assessing an increase or reduction in accidents resulting from investment projects, is satisfactory for a number of reasons. This is so chiefly because they are all inconsistent with the Pareto base of existing allocation theory and benefit-cost analysis. Strict application of the Pareto principle to changes in accidents and fatalities involves a calculation of the compensating variation associated with the changes in risk bearing regarded as external effects. Several of these external effects are discussed at length.

As cost-benefit studies grow in popularity, it is increasingly important to make proper allowance for losses or gains arising from changes in the incidence of death, disablement, or disease caused by the operation of new projects or developments. What is at issue is not the reliability of the current estimates of economic gains or losses arising from the saving or losing of life or health but the appropriateness of the ideal or conceptual measures about which, so far, there is no consensus among economists. I propose, therefore, first to argue that the more familiar concepts employed in evaluating the loss or saving of life are all unsatisfactory and, second, by referring to the basic rationale of economic calculation, to determine how such losses and gains should, in principle, be evaluated.

Since the analysis of saving life is symmetrical with that of losing it, it will simplify the exposition if, initially, we confine ourselves to the analysis of loss of life and limb—or, more briefly, to loss of life alone—indicating the necessary extensions in the latter part of the paper.

I

1. Despite repeated expressions of dissatisfaction with the method, the most common way of calculating the economic worth of a person's life

and, therefore, the loss to the economy consequent upon his decease is that of discounting to the present the person's expected future earnings. A precise expression for the loss to the economy calculated on this method would be L_1, where

$$L_1 = \sum_{t=\tau}^{\infty} Y_t P_\tau^t (1 + r)^{-(t-\tau)} .$$

The Y_t is the expected gross earnings of (or, alternatively, value added by) the person during the tth year, exclusive of any yields from his ownership of nonhuman capital.[1] The P_τ^t is the probability in the current, or rth, year of the person being alive during the tth year, and r is the social rate of discount expected to rule during the tth year. This kind of calculation is occasionally supplemented by a suggestion that auxiliary calculations be made in order to take account of the suffering of the victim, the loss of his utility due to his demise, and/or of the bereavement of his family.[2] More recently, and as an example of the economist's finesse, it has been proposed that such calculations be supplemented by the cost of "premature burial"[3]—the idea being that the present discounted value of the funeral expenses is higher if they are incurred sooner owing to an untimely death.

2. A second method, which might be thought of as more refined than the first, is that of calculating the present discounted value of the losses over time accruing to *others only* as a result of the death of the person at age τ. A precise expression for the loss to the economy based on this method would be L_2, where:

$$L_2 = \sum_{t=\tau}^{\infty} P_\tau^t (Y_t - C_t)(1 + r)^{-(t-\tau)},$$

where C_t is the personal expenditure of the individual during the tth period that is expected at time τ. This kind of measure (sometimes referred

---

[1] For the returns on his (nonhuman) assets continue after his death, or during his disablement.

[2] For example, see Kneese (1966, p. 77) and Ridker (1967, p. 34). The suggestions, needless to remark, have not been taken up. Presumably they are made in response to an uneasy conscience about the methods actually being employed.

[3] The expression occurs in Ridker's book (1967) on the costs of pollution. For those prone to morbid curiosity, the formula used is on page 39, and takes the form

$$C_a = C_o \left[1 - \sum_{n=a}^{\infty} \left(\frac{P_a^n}{(1 + r)^{n-a}} \right) \right],$$

where C_a is the present value of the net expected gain from delaying burial at age a; C_o is the cost of burial; P_a^n is the probability that an individual age a will die at age n, and r is the discount rate. It is not impossible that these calculations were made with tongue in cheek, and, if so, it is perhaps an oversight on his part that he omitted a countervailing consideration; namely, that if the unfortunate person died at a very early age, some useful savings might be effected from the lower cost of a smaller coffin.

to as being based on the "net output" approach in order to distinguish it from the "gross output" approach associated with the L_1 measure), although occasionally mentioned in the literature—for instance, by Devons (1961, p. 107) and Ridker (1967, p. 36)—has not been employed apparently because of the assumed policy implications.

3. A third possible method would repudiate any direct calculation of the loss of potential earnings or spending. Instead, it would approach the problem from a "social" point of view. Since society, through its political processes, does in fact take decisions on investment expenditures that occasionally increase or reduce the number of deaths, an implicit value of human life can be calculated. This approach receives occasional mention—for instance, by Fromm (1965, p. 193) and by Schelling (1968, p. 147)—and, indeed, the appeal to the political, or democratic, process is sometimes invoked to provide guidance on broader issues.[4]

4. The insurance principle is a departure from any of the aforementioned methods. Predicated on the premium a man is willing to pay, and the probability of his being killed as a result of engaging in some specific activity, it is thought possible to calculate the value a man sets on his life. An example is given by Fromm (1965, p. 194).

II

Each of these four possible methods of measuring the loss of life is now briefly appraised.

Method 1, turning on the loss of potential future earnings, can be rationalized only if the criterion adopted in any economic reorganization turns on the value of its contribution to GNP, or, more accurately, to net national product. But although financial journalists manage to convey the contrary impression, maximizing GNP is not an acceptable goal of economic policy. Notwithstanding its usage, most writers have mental reservations about its validity and tend to regard it as only part of the total measurement. For instance, Schelling (1968) makes a distinction

---

[4] Indeed, Rothenberg (1961, pp. 309–36) ends his examination of social welfare criteria by proposing that the democratic process itself be regarded as such a criterion. More recently, Nath (1969, pp. 216–17) proposes that the task of the economist be limited to that of revealing the locus of "efficient" economic production possibilities available to society, leaving it to democracy to select the collection of goods it wishes. If one favors a majority decision rule or some other democratic decision rule for top level choices, the question must arise: On what grounds is this decision rule withheld (in favor of the potential Pareto criterion) at lower levels of *optima*—for instance, in generating a locus of "efficient" collection of goods? A movement from a nonefficient point *inside* the boundary to an efficient point *on* the boundary of production possibilities can claim no more than can a movement from a top-level nonoptimal boundary point to a top-level optimal boundary point. Both of such movements have distributional implications, both meet the "Scitovsky" criterion, and both may be negated by the Kaldor-Hicks criterion.

between the value of likelihood, which is the L_1 measure, and the value of life, which poses a perplexing and possibly unsolvable problem.

The so-called net output method (2) might seem, at first glance, more acceptable than the gross output method. For, taking a cold-blooded attitude, what matters to the rest of society is simply the resulting loss, or gain, to society following the death of one or more of its members. This ex post approach, however, appears to strike some writers as either absurd or dangerous.[5] If accepted, it certainly follows that the death of any person whose L_2 measure is negative confers a net benefit on society. And this category of persons would certainly include all retired people irrespective of their ownership of property. Yet, from this undeniable inference, no dread policy implications follow. If the method were satisfactory on economic grounds, the inference would not, of itself, provide any reason for rejecting it. But the method is not satisfactory for the simple reason that it has no regard for the feelings of the potential decedents. It restricts itself to the interest only of the surviving members of society: it ignores society ex ante and concentrates wholly on society ex post.

As for the method (3) which would build on implicit values placed on human life by the political process, the justification appears somewhat circular even when we ignore the political realities of Western democracies. Assuming that democratic voting alone determines whether or not a particular investment project or part of a project is to be adopted, the idea of deriving quantitative values from the political process is clearly contrary to the idea of deriving them from an independent economic criterion. Where the outcome of the political debate calls upon the economist to provide a quantitative evaluation of the project under consideration, the economist fails to meet his brief insofar as he abandons the attempt to calculate any aspect of the project by reference to an economic criterion and, instead, attempts to extricate figures from previous political decisions.[6] By recourse to a method that refers a question, or part of a question, received from the political process back again to the political process, the economist appears to be concealing some deficiency in the relevant data or some weakness in the logic of his criteria.

Finally, there is method 4 based on the insurance principle. This has about it a superficial plausibility, enough, at any rate, to attract some attention. An early attempt, for instance, was made by Fromm (1965,

---

[5] For example, Devons (1961, p. 108) concludes ironically: "Indeed if we could only kill off enough old people we could show a net gain on accidents as a whole!" As for Ridker (1967, p. 36), the net output method "suggests that society should not interfere with the death of a person whose net value is negative."

[6] Which is not to deny that the economist's criterion or criteria—although independent of the outcome of any particular political process that is sanctioned by the constitution—must be vindicated ultimately by reference to value judgments widely held within the community. The reader interested in this aspect is referred to Mishan (1969a, pp. 13–23).

pp. 193–96) to attribute a value for loss of life raised on the implied assumption of a straight-line relationship between the probability of a person being killed and the sum that he would pay to cover the risk. If, therefore, the premium y corresponding to the additional risk p is known, the value he places on his life is to be reckoned as y/p. Thus, if a man would pay \$100 to reduce his chance of being killed by 1 percent—say, from an existing chance of one-twentieth to two-fiftieths the value he places on his life is to be estimated as \$10,000. (Or, to use Fromm's own calculation, if the probability of being killed in air travel were to be reduced from the existing figure of 0.0000017 per trip of 500 miles to zero, a person who values his life at \$400,000 should be willing to pay sixty-eight cents to reduce the existing risk to zero.)

The implied assumption of linearity, which has it that a man who accepts \$100,000 for an assignment offering him a four-to-one chance of survival will agree to go to certain death for \$500,000, is implausible, to say the least. And, indeed, this linearity assumption was later criticized by Fromm himself (1968, p. 174) when it was incidentally posited by Schelling (1968). But even if it were both plausible and proved, the insurance principle does not yield us the required valuation. For the insurance policy makes provision, in the event of a man's death, only for compensation to *others*. Thus, the amount of insurance a man takes out may be interpreted as a reflection, *inter alia*, of his concern for his family and dependents but hardly as an index of the value he sets on his own life.[7] A bachelor with no dependents could have no reason to take out flight insurance, notwithstanding the fact that he could be as reluctant as the next man to depart this fugacious life at short notice.

III

The crucial objection to each of these four methods, however, is that not one of them is consistent with the basic rationale of the economic calculus used in cost-benefit analysis. If we are concerned, as we are in all allocative problems, with increasing society's satisfaction in some sense, and if, in addition, we eschew interpersonal comparisons of satisfactions, we can always be guided in the ranking of alternative economic arrangements

[7] An ingenious paper by Eisner and Strotz (1961), after some theorizing on the basis of the Neumann-Morgenstern axioms about the optimal amount of insurance a person should buy, addresses itself to the question of why people continue to buy air-accident insurance when ordinary life insurance is cheaper. They suggest, among other things, that flight insurance could be a gamble (related formally to the increasing marginal-utility segment of the income-utility curve), and they point also to the existence of imperfect knowledge, imperfect markets, and inertia. However, the paper does not, and is presumably not intended to, throw any light on this question of the valuation of human life. The observation that a man does not insure his life against some specific contingency cannot be taken as evidence that he is indifferent as between being alive and being dead.

by the notion of a Pareto improvement—an improvement such that at least one person is made better off and nobody is made worse off. A *potential* Pareto improvement,[8] one in which the net gains *can* so be distributed that at least one person is made better off, with none being made worse off, provides an alternative criterion, or definition, of social gain. This alternative, as it happens, provides the rationale of all familiar allocative propositions in economics and, therefore, the rationale of all cost-benefit calculations.[9]

When the full range of its economic effects is brought into the calculus, the introduction of a specific investment project will make some of the community of n members better off on balance, some worse off on balance, the remainder being indifferent to it. If the jth person is made better off, a compensating variation (CV) measures the full extent of his improvement, this CV being a maximum sum V_j he will pay rather than forego the project, the sum being prefixed by a positive sign. Per contra, if the jth person is made worse off by the introduction of the project, his CV measures the full decline of his welfare as a minimal sum V_j he will accept to put up with the project, this sum being prefixed by a negative sign.[10] If, then, in response to the introduction of this specific project, the aggregate sum

$$\sum_j^n V_j > 0$$

(where j runs from 1 to n)—if, that is, the algebraic sum of all n individual CV's is positive—there is a potential Pareto improvement, its positive value being interpreted as the excess of benefits over costs arising from the introduction of the project.[11]

[8] A "potential Pareto improvement" is an alternative and simpler nomenclature than "hypothetical compensation test." The problems associated with the concept are important, but need not concern us here if we accept the fact that cost-benefit analyses take place within a partial context, one in which changes in the prices of all the nonproject goods can be ignored. If this much is granted, the relevant individuals' compensating variations, which is what we are after, will be uniquely determined.

[9] For the arguments that tend to this conclusion, see Mishan (1969, pp. 66–73).

[10] These sums may be calculated as annual transfers or as capital sums according to the method being used in the cost-benefit study. Since the flow of costs and benefits is to be valued at a point of time, consistency would require that the CVs also be reckoned as a capital sum at that point of time. If there are no external effects of saving for future generations, as posited by Marglin (1963), the existence of imperfect capital markets will result in different rates of time preference among the persons concerned. In that case, capitalizing their CVs reckoned as annual sums at some single rate of discount will result in corresponding capitalized CVs which would differ from those chosen directly by these same persons, which latter sums should, of course, prevail.

[11] Within the same broad context, and allowing for sufficient divisibility in the construction of such projects, the corresponding rule necessary to determine the optimal

EVALUATION OF HUMAN LIFE   693

Consistency with the criterion of a potential Pareto improvement and, therefore, consistency with the principle of evaluation in cost-benefit analyses would require that the loss of a person's life be valued by reference to his *CV*; by reference, that is, to the minimum sum he is prepared to accept in exchange for its surrender. For unless a project that is held to be responsible for, say, an additional 1,000 deaths annually can show an excess of benefits over costs *after* meeting the compensatory sums necessary to restore the welfare of these 1,000 victims, it is not possible to make all members of the community better off by a redistribution of the net gains. A potential Pareto improvement cannot, then, be achieved, and the project in question ought not to be admitted.

If the argument is accepted, however, the requirements of consistency might seem to be highly restrictive. Since an increase in the annual number of deaths can be confidently predicted in connection with a number of particular developments—those, for example, which contribute to an increase in ground and air traffic—such developments would no longer appear as economically feasible. For it would not surprise us to discover that, in ordinary circumstances,[12] no sum of money is large enough to compensate a man for the loss of his life.

In conditions of certainty, the logic of the above proposition is unassailable. If, in ordinary circumstances, we face a person with the choice of continuing his life in the usual way or of ending it at noon the next day, a sum large enough to persuade him to choose the latter course of action may not exist. And, indeed, if the development in question unavoidably entailed the death of this specific person or, more generally, a number of specific persons, it is highly unlikely that any conceivable excess benefit over cost, *calculated in the absence of these fatalities*, would warrant its undertaking on the potential Pareto criterion.

It is never the case, however, that a specific person, or a number of specific persons, can be designated in advance as being those who are certain to be killed if a particular project is undertaken.[13] All that can be predicted, although with a high degree of confidence, is that out of a total

---

output of such projects—or, in short periods, the optimal output of the goods of the existing project—takes the simple form that

$$\sum_{j}^{n} v_j = 0 \, ,$$

where v_j is the *CV* of the *j*th person in response to a marginal increment in the size of the industry or (in the short period) the size of its output.

[12] If a man and his family were so destitute and their prospects so hopeless that one or more members were likely to die of starvation, or at least to suffer from acute deprivation, then the man might well be persuaded to sacrifice himself for the sake of his family. But without dependents or close and needy friends, the inducement to sacrifice himself for others is not strong.

[13] Cf. Schelling's remarks (1968, pp. 142–46).

of n members in the community an additional x members per annum will be killed (and, say, an additional ten x members will be seriously injured). In the absence, therefore, of any breakdown of the circumstances surrounding the additional number of accidents to be expected, the increment of risk of being killed imposed each year on any one member of the community can be taken as x/n (and $10x/n$ for the risk of being seriously injured). And it is this fact of complete ignorance of the identity of each of the potential victims that transforms the calculation. Assuming universal risk aversion,[14] the relevant sums to be subtracted from the benefit side are no longer those which compensate a specific number of persons for their certain death but are those sums which compensate each person in the community for *the additional risk* to which he is to be exposed.[15]

In general, of course, every activity will have attached to it some discernible degree of risk (even staying at home in bed bears some risk of mishap—the bed might collapse, the wind might blow the roof in, a marauder might enter). Any change, from one environment to another, from one style of living to another, can be said to alter the balance of risk, sometimes imperceptibly, sometimes substantially. Only the dead opt out of all risk. Yet the actual statistical risk attaching to some activity may be so small that only the hypersensitive would take account of it. In common with all other changes in economic arrangements, there is some *minimum sensible* beyond which an increment, or decrement, of risk will go unnoticed. More important, however, what is strictly relevant to the analysis is not the change in the statistical risk per se but the person's response, if any, to such a change. For the change in risk may go unperceived, and, if perceived, it may be improperly evaluated. Indeed,

[14] Risk aversion is assumed throughout (unless otherwise stated) solely in the interests of brevity. If some people enjoy the additional risk, their CVs will be positive. In general, if the aggregate of the CVs for the additional risk is negative, which is the case for universal risk aversion, there is a subtraction from the benefit side. If, on the other hand, it was positive, there would be an addition to the benefit side.

[15] In a most engaging and highly perceptive paper, Schelling (1968) divides the problem into three parts: (*a*) society's interest, (*b*) an economic interest (in which category a man's contribution to GNP is placed), and (*c*) a "consumer's interest." Discussing this third interest in connection with a lifesaving program, Schelling correctly poses the relevant question: What will people pay for a government program that reduces risk? (p. 142). But being uneasy about the actual measurement of such a sum, and absorbed with other fascinating, though in the context irrelevant, considerations, he does not develop the analysis systematically. Indeed, he goes on later to discuss the value of certain and inescapable loss of life and comes up with the suggestion that college professors would be prepared to pay an amount equal to something between ten and a hundred times their annual income in order to save the life of one of their family. If one is interested solely in the conceptual measure, as I am here, one can make use of the notion of external effects to develop the analysis. Fromm's hypercritical comments (1968), on the other hand, make use of external effects, along with the difficulties of measuring, largely to cast doubt upon this valid part of Schelling's paper.

people do have difficulty in grasping the objective significance of large numbers and, where chance or risk is at issue, they are prone to underestimate it. One chance in 50,000 of winning a lottery, or of having one's house burned down, seems a better chance, or a greater risk, than it is in fact. If so, the existence of gambling and insurance by the same person is explicable without recourse to the ingenious Friedman-Savage hypothesis (1948).

The analysis which follows does not, however, depend upon the veracity of such conjectures. All the reader has to accept is the proposition that people's subjective preferences of the worth of a thing must be counted. In the market place, the price of a good or a "bad" (such as labor input or other disutility) is fixed by the producer, and the buyer or seller determines the amount by reference to his subjective preferences. Where, however, the amount of a (collective) good, or "bad" is fixed for each person—as may be the case with a change in risk—a person's subjective preference can only determine the price he will accept or offer for it; in short, his CV. People's imperfect knowledge of economic opportunities, their imprudence and unworldliness, have never prevented economists from accepting as basic data the amounts people freely choose at given prices. Such imperfections cannot, therefore, consistently be invoked to qualify people's choices when, instead, their preferences are exercised in placing a price on some increment of a good or "bad." True, attempts to observe the change of magnitude when people adjust the price to the change in quantity—rather than the more common assumption that they adjust the quantity to the change in price—does pose problems of measurement. But the problems of measurement must not be allowed to obscure the validity of the concept.

Placed within the broadest possible context then, any additional risk of death, associated with the provision of some new facility, takes its place as one of a number of economic consequences (including employment gains and losses, new purchase and sale opportunities, and the withdrawal of existing ones), all of which affect the welfare of each of the n members of the community.

IV

We shall now consider four types of risk, two of them direct, or physical, risks, the remaining two being indirect, or derivative, risks.

First, there are the direct, or physical, risks that people *voluntarily* assume whenever they choose to buy a product or avail themselves of a service or facility. Inasmuch as such risks are evaluated by each jth person as a CV, equal say to r_{jj}^1, his benefit from the service or facility is estimated net of such risk; that is, after r_{jj}^1 has been subtracted form it. If

Classics in Risk Management I

smoking tobacco causes 20,000 deaths a year, no subtracting from the benefits, on account of this risk, need be entered in a cost-benefit analysis of the tobacco industry inasmuch as smokers are already aware that the tobacco habit is unhealthy. And if, notwithstanding their awareness, they continue to smoke, the economist has no choice but to assume that they consider themselves better off despite the risks. Indeed, the benefits to smokers, net of risk, that is, after subtracting the aggregate,

$$\sum_{j}^{n} r_{jj}^{1} \, ,$$

are reflected in the demand schedule for tobacco. Once the area under the demand curve has been estimated and used as an approximation of the benefit smokers derive from the use of tobacco, any further subtraction for such risks would entail double counting.

Another example will help clarify the principle and will extend the argument. In an initially riskless situation, the jth person's anticipated consumer's surplus on buying a new car can be expressed by

$$C = \int_{0}^{M} \{v(m) - g'(m)\} \, dm + g_{o} - P \, ,$$

where $v(m)$ is the present discounted value of the maximum amounts he will pay (net of all operating costs) for each successive mile for which the car is to be used; $g'(m)$ is the derivative of $g(m)$, the present discounted value of the sum the car will fetch if sold after it has been driven m miles; g_{o} is the discounted present value of the car if he holds it over time without driving it at all; P is the original price of the car (including tax); and M is the total number of miles he expects to drive the car. If we observe that he buys the car, we infer that C_{j} is positive; that, in his own estimation, he is better off with the car than without it.

The introduction, now, of some personal risk associated with driving the car does not alter this inference.[16] Once he is aware of the additional element of risk in driving the car, the consequent reduction in the jth person's welfare is valued at the risk compensation r_{jj}^{1}. If, in spite of the additional risk, the jth person still offers to buy the car, we are compelled to infer that $(C_{j} - r_{jj}^{1}) > 0$; that is, his original consumer's surplus exceeds the risk compensation or, put otherwise, his consumer's surplus net *of risk* is positive. The evaluation of a new automobile plant will, therefore, disregard this type of risk, since the benefits are roughly equal to the

[16] The nice distinction made by Schelling (1968, pp. 132–35) between loss of life and loss of livelihood is, possibly, meaningful, but difficult to capture. Given the "conjuncture" of circumstances in which a man finds himself, there is, in principle, some amount of money that will just induce him to assume a particular risk of being killed. But it is hardly likely that he will be able to apportion that sum as between "life" and "livelihood"—and it is not necessary, in this analysis, that he should be able to do so.

aggregate of consumer's surplus net of risk. Similarly, a cost-benefit study of a highway project which is expected to increase the number of casualties need make no allowance for the expected loss of life provided, again, that this is the only type of risk. For in this case, also, the benefits to be measured are, ultimately, the maximum sums motorists are willing to pay for the new highway system in full cognizance of the additional risks they choose to assume.

Occasionally, as in the automobile example, the risk assumed by each person will depend upon the numbers availing themselves of the service or facility. Since the additional degree of risk generated by all the others are imposed on each one, in addition to the risk he would assume in the absence of all others, the analysis must extend itself to include "external diseconomies internal to the industry."[17] If we let r^1_{ij} stand for the risk-compensation sum required by the jth person for the risk imposed on him by the ith individual, the compensatory sums for the extra risks contributed by all other individuals is given by

$$\sum_i^n r^1_{ij} \qquad (i \neq j) .$$

Now, although these additional risks are imposed on the jth person, they can always be avoided by his refusal to avail himself of the new service or facility. If, however, he decides to avail himself of it, the economist cannot but assume that he believes he is better off with it than without it. Again, therefore, we must assume that

$$\left(c_j - \sum_i^n r^1_{ij} \right) > 0 ,$$

where i now includes j so as to make provision also for the risk that person j would run if he alone enjoyed the new service or facility.[18]

---

[17] The distinction between external effects *internal* to the industry and those *external* to the industry is proposed in Mishan (1965).

[18] The external diseconomies of traffic risk are, therefore, treated exactly as the external diseconomies of traffic congestion. But, as distinct from the problem of estimating the excess benefit of a project of given size, the determination of an *optimal* traffic flow does require intervention by the economist in consequence of these mutual external diseconomies. For the question raised in determining an optimal traffic flow is no longer one of showing that, for a given volume of traffic, total benefits (*net of* risk and congestion) exceed total costs. The question, now, is to *choose* a volume of traffic so as to *maximize* excess benefit over cost, this being realized by equating marginal social benefit to marginal cost. The standard argument is then invoked, namely, that although the effects on all others of risk and congestion grow with each additional car, the jth, or marginal vehicle owner, in deciding whether to use the highway, considers only the term

$$\sum_i^n r^1_{ij}$$

(ignoring the similar congestion term), as indeed does each of the other members, that is, he takes account only of the costs to him of each of the n vehicles on the road,

698   JOURNAL OF POLITICAL ECONOMY

Aggregating over all n members, the net consumer's surplus is

$$\sum_{j}^{n}\left(c_j - \sum_{i}^{n}r_{ij}^1\right),$$

which can be abbreviated to $C - R^1$.

Insofar, then, as additional risks associated with the service or facility are all *voluntarily* assumed, there is no call for intervention in the allocative solution to which the market tends. As for project evaluations, insofar as benefits are calculated by reference to estimates of consumers' surplus, no allowance need be made for additional risk of loss of life. For the sum each person is willing to pay for the services provided by the project is net of all the risks associated with them. However, once we turn from risks that can be voluntarily assumed to *involuntary* risks that cannot be avoided—or, rather, cannot be avoided without incurring expenses—special provision for them has to be made in any cost-benefit analysis.

V

The additional involuntary risks that are imposed on the community as a whole as a by-product of some specific economic activity, and are, therefore, to be regarded as external diseconomies external to the industry, can be separated into three types. Although all three can be inflicted on the same person who could propose a single sum in compensation, it is useful to separate them, there being circumstances where only one or two types of risk are of any importance.

The *direct* involuntary risk of death that is inflicted on the jth person by some specific project can be compensated by the sum r_{jj}^2. For example, the establishment of a nuclear power station and the resulting disposal of radioactive waste materials is held to be responsible for an increase in the annual number of deaths. Again, if supersonic flights over inhabited areas are introduced as a regular service, we can anticipate an increase

---

including his own. What he does *not* take into account is the effect he himself produces on each of the others by his decision to add his vehicle to theirs; which is to say, he ignores the cost

$$\sum_{i}^{n}r_{ji}^1 \qquad\qquad (i \neq j),$$

the costs imposed on each of the intra-marginal vehicles by introducing his own jth vehicle. This latter term, therefore, represents the cost of those external diseconomies generated by the marginal vehicle, diseconomies that are internal to and absorbed by all intramarginal vehicles, and which are properly attributable to the marginal vehicle in determining the optimal flow of traffic.

in the annual number of deaths, at least among the frail, the elderly, and among those suffering from heart ailments.

In addition to this primary risk, there is a secondary risk to which the jth person is exposed, which will arise in other instances. For example, in the absence of legal prohibition, an industry pours "sewage" into the air and increases the incidence of death from a number of lung and heart diseases. Apart from those who are the direct victims of this activity, there will be a number of fatalities arising from infection through others. And this possibility of infection obviously increases the risk since, within a given area, every person becomes a source of risk to every other. In addition, therefore, to the sum r_{jj}^2 to compensate the jth person for the risk imposed on him even if he were the sole inhabitant, he requires also a sum

$$\sum_i^n r_{ij}^2 \qquad\qquad (i \neq j)$$

to compensate for the risk that each of the other $(n - 1)$ persons imposes on him.

There does not seem to be any advantage, however, in upholding this distinction between primary and secondary physical risk. Where the risk of infection through others is acknowledged, it is difficult, if not impossible, to separate primary from secondary risk. In such cases the risk compensation required by each person covers both. We shall, therefore, employ the general term

$$\sum_i^n r_{ij}^2$$

for the jth person (which includes the term r_{jj}^2 for the risk he runs in the absence of others). Aggregating over the n members of the community this total risk compensation is to be valued at

$$\sum_j^n \sum_i^n r_{ij}^2 \,,$$

which can be denoted by R^2.

There are, finally, the *indirect*, or derivative, risks arising from the general concern of each of the n persons with the physical risks, voluntary and involuntary, to which any of the others is exposed. This additional concern to which, in general, each member is prone (as a result of the additional physical risks run by others) has both a financial and a psychic aspect.

a) The financial aspect.—If, on balance, the death of the ith person improves the financial position of the jth person, the additional chance of i's death is a benefit to j, and the risk-compensatory sum r_{ij}^3 is therefore positive. This means that the jth person is willing to pay up to a given sum for the improved chance of his losing some dependent or inheriting some asset—or of inheriting it sooner.[19] If, on the other hand, the death of the ith person would reduce j's real income, the sum r^3_{ij} is negative; that is, the jth person would have to receive a sum of money to compensate him for the increased risk of suffering a reduction in his real income. Although the jth person's financial condition is likely to be affected by the death of only a few members of the community, his risk compensation, on this account, can be written in general as

$$\sum_i^n r^3_{ij} \qquad\qquad (i \neq j) \, .$$

Bearing in mind that most of the terms in the sum will be zero, the total expression will be positive or negative as the increased risk of death run by others makes the jth person on balance better off or worse off.

For this financial risk to which the community as a whole is exposed, the total risk compensation is obtained by aggregating the above expression over the n members to give

$$\sum_j^n \sum_i^n r^3_{ij} \qquad\qquad (i \neq j) \, ,$$

which can be represented by R^3. This sum can, as suggested, be positive or negative according to the way the community as a whole expects to be made financially better off or worse off by the death of others.[20]

b) The psychic aspect.—It is convenient, as well as charitable, to suppose that this concern for the additional risks to which others are exposed entails a reduction in a person's welfare. Thus, the compensatory sum

$$\sum_i^n r^4_{ij} \qquad\qquad (i \neq j)$$

for the jth person's increased risk of bereavement carries a negative sign, being the sum of money necessary to reconcile him to bearing the addi-

---

[19] It might, at first, appear that an asset which is transferred from the deceased to his beneficiaries cancels out, as it does in the L_1 or L_2 measure. But, if transfers are generally omitted from such calculations, it is simply because they take place between living persons: a transfer of $10,000 from person A to person B implies that the sum of their CVs is zero. On our criterion there is neither gain nor loss. However, where the issue is no longer a voluntary transfer of wealth but the risk of an involuntary transfer through death, the case is different. If there is an increased risk of person B losing his life, the CV for that risk is negative; that is, there is some minimum amount of money which will restore his welfare. To person A, however, who cares nothing for B's person but expects to inherit B's vast estate, the increased risk to which B is now exposed is a benefit for which he is willing to pay up to some maximum sum.

[20] Only in an economy in which income was wholly from human capital would the R^3 component be comparable with the L_2 measure. A figure for the latter could be got by subtracting the net *losses* to the surviving members, arising from the death of breadwinners, from the net *gains* to the surviving members, arising from the death of dependents. As for R^3, the better the information, and the more constant the relation between income and utility along the relevant range, the closer the figure would be to the aggregate of the actuarial values of the net expected gain or loss to each

tional risk of death to which his friends and the members of his family are exposed.

The increased risk of bereavement to which the community as a whole is exposed is to be valued at a sum equal to the aggregate

$$\sum_j^n \sum_i^n r_{ij} \qquad\qquad (i \neq j),$$

which sum is abbreviated to R^4.

VI

Simplicity of exposition has restricted the analysis to an increase only in the risk of death. The qualifications necessary for the treatment of an increase also in the risk of injury and disease are too obvious to justify elaboration. Application of the above analysis to a *reduced* risk of death, and to a reduced risk of injury and disease, is perhaps slightly less obvious and it may reassure the reader if its symmetrical nature is briefly illustrated by an example. Just as an increase in the number of accidents and fatalities can be a by-product of some growth in economic activity, so also can a reduction in the number of accidents and fatalities. More familiar, however, is public investment designed primarily to reduce the incidence of disease, suffering, and death. And, although such activity is to be regarded as a collective good, the relationship between collective goods and external effects (which can be thought of as incidental, "non-optional," collective goods and "bads"), is close enough to permit us to make use of our conceptual apparatus without significant modification.

Suppose, then, that the government has a scheme for purifying the air over a vast region, one which is expected to save 20,000 lives annually.[21] The costs of enforcing a clean-air act and of installing preventive devices needed has to be set against the above social benefits. In accordance with our scheme, they are to be evaluated as follows:

1. Since, in this example, the reduced risk of death is a collective good, and not an external economy that is internal to some specific economic activity (as there could be, say, in a development that promoted horticulture, regarded as a healthy occupation), there is no R^1 term. There is here no question of how much a person will pay for some market good after making allowance for the *incidental* reduction of risk. The only good in question here is the collective reduction of risk itself.

2. If the population of the area is 100 million, and the chance of dying from causes connected with air pollution is independent of age, location,

---

person. It is the existence of nonhuman assets, and the possibility of their transfer from deceased to survivors, that adds to the positive value of R^3 and raises it above the L_2 measure.

[21] Again, for simplicity of exposition we omit reference, in this example, to the reduction of suffering or the enjoyment of better health.

occupation, physical condition, or other factors, the risk of death to each person in the region is reduced by 2/10,000. More generally, there is for the jth person a reduction of the risk of death from factors connected with air pollution (including infection by others suffering from air-pollution diseases) for which he is prepared to pay up to

$$\sum_i^n r_{ij}^2 ,$$

which, on our assumption of universal risk aversion, is positive. Aggregating over the n members, the total sum R^2 is, therefore, also positive.[22]

3. A reduction in the risk of death for everyone implies, for the jth person, a reduction in the chance of his being financially worse off or better off in the future. The risk compensation

$$\sum_i^n r_{ij}^3 \qquad\qquad (i \neq j)$$

can therefore be positive or negative. The greater the proportion of aggregate income arising from nonhuman capital, the more likely is the total sum R^3 to be negative for the reduced risk.

4. Finally, there is the reduced risk of the jth person's suffering bereavement over the future, the corresponding risk compensation

$$\sum_i^n r_{ij}^4 \qquad\qquad (i \neq j)$$

being positive. The total sum R^4 will, therefore, also be positive.

Evaluation of the benefits of the government scheme is, then, to be based ultimately on the aggregate of maximal sums that all persons in the region affected are willing to pay for the estimated reduction of the risks of death, an aggregate which can be split usefully into three components, R^2, R^3, and R^4.

[22] It is frequently alleged that at low levels risk can have a positive utility. (In the absence of "income effects" one can, for example, hypothesize a curve relating the person's CV to increasing risk of death. Measuring risk on a horizontal axis, the CV curve is above it for low risk, and below it for all risk exceeding a critical level. As the probability of death rises toward unity, we should expect the curve to increase its rate of decline and become asymptotic to a vertical axis passing through the unity point.) But whether this is so, and the extent to which it is so, would seem to depend upon the activity associated with the risk. Driving at 100 miles per hour increases the risk of a fatal accident. And if some people choose gratuitously to drive at this speed, it is not simply in response to the additional risk per se. It is partly because a test of skill, physical courage, or manhood is involved. Even where skill is absent, as in playing Russian roulette, there is a certain bravado in openly flirting with death. On the other hand, it is hard to imagine a man deriving positive utility from the information that henceforth he is to be exposed—though anonymously, along with millions of others—to an increased risk of death, one over which he has no semblance of choice or control. The risk of increased infection by some new disease or by increased radioactive fallout would be examples. Nevertheless, the question of whether risk, at some levels, has a positive or a negative utility, in any particular case, is an empirical one and does not affect the formal analysis.

VII

A word on the deficiencies in the information available to each person concerning the degree of risk involved. These deficiencies of information necessarily contribute to the discrepancies experienced by people between anticipated and realized satisfactions. For all that, in determining whether a potential Pareto improvement has been met, economists are generally agreed—either as a canon of faith, as a political tenet, or as an act of expediency—to accept the dictum that each person knows best his own interest. If, therefore, the economist is told that a person, A, is indifferent regarding not assuming a particular risk or assuming it along with a sum of money, V, then, on the Pareto principle, the sum V has to be accepted as the relevant cost of his being exposed to that risk. It may be the case that, owing either to deficient information or congenital optimism, person A consistently overestimates his chances of survival. But once the dictum is accepted, as indeed it is in economists' appraisals of allocative efficiency, cost-benefit analysis has to accept V as the only relevant magnitude—this being the sum chosen by A in awareness of his relative ignorance.[23] Certainly all the rest of the economic data used in a cost-benefit analysis or any other allocative study, whether derived from market prices and quantities or by other methods of inquiry, is based on this principle of accepting as final only the individual's estimate of what an article is worth to him at the time the decisoin is to be made. The article in question may, of course, also have a direct worth, positive or negative, for persons other than its buyer or seller, a possibility which requires a consideration of external effects. Yet, again, on the above dictum, it is the values placed on this article by these other persons which will count. Thus, while it is scarcely necessary to urge that more economical ways of refining and disseminating information be explored, the economist engaged in allocative studies traditionally follows the practice of evaluating all social gains and losses solely on the basis of individuals' own evaluations of the relevant effects on their welfare, given the information they have at the time the decision is taken.

VIII

In sum, any expected loss of life or saving of life, any expected increase or reduction in suffering in consequence of economic activity, is to be evaluated for the economy by reference to the Pareto principle; in particular, by reference to what each member of the community is willing to pay or to receive for the estimated change of risk. The resulting aggregate of CVs for the community can be usefully regarded as comprised of four

---

[23] Person A, for example, may find himself disabled for life and rue his decision to take the risk. But this example is only a more painful one of the fact that people come to regret a great many of the choices they make, notwithstanding which they would resent any interference with their future choices.

components, and, of these, R^1—which encompasses all the voluntary risks (where they exist)—can be ignored on the grounds that the benefit to each individual of the direct activity in question (often estimated as equal to the area under the demand curve) is already net of this risk.

The other involuntary components of risk—R^2, R^3, R^4—cannot, in general, be ignored, though one can surmise that with the growth in material prosperity their magnitude will tend to grow. On the other hand, with the growth in the welfare state, and in particular with an increasingly egalitarian structure of real disposable incomes, the financial risk compensation, R^3, will tend to decline. The gradual loosening of family ties and the decline of emotional interdependence should cause the magnitude of the bereavement risk compensation, R^4, to decline also. In a wholly impersonal society in which, for any jth person, the loss of any member of the community is easily replaceable in j's estimation by many others, R^4 will tend to vanish; R^2, however, is wholly selfish in the sense that it depends on people's preference for staying alive. Until such time as a genetic revolution turns men into pure altruists, or pure automatons, ready, like some species of ants, to sacrifice themselves at a moment's notice for the greater convenience of the whole, it can be expected that R^2 will grow over time.

Before concluding, however, it should be emphasized that the basic concept introduced in this paper is not simply an alternative to, or an auxiliary to, any existing methods[24] that have been proposed for measuring the loss or saving of life. It is the only economically justifiable concept. And this assertion does not rest on any novel ethical premise. It follows as a matter of consistency in the application of the Pareto principle in cost-benefit calculations.

Insofar as an immediate application of the concepts to the measurement of loss or saving of life is in issue, one's claims must be more muted· In the attempts to measure social benefits and losses, price-quantity statistics lend themselves better to the more familiar examples in which people choose quantities at given market prices than they do to examples in which people have to choose prices for the given quantities. For one can observe the quantities they choose, at least collectively, whereas one

[24] It is far from impossible that society may choose to refer decisions in matters involving life and death to a representative body or committee and that a decision may be reached that differs from the one which would arise from the consistent application of cost-benefit techniques. Nevertheless, the economist is free to criticize the decision, to point out inconsistencies, and to discover what features, if any, warrant a departure from the Pareto criterion. Consistency, in this instance, requires that the expected change in risk associated with any contemplated scheme be evaluated by reference to the same principle as all other relevant economic gains and losses. To evaluate the welfare effect of risk on some other principle, say, by a voting procedure, entails the adding together of incommensurables. Thus, an implicit figure for the effect of risk on welfare attributable to a decision taken by a smaller group (or even by the whole group), by the method of counting heads, is added to a figure for the other economic effects which, using the Pareto principle, aggregates the valuation of each member determined on a CV basis.

cannot generally observe their subjective valuations. In the circumstances, economists seriously concerned with coming to grips with the magnitudes may have to brave the disdain of their colleagues and consider the possibility that data yielded by surveys based on the questionnaire method are better than none, or better than data obtained by persisting with some of the current measures such as L_1 or L_2. In the last resort, one could invoke "contingency calculations" (Mishan, 1969, p. 70) in order to determine, for example, whether the apparent-excess benefit of a scheme (calculated in the absence of any allowance for the expected increase in fatalities and injuries) is likely or not to exceed any plausible estimate of the evaluation of the increased risk to which people are exposed.

In view of the existing quantomania, one may be forgiven for asserting that there is more to be said for rough estimates of the precise concept than precise estimates of economically irrelevant concepts. The caveat is more to be heeded in this case, bearing in mind that currently used and currently mooted measures of saving life or the loss of life—such as L_1, L_2, L_3, and L_4—have no conceptual affinity with the Pareto basis of cost-benefit analysis.

References

Devons, E. *Essays in Economics.* London: Allen & Unwin, 1961.

Eisner, R., and Strotz, R. H. "Flight Insurance and the Theory of Choice." *J.P.E.* 69, no. 4 (August 1961): 355–68.

Friedman, M., and Savage, L. J. "Utility Analysis of Choices Involving Risks." *J.P.E.* 56, no. 4 (August 1948): 279–304.

Fromm, G. "Civil Aviation Expenditures." In *Measuring Benefits of Government Investment,* edited by R. Dorfman. Washington: Brookings Inst., 1965.

———. "Comment on T. C. Schelling's paper, 'The Life You Save May Be Your Own.'" In *Problems in Public Expenditure,* edited by S. B. Chase, ed. Washington: Brookings Inst., 1968.

Kneese, A. V. "Research Goals and Progress toward Them." In *Environmental Quality in a Growing Economy,* edited by H. Jarrett. Washington: Johns Hopkins Press, 1966.

Marglin, S. "The Social Rate of Discount and the Optimal Rate of Investment." *Q.J.E.* 77, no. 1 (February 1963): 95–111.

Mishan, E. J. "Rent as a Measure of Welfare Change." *A.E.R.* 49, no. 3 (May 1959): 386–94.

———. "Reflections on Recent Development in the Concept of External Effects." *Canadian J. Econ.* 31, no. 1 (February 1965): 3–34.

———. *Welfare Economics: An Assessment.* Amsterdam: North-Holland, 1969.

Nath, S. K. *A Reappraisal of Welfare Economics.* London: Routledge & Kegan Paul, 1969.

Ridker, R. G. *The Economic Costs of Air Pollution.* New York: Praeger, 1967.

Rothenberg, J. *The Measurement of Social Welfare.* Englewood, N.J.: Prentice-Hall, 1961.

Schelling, T. C. "The Life You Save May Be Your Own." In *Problems in Public Expenditure,* edited by S. B. Chase, Jr. Washington: Brookings Inst., 1968.

[3]

Public Policy, Volume 23, No. 4 (Fall 1975)

PROCEDURES FOR VALUING LIVES

RICHARD ZECKHAUSER

I. Introduction: Background and Qualifications, The Analytic Approach and Life Valuation
II. Willingness-to-Pay and the Valuation of Lives: Private Decisions, Public Decisions, Identifying the Affected Parties, Alternative Assessment Procedures
III. The Use and Abuse of Measures of the Value of a Life: The Inadequacy of Potential Pareto Improvements as a Guide for Policy, Frequently Proposed Measures of the Values of Lives
IV. Special Problems in Valuing Lives: Extrapolating Current Statistics to Allow for Productivity Growth, Intergenerational Considerations, Anxiety, Risk-Taking or Risk-Averting Behavior on Number of Lives Lost, Wrong Models and Low Probabilities
V. The Importance of Process: Compensation Paid or Not Paid, Income Distribution, The Portfolio of Injuring Actions
VI. Conclusion

I. *Introduction*

How should we value lives that might be saved, injured, or expended through public or private decision? This perplexing problem of growing policy import has not yielded to the substantial efforts of economists and others. There is no universal agreement on how to value lives; indeed, more surprisingly, no one has even claimed to have found an unequivocal procedure for life valuation. The accumulating evidence suggests that life valuation should not be approached as a search for an elusive number. Even if we divine which marginal curves to cross, or if we conduct an income survey of motorcyclists, or if we see how much is spent to replace a heart valve, no irresistible answers can be expected.

This essay was inspired by and grew out of work performed as a consultant for the Environmental Protection Agency. That agency does not necessarily agree with and bears no responsibility for any views presented here. P. Cook, N. Goldman, N. Jackson, H. Kunreuther, A. Manne, N. Nichols, J. Plummer, C. Riordan, T. Schelling, F. Schoettle, E. Stokey, and J. Yellin provided me with helpful comments.

Lives, for reasons possibly bad but more likely good, are qualitatively different from other commodities that our society produces, expends, or merchandises. Some economists may privately bemoan this fact because it introduces a whole range of analytic complexities. Others may not like it because they think welfare would be improved if apples-and-pears-type valuation procedures were applied to lives. But they are not. The valuation of lives involves and reflects many of the most basic beliefs and institutions of our society. With lives, it is not just the outcome of the valuation process that is important. The legitimacy and acceptability of the process itself may exert a significant influence on welfare.

It might seem, then, that economists would have little to contribute to the life-valuation discussion. This essay argues quite to the contrary. The complexity of the problem enhances the potential contribution of the organizing concepts of the economics discipline. Insights culled from the examination of a number of other sticky issues can be applied with profit. This essay attempts to provide some of these insights.

Background and Qualifications. A theme that emerges from this analysis is that the context in which lives are being sacrificed or saved will affect both the procedures by which lives should be valued, and the valuations themselves. Examples therefore are best chosen from specific contexts. This essay frequently alludes to the life-threatening aspects of low-level ionizing radiation. Risks of damages from radiation are encountered in medical procedures, in association with certain household and industrial devices, as an unwanted byproduct of nuclear-based power generation, and as a possible result of actions such as flight in the stratosphere or the release of aerosols that may partially deplete the ozone layer in our atmosphere.

The evaluation of the risks of low-level ionizing radiation is not a completely scientific investigation. Neither with present knowledge nor in the foreseeable future will it be possible to derive some unambiguous valuation for the potential damages associated with radiation. It should be expected that different policymakers, analysts, and critics will continue to encourage different policies for dealing with these risks. Their disagreements in part will stem from divergent assessments of the value to be

PROCEDURES FOR VALUING LIVES　　　　　　　　　　　421

attached to the losses associated with the genetic and somatic effects of radiation.[1]

It is critical that policymakers realize that there is no unambiguous procedure for valuing a human life. Not only do we lack a general approach that will apply in all circumstances; there is rarely any circumstance for which a specific approach could receive universal approval.[2]

Because there is no possibility for a scientific discovery of the value of a single break in a chromosome or the cancer-induced death of a 40-year-old father of two, the purpose of a study such as this one should be to foster agreement on methodology. The next stage would be to gather some empirical materials that could be fed into such a methodology. With the aid of these supporting materials, some significant narrowing may be achieved in the gaps among the estimates of different assessors. With present knowledge and in the context of the existing debate, great advances can be made merely by securing agreement on ground rules. Indeed, even within the theoretical literature there are extraordinary areas of nonagreement. (The term disagreement is really not appropriate, for the conflicts are rarely addressed. With a few exceptions, such as Mishan's "Evaluation of Life and Limb: A Theoretical

---

[1] Disagreement on factors beyond these further spurs on the debate. (1) There is no consensus on the value of the products that can be produced uniquely or less expensively with the accompaniment of radiation. (2) Though experimental evidence derived from animal experiments and atomic-bomb-survivor studies is narrowing the gaps among many beliefs, scientists are far from agreeing about either (a) the risks of exposure associated with various types of radiation-related devices, or (b) the risks of particular genetic and somatic effects associated with different levels of exposure. What is disturbing about this disagreement is not the fact that it exists, but the biases that it reveals. Individuals who assign significant magnitudes to the types of losses that are potentially incurred tend to express beliefs about physical processes that support the argument that the expected number of such losses will be great, and vice versa. (The debate over the figures presented by Dr. Ernest Sternglass, an individual who has identified exceedingly high health hazards associated with radiation from nuclear power plants, provides an instructive example.) Ideally scientific judgments would be independent of valuations of outcomes.

[2] This failing suggests that many of the propositions that are used as the telling argument against some approach are also without merit. For example, many analysts object to self-valuation-of-life procedures because such procedures fail to take into account the fact that poorer people may in some sense value a dollar more highly. (When we look at dollar benefits, the potential inequity is not so glaring as when we focus attention on potential lives sacrificed.) Whether this would be the telling argument depends on whether these same analysts would accept the procedure if the society had an egalitarian income distribution, or if it were applied, say, in an isolated location where income differences were minor.

Approach" [1971], there has been little attempt to resolve the issues at debate.)

Failure to arrive at unambiguous estimates in the past reflects neither slack efforts nor stunted imagination. The assessment procedure is extraordinarily difficult. This suggests that whatever estimates are derived, whatever procedures are developed to secure estimates, there should be a continuous review process to note their successes and their implications. The valuation process may be simply too complex to reason through from beginning to end. An apparently attractive procedure may lead to valuations that are totally out of line with what seems to be reasonable. If so, it would be worthwhile to retrace the steps of the logic to search for a possible deviation from what was truly intended. It is possible, of course, that the valuation procedure was not in error, and that our original intuition guiding its construction was more finely honed than our expectation regarding the outcomes it would produce. Still, it would seem ill advised to make the valuation process merely a once-around proposition from agreed-upon procedure to accepted result. This may be the way of logicians, but it does not lead to sensible policy analysis.

The Analytic Approach and Life Valuation. Some of the insights gained from analytic approaches to life valuation come not from any individual, but rather from observation of the consensus or divergence of opinion among those professionally involved. (There is striking agreement that this area, ignored until recently, is one in which the economic approach can play a helpful role.) Most analysts would agree that the appropriate value to be placed on a life depends on who is making the decision about the life, who would be paying to save it, and who would benefit if it were saved.

When the decisionmaker is also the payer, the person whose life is at stake, and the predominant beneficiary, there is fairly widespread agreement that his valuation should be the determining one. The analogy is made to market decisionmaking. Whenever the consumer is the only one affected by his purchases, and if markets are functioning perfectly, a socially desirable outcome is achieved by allowing each man to choose for himself.[3] The con-

---

[3] In some contexts the level of risk involved in a particular activity will not be subject to individual choice, but the individual may be able to choose what price,

sensus message from the analysts about such situations is an important one: The government should not intervene.

Disagreements among the analysts would arise when any attempt was made to identify which private decisions about preserving a life entailed at most insignificant externalities. (In this context, it is noteworthy that society does not offer legal sanction to suicide or mercy killing. It is not clear how the considerations that call for societal involvement on those issues extrapolate to situations which involve less extreme sacrifices in probability of survival, as well as require higher resource expenditures.) There would be further disagreements once externalitis to private decisions were identified, and appropriate policies had to be formulated to deal with them.

This essay is directed to the realm of public decisionmaking. The decisions to which it is relevant are those by which a public decisionmaker allocates resources to enhance the probabilities of survival of private citizens. The resources involved may be public, as with highway safety railings; private, as when radiation standards are established for industrial processes; or, as with seatbelt legislation, those of the individual whose survival is affected. Such public decisions implicitly value lives; analysts may be called upon to assist in the valuation process.

Too often when analysts approach the problem of valuing life, they concentrate on philosophical issues which are inherently unresolvable. Sometimes they begin by identifying the difficulties. Then, if they have been scrupulously honest with themselves, they will tend to give up when they discover the most basic problems.

---

if any. he is willing to pay to engage in that activity. Tort recoveries from those who generate the risk would be factored into the effective price to the consumer. A variety of studies growing out of the pioneering work of Coase [1960] has shown that if there are no market imperfections, an efficient outcome will still be achieved by market operations whether the consumer or producer determines the risk level. The argument obviously applies to a number of situations in which environmental disamenities, for example, generate health risks.

A lively literature has developed discussing whether and what types of market imperfections are likely to be encountered in these situations. The imperfections include informational problems (consumers may not know the levels of risk that are involved), thinness of markets (the producer of the risk may have no competitors), and nonconvexities (the losses from further increases in the risk, rather than increasing, go to zero if the consumer chooses to cease engaging in the activity). Posner [1972] discusses the application of the implicit reasoning in the Coase result to a variety of situations involving risk and tort recovery. Polinsky [1974] provides a stimulating review of Posner.

At the other extreme, the analyst grinds out some numbers, however questionable. Such calculations are unlikely to have a positive effect. They will be effectively challenged by politically oriented individuals who oppose the actions they recommend, and by methodologically oriented decisionmakers who recognize inadequacies in their methods of generation.

If recognition of the difficulties leads to a surrender, and if plowing ahead leads to a discarded output, what should be done? Fortunately, a great deal can be accomplished. Most significantly, analysts can provide some basic building blocks so that the ultimate decisionmakers — and decisions are made every day, though frequently by inadvertence — can have some inputs for what they are doing. Sometimes these analytic inputs will make their greatest contribution by bolstering confidence. They may show, for example, that the choice between two options will remain unchanged whether a human life is valued at $X or $100X.

It surely must be of value to an EPA official who is considering just how stringent requirements should be on radiation leakage, for example of industrial equipment, to know (a) how much its potential victims consume over their remaining lifetimes; (b) how highly they value their lives in their implicit decisions about safety; (c) how much is being paid for safety gains in other manufacturing areas; and (d) how much the members of society other than his family will benefit or suffer. The analyst can provide this information.

II. *Willingness-to-Pay and the Valuation of Lives*

Ask an economist how much a commodity is worth to an individual, and the likely answer is: The amount of other resources that he will sacrifice to secure it. The validity of a willingness-to-pay valuation is obvious when individuals are choosing goods for themselves. In the public sphere, however, goods are chosen for others, and payment as such will rarely be secured from the beneficiaries from public decisions. Nevertheless, the willingness-to-pay approach to valuation retains some attractive features. Most particularly, if willingness-to-pay amounts are employed to value outputs, and if programs are sought that provide the maximum excess of benefit over cost, then an efficient outcome will be secured.[4] Conversely, if some selected programs are at variance with the maximization of net benefits using willingness-to-pay valuations, an inefficient outcome will be the inevitable result. As should be expected, the willingness-to-pay approach has been employed by those designing public programs for a range of goods from recreation days to waiting time for medical appointments.

Though lives — or, more precisely, programs to preserve them — are frequent objects of policy choice, willingness-to-pay determinations have not been employed on any widespread basis to guide resource allocation decisions that involve them. This is neither surprising nor disturbing. Human lives have characteristics that differentiate them significantly from the vast array of valued outputs that are derived from public programs. They cannot be produced by traditional industrial processes; property rights for them cannot be secure; and they cannot be legally transferred. For these reasons, among others, they are considered a sacred commodity. For commodities that society refuses to market, it is not evident that the quasi-market measure "willingness-to-pay" is an appropriate indicator of value.

Private Decisions. Might willingness-to-pay be of some limited application? Thomas Schelling, in an elegant essay entitled "The Life You Save May be Your Own" [1968], showed that in many life-preserving contexts information on willingness-to-pay can be profitably and appropriately employed. His object of study, it should be stressed, was the private decisionmaker making choices affecting his own life. The approach he outlined was designed to help individuals get their thinking straight when allocating resources to their own benefit and to the benefit of others who value their continued survival.

Schelling's point is a simple one. If individuals are willing to pay some amount to increase their probability of survival, or conceivably the survival of someone else, then they should be allowed to pay that amount and reap the benefits.[5] If there are other in-

---

[4] Efficiency is interpreted here in terms of Pareto optimality. An outcome is efficient if there is no combination of changes in decisions and transfers of resources that makes some individuals better off without hurting any others.

[5] This assumes that there are no substantial externalities to his life-preservation efforts. Conceivably society would prevent rich victims of kidney disease from purchasing dialysis machines, if lack of machines for the poor would symbolize an

terested parties, and if social arrangements can be worked out so that these others contribute as well, then the sum total that interested individuals are willing to contribute should be spent to that purpose. No necessary connection is implied in Schelling's essay between willingness-to-pay and social value or intrinsic worth. Indeed, willingness-to-pay as it is traditionally employed to gauge the value of the outputs of policy choice is not even the subject of inquiry. Rather, an individual is merely being asked how much he will pay to secure something he values. The recommendation is being made that he be allowed to purchase it.

Public Decisions. The context of the problem changes when the decisionmakers are public, not private, and the lives at stake are not those of the decisionmakers or of others close to them. In general, public mechanisms for allocating resources do not allow for individual purchases by which a citizen who values an output highly can pay more for it and be assured of securing it. Most public resources are generated through tax mechanisms; taxes are rarely imposed on a benefits-received basis.

Still, a rich town may choose to spend more per capita than a poor town on public health or highway safety, thereby offering higher probabilities of survival for its wealthy citizens. It is frequently alleged that within cities with wide disparities in income, health-promoting services such as garbage collection are superior in rich areas. Because the rich would probably pay more for these services, such an outcome — whether the result of political influence, a desire to attract well-to-do citizens, or whatever — is closer to the hypothetical market outcome than an equal provision of services.

What is noteworthy is that to many citizens, including the rich, this unequal provision of services appears inequitable and undesirable. When decisions are made in the public domain, the normative significance of what would be produced by a private market is diminished. This lesson, coupled with observations about the distinctive qualities of life preservation as an output,

---

inequitable society. Legislation discouraging the purchase of heavier, safer cars is now under consideration, primarily because the vehicles use more gasoline, and gasoline is assumed to be priced below its social value. If heavier cars cause those in the other car to be more severely injured when there is a collision, that would provide another externality argument for taxing and thereby discouraging the use of heavier cars.

suggests that determinations of willingness-to-pay will be far from sufficient guides to public decision in the life-preservation area. Nevertheless, willingness-to-pay calculations can provide a useful input to the decisionmaking process. It is no surprise that they provide the motivating philosophy for most analytic approaches to life valuation.

Identifying the Affected Parties. The willingness-to-pay approach suggests that to value lives appropriately it should merely be inquired what individuals would pay in a variety of contexts to save the particular lives at risk. When this process is undertaken, it should be recognized that the "interested parties" may be a diverse group with quite different concerns.

The logical starting place is the individual whose life is to be saved. The reason for starting with him, quite simply, is the expectation that his valuation will likely be the greatest, though this is not necessarily the case.

The second class of individuals who are likely to be interested is the family and friends of the individual. If the potential deceased is a breadwinner, then this will include the primary beneficiaries from his estate. If the individual at risk is a child, it will include people who would be required to support him.[6]

The third category of individuals is society at large, but this will mostly be composed of individuals who have only indirect connections with the potential deceased. (People who are not presently alive may also have an interest. Issues relating to future citizens are discussed below under section IV.) Some indication of the magnitude of society's concern might be given by the amount that the individual would contribute to or drain from society. By this standard, a big taxpayer would be valued more highly than a welfare mother. However, it would seem that in American society, given the expressions of political feeling observed in other circumstances, net dollar contribution is a poor indicator of the valuation of the general society. In most circumstances, following

---

[6] It is possible to tack the even more intractable optimum-population problem onto the valuation-of-life problem. For example, one might inquire about considering the potential offspring of the child. We will leave the unborn beneficiaries of a dead individual out of the analysis. This simplication may not be without consequences. For example, it excludes the unborn children of a newlywed, though it does include the losses of the spouse, who may in turn take into account the losses of unborn children.

the arguments just made, it would be a substantial underassessment.[7]

From an analytic standpoint, a life preserved bears many aspects of any good which offers significant externalities. If the preservation of a specific life were up for sale, and if those who benefited from saving it could be charged in proportion to their benefits, everyone could be made better off if the life were purchased for a price less than the sum of the valuations of all affected parties: the individual himself, his family and friends, and the rest of society.

Alternative Assessment Procedures. Identifying the affected parties is a useful start to get a total willingness-to-pay figure.[8] Next, dollar valuations must be secured. A number of analysts have attempted to make assessments in this direction; their results are instructive, though few of them at this juncture would expect their empirical observations to be put directly into policy application as a well-justified and fair assessment of the value of a life.

Jan Acton [1973] prepared and disseminated a questionnaire which attempted to determine how much individuals would pay for a mobile cardiac unit that would decrease the probability that they would die if they had a heart attack. His results suggested that individuals had difficulty responding to the types of questions he posed, though they provided answers that were not obviously unreasonable. In response to questions about willingness-to-pay to avoid 1/1,000 and 1/500 risks of death, Acton concluded that "large groups of people would be willing to pay $28,000 and

---

[7] Clearly, on average, the actual dollar contribution will be a greater percentage of society's total valuation for individuals with higher net dollar contribution. Weisbrod [1971] estimates internal rates of return for medical research investments treating mortality losses as expected value of future earnings, or for women, expected value of future household services. He observes rates of return varying between 4 and 14%. What is suggested in the text is that if his other assessments are accurate, this is surely a lower bound.

[8] A recent paper by Abt [1975] develops a procedure for assessing the social costs of cancer by identifying the costs to affected parties. Abt classifies the psychosocial costs according to the sufferers: the victims themselves, their families, friends, and caretakers. To make his estimates, he looks at such matters as induced mental illness, sexual loss, family conflict, and isolation. Abt estimates the annual social costs of cancer at about $136 billion, or about $40,000 per victim. His estimate is above and beyond any economic losses. It should be noted that calculations of dollar losses of this sort should not be considered as reductions in GNP. Psychosocial well-being is not included in the GNP measure. If a measure were developed that did include it, the relevant comparison would be between its achieved value and what its value would be if the scourge were eliminated.

$43,000, respectively, for each life saved at the stated probabilities" (pp. 109–110). It should be noted that Acton's question assesses the value of a post-heart attack life, indeed one for which the attack would have been fatal. The quality of such a life and its expected length are likely to be reduced. Its valuation should be diminished accordingly. (In valuing lives, it is important to identify their expected quality and duration should they be preserved.) Richard Thaler and Sherwin Rosen have looked to the labor market to see how it rewards occupations that involve varying risks of injury and death.[9] Inserting appropriate qualifications, they conclude that workers "estimate the value of a life to be in the neighborhood of $200,000" (p. 38). Their interesting methodology begins with consideration of prices revealed in the market, rather than with Acton's interview technique.

Chauncy Starr [1972], operating from the quite different perspective of a physical scientist, has looked at life-saving or life-expending undertakings across a spectrum of activities. Starr draws the important distinction between voluntary and involuntary activities, with the suggestion that free individual choice cannot be expected to yield an efficient outcome when risks are externally imposed, and when individuals cannot inexpensively purchase protection. Starr surveys a potpourri of risks and provides some guidelines for the assessment of alternative categories of risk. The strength of the Starr analysis is that it provides us with useful numerical indicators of the magnitude of present risks and the way these risks may be valued. It stops short, however, of providing us with a coherent methodology that can be employed for setting regulatory standards or more generally in forging public policy.

Recently, Norman Rasmussen at M.I.T. has employed a variant of the Starr approach as one way of conveying the meaning of his assessment of the risks associated with nuclear power generation. He provides the reader with some handy comparisons to dangers associated with other sorts of hazards.[10] The implicit assumption

---

9 See Thaler and Rosen [1974]. Their analysis outlines intelligently many qualifications regarding market observations as a guide to life valuation. Carlson [1963] calculated that flight pay for a U.S. Air Force captain implied a valuation of between $135,000 and $980,000 per life, depending on the type of plane flown.

10 See U.S. Atomic Energy Commission [1974], especially chapters 6 and 7. The relevant comparison would be between the risks of nuclear-based and coal-based

running through the analysis is that there is a portfolio of risks of death or illness, and by seeing just how much a risk under study contributes to the aggregate risk, we can find out whether that risk is worth entertaining. This set of issues is discussed in section V below.

Clearly, the analyst has a great number of suggestive techniques to provide. By gathering assessments of life valuation in two or three different approaches, the policy decisionmaker can attempt to "triangulate" on a final valuation. If the operation of the policy by itself generates information on the number of lives that are sacrificed, and at what price, then the political process may be well equipped to provide updated decisions about the way and the magnitude at which lives should be valued.

III. *The Use and Abuse of Measures of the Value of a Life*

Let us assume that some unequivocal value for a particular life saved in a particular way can be derived. What should be made of it? It has already been suggested that if the preservation of a specific life were up for sale, everyone could be made better off if it were purchased for a price less than the sum of the valuations of all affected parties.

Life preservation, however, is rarely merchandised this starkly. Rather, in a great variety of situations, society or some of its members are called upon to make choices that affect the probabilities that certain lives will be lost. The principle of adding up the valuations of all affected parties still applies. Here the question that should be asked is: In comparison to the status quo, how much would you pay to secure policy X, which among its other consequences will alter risks to lives in the following fashion? If the sum of the honest answers exceeds the cost of policy X, then with the appropriate distribution of charges, that policy could be pursued to everyone's benefit.

---

electric power. To be fair, Rasmussen, the director of the study, was under political constraint not to make his comparison. Energy generation may be the principal area in coming decades when lives are sacrificed through public decision. It is also to be expected that the sharply increased costs of energy will be shared between increased risks to human health and increased costs in more traditional economic resources.

PROCEDURES FOR VALUING LIVES   431

The Inadequacy of Potential Pareto Improvements as a Guide for Policy. The hard question arises if, as is usually the case, there are constraints on assessment possibilities (i.e., side payments), so that it will not be possible to work out charges or payments in conjunction with a policy innovation such that everyone's welfare improves. One school of thought, the so-called Kaldor-Hicks approach now ably represented by Mishan, suggests that the potential for a Pareto improvement is a sufficient guide to action. That is, however charges will be distributed, if the sum of the valuation payments that could be extracted exceeds the cost of the policy, the policy should be followed.

This argument is not logically conclusive. Our society has not shown itself willing to take the required step to make sure that compensation is made. If we merely follow potential Pareto improvements, we may well produce situations that, though Pareto optimal themselves, may with the aid of a social welfare function be shown to be inferior to our starting point.

Figure 1 illustrates this possibility. The dashed curve running

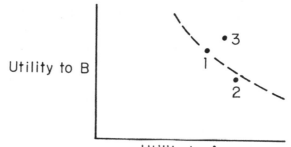

Figure 1. POTENTIAL PARETO IMPROVEMENTS AND THE EVALUATION OF LIFE.
(1)=starting point with loose radiation standards; (2)=point after standards have been tightened, with no compensation paid; (3)= point reached after standards are tightened and compensation is paid.

through the diagram represents one "indifference curve" in a social welfare function. The situation illustrated might relate to a situation in which it is possible to tighten standards on radiation emissions. This will work to the benefit of A, an emissions recipient let us say, and to the detriment of B, who was previously saving funds on radiation control. Moreover, assessments consistent with the figure might show that A would pay $100 to tighten standards, and B would be willing to go along for an $80 side payment. If such transfers could be arranged, matters could be improved for both individuals, with A, for example, providing B with $90, and getting to point 3. But in our society such compensation will rarely be provided, and we will be forced to compare between points 1 and 2. At present we have no unequivocal standards for making that comparison.

It is perhaps worthwhile to make two further points on the virtue of Pareto optimality as a guide to decisions for environmental regulation. First, if the institutional mechanisms are not available to carry out the transfers that would be required to produce a Pareto improvement, it is not appropriate to suggest that the present allocation is not Pareto optimal. Institutional constraints are no less a boundary to welfare than are resource constraints. Second, even where the lack of Pareto optimality can be clearly demonstrated, this need not provoke an undue degree of concern. A situation that misses optimality by a single dollar is considered nonoptimal, just as is a situation for which the efficiency sacrifice should be tallied in the billions of dollars. The first does not really merit our policy concern; the second clearly does.

The Pareto optimality concept has been overstressed in policy discussions perhaps because it is the only unambiguous measure with which economists can provide us. Rarely does it lead to clear policy prescriptions. Between many pairs of alternatives it offers no ranking either way. In those situations for which Pareto optimality does show one alternative to be superior, it gives no indication of the margin of superiority.

To attempt to invoke any of the various measures of the value of lives or disabilities is to attempt to approach Pareto-optimal situations. Fortunately, from the standpoint of analytic simplicity, if the magnitudes of the risks involved are small, and if they are fairly evenly spaced across the population, the distinction between potential Pareto improvements and actual Pareto improvements will not be significant. Whatever measure that individuals would think is an appropriate indicator of their estimated losses will be a roughly appropriate indicator for policy, for the changes that significantly help some at the expense of others are not likely to be encountered.

PROCEDURES FOR VALUING LIVES   433

Frequently Proposed Measures of the Values of Lives

1. DISCOUNTED CONSUMPTION. One frequently employed indicator is to look at discounted consumption as the total gain that an individual receives for remaining alive. There are a variety of objections to this approach. First, it in no way assesses how pleasurable the individual finds his existence, or indeed whether additional funds would make much of a difference. Some individuals commit suicide, after all. Others might be willing to give up a substantial amount in terms of survival probability for an increase in yearly income. The major difficulty with relying on discounted consumption is that it really has no connection with the quantity that is to be determined: willingness to pay for reduced probability of death. Total consumption is determined more by an accounting relationship with lifetime income plus net transfers than it is by any marginal optimization procedure.

2. DISCOUNTED PRODUCTION. An equally popular, though no more compelling, measure of the value of life is discounted production. In theory discounted production takes into account the resources that the society as a whole would lose if the individual ceased to exist.[11] Once again, however, the concept has no connection to tastes or preferences; neither does it include any notion of marginal optimization. Recognizing that the probabilities of death are small, do we really want to prevent a risk-sharing pool of individuals from spending 1 percent of their net production to protect themselves against a 1/10 of 1 percent loss? Admittedly, if sure death were the consequence being prevented, and if no one else cared, discounted production might be the upper bound on valuation. But fortunately that is not the situation, at least where such matters as the control of radiation are concerned. At the time that decisions are made on what levels of control to employ, no individual will be faced with more than a small fraction as a probability of death. This implies that monetary amounts significantly in excess of lost productivity could be extracted to eliminate the radiation peril, at the same time increasing everyone's welfare above what it otherwise would be.[12]

---

[11] Rice and Cooper [1967], employing 1964 data and a 4% discount rate, calculated a present value of earnings figure of $136,121 for white males 25–29 years of age. For nonwhite males over 85 years, the equivalent number was $396.

[12] This suggests that in general more will be paid when environmental risks are

The key to this apparently paradoxical result is the absence of significant income effects. For large probabilities of loss, the constraint on payment imposed by one's discounted lifetime income may become a significant factor in limiting one's willingness to pay. There is an additional, more psychological phenomenon at play as well. Individuals seem to be willing to pay some not insignificant amount to protect themselves against any identified risk, however small its probability.[13] Insurance companies capitalize on this tendency by offering actuarially unfair double indemnity coverage for very unlikely ways of dying. Once the salesman suggests, "And if your death should be by so-and-so," the customer may be willing to expend a few extra pennies to get many extra dollars in case of so-and-so. Assuming away anxiety — and that is a massive assuming away — this course would make sense only if so-and-so were an exceptionally expensive way to die.[14] It may thus be that radiation-induced deaths are particu-

---

spread around the population than when the same risk is concentrated on a few individuals. Yet that seems somewhat contrary to our common sense notions of both risk aversion and equity. The difficulty is that the lottery has been resolved too soon. Some people have already escaped from the risk. To see that our common sense notions were correct, consider two different situations. Situation A offers a 1% probability of death one year from now to each of 100 people. This probability will never be updated. Situation B offers the same 1% probability, but in one day's time it will be announced which two individuals will each incur a ½ probability of death, with the other 98 escaping further risk. Which situation would an individual pay more to avoid? Initially, the amounts probably would not differ. But if there were a two-day wait before any amounts could be collected, situation A would likely produce a greater expected total than situation B.

The examples in the text, in which personal income effects outweigh community concern, are perhaps very typical in areas of environmental control. They raise the question of whether, when victim groups can be identified, we should not revert to a hypothetical question: How would we have decided if the high-risk group had not yet been identified? Consider a society that knew it was to be confronted with an array of environmental risk situations over a series of years. Right now its victim groups are not known. This society could increase the expected welfares of its citizens by agreeing to resolve all future questions as if they had arisen now, before further definition of the suffering groups was carried out. This suggests that there may be advantages to drawing up legislation for environmental control that does not look too closely at the specifics of certain situations. This consideration may be reinforced in a majority rule society. (The counter argument is sometimes made that only intense interests get recognized in our democracy.)

13 See Acton's [1973] work on mobile cardiac units for documentation on this score.

14 Single-trip air travel insurance makes no sense actuarially. Because it represents such a small probability of total death risks, it can hardly be sensible contingency planning. Its big payoff may be relief from anxiety surrounding the risks of a specific event.

larly to be avoided, for the significant chance of large accompanying medical care costs makes them likely to be expensive.

3. NET CONTRIBUTION TO SOCIETY. It is frequently proposed that an individual's life or health be valued by the amount of goods that the remainder of society would lose on net, for example through forgone taxes, were that person to die or become ill. There are two basic objections to this standard. First, it fails to take into account the valuation of some very relevant members of society: the individual and his family. Second, it looks only at the value that society would attach to the individual's economic contribution, and leaves aside measures such as compassion, bereavement, and the fact that society does not like to see its members die.

It is easy to illustrate the incompleteness of this approach. Would we not pay for some measures that were designed to improve the health and well-being of our elder citizens, even though they are a net drain on society's resources? The answer is sometimes given: Yes, but that is why we restrict the application of the net contribution measure to individuals in their productive years, or to those whose productive years stretch before them. That answer is unacceptable. For whatever leads us to have concern for the nonproductive elderly — call it the X factor — would apply to our productive individuals as well. The magnitude of this X factor should be added to the value of the lost productivity to secure any estimate of the value to the society itself. Perhaps the "net contribution to society" approach is based on some empirical observation that among productive individuals the X factor is trivial relative to net contribution. Unfortunately, no evidence is generally given for that claim.

This all implies that net contribution to society should be taken primarily as an indication of a clear lower bound on the value that society in general should place on an individual's life. It should be added to the amount that the individual himself and his family would pay to avoid the risk. If this does not clearly preclude taking the risk, then it would be worthwhile to delve further and see how highly society's noneconomic losses should be tallied.

4. VALUATIONS OF LIVES AND RISKS OF LIVES IN OTHER AREAS OF SOCIETY. It is frequently asserted that we should observe how much

individuals in high-risk occupations, or who live in high-risk areas, charge for assuming these risks. This, it is expected, will give us some indication as to how society should assess the value of removing such a risk for society in general. The comparison is not fully apt, as long as the first class of risks is voluntarily assumed and compensated. The logical problem is that the people who are assuming the risks are those who value them the least in relation to the benefits they get for risking them. They may be the poor, they may be the people whose probability assessments are most in error, they may be the people who legitimately have the lowest probability of being injured, they may be the people who will die soon anyway, or they may be the people who value their own lives the least highly.

Differential benefits may also account for certain individuals or groups accepting voluntary risks of death. Evel Knievel commands a small fortune for engaging in his dangerous activities. People who would otherwise die or suffer greatly are likely to be willing to undergo life-threatening surgery. Individuals who attach great value to their time might take a plane when a boat would be safer. One conclusion is evident. People who choose to engage in activities that place their lives at greater than usual risk are not representative of society in general. If the benefits and costs of taking such risks are independently distributed across the population, then a valuation of lives based on the assessments of those who voluntarily assume risks would tend to be an underestimate.

This brief review makes it evident that there are conceptual and philosophical difficulties inherent in any procedure that attempts to attach a value to life, though conducting assessments with the aid of such procedures may nevertheless be helpful. In many circumstances policy choices may not change substantially if estimates of the value of a life vary by a factor of 10. Getting a valuation that is accurate within a factor of 3 might be very useful.

IV. *Special Problems in Valuing Lives*

Procedures for valuing lives run up against a host of special problems that are unlikely to be encountered with the valuation of traditional commodities. Five of these problems, all of which are of particular interest in relation to valuing the life-threatening consequences of ionizing radiation, are addressed here. The first two are encountered because the impacts of radiation stretch long beyond the year of exposure. The remaining three arise because great uncertainties are involved in predicting the effects of radiation on health.

Extrapolating Current Statistics to Allow for Productivity Growth. Virtually all calculations having to do with the value of human lives rely on current values. If productivity is to serve as some sort of benchmark, they find out, for example, how much a 45-year-old male is earning in 1975. If consumption is to be measured, current consumption levels are computed.

This is obviously an approximation, and if it is expected that per capita income will continue to rise in the United States, the approximation is not a very good one.[15] For purposes of illustration, let us say that discounted consumption is the figure we are after. If the discount rate is 8 percent, a man with a 40-year remaining life span and an annual consumption of $10,000 will have a lifetime discounted consumption value of $128,786. But if that consumption stream is rising at a real rate of 3 percent per year, then his discounted consumption value is $183,568. Obviously, the longer the lifetime, the higher the rate of productivity growth; and the lower the rate of discount, the greater will be the discrepancy (both absolute and percentage) between the approximation and the true value.[16]

If individuals were asked from the beginning what they would be willing to pay to protect themselves against a particular risk, then in theory they would have allowed for their rising income streams, and there would be no need to conduct either the type of corrections just discussed or those that will be mentioned shortly. But there is a significant question as to the capability of individuals to evaluate successfully and equitably their future preferences and welfare. This problem has been referred to in

---

[15] This all abstracts, of course, from the inflation issue. We assume that all numbers are corrected to be measured in terms of real dollars.

[16] The major discrepancies in a variety of real-world situations are likely to relate to probability assessments rather than to computational assumptions. For example, factor-of-10 differences in probability estimates have been on the low side when safety studies of new technologies have been concerned.

the past as inadequate telescopic facility. The term temporal myopia would perhaps be more descriptive.

Even allowing for rising income streams will not be a sufficient correction if the valuation of life is not constant in relation to the stream being observed. In this essay we suggest that consumers' preferences, assuming that they can be educated to understand the intricacies and ramifications of what is happening, should be the guide for policy. This would suggest that the "good," a life secure from a particular type of danger, should be valued like any other commodity. With income streams rising, there is the possibility that the relation between the value attached to life and the size of that stream, or some related stream such as consumption, may change.

Whether this would be the case boils down to the question: What is the income elasticity of demand for the good "reduction of risk to life"? Or to ask a closely related question in lay language: As a person's income goes up, what happens to the fraction of his lifetime income that he will pay to avoid a 1 percent risk of his life? If the answer to this question is that the fraction goes up (in which case the elasticity is greater than one), then even correcting life-evaluation measures by allowing for productivity growth will be an underestimate. If the fraction goes down, it is an overestimate. Hard evidence about this elasticity value does not exist, and information drawn from either longitudinal or cross-sectional studies would be subject to a wide range of statistical problems of interpretation.[17]

Intergenerational Considerations. Economists and policy analysts are frequently called upon to evaluate social policies whose consequences stretch many years into the future. When lives are at risk, particularly if the risks are long lived as they are with contamination from radiation, new complexities may enter. How

---

[17] Observing that richer individuals pay a greater proportion of their funds at a point in time would not be convincing. Because of complications involving relative income position, a man earning $10,000 when the median income is $8,000 is really not in the same situation at all as a man earning $10,000 when the median income has risen to $15,000. There is the additional problem that mere knowledge of market expenditures would not enable us to disentangle supply and demand effects. Individuals are not buying the good "x% increased probability of survival" at some constant price. It should probably be expected that safety expenditures would show diminishing returns, in which case even if the elasticity is greater than one, a man who doubles his income might less than double his expenditures on safety.

should we take into account the feelings of people who are not presently alive? This category can even include those who are already dead. A grandparent near death may benefit when his grandchild's school puts up some safety devices, for he knows that the child's life is less likely to be sacrificed. This raises a question. After this beneficiary dies, should any losses be assigned to him if the devices are removed? If such losses are not tallied, and everyone is watching, the natural consequence is that living individuals will lose faith in contracts that outlast their lives. By weighing in their decisions the preferences that the dead would express, were they here to express them, those presently living may enable themselves to secure enforceable promises from succeeding generations. This is an argument in favor of perpetuities, and against some present legal standards.

This whole discussion may resemble an excursion to fantasyland. But it may have some important consequences with regard to environmental protection, including the control of low-level radiation. If the present generation were confronted with the problem of whether it should proceed with nuclear reactors, in full knowledge that that action would raise the level of radiation for many elements of society, it might decide that it would be willing to forgo this opportunity if that action would protect future societies forever. But it would not be in a position to control the choices of future societies.

Although these future societies might be delighted to be the beneficiaries of the generosity of the present society, they might not be willing to sacrifice their own immediate benefit to provide a less contaminated environment for their successors. It is quite possible indeed that if we could get all future societies to contract together, they might all agree to maintain a policy of purity. But because each must act in isolation, this potential optimal agreement will not be maintainable. This is a familiar, though unfortunate, outcome in many situations. Individuals who are conveying externalities to one another cannot conveniently contract, so an inefficient outcome results. Here the good that provides externalities is the presence of a contamination-free environment.[18] If history continues itself, our descendants will be richer

---

[18] It is worth remarking on the once stirring debate within economics as to whether there is any way to charge future generations for benefits conferred upon them.

than we in pure material goods. This makes it likely that the valuation that they will place on lower genetic deformity rates or cancer incidence, relative, say, to ears of corn or color television sets, will be much greater than that of the average citizen at present. This increase in relative valuation will indeed be magnified if, as may be the case, they are poorer in these environment-related goods, even though richer in other goods.

Most analyses of intergenerational situations relate not to lives but rather to more traditional economic goods. How much should we leave to our descendants in the way of physical capital stock? Environmentalists have taken policy a step further and have made us concern ourselves with the question of what levels of environmental endowments should be provided for the future. But even this question does not begin to get at the types of transfers that are involved with contamination from radiation, or its avoidance.[19]

What right do we have to increase the level of radiation for future generations, and/or what right do we have to contaminate the stock of genetic material by allowing ourselves to be irradiated? Once this question is addressed, we must go a step further and ask whose preferences should be included when these issues are investigated. In our individualistic society, it is traditionally thought that the government's welfare is solely a function of the welfare of its citizens. If we accept this premise, which citizens should count: those alive now, those who will be alive within the near future, or all future citizens?

One frequently heard argument is that the wishes of future citizens should be considered to the extent that they are reflected in the altruistic concerns of those alive today. No individual will

---

There is some possibility for passing charges forward because of the overlap in generations. That is, we can assess today's youngsters at a high rate, for example by drafting them for public service below market wages when they are 18, or by charging them higher social security taxes. This falls under the category of redistribution within the generation of individuals alive at one period of time. But for long-run assessment of charges there are no means for assessing charges on generations not alive. The only thing that can be done is to provide them with less capital stock by way of inheritance. When we think of capital stock, we are accustomed to think in terms of machines or housing. But attention to environmental considerations makes it painfully evident that the purity of the environment and the integrity of the gene pool are two capital stocks of importance.

[19] Most other environmental concerns can be corrected at a price, though that price may be exceptionally high. It is true that restoration, however successful, cannot erase the knowledge that the original situation was at one time despoiled. This raises the difficult question of authenticity.

wish to have a deformed descendant, and anyone should be willing
to pay something to avoid that possibility. There is the significant
issue, however, whether when the links of descent become multi-
generational this sort of altruism does not substantially under-
represent the impacts that will be truly felt.[20] If it does, then
there is at least an a priori basis for arguing that we should think
somewhat differently when we consider imposing on the future
the types of risks associated wih low-level radiation. At the very
least, we should attempt to generate some explicit public debate
on the issue. It may be that broken chromosomes and a radioactive environment passed forward to the future are quite different
from a more advanced technological capability and an increase in
machine tools, the types of forward transfers that are relatively
familiar.

Anxiety. No serious policy analysts are suggesting that radiation
exposure levels will be such that individuals in general will have
a substantial probability of suffering individual damage. Assuming that the physical processes were well understood, a typical
individual might be confronted with a situation in which he was
told that he had an additional 1/10 of 1 percent chance of con-
tracting cancer caused by man-induced radiation sources. We
have a great deal of difficulty thinking about very small probability
levels, and the individual might find it perplexing to distinguish
between 1/10 of 1 percent and 1/100 of 1 percent. Fortunately,
decision and risk analysis can offer some guidelines. We might
ask the individual how much he would pay to avoid a 10 percent
increased chance of cancer. Then we might divide this amount by
100 to get an approximate idea of what a 1/10 of 1 percent chance
is worth.

Though any calculation that can give additional guidance
should be welcomed, it should be recognized that this procedure

---

[20] This observation should be distinguished from the argument that suggests that
the social rate of discount should be lower than private rates. That claim derives
from the belief that our contemporaries value the welfare of an individual's descendants relative to his own more than he does, and that much provision for the
future goes to individuals other than one's descendants. These matters are less at
issue here, except to the extent that individuals take personal risks for which they
themselves are compensated. Whereas a man may be willing to be a radiation
technician, incurring risks to his descendants' gene pools in return for extra compensation, the rest of society may be unhappy letting him take this course. Thus
even if the government is taking into account only the welfare of present citizens,
it may wish to rule out this type of employment.

can be misleading in each of two possible ways. First, it ignores the possibility of income effects. (The income effect in this context has an unusual form: When an individual is put in a position where he must purchase a bigger reduction, he is in effect poorer.) An individual may willingly sacrifice 10 percent of his income to avoid a 1 percent chance of death. He could hardly sacrifice 200 percent of his income to avoid a 20 percent probability of death. This would suggest that if the income effect were the only complicating factor, the produce of 1/100 and the 10 percent answer would be a lower bound on the 1/10 of 1 percent answer.[21]

Second, it fails to consider anxiety. Once a new element of risk is announced, it provides individuals with something to think and worry about.[22] It would seem rather unlikely that a 1/10 of 1 percent risk would generate only 1/10 the anxiety of a 1 percent risk of the same loss. In other words, the amount that would be paid to avoid the anxiety associated with a risk would be very nonlinear with the probability of the risk. For smaller risks it would be proportionately greater.[23]

Because the types of risks that are being discussed in connection with radiation exposure are of the low-probability variety, we must expect the anxiety cost to be a fairly substantial proportion of the amount that an individual would pay to avoid the risk. Mere extrapolation from more significant risks in other areas would not seem to be valid.[24] The medical area would seem likely

---

[21] This ignores problems of valuing money available after death. Legacy dollars in most cases should receive a lower valuation than consumption dollars. This observation provides the basis for the "revolver paradox." A rational bachelor forced to play Russian roulette a single time should pay more for removing one bullet out of two than for removing one bullet out of one. In the former case there is a 1/6 chance (assuming it to be a 6-cylinder revolver) that his payment will diminish his legacy rather than his consumption. That the legacy-consumption argument is not well understood is made evident by the large number of bachelors without dependents who still buy life insurance.

[22] This worrying period would be eliminated if, as is usually assumed when calibrating utilities, all lotteries were resolved immediately. The delay in resolving lotteries on health effects can also introduce planning problems. Spence and Zeckhauser [1972] show that the presence of such problems can make it impossible to generate a traditional von Neumann-Morgenstern utility function. In a forthcoming paper, Shepard et al. [1975] will extrapolate this result to the life-saving context.

[23] Perhaps there is a consciousness threshold. Perhaps noting any changes in small probability risks, even reductions, is bad. It may call attention to something that might otherwise be overlooked.

[24] Traditional decision analysis does not allow for the anxiety concept because it

to provide the best examples of the anxiety-eliminating expenditures that should be borne in mind here. A 40-year-old expectant mother whose future child is at risk from Down's syndrome, a genetic ailment that is detectable by amniocentesis, might welcome that procedure even though she would not have an abortion whatever it reveals. There is a high probability that the results of the test will be negative, and will thereby relieve her anxiety during the course of her pregnancy.

Risk-Taking or Risk-Averting Behavior on Number of Lives Lost. The significance of interpersonal relationships for the valuation of lives should influence society's willingness to accept various categories of risk. Should there be risk aversion related to total number of lives lost? That would imply that society should be more willing to take one chance in 1,000 of losing one life rather than one chance in 10,000 of losing 10 lives. If there were some threshold, say 3 lives, below which the general public was not informed of the loss of life, the one-life loss would not come to the attention of anyone except those immediately involved. Society at large might prefer risk aversion on lives lost when such a limited number of lives was involved. However, if the number of lives lost were multiplied tenfold to 100 and 1,000, the preference of the uninvolved public might reverse to risk-taking. Either the 100 or 1,000 life loss would be regarded as a major catastrophe, but the latter would be only 10 percent as likely to occur and (in the sense that von Neumann-Morgenstern utility functions define intensities of preference) it might not be considered 10 times as bad.

Consideration of the valuations of those immediately involved with those who die might strengthen any societal preference for risk-taking. A happily married childless couple that thought the matter through should almost certainly prefer to take a joint 1/1,000 risk of death rather than each taking it separately. Their risks of death would be the same; but all the unfortunate consequences of widowhood would be eliminated.[25]

---

is assumed that all lotteries are resolved instantaneously. Radiation may not produce its adverse effects, if any, until many years have elapsed. There may be substantial anxiety costs that should be computed in any calculation of social welfare.

[25] Many parents do not fly together in an effort to ensure at least one survivor to bring up the children. This may not be an optimal strategy, even if only the welfare of the children is considered. Depending on adoption or guardianship

The spirit of this example can be carried over into the analysis of risks that are of consequence to the general society. If any explosion wipes out a community of 10,000 individuals, most of the people who would have placed a high value on the lives of those killed will have been killed themselves. By contrast, if an additional 10,000 people are killed in auto accidents, most of the major externality sufferers will still be alive. Other things equal, concentrating the lives lost on a geographic basis reduces the externality loss per death. The general lesson is that at least for those closely connected to individuals with lives at risk, it may be beneficial for society to exhibit risk-preferring behavior.[26]

Wrong Models and Low Probabilities. The assessment of the damages deriving from exposure to radiation, as well as from many other types of health hazards, is made difficult because some of the most significant outcomes may be associated with low probabilities. Much of the difficulty arises because neither individual citizens nor policymakers are well equipped to assess their personal evaluation of low probabilities. Moreover, such probabilities are very difficult to assess on a scientific basis.

If one reads for example the literature on the contamination dangers from nuclear facilities, one discovers that many of the problems are foreseen to occur with probabilities such as 10^{-6} or 10^{-9}. Yet studies on the same subject by environmentally concerned critics may place the risks 1,000 times as high. Even if there is only one chance in 100 that the high-probability critics are correct, computation of the expected probability shows that the danger should be assessed at roughly 11 times the original estimate.

Many of these assessments deal with physical processes that are not yet fully understood; others deal with situations in which a combination of systems must fail, or in which a series of events must turn unfavorable before the unfortunate outcome occurs. The

---

opportunities, it may be preferable to have one chance in 1,000 to be orphaned rather than one in 500 to lose one of two parents.

[26] Many individuals not trained in utility theory and cost-benefit analysis find it difficult to understand this argument or accept its conclusion. This raises a difficult question of elitism. Should paternalistic decisions be made for them, i.e., doing for them what they would likely choose to do if they spent the possibly many hours that would be required to understand the situation fully; or should society respect their expressed preferences?

PROCEDURES FOR VALUING LIVES   445

difficulty may be that certain assessors may portray an optimistic or a pessimistic bias in all of their subjective probabilities.[27] From an analytic standpoint, the danger can be pointed out as deriving from a likely correlation in the errors in assessing probabilities. Say that we have an analyst who is equally likely to be too pessimistic or too optimistic, but we do not know which. Say that the true probabilities of three independent events which must occur if the catastrophe is to befall us are 0.1, 0.2, and 0.4. If the analyst is pessimistic, he will assess these 50 percent too high, as 0.15, 0.3, and 0.6. The probability of the catastrophe will be identified as $0.15 \times 0.3 \times 0.6 = 0.027$. If he is optimistic and assesses them as 50 percent too low, then it will be $0.05 \times 0.1 \times 0.2 = 0.001$. The danger is that if the cutoff probability is, say, 0.01, we will be accepting the unacceptable risk one-half of the time. The opposite result can occur as well. We may be turning down acceptable risks because we assess too pessimistically. (Indeed, the average of the optimistic and pessimistic assessments will be above the true probability.) The important point to recognize is that probability assessments may be substantially in error when compound events are involved.

There is an associated danger worthy of mention. Frequently those who formulate policies involving low-probability events believe that they understand the processes and the means to control them. But the very fact that these are low-probability events means that they are not likely to have had much experience with them, and that they will not accumulate such experience quickly. It is important that policymakers draw the significant distinction between understanding all there is to know at present about a process of control, and knowing all there is to know about it.

---

[27] There is much evidence that individuals are poor probability assessors and perhaps more important, that they underestimate their poorness by assessing probabilities too tightly. See the work by Alpert and Raiffa [1969] on the training of probability assessors. Evidence from psychological experiments indicates that people underestimate dangers when they feel they have some control over a situation. See Otway [1972]. This tendency would introduce a downward bias in the implicit life valuations of those who voluntarily assume risks. Howard Kunreuther and various collaborators, examining evidence on the methods by which individuals insure or protect themselves against natural hazards in both laboratory and field settings, stress problems of perception as they relate to low probability events. Kunreuther develops a bounded rationality model that explains why, for example, individuals in high risk areas do not take out federally subsidized, actuarially favorable insurance. See Kunreuther [1974] for a recent report on this continuing work.

V. *The Importance of Process*

This essay has focused on methods for assessing the values of lives, and the problems inherent in applying such methods. For many societal decisions that affect life-threatening activities, the procedure by which the decision is made may be as important as the actual dollar numbers employed to value the lives involved. Many analysts dismiss too quickly the significance of having an equitable and widely accepted process. (The criminal justice field is an area in which our convictions about the integrity of process have made it difficult for traditional cost-benefit analysts to have much of an impact. It is no surprise that "process" is a watchword of the legal profession.) When process is important, analysts can take any of three tacks. They can labor earnestly to provide the inputs that are required by the process. Alternatively, they can undertake investigations of the outcomes of the process; has it been producing desirable results? Finally, they can examine the process itself, with the hope that by so doing they can improve its performance.

An example of providing the appropriate input might be to suggest to EPA administrators who are attempting to set standards for radiation contamination just how many lives the standards will affect, what it will cost to save those lives (at the margin), and what is being spent to save lives in other environmentally affected areas. The second approach might involve work on the SST, which demonstrated that there was no way to have supersonic or even subsonic flight in the stratosphere without any "detectable influence." The effort, in this instance, would be to get this unintentionally unworkable standard altered. The third approach might be represented by research that would try to determine how EPA should interpret various legalistic phrases of executive orders such as "as low as readily achievable" when they are applied to particular environmental pollutants.

All three of these approaches have the virtue that, rather than ignoring them, they attempt to complement and inform presently accepted procedures for decisionmaking. Not only will the analysis have greater impact than the more myopic approaches being cautioned against; the final outcome may be more attractive. Individuals may far prefer an outcome that they believe has been justly arrived at, to one where some unimpeachable but nevertheless distasteful calculations were the basis of decision. This point about the importance of process is readily supported by elementary economics. (1) Most of the decisions that we are making in the area of environmental protection, and certainly with regard to the regulation of low-level radiation, though they may cost or save great numbers of absolute lives, can have at most a marginal impact on total life expectancy in the society.[28] (2) The dollars that we will be spending because we tighten standards on radiation can run into the billions or even tens of billions of dollars. Still, this expenditure is unlikely to be more than a small percentage of our GNP. (3) The basis for decisions is not a variable that takes continuous values between fully acceptable and unacceptable. Either we are following some procedures that have general adherence, or we are not. The use of an acceptable process for environmental decisionmaking is what has elsewhere been labeled an "on-off" variable.[29] If we can keep this variable "on" in return for less than extreme sacrifices on either one of the first two variables, then we may be gaining an extraordinary amount at small cost.

The attractiveness of a process for making policy choices will be enhanced the more closely it accords with valued beliefs. When risks of lives are involved, an important valued belief is that society will not give up a life to save dollars, even a great many dollars. Rarely is this belief, widely held albeit mistaken, put to a clear test. When it is, it may be desirable for society to spend an inordinate amount on each of a few lives to preserve a comforting myth. Such a myth-preserving action was taken when the federal government assumed the costs of renal dialysis. The specific individuals who would have died in the absence of the government program were known. The lives at stake in this policy context were identified lives. They can be contrasted with the nonpersonalized, statistical lives that are saved, for example, by expenditures to construct highway safety barriers. If lives are sacrificed for dollars, the valued belief that society will not make such sacri-

---

28 It is sometimes asserted that a primary health effect of exposure to radiation is an increase in spontaneous abortions, stillborns, and infant mortalities. If life expectancy were computed from conception, rather than from birth, radiation would have a significant effect on this widely discussed indicator.

29 See Zeckhauser [1973].

fices is more likely to be jeopardized when the specific identities of the victims are known. An effort to preserve this valued belief may explain in part the frequently noted difference between the resources expended to save statistical and identified lives. Society, acting collectively, shows itself willing to pay much more to save the latter.

Counterexamples do exist, however. If we knew that on average one maiden would be snatched by the dragon, and if the dragon could be dissuaded from his snatching by a $1 million payment, we might well make that payment. Here the life that would be saved would be statistical in the sense that we would never know which maiden turned out to be the beneficiary of our expenditure. A more realistic example might be the maintenance at a local hospital of a medicine for a rare but swiftly fatal disease.

Acceptance of the importance of process in life valuation can have some discomforting implications, particularly for those who are trained to the use of analysis. We may find that we are spending $100,000 to save a life in one area, but sacrificing lives in others that could be saved for an expenditure of $10,000. The consequence is that with a reallocation of resources toward the latter area we could have both more lives and more money. Yet, if the decisions in the two areas were well accepted by the society, then it might be preferable not to change. Lives and dollars are sacrificed in return for more satisfaction with the ways these decisions have been made. Agreement on process enables society to avoid what might be difficult conflicts involving equity.

How could this "inefficient" situation have come about? The answer is simple. Procedures are developed and generated by different groups of individuals, for different purposes, and there is rarely much of an attempt to keep them all consistent, at least with respect to the ways lives are valued at the margin. If the state of industrial progress remained constant for a few decades, and if levels of environmental degradation were frozen for the same period, the opportunity to bring these standards into conformity with one another might develop. But those who are attempting to rationalize procedures and make them consistent will soon find that new targets arise constantly and that old ones move significantly, indeed sometimes swiftly. At any one point in time, there will be substantial inconsistencies. (What this suggests, per-

PROCEDURES FOR VALUING LIVES   449

haps, is that efforts to derive standards for one policy area based
on the way lives or illnesses have been implicitly priced in another
will not bear significant fruit. This is a matter on which more
will be said later.)

Once the importance of process is recognized, the next logical
step is to inquire what possible regulatory mechanisms are available. It is not the purpose of this essay to detail the way in which
regulatory mechanisms might work, but it is imperative to note
that the relationship between appropriate valuation and regulatory process is multifaceted, and that standards for valuation
should never be drawn up until it is understood how they will be
employed.

The first natural question, particularly within our capitalist
society, is, Why should there be any need for regulation whatsoever? To some people the need for regulation may be so obvious
that they tend to ignore this question. That is not a satisfactory
stance. Unless we understand why we might wish to regulate, we
will be unable to arrive at an appropriate regulatory standard or
an efficacious regulatory mechanism. One possibility, perhaps
favored by economists enamored with the purity of the core of
their discipline, is that radiation be recognized as just another
costly input of production processes. If flights by SSTs deplete
the ozone layer, leading to increased ultraviolet radiation and
higher incidence of skin cancer, then this radiation dose is the
cost of obtaining swifter travel.[30]

The ultraviolet radiation example makes it clear why damage
from radiation cannot be treated as a market-traded good. In the
absence of governmental intervention, the cost is borne by all
members of society, not just the purchasers of air travel. Still this
is no more than the traditional notion of an external diseconomy
or public bad, and economists have developed many techniques

[30] There is much debate on the manner in which this radiation should be valued
as an input. If expenditures could be made that would lead to the same speed and
comfort for the plane, but lesser ozone depletion, hence less of an increase in radiation, then the magnitude of the marginal expenditure relative to the savings in
radiation would indicate how much we were saving from using radiation as an input.
In many instances, we will not be operating over a range where such tradeoffs exist.
It may be prohibitively expensive to undertake actions that have a significant effect
in diminishing radiation damage without in some other way lessening effectiveness.
Then there will be no clear indication of what the input is saving us, though it
will be possible to establish an upper or a lower bound.

for dealing with these externalities. One possibility would be to employ the equivalent of effluent charges for the contamination. But this approach would not get around the problem of valuing human lives and health. It might also be regarded as unfavorable in and of itself. Though the difference as measured in eventual lives and dollars expended may be slim, it may seem more desirable for our government to protect us against a form of pollution by establishing standards than by selling rights to take lives, even though the victims' identities would never become known. If, as would seem desirable, the standards are established in cognizance of the economic costs of tightening emissions controls, then there may be no difference between the two sets of outcomes. But the weight of government pressures, and therefore the public recognition of the process, may be very different.[31]

Even though we may not wish to implement an effluent charge scheme in practice, consideration of the capabilities and drawbacks of such a scheme may be a way of gaining further insight into what procedures we should like to employ in valuing health and life when we do adopt a standards approach. An alternative approach, also worthy of consideration as a means of getting our thinking straight, would be to look at compensation arrangements. This approach could be implemented in a variety of ways. We might look to the courts to see how that particular institution within society is valuing lives. This information might be complemented by research assessing the willingness of individuals to risk their lives depending on the compensation amounts that would be paid.[32]

There are a variety of problems with the use of compensation measures as a means of assessing life valuation. First and foremost, determinations in court do not represent anything close to an analytic thinking process, neither is there even consistency across time or across jurisdictions in the determination of financial amounts for damages.[33]

31 Actually, if the standards are not appropriately calibrated in each area on a cost-effective basis, then the standards approach may result in more lives being sacrificed at any particular economic price. Drawing on the arguments above, however, it may be felt that this loss of efficiency is merited in moving toward the more attractive standards approach.

32 In some sense, this would be equivalent to looking at the wages of sandhogs or steeplejacks to see how risks or deaths were valued.

33 A very few lawyers have been credited with raising, by a remarkable multiple,

PROCEDURES FOR VALUING LIVES   451

Part of the difficulty is that the legal process is not well suited to deal with probabilistic phenomena.[34] Consider a hypothetical case. A woman who lives in the neighborhood of a radiation-emitting facility contracts cancer and dies. It is discovered that her mother, who did not live in that neighborhood, had died of a similar malignancy. It is understood that there is a relationship between this type of cancer and radiation. But there is also a well-known hereditary tendency toward this particular cancer. Even if there were an unambiguous way to place a valuation on the woman's life, our courts as presently constituted would probably be unwilling to rule on whether and to what extent the radiation increased the probability of the cancer's occurrence. Admittedly, this same difficult assessment procedure would be required before any standards for environmental protection could be devised, but regulatory agencies are likely to be better equipped than courts to assess damages when causality can at best be interpreted on a probabilistic basis.

A second problem associated with any reliance on observed compensation arrangements as a means of establishing appropriate levels of emission, or as a more general guideline for policy judgments, is the issue of who must compensate whom. There has been an extensive debate in the economics literature about the consequences of granting the polluter as opposed to the recipient of the pollution, original rights. For example, should it matter to ultimate resource allocation whether (a) those who are the sufferers from radiation pollution are presented with a no rights situation, their choice being whether to move, insulate, or bribe the polluter to diminish the contamination; or (b) these individuals are guaranteed the right to a pollution-free environment, where any nonnatural contaminator would have to pay them for undertaking risks? If the conclusion is that it does not matter, then except as it affects one-time, lump-sum transfers of income in response to a shift in a benchmark, policymakers need not concern

---

the amounts that have been paid for various malpractice or negligence injuries. We would hardly want governmental standards to move substantially up or down in response to certain vagaries within the legal system.

[34] A good example is provided by the concept of contributory negligence in tort law. In other than no-fault states, if it can be shown that a person contributed to the likelihood of an accident, his rights of recovery are forfeited. See Posner [1974] and Diamond [1974] for discussions of economic models of the operation of the tort system.

themselves with who gets rights or where standards are set. It would be essential for efficiency, however, that some benchmark be established; from it, polluters and recipients could purchase higher or lower pollutant levels.[35]

But there have been no clear benchmarks in the real world, much less payments for deviations from them. Furthermore, there are inordinate transactions costs (costs in time and money required to make and enforce contracts) associated with any attempts to implement schemes of this sort. This implies that observed market-produced outcomes should not be employed automatically as guides for policy. That a particular polluter has been allowed to continue in his contaminating ways may not reveal that the damaged recipients value their losses less than his gains; rather it may reflect the fact that they have a very difficult time getting together payments that would enable them to compensate him for polluting less. For example, the tens of thousands of individuals who have suffered from taconite disposal in Lake Superior, or the millions of people who may feel their welfare diminished because of a few nations' policies of overwhaling, have no natural unit of organization. Even if these affected individuals value their losses much more highly than the polluters' or whalers' gains, and even if they would be willing to pay to reverse this situation if such a choice were presented to them, there is no obvious way that these actions can be taken. Finally, because there is a possibility that some activities will be shut down or come into being, depending on which side is granted property rights, allocation schemes may be merely locally optimal, not globally optimal. The social optimum may be quite far from what would be produced.[36] If we allow a nuclear power station to locate in a populated area, without paying compensation, many citizens may leave. An ex post examination of marginal benefit and marginal cost may show the two quantities to be in equilibrium. What is not obvious is the amount that the departers would have paid if they could have stayed in

---

[35] The classic article on this subject is Coase [1960].

[36] This misallocation problem is associated with a nonconvexity in the loss function of the pollution recipient. Once the radiation level gets so high that it is resource saving for him to cease operations, his marginal losses from increased radiation fall to zero. Conversely, once control standards reach a level that a polluter can no longer profitably operate, it will no longer cost him anything if standards are raised still further. See Starrett and Zeckhauser [1974].

their old surroundings. In the industrial equivalent to this example, the firm that is injured by the contamination may cease operation, in which case its marginal loss from further pollution becomes zero. An after-the-fact look at marginal losses will not reveal this firm's preference for a less polluted situation.

Market solutions, or any attempt to simulate them, run into difficulty in another area. Not all beneficiaries or losers from whatever contract is drawn will be available to participate. First, because some forms of radiation spread over substantial geographic areas, there may be millions of individuals affected by some particular tightening or relaxation of control. They could not possibly coordinate themselves, particularly because they are likely to be members of different political jurisdictions. A quite different version of this problem arises with particular virulence when damage from radiation is concerned. Many of the potential sufferers are not even present on earth to have their interests represented; some may suffer by losing the opportunity to be born. The intergenerational equity issue is of sufficient magnitude to have received separate treatment earlier in this essay.

Compensation Paid or Not Paid. The economics literature relating to the valuation of unfortunate events concentrates heavily on the issue of compensation. The conceptual framework emerging from compensation considerations stresses two issues. First, if risks can be individually transferred, and confined only to those who wish to assume them, then individual valuations will reflect the values of the risks. Thus, for example, we observe that dangerous occupations are paid more than safe modes of employment that require similar skill levels. Second, if employers or any parties who impose risks on others are forced to pay compensation, they will impose only those risks that are economically worthwhile. Questions have been raised elsewhere in this essay as to whether such markets can be expected to perform appropriately, or whether individuals can calibrate risks involving small probabilities.

A quite different class of considerations suggests that compensation will rarely be an appropriate means to deal with a risk. This has the important implication that statistics on insurance amounts, for example, will have no significance in determining how much individuals value nonmonetary risks. Because so much of the literature on insurance deals with losses that are primarily financial, this point is readily overlooked.

Consider a woman who is confronted with the risk of breast cancer, with the likely consequence of a mastectomy. Leave aside for the moment the possibility of the spread of the cancer. The woman is offered the opportunity to pay $5,000 for a medical treatment to reduce the risk of this cancer by 5 percent. She accepts the opportunity, implying in some sense that she values the event nonremoval of her breast at $100,000. This same woman is next told that there is still a 5 percent chance that she will need to undergo this operation, the treatment reducing the original probability from 10 to 5 percent. She is offered the opportunity to purchase actuarially fair insurance, in which each premium dollar is converted to $20 of coverage. Should she purchase this insurance, say $100,000 worth for $5,000? The answer is no, unless breast removal in some way affects her marginal utility of money. If she expects her employment, marital situation, etc. to remain the same, it would be quite rational for her to insure no more than the medical expenses of this operation. This example calls into question the common assertion that, if there were a grave risk, then people would insure against it.[37]

There is even the question of whether relatively sophisticated organizations such as labor unions can represent their constituents on a rational basis when it comes to protecting them against environmental hazards such as radiation. First, union leaders may not wish to have salary increases or premiums identified as risk pay. They may not want to appear to be in the business of selling their members' lives or health. Also, they may wish to take credit for achieving wage gains through superior bargaining capability. Second, it is frequently as much in the interest of the union to overlook dangerous situations as it is for management. In a number of instances in marginal employment situations, it has been alleged that unions may have collaborated with management in discouraging the rigorous application of various government protective standards. (The fear, of course, is that there would not be a marginal readjustment, but because of institutional rigidities

---

[37] See Zeckhauser [1973] for further discussion of why one might not insure goods that are valued highly. Cook and Graham [1974], employing a rigorous methodology, have placed this argument in a more general context.

producing downward inflexibility of wages, the firm would go out
of business. Nudging up a standard could produce a substantial
loss.) Third, there is the straightforward question: Can a union
adequately conduct the analysis that shows how risky its profession
might be? The numbers may be small, the time lags until effects
show up extensive, and the incentive to fool oneself significant.
Finally, neither the union nor its members bear the full cost
of any disability. As the American experience with coal miners
shows, some significant portion of financial expenses associated
with occupational disability will eventually be borne by society
as a whole. When nonfinancial externalities are taken into account, society's total burden may seem substantially greater.

Income Distribution. One of the most troubling areas relating
to the life and health evaluation issue is the need to take income
distribution into account. Yet it seems that this issue is sometimes
introduced as a red herring. One is often told that a certain procedure is unacceptable because it does not concern itself with
distributional implications, or because it would value the lives of
the poor less than the lives of the rich. These objections could
conceivably be telling, but only if the objector would accept the
particular procedures if there were a totally egalitarian income
distribution. But such acceptance would frequently not be forthcoming, and the distribution-based objection is perhaps merely
the most convenient one at hand.[38]

What about the cases in which income distribution or lack of
attention to it may be a decisive issue? First, consistent with the
theme set forth above, process is important. If the lives or dollars
involved, though consequential, are not significant in relation to
the total magnitudes for society, then we may strongly object to a
scheme that appears to disadvantage the poor, or certain ethnic
groups, or people who live in particular places, however efficient
the scheme may appear. This issue relates to the whole question
of efficient and inefficient transfers, whether compensation will be
paid for losses incurred, and ex ante versus ex post welfare assessments. For purposes of present discussion, let us assume that a

[38] A problem can arise, of course, when there are two objections, either of which
alone would be decisive. For example, an approach might be thought to be unacceptable both because it ignored distributional questions and also because it required an unobtainable amount of information. By the criterion above, neither
objection would be identified as telling.

poor man would pay up to $5,000 to eliminate a particular risk on his life, and that a rich man would pay up to $50,000. A policy question arises in which there is the opportunity to spend $10,000 to eliminate such a risk on either of the two men, $20,000 to eliminate it on both of them.

If income transfers could be made without cost, it would be nonoptimal not to leave the life of the poor man at risk while eliminating the risk for the rich man.[39] With the $10,000 saved, we could give the poor man his indifference price for continued exposure to the risk plus a $5,000 bonus. The rich man could be charged part of his $40,000 surplus.[40]

Now income transfer schemes are rarely undertaken to compensate for particular low-level risks that are imposed on individuals, so this sort of transfer cannot be expected to take place.[41] Still there are societal policies that work to some extent in this direction. For example, tax assessments may be revised downward in areas that are newly polluted. If public policymakers really followed the individualistic ethic, then they would monitor who gains and who loses on average and at the margin from each policy measure. Then by adjusting policies so that the relative weights placed on different income groups are consistent, a more equitable income distribution could be achieved in an efficient manner. The policies that redistribute the most for a given efficiency loss would carry the heaviest redistributional load.[42] In contrast to the present situation, in which some poorly chosen redistributional efforts incur tremendous efficiency losses, the poor would be substantially better off, and so would the rest of society.

[39] This issue has shown up in different nations' preferences for reactor safety standards. India prefers to have lower standards than the United States, and to facilitate such a choice she opposes any uniform international standards.

[40] This leaves aside the problem of income effects which could produce a divergence between the buying and selling prices for the lotteries. If the probabilities involved were small, then so would be the actuarial amounts, and income effects would likely be negligible.

[41] The inability to assess sufficient externality charges frequently prevents an efficient outcome from being achieved. A firm wishing to build a nuclear plant in a small town could assume most of the burden of the town's taxes. It could even be exploited by being assessed for previously unthought-of public goods. But it probably cannot legally go around giving each citizen a cash handout, even though it and the citizens might welcome such an outcome. The result may be that the plant will be excluded from the community even though it would be willing to pay more than the townspeople's valuation of the risks it created.

[42] Even if substantial redistribution is being achieved, an efficient mix of redistributional policies is likely to include some that are outright regressive.

Attention to problems of distribution can affect our willingness to allow the free market to operate. If we are confronted with the decision, let us say, of whether to allow certain individuals to engage in high-risk professions, it may well be argued that this is unfair because the poor will be induced to pursue those professions. But are they not better off to have the opportunity available to them? Provided that they understand the risks they are taking, the answer is yes. What of the objection that we should introduce social policies that reduce their poverty and that would therefore remove their incentive to assume these risks? That objection may be valid, but until those policies are introduced, we should not further reduce the welfare of the poor by denying them occupations just because middle-class individuals would not be willing to accept them.[43] Anatole France remarked on a variety of prohibitions that discriminate against the poor in this manner: "The law, in its majestic equality, forbids the rich as well as the poor to sleep under bridges, to beg in the streets, and to steal bread."

The whole issue of denying the poor risks that they view as acceptable gets tied up with our perceptions of the income distribution. If we observe that poor people have to sell themselves into potential physical infirmities, we are forced to recognize that the income distribution is much more uneven or much more consequentially uneven than we have previously perceived. Prohibitions of this sort may be a way of salving the conscience of the middle class at the expense of the welfare of the poor. To the extent that it clouds perceptions about inequalites in the income distribution, it may do the poor a double disservice.

The Portfolio of Injuring Actions. The particular policies that should be undertaken with regard to the control of societal actions that increase low-level ionizing radiation should depend on the

---

[43] James Plummer suggested to me the interesting and relevant example as to whether we should let relatively impoverished American Indians mine for uranium. If so, should the premium they receive be what it takes to get them to undertake the work, or what it would take to induce a slightly less impoverished group to supply the labor? (The problem would become even more complex and ethically debilitating if we observed that the risks are lesser for low income groups because they are likely to die of other causes before the radiation contamination takes its toll.) A key question is whether choice of life risk by such disadvantaged groups can ever be uncoerced. This issue has received significant attention recently in the discussion of whether prisoners can be said to give informed consent to a variety of dangerous medical procedures.

life-, health-, and gene-threatening actions being taken elsewhere. They should be looked at as part of a total portfolio.

This statement is likely to receive a "well, sure" nodding approval from individuals who think in microeconomic concepts, employing such terms as income effects and convexity of indifference curves. They could argue: "Of course, the relative value of a life will depend on how much one is spending already on the saving of lives, and on how many lives are at risk. Lives can be traded off for any commodity." This argument may be technically correct, but that is not the factor of great consequence here. An example makes the point. If the installation of air bags were to reduce the rate of auto fatalities by 90 percent, it is not likely that we would want to spend appreciably less per life saved on industrial safety.[44]

The major reason a portfolio approach is important is the strong interrelationship of our fears of catastrophe, our anxieties, our relative guilt feelings about errors of omission and commission, and like components of welfare that produce very nonlinear responses. Say, for example, that our society were willing to send astronauts on one-way trips to the moon on the theory that the additional millions of dollars required to get them home were worth more than the lives involved. This, it would seem, would lay bare our willingness to operate on the principle of sacrificing lives for a price. We would feel very uncomfortable as we received radio or television reports of the astronauts' demise.

In situations in which the lives-for-dollars tradeoff can be fuzzed over, decisions to sacrifice lives can be less discomforting. For example, our level of discomfort might not be noticeably increased if we took actions allowing workers to be exposed to higher levels of radiation in return for higher wages, or risking increased radiation in return for faster flight through the stratosphere, or producing a greater risk of radiation contamination in return for the dollar gains from the operation of nuclear plants.

Given the widespread public education and lobbying efforts related to radiation exposure, and the extensive concern within government circles, it is unlikely that a sacrifice of lives in this

---

44 Indeed, the amount might even increase, for the "saved" worker would be less likely to die in an auto accident in the future. After the installation of air bags, more of an expected lifetime is being saved when a life is preserved.

PROCEDURES FOR VALUING LIVES   459

area will melt into the background, with the lives-for-dollars tradeoff fuzzed over. It is much more likely to be a sacrifice that is cited and bemoaned.[45]

To look at the positive in this sometimes rather dreary story, we may also wish to examine the corrective possibilities that are available. Genetic counseling procedures and improved capabilities for detection of defects may enable society to overcome some of the more tragic consequences of exposure to radiation.[46] This possibility, of course, raises extraordinarily delicate issues about tampering with genes, the sanctity of life, and the whole societal pattern of reproduction. These issues merit attention in their own right. The important methodological point to be grasped for the moment is that the corrective devices available may influence the magnitude of the risks we wish to take. Some observers may suggest, quite correctly, that this implies when we improve our capabilities to deal with radiation, we will in essence give those who pollute the environment with radiation more of a license to pollute.

The portfolio approach to the evaluation of life-saving and life-threatening measures suggests that merely relying on expected numbers of lives saved or sacrificed and monies available for other goods may give a wholly unrealistic impression of welfare. How people feel about the society in which they are living matters a tremendous amount. Is the government affording them adequate protection? Are large corporations being allowed to foul portions of the environment which by right should be common resources? What sorts of compensation schemes are being carried out? The questions might continue, but the basic point is clear. Because of factors quite apart from dollars and lives, a society may prefer a

---

[45] Our society may have reached or may soon reach the point where it is no longer worth attempting to preserve the myth that life is priceless. Once the myth is abandoned, attitudes toward exposure to radiation and many other issues involving life preservation may shift rapidly.

[46] Changes in detection capabilities may also alter the performance of regulatory standards. The much debated Delaney amendment prohibits the use in food of materials that in any concentration can be shown to induce cancer in animals or humans. As testing and detection procedures improve, this standard will ban many ingredients that it would be preferable not to prohibit. If process is a strong consideration, an argument can be made in support of the Delaney approach. In comparison to judgmental cost-benefits methods, it offers substantial reassurance to the general public in return for the inappropriate banning of a few substances. When such banning becomes extreme, a shift to a cost-benefit approach would clearly be called for.

set of policies that produces point B to one that produces point A in Figure 2. The points are purposefully selected so that it is not a variation in the lives that are lost that can explain the preference

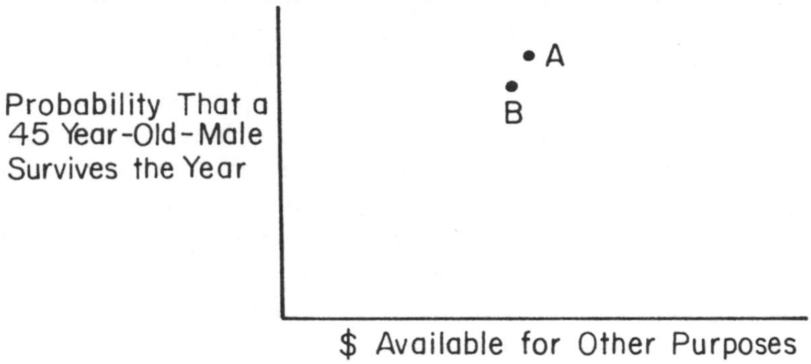

Probability That a
45 Year-Old-Male
Survives the Year

$\bullet$ A

$\bullet$
B

$ Available for Other Purposes

Figure 2. THE ATTRACTIVENESS OF PROCESS IN THE EVALUATION OF LIFE

for the apparently dominated point. Rather, it may relate to the way in which decisions were achieved, the way compensation was carried out, and the like. The omitted dimension is the attractiveness of the processes through which lives were saved and expended.[47]

It is not possible to disentangle completely the attractiveness of a process and the quality of the outcomes that it generates. If a choice procedure usually (though not always) leads to the right results, protects against extremely serious mistakes, and has a logic and internal consistency that supports its integrity, then the procedure itself is likely to be well regarded. If the procedure occasionally selects an inefficient outcome, such as point B over point A in Figure 2, that may turn out to be a cheap price to pay for acceptable process. It would seem unwise to tamper with the procedure on the few occasions when it makes such selections.

[47] This is not to imply that we should accept all circumstances in which we find society simultaneously sacrificing both dollars and lives. There may be no compensating gains in process, or indeed on any other valued dimension. Society may just be making poor choices.

Because small probabilities are involved, it is often difficult to predict the benefits from policies designed to save lives. This, coupled with the fact that many decisionmakers are involved, makes poor choices easy to make. Fortunately, the total conceivable sacrifice is limited because most of the life saving and life losing in our society is totally out of the hands of those who run the government. This fact probably increases the relative importance of process as a valued attribute of government decisionmaking that affects risks to lives.

PROCEDURES FOR VALUING LIVES   461

To do so would likely undermine its legitimacy.[48] On the other
hand, procedures that regularly lead to inferior outcomes are
less likely to be respected and cherished, in part for that very
reason, at least over the long run. This is not to assert that when
assessing the attractiveness and legitimacy of a process the members of society are likely to be guided predominantly by the outcomes that they observe or predict it will produce. It is more
likely that they will apply as well criteria such as: Does the procedure pay attention to all lives that are threatened? Does it
appear that resource costs are appropriately recognized in its de-
liberations? Are its methods consistent across choice situations?
Evaluations that employ criteria such as these will favor procedures that on the whole will perform effectively. This suggests that
attractive procedures can be found that will generate efficient outcomes with a degree of regularity.

VI. *Conclusion*

Many of the most important issues confronting society directly or
indirectly involve the valuation of lives. A number of these issues,
such as the choice of technologies for generating electricity, the
levels of stringency to be applied in environmental protection, or
the promotion of transit modes to compete with the automobile,
lie somewhat outside the traditional health-care field. Observing
this range of contexts, an economist's first impulse is to attempt
to ensure that the values assigned to the preservation of the same
life in different areas are constant. His approach here may derive
from the belief that if risk avoidance could somehow be packaged
and sold to individuals, informed consumer sovereigns would reflect such constancy in their own purchases.

---

[48] Thomas Schelling provided me with a helpful analogy from the sports world:
"If something happens in a sports event that the umpire or referee does not see,
and the result is an outcome that leaves everybody feeling bad, it may nevertheless
be recognized that if the umpire didn't see it he can't call it as though he did.
He may know as well as everybody else that it had happened; indeed with instant
replay it may be beyond dispute. But people may believe that it is so important
that umpires only call what they see, and even believe that the institution of the
umpire will gradually be eroded if instant replay is brought in on appeal, that
they'd just rather let these occasional egregious mistakes go ahead, just as a series-
winning fluke home run will not be called back if a seagull hits the ball high in the
air and keeps it from going foul at the last minute." Personal communication,
February 4, 1975.

Because society does not confront policy issues involving protection against risks on an individual-by-individual basis, results derived from the paradigm suggesting what individuals' isolated consumption choices would be may not apply. This suggests that estimates of the values of lives inferred from market transactions may not be appropriate guides for government decisionmakers. Indeed, this essay argues that once life valuation is made subject to collective choice, much more than lives and dollars may enter into individuals' valuation functions. Most significantly, the way choices are made may be of vital concern. That is, process may matter. (Economists may bemoan this fact, but particularly given their professional predilection to take consumers' preferences as given in other contexts, they should not dismiss it.)

Procedures for valuing lives must be developed that appropriately reflect not only considerations of process, but also such matters as anxiety, income distribution, and possibilities for compensation. This is a challenging assignment; it should be approached realistically. The search should be for significant insights, useful benchmarks, and helpful guidelines, not unequivocal answers. Present procedures are sufficiently haphazard that even a much qualified analytic approach can provide substantial benefits.

REFERENCES

Abt, Clark C. "The Social Costs of Cancer." Unpublished manuscript, Abt Associates Inc., Cambridge, Mass., 1975.

Acton, Jan. "Evaluating Public Programs to Save Lives: The Case of Heart Attacks." RAND Corporation, R–950–RC, 1973.

Alpert, Marc, and Howard Raiffa. "A Progress Report on the Training of Probability Assessors." Unpublished manuscript, Kennedy School of Government, Harvard University, 1969.

Carlson, Jack W. "Valuation of Life Saving." Ph.D. thesis, Department of Economics, Harvard University, 1963.

Coase, R. H. "The Problem of Social Cost." *Journal of Law and Economics* 3: 1–44, 1960.

Cook, Philip J., and Daniel A. Graham. "The Demand for Insurance and Protection: The Case of Irreplaceable Commodities." Unpublished manuscript, Duke University, 1974.

PROCEDURES FOR VALUING LIVES   463

Diamond, Peter. "Accident Law and Resource Allocation." *The Bell Journal of Economics and Management Science 5* (Autumn): 366–405, 1974.

Kunreuther, Howard. "Protection Against Natural Hazards: A Lexicographic Approach." Discussion Paper 45, Fels Center of Government, University of Pennsylvania, 1974.

Mishan, E. J. "Evaluation of Life and Limb: A Theoretical Approach." *Journal of Political Economy* 79: 687–705, 1971.

Otway, H. J. "The Quantification of Social Values." Presented at symposium Risk Versus Benefit Analysis: Solution or Dream, Los Alamos Scientific Laboratory, Los Alamos, New Mexico, February 1972, LA–4860–MS.

Polinsky, A. Mitchell. "Economic Analysis as a Potentially Defective Product: A Buyer's Guide to Posner's Economic Analysis of Law." *Harvard Law Review* 87 (8): 1655–1681, 1974.

Posner, Richard. *Economic Analysis of the Law*, Boston: Little, Brown, 1972.

Rice, D. P., and B. S. Cooper. "The Economic Value of Human Life." *American Journal of Public Health* 57: 1954–66, 1967.

Schelling, Thomas. "The Life You Save May Be Your Own." In S. B. Chase (ed.), *Problems in Public Expenditure Analysis.* Washington, D.C.: Brookings, 1968.

Shepard, D. S., J. S. Pliskin, and M. C. Weinstein. "The Non-Existence of Reduced-Form Utility Functions: Problems in Valuing Lotteries on Length of Life." Unpublished manuscript, Harvard University, 1975.

Spence, Michael, and Richard Zeckhauser. "The Effect of the Timing of Consumption Decisions and the Resolution of Lotteries on Income." *Econometrica* 40 (March): 401–403, 1972.

Starr, Chauncey. "Benefit-Cost Studies in Sociotechnical Systems." In Committee on Public Engineering Policy, National Academy of Engineering, *Perspectives on Benefit-Risk Decision Making.* Washington, D.C. 1972, pp. 17–42.

Starrett, David, and Richard Zeckhauser. "Treating External Diseconomies — Markets or Taxes?" In John W. Pratt (ed.), *Statistical and Mathematical Aspects of Pollution Problems.* New York: Dekker, 1974, pp. 65–84.

Thaler, Richard, and Sherwin Rosen. "The Value of Saving a Life: Evidence from the Labor Market." Discussion Paper 74–2, Department of Economics, University of Rochester, 1974.

U.S. Atomic Energy Commission. "Reactor Safety Study: An Assessment of Accident Risks in U.S. Commercial Nuclear Power Plants." WASH–1400, August 1974, especially chapters 6 and 7.

Weisbrod, Burton. "Costs and Benefits of Medical Research: A Case Study of Poliomyelitis." *Journal of Political Economy* 79: 527–544, 1971.

Zeckhauser, Richard. "Coverage for Catastrophic Illness." *Public Policy* 21 (Spring): 149–172, 1973.

[4]

COMPENSATING WAGE DIFFERENTIALS AND PUBLIC POLICY: A REVIEW

ROBERT S. SMITH

THE theory of compensating wage differentials, originally conceived by Adam Smith, has existed in its original form for over 200 years. The theory suggests that jobs with disagreeable characteristics will command higher wages, other things equal, because "the whole of the advantages and disadvantages of the different employments of labor and stock must, in the same neighborhood, be either perfectly equal or continually tending toward equality."[1] Like most other predictions of microeconomic theory, those suggested by Smith's theory awaited the availability of large data sets and high-speed computing in order to be empirically tested.

This paper will summarize the concepts of compensating wage differentials recently developed in the context of hedonic price theory, review the relevant empirical studies, and draw inferences for public policy. The paper will focus exclusively on the predicted trade-off between wages and disagreeable *job* characteristics. Differentials arising from educational investments, race, sex, or other individual characteristics, which could also be treated as compensating variations, will be ignored here. (They have been widely examined elsewhere.) The growing body of literature on the trade-offs between wages and nonwage forms of compensation will also be ignored.[2]

This paper reviews the theory of compensating wage differentials associated with disagreeable job characteristics and the empirical tests that have been made of that theory. The review of the theory is confined to graphical analysis, and it is intended to make the major implications of hedonic price theory available to a wide audience. Data sources and theoretical underpinnings are stressed in the empirical review section, where it is concluded that only for the risk of death on the job are the findings consistently supportive of the theory. The policy implications of that conclusion are then discussed.

Robert S. Smith is Associate Professor at the New York State School of Industrial and Labor Relations at Cornell University. This paper was prepared under a National Science Foundation grant. The author is grateful for lengthy discussions with Robert Hutchens and helpful comments from Charles Brown, Ronald Ehrenberg, Daniel Hamermesh, Hirschel Kasper, Ed Lazear, Walter Oi, Cordelia Reimers, Sherwin Rosen, and Kip Viscusi.—EDITOR

[1]Adam Smith, *The Wealth of Nations* (New York: Modern Library, 1937), p. 100.

[2]See, for example, Ronald Ehrenberg, "Retirement System Characteristics and Compensating Wage Differentials in the Public Sector," mimeo (Ithaca, N.Y.: Cornell University, 1978); Randall Weiss and Bradley Schiller, "The Value of Defined Benefit Pension Plans: A Test of the Equalizing Differences Hypothesis," mimeo (College Park, Md.: University of Maryland, 1976); Jack Whiting, "Compensating Wage Differentials and Pension Coverage," Ph.D. dissertation, Cornell University, (in process).

Industrial and Labor Relations Review, Vol. 32, No. 3 (April 1979). © 1979 by Cornell University.
0019-7939/79/3203-0339$00.75

The Theory of Compensating Wage Differentials

When a worker is hired, employer and employee agree to a single wage rate for a job containing numerous dimensions. These dimensions—such as pace of work, probability of injury, and unpleasantness of tasks—are elements of both the demand and supply functions relevant to the job. Therefore, the wage rate embodies a series of implicit prices at which each of these job characteristics is bought and sold—prices we shall call compensating wage differentials. The nature of these differentials suggests that the theory of hedonic prices, perhaps most usefully outlined by Rosen,[3] is the most appropriate framework of analysis.

Following Rosen, consider jobs in which all aspects but one are at their market-clearing (implicit) prices and quantities. For purposes of illustration, assume that the only job characteristic for which equilibrium value has yet to be determined is the risk of injury. Firms can supply safer jobs if they undertake the expenses necessary to reduce risk; but to maintain a given profit level they will only reduce risk if they can simultaneously reduce the wage (all other job characteristics being determined). Assuming that firms order their risk prevention projects inversely to costs, greater safety (at constant profits) will be provided only at ever-increasing wage reductions. This assumption is reflected in Figure 1 by drawing as concave from below the relationship between job risk and the wage rate a firm is willing to pay at a given profit level (curve AA represents the relationship for firm A, for example).

Because firms differ in their optimum technologies or face different product or factor prices, they will not all have the same set of isoprofit curves. Firms B and C in Figure 1, for example, find it more costly at the margin to achieve a given level of safety than does firm A.[4] If there is a large number

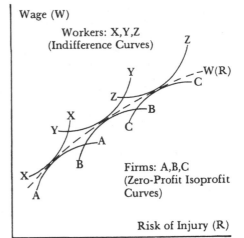

Wage (W)

Workers: X,Y,Z
(Indifference Curves)

Firms: A,B,C
(Zero-Profit Isoprofit Curves)

Risk of Injury (R)

Figure 1.

of firms operating at the long-run competitive equilibrium, the envelope of the wage-risk offer curves (at zero profits) will trace out what Rosen calls the "market clearing implicit price" curve. This envelope—W(R) in Figure 1—has a positive slope and will be concave from below, Rosen argues, if there are increasing marginal costs of supplying safety across firms or industries and it is impossible to "untie" any package of job characteristics and sell safety separately.[5]

Workers are assumed to have utility functions in which wage goods and all "pleasant" job characteristics—including job safety—enter positively. Again, if the levels of all job characteristics except that of safety have been optimized, it is possible to draw worker indifference curves showing, for given levels of utility, the trade-off each worker is willing to make between wages and risk levels. These indifference curves, which are shown in Figure 1 (see XX, for example) are convex from below, reflecting

---

[3]Sherwin Rosen, "Hedonic Prices and Implicit Markets," *Journal of Political Economy*, Vol. 82, No. 1 (January-February 1974), pp. 34-55.

[4]The firms depicted in Figure 1 can be in either the same or different industries, as long as they compete in the same labor market for workers. For example, at

low levels of risk firm A can afford to pay a higher wage (in competitive equilibrium) than firm B and C. Thus, *at low levels of risk* firm A, no matter what its product, can dominate B and C in attracting workers (and therefore in producing).

[5]Rosen, "Hedonic Prices," p. 51.

the usual assumptions about marginal rates of substitution. Workers are assumed to vary in their tastes for job safety, with worker X requiring (at any wage rate) larger wage increases for given reductions in safety than workers Y and Z. Each worker maximizes utility at the point where an indifference curve is tangent to the market clearing implicit price curve, W(R). Thus workers who value safety highly (worker X) tend to accept jobs with firms that can offer it most cheaply (firm A). Workers placing the least value on safety (worker Z) find it optimal to take employment with firms offering the highest wages and the least safety (firm C).

It is important to note that, according to the above theory, when employers have different offer functions and workers different preferences, single-stage estimates of compensating wage differentials will trace out only the market clearing envelope curve. The fact that we cannot in general estimate underlying demand or supply functions for job characteristics limits the usefulness of compensating differentials for policy purposes, as we shall see below.

Two other theoretically-based issues of importance for research on compensating differentials deserve mention. First, the market clearing envelope curve can shift over time in response to changes in the relative profitability of production at each level of risk. These changes can come about because of technological innovation, or they can arise in the process of firms' responses to changed consumer or worker preferences. As an example, suppose worker preferences change such that the number of workers like X increases at the expense of the number of those like Z. Capital will flow from C firms to A firms in response to profit changes caused by C's new relative difficulty in hiring a work force. If the new entrants among A-type firms increase the cost or reduce the price of output in that industry, the new zero-profit curve for A's will lie below the old one in Figure 1.[6] If the reverse happens to firms like C, the new market equi-

librium curve will take on a steeper slope than the old one.

Second, more than one wage rate will prevail at any level of risk if workers vary in productivity (perhaps because of acquired human capital) at that risk level and there is no noncostly way to eliminate the productivity differences. While this point appears to say little more than that wages are affected by factors other than risk, it does serve to remind us that in general there will be more than one market equilibrium curve and that these curves need not have the same slope at each level of risk. Empirical work can take account of slopes that may differ by interacting job characteristics variables with other variables influencing wages.

Empirical Studies

Studies of compensating wage differentials attempt to test the theory by selecting disagreeable job characteristics and identifying positive wage differentials associated with them. If a predicted relationship fails to appear, however, it is sometimes tempting to conclude that the measured job characteristic is not in fact disagreeable to the marginal worker—a conclusion that suggests the researcher has formulated a hypothesis that cannot be disproved. The heterogeneity of worker tastes therefore poses an additional difficulty for good research in this area. Besides the normal requirements of, first, data that are relatively free of measurement error and that include all important variables and, second, estimating equations and techniques that make full use of theoretical insights, there is a third essential ingredient: the ability to specify unpleasant job characteristics a priori.

Data. There are two general types of data used in attempts to measure compensating wage differentials, each with its own strengths and problems. One approach is to build a data set around a large, ongoing sample containing information on individual characteristics and earnings, and then to take data on job characteristics from other

---

[6]Put differently, the increase in X-type workers initially depresses wages in the industry in which they work. The inflow of capital tends to push the wage back up, but the increased costs or reduced prices in

the industry terminate the wage increase before wages are restored to their old level.

sources and match them to individuals in the sample through industry or occupational codes. Current Population Survey data have been merged, for example, with data on occupational characteristics from the Dictionary of Occupational Titles,[7] actuarial data on excess deaths by occupation,[8] and injury rates by industry.[9] Data from the Census of Population have been combined with industry-by-occupation injury rates from Workers' Compensation sources by Dillingham and by McLean, Wendling, and Neergaard.[10] The National Longitudinal Survey has been similarly used.[11] Matching (necessarily) *average* job characteristics to individuals who may not possess jobs with those characteristics introduces an errors-in-variables problem that tends to bias the tests against finding compensating wage differentials. Efforts to reduce this kind of measurement error, such as the use of occupation/industry cells to compute average job characteristics, usually result in other sample restrictions. Dillingham and McLean, Wendling, and Neergaard, for example, had to confine their analyses to one state each.

A second type of data base contains self-reported, individual-specific job characteristics in addition to the usual data collected

for individuals. The 1969-70 Survey of Working Conditions and the 1972-73 Quality of Employment Survey contain self-assessed qualitative measures of job dangers, work pace, freedom in the job, and so forth, and they have been widely used.[12] The 1975-76 Time Use Survey, which contains self-reported measures of work effort and freedom to obtain time off from work, has also been used.[13] A longitudinal data set with self-reported measures on job freedom, enjoyability, and stability—the Panel Study of Income Dynamics—has been used by Duncan.[14]

While the data on job characteristics in the above samples are individual-specific, they may suffer from a lack of comparability across individuals because of their subjectivity. Workers dissatisfied with their jobs (perhaps because of relatively low pay) may report the existence of disagreeable characteristics more satisfied workers may not report—a problem raised by Hamermesh.[15] Similarly, workers' social background or their degree of aversion to risk may affect their perception of (say) hazards such that subjective and objective measures of job dangers will not correspond across a given sample. Viscusi investigates this possibility; he finds that while neither large increases nor decreases from the average industry injury rate bring proportionately large changes in the probability of reporting one's job as dangerous, the two measures of danger yield substantially the same evidence of (significant) compen-

[7]Robert E. B. Lucas, "Working Conditions, Wage Rates, and Human Capital: A Hedonic Study," Ph.D. dissertation, M.I.T., 1972.

[8]Richard Thaler and Sherwin Rosen, "The Value of Saving a Life: Evidence from the Labor Market," in Nestor Terleckyj, ed., *Household Production and Consumption* (New York: National Bureau of Economic Research, 1975).

[9]Robert S. Smith, "Compensating Wage Differentials and Hazardous Work," Technical Analysis Paper No. 5 (Washington, D.C.: Office of the Assistant Secretary for Policy, Evaluation, and Research, U.S. Department of Labor, 1973); and Craig Olson, "Trade Unions, Wages, Occupational Injuries, and Public Policy: An Empirical Analysis," Ph.D. dissertation, University of Wisconsin, (in process).

[10]Alan Dillingham, "The Injury Risk Structure of Occupations and Wages," Ph.D. dissertation, Cornell University (in process); and Robert McLean, Wayne Wendling, and Paul Neergaard, "Compensating Wage Differentials for Hazardous Work: An Empirical Analysis," *Quarterly Review of Economics and Business*, forthcoming.

[11]Charles Brown, "Equalizing Differences in the Labor Market," *Quarterly Journal of Economics*, forthcoming.

[12]For example, see Greg Duncan, "Earnings Functions and Nonpecuniary Benefits," *Journal of Human Resources*, Vol. 11, No. 4 (Fall 1976), pp. 462-83; Daniel S. Hamermesh, "Economic Aspects of Job Satisfaction," in Orley Ashenfelter and Wallace Oates, eds., *Essays in Labor Market Analysis* (New York: John Wiley and Sons, 1978), pp. 53-72; W. Kip Viscusi, "Wealth Effects and Earnings Premiums for Job Hazards," *Review of Economics and Statistics*, Vol. 60, No. 3 (August 1978), pp. 408-16.

[13]Greg Duncan and Frank Stafford, "Do Union Members Receive Compensating Differentials?" mimeo (Ann Arbor: Institute for Social Research and Department of Economics, University of Michigan, 1978).

[14]Duncan, "Earnings Functions."

[15]Hamermesh, "Economic Aspects."

COMPENSATING WAGE DIFFERENTIALS   343

sating differentials.[16] While Viscusi's results are heartening, it must be remembered that danger is probably viewed on a more standard basis by workers than are many other job characteristics, such as stress or pace.

The use of longitudinal data on individuals has been proposed as a means of controlling for the problem of unmeasured personal characteristics common to cross-sectional data sets,[17] and might also appear attractive in mitigating the problems of idiosyncratic subjectivity. Using the analysis of individual-specific wage changes to test the theory of compensating differentials, however, is subject to the difficulty that market equilibrium curves can shift and change shape between survey dates. Even though it may initially appear plausible that the curves can be assumed stable over relatively short periods, analysis of longitudinal data nevertheless relies heavily on job changers to provide the variance required in the dependent and independent variables. For the analysis to identify the shape of the market equilibrium curve, it must be true (a) that job changers move from an old equilibrium point to a new one, and (b) that whatever changes in employee preferences or employer technologies cause some workers formerly in equilibrium to change jobs occur in so few cases that the market equilibrium curve is unaffected. Although studies using other types of data also typically require that workers be in equilibrium, longitudinal data must satisfy condition (b) as well. The possibility of shifts in the market equilibrium curve thus diminishes to some unknown extent the confidence one can place in the estimates of compensating differentials derived from longitudinal data.

Consistency with Theory. Most tests for compensating wage differentials fail to utilize available theory fully. With the exception of Dillingham, Lucas, Olson, and Thaler and Rosen, the research on this topic has not allowed for the existence of multiple market equilibrium curves of different

slopes. In addition, although there is a reasonable possibility that the envelope curve will be concave from below, only three studies allow for the possibility of this concavity.[18] Some of the other studies constrain the relationship to be linear, while most force the estimated envelope curve to be convex. The latter shape is produced by regressing the logarithm of the wage rate on the level of job characteristics, and it is sometimes done in the mistaken belief that the researcher is estimating worker indifference curves rather than the market equilibrium envelope.[19]

Finally, because regressing wages on job characteristics is an attempt to locate a series of demand-supply tangencies rather than the demand or supply isoquants themselves, there is nothing improper (contrary to McLean, Wendling, and Neergaard) about the use of single-equation estimating models. Rosen suggests a two-step procedure for estimating the demand or supply isoquants after the envelope has been estimated,[20] but the data requirements for identification purposes are so formidable that attempts to use his suggested procedure have not proven successful.[21]

Disagreeable Job Characteristics. Testing the theory of compensating differentials requires a priori specification of disagreeable job characteristics, but worker tastes are so heterogeneous that such a priori specification is usually treacherous. Whether jobs that are physical, repetitive, or have little freedom, for example, are unpleasant to the marginal worker (other things equal) is highly uncertain. Therefore, tests of the theory using these characteristics must

---

[16]Viscusi, "Wealth Effects."

[17]Brown, "Equalizing Differences."

[18]Thaler and Rosen, "Value of Saving a Life"; Olson, "Trade Unions"; Cento G. Veljanovski, "The Economics of Job Safety Regulation: Theory and Evidence," Part I (Oxford: Centre for Socio-Legal Studies, Wolfson College, 1978).

[19]Self-reported data on job characteristics, being qualitative in nature, are usually reported on a dichotomous basis—which precludes the use of polynomial terms to generate nonlinearities. In fact to allow for a concave relationship requires the use of uncommon functional forms, such as regressing the square of wages on the independent variables.

[20]Rosen, "Hedonic Prices."

[21]Whiting, "Compensating Wage Differentials."

necessarily be inconclusive. We thus begin our survey of results with the job characteristics most certain to be considered disagreeable to the marginal worker: occupational injuries.

Risk of injury or death. Perhaps the most persuasive tests of the theory are those using some measure of the risk of injury or death on the job. It can be plausibly assumed that everyone would be willing to pay at least some positive sum to avoid injuries. Furthermore, although some researchers use ordinal measures of job hazards, injury rates are susceptible to being objectively measured on a cardinal scale. This characteristic not only permits greater variance in the

independent variables and correspondingly better estimates than can be obtained using dichotomous variables; it also allows the calculation of wage differentials per injury or death that can be compared across a variety of studies.

The results of studies using some measure of job hazards as an independent variable are summarized in Table 1. About half the authors use a dichotomous measure of hazards; in some cases this measure is self-reported and in others it is derived from occupational characteristics contained in the Dictionary of Occupational Titles. Taken as a whole the results using 0-1 variables are rather ambiguous, which is not surprising

Table 1. Signs and Significance of Estimated Compensating Wage Differentials for Dangerous Jobs.[a]

Study	Hazardous Job (0,1)	Injury Rate	Risk of Death	Approximate % Risk Differential for Average Worker in Sample [c]	Willingness to Pay for 1/1000 Reduction in Risk of Death [d]	
					Per Worker ($)	Per 1,000 Workers ($)
Brown [e]	−		+*	1	400–600	.4–.6 Million
Chelius [f]	−					
Dillingham	+		+*	1	200	.2 Million
Gordon Railroad Maintenance of Way Workers	−		+			
Engineers and Trainmen	+*		+	8		
Hamermesh	− (Materials)[g] + (Equipment)[g] + (Misc.)[g]					
Lucas	+*			3-4		
McLean, Wendling, and Neergaard			+*	20		

Table 1 (Cont.). Signs and Significance of Estimated Compensating Wage Differentials for Dangerous Jobs.[a]

Study	Hazardous Job (0,1)	Injury Rate[b]	Risk of Death	Approximate % Risk Differential for Average Worker in Sample[c]	Willingness to Pay for 1/1000 Reduction in Risk of Death[d]	
					Per Worker ($)	Per 1,000 Workers ($)
Olson		+*	+*	3 (Injury) 4 (Death)	3,500	3.5 Million
Quinn[h]	+					
Smith (1973)		−	+*	3-4	2,000	2 Million
(1976)			+*	2-3	1,500	1.5 Million
Thaler-Rosen			+*	4	200-300	.2-.3 Million
Veljanovski[f]		−	+*	2-3	1,900-2,700	1.9-2.7 Million[i]
Viscusi (August 1978)	+*g	+*		6 5-6		
(Summer 1978)	+	+	+*	2-3	1,500	1.5 Million

[a] Results are generally for white, male workers in blue-collar jobs.

[b] When the risk of death is included in the equation, the relevant injuries are nonfatal; otherwise the data include fatalities.

[c] This column contains the risk-related compensating differential as a percentage of average wages for a worker facing the average level of risk in each sample. It is calculated only for statistically significant, positive compensating differentials.

[d] Workers who forgo higher wages to take safer work are said to be "willing to pay" for greater safety. The total sum of what 1,000 workers are willing to pay for a 1/1000 reduction in the risk of death can be thought of as what they are collectively willing to pay to avoid one death. Where applicable, calculations are at the sample means of wages and risk.

[e] Only Brown's cross-sectional results are reported here. These results are estimated using several years of data under the implicit assumption that the market envelope curve remains stationary over time. The results of his study of individual changes in wages and risk over time are not reported in this table.

[f] Earnings data are averages for firms or industries in this study. In other studies the earnings are for individuals.

[g] Self-reported hazard variable.

[h] This study used data for white males ages 58– 63.

[i] These figures are based on 1971 data for British industries, converted to dollars at the 1971 exchange rate of 2.4 dollars per pound.

*Indicates statistical significance at the conventional .05 level (one-tail tests). The negative coefficients in the Brown, Chelius, and Veljanovski studies are at least twice their standard errors.

Sources: See Appendix.

given the crude dichotomy created between "safe" and "dangerous" jobs.

From the slightly more numerous studies using the risk of injury or death, or both, as measures of job risk, some preliminary conclusions can be offered. First, outside of the Gordon study, which used data from a small sample of firms,[22] all studies using a "risk of *death*" variable find it to have a positive and statistically significant coefficient. Results with respect to the risk of injury are less clear cut. Perhaps the variation in expected uncompensated losses from injury is small not only relative to that from death, but also relative to random variations in the wage rate—a situation that makes it difficult to filter out injury-related differentials.

Second, the death-related wage differential paid to the average worker in each relevant study is estimated to be in the narrow band of 1-4 percent of earnings. Unfortunately, the level of risk faced by the workers in the studies varies considerably, so that the narrow band of average differentials implies wide variation in the total wage compensation associated with an additional occupational death. Both the Smith and Thaler-Rosen studies, for example, suggest average differentials of 3-4 percent, but because the workers in the latter study face a level of risk eight times greater than those in the former, the estimated differential per unit reduction in risk is different by one order of magnitude.[23]

Third, studies using death rates by industry (Olson, Smith, Veljanovski, and Viscusi) estimate much larger wage-risk trade-offs than studies using risks by occupation (Brown, Dillingham, and Thaler-Rosen). It is possible that these differences are related to the fact that the average risk of death is two to eight times larger in the occupational than in the industry studies. It is also possible, however, that safe occupations (say) in dangerous industries get paid more than equally safe occupations in safe industries. Put differently, there may be

within-industry wage spillovers (perhaps created by the presence of industrial unions) from jobs with the risk level most typical of the industry to those with less typical risk levels in the industry. If so, the dominant jobs in an industry are more likely to be in equilibrium than the atypical jobs[24]— which suggests that the market-clearing envelope should be estimated using just the "dominant" occupation in each industry.

Other job characteristics. A summary of findings from studies attempting to test the theory of compensating differentials using job characteristics other than risk of injury or death is displayed in Table 2. Given the variety of human preferences, it is doubtful that characteristics such as physical work, repetitiveness, fast work pace, machine work, and supervisory responsibilities can be claimed, a priori, to be disagreeable at the margin. Hence, most of these results say very little about the predictive power of the theory.

Of all the characteristics listed in Table 2, job insecurity and hard or stressful work probably come closest to being a priori specifiable as unpleasant. Focusing on these two characteristics, we find no consistent support for the theory: significantly positive coefficients are found in only three out of eight cases. The one significantly negative result is disturbing, but it may be merely a self-reporting problem—where low-wage, unhappy workers may have a greater tendency to report their jobs as insecure. Even so, one cannot claim that the results to date form a substantial set of findings consistent with the theory.

Antos and Rosen provide a further test of the theory.[25] They relate teacher wages to proxies for the difficulties of their job, finding significantly positive wage differentials for lack of student ability and high student drop-out rates.

---

[22]Kenneth Gordon, "Accident Rates and Wages on U.S. Class I Railroads," Ph.D. dissertation, University of Chicago, 1973.

[23]Smith, "Compensating Differentials"; and Thaler and Rosen, "Value of Saving a Life."

---

[24]The "key wages" theory by Dunlop supports the notion that equilibrium and nonequilibrium wages can coexist in the presence of union power. See John T. Dunlop, *The Theory of Wage Determination* (London: The Macmillan Co., 1964).

[25]Joseph Antos and Sherwin Rosen, "Discrimination in the Market for Public School Teachers," *Journal of Econometrics*, Vol. 3 (1975), pp. 123-50.

COMPENSATING WAGE DIFFERENTIALS   347

Table 2. Estimated Wage Differentials for Selected Job Characteristics.

Study	Physical Work	Repetitive	Fast Pace	Lacks Freedom	Hard or Stressful	Job or Income Insecurity	Machine Work	Supervise Others
Abowd-Ashenfelter						— b		
Bluestone	— *							
Brown	—	— *			+			
Duncan (1976)[c]				+ e		+ e		
Duncan-Stafford [c,d]				+	+*		+*	
King						¦*		
Lucas	— *	+*						+*
Quan[c]	—		+	—	—			
Quinn	—				+*			
Viscusi (August 1978)			+*	—		— *		+*

[a] Results, where possible, are for white male workers in blue-collar jobs.
[b] This study generally finds positive and insignificant wage variations associated with the extent to which working hours are constrained to be less than desired but finds the reported negative differentials associated with the *variation* in the constraint.
[c] Job characteristics in this study are self-reported.
[d] Only those results for nominal wages are reported in this table to maximize comparability with other studies.
[e] No significance test can be performed in this case because the canonical correlation technique was used to make the estimates.
*Indicates the estimated coefficient is at least twice its standard error.
Sources: See Appendix.

Overall Assessment of the Tests. Tests of the theory of compensating differentials, to date, are inconclusive with respect to every job characteristic except the risk of death. This is partly a function of the relatively few studies completed in the field and partly of several deficiencies in virtually all the studies completed. All but three have estimated a market-clearing envelope curve that is either linear or convex, and only a few allow for the possibility of multiple envelopes with different slopes. The self-reported data used in many may have serious problems of comparability across individuals, and heterogeneity of tastes causes difficulties in specifying disagreeable characteristics a priori even in cases in which such

characteristics can be objectively measured. Furthermore, the scatter and pattern of estimated differentials associated with the risk of death challenge the presumption that equilibrium quantities have been estimated even in these generally "successful" tests. In all, one must conclude that empirical testing of the theory is still in its infancy.

Policy Implications

Evidence that workers are generally compensated by "the market" for unpleasant job characteristics would be useful to policy makers motivated to correct workplace ills, whether they be health hazards, poor pension practices, or the confinement of women and minorities to jobs with particular characteristics. Unfortunately, empirical tests of the theory of compensating wage differentials are largely inconclusive thus far. The one area in which reasonably satisfactory evidence of compensating differentials has been found—the risk of death—nevertheless represents the single most important area of their application to public policy. We therefore deal now with applying estimated wage differentials for the risk of death to the problem of measuring the benefits of government lifesaving programs.

The propriety of attempting to quantify the benefits of programs to save lives is debatable only among noneconomists and will not be dealt with in this paper.[26] What is debatable among economists, although increasingly less so, is just what measure of benefits to use. The most widely used method, in both current and past practice, is to place a value on lives saved equal to the discounted lifetime earnings streams preserved. This method has been attacked by several analysts as both underestimating the losses attached to death and being inconsistent with the "willingness to pay" criterion underlying cost-benefit analysis.[27]

Two general approaches have been taken to estimate the willingness of people to pay for reductions in the risk of death. One is the survey method in which people are asked to respond to hypothetical questions. Acton, for example, asked people about their willingness to pay for equipment that would reduce heart attack fatalities; he estimates that they are willing to pay $28 for measures to reduce their chances of death by one per 1,000.[28] Murphy uses a technique

that seeks to ascertain the value people put on the various ways in which they spend their time.[29] He estimates that workers would be willing to pay $2,000 for a one per 1,000 reduction in the risk of death. Jones-Lee, who analyzes 16 individuals' responses to hypothetical questions about air travel, finds that 13 indicate a "willingness to pay" of between $1,200 and $6,000 for a one per 1,000 reduction in the death rate.[30] While Acton's estimates can be criticized on the grounds that they are substantially below expected losses of discounted future earnings for most people,[31] all these studies suffer from the methodological problem of asking about hypothetical behaviors in situations in which the costs and benefits of a choice will not actually be borne by those in the sample.

A second way of estimating willingness to pay for lifesaving programs is to infer it from the actual behavior of individuals at risk. Although Blomquist has come up with an estimate (of $200 for a one per 1,000 reduction in the death rate) based on seatbelt usage,[32] the predominant technique has been to infer willingness to pay for reduced levels of risk from compensating wage differentials. However appealing this might be, given the number of studies available, more than the usual care ought to be taken in making such inferences.

Theoretical Problems. It must be remembered that the estimates of compensating differentials only trace out a market-clearing envelope curve, not worker indifference (willingness to pay) curves. Because the

---

[26]See Robert S. Smith, *The Occupational Safety and Health Act: Its Goals and Its Achievements* (Washington, D.C.: The American Enterprise Institute for Public Policy Research, 1976), Chaps. 2 and 3, for one set of arguments in favor of such quantification.

[27]See, for example, E. J. Mishan, "Evaluation of Life and Limb: A Theoretical Approach," *Journal of Political Economy*, Vol. 79, No. 4 (July/August 1971), pp. 687-705; Richard Zeckhauser and Donald Shepard, "Where Now for Saving Lives?" *Law and Contemporary Problems*, Vol. 40, No. 4 (Autumn 1976), pp. 5-45.

[28]Jan Paul Acton, "Evaluating Public Programs

to Save Lives: The Case of Heart Attacks," Report R-950-RC (Santa Monica, Calif.: The Rand Corporation, 1973).

[29]John F. Murphy, "Sore Throat Management—Decision Analysis Using Pleasant Hour Equivalents," mimeo (East Lansing: Department of Medicine, Michigan State University, 1978).

[30]M. W. Jones-Lee, *The Value of Life: An Economic Analysis* (Chicago: University of Chicago Press, 1976).

[31]One thousand workers, each paying $28 for a 1/1000 reduction in risk of death, are collectively willing to pay only $28,000 for measures that would save one life.

[32]Glenn Blomquist, "Value of Life: Implications of Automobile Seat Belt Use," Ph.D. dissertation, University of Chicago, 1977.

latter curves are tangent to the envelope, the slope of the envelope at a given level of risk is equal to the willingness of workers to pay, but only for small changes in risk and only for those workers choosing that level of risk. The heterogeneity of worker tastes and the nonmarginal character of many governmental lifesaving programs suggest that using compensating differentials to estimate the benefits of lifesaving programs will result in some predictable biases.

One set of biases results from the heterogeneity of worker preferences. Theory implies that if the wage-risk trade-off of workers knowingly choosing high-risk jobs is used to estimate the willingness to pay of beneficiaries choosing lower risks, benefits will be understated. Benefits, therefore, must be calculated for specific groups of beneficiaries and must, in addition, be based on their trade-offs between wages and known risks. The latter point deserves some attention.

The theory and empirical tests outlined in this paper assume workers know, at least roughly, the risk of death (say) on various jobs and can therefore make choices about wages and risks. All the studies on compensating differentials for the risk of death use data on traumatic deaths or known excess death rates—data where the assumption of worker knowledge is plausible. The government, on the contrary, often mandates lifesaving programs for situations in which doctors and actuaries are largely ignorant of risks (as in the case of vinyl chloride and coke oven emissions). Thus, a worker may choose a job in which the known risk of death is X and later a government standard may be proposed with the knowledge that the actual risk is X + Y. The considerations discussed here suggest that when the benefits of reducing Y to zero (say) are estimated, the willingness to pay calculations should be based on the beneficiaries' *known* risk level of X, not X + Y. Risk level X is the level workers think they are choosing, and it is the one which reveals their wage-risk trade-off.

The second set of biases arises because of the (unknown) diminishing marginal rate of substitution between safety and wage goods. The *observed* marginal rate of substitution for any given group of workers will always be greater than that which will prevail after a nonmarginal increase in safety, thus leading to an inevitable overestimate of benefits. In Figure 2, for example, the trade-off at the observed risk level A implies that workers depicted are willing to take a wage cut of up to W_1W_3 to achieve a reduction of AB in risk, whereas in fact they are only willing to take a cut of up to W_1W_2. The resulting overstatement of benefits is somewhat reassuring, however. The consequences of decisions affecting job-related mortality are reversible in one direction but not in the other. Thus, if society is generally risk averse, and if errors in the estimation of benefits are unavoidable, we would rather overstate the benefits of lifesaving programs than understate them.

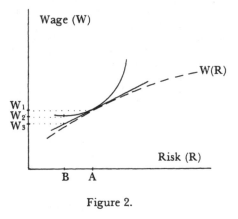

Figure 2.

Finally, it must be remembered that for estimates of compensating wage differentials to be useful in evaluating the benefits of lifesaving programs, labor markets must function perfectly with respect to the risks analyzed. If this is true, government-mandated lifesaving programs can only have net benefits if they are addressed to risks that are largely unknown or misperceived.[33] If the

---

[33]Many of the standards proposed by the Occupational Safety and Health Administration are addressed to problems of job-related diseases, in which long latency periods inhibit knowledge of risks.

labor market does not function well, then estimated compensating differentials are not trustworthy indicators of the value of lifesaving programs.

Empirical Problems. Several empirical issues suggest a good deal of caution in using existing estimates of wage-risk trade-offs for policy purposes. Few studies have permitted estimates of the envelope curve to be concave, little attention has been given to the possibilities of multiple envelopes, and errors-in-variables problems potentially create a downward bias in the estimated differentials. Furthermore, there are wide variations in the results depending on whether industry or occupational risk is used—raising the issue of whether equilibrium relationships have in fact been estimated. One difficulty in trying to decide which of the existing estimates come closest to the actual wage-risk function is that, outside of future discounted earnings, there is no objective measure of death-related losses. Even the smallest estimated aggregate values of saving a life are twice the discounted stream of earnings for workers in the sample, and thus all estimates are in the range of plausibility. We can only hope that from a variety of future estimates on different data sets a consensus will develop.

Can the existing estimates be of immediate help to policy makers? Considering the discounted lifetime earnings of the average worker at risk, and given that four separate studies (including Blomquist) found an average per-worker willingness to pay of $200-$500 for a one per 1,000 reduction in the death rate, a plausible lower bound on the aggregate value workers attach to saving a life seems to lie on the average in the $200,000-$500,000 range.[34] Acton's study aside, all the other estimates of the aggregate willingness to pay tend to be in the range of $1.5-$3.0 million. These estimates indicate how far away the upper bound may be for average workers.[35]

The value of these seemingly disparate estimates for policy purposes lies in the fact that the range of lifesaving values implied by governmental programs is even more disparate. As Table 3 suggests, the Department of Transportation is clearly using a lifesaving value near the lower bound, implying there is no danger it is overstating benefits of its safety programs but that there is a danger it is understating them. On the other hand, if we adopt as an upper-bound estimate a value equal to that of the highest one estimated for the United States (erring, it is hoped, on the side of overstatement), the resulting $3.5 million figure suggests that all of the Occupational Safety and Health Administration's standards listed in Table 3 are of questionable social value unless the more optimistic assumptions are valid. The benefits of the power mower standard, in contrast to the others, are squarely in the range of estimated values.

Thus, while the estimated values of lifesaving are distinctly bimodal and disparate, the studies to date do begin to provide a feel for the range into which a future consensus estimate is likely to fall. As crude as the range is, it is interesting to note that using it to evaluate the programs in Table 3 would have called into serious question decisions made in six of seven government safety proposals. Perhaps this best indicates the value of existing estimates of compensating wage differentials for policy purposes.

---

[34]Preliminary estimates by Richard J. Arnold, "The Value of Saving a Life: Wage-Risk Premiums with Adjustments for Workmen's Compensation," mimeo (Urbana: Department of Economics, University of Illinois, in process), also suggests values in this range.

---

[35]There are hints in the Thaler-Rosen and Olson studies that compensating differentials for risk of death are significantly larger for union than nonunion workers. The reasons for this are not clearly understood, and to the author's knowledge no study to date has investigated them. For policy purposes, it is important to know if the larger differentials are monopolistic rents or if they represent values closer to equilibrium (because unions provide better information on risks or give their members alternatives to quitting in situations where working conditions are nonoptimal). This important issue is outside the scope of this paper.

COMPENSATING WAGE DIFFERENTIALS   351

Table 3. Implicit Values Placed on Saving a Life in Selected Government Policies.

Agency or Program	Cost or Value per Life Saved [a] (Millions of Dollars)
Department of Transportation, Occupant Crash Protection ,and. Highway Safety Programs	$0.3
Occupational Safety and Health Administration Vinyl Chloride Standard	5—10
Coke Oven Emissions Standard	4—158
Deep Sea Diving Standards	15—39
Inorganic Arsenic Standard	1—9
Acrylonitrile Standard (High Threshhold)	2—8
(Low Threshhold)	3—625
Consumer Product Safety Commission Power Mower Standard	0.3—2

[a] The figures in this column, with the exception of the first, are obtained by dividing lives saved per year into yearly program costs. In doing so, we have attempted to adjust the figures for the benefits of reduced morbidity. In most cases, the range of estimates reflects "high" and "low" estimates of impact on mortality.

Sources:

James Miller, "Exposure to Inorganic Arsenic Proposed Standard," statement before the Occupational Safety and Health Administration on behalf of the Council on Wage and Price Stability, Washington, D.C., 1976.

James Miller, "Occupational Exposure to Acrylonitrile," statement before the Occupational Safety and Health Administration on behalf of Vistron Corporation, Washington, D.C., 1978. Data on power mower standard also come from this source.

John Morrall, "Exposure to Coke Oven Emissions Proposed Standard," statement before the Occupational Safety and Health Administration on behalf of the Council on Wage and Price Stability, Washington, D.C., 1975.

Charles Perry and Randall Outlaw, "Safe and Healthful Working Conditions—The Vinyl Chloride Experience" (Philadelphia: University of Pennsylvania, 1978).

U.S. Department of Transportation, "Occupant Crash Protection [and] Highway Safety Program Standards," *Federal Register*, Vol. 41 (Washington, D.C.: G.P.O., June 14, 1976), pp. 24,070-24,079.

U.S. Executive Office of the President, Council on Wage and Price Stability, "Commercial Driving Standards," statement before the Occupational Safety and Health Administration and the Coast Guard, Washington, D.C., 1977.

Appendix

Empirical Studies of Compensating Wage
Differentials for Unpleasant Job Characteristics

John Abowd and Orley Ashenfelter, "Unemployment and Compensating Wage Differentials," mimeo (Princeton: Princeton University, June 1978).

Joseph Antos and Sherwin Rosen, "Discrimination in the Market for Public School Teachers," *Journal of Econometrics*, Vol. 3 (1965), pp. 123-50.

Richard J. Arnold, "The Value of Saving a Life: Wage-Risk Premiums with Adjustments for Workmen's Compensation" (Urbana, Ill.: University of Illinois, Department of Economics, in process).

Barry Bluestone, "The Personal Earnings Distribution: Individual and Institutional Determinants," Ph.D. dissertation, University of Michigan, 1974.

Charles Brown, "Equalizing Differences in the Labor Market," *Quarterly Journal of Economics*, forthcoming.

James Chelius, "The Control of Industrial Accidents: Economic Theory and Empirical Evidence," *Law and Contemporary Problems*, Vol. 38, No. 4 (Summer-Autumn 1974), pp. 700-29.

Alan Dillingham, "The Injury Risk Structure of Occupations and Wages," Ph.D. dissertation, Cornell University, in process.

Greg Duncan, "Earnings Functions and Nonpecuniary Benefits," *The Journal of Human Resources*, Vol. 11, No. 4 (Fall 1976), pp. 462-83.

Greg Duncan and Frank Stafford, "Do Union Members Receive Compensating Wage Differentials?" (Ann Arbor, Mich.: Institute for Social Research and Department of Economics, University of Michigan, 1978).

Kenneth Gordon, "Accident Rates and Wages on U.S. Class I Railroads," Ph.D. dissertation, University of Chicago, 1973.

Daniel S. Hamermesh, "Economic Aspects of Job Satisfaction," in Orley Ashenfelter and Wallace Oates, eds., *Essays in Labor Market Analysis* (New York: John Wiley and Sons, 1978).

Allan King, "Occupational Choice, Risk Aversion, and Wealth," *Industrial and Labor Relations Review*, Vol. 27, No. 4 (July 1974), pp. 586-96.

Robert E. B. Lucas, "Working Conditions, Wage Rates, and Human Capital: A Hedonic Study,"

Ph.D. dissertation, M.I.T., 1972.

Robert McLean, Wayne Wendling, and Paul Neergaard, "Compensating Wage Differentials for Hazardous Work: An Empirical Analysis," *Quarterly Journal of Economics and Business*, forthcoming.

Craig Olson, "Trade Unions, Wages, Occupational Injuries, and Public Policy: An Empirical Analysis," Ph.D. dissertation, University of Wisconsin, in process.

Nguyen Quan, "The Impact of Unionism on the Size Distribution of Earnings of Industrial Workers," Ph.D. dissertation, Michigan State University, in process.

Joseph Quinn, "The Microeconomics of Early Retirement," Ph.D. dissertation, M.I.T., 1975.

Robert S. Smith, "Compensating Wage Differentials and Hazardous Work," Technical Analysis Paper No. 5 (Office of the Assistant Secretary for Policy, Evaluation, and Research, U.S. Department of Labor, August 1973).

Robert S. Smith, *The Occupational Safety and Health Act: Its Goals and Its Achievements* (Washington, D.C.: The American Enterprise Institute for Public Policy Research, 1976).

Richard Thaler and Sherwin Rosen, "The Value of Saving a Life: Evidence from the Labor Market," in Nestor Terleckyj, ed., *Household Production and Consumption* (New York: National Bureau of Economic Research, 1975).

Cento G. Veljanovski, "The Economics of Job Safety Regulation: Theory and Evidence: Part I—The Market and Common Law," (Oxford: Centre for Socio-Legal Studies, Wolfson College, September 1978).

W. Kip Viscusi, "Labor Market Valuations of Life and Limb: Empirical Evidence and Policy Implications," *Public Policy*, Vol. 26, No. 3 (Summer 1978), pp. 359-86.

W. Kip Viscusi, "Wealth Effects and Earnings Premiums for Job Hazards," *Review of Economics and Statistics*, Vol. 60, No. 3 (August 1978), pp. 408-16.

[5]

WORKERS' COMPENSATION: WAGE EFFECTS, BENEFIT INADEQUACIES, AND THE VALUE OF HEALTH LOSSES

W. Kip Viscusi and Michael J. Moore*

Abstract—Using the 1977 Quality of Employment Survey in conjunction with BLS risk series and state workers' compensation benefit formulas, the authors assess the labor market implications of workers' compensation. Higher levels of workers' compensation benefits reduce wage levels, and controlling for workers' compensation raises estimates of compensating differentials for risk. The rate of trade-off between wages and workers' compensation suggests that benefit levels provide suboptimal levels of income insurance, abstracting from moral hazard considerations. The value of nonmonetary losses from job injuries (including pain and suffering and nonwork disability) is estimated to be $17,000–$26,000.

I. Introduction

ALTHOUGH there has been a decade of literature on empirical estimates of compensating differentials for job hazards,[1] it is only recently that analysts have begun to focus on the role of the workers' compensation system in affecting these differentials.[2] From a conceptual standpoint one would expect workers' compensation to play a significant role since the employer can compensate workers for job risks either through ex ante compensation (compensating wage differentials) or ex post compensation (such as workers' compensation benefits). The relative importance of the two forms of compensation depends on the degree to which workers wish to insure the income risks of job injury—a value that hinges on factors such as the degree of wage loss

Received for publication July 15, 1985. Revision accepted for publication May 23, 1986.

* Northwestern University and Duke University, respectively.

Helpful comments and data were received from John F. Burton, Jr., John Worrall, Alan Krueger, and seminar participants at several universities. The University of Chicago Center for the Study of the Economy and the State and the Duke University Fuqua School of Business provided partial research support.

[1] See, for example, the studies by Brown (1980), Duncan and Holmlund (1983), Olson (1981), Smith (1976), Thaler and Rosen (1976), and Viscusi (1978, 1983). Also see the reviews by Bailey (1980), Rosen (1985), Smith (1979), and Viscusi (1983). The literature began with Adam Smith (1776).

[2] Recent empirical work includes studies by Arnould and Nichols (1983), Butler (1983), and Dorsey and Walzer (1983). Also see the broader perspectives by Chelius (1977), Darling-Hammond and Kniesner (1980), Ehrenberg (1985), and Oi (1973) as well as the volumes edited by Worrall (1983) and by Worrall and Appel (1985).

and the effect of the accident on the marginal utility of consumption.

One could omit workers' compensation from wage equations if there were uniformity in the benefit levels. There are, however, substantial variations both by state and according to the worker's wage level. For example, the usual formula for temporary and permanent total disabilities provides for two-thirds wage replacement with a benefit cap, so that lower paid workers effectively receive more benefits. The principal state differences are with respect to features such as benefit caps, benefit floors, and time limits for benefit payment.

In view of this variation, one would expect the level of workers' compensation to play an important role in analyses of the compensation package. Although research results to date are somewhat mixed, they suggest evidence of two types of influences. First, workers are willing to trade off additional wage compensation for higher workers' compensation benefits. Second, inclusion of a workers' compensation variable raises estimates of the trade-off between wages and job risks.

Thus far there has been no link between empirical issues of this type and the more policy-oriented themes in the workers' compensation literature. A continuing perceived need that has been in the forefront of job safety policy since *The Report of the National Commission on State Workmens' Compensation Laws* (1972) has been determination of the adequacy of existing workers' compensation benefit levels.[3] Nominal workers' compensation earnings replacement rates have traditionally been below 1.0 except for very low income workers whose wages are exceeded by a benefits floor. (Replacement rates taking into account the benefits' favorable tax status are higher.) Whether partial compensation is optimal is, however, more difficult to ascertain. If a job injury lowers the

[3] This theme of inadequate benefits has continued to be emphasized in the more recent work by the former Chairman of the National Commission on State Workmens' Compensation Laws, John Burton. See particularly Burton (1978).

worker's marginal utility of consumption for any given consumption level, as is often assumed in the health literature, then less than full compensation is desirable.[4] A worker would not choose to equalize income levels in the healthy and injured states if the injury impaired his ability to derive utility from the expenditures. How far below 1.0 the optimal replacement rate should be and whether current replacement rates are optimal remain open issues.

Obtaining a general sense of whether workers' compensation benefits are adequate is particularly important since this wage benefit component is not the result of a voluntary market transaction. States set the benefit floors for different classes of injury so that it is not possible to infer that actual benefits are necessarily efficient. Firms cannot reduce the benefit levels, and the transactions costs involved in setting up a separate program to augment existing benefit levels may discourage efforts to overcome the shortcomings that arise from inadequate benefits.

The purposes of this paper are threefold. First, the theoretical framework we develop enables us to assess the economic implications of the trade-off between wages and workers' compensation. We explore this trade-off using data from the 1977 Quality of Employment Survey coupled with information on industry risk levels and state workers' compensation benefits. Second, we refine the empirical estimates of the effect of workers' compensation on wage levels and on compensating differentials for job risks. Our analysis differs from previous studies in that the workers' compensation variable is worker-specific rather than a state benefit average, and it incorporates the favorable tax status afforded benefits. In addition, the diversity of the risk measures and the set of other nonpecuniary characteristics included is broader than in earlier studies. In particular, we include an individual-specific measure of job hazards in a number of our estimated equations.

As a final product of this research we generate the first implicit values of the nonpecuniary aspects of job injuries that have ever been obtained. This general area of concern, often referred to as the cost of pain and suffering and nonwork disability, has thus far not been amenable to estimation.

---

[4] See Viscusi (1979, 1980).

We develop the theoretical framework for the subsequent analysis in section II. Section III provides an overview of the data and the empirical framework, which can be viewed as a straightforward extension of the compensating differential approach. In section IV we report our empirical results and explore their implications.

II. Conceptual Framework

The focus of the empirical analysis is on the trade-off between wages and workers' compensation in the total compensation package for hazardous jobs. For much the same reason that we observe positive compensating wage differentials for job risks and other unpleasant job attributes, we should observe negative wage differentials for beneficial aspects of the overall compensation package, such as workers' compensation. The purpose of this section is not to reiterate this basic result, which is a direct generalization of the work of Adam Smith, but rather to investigate the properties of the trade-off between wages and workers' compensation. In particular, what is the efficient rate of substitution between these two compensation components? The expression we derive for this trade-off provides the benchmark in the subsequent empirical work for ascertaining whether workers' compensation levels are appropriate.

The formulation of the model, which entails very few restrictive assumptions, parallels the health state utility function approach of Viscusi (1978). Suppose that there are two possible health states. In state 1 the worker is healthy and experiences utility $U^1(x)$ from any given consumption level x. In state 2 the worker experiences a job injury and has utility $U^2(x)$. For any given level of consumption, the worker would rather be healthy than not ($U^1(x) > U^2(x) > 0$), has a greater marginal utility of consumption when healthy than when injured ($U_x^1(x) > U_x^2(x) > 0$), and has a diminishing marginal utility of consumption ($U_{xx}^1, U_{xx}^2 < 0$).

Let p denote the risk of an on-the-job injury, that is, the probability that state 2 prevails. Similarly, $1 - p$ is the probability that the worker remains healthy. Let w_1 be the wage the worker is paid when he is healthy and w_2 be the level of workers' compensation when the worker is injured. For simplicity all other income the worker receives when injured, such as social security benefits, is subsumed into the functional form of $U^2(x)$.

As Worrall and Butler (1985) document, such supplementary benefits are a significant source of income support. While the level of such benefits affects the welfare of workers, there is no loss in generality in excluding them from the analysis by incorporating them into $U^2(x)$, provided that the assumptions above are satisfied. Unlike workers' compensation, social security benefits are not merit rated to any degree so that there is no trade-off between wages and benefits within the particular job contract. The benefit value does, however, have an indirect effect by raising the level of $U^2(x)$ and possibly altering its shape. The analysis below addresses the worker's welfare net of any such influences. Viewed somewhat differently, it addresses the adequacy of workers' compensation benefits, given the existence of these other social insurance programs.[5]

To facilitate the conceptual analysis, assume all disabilities are temporary and total. Unlike earlier analyses of workers' compensation, this model and the subsequent empirical analysis explicitly recognize its favorable tax status. There is a proportional tax rate t on wages w_1. We assume that the role of assets in affecting consumption is subsumed in the functional form of the utility functions, so that consumption levels in states 1 and 2 are $(1 - t)w_1$ and w_2.

The focus here is on the rate of substitution between wages and workers' compensation for a worker at a job with risk p. Analytically, the initial part of the development follows Diamond (1977) and Viscusi (1980). The worker's expected utility is given by

$$(1 - p)U^1((1 - t)w_1) + pU^2(w_2) = G. \quad (1)$$

The rate of trade-off between wages and workers' compensation that maintains the worker's level of welfare is

$$\frac{dw_1}{dw_2} = \frac{-\partial G/\partial w_2}{\partial G/\partial w_1} = \frac{-pU_x^2}{(1 - p)(1 - t)U_x^1}. \quad (2)$$

<hr>

[5] This discussion addresses a homogeneous class of injuries. If social security benefits vary by injury severity, the net effect is to raise the level of $U^2(x)$ for these more heavily compensated injuries. The empirical analysis will address whether there is any remaining benefits gap, where in effect the higher social security benefits can be viewed as making classes of injuries less severe.

If the job risk p equals zero then dw_1/dw_2 also equals zero. The existence of a trade-off between wages and workers' compensation consequently hinges on the existence of some risk that state 2 will prevail.

In a situation in which the tax rate is zero and there is workers' compensation insurance available on an actuarially fair basis, from Viscusi (1979) we have the result that income will be allocated across the two states so that U_x^1 equals U_x^2. In this perfect markets case, equation (2) reduces to

$$\frac{dw_1}{dw_2} = \frac{-p}{1 - p}.$$

For the workers in the sample considered below, and using the lost workday case injury rate as the value of p, this condition implies a trade-off of -0.04. In effect, workers will sacrifice 4 cents of compensation (i.e., wages, fringes, etc.) when healthy for an additional 1 dollar in compensation when injured (i.e., workers' compensation) if there are no taxes and if insurance is available on an actuarially fair basis.

The manner in which these relationships are altered under the existing compensation system can be ascertained by assuming that the government has structured the compensation system optimally. Observed deviations from these conditions can then be used to determine whether compensation levels are appropriate and, if not, how they differ from the optimal amount.

In addition to the presence of tax rates, actual social insurance schemes have associated administrative costs so that under standard loading procedures with imperfect markets the schemes are not actuarially fair. Suppose that the degree of insurance loading is such that for each dollar of expected compensation in state 2 the insured worker must sacrifice $1 + a$ dollars of compensation in state 1. Furthermore, the worker must break even on an actuarial basis given this degree of loading. The total limit on expected reimbursement, including the administrative costs of insurance, is the worker's marginal product, z. For a competitive firm, the marginal worker's marginal product equals his expected wages and workers' compensation benefits plus an additional fee, apw_2, to cover the administrative costs of all benefits received. The actuarial constraint is consequently

$$(1 - p)w_1 + (1 + a)pw_2 - z = 0. \quad (3)$$

252   THE REVIEW OF ECONOMICS AND STATISTICS

The optimal insurance scheme is obtained by maximizing the worker's expected utility subject to equation (3), or

$$\max_{w_1, w_2, \lambda} V = (1 - p)U^1((1 - t)w_1) + pU^2(w_2)$$
$$- \lambda[(1 - p)w_1 + (1 + a)pw_2 - z],$$

which yields

$$\lambda = (1 - t)U_x^1 = U_x^2/(1 + a),$$

or

$$U_x^2 = (1 - t)(1 + a)U_x^1. \qquad (4)$$

The presence of taxes and deviations from actuarially fair rates lead to optimal levels of insurance that do not equate the marginal utility of income in two health states unless $(1 - t)(1 + a)$ equals one. An appropriate combination of tax rates and insurance loading could produce this outcome. If $(1 - t)(1 + a)$ exceeds one, as when tax rates are low and the degree of insurance loading is high, then the optimal marginal utility of consumption in state 2 will be greater than in state 1. To produce this higher marginal utility in state 2 one must decrease the level of consumption in state 2. This result is expected since shifting resources to state 2 is more costly in the presence of taxes and actuarially unfair insurance rates, leading to a lower level of state 2 consumption and a higher associated marginal utility. Similarly, if $(1 - t)(1 + a)$ is below 1, U_x^1 will exceed U_x^2.

The principal issue considered here is how, given optimal workers' compensation benefit conditions as characterized by equation (4), the trade-off between compensation in the two states is affected. Substituting the value of U_x^2 from equation (4) into equation (2), we have

$$\frac{dw_1}{dw_2} = \frac{-p(1 - t)(1 + a)U_x^1}{(1 - p)(1 - t)U_x^1} = \frac{-p(1 + a)}{1 - p}. \qquad (5)$$

With current levels of insurance loading, beneficiaries receive approximately 80 cents of each dollar of insurance premiums, according to calculations based on the net earned premium valuation method in Burton and Krueger (forthcom-

---

[6] This result is derived in Viscusi (1979), who also cites related formulations in the medical insurance literature. It should be noted that this result only pertains to earnings replacement. Medical expenditures that may enhance the chance of returning to good health are an entirely different issue.

ing).[7] The average value of dw_1/dw_2 for both the risk level in our sample and for the typical manufacturing worker will consequently be -0.05. Workers should be willing to trade off 5 cents of wages per additional dollar of workers' compensation benefits.

If the level of workers' compensation benefits is suboptimal, as a variety of observers have suggested, then the observed rate of trade-off should exceed 5 cents per dollar. Similarly, if benefit levels are excessive, then the observed trade-off of wages that workers are willing to sacrifice for more workers' compensation will be below this level. In the subsequent empirical analysis we ascertain how estimated rates of compensation substitution compare with the reference point provided by equation (5).

It should be noted, however, that these tests for optimality pertain only to the private valuation by the worker. The analysis does not address the role of his neglect of the external altruistic concern of society in his own welfare when making his job choice. If, however, benefits are found to be too low, consideration of these altruistic interests will simply reinforce the result.

A factor that works in the opposite direction is that of the adverse incentives or moral hazard problems associated with insurance. If workers' compensation leads workers to be less careful in avoiding accidents, then the efficient level of insurance will be lower. As a result, observing that insurance is inadequate from the standpoint of meeting workers' financial insurance needs might not necessarily imply that the outcome is inefficient if there is a significant moral hazard problem. Other causes of an observed excess of the estimated rate over our optimal rate include the option value of risky jobs (Viscusi, 1979) and the value of leisure during injury-induced layoffs.

III. Empirical Formulation and Sample Characteristics

The Data Base

The data used to estimate the model are drawn from the 1977 Quality of Employment Survey (QES) in which respondents were asked about

---

[7] Although their paper focuses on 1983, similar calculations by Burton for other years suggest that the ratio of losses incurred to the net cost to policy holders has been in the 0.80 range in recent years.

their 1976 employment experiences.[8] The subsample that we examine contains 485 observations, consisting of non-farm heads of households who were not self-employed and who worked at least twenty hours a week in the year of the survey. The 1977 QES and its two antecedents (e.g., the 1969–70 Survey of Working Conditions) are unique in the variety of individual-specific information provided about working conditions. It is also possible to match objective measures of workplace hazards to sample members based on their industry and to assign workers' compensation benefit levels to workers based on their state of residence. Finally, unlike its earlier counterparts, the 1972 73 QES and the 1969–70 Survey of Working Conditions, the hourly wage can be calculated in the 1977 QES. Thus, estimates of compensating wage differentials are not confounded by hours effects.

The two central variables in this study are the job risk and workers' compensation variables. We capture the health and safety risks to which the worker is exposed in three different ways. First, the survey includes subjective, individual-specific responses to a series of questions concerning exposure to job hazards. If a worker cited any health and safety risks of his job, the binary *DANGER* variable assumes a value of 1. The remaining two risk variables are based on the U.S. Bureau of Labor Statistics (1979) data on industrial injuries and illnesses, which are matched to workers by three-digit industry code. These two variables are *RISKLW* and *RISKTR*, and they represent the rates of lost workday cases and total recorded cases of injury and illness per 100 workers, respectively. It has long been observed that each of these measures is potentially affected by errors-in-variables bias. The paper by Moore and Viscusi (1985) explores this problem, however, and finds no evidence of a statistically significant measurement error bias, or evidence of endogeneity of the risk variable.

The second variable of interest is the measure of workers' compensation benefits. The measure we constructed took into account not only the favorable tax status of workers' compensation benefits but also the manner in which the benefit formulas

pertained to the particular individual rather than to the average worker. This is especially important because benefit caps lead to a lower replacement rate for more affluent workers, while benefit floors can dramatically increase replacement rates for low wage workers. To appreciate the difference between replacement rates estimated for average workers and those used here, one need only consider the ranges of rates derived in both cases. If the replacement rate across states is analyzed for the average workers in the sample, one finds that it varies between about 40% and 105%, while at the individual level the replacement rate goes from 18% to as high as 200%. It is also noteworthy that the mean replacement rate across all individuals in the sample increases from 0.55 to 0.83 when taxes are considered.

The worker-specific replacement rates including recognition of tax factors differ from those in the literature in differing degrees. Dorsey and Walzer (1983) use an industry and state-specific rate based on insurance premiums that is then matched to workers using Census industry codes. Butler (1983) uses two measures, each at the industry level. The first is actual benefits paid for death, temporary total disability, and other injury categories that are included as regressors in a pooled time series–cross section regression of industry average wages on human capital, injury and death rates, actual benefits, and other variables. His second measure is the industry average replacement rate for each year, which corresponds more closely to expected benefits and is consequently better suited to the theoretical model. Arnould and Nichols (1983) use state gross replacement rates from the *Compendium on Workmen's Compensation* (Rosenblum, 1973) matched to workers in the 1970 census 1/10,000 sample. Finally, Ruser (1985) uses an individual-specific measure similar to ours, but he does not include the effect of tax status on the replacement rate.

Each of these measures yields mixed results. Compensating differentials are often insignificant, and sometimes wrong-signed. Likewise, the workers' compensation effects are usually weak. Dorsey and Walzer, in fact, find a positive relationship between wages and workers' compensation in the union portion of their sample. This finding is not replicated by Ruser. Note also that insurance premiums should be positively related to accident rates and are less likely to reflect the negative effect of ex ante insurance on wages.

---

[8] There were major changes in the workers' compensation benefit formulas in the 1970s so that, to the extent that there is a lag in the wage adjustment, the full equilibrium effects of the revisions may not be apparent. The results consequently may understate the equilibrium wage response to higher benefits.

Each of the previous studies attempts to identify an additive effect of workers' compensation on wages, and in some instances an interactive effect with job risks as well. In the purely additive models, workers' compensation variables usually have the expected negative signs, and are sometimes significant. The addition of higher-order terms consistently results in a dilution of this result. The interactive effects are usually negative, but are seldom significantly different from zero.

This previous research, although suggestive, appears to suffer from two principal shortcomings. First, as shown in section II above, workers' compensation affects wages only at positive risk levels, thus making an interactive model theoretically appropriate. Second, most of the aforementioned studies measure individual insurance levels with substantial error.

The replacement rate variable to be used in the subsequent analysis—*WORKCOMP*—is similar to that used by Topel (1984) to measure unemployment insurance benefits. Unfortunately, there is no single benefits measure that is ideal. States have often complex benefit formulas that provide for lump sum benefits and benefits depending on the duration of the disability. The waiting periods for these benefits may vary, and there are differences in the benefit structure according to the degree and type of disability, or whether a fatality was involved.

The approach we adopted was to base our benefits variable on the benefit formulas for temporary total disability by state.[9] This benefit category accounts for three-fourths of all claims and one-fifth of all cash benefits.[10] The formulas for permanent total disability are almost identical, except that the duration of these benefits is greater. Similarly, the large claims category of permanent partial disability benefits is positively correlated with temporary total disability.[11] Ideally, one

might wish to obtain actuarial valuation of expected benefit levels by state, but such calculations are a substantial research task for which we did not have access to the pertinent data. Because of the positive correlation among benefit categories, we will use the temporary total benefit formulas as a proxy for state differences in workers' compensation benefit levels.

Where it was appropriate to do so, we adjusted the benefit levels using information on the survey respondents' marital status and number of dependents, and entered the resulting benefit figure as the numerator in the replacement ratio R_i:

$$R_i = \frac{b_i}{w_i(1 - t_i)}.$$

Since benefits are not taxed, the tax rate does not appear in the numerator of the expression for R_i. The denominator in R_i is the after-tax wage, $w_i(1 - t_i)$, where w_i is the weekly wage and t_i the marginal tax rate. We used the earnings, hours, and weeks worked information in the QES to calculate a wage variable. In computing the tax rate, we assume that all workers took the standard deduction, with the number of exemptions based on the reported number of dependents.[12]

Unlike previous measures of workers' compensation replacement rates, the value of R_i is individual-specific and includes the effects of taxes. As a result, it more closely measures the actual rate workers use in making their decisions. As noted by Topel for the analogous unemployment compensation situation, observable determinants of w_i and t_i render R_i endogenous. To correct for this endogeneity, we regress R_i on a vector of characteristics (Z_i) and state dummy variables.[13] The variable *WORKCOMP*, which is the predicted value of R_i, serves as the exogenous measure of the replacement ratio.

A detailed list of variable definitions appears in table 1, and table 2 summarizes the means and standard deviations. The dependent variable in the subsequent analysis is the worker's hourly wage (*WAGE*) or its natural logarithm. Each equation also includes a set of variables pertaining

---

[9] U.S. Chamber of Commerce (1976).

[10] See Price (1984).

[11] These correlations are reported in unpublished work by John Burton and Alan Krueger. Using a sample of 31 states, Burton and Krueger have found that the logarithm of temporary total disability benefits has a correlation coefficient of 0.58 with the logarithm of permanent total disability benefits, 0.64 with the logarithm of fatality benefits, and 0.38 with permanent partial benefits. Their research effort takes into account benefit maximums, minimums, replacement rates, and durations. In contrast, our measure abstracts from duration but is otherwise an accurate measure of both temporary total disability and permanent total disability.

[12] Tax rates are from Commerce Clearing House, Inc. (1976a, b).

[13] The variables Z_i include the number of dependents, a marital status dummy variable, and all exogenous variables in the wage equation.

WORKERS' COMPENSATION　　　　　　　　255

TABLE 1.—VARIABLE DEFINITIONS

WAGE	Computed hourly after-tax wage measure.
FEMALE	Sex dummy variable (d.v.): 1 if female, 0 otherwise.
BLACK	Race d.v.: 1 if worker is black, 0 otherwise.
HEALTH	Severity of health limitation d.v.: 1 if limiting physical or nervous condition has created either sizable or great problems in working on or in getting jobs, 0 otherwise.
EXPER	Experience variable: Years worked for pay since age 16.
*EDLT*12	Education d.v.: 1 if worker did not finish high school, 0 otherwise.
*EDEQ*12	Education d.v.: 1 if worker finished high school, 0 otherwise.
EDSC	Education d.v.: 1 if worker has some college education, 0 otherwise.
EDCP	Education d.v.: 1 if worker has at least a college degree, 0 otherwise.
MTAX	Marginal tax rate.
DANGER	Hazardous working conditions d.v.: 1 if worker answered "yes" to "does your job at any time expose you to what you feel are physical dangers or unhealthy conditions," 0 otherwise.
RISKLW	BLS industry hazard variable: annual rate of injuries and illnesses involving lost workdays.
RISKTR	BLS industry hazard variable: total annual rate of injuries and illnesses.
WORKCOMP	Workers' compensation replacement rate: Benefit level/($WAGE(1 - MTAX)$).
FAST	Work pace d.v.: 1 if job requires worker to work very fast a lot, 0 otherwise.
NODEC	Absence of worker decisions on job d.v.: 1 if it is not at all true that the worker makes a lot of decisions on the job, 0 otherwise.
OVERT	Overtime work d.v.: 1 if worker works overtime often, 0 otherwise.
SECURE	Job security d.v.: 1 if it is very true that the worker's job security is good: 0 otherwise.
SIZE	Firm size: Midpoints assigned to intervals for number of workers at the firm (hundreds of workers).
SUPER	Super d.v.: 1 if worker supervises anyone as part of his job, 0 otherwise.
TRAIN	Training program d.v.: 1 if employer makes available a training program to improve worker skills, 0 otherwise.
UNION	Union status d.v.: 1 if worker belongs to a union or employee's association, 0 otherwise.
NEAST	Northeast region d.v.: 1 if worker lives in northeastern United States, 0 otherwise.
SOUTH	Southern region d.v.: 1 if worker lives in southeastern U.S., 0 otherwise.
NCENT	North Central region d.v.: 1 if worker lives in north central U.S., 0 otherwise.
WEST	Western region d.v.: 1 if worker lives in western U.S., 0 otherwise.
URBAN	Urban area d.v.: 1 if worker lives in a major SMSA, 0 otherwise.
PROF	Professional and technical d.v.: 1 if worker reports occupation as professional or technical, 0 otherwise.
MGR	Manager and administrator d.v.: 1 if worker reports occupation as manager or administrator, 0 otherwise.
SALES	Sales d.v.: 1 if worker reports occupation as sales, 0 otherwise.
CLERK	Clerical d.v.: 1 if worker reports occupation as clerical, 0 otherwise.
CRAFT	Craftsmen and foremen d.v.: 1 if worker reports occupation as craftsman or foreman, 0 otherwise.
OPER	Operative d.v.: 1 if worker reports occupation as non-transport operative, 0 otherwise.
TRANS	Transport operative d.v.: 1 if worker reports occupation as transport equipment operative, 0 otherwise.
UNSK	Unskilled d.v.: 1 if worker reports occupation as unskilled laborer, 0 otherwise.
SERVE	Service d.v.: 1 if worker reports occupation as private household services, 0 otherwise.

to the worker's personal characteristics, such as the worker's sex (*FEMALE* dummy variable—d.v.), race (*BLACK* d.v.), presence of health impairments (*HEALTH* d.v.), years of work experience since the age of 16 (*EXPER*), and whether the worker has less than 12 years of schooling (*EDLT*12 d.v.), exactly 12 years (*EDEQ*12 d.v), some college (*EDSC* d.v.), or has completed at least a college degree (*EDCP* d.v.).

Pertinent job characteristics include the worker's marginal tax rate (*MTAX*), which was used in constructing the *WORKCOMP* variable, the subjective risk assessment variable (*DANGER* d.v.), the lost workday accident rate (*RISKLW*), the total recorded injury and illness rate (*RISKTR*), the predicted value of the workers' compensation replacement rate (*WORKCOMP*), whether the job requires the worker to work fast (*FAST* d.v.), whether the job permits the worker to make deci-

sions (*NODEC* d.v) whether the worker works overtime often (*OVERT* d.v.), whether the worker has good job security (*SECURE* d.v.), the number of employees at the workplace (*SIZE*), whether the worker is a supervisor (*SUPER* d.v.), whether the employer offers a training program (*TRAIN* d.v.), and whether the worker is a union member (*UNION* d.v.). Occupation dummy variables (*PROF, MGR, SALES, CLERK, CRAFT, OPER, TRANS, UNSK, SERVE*) were entered to control for unobservable occupation-specific characteristics. The particular set of nonpecuniary rewards variables that was selected closely followed the group utilized in the earnings equations for the earlier Survey of Working Conditions results reported in Viscusi (1978).

Finally, we included a set of regional dummy variables for whether the respondent lived in the Northeast (*NEAST* d.v.), in the South (*SOUTH*

TABLE 2.—SAMPLE MEANS AND STANDARD DEVIATIONS
(N = 485)

Variable	Means	Standard Deviation
WAGE	7.676	3.779
FEMALE	0.162	0.369
BLACK	0.068	0.252
HEALTH	0.029	0.167
EXPER	20.901	12.078
EDLT12	0.191	0.393
EDEQ12	0.351	0.477
EDSC	0.226	0.419
EDCP	0.232	0.423
MTAX	0.264	0.095
DANGER	0.798	0.402
RISKLW	3.810	2.418
RISKTR	9.738	5.627
WORKCOMP	0.835	0.315
FAST	0.162	0.369
NODEC	0.016	0.127
OVERT	0.347	0.477
SECURE	0.427	0.495
SIZE	6.698	10.265
SUPER	0.351	0.478
TRAIN	0.511	0.500
UNION	0.341	0.474
NEAST	0.200	0.400
SOUTH	0.284	0.451
NCENT	0.337	0.473
WEST	0.179	0.384
URBAN	0.259	0.438
PROF	0.216	0.412
MGR	0.136	0.343
SALES	0.047	0.212
CLERK	0.092	0.290
CRAFT	0.219	0.414
OPER	0.127	0.334
TRANS	0.062	0.241
UNSK	0.046	0.209
SERVE	0.055	0.229

d.v.), in the North Central (*NCENT* d.v.), in the West (*WEST* d.v.), and in an urban area (*URBAN* d.v.). Detailed industry and occupation responses for each worker also made it possible to create pertinent job-related dummy variables and to merge the BLS risk data with the sample information at the three-digit industry level.[14] Overall, the sample was broadly representative of the working population.

The wage equations differ in three ways. First, the functional form of the dependent variable, which is theoretically arbitrary, is either *WAGE* or ln *WAGE*. The second distinction among the regressions is in the nature of the job hazard measure. As described above, there are three of these,

[14] In only a few cases was it necessary to use two-digit risk measures.

DANGER, *RISKLW*, and *RISKTR*. Third, the manner in which the *WORKCOMP* variable enters varies, partly for purposes of comparison with previous research. We first omit *WORKCOMP* from the regressions, then enter it separately to provide a comparison with earlier research. Finally, the theoretically preferable interaction of *WORKCOMP* with the *RISK* variables is included. Not reported below are results from regressions in which the *WORKCOMP* variable is entered both interactively and additively. The additive term was never significant in any of these, while the interactive term performed well.

For example, the three ln *WAGE* equations for person i using $RISKLW_i$ as the hazard measure are[15]

$$\ln WAGE_i = \sum_k \beta_k X_{ik} + \gamma RISKLW_i + \epsilon_i, \quad (6)$$

$$\ln WAGE_i = \sum_k \beta_k X_{ik} + \gamma RISKLW_i$$
$$+ \mu WORKCOMP_i + \epsilon_i \quad (7)$$

and

$$\ln WAGE_i = \sum_k \beta_k X_{ik} + \gamma RISKLW_i$$
$$+ \delta RISKLW_i \times WORKCOMP_i$$
$$+ \epsilon_i. \quad (8)$$

Equation (6) corresponds to the usual hedonic wage regression that fails to account for insurance. Equation (7) is similar to those estimated by several other investigators. In Arnould and Nichols (1983), inclusion of the workers' compensation variable boosted the value of the risk coefficient by 12% and was associated with a statistically significant wage reduction, as expected. These modest effects may stem in part from their use of the death risk as a proxy for compensable job-related injuries, which is likely to be a less pertinent measure than the lost workday risk. Dorsey and Walzer (1983) adopted a similar formulation using BLS injury rate data and found a substantial positive effect on the job risk premium for nonunion workers and a negative effect for union workers.[16] Another approach that has appeared in papers by Ruser

[15] The variables X_{ik} are *EXPER*, $EXPER^2$, *FEMALE*, *BLACK*, *HEALTH*, *UNION*, education dummy variables, *FAST*, *NODEC*, *SECURE*, *SUPER*, *OVERT*, *TRAIN*, *SIZE*, *URBAN*, and region and occupation dummy variables.
[16] In our exploratory runs to be reported in a future study on unions we found an effect of workers' compensation for both union and nonunion subsamples of the QES.

(1985) and Butler (1983) is to include both a separate workers' compensation variable and one that has been interacted with the risk level, but their results are usually not statistically significant or have the wrong signs. It is worth noting that all previous research has omitted other workplace characteristics, a potential source of bias. Moreover, the individual-specific hazard variable *DANGER* has heretofore not been used in a study including workers' compensation.

IV.   Compensating Differential Estimates

The focus of our empirical analysis is on a series of equations including different combinations of risk and workers' compensation variables. The basic structure of the wage equation is, however, unchanged. In table 3 we report detailed estimates for a representative ln *WAGE* equation with the *RISKLW* variable and the interaction of this risk variable with *WORKCOMP*. This specification is the most important, since it is the lost workday accident rate and its interaction with the workers' compensation variable that best reflect the impact of the workers' compensation system.

Overall, the equation and its *WAGE* equation counterpart perform in the expected manner. There is a positive but diminishing effect of work experience on earnings. Workers in the college-educated group tend to earn more income, as do union members. Moreover, the performance of the explanatory variables such as union status is quite robust with respect to specification of the risk variables.

The focus of the analysis is on the various risk and workers' compensation measures. Results for the different combinations of risk and compensation variables utilized appear in table 4. In each case we first included a risk variable by itself, then with the interaction with the workers' compensation variable, and finally with a workers' compensation variable not interacted with the risk. Although we estimated eighteen equations in all, the principal patterns of influence were common across all of these variants. In 10 of 12 cases, inclusion of the workers' compensation variable boosted the statistical significance of the risk variable alone. Inclusion of workers' compensation (not interacted with job risk) had little effect on the risk variable coefficient. This was not the case for the interactive regressions 2, 5, and 8. Finally, the workers' compensation variable was con-

TABLE 3.— ESTIMATES OF ln *WAGE* EQUATIONS
(*t*-ratios in parentheses)[a]

Independent Variable	Coefficient (*t*-ratio)
FEMALE	−0.230
	(−4.545)
BLACK	−0.124
	(−1.834)
HEALTH	−0.210
	(−2.156)
EXPER	0.031
	(5.576)
EXPERSQ	−0.001
	(−4.773)
*EDLT*12	−0.098
	(−2.028)
EDSC	−0.018
	(−0.394)
EDCP	0.185
	(3.314)
RISKLW	0.041
	(2.946)
RISKLW × WORKCOMP	−0.031
	(−2.079)
FAST	−0.068
	(−1.549)
NODEC	0.140
	(1.092)
OVERT	−0.042
	(−1.208)
SECURE	0.085
	(2.564)
SIZE	0.007
	(3.931)
SUPER	0.069
	(1.761)
TRAIN	0.049
	(1.353)
UNION	0.160
	(4.218)
NCENT	0.036
	(0.761)
SOUTH	−0.013
	(−0.275)
WEST	0.142
	(2.614)
URBAN	0.182
	(4.599)
PROF	0.210
	(2.132)
MGR	0.236
	(2.375)
SALES	0.201
	(1.780)
CLERK	0.028
	(0.283)
CRAFT	0.096
	(1.073)
OPER	0.008
	(0.094)
TRANS	0.005
	(−0.052)
SERVE	−0.290
	(−2.704)
$\bar{R}^2$	0.477

[a] Critical *t*-values are 1.64 (5% confidence level), and 1.96 (1% level) for one-tailed tests.

THE REVIEW OF ECONOMICS AND STATISTICS

TABLE 4.—SUMMARY OF RISK AND WORKERS' COMPENSATION COEFFICIENTS (*t*-ratios in parentheses)[a]

Independent Variable	Equation Number								
	1	2	3	4	5	6	7	8	9
WAGE Equations									
RISKLW	0.099 (1.528)	0.282 (2.319)	0.101 (1.599)	—	—	—	—	—	—
RISKTR	—	—	—	0.037 (1.310)	0.113 (2.249)	0.038 (1.353)	—	—	—
DANGER	—	—	—	—	—	—	0.270 (0.715)	1.057 (1.659)	0.252 (0.660)
RISKLW × WORKCOMP	—	−0.230 (1.777)	—	—	—	—	—	—	—
RISKTR × WORKCOMP	—	—	—	—	−0.096 (−1.828)	—	—	—	—
DANGER × WORKCOMP	—	—	—	—	—	—	—	−0.999 (−1.534)	—
WORKCOMP	—	—	−0.606 (−1.075)	—	—	−0.610 (−1.083)	—	—	−0.560 (−0.993)
$\bar{R}^2$	0.374	0.374	0.372	0.373	0.411	0.371	0.372	0.371	0.369
ln WAGE Equations									
RISKLW	0.017 (2.214)	0.041 (2.946)	0.017 (2.256)	—	—	—	—	—	—
RISKTR	—	—	—	0.007 (2.017)	0.018 (2.945)	0.007 (2.064)	—	—	—
DANGER	—	—	—	—	—	—	0.029 (0.651)	0.148 (2.008)	0.026 (0.596)
RISKLW × WORKCOMP	—	−0.031 (−2.079)	—	—	—	—	—	—	—
RISKTR × WORKCOMP	—	—	—	—	−0.012 (−2.188)	—	—	—	—
DANGER × WORKCOMP	—	—	—	—	—	—	—	−0.153 (−2.013)	—
WORKCOMP	—	—	−0.080 (−1.225)	—	—	−0.081 (−1.241)	—	—	−0.074 (−1.212)
$\bar{R}^2$	0.479	0.477	0.474	0.478	0.477	0.473	0.474	0.472	0.469

[a] Critical *t*-values are 1.65 (5% confidence level) and 1.96 (1% level) for one-tailed tests.

sistently negative and statistically significant in the interacted version.

The Implicit Value of Job Injuries

Although addition of the interactive *WORK-COMP* variable greatly boosts the coefficient on the job risk variable, after taking into account the role of both the risk and the interaction term there is not a large difference in the implicit value of job injuries when evaluated at current workers' compensation levels. The implicit value of a lost work-day accident remains at $43,000 for the ln *WAGE* equation and rises from $32,000 to $36,000 for the *WAGE* equation upon inclusion of the interaction term.[17] Each of these is consistent with past estimates of the implicit value of injuries, as found in Viscusi (1979, 1983).

[17] All estimates are in 1984 dollars.

These estimates, however, do not take into account the depressing influence that workers' compensation has on the level of risk premiums. If workers' compensation benefits dropped to zero, the required wage premium would rise substantially because of the income risks workers would face. One measure of this increase is the increased implicit value of a job injury, which would rise to $96,000 for the wage equation and to $112,000 for its log wage counterpart. Similarly, full earnings replacement would lead to implicit values of injuries of $17,000 for the wage equation and $26,000 for the semilogarithmic form.

Although extrapolations of this nature are not as reliable as are estimates pertaining to current levels of compensation, the overall spirit of the results is clear. If there were no program providing earnings replacement to injured workers, the level of risk premiums would increase greatly. The reduction in risk premiums from additional increases in workers' compensation is much more modest.

The results for the full compensation case are of interest in their own right since they isolate the earnings risk from the health status risk associated with job injuries. The findings here imply that at least half of current implicit valuations of injuries represent implicit values of the nonmonetary aspects of injuries. In effect, the $17,000 and $26,000 estimates presented above represent the value of the nonmonetary health losses associated with accidents.

These results are the first estimates of nonpecuniary health impacts that have ever been obtained. These valuations pertain both to the value of pain and suffering and the more general welfare losses from what Burton (1983) has termed "nonwork disability." To the extent that analysts wish to place a value on these nonmonetary considerations for policy evaluation or in a judicial proceeding, these empirical estimates provide a beginning for the process of trying to assess these amounts, which in the past have been based entirely on speculation. At current compensation levels, about half of the compensation for injuries is for nonpecuniary consequences. If, however, there were no income replacement program, the relative importance of the health aspects would be far less.

Are Benefits Levels Optimal?

The fundamental and more immediate policy concern to which this paper is addressed is whether there is an adequate level of earnings replacement under the workers' compensation system. The results most pertinent to an assessment of the rate of substitution between wages and workers' compensation are in column 2 of table 4, which includes both *RISKLW* and the interaction of this variable with *WORKCOMP*. The lost workday accident rate is the risk variable that most closely corresponds to the probability of receiving workers' compensation benefits for temporary total disability or permanent total disability. Similarly, *WORKCOMP* is the appropriate measure of insurance.

The interaction term approach to assessing the role of workers' compensation is preferable be-

cause the expected value of workers' compensation coverage hinges on the risk level. Workers in completely safe jobs receive no benefits from the existence of such a compensation scheme. The expected benefits are the products of the risk level and benefits level, where in this case we use the replacement rate as the benefit variable. The interaction variable appears in columns 2, 5, and 8 of table 4.

The rate of substitution between wages and workers' compensation implied by these equations is quite substantial. Based on the empirical results, one can calculate how changes in the benefit formula affect the wage level. For both the *WAGE* and ln *WAGE* equations an additional 1 dollar in workers' compensation benefits leads to a 12 cent reduction in wages. In each case, the rate of substitution is more than twice the 5 cent per dollar trade-off one would expect given current rates of insurance loading and injury rates. Moreover, the 4 cent per dollar trade-off that would be optimal with actuarially fair insurance is even further below the observed trade-off rates.

Not only is there substitution between wages and worker's compensation, but workers are willing to sacrifice more wages when healthy than would be dictated by the added insurance costs. Taken at face value, these results imply that existing levels of workers' compensation benefits are suboptimal from the standpoint of insuring income levels. Such underprovision of benefits may nevertheless be efficient if moral hazard is an important concern. Recent evidence in Butler and Worrall (1983) suggests that the elasticity of injuries with respect to the level of benefits may be substantial. Their finding of a strong interstate correlation of workers' compensation benefits and reported injury rates is suggestive, but it has never been resolved whether this result is a reporting phenomenon or a reflection of an actual difference in injury rates.

Several other implications of the results are also noteworthy. First, we have calculated the benefit levels necessary to provide full insurance to equate the marginal utility when healthy and when injured and found that an increase of $111 from the weekly average of $266 would achieve this result. Second, and finally, it is not possible to calculate the benefit level necessary to reach the desired wage trade-off of 5 cents per dollar of benefits. This requires information on preferences, which is not available from hedonic wage equations such as we have estimated here.

V. Conclusion

The workers' compensation variable proved to be of fundamental importance in analyzing the structure of job risk compensation for workers in the Quality of Employment Survey. Higher levels of workers' compensation lead to a reduction in the base wage level that workers are paid. In addition, the size of the estimated risk–wage trade-off is enhanced by inclusion of a workers' compensation variable, thus strengthening findings in the compensating differential literature. Overall, the strongest results were those for which the workers' compensation variable interacted with the job risk measure, as should be expected.

Two of the implications of the results extend to concerns of a much broader nature. First, the observed rate at which workers are willing to trade off base wage rates for higher levels of workers' compensation greatly exceeds the actuarial rate of trade-off, even taking into account administrative costs. These results suggest that benefit levels in 1976 were suboptimal, provided that one abstracts from moral hazard considerations.

Finally, the results suggest that a large portion of compensating differentials for job hazards is for the nonmonetary aspects of the potential loss. However, if there were no workers' compensation system the role of income losses would predominate. The estimate that job hazards have an associated health impact of $17,000 to $26,000 is the first estimate of the role of the nonmonetary costs of job risks. In this case it is clear that welfare implications of job risks extend well beyond their financial implications.

REFERENCES

Arnould, Richard J., and Len M. Nichols, "Wage–Risk Premiums and Workers' Compensation: A Refinement of Estimates of Compensating Wage Differential," *Journal of Political Economy* (1983), 332–340.

Bailey, Martin J., *Reducing Risks to Life: Measurement of the Benefits* (Washington, D.C.: American Enterprise Institute, 1980).

Brown, Charles, "Equalizing Differences in the Labor Market," *Quarterly Journal of Economics* 94 (1) (1980), 113–134.

Burton, John F., "Wage Losses from Work Injuries and Workers' Compensation Benefits: Shall the Twain Never Meet," in *1978 Convention Proceedings of IAIABC* (Quebec City: International Association of Industrial Accident Boards and Commissions, 1978), 74–83.

——, "Compensation for Permanent Partial Disabilities," in John D. Worrall (ed.), *Safety and the Work Force: Incentives and Disincentives in Compensation* (Ithaca: Industrial and Labor Relations Press, 1983), 18–60.

Burton, John F., and Alan B. Krueger, "Interstate Variations in the Employers' Cost of Workers' Compensation, with Particular Reference to Connecticut, New Jersey, and New York," in James R. Chelius (ed), *Current Issues in Workers' Compensation* (Kalamazoo: Upjohn Institute, forthcoming).

Butler, Richard J., "Wage and Injury Rate Response to Shifting Levels of Workers' Compensation," in John D. Worrall (ed.), *Safety and the Work Force: Incentives and Disincentives in Compensation* (Ithaca: Industrial and Labor Relations Press, 1983), 61–86.

Butler, Richard J., and John D. Worrall, "Workers' Compensation: Benefit and Injury Claims Rates in the Seventies," this REVIEW 65 (4) (1983), 580–599.

Chelius, James, *Workplace Safety and Health: The Role of Workers' Compensation* (Washington, D.C.: American Enterprise Institute, 1977).

Commerce Clearing House, *State Tax Handbook* (Chicago: Commerce Clearing House, 1976a).

——, *1976 U.S. Master Tax Guide* (Chicago: Commerce Clearing House, 1976b).

Darling-Hammond, Linda, and Thomas J. Kniesner, *The Law and Economics of Workers' Compensation*, Rand Institute for Civil Justice Report R-2716-ICJ (1980).

Diamond, Peter, "Insurance Theoretic Aspects of Workers' Compensation," in *Natural Resources, Uncertainty, and General Equilibrium Systems* (New York: Academic Press, 1977), 67–89.

Dorsey, Stuart, and Norman Walzer, "Workers' Compensation, Job Hazards, and Wages," *Industrial and Labor Relations Review* (4) (1983), 642–654.

Duncan, Greg, and Bertil Holmlund, "Was Adam Smith Right After All? Another Test of the Theory of Compensating Wage Differentials," *Journal of Labor Economics* (4) (1983), 366–379.

Ehrenberg, Ronald G., "Workers' Compensation, Wages, and the Risk of Injury," National Bureau of Economic Research Working Paper No. 1538 (1985).

Krueger, Alan B., and John F. Burton, Jr., "Interstate Differences in the Employers' Costs of Workers' Compensation: Magnitudes, Causes, and Cures," Working Paper Cornell University (1983).

Moore, Michael J., and W. Kip Viscusi, "Specification and Estimation of Models of Compensation for Job Hazards," Center for the Study of Business Regulation Working Paper, Duke University (1985).

Oi, Walter, "An Essay on Workmens' Compensation and Industrial Safety," in *Supplemental Studies for the National Commission on State Workmen's Compensation* (Washington, D.C.: U.S. Government Printing Office, 1973).

Olson, Craig, "An Analysis of Wage Differentials Received by Workers in Dangerous Jobs," *Journal of Human Resources* 16 (2) (1981), 167–185.

Price, Daniel N., "Workers' Compensation: 1976–80 Benchmark Revisions," *Social Security Bulletin* (7) (1984), 3–23.

The Report of the National Commission on State Workmens' Compensation Laws (Washington, D.C.: U.S. Government Printing Office, 1972).

Rosen, Sherwin, "The Theory of Equalizing Differences," Economics Research Center/NORC Working Paper 85-3 (1985).

Rosenblum, Marcus (ed.), *Compendium on Workmen's Com-*

WORKERS' COMPENSATION   261

pensation (Washington, D.C.: U.S. Government Printing Office, 1973).

Ruser, John, "Workers' Compensation Benefits and Compensating Wage Differentials," U.S. Bureau of Labor Statistics (1985).

Smith, Adam, *The Wealth of Nations* (New York: Modern Library, 1776, reprint ed. 1937).

Smith, Robert S., *The Occupational Safety and Health Act: Its Goals and Achievements* (Washington, D.C.: American Enterprise Institute, 1976).

_____, "Compensating Differentials and Public Policy: A Review," *Industrial and Labor Relations Review* 32 (1979), 339–352.

Thaler, Richard, and Sherwin Rosen, "The Value of Saving a Life: Evidence from the Labor Market," in N. Terleckyj (ed.), *Household Production and Consumption* (New York: Columbia University Press, 1976).

Topel, Robert H., "Equilibrium Earnings, Turnover, and Unemployment: New Evidence," *Journal of Labor Economics* (4) (1984), 500–522.

U.S. Bureau of Labor Statistics, *Occupational Injuries and Illnesses in the United States by Industry*, Bulletin 2019 (Washington, D.C.: U.S. Department of Labor, 1979).

U.S. Chamber of Commerce, *Analysis of Workers' Compensation Laws*, 1976 edition (Washington, D.C.: U.S. Chamber of Commerce, 1976).

Viscusi, W. Kip, "Wealth Effects and Earnings Premiums for Job Hazards," this REVIEW 60 (3) (1978), 408–416.

_____, *Employment Hazards: An Investigation of Market Performance* (Cambridge: Harvard University Press, 1979).

_____, "Imperfect Job Risk Information and Optimal Workmen's Compensation Benefits," *Journal of Public Economics* 14 (1980), 319–337.

_____, *Risk by Choice: Regulating Health and Safety in the Workplace* (Cambridge: Harvard University Press, 1983).

Worrall, John D., *Safety and the Work Force: Incentives and Disincentives in Compensation* (Ithaca: Industrial and Labor Relations Press, 1983).

Worrall, John D., and David Appel, *Workers' Compensation Benefits: Adequacy, Equity, and Efficiency* (Ithaca: Industrial and Labor Relations Press, 1985).

Worrall, John D., and Richard J. Butler, "Some Lessons of Workers' Compensation," paper presented at U.S. Department of Education Conference on Disability (1985).

[6]

Journal of Risk and Uncertainty, 4:213–219 (1991)
© 1991 Kluwer Academic Publishers

Altruism and the Value of Other People's Safety

M. W. JONES-LEE*
Department of Economics, University of Newcastle upon Tyne, NE1 7RU England

Key words: altruism, safety, willingness-to-pay

Abstract

This article considers the manner in which people's altruistic concern for other people's safety should be incorporated in willingness-to-pay based values of statistical life and safety. It is shown that, within a utilitarian framework, the traditional prescription that such values should take full account of people's willingness to pay for others' safety is valid *if and only if* altruism is exclusively *safety-focused*, in the sense that while i is concerned for j's safety, he is quite indifferent to other determinants of j's utility.

During recent years there has been a substantial growth of interest in the *willingness-to-pay* approach to the valuation of safety. Indeed, some public-sector and related agencies have now explicitly espoused this approach in preference to more traditional alternatives based on lost output.[1] It therefore seems surprising that an important issue of principle related to the willingness-to-pay approach has remained unresolved and—to the best of this author's knowledge—has been given only scant attention in the literature. The issue alluded to is, quite simply, whether and how people's altruistic concern for others' safety ought to be accommodated within the willingness-to-pay framework.

The traditional prescription, advocated by, among others, Mishan (1971), Needleman (1976), Jones-Lee (1976) and, more recently, Viscusi et al. (1988), is that values of statistical life and safety should reflect not only the amounts that people would be willing to pay for improvements in their own safety, but also the amounts that they would be willing to pay for improvements in the safety of other people.

However, Bergstrom (1982) provided a simple but conclusive proof of the proposition that if altruism (or benevolence) takes the "pure" form of concern for other people's utility, then from a utilitarian perspective it is unequivocally inappropriate to include a term reflecting willingness to pay for other people's safety in willingness-to-pay based values.[2] The purpose of this article is to extend Bergstrom's important result by showing that, within a utilitarian framework, the Mishan/Needleman/Jones-Lee/Viscusi et al. prescription is valid in its full-blown form *if and only if* altruism is exclusively safety-focused, in the sense that individual i's concern for j's welfare is solely related to j's safety

*The idea explored in this article arose in the course of work conducted under contract to the U.K. Department of Transport. The Department, of course, bears no responsibility for views expressed in the article. I am grateful to Ted Bergstrom and Ian Dobbs for helpful comments and suggestions.

and not to other determinants of j's well-being. As such, it would appear that the appropriate way in which to incorporate altruistic concern for other people's safety in public-sector decision making depends on the precise form that such concern takes. To the extent that the willingness-to-pay approach is enjoying increasing currency as a real policymaking tool, it is therefore clear that empirical research on the nature of this sort of concern is urgently needed.

The argument is developed by first setting up a general model of constrained social welfare maximization in the context of physical risk. This general model accommodates, as special cases, *pure selfishness*, in which people care only about their own well-being; *pure altruism*, in which people are also concerned about other people's utility (and, in particular, respect their preferences); and finally, *safety-focused altruism*, in which altruism relates exclusively to other people's safety. The cases of pure selfishness and pure altruism, having already been analyzed elsewhere in the literature, are not considered in detail here, though the results for these two cases are given as reference points. In the case of safety-focused altruism, however, a proof of the "necessity and sufficiency" result referred to above is developed in full.

For the sake of simplicity, the analysis will deal only with the risk of death during a single forthcoming period, will ignore niceties such as life insurance and bequest motives, and will focus upon first-best optimality. Some remarks will, however, be made concerning the impact of relaxing these simplifying assumptions.

1. The general case

Consider a society of n individuals, indexed by $i = 1 \ldots n$, whose preferences over own and others' survival probabilities, $\pi_1 \ldots \pi_n$, and levels of wealth, $w_1 \ldots w_n$, are representable by (differentiable and generally well-behaved) utility functions[3]

$$u_i = u_i(\pi_1, w_1, \ldots, \pi_n, w_n), \qquad i = 1 \ldots n, \tag{1}$$

where u_i is strictly increasing in π_i and w_i and is nondecreasing in its other arguments. Notice that in the case of a von Neumann–Morgenstern expected utility maximizer, u_i would be *linear* in $\pi_1 \ldots \pi_n$. Suppose, furthermore, that survival probabilities are all differentiable, increasing, and strictly concave functions of the public safety expenditure, s, financed by lump-sum taxes, t_i, levied on the n individuals. For the case in which social choices are made so as to maximize a utilitarian social welfare function, optimal levels of s and t_i will be given by the solution to[4]

$$\max_{s, t_i} \sum_i a_i u_i(\pi_1, w_1 - t_1, \ldots, \pi_n, w_n - t_n) \qquad \text{subject to } s = \sum_i t_i,$$

where the a_i are positive distributional weights.

ALTRUISM AND THE VALUE OF OTHER PEOPLE'S SAFETY   215

Setting up the Lagrangean

$$L = \sum_i a_i u_i(\pi_1, w_1 - t_1, \ldots, \pi_n, w_n - t_n) + \lambda(s - \sum_i t_i), \tag{2}$$

where λ is a Lagrange multiplier, necessary conditions for a constrained optimum will then include[5]

$$\sum_i \sum_j a_i u_{i\pi_j} \frac{d\pi_j}{ds} + \lambda = 0, \tag{3}$$

where $i, j = 1 \ldots n$, and $u_{i\pi_j}$ denotes the partial derivative of u_i with respect to π_j, and

$$- \sum_j a_j u_{jw_i} - \lambda = 0, \qquad i = 1 \ldots n, \tag{4}$$

where u_{jw_i} denotes the partial derivative of u_j with respect to w_i.

Notice that this formulation of the problem is sufficiently general to encompass, as special cases, 1) pure selfishness, in which $(\forall j \neq i) u_{i\pi_j}, u_{iw_j} = 0$; 2) pure altruism, in which $(\forall j \neq i) \frac{u_{i\pi_j}}{u_{iw_j}} = \frac{u_{j\pi_j}}{u_{jw_j}}$, so that i's marginal rate of substitution[6] of w_j for π_j is equal to j's marginal rate of substitution of "own" wealth for "own" survival probability; and finally 3) safety-focused altruism, in which $(\forall j \neq i) u_{iw_j} = 0$ and $(\exists j \neq i) u_{i\pi_j} > 0$, so that while i may be concerned for j's survival probability, he is quite indifferent to other determinants of j's well-being.

2. Pure selfishness and pure altruism

Denote the ith individual's marginal rate of substitution of own wealth for own survival probability by m_{ii}. Within the context of a constrained social-welfare-maximizing model such as that set out above, Dehez and Drèze (1982) and Bergstrom (1982) have shown that, provided m_{ii} and $\frac{d\pi_i}{ds}$ are uncorrelated across the n individuals, a necessary condition for constrained social welfare maximization, given pure selfishness, is that

$$\frac{1}{n} \sum_i m_{ii} = \frac{ds}{d \sum_i \pi_i}. \tag{5}$$

This is, of course, the standard willingness-to-pay result, which requires that public-safety expenditure should be carried out to the point at which the *value of statistical life*—defined as the population mean of m_{ii}—is equal to the marginal cost of saving one statistical life, $\dfrac{ds}{d \sum_i \pi_i}$.

Furthermore, as already noted, Bergstrom (1982) has shown that in the case of pure altruism, the necessary condition for constrained social welfare maximization is *identical* to that given in equation (5). This means that, given pure altruism, *no modification* is required to the standard definition of the value of statistical life.

3. Safety-focused altruism

In stark contrast to the results for pure selfishness and pure altruism just summarized, the Mishan/Needleman/Jones-Lee/Viscusi et al. prescription is to the effect that the value of statistical life should be set equal to $\frac{1}{n} \sum_i \sum_j m_{ij}$, where m_{ii} is as defined above and $m_{ij}(j \neq i)$ denotes the ith individual's marginal rate of substitution of "own" wealth, w_i, for j's survival probability, π_j. Public-safety expenditure would then be undertaken up to the point at which this augmented value of statistical life, rather than the population mean of m_{ii}, is equal to the marginal cost of saving one statistical life. In this section it will be shown that this prescription is valid within the context of the general social-welfare-maximizing framework set up in section 1 *if and only if* $(\forall j \neq i)u_{iw_j} = 0, i = 1 \ldots n$—that is, altruistic concern, if it exists, *is exclusively safety-focused.*

From equation (4) it follows that

$$a_i = \frac{-\lambda - \sum_{j \neq i} a_j u_{jw_i}}{u_{iw_i}}, \qquad i = 1 \ldots n. \tag{6}$$

Substituting from equation (6) into equation (3) then gives

$$\sum_i \sum_j \frac{(\lambda + \sum_{j \neq i} a_j u_{jw_i})}{\lambda} \frac{u_{i\pi_j}}{u_{iw_i}} \frac{d\pi_j}{ds} = 1. \tag{7}$$

Furthermore, $\frac{u_{i\pi_j}}{u_{iw_i}} = m_{ij}$, so that provided $\left[\frac{(\lambda + \sum_{j \neq i} a_j u_{jw_i})}{\lambda} m_{ij}\right]$ and $\frac{d\pi_j}{ds}$ are uncorrelated—which would seem to be the natural counterpart to the condition employed in the Dehez and Drèze and Bergstrom analyses—then the necessary condition for constrained social welfare maximization given in equation (7) can be written as

$$\sum_i \frac{1}{n} \left(\sum_j \alpha_i m_{ij} \right) \left(\sum_j \frac{d\pi_j}{ds} \right) = 1, \tag{8}$$

or, equivalently, as

$$\frac{1}{n} \sum_i \sum_j \alpha_i m_{ij} = \frac{ds}{d \sum_j \pi_j}, \tag{9}$$

where

$$\alpha_i = \frac{\lambda + \sum_{j \neq i} a_j u_{jw_i}}{\lambda}. \tag{10}$$

ALTRUISM AND THE VALUE OF OTHER PEOPLE'S SAFETY   217

Now it is clear from equation (3) that $\lambda < 0$ and from equation (4) that $0 \leq \sum_{j \neq i} a_j u_{jw_i} <$ $|\lambda|$. Thus from equation (10), given $(\forall j \neq i) \, u_{jw_i} \geq 0, i = 1 \ldots n,$

$$[(\exists j \neq i) u_{jw_i} > 0] \Leftrightarrow 0 < \alpha_i < 1, \tag{11}$$

and

$$[(\forall j \neq i) u_{jw_i} = 0] \Leftrightarrow \alpha_i = 1. \tag{12}$$

From equations (9), (11), and (12), it follows that the value of statistical life—to be equated to the marginal cost of saving one statistical life—will be equal to $\frac{1}{n} \sum_i \sum_j m_{ij}$ (the Mishan/Needleman/Jones-Lee/Viscusi et al. prescription) *if and only if* $(\forall j \neq i) u_{jw_i}$ $= 0, i = 1 \ldots n$—which is, of course, equivalent to $(\forall j \neq i) u_{iw_j} = 0, i = 1 \ldots n$—that is, *if and only if* altruism is exclusively safety-focused. Under all other circumstances, the appropriate value will be *smaller* than this figure by an amount determined by the magnitude of u_{iw_j}. In particular, as shown by Bergstrom, if u_{iw_j} is set in relation to $u_{i\pi_j}$ so as to respect j's marginal rate of substitution of w_j for π_j (the case of pure altruism), then the value of statistical life is given by $\frac{1}{n} \sum_i m_{ii}$, as in the case of pure selfishness.

4. Concluding remarks

While Bergstrom's result has been on the record, as it were, for the better part of the last decade—or, for the more perceptive interpreters of Edgeworth's propositions, for more than a century—this important and somewhat counterintuitive finding has received surprisingly little attention in the literature.[7] Nonetheless, the result would appear to be quite robust and, should altruism take the form that many circumspect humanitarians would probably expect it to, entails that values of statistical life and safety should definitely *not* include a sum reflecting people's willingness to pay for others' safety, *in spite of the fact that this sum is strictly positive*. In particular, as this article has shown, inclusion of such a sum in the manner prescribed by Mishan/Needleman/Jones-Lee/Viscusi et al. is appropriate, within a utilitarian framework, *if and only if* altruism is exclusively focused upon other people's safety. The intuitive explanation for this initially somewhat puzzling result is that to push values of safety beyond the level implied by people's willingness to pay for their *own* safety would result in an overprovision of safety relative to the other determinants of their utility. Such an increase in values of safety would therefore be considered as desirable *only* by people who *disregard* those factors besides safety that contribute to other people's utility.

But what form does altruistic concern for others' safety typically take? This is an essentially empirical question to which, currently, this author does not have an answer. Nonetheless, one can speculate about how things might turn out. For example, introspection and casual questioning of colleagues suggests that if people do display altruism, then for family and friends it probably takes a form closer to the pure type of concern for general well-being or utility (including safety), whereas for those more distantly removed, the safety-focused version seems more plausible. However, this is merely a conjecture, and a definitive resolution to the question considered in this article must await the results of urgently needed empirical work on the precise nature of altruism in the safety context. It is hoped that this article will have served to highlight the nature of the key issues that will have to be addressed by such empirical work.

Finally, what would be entailed by relaxation of the simplifying assumptions underpinning the characterization of the constrained social-welfare-maximizing problem? A multiplicity of future periods would plainly change nothing of substance in the argument. The introduction of bequest motives and opportunities to purchase life insurance would also merely have the effect of rendering expressions for marginal rates of substitution of wealth for risk rather more complex. Finally, introduction of second-best constraints, such as taxes that are related to income or wealth, would also almost certainly do little to alter the substance of the conclusions reached—at least insofar as they pertain to the implications of pure as opposed to safety-focused altruism.[8]

Notes

1. For example, the U.K. Department of Transport recently abandoned its former gross-output based approach to the valuation of avoidance of a road fatality in favor of the willingness-to-pay approach, thereby effectively doubling the value concerned. It is understood that other government agencies in Europe and the U.S.A. are in a similar position.
2. Bergstrom's conclusion is, in fact, closely related to an argument first advanced by Edgeworth (1881), p. 53, n. 1, and developed more recently by Collard (1975) and Archibald and Donaldson (1976).
3. Given the additive form of the social welfare function employed in this article, it is clearly essential to regard the u_i as being *cardinal* measures, unique only up to affine transformations. Application of any such transformation would then require a corresponding adjustment to the distributional weights, a_i, referred to below. If, by contrast, one wished to treat the u_i as merely ordinal measures, unique only up to increasing monotonic transformations, then it would be necessary to specify the social welfare function as $w = f(u_1, \ldots, u_n)$—presumably with f increasing in all u_i—and application of any admissible transformation to the u_i would then require a corresponding respecification of f. Notice that with the u_i treated as ordinal measures, the argument developed in this article would be quite unaffected, save that in equation (3) onwards the distributional weights, a_i, would be replaced by the appropriate partial derivatives of f.
4. This way of setting up the optimal safety expenditure problem is based on the approach proposed by Bergstrom (1982) and Dehez and Drèze (1982).
5. Second-order conditions for a constrained optimum are fulfilled as a result of the assumed properties of $u_i(w_i)$ and $\pi_i(s)$.
6. That is, the *modulus* of the rate at which i is willing to trade w_j for π_j at the margin.
7. Viscusi et al., however, do allude to a distinction between what is effectively safety-focused altruism and other forms. See Viscusi et al. (1988).
8. For a discussion of the way in which second-best considerations affect the results of a constrained social-welfare-maximization exercise in the safety context, see Jones-Lee (1989), pp. 15, 16.

References

Archibald, G. C. and D. Donaldson. (1976). "Non-Paternalism and the Basic Theorems of Welfare Economics," *Canadian Journal of Economics* 9, 492–507.

ALTRUISM AND THE VALUE OF OTHER PEOPLE'S SAFETY   219

Bergstrom, T. C. (1982). "When is a Man's Life Worth More than His Human Capital?" In M. W. Jones-Lee (ed.), *The Value of Life and Safety: Proceedings of a Conference held by the Geneva Association*. Amsterdam: North Holland, pp. 3–26.

Collard, D. (1975). "Edgeworth's Propositions on Altruism," *Economic Journal* 85, 355–360.

Dehez, P. and J. H. Drèze. (1982). "State-Dependent Utility, the Demand for Insurance and the Value of Safety." In M. W. Jones-Lee (ed.), *The Value of Life and Safety: Proceedings of a Conference held by the Geneva Association*. Amsterdam: North Holland, pp. 41–65.

Edgeworth, F. Y. (1881). *Mathematical Psychics*. London: C. Kegan Paul and Company.

Jones-Lee, M. W. (1976). *The Value of Life: An Economic Analysis*. London: Martin Robertson, and Chicago: University of Chicago Press.

Jones-Lee, M. W. (1989). *The Economics of Safety and Physical Risk*. Oxford: Basil Blackwell.

Mishan, E. J. (1971). "Evaluation of Life and Limb: A Theoretical Approach," *Journal of Political Economy* 79, 687–705.

Needleman, L. (1976). "Valuing Other People's Lives," *Manchester School* 44, 309–342.

Viscusi, W. K., W. A. Magat, and A. Forrest. (1988). "Altruistic and Private Valuations of Risk Reduction," *Journal of Policy Analysis and Management* 7, 227–245.

[7]

Journal of Economic Literature
Vol. XXXI (December 1993), pp. 1912–1946

The Value of Risks to Life and Health

By W. KIP VISCUSI

Duke University

Susan Jakubiak and three anonymous referees provided detailed and helpful comments. Many of the themes of this paper are developed more fully in Viscusi (1992a).

1. Introduction

HEALTH AND SAFETY RISKS comprise one aspect of our lives that we would all like to eliminate. Even if we set out to provide a risk-free existence, however, our efforts would be constrained by our economic resources. If the entire American GNP were devoted to preventing fatal accidents, we would be able to spend an average of only $55 million per fatality. There are also other demands on these resources, ranging from food to recreation, which will reduce the funds available for risk reduction.

One possible approach is to set the risk reduction priorities based on the magnitude of the hazard. Table 1 lists a series of risks involving market processes and individual decisions that have been the focus of economic analyses to be considered below. The vigilance that individuals and society should devote to reducing these risks is not, however, governed solely by their size. Risks thought to be amenable to technological improvements, such as motor vehicle safety, have attracted the greatest attention. Risks be-

yond our control have merited comparatively modest risk reduction efforts.

Scientists estimate that we face an annual fatality risk from asteroid impact—the "doomsday rock"—of 1/6,000 (*New York Times*, June 18, 1991, p. B5). Yet, few would argue that we should abandon efforts to reduce smaller risks, such as those posed by jobs and home accidents, and reallocate these funds to fending off asteroids.[1] The key issue is the risk reduction that is achievable for any given expenditure and the value society places on this risk reduction.

The government faces a variety of opportunities to reduce risk.[2] Airplane cabin fire protection costs $200,000 per life saved; automobile side door protection standards save lives at $1.3 million each; Occupational Safety and Health Administration (OSHA) asbestos regula-

---

[1] Some scientists have begun speculating on the feasibility of such risk reductions. For example, some have suggested the use of nuclear weapons to alter the path of an asteroid. Thus far, it appears that less flamboyant policies, such as improved guardrails on highways, would be more cost-effective.

[2] For a review of the federal guidelines on the valuation of health risks, see the U.S. Office of Management and Budget (1988, 1990).

Viscusi: *The Value of Risks to Life and Health*   1913

TABLE 1

Source of Risk	Annual Fatality Risk
Cigarette smoking (per smoker)	1/150
Cancer	1/300
Motor Vehicle Accident	1/5,000
Asteroid (doomsday rock)	1/6,000
Work Accident (per worker)	1/10,000
Home Accident	1/11,000
Poisoning	1/37,000
Fire	1/50,000
Aviation Accident (passenger deaths/ total population)	1/250,000

Source: National Safety Council (1990); and further calculations by Viscusi (1992a, 1992b): the smoking risk estimates are averaged over the entire smoking population. The average smoker consumes 1.5 packs per day.

tions save lives at $89.3 million each; Environmental Protection Agency (EPA) asbestos regulations save lives at $104.2 million each; and a proposed OSHA formaldehyde standard cost $72 billion per life saved (John Morrall 1986).[3] Which of these different policies should be pursued, and which provide benefits that are not commensurate with their costs?

In a democratic society, the appropriate starting point for analyzing these tradeoffs is the value individuals bearing the risk place on the improved safety.[4] Over the past two decades, there has developed a substantial literature on the value of these risk-money tradeoffs. The greatest emphasis has been on the trade-

off involving mortality risks and wages. These labor market studies have addressed the implicit values of life of workers in many countries, including the United States, the United Kingdom, Australia, Canada, and Japan. Straightforward extensions of these models have included a measure of nonfatal risks faced by the worker, enabling analysts to impute an implicit value per statistical injury in the workplace. Economists have also analyzed the price-risk tradeoff for a variety of consumer products. In situations in which no market data are available, such as some environmental risks, one can use surveys to derive a market value if a market for the good existed. This paper explores these different approaches to establishing appropriate economic values for risks to life and health.

2. *Estimating the Value of Life Using Labor Market Data*

The dominant approach to obtaining estimates of the risk-dollar tradeoff uses labor market data on worker wages for risky jobs to infer attitudes toward risk. The theory underlying this analysis extends back to Adam Smith (1776), who observed that risky or otherwise unpleasant jobs will command a compensating wage differential.

Basic Elements of the Hedonic Wage Methodology

The main empirical approach to assessing risk tradeoffs in the labor market has utilized a methodology known as "hedonic" (i.e., quality-adjusted) wage equation.[5] Controlling for other aspects

---

[3] These estimates reported by Morrall (1986) are for new government regulations. For example, the 1986 OSHA asbestos standard that cost $89.3 million per life was more stringent than the 1972 OSHA standard, which cost $7.4 million per life.

[4] This principle is the same as in other benefit valuation contexts. The primary matter of interest is society's willingness to pay for the benefits generated by the policy. Thomas Schelling (1968) first presented the willingness-to-pay approach in the life-saving context.

[5] A forerunner of this line of work is the research on hedonic price indexes by Zvi Griliches (1971). Sherwin Rosen (1986) provides a survey of this approach focusing on nonpecuniary job attributes in general, where health and safety risks represent a special case. See also Richard Thaler and Rosen (1976), Robert Smith (1979), and Viscusi (1979). Schelling (1968) first outlined the proper use of value of life estimates.

1914   *Journal of Economic Literature, Vol. XXXI (December 1993)*

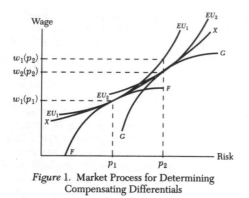

Figure 1. Market Process for Determining
Compensating Differentials

of the job, what is the wage premium workers receive for risk? These premiums are the result of the interaction of labor demand by firms and labor supply decisions by workers.

Providing greater workplace safety is costly to the firm. To maintain the same level of profits along some isoprofit curve, the firm must pay a lower wage rate to offset the cost of providing a safer work environment. The firm's wage offer curve consequently will be an increasing function of the risk. The offer curves for two different firms appear in Figure 1 as FF and GG. For any given risk level, workers will prefer the market offer curve with the highest wage level.

The characteristics of the supply side of the market are defined by several mild restrictions on preferences. Consider a formulation using a von Neumann-Morgenstern expected utility model with state-dependent utilities. Suppose that $U(w)$ denotes the utility of being healthy and $V(w)$ denotes the utility of being injured. Post-injury workers' compensation benefits are usually a function of w, where the exact relationship is subsumed into the functional form for $V(w)$.[6] The

only critical assumptions required for workers to demand compensating differentials for risk are that one would rather be healthy than not $[U(w) > V(w)]$ and the marginal utility of income is positive $[U'(w), V'(w) > 0]$. It is not necessary to assume that individuals are risk-averse $[U'', V'' < 0]$ in their attitude toward financial gambles.[7]

Workers will select the available wage-risk combination from the schedule WW that yields the maximum expected utility. For worker 1 in Figure 1 the optimal job risk is at the point where the worker's constant expected utility locus EU_1 is tangent to FF, and for worker 2 it is where EU_2 is tangent to GG.

The slope of the EU_1 and EU_2 curves can be readily verified. Wage-risk combinations that maintain a worker's constant expected utility level consist of the points that satisfy

$$Z = (1 - p)U(w) + pV(w).$$

The wage-risk tradeoff along this curve is given by

$$\frac{dw}{dp} = -\frac{Z_p}{Z_w} = \frac{U(w) - V(w)}{(1 - p)U'(w) + pV'(w)} > 0,$$

or the required wage rate increases with the risk level.

The points (p_1, w_1) and (p_2, w_2) in Figure 1 represent the points of tangency of the two constant expected utility loci with the market wage opportunities. These are the points that are observable using labor market data. In effect, economists only observe particular wage-risk choices of different workers at points of tangency with the market opportunities curve.

The econometric task is to estimate the locus of these wage-risk tradeoffs for the

---

[6] If there is no dependence of benefits on w, $V'(w) = 0$. So long as $U'(w) > 0$, the results below will hold.

[7] Risk neutrality ($U'', V'' = 0$) always leads to the results below. If individuals are risk lovers, the second-order conditions may not be met. See Viscusi (1979).

entire market. In effect, the hedonic wage studies fit a curve XX through points such as these and estimate the market locus of wage-risk tradeoffs.

The observed (p_i, w_i) reflect the influence of both supply and demand on the market equilibrium for the entire set of workers.[8] The estimated rate of tradeoff $\partial w / \partial p$ equals the slope of constant expected utility loci that are tangent to XX, thus providing a local measure of the wage-risk tradeoff for marginal changes in risk. For any given worker located along XX, the estimated slope simultaneously reflects the marginal willingness to accept risk and the marginal willingness to pay for greater safety. The points on XX also represent the points of tangency of firms' offer curves with workers' constant expected utility loci. The slope for the firm reflects both the marginal cost of greater safety and the marginal cost reductions from an incremental increase in risk. The slope at any point $\partial w_i / \partial p_i$ consequently represents the marginal supply price as well as the marginal demand price of risk for both the worker and firm located at that point. Econometric models that estimate a linear XX assume that the observed tradeoff rates are the same at all levels of risk.

The shape of the estimated locus of tradeoffs depends on the mix of firms and workers. The situation illustrated in Figure 1 consists of heterogeneous workers and firms. If all workers were homogeneous and, for example, had a constant expected utility locus EU_1, then the observed market combination (p_i, w_i) would consist of a series of points along EU_1 that were tangent to different firms' offer curves. The resulting estimates of XX would then approximate EU_1, and the

local tradeoff rate would characterize every worker's wage-risk tradeoff at that particular risk level. Similarly, consider the case of homogeneous firms, where all firms have offer curves FF. If there are heterogeneous workers, the market tradeoff curve XX would approximate the firm's offer curve, and its slope would approximate the marginal cost of altering job risks at that risk level.

With heterogeneous workers and heterogeneous firms, as in Figure 1, XX does not provide estimates of either the offer curves or constant expected utility loci. Rather, XX reflects only a set of tangencies between different firms' offer curves and different workers' constant expected utility loci. The value of $\partial w_i / \partial p_i$ at any given point (p_i, w_i) is the local tradeoff that is pertinent to the particular worker and firm located at that risk level. The estimated tradeoff rate at different levels of risk reflects other job-worker matches.

The estimated local tradeoffs may be a misleading index of the wage differentials required to maintain a worker's constant expected utility in the presence of a major change in risk because workers' risk preferences may differ. Worker 2 is willing to accept risk p_2 for $w_2(p_2)$. However, worker 1 will require a higher amount of wage compensation $w_1(p_2)$ along EU_1 to face the risk level p_2 than worker 2 requires on EU_2. If the estimated wage-risk tradeoff curve XX for the market were linear, then the estimated rate of tradeoff would be the same for all workers whose indifference curves are tangent to XX. However, even for a linear locus of tangencies XX, for changes of more than a marginal amount from the current risk level, the worker's wage-risk tradeoff will not be the same because the pertinent tradeoff value must be measured along a constant expected utility locus, not the estimated market tradeoff curve.

[8] Inframarginal workers earn an economic rent. The wage-risk tradeoff of the marginal worker is instrumental in establishing the wage rate the firm must pay and consequently the value of the risk reduction.

General Specification Issues

The basic approach in the literature is to specify a wage equation which characterizes the line XX in Figure 1, or

$$w_i = \alpha + \sum_{m=1}^{M} \psi_m x_{im} + \gamma_0 p_i$$
$$+ \gamma_1 q_i + \gamma_2 q_i WC_i + u_i, \quad (1)$$

where w_i is worker i's wage rate (or its natural logarithm), α is a constant term, the x_{im} are different personal characteristic and job characteristic variables for worker i ($m = 1$ to M), p_i is the fatality risk of worker i's job, q_i is the job's nonfatal risk, WC_i reflects the workers' compensation benefits that are payable for worker i's job injury, u_i is a random error term reflecting unmeasured factors that influence the wage rate, and the remaining terms are coefficients to be estimated.[9] The x_{im} values play a key role in that different worker characteristics, such as education, will affect the firm's offer curve, the market opportunity locus, and worker preferences.[10] Figure 1 pertains to a group of workers who have identical productivity, but different preferences. Some researchers have interacted various x_{im} variables with the risk variables to capture the role of different markets for workers that differ in terms of their market opportunities.[11] Interactive terms, such as education and risk, reflect the joint influence of possible differences in worker preferences as well as differences in firms' offer curves for workers with different educational attainment. Alternative econometric ap-

proaches involving the use of structural equation systems have also been used to isolate the wage-risk tradeoff controlling for other aspects of the job and the worker.[12]

Efforts to estimate variants of equation (1) before the 1970s were largely unsuccessful because of the absence of detailed micro data sets on individual worker behavior. Large individual data sets on worker behavior generally include a more extensive set of demographic and job characteristic variables than industry data. Moreover, the values of these variables are matched to a particular worker rather than being averaged across the entire industry. If there is also available job risk data by individual (e.g., self-assessed risk data) or by occupation, one will have information on actual points (p_i, w_i) selected in individual job choices rather than an average of such points

---

[9] A fuller version of the model also could include annuity benefits in the event of a fatality.

[10] See Thaler and Rosen (1976), especially pp. 283–286.

[11] Although these interactions are usually to capture productivity-related influences, discrimination-based effects may also be influential as well. In any event, these interactive effects will reflect the joint influence of worker and firm variations.

[12] More recently, some economists have estimated structural equation systems. See, in particular, James Brown (1983), Shulamit Kahn and Kevin Lang (1988), Jeff Biddle and Gary Zarkin (1988), Viscusi and Michael Moore (1989), Moore and Viscusi (1990b, 1990c), and Joni Hersch and Viscusi (1990). These models, which will be discussed further below, consist of two-equation systems for which researchers have augmented equation (1) with variables such as regional variables that ideally serve to identify the market wage opportunities locus, and there is a second equation defined by the tangency of worker preferences with this market opportunities locus.

In particular, one estimates the nonlinear equation obtained after equating $\partial w/\partial p$ on both a constant expected utility locus and the market wage frontier. For this approach to be feasible, one must assume a specific functional form for the utility function. The use of regional economic variables to identify the market opportunities locus assumes that the regional differences reflect differences in economic conditions and perhaps technologies as well (e.g., logging in the Pacific Northwest, petroleum exploration in Texas and Alaska, etc.) If, however, individual preferences also vary across regions, then $\partial w/\partial p$ may also vary systematically across regions. At the current stage of development, it is not clear whether the strong estimation assumptions of structural models are satisfied to a sufficient degree to yield reliable estimates that will be robust across data sets. The emphasis here will be on traditional hedonic wage estimation because many of the econometric issues are common to the structural models as well.

across heterogeneous workers in an industry.[13]

Estimation using industry-wide data sets often encountered difficulty in distinguishing the positive wage premium for job risks. The reliance on aggregative industry data pools workers with heterogeneous preferences and firms with perhaps quite different offer curves so that the estimated tradeoffs at any particular risk level cannot be linked to any worker's preferences or any firm's offer curve. In contrast, micro data sets give information pertinent to one (p_i, w_i) point in resulting from the decisions of a single firm and worker.

One source of variation lost with aggregation is that due to differences in lifetime wealth. A negative relation between wealth and risk arises for two reasons. First, differences in worker preferences will influence this relationship because job safety is a normal economic good.[14] More affluent workers will select a lower risk level from any given wage offer schedule. The wage w_i that a worker requires to accept any given risk p_i will increase with wealth, and the wage-risk tradeoff $\partial w/\partial p$ will also increase with wealth. Employees also will have more incentive to protect their more highly skilled employees because they have a greater investment in their training.

Overall, as John Stuart Mill observed, the best jobs in society will tend to be the highest paid. However, this does not imply that there are no compensating differentials for any particular position, only that there is a broader societal wealth

effect at work that will make it difficult to disentangle the wage-risk tradeoff that is present. Use of individual level data that includes measures of worker education, experience, and other productivity-related variables isolates the additional compensation workers of a given productivity will receive for jobs posing greater risk. It cannot be determined, however, whether observed differences in risk tradeoff rates reflect heterogeneity in firms' offer curves for workers with different characteristics.

The Wage Variable

It is instructive to consider each of the components of equation (1) in turn. The dependent variable is the worker's hourly wage rate. In practice, researchers have often been forced to use other income measures, such as the worker's annual income or a constructed wage value using information on weeks and average hours worked. What is particularly relevant to the worker is not the gross wage but rather the aftertax wage from a particular job. For most labor market studies this distinction is not of great consequence because the main effect of taxes is not too dissimilar from scaling up the wage rate by a factor of proportionality if workers' income levels and tax rates do not differ substantially. However, if the equation also includes a workers' compensation variable, as in the case of equation (1), then the workers' compensation benefits and the wage rate should be expressed in comparable aftertax terms so as to measure the wage effects of workers' compensation correctly.

Job Risk Measures

For most purposes, the most important of the explanatory variables is the fatality risk variable p that is the basis for estimating the worker's fatality risk-money tradeoff. The ideal risk measure would

[13] Note that a firm's offer curve *FF* in Figure 1 for one class of workers may differ than its offer curve for a different group of workers.

[14] See Thaler and Rosen (1976), Michael Jones-Lee (1976), Viscusi (1979), and Viscusi and William Evans (1990). Researchers have attempted to capture the role of wealth through interactive risk x wealth variables, where wealth has been measured directly and captured through various proxies for lifetime wealth, such as education.

1918   *Journal of Economic Literature, Vol. XXXI (December 1993)*

reflect subjective assessment of the fatality risk of the job by both the worker and the firm. In practice, researchers have a less perfect measure. Most studies have used information from available national data sets that typically provide information on several thousand workers and their jobs. These data sets include detailed information pertaining to the worker's demographic characteristics (age, race, sex, years of schooling, health status, marital status, etc.), nature of employment (wage rate, hours worked, industry, occupation, union status, years of experience, etc.), and place of residence. The University of Michigan Survey of Working Conditions and Quality of Employment Survey also included information on the worker's job attributes, as perceived by the worker. Among these variables is whether the worker believes he faces hazards on his particular job. Usually, researchers have matched objective measures of the industry or occupation risk to the worker based on his job classification.

The degree of refinement of these risk variables varies. The pre-1971 Bureau of Labor Statistics (BLS) death risk data are published for three-digit Standard Industrial Classification (SIC) codes. Manufacturing and nonmanufacturing industries are both represented.[15] After 1971, the BLS published death risk data for one-digit SIC codes so that the available data became more aggregative. Unpublished death risk data by two-digit SIC code are also available from the agency. The National Institute of Occupational Safety and Health (NIOSH) death risk data are available by one-digit SIC industry codes for each of the states. The Society of Actuaries fatality data are based on occupational fatality risks rather than industry risks, and 37 occupations are represented in these data. The performance of these

---

[15] Government employees are not, however, included in the BLS or NIOSH data.

different measures differs, as will be explored below.

A fundamental issue is how systematic biases in individual risk perception affect the market processes that give rise to the compensating wage differential estimates.[16] A sizable literature in psychology and economics has documented biases in individual assessments of risk. Individuals tend to overestimate low probability events, such as the chance of being struck by lightning, and to underestimate risks of high probability events, such as the chance of dying from heart disease (see Baruch Fischhoff et al. 1981).

Because these biases are systematic, we know a great deal about their consequences. In particular, the relationship between perceived risks and actual risks is similar to that displayed in Figure 2. The perceived probability line *CD* lies above the actual probability level for

---

[16] Labor market estimates focus on the wage that workers require to accept risks, whereas policy evaluations are based on willingness to pay for risk reduction. For sufficiently small risk changes, willingness-to-pay and willingness-to-accept values should be equal. One experimental study—Viscusi, Wesley, Magat, and Joel Huber (1987)—found substantial differences in these valuations for risk changes on the order of 5/10,000. When presented with risk changes in a survey context, individuals may require a large financial inducement to accept an increase in risk from their accustomed risk level that greatly exceeds their willingness to pay for incremental reductions in risk even though those tradeoff rates should be identical.

The source of this influence appears to be a perception bias on the part of survey respondents in which they overreact to newly identified risks. The survey results in Viscusi and Charles O'Connor (1984) and Shelby Gerking, Menno deHaan, and William Schulze (1988) suggest that these effects may not be as great for job safety contexts, perhaps in part because workers' familiarity with job risks make them less alarmed by information regarding a minor increase in risk. Explicit estimates that do this in the case of worker injury risks are provided in Viscusi and Evans (1990). Indeed, this effect is borne out in the behavior of society at large in terms of the frequent overreaction to small, but highly publicized risks. If, however, the risk changes are of more than a modest incremental amount, then the curvature of the constant expected utility locus shown in Figure 2 will also affect the tradeoff rate.

Viscusi: *The Value of Risks to Life and Health*   1919

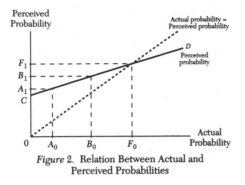

Figure 2. Relation Between Actual and
Perceived Probabilities

small risks and under this amount for
large risks. The role of risk perceptions
is to decrease the risk change that individuals associate with any incremental
change in the risk. Thus, in the case of
a job that poses some specific incremental risk $A_0 B_0$ to the worker in Figure 2,
the worker will perceive this incremental
increase to be a lower amount $A_1 B_1$ and
will consequently demand less compensation than he otherwise would.[17] In
terms of the estimated compensating differential, workers will demand less compensation per unit of actual risk that they
face because the risk increase is greater
than they believe it to be. The value of
$\partial w/p$ will be smaller at any given value
of p (see Viscusi 1990), thus influencing
the market equilibrium locus that is estimated. The net effect on the estimated
value of XX depends on how these
changes in the EU_i interact with the
available offer curves. In addition, random measurement error in the risk variable would tend to bias the estimated
tradeoffs downward, but systematic measurement error could lead to a bias in
either direction.[18]

To isolate the wage premium for risk,
the wage equation should include other
attributes of the worker's job. Jobs that
are risky tend to be unpleasant in other
respects. One such variable is the other
component of job risk—the nonfatal risk
q indicated in equation (1). Inclusion of
this variable is sometimes difficult either
because of the correlation between the
death risk variable and the nonfatal risk
measures or because the differences in
the data sources and the reference populations for which these data have been
gathered may make it difficult to include
both variables simultaneously. As a result, few studies in the literature include
both risk measures. The exclusion of the
nonfatal injury variable may lead to an
upward bias in the estimated coefficient
for the fatality risks if the death risk variable's coefficient captures the omitted influence of the premiums for nonfatal
risks, which should be positively correlated with fatality risks.[19] In addition, a
bias may result if the probability of injury
is positive but the death risk is zero.

Another key risk-related variable is the
workers' compensation variable indicated
by qWC in equation (1). What is pertinent to the worker is the expected workers' compensation benefit.[20] Most of the
early studies in the compensating differential literature did not include a workers' compensation variable, but it has
been included in several recent studies
discussed below. This ex post compensation variable ideally will be in terms of
the expected workers' compensation
benefit or some other form (e.g., expected rate of replacement of lost earn-

---

[17] For a more formal exploration of these issues,
see Viscusi (1990).
[18] Comparison of the BLS and NIOSH data in
Moore and Viscusi (1988a) suggests that the measurement error is not random in the case of the BLS
data, if we use the NIOSH data as the reference
point. Other biases also may be present, such as an

upward bias that arises if the study omits other nonpecuniary attribute variables.
[19] Viscusi (1978a) presents estimates with and without such control variables.
[20] More formally, what the worker is truly concerned with is the insurance premium he is willing
to pay for workers' compensation benefits. The expected workers' compensation value captures this for
a risk-neutral worker.

1920   *Journal of Economic Literature, Vol. XXXI (December 1993)*

ings) that takes into account the probability that the worker will actually collect the benefits. If the worker faces a job that poses zero risk, then workers' compensation benefits offer no expected welfare benefit, and consequently there will be no compensating differential.

A related issue is the role of worker uncertainty. Apart from the fact that we do not know exactly what workers' risk perceptions are, there is the additional problem that these perceptions may not be precise. Thus, workers have a subjective risk perception pertaining to the hazards posed by a job, but these perceptions may not be as tight as an objective probability.

The main consequence of this uncertainty for workers is to increase the likelihood of a worker quitting once he learns about the adverse properties of a job and revises his prior risk beliefs. This quit effect can be viewed as a generalization of the theory of compensating differentials to a situation of worker uncertainty and adaptive behavior (Viscusi 1979; Viscusi and O'Connor 1984). One measure of the magnitude of this effect is that if all industries eliminated their job risks, holding constant other aspects of the job including wages, it would reduce the manufacturing industry quit rates by one-third.[21] On a theoretical basis, the opportunity for learning and adaptive behavior should lead workers to demand less compensation per unit risk than they would if they were fully informed about the probabilities even if this information did not alter the assessed risk level (see Viscusi 1979). The reasoning behind this result is that workers in a sequential job

choice situation should prefer the less precisely understood risk because they can quit if they acquire sufficiently unfavorable information about the risk, and they can remain on the job if they acquire favorable information. Employers may also respond to this quitting by raising worker wages to retain experienced workers who are aware of the risk. Empirically, the net effect is that more experienced workers on hazardous jobs receive higher compensating differentials (see Viscusi and Moore 1991).

Recognition of the Duration of Life

The standard hedonic wage equation includes the probability of death, but the amount and quality of life at risk differs.[22] For the typical healthy worker, the major difference across individuals will be in terms of the quantity of life at risk. A 20-year-old worker faces a more substantial loss from a given fatality risk than a 60-year-old worker. An offsetting influence that should also be taken into account is that there may be age-related differences in the proclivity toward risk taking, some of which may be attributable to differences in family structure. Age clearly is a factor that may potentially affect where along the market equilibrium curve XX a worker is located. If XX is nonlinear, then age may also affect the slope. Worker age may also influence the offer curves workers face as well.[23]

The simplest approach to addressing the life duration issue is to include a fatality risk variable interacted with worker age, i.e., $p \times$ worker age. This approach is used in Thaler and Rosen (1976) and

---

[21] Wages, of course, would also change in a competitive market. This estimate is based on the implications of quit rate regressions using data from the University of Michigan Panel of Income Dynamics, as reported in Viscusi (1979). The one-third figure (more precisely, 35% is calculated using these results in Viscusi 1983, pp. 67, 182).

[22] Richard Zeckhauser and Donald Shepard (1976) develop a quality-adjusted value-of-life concept to recognize quantity and quality differences. Economists have had more success at estimating quantity differences than quality differences.

[23] Although the earlier models with age interaction terms did not attempt to sort out both sets of influence, the structural models discussed below attempt to do this.

Viscusi (1979), with evidence of a significant negative age-risk interaction.

A refinement of this approach is to include a variable that reflects the expected years of life lost, such as $p \times$ life expectancy. This variable would capture two influences at work. First, younger workers have a longer future life at risk. Second, as we age, the expected date of death conditional upon our age is pushed out.

Although the life expectancy approach represents a refinement of simply interacting worker age with death risks, it does not recognize the role of discounting with respect to the years of life at risk. Instead of estimating the coefficient for a variable pertaining to the worker's life expectancy, one would prefer to estimate the discounted loss in life expectancy, so that the job risk variable takes the form $p(1 - e^{-rT})/r$, where r is the rate of discount and T is the remaining period of life. Assuming that the only affect of age is to influence the character of worker preferences, not firms' offer curves for risky jobs, estimation of such a model yields an estimate of the implicit value of life, the implicit value per discounted expected life year lost, and the rate of time preference that workers use in discounting years of life. Including the discounted expected loss in life expectancy in equation (1) in lieu of the job risk variable p produces an estimated rate of time preference of 10–12 percent with respect to expected life years (Moore and Viscusi 1988b). As in the case of wage-risk tradeoffs, the presence of heterogeneity of worker preferences will make this estimate a nonlinear weighted average of the individual workers' preferences.[24]

[24] Some of the more important sources of heterogeneity can be ascertained through interaction terms. For example, college-educated workers exhibit lower rates of time preference than those with less education, as one might expect.

A more elaborate alternative is to develop a model of lifetime job choice from which is derived a functional form for the worker's decision to engage in potentially hazardous work. Rosen (1988) and a series of papers by Viscusi and Moore (1989) and Moore and Viscusi (1990a, 1990b, 1990c) have explored these models. By using a structural model of the job choice process, these analyses ideally distinguish differences in worker preferences from worker characteristics that affect the market offer curve available to these workers.

Two general approaches have proven estimable.[25] One is to estimate a standard life-cycle consumption model, with the main difference being that the model recognizes that there is a probability in each period that the consumption stream may be terminated. The alternative is to construct a lifetime decision model, where the worker selects the optimal job risk from the wage offer curve, where this risk affects the probability of death in each period. One example of the latter approach is the Markov decision model in Viscusi and Moore (1989).[26] In selecting their optimal job risks, workers determine their life expectancy.[27] After assuming an explicit functional form for the

[25] Rosen's (1988) paper does not estimate the life cycle model directly, but uses the results of Thaler and Rosen (1976) in conjunction with the model to obtain estimates of the key components of interest.

[26] This variant of the model will exclude causes of death other than one's job to simplify the exposition.

[27] More specifically, let the utility of death equal to zero and assume that the worker faces a time-invariant sequence of lotteries on life and death. To recognize the dependence of the job risk data on worker i's reported industry j, p_{ij} will be used to denote the pertinent fatality risk level. Worker i selects the optimal death risk p_{ij} from the available opportunities locus $w(p_{ij})$ to maximize discounted expected lifetime utility

$$G = U(w(p_{ij}))(1 - p_{ij}) \sum_{t=1}^{\infty} [\beta(1 - p_{ij})]^{t-1},$$

where t indexes time periods and β is the discount factor (the inverse of 1 plus the interest rate).

utility function (i.e., a constant relative risk aversion utility function, $a + bw^c$), Viscusi and Moore (1989) estimate a two-equation structural system based on the local tradeoff implied by the optimization problem in which the worker selects the optimal fatality risk, and a wage equation characterizing the market opportunities locus.[28] For worker i in industry j with market opportunities affected by variables x_{im}, the market implicit price equation takes the form

$$\ln w_i = \sum_{k=1}^{4} (\phi_k R_{ik} p_{ij} + \delta_k R_{ik} p_{ij}^2)$$

$$+ \sum_{m=1}^{M} \psi_m x_{im} + \epsilon_i \quad (2)$$

where the R_{ik} are regional dummy variables, the first summation is over the four geographical regions, ϵ_1 is a random error term, and ϕ_k, δ_k, ψ_m are coefficients to be estimated.[29] The worker decision equation generated by this particular model is

$$\ln w_i = (1 - \beta)(1 - p_{ij}) \frac{\partial \ln w_i}{\partial p_{ij}}$$

$$+ \sum_{n=1}^{N} \alpha_k x_{ik} + \epsilon_2, \quad (3)$$

where β is the discount factor $1/(1 + r)$ to be estimated, ϵ_2 is a random error

term, and the α_k are coefficients on the taste-shifter variables to be estimated. The value of $\partial \ln w_i/\partial p_{ij}$ is computed from the first stage market wage equation. This general estimation approach follows the procedure advocated by Kahn and Lang (1988) and Biddle and Zarkin (1988) to estimate structural hedonic systems.

In all such models, the worker selects the optimal job risk p_{ij} from among a schedule of wage-risk combinations in the workplace. From this optimization problem is derived an explicit functional form that relates the worker's rate of tradeoff $\partial w_i/\partial p_{ij}$ to various aspects of the job choice problem, including the job risk $p_{ij,}$ the discount rate, and in models based on a finite time horizon, the worker's remaining life. Some models also include a probability of death from causes other than the job to reflect the fatality risks that a worker faces throughout his life. This nonlinear equation (3) is coupled with a second market wage equation (2) to complete the structural equation system. The estimated discount rates range from 1 to 14 percent, which are broadly consistent with financial rates of return that one might use as a reference point in assessing the rationality of inter-temporal choices.

Estimation of Utility Functions

Knowledge of the shape of worker utility functions rather than a local tradeoff rate along a constant expected utility locus would provide the basis for more detailed judgments. For example, it makes possible analysis of variations in the value of life with respect to income levels and assessments of valuations of nonmarginal changes in risk. The utility function models are based on two different state-dependent utility functions. In the good health state 1, the utility function is $U(w)$, and in the ill health state, the utility function is $V(y)$, where y is the benefit paid upon death. One can make y a function

[28] Identification remains an issue. Regional dummy variables are used to identify the market wage equation based on the assumption that these variables indicate geographically distinct labor markets, but do not affect worker preferences. These regional variables include interactions with the linear and quadratic job risk variables. This identification issue is present in hedonic price models as well. See Dennis Epple (1987).

[29] This equation differs from equation (1) in that the death risk and (death risk)² variables are included by region. The nonpecuniary risk variable q and its interaction with workers' compensation does not appear because the NIOSH risk data pertain to fatalities only. More generally, the hedonic wage equation focuses on both supply and demand factors, whereas structural models attempt to distinguish factors reflecting tastes and opportunities using separate equations for each.

of w. In the case of fatality risks, $V(y)$ represents the worker's bequest function, which can equal zero if the worker has no beneficiaries.

Estimating utility functions involves a quite different estimation procedure than the hedonic wage equation approach, and it utilizes a different type of data as well. The concern is no longer with tracing out the locus of tangencies involving a firm's offer curve and an individual worker's constant expected utility locus. Rather, the focus is on information provided by two or more points along a particular worker's constant expected utility locus. Because natural market experiments do not provide such information, researchers have used survey evidence regarding the stated compensating differentials that the worker would require if faced with a change in job risk. This procedure leads to estimates of the state-dependent, von Neumann-Morgenstern utility functions $U(w)$ and $V(y)$ up to a positive linear transformation.

Viscusi and Evans' (1990) procedure uses worker survey data from four chemical firms that provides information on two equivalent jobs a and b along a constant expected utility locus, such as EU in Figure 3. This curve is tangent to the market offer curve ABC. The worker reports his current wage rate w_a and his assessed job risk q_a using a linear scale comparable to the BLS injury risk metric. The worker is then given a hazard warning for a chemical and told that this chemical would replace the chemicals with which he now works.[30] The worker then assesses the risk q_b associated with the transformed job and the wage rate w_b he would require to remain on EU. The income replacement after an injury, y_a

Figure 3. The Market Offer Curve and the Worker's Expected Utility Locus

and y_b, can be computed using w_a, w_b, and workers' compensation benefit formulas for the worker's state of residence. The survey addresses the components of the following equality:

$$(1 - q_a)U(w_a) + q_aV(y_a)$$
$$= (1 - q_b)U(w_b) + q_bV(y_b). \quad (4)$$

All the elements of equation (4) are observable except for U and V. One must impose some structure on the utility functions to make estimations of them feasible. If we assume a specific functional form for the utility functions (e.g., logarithmic) or use a Taylor's series approximation to the general utility function, then we can solve equation (4) for the wage increase required by the worker to face the new risk, yielding an equation that can be estimated with nonlinear regression methods.[31] If we observe more than two points on a constant expected

---

[30] The chemicals used were TNT, asbestos, chloroacetophenone, and sodium bicarbonate. The warnings conformed with current industry practice given the properties of these chemicals. The original survey results appear in Viscusi and O'Connor (1984).

[31] Let $w_b = (1 + \delta)w_a$, where δ is the percentage wage premium for the higher risk on job b. The dependent variable in the model is δ. For the first-order Taylor's series expansion variant of the model, the parameters to be estimated are $\beta_1 = U(w_a) - V(w_a)$, $\beta_2 = U'(w_a)$, and $\beta_3 = V'(w_a)$. Thus, the estimation focuses on three parameters that characterize the nature of worker preferences. With no loss of generality one can set $\beta_2 = 1$ because von Neumann-Morgenstern utility functions are not altered by a positive linear transformation, leaving two parameters to be estimated. One can also make β_1 and β_3 functions of personal characteristics, such as education. See Viscusi and Evans (1990) for further details.

utility locus, as in Evans and Viscusi (1991), then we have an ability to estimate utility functions characterized by a larger number of parameters.

The utility function estimation procedure can explicitly recognize the role of individual heterogeneity by making the parameters of the utility function dependent on worker characteristics.[32] This ability to distinguish differences in preferences stems in part from use of data that does not confound the influence of worker and firm decisions. Only the information on multiple points (p_i, w_i) along the worker's constant expected utility locus is used. Estimates involving variation across a broad sample of worker characteristics makes possible the estimation of the dependence of the utility function parameters on personal characteristics.

3. *Review of Risk Tradeoffs in the Labor Market Literature*

Although the methodology for estimating the labor market value of life is straightforward, the empirical estimates differ substantially. Table 2 summarizes 24 principal labor market studies of the implicit value of life, where these valuation estimates are all in December 1990 dollars. These studies appear in chronological order. Robert S. Smith (1974) used industry-level data to estimate wage premiums for risk, but the other studies in Table 2 used individual worker data. The advent of large micro data sets on individual worker behavior enabled economists to isolate the role of job risks from factors such as education and experience. As Charles Brown (1980) has observed, even large micro data sets do not always resolve these estimation prob-

lems. Potentially substantial measurement error arises when the researcher creates the nonpecuniary characteristic variables by matching to the worker objective measures of job attributes, such as fatality rates, based on the worker's industry or occupation.[33]

The studies listed in Table 2 differ in a variety of respects, including the data sets as well as the wage equation specification. The initial studies in the literature consisted almost entirely of simple regressions of wage rates on risk levels, possibly interacted with worker age. Beginning with Moore and Viscusi (1988b) there was an attempt to estimate the tradeoff for discounted expected life years lost. The starkest difference among the studies consists of the structural estimation approach that is employed in differing degrees in some of the most recent studies listed in the table.[34]

The structural models focusing on the duration of life at risk assist in illuminating aspects of the lifetime job choice problem, such as workers' implicit rate of discount. However, the additional information comes at a cost. The estimation procedures often are quite complicated, and considerably greater demands are placed on the data. The risk-dollar tradeoff estimates have been less robust for these models than more straightforward estimation approaches, such as those following equation (1). As a result, I place greater emphasis upon the more conventional wage equation estimates of the risk-wage tradeoff than on the find-

---

[32] For the logarithmic utility function case, one might, for example, set the utility of injury equal to $\ln(w)$, and the utility of good health equal to $(\alpha + \beta_1 \text{ Education} + \beta_2 \text{ Age} + \beta_3 \text{ Sex})\ln(y)$.

[33] It should be noted that Charles Brown's (1980) effort entailed an ambitious matching of detailed information from the *Dictionary of Occupational Titles* to the workers. Another innovation is that he used panel data from the National Longitudinal Survey Young Men's sample to link wage changes to changes in job characteristics in an effort to control for omitted differences in worker ability.

[34] There were antecedents to these structural models, but not involving fatality risks. See James N. Brown (1983), Kahn and Lang (1988), and Biddle and Zarkin (1988).

ings yielded by the structural estimation models.

Although many of the studies listed in Table 2 consist primarily of replications and consistency checks on earlier results, there have been a number of important innovations in the literature. The columns in Table 2 summarize several salient dimensions of these studies. All except four of the studies rely upon large U.S. data sets, and all but two of these studies use national surveys of worker behavior.

Choice of the Job Risk Variable

Because all of these surveys include most of the demographic and job characteristic information needed to estimate the wage equation, the main distinguishing feature is the manner in which the risk variable is created. None of the sets of survey data listed includes any objective measure of the risks posed by the worker's particular job. Nor do the risk data distinguish which injuries are attributable to the job environment and which arise solely from worker actions.[35] The University of Michigan's Survey of Working Conditions and Quality Employment Survey each include a subjective risk variable, which ascertained whether the worker views the job as posing dangerous or unhealthy conditions.[36] The subjective risk perception variable p_s, which is a 0–1 dummy variable

for whether the worker's job poses any health and safety risks, can be interacted with some objective measure of the risk p_0 to create a potentially more refined estimate of the risk variable ($p_s \times p_0$), as in Viscusi (1978a, 1979) and Moore and Viscusi (1988b).

Gegax, Gerking, and Schulze (1991) use a continuous measure of the worker's subjective risk of fatality derived from an interview approach analogous to the Viscusi and O'Connor (1984) study of nonfatal job injuries. However, the risk scale they presented to workers ranged from 1/4,000 to 10/4,000.[37] Because the average U.S. fatality risk of 1/10,000 lies outside the range, the risk interval used was likely to generate overestimates of the job risk. Not surprisingly, their respondents' assessed job risks were very high; their white-collar subsample assessed the annual job fatality risk as 1/2,000.[38]

The dominant approach followed in the literature is to rely upon some published measure of the risk level by occupation or industry, and then to match this risk variable to the worker in the sample using information provided by the respondent. The study by Thaler and Rosen (1976) used Society of Actuaries data pertaining to the risk associated with different occupations, as did Charles Brown (1980) and Arnould and Nichols (1983). These data pertain primarily to high risk occupations with average annual risks of death on the order of 1/1,000—roughly ten times the average for the U.S. work-

---

[35] Making such distinctions is difficult because workplace technologies and worker safety precautions jointly determine the risk. If all accidents were due to worker carelessness and would have arisen in all other contexts in which the worker was employed, then no wage premiums for risk would be observed.

[36] These data sets have been analyzed by Viscusi (1978a, 1979), Dillingham (1985), Leigh (1987), and Moore and Viscusi (1988b), but not all of these researchers have used the subjective risk variable. Also see the nonfatal risk study of Biddle and Zarkin (1988). None of the data sets include measures of the employer's perceptions, which are relevant to the shape of the offer curve.

[37] Respondents could select one of ten integer responses ranging from 1/4,000 to 10/4,000. The average U.S. job fatality risk is not in this range.

[38] The upward bias in risk assessments in turn will tend to produce low estimates of the value of life, as appears to be the case. The higher value-of-life estimates for changes in risk generated by the same survey instrument, as reported in Gerking, deHaan, and Schulze (1988), are also consistent with overestimation of the base job risk level.

TABLE 2
SUMMARY OF LABOR MARKET STUDIES OF THE VALUE OF LIFE

Author (Year)	Sample	Risk Variable	Mean Risk	Nonfatal Risk Incl?	Workers' Comp Incl?	Avg Income Level (1990 U.S. $)	Implicit Value of Life ($ million)	Implicit Value of Life for Air Travelers ($ million)
R. S. Smith (1974)	Industry data: Census of Manufacturers, U.S. Census, Employment and Earnings	Bureau of Labor Statistics (BLS)	NA	Yes	No	22,640	7.2	11.0
Thaler & Rosen (1976)	Survey of Economic Opportunity	Society of Actuaries	0.001	No	No	27,034	0.8	1.0
R. S. Smith (1976)	Current Population Survey (CPS), 1967, 1973	BLS	0.0001	Yes, not signif.	No	NA	4.6	NA
Viscusi (1978a, 1979)	Survey of Working Conditions, 1969–1970 (SWC)	BLS, subjective risk of job (SWC)	0.0001	Yes, signif.	No	24,834	4.1	5.7
Charles Brown (1980)	National Longitudinal Survey of Young Men 1966–71, 1973	Society of Actuaries	0.002	No	No	NA	1.5	NA
Viscusi (1981)	Panel Study of Income Dynamics, 1976	BLS	0.0001	Yes, signif.	No	17,640	6.5	12.8
Craig Olson (1981)	CPS 1978	BLS	0.0001	Yes, signif.	No	NA	5.2	NA
Alan Marin & George Psacharopoulos (1982)	U.K. Office of Population Censuses and Surveys, 1977	Occupational Mortality U.K.	0.0001	No	No	11,287	2.8	8.1
Richard Arnould & Len Nichols (1983)	U.S. Census	Society of Actuaries	0.001	No	Yes	NA	0.9	NA
Richard Butler (1983)	S.C. Workers' Compensation Data 1940–69	S.C. Workers' Compensation Claims Data	0.00005	No	Yes	NA	1.1	NA
J. Paul Leigh & Roger Folsom (1984)	Panel Study of Income Dynamics, 1974; Quality of Employment Survey (QES) 1977	BLS	0.0001	Yes	No	27,693, 28,734	9.7 10.3	11.0 11.7
V. Kerry Smith and Carol Gilbert (1984)	CPS 1978	BLS	NA	No	No	NA	0.7	NA
Alan Dillingham (1985)	QES 1977	BLS; Constructed by author	0.000008, 0.00014	No	No	20,848	2.5–5.3; 0.9	4.2–8.8; 1.5

Study	Data	Data source	Risk			Income	Value	Value
Leigh (1987)	QES 1977; CPS 1977	BLS	NA	No	No	NA	10.4	NA
Moore & Viscusi (1988a)	Panel Study of Income Dynamics, 1982	BLS, NIOSH National Traumatic Occupational Fatality Survey	0.00005, 0.00008	No	Yes	19,444	2.5, 7.3	4.6, 13.4
Moore & Viscusi (1988b)	QES 1977	BLS, discounted expected life years lost; subjective risk of job (QES)	0.00006	No	Yes	24,249	7.3	10.5
John Garen (1988)	Panel Study of Income Dynamics, 1981–82	BLS	NA	Yes	No	NA	13.5	NA
Jean-Michel Cousineau, Robert Lacroix & Anne-Marie Girard (1988)	Labor, Canada Survey, 1979	Quebec Compensation Board	0.00001	No	No	NA	3.6	NA
Viscusi & Moore (1989)	Panel Study of Income Dynamics, 1982	NIOSH National Traumatic Occupational Fatality Survey, Structural Markov Model	0.0001	No	No	19,194	7.8	14.1
Moore & Viscusi (1990a)	Panel Study of Income Dynamics, 1982	NIOSH National Traumatic Occupational Fatality Survey, Structural Life Cycle Model	0.0001	No	No	19,194	16.2	29.4
Moore & Viscusi (1990b)	Panel Study of Income Dynamics, 1982	NIOSH National Traumatic Occupational Fatality Survey, Structural Integrated Life Cycle Model	0.0001	Yes	Yes	19,194	16.2	29.4
Thomas Kniesner and John Leeth (1991)	Two-digit mgf. data, Japan. 1986	Yearbook of Labor Statistics, Japan	0.00003	Yes	No	34,989	7.6	7.5
	Two-digit mfg. data, Australia, by state, 1984–1985	Industrial Accident data, Australia	0.0001	Yes	Yes	18,177	3.3	6.3
	CPS U.S., 1978	NIOSH (National Traumatic Occupational Fatality Survey)	0.0004	Yes	Yes	26,226	0.6	0.8
Henry Herzog & Alan Schlottman (1987)	U.S. Census, 1970	BLS	NA	No	No	NA	9.1	NA
Douglas Gegax, Gerking, and Schulze (1991)	Authors' mail survey, 1984	Worker's assessed fatality risk at work	0.0009	No	No	NA	1.6	NA

Note: All values are in December 1990 dollars

NA = Not available

place. To the extent that workers who select themselves into high risk jobs have a lower risk-dollar tradeoff than workers in higher risk jobs, one would expect to obtain lower value-of-life estimates in studies that use these data, as Thaler and Rosen (1976) recognize.[39] In addition, the Society of Actuaries data pertain to all incremental mortality risks associated with people in 37 different occupations, not simply the job-specific risk. Thus, this variable also reflects risks other than those on the job, which would not be compensated through the wage mechanism. Actors, for example, have a very high mortality rate.

The lower value-of-life estimates obtained using the Society of Actuaries data rather than data for workers in less risky jobs is consistent with the self-selection of individuals with low risk-dollar tradeoffs into the most hazardous pursuits. The substantial variation in the value-of-life estimates in Table 2 with the risk level, which is a consequence of the joint influence of worker and firm heterogeneity, suggests that one should exercise substantial caution in extrapolating estimates across risk ranges.

Twelve of the studies listed in Table 2 use the BLS risk data based on the risks associated with different industries. The BLS risk measure is positively correlated with workers' subjective risk assessments in the Survey of Working Conditions. Moreover, the BLS objective industry risk measure and the worker-specific subjective risk variable yield estimates of the annual risk premium that are not significantly different from one another (see Viscusi 1979a; Viscusi and O'Connor 1984; and Gerking, deHaan, and Schulze 1988).

The BLS risk measure has changed

[39] Some initial efforts to address the role of these worker differences included the interaction of the risk variable with demographic characteristic variables.

over time.[40] After the advent of the OSHA, the reporting system for all injuries changed so that BLS risk data beginning in 1972 are not comparable with the earlier data. Studies such as Robert S. Smith (1974, 1976) and Viscusi (1978a, 1979) use the pre-OSHA industrial fatality data, whereas more recent studies using BLS data have relied upon the post-OSHA data.

The main deficiency of industry-based data is that they pertain to industry-wide averages and do not distinguish among the different jobs within that industry; perceptional differences in risk are also not recognized. To promote greater pertinence of the risk measures to the jobs in the survey, some researchers have restricted the sample composition by, for example, limiting it to males or blue-collar workers, for whom the risk data are more relevant.[41] Additional limitations of the BLS data are that the reporting may not be complete, and occupational diseases are underrepresented.

The National Institute of Occupational Safety and Health sought to reduce the measurement error associated with the industry level fatality data through its National Traumatic Occupational Fatality Survey. This survey yielded new data on industrial fatality rates that have been

[40] An interesting and so far unexplored issue is whether the change in the BLS reporting system altered the risk data in a manner that affected workers' risk beliefs. The most that is available is a comparison of the wage premiums generated by the different risk measures.

[41] Many studies have obtained significant estimates of wage premiums without such restrictions. However, there remains an important need both for better risk measures as well as more detailed assessments of the value of other nonpecuniary aspects of the job so that the estimates will represent premiums for risk rather that job attributes correlated with risk. The Quality of Employment Survey and Survey of Working Conditions do provide detailed nonpecuniary attribute data, but the risk variable is categorical (does the worker's job expose him to dangerous or unhealthy working conditions?) rather than continuous.

TABLE 3
FATALITY RATE DATA BY INDUSTRY

Industry	BLS Fatality Rate per 100,000 Employees	NIOSH Fatality Rate per 100,000 Employees
Mining	35.4	30.1
Construction	23.9	23.1
Agriculture, Forestry, and Fisheries	17.5	20.3
Transportation, Communication, Electricity	16.8	19.5
Manufacturing	4.2	4.2
Retail Trade	2.9	1.8
Wholesale Trade	2.9	1.1
Services	2.4	2.9
Finance, Insurance, Real Estate	1.9	1.3
Public Sector	NA	NA

Source: Bureau of Labor Statistics (1985), using data for 1982–1983 combined; and data from the National Institute for Occupational Safety and Health (1987). NA = Not Available

used in four recent studies by Moore and myself, which are reported at the end of Table 2, and by Kniesner and Leeth (1991).

Table 3 summarizes the BLS and NIOSH fatality rates per 100,000 workers for major industry groups. The overall size of the risk is on the order of 1/10,000, with agriculture, mining, construction, and transportation representing above average risk industries. The direction of the risk differences between the BLS and NIOSH data varies by industry. Differences in sampling procedure may account for the discrepancy. The BLS data are based on a sample of industry reports to the agency, whereas the NIOSH data are based on a comprehensive census of death certificates to identify job-related fatalities. In practice, the main difference is that estimates of the wage-risk tradeoff based on NIOSH data are roughly twice as large as those of the BLS data, which

is consistent with the effect of greater random measurement error with the BLS measure offsetting the influence of the underreporting of injuries with the BLS data.[42]

Nonfatal Risks and Other Job Attributes

An important dimension on which the studies in Table 2 differ is the set of other job characteristic variables included in the equation. Omission of nonpecuniary attributes of the job may bias the estimated risk coefficient. Most studies attempt to control for these influences using sets of occupational or industry dummy variables. In addition, several of these studies include a measure of the nonfatal risk associated with the job.

The studies by Viscusi (1978a, 1979) were the first to obtain an estimate of a statistically significant value of compensation for injuries as well as fatalities. These studies also included a comprehensive set of nonpecuniary job characteristics, including whether the worker was a supervisor, the speed of work, whether the worker made decisions on the job, whether the job requires the worker not make mistakes, job security, overtime work, worker training, and a dummy variable for the worker's occupation.

The chief recent addition to the wage equation has been the inclusion of a workers' compensation variable, beginning with the studies by Butler (1983) and by Arnould and Nichols (1983). In practice, inclusion of this variable has raised the estimated wage-risk tradeoff. Although most studies in the literature have used state average benefit mea-

[42] See Moore and Viscusi (1988a). Suppose that we observe q_i^* instead of measuring the actual risk of q_i, where $q_i^* = q_i + v_i$. The usual random measurement error model assumption is that v_i has zero mean and constant variance, in which case the coefficient on q_i^* will be biased downward from its true value.

sures, Viscusi and Moore (1987) and their subsequent work included an individual-specific workers' compensation variable calculated based on the state benefit formulas in conjunction with the worker's demographic characteristics. This variable was interacted with the risk on the worker's job so that it was the expected workers' compensation benefit (or more specifically, the expected rate of replacement of lost earnings), which is a more pertinent measure than the overall state benefit average.

Survey Differences in Worker Earnings Levels

As the average earnings level data in Table 2 indicate, the sample composition has varied considerably. This distinction is important because what these studies yield is an estimate of the implicit wage-risk tradeoff that is pertinent to a particular segment of the population and cannot necessarily be generalized to the population at large. The standard ex post measure of economic damages for accidents—the present value of earnings—varies proportionally with income. One would also expect some earnings variation in the wage-risk tradeoffs, which are related to the compensation required for injury prevention. In particular, if w, p, and q are defined in terms of annual earnings and annual risk, then the tradeoff $\partial w/\partial p$ is the implicit value per statistical life and $\partial w/\partial q$ is the implicit value per statistical injury. Viewed somewhat differently, the statistical value of life is the total amount of compensation n workers would require to face one expected death from their group, where n is a large number. The implicit values of life evaluated at the sample mean risk levels appear in the second-to-last column of Table 2. Using survey data that provided information on the two points along EU indicated in Figure 3, Viscusi and Evans (1990) calculated the elasticity of $\partial w/\partial q$ with re-

spect to earnings, which was approximately 1.0. The calculations below assume that a unitary income elasticity also pertains to $\partial w/\partial p$.

To see how one might apply the value-of-life estimates to a different group, suppose that we are valuing the benefits from improved aviation safety. The average passenger on a U.S. airline has a median income level of $32,840, which is considerably higher than the income levels listed in Table 2 (see The Gallup Organization 1989). Extrapolating Thaler and Rosen's (1976) values to this income group would yield a value per life of $1.0 million.[43] Those in Viscusi (1978a, 1979) would rise to $5.7 million. The results from the U.K. by Marin and Psacharopoulos (1982) would be even higher—$8.1 million—even though their estimates for workers in the U.K. are lower than in most studies of U.S. workers. The final column in Table 2 summarizes the implied value-of-life estimates for the typical airline passenger.

The Value-of-Life Range

As the implicit value-of-life estimates in Table 2 indicate, the estimated wage-risk tradeoff varies considerably across data sets and methodologies. Some heterogeneity is expected. The value of life is not a universal constant, but reflects the wage-risk tradeoff pertinent to the preferences of the workers in a particular sample. The mix of workers in these samples is quite different. The majority of the estimates in Table 2 are in the $3 million—$7 million range.

The results that I place the greatest reliance on for the typical worker are those in Viscusi (1978a, 1979), which include the most comprehensive set of non-

---

[43] These calculations used the income levels and value of life estimates reported in Table 2 and scaled up the estimates proportionally with the income of airline passengers relative to the average sample member's income.

pecuniary characteristic variables, and the NIOSH data results in Moore and Viscusi (1988a). Other studies are better suited to estimating the value of life for workers in high risk jobs (Thaler and Rosen 1976) or workers in other countries.

Perhaps the best way to interpret these studies is that there is a value-of-life range that is potentially pertinent. The wage-risk relationship is not as robust as is, for example, the effect of education on wages.[44]

4. The Implicit Value of Injury Based on Labor Market Studies

Estimation Issues

As in the case of fatalities, the principal source of evidence on risk-dollar tradeoffs for nonfatal injuries is labor market data. The procedure for measuring the wage premium for nonfatal risks parallels that for fatalities.

Ideally, one would like to distinguish the compensation for fatality risks from that for nonfatal risks. In practice, estimation of significant wage premiums for both a fatal risk measure and a nonfatal risk measure has proven difficult.

Two types of problems arise. First, if there is a strong positive correlation between fatal and nonfatal risk measures for the industry, which are then matched to the individual worker, then it will be hard to disentangle the premiums associated with each of these risk measures. Second, recent studies have begun to rely upon the NIOSH fatal accident data rather than the BLS accident data. Because there is no nonfatal injury variable counterpart to the NIOSH data, whereas there was such a counterpart for the BLS data, there is no ideal pair of variables

gathered by government agencies that covers both classes of accidents. Attempts to include a NIOSH fatality risk variable in equations with BLS nonfatal risk measures have thus far not led to significant estimates for both sets of coefficients, perhaps due in part to the different reporting bases and methodologies used in gathering these accident statistics. Exclusion of the fatality risk measure from a nonfatal risk equation will tend to bias the estimates of the fatality risk premium upward, whereas random measurement error that arises from matching up an industry injury risk measure to an individual based on the reported industry will tend to bias the estimated value of the injuries downward.

Estimates of Wage-Injury Risk Tradeoffs

Table 4 summarizes 17 studies that have estimated statistically significant wage premiums for job injury risk, where these are the $\partial w / \partial q$ values evaluated at the mean sample risk.[45] For 14 of these 17 studies it is possible to compute an implicit value of job injuries based on the data presented by the authors.[46]

The studies in Table 4 do not pertain to a homogeneous class of nonfatal injuries. In some cases, the injuries reflect only those accidents that led to a loss in work, whereas in other instances less se-

---

[44] One possible policy approach might be to calculate the discounted costs per expected life saved and then to ascertain whether this figure is reasonable given the range of plausible value of life estimates that have been obtained in the literature.

[45] Some researchers have reported that statistically significant estimates could not be obtained. For example, Moore and Viscusi (1990a) estimated significant premiums for fatalities but not for nonfatal injuries when the BLS nonfatal accident risk variable was added to a regression including the NIOSH death risk variable. The different sources for and definitions of the two risk measures create potential problems of multicollinearity.

[46] For example, one cannot estimate the implicit value of an injury for a log wage equation without knowing the average wage level in the sample. Daniel Hamermesh and John Wolfe (1990) obtain significant estimates of the wage premiums for the frequency and duration of injuries, but they do not report an estimate of the implicit value of an injury. They do find a stronger effect of injury duration than injury frequency.

TABLE 4

SUMMARY OF LABOR MARKET STUDIES OF JOB INJURIES

Author (Year)	Sample	Nonfatal Risk Variable	Mean Injury Risk	Fatality Risk Included?	Workers' Comp Included?	Average Income Level ($1990)	Implicit Value of Injury	Implicit Value of Injury for Air Traveler ($ millions)
Viscusi (1978a, 1979)	Survey of Working Conditions, 1969–1970	BLS nonfatal injury rate, 1969 (pre-OSHA)	.032	Yes	No	$24,800	$20,038–$38,560	$26,450–$50,899
Viscusi (1978b)	Survey of Working Conditions, 1969–1970	BLS nonfatal injury rate, 1969 (pre-OSHA)	.032	No	No	$24,800	$47,993–$49,322	$63,351–$65,105
Olson (1981)	Current Population Survey, 1973	BLS total lost workday accident rate, 1973	.035	Yes	No	$27,686	$18,725–$25,194	$22,283–$29,981
Viscusi (1981)	Panel Study of Income Dynamics, 1976	BLS lost workday injury rate, 1976	.032	Yes	No	$23,656	$46,200	$64,136
Butler (1983)	S.C. Workers' Compensation data, 1940–1969	S.C. workers' compensation injury days data	.061 (claims rate)	No	Yes	$12,403	$730/day or $13,140 for an 18 day injury	$1,933/day
Dorsey & Walzer (1983)	Current Population Survey, 1978	BLS nonfatal lost workday injury incidence rate, 1976	.030	Yes, in some equations	Yes	NA	Not reported, can't calculate	NA
Smith, V. K. (1983)	Current Population Survey, 1978	BLS work injury rate	.078	No	No	$25,338	$27,675	$35,869
Leigh & Folsom (1984)	Panel Study of Income Dynamics, 1974; Quality of Employment Survey, 1977	BLS nonfatal injury rate	.074, .066	Yes	No	$27,693, $28,734	$77,547–$89,403	$92,281–$106,390
Viscusi & O'Connor (1984)	Authors' chemical worker survey, 1982	Workers' assessed injury and illness rate	.10	No	No	$29,357	$13,810–$17,761	$15,467–$19,892

TABLE 4 (Continued)
SUMMARY OF LABOR MARKET STUDIES OF JOB INJURIES

Author (Year)	Sample	Nonfatal Risk Variable	Mean Injury Risk	Fatality Risk Included?	Workers' Comp Included?	Average Income Level ($1990)	Implicit Value of Injury	Implicit Value of Injury for Air Traveler ($ millions)
Viscusi & Moore (1987)	Quality of Employment Survey, 1977	BLS lost workday injury rate, BLS total injury rate	.038, .097	No	Yes	$33,928	$55,100 lost workday accident; $21,800 for nonpecuniary loss-lost workday accident; $35,400 per accident	$53,447 lost workday accident; $21,146 for nonpecuniary loss-lost workday accident; $34,338 per accident
Biddle & Zarkin (1988)	Quality of Employment Survey, 1977	BLS nonfatal lost workday injury incident rate, 1977	.037	No	No	$32,889	$131,495 (willing to accept), $121,550 (willing to pay)	$131,299 (willing to accept), $121,368 (willing to pay)
Cousineau, Lacroix & Girard (1988)	Labor Canada Survey, 1979	Quebec compensation board occupational injury rates	.069	Yes	No	NA	Not reported, can't calculate	NA
Garen (1988)	Panel Study of Income Dynamics, 1981–1982	BLS nonfatal injury rate, 1980–1981	NA	Yes	No	NA	$21,021	
Hersch & Viscusi (1990)	Authors' survey in Eugene, OR 1987	Workers' assessed injury rate using BLS lost workday incidence rate scale	.059	No	No, same state	$17,078	$56,537 (full sample); $30,781 (smokers); $92,245 (seatbelt users)	$108,551 (full sample); $59,100 (smokers); $177,110 (seatbelt users)
Viscusi & Evans (1990)	Viscusi and O'Connor chemical worker survey, 1982	Utility function estimates using assessed injury and illness rate	.10	No	No	$29,482	$18,547 (marginal risk change); $28,880 (certain injury)	$20,660 (marginal risk change); $32,169 (certain injury)
Michael French & David Kendall (1992)	Current Population Survey, 1980, railroad industry only	Federal Railroad Administration injury data	.048	No	No	$36,097	$38,159	$34,716
Kniesner & Leeth (1991)	Current Population Survey, 1978	BLS lost workday accident rate	.055	Yes	Yes	$26,268	$47,281	$57,110

vere injuries may be included. There are other differences as well, as some sets of injury data pertain to average reported industry risk levels, whereas others are subjectively assessed injury risks.

The first of the injury variables used was the BLS injury rate data gathered before the advent of the OSHA and the institution of the new reporting system (see Viscusi 1978a, 1978b, 1979). The second injury variable used is the total BLS reported accident rate. Studies using these data capture all job injuries, including those that are not severe enough to lead to the loss of a day of work (see Viscusi 1981; Olson 1981; V. K. Smith 1983; Leigh and Folsom 1984; Viscusi and Moore 1987; and Garen 1988). To capture injuries of greater severity, some studies have used only the lost workday injury component of the reported BLS nonfatal accident statistics (see Viscusi and Moore 1987; and Kniesner and Leeth 1991).

Two studies have used subjective risk perception variables based on workers' assessed risk, where the risk scale presented to the workers was patterned after the BLS objective risk measure described above. Viscusi and O'Connor's (1984) reference scale was based on the overall reported BLS injury rate, and Joni Hersch and Viscusi's (1990) scale was based on the BLS lost workday accident rate. These two studies provide the values of workers' subjective risk perceptions that are the counterparts of the two currently maintained BLS injury rate series.[47]

The two exceptions to the standard he-

donic wage equation approach are those that have attempted to explore more fully the character of individuals' utility functions. Biddle and Zarkin (1988) attempted to impose greater structure on the estimation process by taking into account the constraints imposed by the tangency of individual utility functions with the market offer curve. They jointly estimate a two-equation structural system similar in spirit to that described above for Viscusi and Moore (1989). The first equation is the hedonic income locus— the envelope of the firms' isoprofit curves for the annual income offers Y for jobs of different risk. The second equation is the first-order condition that equates $\partial Y/\partial p$ for the hedonic income locus and the worker's utility function, which they assume to be a translog utility function.

The other nonfatal risk study that does not consider a standard wage equation is Viscusi and Evans (1990). They explicitly estimate individual utility functions in good and ill health following Equation (4) using survey data in which responses to a hazard warning and baseline job information make it possible to observe two points along a constant expected utility locus.

Several additional insights are provided by knowledge of the individual utility functions. First, job accidents lower the marginal utility of income.[48] Job injuries consequently alter the structure of preferences and cannot be treated as tantamount to a monetary loss. Their estimates imply that less than full insurance of income loss (i.e., 85 percent replacement rate) is optimal. Second, differences between willingness-to-accept values for risk increases and willingness-to-pay amounts for risk reductions of a magnitude of .01 are very minor—under

---

[47] Two other studies have used other risk data that are more specific in nature. Butler (1983) analyzed employment data for South Carolina workers using workers' compensation data for injuries that are severe enough to be filed in the workers' compensation system in South Carolina. French and Kendall (1992) relied upon Federal Railroad Administration injury rate data to derive estimates of the implicit value of job injuries.

[48] For the logarithmic utility function cases Viscusi and Evans (1990) found that $U(w) = 1.077 \log w$ and $V(y) = \log y$, where the coefficient for $\log y$ was constrained to be unity (no loss of generality).

one percent. The extent of the risk change is, however, consequential, as the implicit value per statistical injury is much greater for large increases in risk.[49] Third, the paper estimated the elasticity of the value of job injuries (measured in terms of the risk-dollar tradeoff $\partial w/\partial q$) with respect to earnings as being approximately 1.0.[50] This estimate was the basis for the extrapolation of the value of injury statistics to reflect other earnings levels in Table 2 and Table 4. Injury valuation results for individuals with income comparable to that of airline passengers appear in the final column of Table 4.

The wage-risk tradeoffs tend to be greater for more severe types of injuries. Most of the estimates based on data for all injuries regardless of severity are clustered in the $25,000–$50,000 range. The values obtained using the lost workday injury variable tend to be somewhat greater. This risk measure excludes temporary injuries that are not sufficiently severe to lead to loss of one or more days of work. The value of lost workday injuries is in the area of $50,000, or at the high end of the range for estimates for the implicit value of injuries overall. The subjectively assessed counterparts of the total injury rate in Viscusi and O'Connor (1984) and the lost workday risk in Hersch and Viscusi (1990) also are consistent with these patterns.

Hersch and Viscusi's (1990) study also provides estimates of differences in the implicit value of risk for different segments of the population, illustrating the influence of differences in preferences on estimated wage-risk tradeoffs. Their analysis used both a conventional wage equation as well as a two-equation structural model. Revealed differences in risk-taking behavior affect the risk premium estimates in the expected direction, as the implicit value of injury is $30,781 for smokers, $56,537 for the full sample, and $92,245 for seat belt users.

The two studies that report estimated implicit values of injury obtained using other types of data also yield similar estimates. After adjusting for income level differences, Butler's (1983) results for the typical airplane passenger imply an injury value of $34,794. The study of railroad worker injuries by French and Kendall (1991) yields an implicit value per injury of $38,200—or $34,716 for the typical airplane passenger's income level—which is very much in the range of the aforementioned studies of job injury.

5. Other Market Evidence on Implicit Tradeoffs

Other market transactions could be used to estimate the tradeoff value. In our consumption, transportation, and recreational activities, we take a variety of risks. If the risk component and the offsetting benefits of these activities is identified, then the money-risk tradeoff may be estimated.

The advantage of labor market studies is that we observe the workers' incomes and wages, and we have available risk measures that distinguish risk levels across individuals. The main disadvantage of the nonlabor market studies is that either the risk facing the individual or the monetary value of the attribute (e.g., travel time) is not observed so that the researcher must impute at least one

---

[49] For an annual accident probability change of +.01, the implicit value of injury is $13,401 (logarithmic utility) and $9,299 (Taylor's series), and for a risk increase of +.915, these values rise to $20,777 and $16,213 respectively. Valuations are in 1982 prices.

[50] If we let w represent annual earnings, z be defined as $\partial w/\partial q$, then the income elasticity of the value of injuries ν is given by $\nu = \frac{w}{z}\frac{\partial z}{\partial w}$. For logarithmic utility functions, $\nu = 1.10$, and for a second-order Taylor's series approximation to a general utility function, $\nu = .67$.

TABLE 5

SUMMARY OF VALUE OF LIFE STUDIES BASED ON TRADEOFFS OUTSIDE THE LABOR MARKET

Author (Year)	Nature of Risk, Year	Component of the Monetary Tradeoff	Average Income Level	Implicit Value of Life ($ millions)
Debapriya Ghosh, Dennis Lees, & William Seal (1975)	Highway speed-related accident risk, 1973	Value of driver time based on wage rates	NA	.07
Glenn Blomquist (1979)	Automobile death risks, 1972	Estimated disutil-ity of seat belts	$29,840	1.2
Rachel Dardis (1980)	Fire fatality risks without smoke detectors, 1974–1979	Purchase price of smoke detectors	NA	0.6
Paul R. Portney (1981)	Mortality effects of air pollution, 1978	Property values in Allegheny Co., PA	NA–value of life for 42-year-old male	0.8
Pauline Ippolito & Richard Ippolito (1984)	Cigarette smoking risks, 1980	Estimated mone-tary equivalent of effect of risk information	NA	0.7
Christopher Garbacz (1989)	Fire fatality risks without smoke detectors, 1968–1985	Purchase price of smoke detector	NA	2.0
Atkinson & Halvorsen (1990)	Automobile acci-dent risks, 1986	Prices of new auto-mobiles	NA	4.0

Note: All values in December 1990 dollars.

component of the tradeoff. These studies consequently provide a less direct and probably less reliable measure than labor market estimates.

Nevertheless, even if the labor market estimates are more accurate reflections of the market tradeoff, the evidence from product markets is valuable as well. Obtaining estimates of the value of life and health in a variety of risk contexts should enhance our confidence in the existence of such tradeoffs. Moreover, because these different risk contexts often involve individuals with different preferences facing different magnitudes of risk than those posed by jobs, this evidence is of independent interest.

Table 5 summarizes the components of seven different studies in the literature. The tradeoffs involve the choice of highway speed, installation of smoke detectors, cigarette smoking, property values, and automobile safety. Many of these choices involve discrete safety decisions. Will the consumer purchase a smoke detector? Such studies provide a lower bound on the value of life, but will not provide information about the consumer's total willingness to pay for safety, because with such discrete decisions consumers are not pushed to the point where the marginal cost of greater safety equals its marginal valuation.

A major difference among the studies is the observability of the monetary component of the tradeoff. An example of a study that closely parallels the labor market analysis in terms of having reliable information on the monetary component of the tradeoff is that of Scott E. Atkinson and Robert Halvorsen (1990). The dependent variable in their hedonic price model is the car's purchase price, which is the analog of the wage variable. The explanatory variables consist of product market counterparts of the job characteristics (e.g., *Consumer Reports* ratings of comfort, EPA fuel efficiency ratings) and individual characteristics (e.g., age and gender of drivers). The risk variable is the occupant fatality rate for the automobile model, and the coefficient of this variable defines the price-risk tradeoff, which they estimate to be $4.0 million per life. Their study provides the most comprehensive analysis of risk-dollar tradeoffs outside the labor market.

Many of the other studies use imputed values of the monetary component of the risk tradeoff, potentially introducing another source of error. Consider, for example, Glenn Blomquist's (1979) imaginative analysis of the decision to wear a seat belt. The risk involved pertains to the reduced risk of fatality associated with the wearing of seat belts. Before the advent of state mandatory seat belt laws, only 17.2 percent of the population always used seat belts, 9.7 used the belt most of the time, 26 percent used the belts sometimes, and 46.6 percent never used seat belts.[51] The major issue in this analysis is the value attached to the time and inconvenience costs of wearing a seat belt, which are not directly observable.

The monetary component of the risk tradeoff analyzed by Blomquist (1979) is the value of time required to buckle a seat belt, which he estimates at eight seconds per use. Valued at the driver's wage rate, he estimates the annual disutility cost to be $45.[52] Blomquist's value-of-life estimate is lower than most labor market estimates, perhaps in part because of the presence of other nonpecuniary costs (e.g., discomfort) and possible driver underestimation of the risk reduction of seat belt use. For example, Arnould and Henry G. Grabowski (1981) find that these precautions are suboptimal, given the benefits and costs of seat belt use.[53] One explanation for possibly suboptimal precautionary behavior is that the perceived risk function is flatter than the actual risk perception function in Figure 2. Risk reductions from B_0 to A_0 are viewed as being a smaller amount—from B_1 to A_1. Such misperceptions will lead individuals to take a suboptimal amount of precautions. Market estimates will understate the implicit value of life that would prevail if individuals were fully rational or informed.

Capital market contexts also may provide evidence on the value of life. Ivy Broder (1990) found that industrial fatalities such as airplane crashes and hotel fires were valued by stockholders at $50 million per death. This high estimate reflects private valuations of risk by consumers of the firm's products, the total cost of tort awards, and possibly a lowered assessment of the overall quality of the firm's operations as well.

6. Surveys and Contingent Valuations

Market-based evidence on risk tradeoffs offers the considerable strength that it is based on the actual risk-taking decisions individuals make. Revealed preferences toward risk are a potentially

---

[51] These 1983 data are for persons five years old and over. See the U.S. Department of Commerce, (1986), p. 604.

[52] This approach is similar in spirit to the approach used in highway speed-travel time tradeoff analysis of Ghosh, Lees, and Seal (1975).

[53] Their analysis does not address the nonpecuniary costs of seat belts, however, and consequently is not conclusive.

useful basis for inferring the price that individuals attach to improved safety.

The above review of these estimates identified a series of potential shortcomings. Chief among these are the following. First, the tradeoff values are pertinent only in a local range.[54] Analysis of nonincremental risk changes or other fundamental policy questions, such as how the local tradeoff rate will change if the individual's base level of risk is altered, cannot be addressed. Second, there remain substantial estimation issues regarding the identification and meaning of the risk premium estimates. The usual studies of a single risk-wage tradeoff, for example, ignore the substantial heterogeneity across individuals in their attitudes toward risk. Third, there is an important class of econometric problems pertaining to whether the researcher has in fact isolated the risk-money tradeoff. In the case of labor market studies, there are other nonpecuniary aspects of the job correlated with riskiness that one must also take into account to isolate the risk tradeoff. Many of the product market studies encounter similar difficulties, with the added complication that it is often necessary to impute the monetary component of the tradeoff. Furthermore, all of these results are premised on an assumption of individual rationality. If individuals do not fully understand the risk and respond to risks in a rational manner, then the risk tradeoff that people are actually making may not be those that researchers believe they are making based on objective measures of the risk. Finally, market studies of risk are limited to a narrow range of health outcomes.

Survey methods that elicit individual willingness to pay for greater safety or compensation required to bear an in-

crease in the risk level may avoid these problems. Figure 3 illustrates a market wage opportunities frontier *ABC* and the worker's highest constant expected utility locus *EU*, which is tangent to the market opportunities frontier. The most that can be achieved with a well designed labor market study is an evaluation of the local tradeoff at a point such as *B*. In contrast, a survey that asks an individual what wage increase is needed to bear an increase in risk level from q_a to q_b will provide information on two points *B* and *D* on a constant expected utility locus. The wage increment in this context will truly be a compensating differential that maintains the individual's utility at a constant level. Moreover, the risk increments between q_a and q_b can be designed to analyze risk changes of any magnitude.

Perhaps most important, information pertaining to two or more points along a constant expected utility locus permits the estimation of the utility functions governing behavior. With knowledge of these utility functions, all pertinent questions regarding risk valuation may be addressed, thereby greatly extending the range of issues that can be explored.

The character of the influence of health impacts on the utility function is an important matter of concern. If, for example, adverse health effects lower the marginal utility of income in the ill health state, then less than full income replacement following these losses is optimal. The entire structure of the optimal social insurance efforts consequently hinges on the character of utility functions.

Viscusi and Evans' (1990) results mentioned earlier found that the typical job injury lowered both the absolute level of utility and the marginal utility of income. Moreover, the character of this effect differed from what would have occurred if the job injury was tantamount to a monetary loss equivalent (i.e., $V(w)$

---

[54] It should be noted, however, that use of the two-stage structural hedonic approach with market data can address nonmarginal risk changes as well.

$= U(w - L)$, where L is some monetary loss value equivalent of the injury).

In contrast, different kinds of results are implied by using survey data on minor health effects, in particular, temporary poisonings and other injuries related to use of household chemical products. For minor health effects, the hypothesis that these health outcomes are tantamount to a monetary loss equivalent cannot be rejected (Evans and Viscusi 1991). In situations such as this where the health outcome does not affect the marginal utility of income, full insurance of losses is optimal. Moreover, assessment of the valuations of different incremental changes in the risk of loss is straightforward once we know that the health outcome is valued at some fixed monetary amount.

Three basic survey methodologies have been used to assess points such as B and D in Figure 3. All of these involve eliciting responses to a simulated market context using variants of a procedure known as "contingent valuation," which ascertains individual preferences contingent upon some hypothetical market scenario.

The first such technique is a direct contingent valuation method. A survey might ask respondents directly how much of a wage increase they would require to accept a given risk increase. A variant on this approach is to proceed in iterative fashion. Rather than seeking a response to an open-ended question, the willingness-to-pay value may be adjusted until the respondent indicates indifference.

A second technique involves presenting subjects with pairwise comparisons. In the job risk case, for example, Job 1 might consist of a wage-risk combination of (p_1, w_1), and Job 2 might consist of a wage-risk package of (p_2, w_2). Subjects could indicate their preference between these two jobs, and the packages could

be manipulated until indifference is achieved.

The third approach is to offer lotteries and to elicit preferences with respect to a reference lottery. For example, Viscusi, Magat, and Huber (1991) analyze the value of chronic bronchitis by ascertaining the equilibrating probability, s, that establishes indifference between bronchitis and a lottery on life and death, where

$$U(\text{Chronic Bronchitis}) = sU(\text{Life}) + (1 - s)V(\text{Death}).$$

Choice of the particular survey method depends in large part on which will elicit the most reliable statement of preferences, and thus far no consensus has developed.

One of the main advantages of survey-type approaches is that the analysis need not be constrained by the availability of market data. Consider, for example, the range of health outcomes addressed in Tables 6 and 7. The value-of-life estimates in Table 6 are perhaps the most homogeneous because they all pertain to different classes of accidental deaths or acute outcomes such as heart attacks. The morbidity effects in Table 7 are much more diverse, ranging from coughing spells and hand burns to nerve disease and cancer. A principal benefit of survey methodologies is that they provide insight into classes of outcomes that cannot be addressed with available market data. One such benefit category is altruistic benefits, which by their very nature will not be reflected in market risk-taking decisions (see Viscusi, Magat, and Anne Forrest 1988).

A major concern with survey valuations of health risks is that the responses will be reliable only to the extent that individuals understand the tasks to which they are responding. A matter of particular concern is the processing of risk information presented in survey context.

TABLE 6
SUMMARY OF VALUE OF LIFE ESTIMATES BASED ON SURVEY EVIDENCE

Author (Year)	Nature of Risk	Survey Methodology	Average Income Level	Implicit Value of Life ($ millions)
Jan Acton (1973)	Improved ambulance service, post-heart attack lives	Willingness to pay question, door-to-door small (36) Boston Sample	NA	.1
Jones-Lee (1976)	Airline safety and locational life expectanty risks	Mail survey willingness to accept increased risk, small (30) U.K. sample, 1975	NA	15.6
Gerking, deHaan, & Schulze (1988)	Job fatality risk	Willingness to pay, willingness to accept change in job risk in mail survey, 1984	NA	3.4 willingness to pay, 8.8 willingness to accept
Jones-Lee (1989)	Motor vehicle accidents	Willingness to pay for risk reduction, U.K. survey, 1982	NA	3.8
Viscusi, Magat, & Huber (1991)	Automobile accident risks	Interactive computer program with pairwise auto risk-living cost tradeoffs until indifference achieved, 1987	43,771	2.7 (median) 9.7 (mean) (1987)
Ted Miller & Jagadish Guria (1991)	Traffic safety	Series of contingent valuation questions, New Zealand Survey, 1989–1990	NA	1.2

Note: All values in December 1990 U.S. dollars.

Consider two different valuation studies of the same health outcome using surveys involving different risk levels. The first of the studies reported in Table 7, by Viscusi, Magat, and Huber (1987), focuses on individuals' valuations of the risks from bleach and drain opener, chloramine gassings, child poisonings, and hand burns, among others. These morbidity effects are by no means catastrophic, but the estimated values the respondents attach to them are in excess of $1 million in three cases.

Viscusi, Magat, and Huber (1987) dealt with a similar class of injuries but addressed a much more comprehensible risk level—on the order of 15/10,000 annually. The value of the morbidity effects such as skin poisonings and chloramine gassing is in a more reasonable range, as the health effects assessed in this study range in value from $700 to $3,500.

The discrepancy in the studies can be traced to the difficulties posed by the small risks in the first study. Individuals who are willing to pay one dollar to reduce the risk of bleach gassing by 1/1,000,000, will exhibit an implicit value

TABLE 7
SUMMARY OF VALUATIONS OF NONFATAL HEALTH RISKS

Author (Year)	Survey Methodology	Average Income Level	Nature of Risk	Value of Health Outcome
Mark Berger et al. (1987)	Contingent valuation interviews with 119 respondents, 1984–1985	NA	Certain outcome of one day of various illnesses	$98 (coughing spells), $35 (stuffed-up sinuses), $57 (throat congestion), $63 (itching eyes), $183 (heavy drowsiness), $140 (headaches), $62 (nausea)
Viscusi & Magat (1987)	Paired comparison and contingent valuation interactive computer survey at mall, hardware store, 1984	$39,768	Bleach: chloramine gassings, child poisonings; drain opener: hand burns, child poisonings	$1.78 million (bleach gassing), $0.65 million (bleach poisoning), $1.60 million (drain opener hand burns), $1.06 million (drain opener & child poisoning)
Viscusi, Magat, & Huber (1987)	Contingent valuation computer survey at mall, hardware stores, 1986	$42,700	Morbidity risks of pesticide and toilet bowl cleaner, valuations for 15/10,000 risk decrease to zero	Insecticide $1,504 (skin poisoning), $1,742 (inhalation), $3,489 (child poisoning), toilet bowl cleaner $1,113 (gassing), $744 (eye burn), $1,232 (child poisoning)
Viscusi, Magat, & Forrest (1988)	Contingent valuation computer survey at mall, hardware stores, 1986	$44,554	Insecticide inhalation-skin poisoning, inhalation-child poisoning	Inhalation-skin poisoning $2,538 (private), $9,662 (NC altruism), $3,745 (U.S. altruism); Inhalation-child poisoning $4,709 (private), $17,592 (NC altruism), $5,197 (U.S. altruism)
Evans & Viscusi	Contingent valuation computer survey at mall, hardware stores, 1986	$32,700	Morbidity risks of pesticides and toilet bowl cleaner; utility function estimates of risk values. T values pertain to marginal risk-dollar tradeoffs, and L values pertain to monetary loss equivalents.	Insecticide: $761 ($T$), $755 ($L$) (skin poisoning); $1,047 ($T$), $1,036 ($L$) (inhalation-no kids); $2,575 ($T$) (inhalation-children) $1,748; $3,207 ($T$), $2,877 ($L$) (child poisoning); toilet bowl cleaner $633 ($T$), $628 ($L$) eye burn; $598 ($T$), $593 ($L$) gassing (no kids); $717 ($T$), $709 ($L$) gassing (children); $1,146 ($T$), $1,126 ($L$) child poisoning

1942   *Journal of Economic Literature, Vol. XXXI (December 1993)*

TABLE 7 (Continued)

Author (Year)	Survey Methodology	Average Income Level	Nature of Risk	Value of Health Outcome
Magat, Viscusi, & Huber (1991)	Risk-risk computer survey at mall, 1990	$35,700	Environmental risk of nonfatal nerve disease, fatal lymphoma, nonfatal lymphoma	$1.6 million (nerve disease), $2.6 million (nonfatal lymphoma), $4.1 million (fatal lymphoma)
Viscusi, Magat, & Huber (1991)	Risk-risk and risk-dollar computer survey at mall, 1988	$41,000	Environmental risk of severe chronic bronchitis morbidity risk	.32 fatality risk or $904,000 risk-risk; $516,000 risk-dollar
Alan Krupnick & Maureen Cropper (1992)	Viscusi-Magat-Huber (1991) survey for sample with chronic lung disease, 1989	$39,744	Environmental risk of severe chronic bronchitis morbidity risk	$496,800–$691,200 (median)

for the injury of $1 million, but this response may not reflect the underlying risk-dollar tradeoff so much as it does the inability of individuals to deal with extremely low probability events. As the risk levels in Table 1 indicate, the usual range of experience with risk is with hazards of much greater frequency. The evidence in the psychology and economics literature sketched in Figure 2 indicates there is a tendency to overestimate the magnitude of very low probability events, particularly those called to one's attention. Survey methodologies may elicit individual valuations as perceived by the respondent, but one must ensure that what is being perceived is accurate. Errors in risk perceptions may be a particularly salient difficulty.

A final concern with respect to survey valuations is whether the respondents are giving honest and thoughtful answers to the survey questions. In practice, truthful revelation of preferences has proven to be less of a problem than has the elicitation of meaningful responses because of a failure to understand the survey task. Strategic misrepresentation can also be addressed by using a survey mechanism that is designed to elicit a truthful expression of preferences, such as hypothetical voting on a political referendum.

7. Policy Implications

Although the value-of-life literature is now roughly two decades old, the essential approach became well established in the 1970s. The appropriate measure of the value of life from the standpoint of government policy is society's willingness to pay for the risk reduction, which is the same benefit formulation in all policy evaluation contexts.

Economists have had the greatest success in assessing the risk-money tradeoff using labor market data. Although the tradeoff estimates vary considerably depending on the population exposed to the risk, the nature of the risk, individuals' income level, and similar factors, most of the reasonable estimates of the value of life are clustered in the $3 million–$7 million range. Moreover, these estimates are for the population of exposed workers, who generally have lower incomes

Viscusi: *The Value of Risks to Life and Health* 1943

than the individuals being protected by broadly based risk regulations. Recognition of the positive elasticity of the value of life with respect to worker earnings will lead to the use of different values of life depending on the population being protected. Taste differences may also enter, as smokers and workers in very hazardous jobs, for example, place lower values on health risks.

The 1980s marked the first decade in which use of estimates of the value of life based on risk tradeoffs became widespread throughout the Federal government. Previously, agencies assessed only the lost present value of the earnings of the deceased, leading to dramatic underestimation of the benefit value. In large part through the efforts of the U.S. Office of Management and Budget, agencies such as OSHA and EPA began incorporating value-of-life estimates in their benefit evaluations.[55] Policy makers' recognition of the nonpecuniary aspects of life is an important advance.

Given the range of uncertainty of the value-of-life estimates, perhaps the most reasonable use of these values in policy contexts is to provide a broad index of the overall desirability of a policy. In practice, value-of-life debates seldom focus on whether the appropriate value of life should be $3 million or $4 million— narrow differences that cannot be distinguished based on the accuracy of current estimates and the potential limitations of individual behavior underlying these estimates. However, the estimates do provide guidance as to whether risk reduction efforts that cost $50,000 per life saved or $50 million per life saved are warranted. The threshold for the Office of Management and Budget to be successful in rejecting proposed risk regula-

tions has been in excess of $100 million (see Viscusi 1992a). It is in addressing the most extreme policy errors that the estimates will be most useful, as opposed to pinpointing the value of life that should guide policy decisions.

A needed major change is to establish an appropriate schedule of values of life that is pertinent for the differing populations at risk. The quantity of life at risk often varies quite widely, as do individual attitudes toward these risks. Policies that protect groups who incur risks voluntarily should be treated quite differently from policies that protect populations who bear risks involuntarily or who have a very high aversion to incurring health risks. Differences also arise on a temporal dimension. Valuation of health risks to future generations is assuming greater policy importance, but these values will not be the same as for those currently alive.

Broad gaps in our knowledge remain, particularly with regard to risks other than accidental fatalities. How, for example, should we value genetic risks and increased life extension for AIDS victims, as compared with other health outcomes? The class of health outcomes of policy interest is much broader than acute fatal injuries and lost workday accidents, which have been the main targets of analysis. Survey evidence on attitudes toward risk can potentially expand the range of health outcomes that we can value, but there is a continuing need to assess the validity of these benefit measures.

REFERENCES

Acton, Jan P. *Evaluating public programs to save lives: The case of heart attacks*, R-950-RC. Santa Monica: The Rand Corporation, 1973.

Arnould, Richard J. and Grabowski, Henry G. "Auto Safety Regulation: An Analysis of Market Failure," *Bell J. Econ.*, Spring 1981, *12*(1), pp. 27–48.

Arnould, Richard J. and Nichols, Len M. "Wage-Risk Premiums and Workers' Compensation: A Re-

---

[55] Indeed, the U.S. Office of Management and Budget (1990, pp. 661–63) has developed explicit guidelines on the use of implicit values of life and health.

1944   *Journal of Economic Literature, Vol. XXXI (December 1993)*

finement of Estimates of Compensating Wage Differential," *J. Polit. Econ.*, Apr. 1983, 91(2), pp. 332–40.

ATKINSON, SCOTT E. AND HALVORSEN, ROBERT. "The Valuation of Risks to Life: Evidence from the Market for Automobiles," *Rev. Econ. Statist.*, Feb. 1990, 72(1), pp. 133–36.

BERGER, MARK C. ET AL. "Valuing Changes in Health Risks: A Comparison of Alternative Measures," *Southern Econ. J.*, Apr. 1987, 53(4), pp. 967–84.

BIDDLE, JEFF E. AND ZARKIN, GARY. "Worker Preferences and Market Compensation for Job Risk," *Rev. Econ. Statist.*, Nov. 1988, 70(4), pp. 660–67.

BLOMQUIST, GLENN. "Value of Life Saving: Implications of Consumption Activity," *J. Polit. Econ.*, June 1979, 87(3), pp. 540–58.

BRODER, IVY E. "The Cost of Accidental Death: A Capital Market Approach," *J. Risk Uncertainty*, Mar. 1990, 3(1), pp. 51–63.

BROWN, CHARLES. "Equalizing Differences in the Labor Market," *Quart. J. Econ.*, Feb. 1980, 94(1), pp. 113–34.

BROWN, JAMES N. "Structural Estimation in Implicit Markets," in *The measurement of labor cost.* Ed.: JACK E. TRIPLETT. Chicago: U. of Chicago Press, 1983, pp. 123–51.

BUTLER, RICHARD J. "Wage and Injury Rate Responses to Shifting Levels of Workers' Compensation," in *Safety and the work force.* Ed.: JOHN D. WORRALL. Ithaca: ILR Press, 1983, pp. 61–86.

COUSINEAU, JEAN-MICHEL; LACROIX, ROBERT AND GIRARD, ANNE-MARIE. "Occupational Hazard and Wage Compensating Differentials." U. of Montreal Working Paper, 1988.

DARDIS, RACHEL. "The Value of a Life: New Evidence from the Marketplace," *Amer. Econ. Rev.*, Dec. 1980, 70(5), pp. 1077–82.

DILLINGHAM, ALAN. "The Influence of Risk Variable Definition on Value-of-Life Estimates," *Econ. Inquiry*, Apr. 1985, 23(2), pp. 277–94.

DORSEY, STUART AND WALZER, NORMAN. "Workers' Compensation, Job Hazards, and Wages," *Ind. Lab. Relat. Rev.*, July 1983, 36(4), pp. 642–54.

EPPLE, DENNIS. "Hedonic Prices and Implicit Markets: Estimating Demand and Supply Functions for Differentiated Products," *J. Polit. Econ.*, Feb. 1987, 95(1), pp. 59–80.

EVANS, WILLIAM N. AND VISCUSI, W. KIP. "Estimation of State-Dependent Utility Functions Using Survey Data," *Rev. Econ. Statist.*, Feb. 1991, 73(1), pp. 94–104.

FISCHHOFF, BARUCH ET AL. *Acceptable risk.* Cambridge: Cambridge U. Press, 1981.

FRENCH, MICHAEL T. AND KENDALL, DAVID L. "The Value of Job Safety for Railroad Workers," *J. Risk Uncertainty*, May 1992, 5(2), pp. 175–85.

GALLUP ORGANIZATION. *Air travel survey, 1989,* produced for Air Transport Association of America. Princeton: Gallup Organization, 1989.

GARBACZ, CHRISTOPHER. "Smoke Detector Effectiveness and the Value of Saving a Life," *Econ. Letters,* Dec. 1989, 31(3), pp. 281–86.

GAREN, JOHN E. "Compensating Wage Differentials

and the Endogeneity of Job Riskiness," *Rev. Econ. Statist.*, Feb. 1988, 70(1), pp. 9–16.

GEGAX, DOUGLAS; GERKING, SHELBY AND SCHULZE, WILLIAM. "Perceived Risk and the Marginal Value of Safety," *Rev. Econ. Statist.*, Nov. 1991, 73(4), pp. 589–96.

GERKING, SHELBY; DEHAAN, MENNO H. AND SCHULZE, WILLIAM. "The Marginal Value of Job Safety: A Contingent Valuation Study," *J. Risk Uncertainty*, June 1988, 1(2), pp. 185–99.

GHOSH, DEBAPRIYA; LEES, DENNIS AND SEAL, WILLIAM. "Optimal Motorway Speed and Some Valuations of Time and Life," *Manchester Sch. Econ. Soc. Stud.*, June 1975, 43(2), pp. 134–43.

GRILICHES, ZVI, ed. *Price indexes and quality change.* Cambridge: Harvard U. Press, 1971.

HAMERMESH, DANIEL S. AND WOLFE, JOHN R. "Compensating Wage Differentials and the Duration of Wage Loss," *J. Labor Econ.*, Jan. 1990, 8(1), Part 2, pp. S175–97.

HERSCH, JONI AND VISCUSI, W. KIP. "Cigarette Smoking, Seatbelt Use, and Differences in Wage-Risk Tradeoffs," *J. Human Res.*, Spring 1990, 25(2), pp. 202–27.

HERZOG, HENRY W., JR. AND SCHLOTTMANN, ALAN M. "Valuing Risk in the Workplace: Market Price, Willingness to Pay, and the Optimal Provision of Safety," *Rev. Econ. Statist.*, Aug. 1990, 72(3), pp. 463–70.

IPPOLITO, PAULINE M. AND IPPOLITO, RICHARD A. "Measuring the Value of Life Saving from Consumer Reactions to New Information," *J. Public Econ.*, Nov. 1984, 25(1/2), pp. 53–81.

JONES-LEE, MICHAEL W. *The value of life: An economic analysis.* Chicago: U. of Chicago Press, 1976.

―――. *The economics of safety and physical risk.* Oxford: Basil Blackwell, 1989.

KAHN, SHULAMIT AND LANG, KEVIN. "Efficient Estimation of Structural Hedonic Systems," *Int. Econ. Rev.*, Feb. 1988, 29(1), pp. 157–66.

KNIESNER, THOMAS J. AND LEETH, JOHN D. "Compensating Wage Differentials for Fatal Injury Risk in Australia, Japan, and the United States," *J. Risk Uncertainty*, Jan. 1991, 4(1), pp. 75–90.

KRUPNICK, ALAN J. AND CROPPER, MAUREEN L. "The Effect of Information on Health Risk Valuations," *J. Risk Uncertainty*, Feb. 1992, 5(1), pp. 29–48.

LEIGH, J. PAUL. "Gender, Firm Size, Industry, and Estimates of the Value-of-Life," *J. Health Econ.*, Sept. 1987, 6(3), pp. 255–73.

LEIGH, J. PAUL AND FOLSOM, ROGER N. "Estimates of the Value of Accident Avoidance at the Job Depend on the Concavity of the Equalizing Differences Curve," *Quart. Rev. Econ. Bus.*, Spring 1984, 24(1), pp. 56–66.

MAGAT, WESLEY A.; VISCUSI, W. KIP AND HUBER, JOEL. "The Death Risk Lottery Metric for Health Risks: Cancer and Nerve Disease." Duke U. Working Paper, 1991.

MARIN, ALAN AND PSACHAROPOULOS, GEORGE. "The Reward for Risk in the Labor Market: Evidence from the United Kingdom and a Reconciliation with Other Studies," *J. Polit. Econ.*, Aug. 1982, 90(4), pp. 827–53.

MILLER, TED. "The Plausible Range for the Value of Life—Red Herrings Among the Mackerel," *J. Forensic Econ.*, Fall 1990, 3(3), pp. 17–39.

MILLER, TED AND GURIA, JAGADISH. "The Value of Statistical Life in New Zealand." Report to the Ministry of Transport, Land Transport Division, 1991.

MISHAN, EZRA J. "Evaluation of Life and Limb: A Theoretical Approach," *J. Polit. Econ.*, July/Aug. 1971, 79(4), pp. 687–705.

MOORE, MICHAEL J. AND VISCUSI, W. KIP. "Doubling the Estimated Value of Life: Results Using New Occupational Fatality Data," *J. Policy Anal. Manage.*, Spring 1988a, 7(3), pp. 476–90.

———. "The Quantity-Adjusted Value of Life," *Econ. Inquiry*, July 1988b, 26(3), pp. 369–88.

———. "Promoting Safety through Workers' Compensation," *Rand J. Econ.*, Winter 1989, 20(4), pp. 499–515.

———. *Compensation mechanisms for job risks.* Princeton: Princeton U. Press, 1990a.

———. "Discounting Environmental Health Risks: New Evidence and Policy Implications," *J. Environ. Econ. Manage.*, Mar. 1990b, 18(2) Part 2, pp. S51–62.

———. "Models for Estimating Discount Rates for Long-Term Health Risks Using Labor Market Data," *J. Risk Uncertainty*, Dec. 1990c, 3(4), pp. 381–401.

MORRALL, JOHN F. III. "A Review of the Record," *Regulation,*, Nov./Dec. 1986, 10(2), pp. 25–34.

NATIONAL INSTITUTE FOR OCCUPATIONAL SAFETY AND HEALTH. "National Traumatic Occupational Fatalities, 1980–1984." Apr. 27, 1987.

NATIONAL SAFETY COUNCIL. *Accident facts.* Chicago: National Safety Council, 1990.

OLSON, CRAIG A. "An Analysis of Wage Differentials Received by Workers on Dangerous Jobs," *J. Human Res.*, Spring 1981, 16(2), pp. 167–85.

PORTNEY, PAUL R. "Housing Prices, Health Effects, and Valuing Reductions in Risk of Death," *J. Environ. Econ. Manage.*, Mar. 1981, 8(1), pp. 72–8.

ROSEN, SHERWIN. "The Theory of Equalizing Differences," in *Handbook of labor economics.* Eds.: ORLEY ASHENFELTER AND RICHARD LAYARD. Amsterdam: North-Holland, 1986, pp. 641–92.

———. "The Value of Changes in Life Expectancy," *J. Risk Uncertainty*, Sept. 1988, 1(3), pp. 285–304.

SCHELLING, THOMAS C. "The Life You Save May Be Your Own," in *Problems in public expenditure and analysis.* Ed.: SAMUEL B. CHASE, JR. Washington, DC: Brookings Institute, 1968, pp. 127–62.

SMITH, ADAM. *The wealth of nations.* New York: Modern Library, [1776] 1937.

SMITH, ROBERT S., "The Feasibility of an 'Injury Tax' Approach to Occupational Safety," *Law Contemp. Probl.*, Summer–Autumn 1974, 38(4), pp. 730–44.

———. *The occupational safety and health act.* Washington, DC: American Enterprise Institute, 1976.

———. "Compensating Wage Differentials and Public Policy: A Review," *Ind. Lab. Relat. Rev.*, Apr. 1979, 32(3), pp. 339–52.

SMITH, V. KERRY, "The Role of Site and Job Characteristics in Hedonic Wage Models," *J. Urban Econ.*, May 1983, 13(3), pp. 296–321.

SMITH, V. KERRY AND GILBERT, CAROL. "The Implicit Risks to Life: A Comparative Analysis," *Econ. Letters*, 1984, 16, pp. 393–99.

THALER, RICHARD AND ROSEN, SHERWIN. "The Value of Saving a Life: Evidence from the Market," in *Household production and consumption.* Ed.: NESTOR E. TERLECKYJ. Cambridge: NBER, 1976, pp. 265–98.

TORRANCE, GEORGE W. "Measurement of Health State Utilities for Economic Analysis: A Review," *J. Health Econ.* Mar. 1986, 5(1) pp. 1–30.

U.S. BUREAU OF LABOR STATISTICS. *Occupational injuries and illness in the United States by industry, 1983.* Washington, DC: U.S. GPO, 1985.

U.S. DEPARTMENT OF COMMERCE. *Statistical abstract of the United States.* Washington, DC: U.S. GPO, 1986.

U.S. OFFICE OF MANAGEMENT AND BUDGET. *Regulatory program of the United States Government, April 1, 1988—March 31, 1989.* Washington: U.S. GPO, 1988.

———. *Regulatory program of the United States Government, April 1, 1990—March 31, 1991.* Washington, DC: U.S. GPO, 1990.

VISCUSI, W. KIP. "Labor Market Valuations of Life and Limb: Empirical Estimates and Policy Implications," *Public Policy*, Summer 1978a, 26(3), pp. 359–86.

———. "Wealth Effects and Earnings Premiums for Job Hazards," *Rev. Econ. Statist.*, Aug. 1978b, 60(3), pp. 408–16.

———. *Employment hazards: An investigation of market performance.* Cambridge: Harvard U. Press, 1979.

———. "Occupational Safety and Health Regulation: Its Impact and Policy Alternatives," in *Research in public policy analysis and management*, Vol. 2. Ed.: J. CRECINE. Greenwich, CT: JAI Press, 1981, pp. 281–99.

———. *Risk by choice: regulating health and safety in the workplace.* Cambridge: Harvard U. Press, 1983.

———. "The Valuation of Risks to Life and Health: Guidelines for Policy Analysis," in *Benefits assessment: the state of art.* Eds.: JUDITH D. BENTKOVER, VINCENT COVELLO, and JERYL MUMPOWER. Dordrecht, Holland: Reidel Publishers, 1986, pp. 193–210.

———. "Prospective Reference Theory: Toward an Explanation of the Paradoxes," *J. Risk Uncertainty*, Sept. 1989, 2(3), pp. 235–63.

———. "Sources of Inconsistency in Societal Responses to Health Risks," *Amer. Econ. Rev.*, May 1990, 80(2), pp. 257–61.

———. *Fatal tradeoffs: public and private responsibilities for risk.* New York: Oxford U. Press, 1992a.

———. *Smoking: making the risky decision.* New York: Oxford U. Press, 1992b.

VISCUSI, W. KIP AND EVANS, WILLIAM N. "Utility

Functions That Depend on Health Status: Estimates and Economic Implications," *Amer. Econ. Rev.*, June 1990, *80*(3), pp. 353–74.

VISCUSI, W. KIP AND MAGAT, WESLEY A. *Learning about risk: Consumer and worker responses to hazard information.* Cambridge: Harvard U. Press, 1987.

VISCUSI, W. KIP; MAGAT, WESLEY A. AND FORREST, ANNE. "Altruistic and Private Valuations of Risk Reduction," *J. Policy Anal. Manage.*, Winter 1988, *7*(2), pp. 227–45.

VISCUSI, W. KIP; MAGAT, WESLEY A. AND HUBER, JOEL. "An Investigation of the Rationality of Consumer Valuations of Multiple Health Risks," *Rand J. Econ.*, Winter 1987, *18*(4), pp. 465–79.

——. "Pricing Environmental Health Risks: Survey Assessments of Risk-Risk and Risk-Dollar Trade-Offs for Chronic Bronchitis," *J. En-*

viron. Econ. Manage., July 1991, *21*(1), pp. 32–51.

VISCUSI, W. KIP AND MOORE, MICHAEL J. "Workers' Compensation: Wage Effects, Benefit Inadequacies, and the Value of Health Losses," *Rev. Econ. Statist.*, May 1987, *69*(2), pp. 249–61.

——. "Rates of Time Preference and Valuations of the Duration of Life," *J. Public Econ.*, Apr. 1989, *38*(3), pp. 297–317.

——. "Worker Learning and Compensating Differentials," *Ind. Lab. Relat. Rev.*, Oct. 1991, *45*(1), pp. 80–96.

VISCUSI, W. KIP AND O'CONNOR, CHARLES. "Adaptive Responses to Chemical Labeling: Are Workers Bayesian Decision Makers?" *Amer. Econ. Rev.*, Dec. 1984, *74*(5), pp. 942–56.

ZECKHAUSER, RICHARD AND SHEPARD, DONALD. "Where Now for Saving Lives?" *Law Contemp. Probl.*, Autumn 1976, *40*, pp. 5–45.

Journal of Risk and Uncertainty, 13:263–275 (1996)
© 1996 Kluwer Academic Publishers

The Value of Private Safety Versus the Value of Public Safety

MAGNUS JOHANNESSON
Department of Economics, Stockholm School of Economics, Box 6501, S-113 83 Stockholm, Sweden

PER-OLOV JOHANSSON
Department of Economics, Stockholm School of Economics, Box 6501, S-113 83 Stockholm, Sweden

RICHARD M. O'CONOR
Department of Economics, Stockholm School of Economics, Box 6501, S-113 83 Stockholm, Sweden

Abstract

In this study, one group of respondents is offered to purchase a safety device to be installed in their cars, while another group is offered a public safety program (improved road quality) which results in the same size risk reduction. In terms of the value of a statistical life, our results are very reasonable. However, the WTP for the private safety device is *higher* than the WTP for the public safety measure. Drawing on a model developed by Jones-Lee (1991), we show that some types of altruists may, but need not, be willing to pay more for a private risk reduction than for a uniform risk reduction of the same magnitude. Still, our empirical results are surprising, and further empirical research seems warranted.

Key words: safety, willingness to pay, altruism, environment, traffic

JEL Classification: D61, D91, H51, I10, I12

It is often claimed that people are concerned not only with their own welfare but also with the welfare of others. Even if a person is unaffected by a particular project, he may be concerned about the project's impact on the welfare of others, i.e., express altruistic concerns.[1] Such altruistic concerns are usually not valued on the market and are hence difficult to capture using market data, i.e., it is difficult to estimate from market data the *total* monetary value which people place on changes in morbidity and mortality risks, for example. The contingent valuation method, CVM for short, has therefore become an important tool for evaluating health outcomes and other changes caused by pollution and programs such as public safety expenditures and medical treatments.

In a recent article, Milgrom (1993), drawing on results derived by Bergstrom (1982), has argued forcefully that one can ignore altruistic components in a social cost-benefit analysis. In terms of a project affecting people's safety, Milgrom thus implicitly claims that one should ask people about their willingness to pay for changes in their *own* safety. Moreover, in two recent articles, Jones-Lee (1991, 1992) has derived a set of results on the valuation of a statistical life in the presence of different kinds of altruism; the value of a statistical life is the aggregate WTP for a project expected to save one life. In particular, Jones-Lee shows that one should take full account of people's willingness to pay for the safety of others if and only if altruism is exclusively safety-focused, in the sense that people care about the safety of others but ignore other dimensions of their welfare. If altruism is pure in the sense that people care about the level of welfare attained by others, one can simply ignore WTP for improvements in the safety of others, i.e., concentrate on the value of statistical life. The intuition behind this result is that the pure altruist values both benefits and costs that accrue to others (the overall change in utility). These benefits and costs net out if we are close to a social welfare optimum.

In CVM experiments, people typically pay a uniform amount of money for a public (safety) project. In this article, we show that a pure altruist's *total* WTP for such a project can exceed or fall short of his WTP for a change in his own safety, depending on whether he believes that his own WTP falls short of or exceeds the WTP of others. Let us assume that he is willing to pay t for a ceteris paribus increase in his own safety. His total WTP for a uniform public risk reduction of the same magnitude will fall short of t if he believes that others are willing to pay less than t but will still be forced to pay that amount (t) for the project. This is because those other individuals, for whom he cares, will then experience a lower utility if the program is implemented. In turn, this decrease in the utility of others reduces the pure altruist's WTP for the public safety project. To our knowledge, this fact has been overlooked by previous authors within the field.

We also report an empirical study, in which automobile owners are asked about their WTP for private and public measures aimed at reducing traffic risks. In previous empirical studies, such as Jones-Lee et al. (1985) and Viscusi et al. (1988), respondents have been asked about their WTP for improvements in their own safety due to a private safety measure. Altruistic components of value were elicited with a second valuation question concerning respondents' WTP for a public safety program. The drawback of this approach is that the answer to a second valuation question may be influenced by the answer to the first valuation question.

For this reason, we use two different samples of respondents. One group of car owners is asked a dichotomous choice question concerning their WTP for a private safety device that reduces, by x percent, the risk of a traffic fatality for those travelling in the car. A second group of car owners are asked a similar WTP question concerning a public safety measure: improved road quality that reduces, by x percent, their own risk (and the risk for all other road users) of a traffic fatality. By design, the two proposals differ only with respect to who receives the benefits of the risk reduction: the car owners and his passengers, in the case of the private safety device, or all road users, in the case of the public program. Any difference between the WTP for the measures should thus be attributable to inter-household altruistic motives (since we are able to control for the perceived impact of the public safety project on the environment). Respondents are also asked about their perceived relative risks of a traffic fatality in order to test if WTP increases with the perceived risk level.

This article is structured as follows. Section 1 presents a theoretical model used as a point of departure for the empirical study. In section 2, we present the methodological approach used in the empirical part of the study, while section 3 presents the results of the empirical study. The article ends with some concluding remarks.

1. The theoretical framework

The Hicks–Allais type of model used in this section is due to Jones-Lee (1991, 1992). It is a simple single-period model in which individuals, as viewed from the beginning of the period, face two possible future states of the world: being alive or being dead. Given the purpose of this article, using such a simplified model saves us from an unnecessarily complex mathematical presentation without loss of generality. It is assumed that individuals have preferences over their own survival probabilities and levels of wealth, and those of others. We also assume that individuals are concerned about the quality of the environment. The reason for introducing this assumption is the fact that we are considering projects which may affect pollution of the environment. In order to simplify the notation, we aggregate individuals into two broad categories: the considered individual (including any of his household members), in what follows denoted as individual No. 1, and all other individuals, in what follows denoted as individual No. 2. The well-behaved cardinal utility function of the considered individual (household) is written as follows:

$$V_1 = V_1(\pi_1, y_1, \pi_2, y_2, z) \tag{1}$$

where π_1 is a vector of the survival probabilities of the individuals belonging to the household of the considered individual, and y_1 is his (or alternatively his household's) wealth; while π_2 and y_2 are the corresponding figures for the second individual, and z is an index reflecting environmental quality. The function $V_1(.)$ is assumed to be strictly increasing in π_1 and y_1, and nondecreasing in π_2, y_2, and z. As noted by Jones-Lee (1992, p. 82), this formulation of the utility function is sufficiently general to include as special cases virtually all of the main approaches to the treatment of choice under uncertainty, for example, the expected utility approach. Note also that if the considered individual (household) is purely selfish, then $\partial V_1(.)/\partial \pi_2 = 0$ and $\partial V_1(.)/\partial y_2 = 0$, while they are strictly positive if he is a pure altruist.[2] If $\partial V_1(.)/\partial \pi_2 > 0$ while $\partial V_1(.)/\partial y_2 = 0$, the individual is said to be a paternalistic or safety-focused altruist, since he cares about only one aspect of others well-being, namely, their safety (here ignoring environmental quality). It should be pointed out, however, that safety-focused altruism is just one (rather extreme) form of paternalistic altruism. For example, another (equally extreme) form of paternalistic altruism is wealth-focused altruism, in which one cares only about others income or wealth and is indifferent to variations in their safety.

In what follows, we will concentrate on inter-household altruism. This seems to be the form of altruism of which people most often think when they refer to altruistic motives, for example, within public safety and environmental contexts. Let us now consider two different traffic safety projects which both change survival probabilities from π_{h0} to π_{h1} for $h = 1, 2$, where a subscript 0 (1) refers to before project (with project) values. The first project or measure is purely private but affects all users of a car in the same way, such as an airbag which can be purchased in the market and provides a uniform risk reduction for the driver and his passengers. The second project is a pure public safety measure, such as improving the quality of roads in the country. This public safety program is assumed to cause a uniform risk reduction for all road users.

The considered individual, who in the empirical study is a car owner, is asked about his/her willingness to pay for the two projects.[3] Firstly, we inquire about his/her willingness to pay for a purely private safety measure. Secondly, he/she is asked about his/her WTP for the public safety project. In the latter case, the payment vehicle is a uniform tax increase for all car owners. Using (1), we arrive at the following two money measures:

$$V_1(\pi_{11}, y_{10} - p_1, \pi_{20}, y_{20}, z_0) = V_{10} \tag{2}$$

$$V_1(\pi_{11}, y_{10} - t_1, \pi_{21}, y_{20} - t_1, z_0) = V_{10}$$

where V_{10} is the initial (i.e., pre-project) level of utility of the considered individual, p_1 is his willingness to pay (noncontingent compensating variation) for the individual or private safety measure,[4] and t_1 is his noncontingent compensating variation for the public safety measure *provided* everybody else pays t_1 for the project in question: Recall that, by construction, every car owner must pay the same tax.

By assumption, the two safety measures affect all members of a household in the same way. Thus, if there is a difference between p_1 and t_1, it must be due to some kind of inter-household altruism (holding environmental quality z constant). A pure altruist would report $p_1 < t_1$ if the tax t_1 is such that the welfare of the second individual is improved. This is so because a pure altruist positively values the fact that the welfare of the second individual is increased by the public safety project. However, if he believes that t_1 approximates the willingness to pay of the second individual (t_2), it holds that $p_1 = t_1$. The reason is simply the fact that if $t_1 = t_2$, then the second individual remains at his initial level of utility. In this case, in both lines of (2), the second individual stays at his initial level of utility. Thus, it must hold that $p_1 = t_1$ if the first individual is a pure altruist and $t_1 = t_2$. Finally, if $t_1 > t_2$, it holds that $p_1 > t_1$. In other words, $p_1 > t_1$ if $t_1 > t_2$, while $p_1 \leq t_1$ if $t_1 \leq t_2$. To the best of our knowledge, previous authors asking people to pay for non-use or passive use values have overlooked this complication of using a uniform tax as the payment vehicle when individuals are pure altruists. Our rough way of handling this complication in the empirical study is by asking a follow-up question, where we inquire whether respondents believe that they are willing to pay more or less than the average car owner.

If the considered individual is a safety-focused altruist, then $p_1 < t_1$, since such a person cares only about a project's impact on the survival probabilities of others, i.e., does not care about the utility/wealth of others per se, and the second-line project, but not the first-line project, in (2) raises the survival probability of others. On the other hand, if he is a wealth-focused altruist, he would report $p_1 > t_1$, since the public safety program reduces the wealth of those he cares for. Finally, if he is strictly selfish, then $p_1 = t_1$.

Our valuation questions refer to a percentage reduction of the risk of being killed in a traffic accident. This fact means, ceteris paribus, that the WTP for the private measure, i.e., p_1, should be larger, the larger are the risks which the individual faces in traffic. Similarly, *if* the high-risk road user believes that he gains more from the considered public safety program than the average road user, he will report a WTP, which, ceteris paribus, exceeds the average WTP. By asking individuals about the traffic risks which they face, we can test these hypotheses.

A project improving the quality of roads may increase traffic and hence increase pollution. If people who are concerned about the magnitude of z (see (1)) believe that the considered public safety program will reduce environmental quality, their WTP will be lower than t_1 in (2). However, by asking respondents if they believe that the considered program will affect the quality of the environment, we are able to test this hypothesis. This concludes the presentation of the theoretical framework of the study.

2. Methods

Our valuation questions were included in a general population telephone survey of 2,000 individuals aged 16 years and older in Sweden. Only car owners in a household with one car received our questions. In total 1,067 car owners were interviewed. The survey was carried out by a professional survey firm (SIFO AB) in September/October 1995.

The sample was randomly divided into two subsamples which each received one of the valuation questions. The respondents in the first subsample were asked about their willingness to pay for a private safety device:

"In Sweden 600 persons die annually in traffic. A possible measure to reduce the traffic risk is to equip cars with safety equipment, such as airbags.

Imagine a new type of safety equipment. If this equipment is installed in your car, the risk of dying in a traffic accident will be cut in half for you and everyone else travelling in the car. This safety equipment must be reinstalled each year to work.

Would you choose to install this safety equipment in your car if it will cost you SEK *B* per year?

.... YES

... NO"

The 600 road deaths refer to all road users. The respondents in the second subsample were asked about their willingness to pay for a public safety measure. This question was intended to be identical to the first with the exception that now the risk would be reduced by 50% for *all road users*. This question was phrased in the following way:

"In Sweden 600 persons die annually in traffic. The number of deaths can be reduced if we devote more resources to preventing traffic accidents. We can, for instance, straighten out bends, build safer crossings, and increase the supervision of traffic.

Imagine a program that halves your, but also other road users', risk of dying in a traffic accident. Are you willing to pay SEK *B* per year more in taxes on your car for this program?

.... YES

.... NO"

In both willingness-to-pay questions, the following six bids were used in SEK (Swedish Crowns; $1 = SEK 6.60, £1 = SEK 10.20 in January 1996): 200, 1,000, 2,000, 5,000, 10,000, and 20,000.

In a follow-up to the yes/no question, we asked respondents who answered "yes" if they were "fairly sure" or "absolutely sure" that they would pay. Our hypothesis is that only those individuals who are certain of their yes response would be likely to pay in a real decision situation. This approach allows a more conservative estimation of willingness to pay where only the respondents that are certain of their yes response are interpreted as truly accepting the bid. Ready et al. (1995) found that replacing the pure binary yes/no alternatives by several yes/no alternatives (yes definitely, yes probably, etc.) may affect the overall proportion of yes answers. Our approach, where we ask a pure binary yes/no question and then follow up by inquiring whether the yes answer is certain or uncertain, avoids this complication. Johannesson et al. (1995), in an experiment, found that the real average WTP (for a particular brand of chocolate) was overestimated by the conventional hypothetical binary yes/no question but underestimated if only absolutely sure yes responses were considered as corresponding to a purchase decision in a real situation. With the exception of the follow-up question, that experiment is a replication of the experiment reported in Cummings et al. (1995). In this study, we estimated the WTP both in accordance with the standard interpretation of the yes responses and the more conservative interpretation of the yes responses.

We also asked the respondents if they thought that their risk of being killed in a traffic accident was lower, the same, or higher than that of the average driver. This question was included to test the hypothesis that willingness to pay increases with the perceived risk level.

A problem in comparing the willingness to pay between the private and the public safety measures is that respondents may believe that the public program has effects other than risk reduction. One possibility is that respondents expect the public program to affect the environment (through an impact on traffic volume, for example). To account for this possible confounding effect, we included a question about the perceived impact of the public safety program on the environment. The respondents were asked if they thought the program would improve, worsen, or have no effect on the environment. Information about the following socioeconomic variables—age, sex, education, household size, and household income—was also collected in the survey.

3. Results

For the private safety measure, 82% agreed to pay the lowest bid of SEK 200 in the study, and 9% agreed to pay the highest bid of SEK 20,000. If only "absolutely sure" responses are counted, these proportions decrease to 66% and 1%, respectively. For the public safety measure, 63% agreed to pay the lowest bid of SEK 200 in the study, and 7% agreed to pay the highest bid of SEK 20,000. If only "absolutely sure" responses are counted, these proportions decrease to 43% and 3%, respectively. Of all respondents answering "yes," 52% were "absolutely sure" of their responses.

In estimating the probability of agreeing to pay a specified amount of money B in exchange for the considered project, i.e., a change in the survival probability from π_{h0} to π_{h1} for $\forall h$, we assume a logistic model. The acceptance probability P is written as follows:

$$P = F(B) = 1/[1 + e^{-\Delta v}], \tag{3}$$

where $F(B)$ is the "survivor" function yielding the probability of accepting to pay at least $\$B$ in exchange for the project, and Δv is the change in utility caused by the considered improvement in safety if the person pays $\$B$ for the improvement. In what follows, we assume a linear approximation of the change in utility: $\Delta v = \gamma_0 + \gamma_1 B + \gamma_2 S$, where γ_0 is interpreted as the change in utility caused by a ceteris paribus improvement in safety, S is a vector of socioeconomic factors, and γ_i for $i = 0,..., 2$ are parameters to be estimated. Since we have three categories, i.e., those who are absolutely sure that they agree to pay a particular amount of money in exchange for the considered project, those who are fairly sure of their yes responses, and those rejecting the project at the proposed price, we have estimated ordered as well as conventional logistic models (i.e., with separate regressions for the standard and the conservative interpretations of the yes answers, respectively). In table 1, the results of the ordered logit regressions of the intention to pay for the risk reduction are shown. The conventional models produce similar results and are therefore not reported here, but the results are available from the authors.

The intention to pay for the safety measure based on the three possible responses was used as a dependent variable (with $1 =$ reject to pay, $2 =$ fairly sure yes response, $3 =$ absolutely sure yes response). The regressions were estimated using maximum likelihood methods (in Stata). We report two goodness-of-fit measures: the percentage of correctly predicted responses and the likelihood ratio index (Greene, 1993).

The bid is highly significant with an expected negative sign in both the regression for the private safety measure and the regression for the public safety measure. Income is also highly significant in both regressions, showing that the probability of accepting a given bid increases with income. Other socioeconomic variables are not statistically significant, with the exception of sex in the regression for the public safety measure (indicating that the probability of agreeing to pay for the public safety program is higher for women than for men).

Table 1. Results of ordered logit regression of the intention to pay for a safety measure (ordered response: 1 = rejects to pay, 2 = fairly sure yes response, 3 = absolutely sure yes response). Standard errors are shown within parentheses

Regressor variable	Safety measure	
	Private	Public
Bid	−0.00024***	−0.00017****
	(0.000032)	(0.000028)
Sex[a]	−0.11	0.48**
	(0.23)	(0.24)
Age	−0.012	0.00013
	(0.0076)	(0.00049)
Household size	0.079	−0.026
	(0.14)	(0.22)
Education[b]	−0.058	−0.057
	(0.28)	(0.27)
Household income[c]	0.032**	0.050***
	(0.014)	(0.015)
Average risk[d]	0.28	0.092
	(0.25)	(0.24)
Higher than average risk	0.96*	0.50
	(0.49)	(0.46)
No effect on the environment[e]		−0.26
		(0.45)
Improved environment		0.69
		(0.44)
Cut 1[f]	−0.26	1.58***
	(0.61)	(0.59)
Cut 2[g]	0.73	2.90***
	(0.62)	(0.61)
No. of obs.	389	410
Log-likelihood	−290.95	−289.52
Individual prediction (%)	69.64	70.00
Likelihood ratio index	0.19	0.15

***,**,* = Significant at 1%, 5%, and 10% levels (two-tailed test).
[a]: 1 = woman, 0 = man.
[b]: 1 = ≥high school, 0 = otherwise.
[c]: Thousand SEK/month (pre-tax).
[d]: lower than average risk baseline category.
[e]: worsened environment baseline category.
[f]: $= -\gamma_0$; standard interpretation of the yes responses
[g]: $= -\gamma_0$; conservative interpretation of the yes responses.

The dummy variable indicating the group who perceives their traffic risk to be average has the expected positive sign in both regressions (lower than average is the omitted category), but is not statistically significant. The dummy variable for the group with a higher than average perceived risk also has an expected positive sign, but is only statistically significant in the regression for the private safety measure. Perhaps, it is more difficult for a respondent to relate his own risk level or behavior as a driver to a national

THE VALUE OF PRIVATE SAFETY VERSUS THE VALUE OF PUBLIC SAFETY   271

public safety program than to a private safety device. The dummy variable for the perceived effect on the environment included in the regression for the public safety measure is not statistically significant according to a two-tailed test. (The coefficient for an improved environmental quality is significant according to a one-tailed test. Such a test is appropriate if the hypothesis is that an improved environmental quality increases the acceptance probability. Moreover, there are only about 35 observations in the baseline category. The coefficient of a dummy, taking on the value one if the environment is improved and zero if not, is positive and significant at the 1% level according to a two-tail test.)

We have used the parameters reported in table 1 to estimate the mean WTP for the two programs. However, as can be seen from (3), the regression equations predict that a certain proportion of respondents have a negative WTP, since P will approach one as B approaches minus infinity. However, safety equipment is a private commodity, which you freely may or may not elect to buy. For this reason, we rule out a negative WTP in the estimation of the mean WTP for the private safety measure. WTP is set equal to zero for the proportion of respondents who are predicted to have a non-positive WTP. In the case in which the WTP is non-negative, but in which the probability of a zero WTP is strictly positive, the mean willingness to pay is equal to (see Johansson, 1995; O'Conor, 1995):

$$p^M = \int_0^\infty [1/(1 + e^{-(\gamma_3 + \gamma_1 B)})] dB = -(1/\gamma_1) \, ln[1 + e^{\gamma_3}], \qquad (4)$$

where p^M denotes the mean WTP for the private safety measure and γ_3 denotes the magnitude of the constant term in (3) when the elements of S are assigned particular values. We have used (4) to estimate the mean WTP, denoted t^M, for the public safety measure as well.

The results are reported in table 2. The mean WTP for a program was estimated with the explanatory variables set at their sample means. Thus, we are estimating WTP for an average respondent across the two programs. The standard error of the mean WTP was estimated using a Taylor series approximation (Kmenta, 1986). To test if there was a statistically significant difference in the mean WTP, we used a two-tailed independent samples t-test (Newbold 1991).

The mean WTP for the private safety measure is about SEK 4,700 based on the standard estimation, and about SEK 2,400 based on the conservative estimation. The mean WTP for the public program is about SEK 3,900 based on the standard estimation, and about SEK 1,300 for the conservative estimation. For the conservative (standard) estima-

Table 2. The estimated mean willingness to pay (WTP) for private and the public safety measures. Standard errors are reported within parentheses. In SEK ($1 = SEK 6.60, £1 = SEK 10.20 in January 1996).

WTP estimation	Safety measure		WTP difference
	Private (p^M)	Public (t^M)	($p^M - t^M$)
Standard	4,687 (499)	3,903 (504)	784 (709)
Conservative	2,403 (315)	1,322 (233)	1,081 (392)***

***Significant at the 1% level (two-tailed test).

tion, the WTP for the private safety measure is (not) significantly higher than the WTP for the public safety measure. We also estimated the mean WTP based on a regression using only the bid on the right-hand side so that no respondents are excluded due to missing values of the explanatory variables. This estimation led to similar WTP amounts as those reported in table 2, but WTP differed significantly between the two programs according to the standard estimation (at the 10% level), as well as the conservative interpretation of affirmative responses. Additionally, we estimated the mean WTP for the public safety measure, given that there would be no impact on the environment (by setting the dummy variable on the environmental change to zero when using (4)). This led to a somewhat lower estimate of mean WTP for the public safety measure and, as a result, WTP differs significantly between the public and the private safety measure for both the standard and the conservative interpretations of yes responses.

Based on estimates of willingness to pay for the risk reduction, the implied value of a statistical life can also be estimated. If we assume that our respondents and their household members (or other car passengers) face the same death risks in traffic as the average Swede, the value per statistical life varies between SEK 30 million ($4.5 million) and SEK 59 million ($8.9 million) for private risk reduction.[5] For public risk reduction, the value per statistical life varies between SEK 17 million ($2.6 million) and SEK 49 million ($7.4 million). These estimates are on the same level as other estimates in the literature (Viscusi 1992, 1993). It should be stressed that these estimates assume that the respondents (which are car owners in households with one car) report household willingness to pay rather than their individual WTP. This assumption is very reasonable for Sweden, since most Swedish households have a joint budget (a fact that is not necessarily true for other countries). This is also confirmed by the strong influence of household income on the acceptance probability (see table 1). However, if a subset of respondents have reported their individual WTP, our estimate of the value of a statistical life provides only a lower bound for its "true" value (while its upper bound is approximately twice the magnitude reported above). In any case, we can see no strong reason why there should be a difference with respect to which WTP measure is reported between the two subsamples. Thus, the magnitude of the value of a statistical life for private risk reduction relative to the value of a statistical life for public risk reduction should be unaffected by the assumption whether an individual or a household WTP is reported.

The equations in table 1 can also be used to estimate the willingness to pay of individuals at different perceived risk levels. The dummy variable for perceived risk reduction is only statistically significant for private risk reduction. For private risk reduction, the standard (conservative) WTP is SEK 4,200 (SEK 2,100) for the individuals with a lower than average perceived risk, and SEK 7,200 (SEK 4,200) for individuals with a higher than average perceived risk. Thus, the perceived initial risk level has a strong impact on the WTP for a risk reduction. Overall, the respondents seem to underestimate their own risks. About 40% think that they have a lower than average risk, and 7% think that they have a higher than average risk. The remaining 53% think that they face about the same risk as the average Swedish driver.

In the case of a public safety measure, everyone is "forced" to pay, even if his/her WTP is negative, because, for example, he/she believes that the program will have a strong negative impact on the environment. For this reason, in one variation, we allow WTP $\in$ $(-\infty, +\infty)$ as is, in fact, predicted by (3). Then, the average WTP is equal to $t^{Ma} = -\gamma_3/\gamma_1$, where t^{Ma} denotes the mean WTP for the public safety measure (see Johansson, 1995, for details). In this case, the mean WTP for the public safety program is either approximately zero (standard estimation) or negative (conservative estimation).

4. Concluding remarks

In the present study, the average WTP for the private safety device exceeds the average WTP for the public safety measure, a result that deserves some comment. According to our theoretical model, a pure altruist will report $p_1 > t_1$ if his WTP exceeds the WTP of others. Of our respondents, 33% (24%) believed that their own WTP exceeds (falls short of) the average WTP for the public safety measure, while 43% believed that their WTP is about the same as the average WTP. Thus, there is a tendency to overestimate one's own WTP relative to the WTP of others. This tendency should, ceteris paribus, cause the average WTP for the public safety program to fall short of the average WTP for the private safety device if respondents are pure altruists (see section 1 for details). Similarly, wealth-focused altruists will report $p_1 > t_1$, a fact which further lowers t^M relative to p^M, where a superscript M denotes the average or mean WTP. However, we don't know if these two groups of altruists "outweigh" the safety-focused altruists (for whom $t_1 > p_1$) to such an extent that p^M is (significantly) higher than t^M.

The result $p^M > t^M$ is not due to an expected negative environmental impact of the public safety program. About 90% of the respondents believed that the proposed public safety measure would either improve environmental quality or leave it unchanged. Possibly, the payment vehicle for the public safety measure, i.e., a tax increase for car owners, is considered to be unfair. After all, the proposed measure will increase safety for both car owners and other kinds of road users. Car owners in Sweden are heavily taxed and may feel that they already are subsidizing other road users. Since all car owners would have to pay the tax, there is also a demand effect. Some people would choose to sell their cars in response to a higher "car price," a fact which, ceteris paribus, reduces the average WTP. There is, of course, also the possibility that the valuation question failed for one reason or the other. In addition, the sample of respondents is quite small, implying that our results may be due to random factors which would "net out" if the sample size were increased. On the other hand, according to the results reported in table 1, the two valuation questions seem to have worked. In particular, the probability of acceptance is sensitive to the magnitude of the bid, to the level of income, to the risk level faced by the respondent, and to the perceived environmental impact of the public safety program.

Our results contrast sharply with those reported in some previous studies of the value of risk reductions. Both Jones-Lee et al. (1985) and Viscusi et al. (1988) report a positive mean WTP for altruistic concerns. However, there are several important differences between these studies and the one reported here. First, both Jones-Lee et al. (1985) and Viscusi et al. (1988) use open-ended question formats, while we use a closed-end format. Second, in contrast to earlier studies, we specify how much other households, besides the respondent's, must pay for the public safety program; the payment vehicle is a uniform tax on cars. Third, in order to avoid the possibility of a kind of "anchoring" effect, where the answer to the second question (typically the altruism question) is influenced by the answer to the first question (typically the private risk reduction question), our respondents were asked only one valuation question, not two or more as is the case in previous studies. Fourth, in contrast to Viscusi et al. (1988), in the public safety valuation question we did not translate the risk reduction caused by the public safety program into the number of fatalities avoided. The reason was that we feared that including such information in one but not the other of the valuation questions could cause a difference in the respondents' perceptions of the magnitudes of the programs. Thus, there are important differences between the studies, a fact which, at least in part, may explain the different results.

Jones-Lee et al. (1985) found a positive mean WTP for altruistic concerns for other car occupants (i.e., presumably intra-household altruism rather than inter-household altruism). However, the Jones-Lee et al. study also had a pure public goods question in which the value of a statistical life implied by the mean response was much lower than in the private goods question. Jones-Lee et al. interpreted this difference as evidence of free-rider effects, an interpretation that may be relevant for the results in the present study. That is, without a detailed attitudes survey which fully captures the reasons behind a person's response to our valuation question, we cannot rule out the possibility that the differences reported in table 2 are attributable to a public goods free-rider effect rather than to pure altruism and perceived overpayment by others or wealth-focused altruism. However, a respondent may overstate or understate his true WTP based on strategic considerations, depending on what part of the project, e.g., its magnitude or his own payment obligation, he expects to affect. Thus, in general, it is unclear whether strategic behavior would tend to increase or decrease mean WTP. Moreover, in contrast to Jones-Lee et al. (1985), we use a closed-end valuation technique. With such an approach, it is not obvious that strategic behavior can be expected to influence the outcome of the valuation experiment. Although we cannot completely rule out the possibility that our results are affected by some kind of strategic behavior, the empirical results are striking and highlight the theoretical complication of using a uniform tax as a payment vehicle in public good valuation surveys.

Acknowledgment

We are grateful to an anonymous referee for detailed comments and suggestions. This research was financially supported by the Swedish Council for Social Research.

Notes

1. There are also theories of impure altruism, for example, Andreoni's (1990) theory of warm-glow giving, but these approaches are not addressed here.
2. A pure altruist respects the preferences of others. This means that $(\partial V_1(.)/\partial \pi_2)(\partial V_1(.)/\partial y_2) = (\partial V_2(.)/\partial \pi_2)(\partial V_2(.)/\partial y_2)$.

3. In the empirical analysis, we use different samples for the two (dichotomous-choice) questions in order to avoid an "anchoring" effect, i.e., the problem that the answer to a second WTP question is influenced by the answer to the first question.
4. This is a discrete commodity, i.e., it is either purchased or not, explaining the fact that we have chosen to deduct p_1 (times one) from income.
5. The value of a statistical life is here defined as the mean household WTP (from table 2) divided by (300/3,700,000). There are about 3.7 million households in Sweden, and halving the risk of dying in a road accident would save 300 lives. We use average household data, since no death risk data are available for households with one car.

References

Andreoni, James. (1990). "Impure Altruism and Donation to Public Goods: A Theory of Warm Glow Giving," *Economic Journal* 100, 464–477.

Bergstrom, Theodore C. (1982). "When is A Man's Life Worth More Than His Human Capital?" In Michael W. Jones-Lee (ed.), *The Value of Life and Safety*. Amsterdam: North-Holland.

Cummings, Ronald G., Glenn W. Harrison, and Elisabet F. Rutström. (1995). "Homegrown Values and Hypothetical Surveys: A Comment." *American Economic Review* 85, 260–266.

Greene, William H. (1993). *Econometric Analysis*, 2nd ed. New York: Macmillan.

Johannesson, Magnus, Bengt Liljas, and Per-Olov Johansson. (1995). "An Experimental Comparison of Dichotomous Choice Contingent Valuation Questions and Real Purchase Decisions." Mimeo, Stockholm School of Economics.

Johansson, Per-Olov. (1995). *Evaluating Health Risks: An Economic Approach*. Cambridge: Cambridge University Press.

Jones-Lee, Michael W. (1992). "Paternalistic Altruism and the Value of a Statistical Life," *Economic Journal* 102, 80–90.

Jones-Lee, Michael W. (1991). "Altruism and the Value of Other People's Safety," *Journal of Risk And Uncertainty* 4, 213–219.

Jones-Lee, Michael W., M. Hammerton, and P. R. Philips. (1985). "The Value of Safety: Results of a National Sample Survey," *Economic Journal* 95, 49–72.

Kmenta, Jan. (1986). *Elements of Econometrics*, 2nd ed. New York: Macmillan.

Milgrom, Paul. (1993). "Is Sympathy an Economic Value? Philosophy, Economics, and the Contingent Valuation Method." In Jerry A. Hausman (ed.), *Contingent Valuation: A Critical Assessment*. Amsterdam: North-Holland.

Newbold, Paul. (1991). *Statistics for Business and Economics*, 3rd ed. Englewood Cliffs, NJ: Prentice-Hall.

O'Conor, Richard M. (1995). "Consumer-patient Valuation of Drug Safety and Efficacy." Doctoral dissertation: University of Kentucky.

Ready, Richard C., John C. Whitehead, and Glenn C. Blomquist. (1995). "Contingent Valuation When Respondents are Ambivalent," *Journal of Environmental Economics and Management* 29, 181–196.

Viscusi, W. Kip. (1993). "The Value of Risks to Life and Health," *Journal of Economic Literature* 31, 1912–1946.

Viscusi, W. Kip. (1992). *Fatal Tradeoffs. Public & Private Responsibilities for Risk*. New York: Oxford University Press.

Viscusi, W. Kip, Wesley A. Magat, and Anne Forrest. (1988). "Altruistic and Private Valuations of Risk Reduction," *Journal of Policy Analysis and Management* 7, 227–245.

[9]

Journal of Risk and Uncertainty, 14:235–257 (1997)
© 1997 Kluwer Academic Publishers

Explaining the "Identifiable Victim Effect"

KAREN E. JENNI
Department of Engineering and Public Policy, Carnegie Mellon University

GEORGE LOEWENSTEIN
Department of Social and Decision Sciences, Carnegie Mellon University

Abstract

It is widely believed that people are willing to expend greater resources to save the lives of identified victims than to save equal numbers of unidentified or statistical victims. There are many possible causes of this disparity which have not been enumerated previously or tested empirically. We discuss four possible causes of the "identifiable victim effect" and present the results of two studies which indicate that the most important cause of the disparity in treatment of identifiable and statistical lives is that, for identifiable victims, a high proportion of those at risk can be saved.

Key words: value of life, identifiable victims

JEL Classification: J-17

> "There is a distinction between an individual life and a statistical life. Let a 6-year-old girl with brown hair need thousands of dollars for an operation that will prolong her life until Christmas, and the post office will be swamped with nickels and dimes to save her. But let it be reported that without a sales tax the hospital facilities of Massachusetts will deteriorate and cause a barely perceptible increase in preventable deaths—not many will drop a tear or reach for their checkbooks." (Schelling, 1968)

> "The death of a single Russion soldier is a tragedy. A million deaths is a statistic." Joseph Stalin (quoted in Nisbett and Ross, 1980:43)

In late 1987, eighteen-month old Jessica McClure spent 58 hours trapped in a well, and Americans responded with sympathy, a tremendous rescue effort, and money. The McClures received over $700,000 in donations for "baby Jessica" in the months after her rescue, and eventually a popular television movie, "Everybody's Baby: The Rescue of Jessica McClure," was made about the incident (People Weekly, November 2, 1987; April 16, 1990; Variety, May 31, 1989). At the time, there was no question but that everything possible should and would be done to rescue the child; cost was no object. If similar resources were spent on preventative health care for children, hundreds of lives could be saved. Yet it is difficult to raise money for efforts directed at saving such "statistical" victims.

The story of "baby Jessica" is simply one example of the "identifiable victim effect:" society is willing to spend far more money to save the lives of identifiable victims than to save statistical victims. This has been remarked upon in treatises on public policy (Gore, 1992), in scholarly works (Schelling, 1968; Calabresi and Bobbitt, 1978; Viscusi, 1992; Whipple, 1992), the medical literature (Redelmeier and Tversky, 1990) and the popular press (Toufexis, 1993).

The identifiable victim effect plays a role in many important policy issues. Recently, it has received special prominence in the national debate over funding priorities for health care, where expensive measures are often taken for identified individuals, but funding for preventative care seems to be lacking. For example, a recent effort to separate conjoined twins, whose probability of surviving the operation was estimated to be less than 1%, was used in some media to highlight the discrepancies between extravagant health care funding for "last-ditch efforts ... to save the few" and modest funding for basic and preventative care that would benefit the many (Toufexis, 1993). In debates over the North American Free Trade Agreement, opponents could identify specific individuals who would lose their jobs if the agreement was approved, whereas proponents could refer only to the additional "statistical" jobs that would presumably result (Goodman, 1993). Identifiable victims need not be human: in 1988 a multi-national effort spent millions to rescue three grey whales trapped under the Arctic ice cap, while at the same time the Japanese whaling industry was spending millions to locate and harvest whales (Linden, 1988).

Identifiable victims seem to produce a greater empathic response, accompanied by greater willingness to make personal sacrifices to provide aid. One might think, therefore, that the large literature on empathy, altruism, and helping behavior would provide clues about why identifiable victims are treated differently from statistical victims. However, the literature on helping behavior focuses almost exclusively on the factors that cause people to aid identified victims (see, e.g., Latané and Darley, 1970, or Piliavin et al., 1981), and much of this literature looks at factors, such as the number of potential aiders and the costs of providing aid, that are not obviously relevant to the problem of why identifiable and statistical victims are treated differently. Likewise, the literature on empathy and altruism has been concerned primarily with the question of whether "true"—that is selfless—empathy actually exists (see, e.g., Cialdini et al., 1987, and Batson et al., 1991), which again seems to have little relevance to the question of why identifiable and statistical victims produce such a different response. We have not seen any explicit treatment of the identifiable victim effect in either literature.

In those literatures where it has been discussed, the distinction between identifiable and statistical victims is typically treated as a simple dichotomy, and the frequency with which it is mentioned reinforces this view. However, the simplicity of the distinction is deceptive: in practice, there are several differences between identifiable and statistical victims, any one of which could account for their differential treatment.

Our goal in this paper is to gain a better understanding of the psychological underpinnings of the identifiable victim effect. We do not attempt to explain the effect at a deeper level—e.g., to explain at an evolutionary level how or why humans have come to respond more strongly to identifiable than to statistical victims. Based on discussions with colleagues and a combing of the literature, we came up with four factors that differ between statistical and identifiable victims that could potentially account for their differential treatment. Although we do find that one of these factors appears to be an important cause of the effect, it is possible that other factors we have not identified also play a role.

In what follows, we first discuss these four differences between identifiable and statistical victims which may be responsible for the effect. We then discuss the normative status of the effect in relation to each of the four possible causes. Finally, we present findings from two studies designed to test the four possible causes and to determine whether, if supported, they are consciously endorsed.

1. Potential causes of the identifiable victim effect

1.1. Vividness

When an identifiable person is at risk of death, the media tell us a lot about them, and we may come to feel that we know them[1]. Research on "vividness" has shown that specific, concrete examples have far greater influence on what people think and how they behave than more comprehensive but pallid statistical information (Nisbett and Ross, 1980). Situations with identifiable victims are often characterized by all the major factors that convey vividness: the stories are very emotional (victims featured in the media are often particularly sympathetic, helpless, or blameless), we see visual images of the victim in newspapers and on television, and we see the events unfold in real-time—without the emotional distance provided by a historical perspective. For example, we see the picture of the small girl who is trapped in the well, interviews with her tearful parents on television, and live coverage of the desperate attempt to rescue her. These vivid details may result in a perceived familiarity with the victim, making it seem more important to undertake extraordinary measures to save that person. As Schelling (1968) expresses it, "the more we know, the more we care."

Indeed, many public relations and marketing tactics seem to be premised on the view that the vividness of an identifiable victim will enhance the public's desire to "do something" about the problem. For example, the "poster child" for MS fund raising, and the pictures and life stories that accompany requests for money to prevent malnutrition point to a widespread belief that concrete details increase the public's concern. Likewise, arguments for and against the proposed "three strikes and you're out" federal sentencing policy rely on vividness to create sympathy for their position: arguments for implementing such a system discuss specific victims of violent crimes who would not have been victimized had the "three strikes" policy been in place (Skelton, 1993), whereas arguments against the policy focus on relatively harmless three-time offenders who would face lifetime incarceration (Egan, 1994).

1.2. Certainty and uncertainty

A second distinction between identifiable and statistical victims is that identifiable deaths are usually certain to occur if action is not taken, whereas statistical deaths, by definition, are probabilistic. Since they are certain to occur if action is not taken, the subjective importance of identifiable deaths may be enhanced by the "certainty effect"—the tendency to place disproportionate weight on outcomes that are certain relative to those that are uncertain but likely (Kahneman and Tversky, 1979). In addition, there is compelling evidence that people are typically risk-seeking for losses (Kahneman and Tversky, 1979; Tversky and Kahneman, 1981, 1986; Cohen, Jaffrey, and Said, 1987). Risk-seeking for losses implies that a certain loss is seen as worse than an uncertain loss with the same expected value. For example, most people prefer a 50:50 chance of losing $100 or losing nothing to a certain loss of $50. Risk-seeking for losses has been demonstrated for non-monetary losses as well: in one well-known study (Tversky and Kahneman, 1981), subjects were given two identical scenarios in which lives were at risk and were asked to choose between two treatment options. In one case, the scenarios were worded in terms of lives saved (gains), and in the other they were worded in terms of lives lost (losses). Consistent with the prediction that people are risk-seeking for losses, most subjects in the lives lost condition chose the riskier treatment option. Risk-seeking for losses implies that the number of certain (identifiable) fatalities that is deemed "equivalent" to uncertain (statistical) fatalities is less than the expected number of statistical deaths. Both the certainty effect and risk seeking for losses, therefore, may contribute to the tendency to treat identifiable (and thus certain) victims as more worthy of attention than statistical victims.

1.3. Proportion of the reference group that can be saved

Public perceptions of risk are responsive to the distribution of risk among the population as well as to the absolute level of risk (Slovic, Fischhoff, and Lichtenstein, 1980). In general people are more concerned about risks that are concentrated within a geographic region or population than about those that are dispersed (National Research Council, 1989). This concern with the concentration of risk may help to explain the identifiable victim effect: identifiable victims represent highly concentrated distributions of risk within a specific reference group. In effect, identifiable victims become their own reference group, creating a situation where *n* out of *n* people will die if action is not taken. For example, if 120 people are likely to die in a plane crash this year, these are only 120 people out *of the millions who fly*. Once a plane carrying 120 passengers crashes with all aboard lost, however, these are 120 fatalities out of the 120 *on board the plane*.

There is considerable evidence that, holding the number of victims constant, people's concern increases as the applicable reference group shifts. For example, people are less tolerant of the risks of vaccination when there is a smaller "risk group" for vaccine side effects, even when members of that risk group could not be identified *a priori* (Ritov and Baron, 1990). Similarly, economic studies of the "value of life" have found that the value of avoiding death or injury increases as the baseline probability of death or injury increases (Weinstein, Shepard, and Pliskin, 1980; Viscusi and Evans, 1990; Horowitz and Carson, 1993). Willingness to pay for small reductions in risk can be extrapolated to calculate a value of life. For example, the value of life can be calculated as 10 times the willingness to pay to avoid a 10% chance of death, or as 100 times the willingness to pay to avoid a 1% chance of death. The willingness to pay to avoid a 10% chance of death is greater than ten times the willingness to pay to avoid a 1% chance of death, resulting in a higher overall value of life when the baseline risk is high. Since a high proportion of the reference group at risk implies a high probability of fatality, or high baseline risk, for each member of the risk group (e.g., if 25 out of 100 will die the baseline risk for each member of the reference group is 0.25, but if 25 out of 50,000 will die, the baseline risk for each member of the reference group is 0.0005), these findings are consistent with an increase in concern about fatalities when the reference group is small relative to the number at risk.

According to the proportion of the reference group at risk explanation, there is not a strict dichotomy between identifiable and statistical lives. Instead, identifiable victims lie at one end of a continuum running from low probability risks spread over the entire population (statistical deaths) to certain death for every member of the population (identifiable deaths).

1.4. Ex post *versus* ex ante *evaluation*

Identifiable victims are actual people who are very likely to die or be injured, whereas statistical victims are, as the term implies, simply statistics. In other words, with identifiable victims, both they and we know, at the time we have to decide what to do, that they are likely to die as the result of a preventable or addressable cause. The decision about rescuing an identifiable victim, or the evaluation of the value of rescuing the victim, is usually made *ex post*, or after, the occurrence of some risk-producing event. In contrast, the evaluation of the value of addressing risks to statistical victims is usually made *ex ante*, or before the risk-producing event has occurred. (Weinstein, Shepard, and Pliskin, 1980). The *ex post/ex ante* distinction appears to be the identifiable victim effect itself, after other factors that covary closely with the identifiable/statistical discrepancy—i.e., vividness, certainty, and the proportion of the reference group at risk—have been eliminated.

Ex post evaluation makes it more difficult to apply cost-benefit principles in deciding what to do, and instead makes issues of responsibility and blame salient. Once a victim has been identified *ex post*, people can no longer "withdraw to a naked statistical analysis of the cost-effectiveness of the effort," whereas people have few reservations about doing so *ex ante* (Gillette and Hopkins, 1988). In addition, peoples' perceptions and judgments of "risk" depend in part on the saliency of blame (Douglas, 1992). The possibility for the recognition of responsibility, and thus the attribution of blame, is clear in the *ex post* case and almost absent in the *ex ante* case.

2. Normative status of the identifiable victim effect

Scholars are divided about the identifiable victim effect's normative status. Emphasis on saving identifiable victims has been deplored as irrational (MacLean, 1986; Whipple, 1992), and praised as humanizing (Glover, 1977; Calabresi and Bobbitt, 1978; Gibbard, 1986; Gillette and Hopkins, 1988). For example, MacLean (1986) argues that activities undertaken to rescue identifiable victims, when compared to the efforts spent to reduce statistical risks, "defy economic or even risk-minimizing sense," whereas Gibbard (1986) asserts that it is immoral not to act when identifiable lives can be saved. Although the normative status of the effect may not be important for individual decision making, it is extremely important when identifiable victims are used to justify or defend specific policy decisions. How should the sympathy we feel for identifiable victims affect public policy?

The normative defensibility of the effect depends, in part, on its cause. For example, since people generally obtain more information about, and see more vivid descriptions of, identifiable victims than statistical victims, identified victims may be seen as more familiar. Although people might reasonably respond in a more emotional fashion to familiar or vivid victims, it is less reasonable to endorse a *policy* that gives higher priority to more familiar victims, all else held equal, than to less familiar victims. This view would amount to allowing media coverage to determine aid allocation.

The normative status of the effect of certainty lies in a grey area. Although many people display an analogous pattern of behavior when deciding between certain and uncertain monetary losses, it is not clear whether risk seeking for losses is a principle that people do, or should, consciously endorse or, if so, whether that the same principle should apply to decisions involving lives. Indeed, it is always possible to reframe a decision involving tradeoffs between numbers of deaths as one involving saving lives.

There may be normative arguments for being concerned with the distribution as well as the absolute magnitude of potential harm. MacLean (1986) believes that we should "distribute risks of death equally or in proportion to the distribution of expected benefits." Along similar lines, several moral philosophers argue that "fairness" or equity is a critical factor both in defining justice and in evaluating risks (Rawls, 1971, 1993; Shrader-Frechette, 1991; Raynor, 1992), a view which is especially cogent in light of the environmental justice movement, and the claim that the risks of hazardous waste disposal and pollution are borne disproportionately by minorities and by the poor (Bullard, 1993; Cushman, 1994).

However, in other situations taking the risk distribution into account seems less defensible. Given that reference group size is often a matter of framing—a reference group of arbitrary size can be specified for virtually any hazard—a blanket endorsement of a policy that treats fatalities differently based on what proportion of the reference group they compose is normatively dubious. For example, it probably makes no sense to treat a disease that kills 100% of the 10% of the population susceptible to it differently from one that kills 10% of the 100% of the population susceptible to it. However, some reference groups may be more normatively defensible than others. Thus, even after careful consideration, one might be more upset about a disease that kills an entire family or people in a small geographic area than one that kills a similar number of victims from around the country.

The normative status of the distinction between *ex post* and *ex ante* evaluation of risks is also ambiguous. Although *ex post* evaluation of identifiable victims may bring into play powerful emotions that do not apply to statistical victims, it is not clear what role those reactions should play in making policy decisions.

These four possible causes of the identifiable victim effect are, it seems, differentially defensible. Thus shedding light on which, if any, of these causes are responsible for the effect will also help to determine its normative status. In addition, it is not clear whether the identifiable victim effect is the result of a reasoned response, or if it is a gut-level, instinctive response. Whatever the cause of the identifiable victim effect, it would be interesting to ascertain whether people embrace it as a principle of decision making. That is, do we value identifiable lives more than statistical lives unconsciously and possibly unintentionally, or do we continue to value identifiable lives more after reflection? The answer to this question may also reflect on the normative status of the effect.

3. The studies

Our first goal was to determine which of these four potential causes, if any, contribute to the identifiable victim effect. In both studies, subjects read risk and accident scenarios in which each cause was either present or absent, and then rated the importance of saving the victim(s)[2]. In the first study we had a second goal: to determine if people continue to distinguish between identifiable and statistical victims when faced with an explicit choice between saving identifiable versus statistical lives. To address this question, we included two judgment conditions: rating and direct comparisons.

3.1. Study 1

Method. To test the various explanations for the identifiable victim effect, and to determine whether, if supported, they are consciously endorsed, we developed sets of scenarios in which the four causal factors were manipulated. We asked subjects to judge the importance of reducing risks in each, by having them either rate or compare the scenarios.

To investigate whether the identifiable victim effect is unconscious, or whether it persists in the face of obvious comparisons of identifiable and statistical victims, we tested subjects in two conditions. In the *rating* condition, subjects saw the scenarios in random order, with scenarios related to the same explanation separated by other questions. They rated the importance of eliminating risks in each scenario (compared to other risks for which the government has responsibility) on a one-to-five scale, where 1 was "not deserving of attention," and 5 was "one of the most important." In the *direct comparison* condition, subjects read the scenarios designed to test a single explanation together, and chose the situation in which it was more important to eliminate the risk. "Equally important" was given as an option. The direct comparison version makes it clear to subjects that the same number of lives could be saved in each case, and makes the manipulation highly salient. Given this salience, we can assume that any choice other than indifference is the result of a conscious judgment on the part of subjects about the importance of the distinction. In the rating condition, on the other hand, subjects were unaware of what was special about the scenarios they viewed. For example, those who were exposed to a victim described in detail to increase vividness were not aware that there was another condition in which details were not provided. Thus, they would have a much harder time avoiding a gut-level response, even if they believed that normatively it should not affect their judgments.

If a particular effect operates unconsciously and unintentionally, differences caused by the manipulation should be evident in the rating condition but not in the direct comparison condition. Alternatively, if the asymmetry is consciously endorsed, we would expect it to be equally strong in both the rating and the comparison groups, or possibly even stronger in the latter.

To test whether vividness increases the apparent importance of undertaking a rescue attempt, we presented two scenarios involving a traffic accident in which a victim was injured and required immediate, possibly expensive, medical help. The two scenarios are presented in the first panel of Table 1. The two situations are identical except that in one case no information about the victim was provided, and in the other case we provided a brief description of the victim. If vividness is a critical factor in making decisions about life-saving actions, subjects should rate it as more important to save the vividly described victim than the anonymous victim.

Testing the effect of uncertainty is complicated by the fact that (at least) two types of uncertainty might be relevant—uncertainty about whether a specific individual will become a victim, and uncertainty about whether that individual, once a victim, will die. In this first study, the effect of certainty versus uncertainty was examined with two scenarios in which the expected number of fatalities from a contaminated food source was held constant (at ten), but in one case the deaths are certain to occur if action is not taken, and in one case they are probabilistic. In the probabilistic case, the scenario explicitly stated that fewer or more than ten may die. These scenarios are shown in Table 2. If people are risk seeking when it comes to deaths, we would expect most subjects to find it more important to prevent the ten certain deaths than to prevent the ten probabilistic deaths.

To test whether the proportion of the risk group that can be saved affects subjects' preferences for risk-reducing projects, we developed two scenarios involving traffic fatalities and different at-risk populations. Table 3 presents these two scenarios. In both, "exactly" 25 lives could be saved by a new safety program, but the number of people specified as being at risk was 50,000 in one case and 25 in the other. According to the proportion-of-the-reference-group hypothesis, the problem should be seen as more severe as the percentage of the reference group at risk increases, so that saving 25 out of 25 at risk will be considered more important than saving 25 out of 50,000.

Finally, to test whether people believe that *ex post* decisions to save lives are more important than *ex ante* decisions to protect them, we developed two parallel scenarios where one individual was at risk from a pesticide being field-tested (see Table 4). The scenarios differed only in whether action could be taken before or after the pesticide had

Table 1. Scenarios testing the effect of vividness.

Study 1

[Anonymous] There has been a traffic accident on a remote section of the highway, and a person has been seriously injured. This person requires a helicopter rescue and immediate medical treatment to save his life.

[Vivid] There has been a traffic accident on a remote section of the highway, and a young secretary has been seriously injured. The secretary was traveling by herself, on her way to spend the weekend with her parents. She requires a helicopter rescue and immediate medical treatment to save her life.

Study 2

The 1994 earthquake in Southern California caused approximately 34 deaths, thousands of injuries, over a billion dollars of structural damage to buildings, and seriously damaged six of the major freeways in the region. Two days after the earthquake, rescue workers discovered a victim trapped in a collapsed parking garage located very near Highway 17. The news story reproduced below describes the rescue efforts that were undertaken at the time.

Example of news story with a "described" victim
Rescue Workers Find Quake Survivor
Efforts to remove survivor underway

Los Angeles, Calif. Jan. 15. Rescue workers were losing hope. It's not possible, not in that wreckage. There couldn't be anyone alive in there.

A few still hoped. Perhaps, they thought, as they probed the wreckage of the municipal parking garage at the 23rd Ave. exit of Highway 17 with high-tech survivor, and are working as quickly as possible to sort through the rubble to reach him.

Don Grisom, the attendant at the parking garage, remembers waving to Bob Wright as he went to his car shortly before 3 pm. Then the earthquake struck and the garage collapsed. Mr. Grisom was able to run to safety, but saw Mr. Wright just getting into his car as the building began to come down. Mr. Wright, 42, is a local high school teacher and basketball coach. His wife, Mary, has not left the equipment, perhaps some-

one could have survived the collapse.

Finally, just after 6 am, a worker using a special fiber optic camera to search parts of the garage that are currently inaccessible spotted a hand moving in the window of a car. Someone was alive in that mountain of rubble—imprisoned in a tomb of concrete, but alive nonetheless. Scene since she heard her husband might be trapped inside. She is ecstatic that he has been found, but is very concerned. "It's frightening," she says, "But Bob is strong and has an incredible zest for life. I know he will hold on for me and for Jimmy [the couple's 3 year old son]. I am hoping and praying for him, and I'm sure he is going to be OK."

While rescue workers are cautiously optimistic, the survivor appears to be pinned in his car, underneath tons of concrete and

Search of the partially collapsed parking structure began yesterday afternoon, after a parking attendant, who miraculously escaped the collapsing garage during the earthquake, remembered seeing a man walk into the garage to pick up his car at about 3 pm, minutes before the quake hit.

Workers and paramedics have made voice contact with the steel rubble, and in a particularly unstable section of the collapsed structure. Before full-scale extraction measures can begin, parts of the building must be stabilized. City engineers are on the site directing the stabilizing work, but are unsure how long it will be before they will be able to remove the survivor. However, rescuers are also working to create an access route so paramedics can reach the survivor quickly and attend to any critical injuries.

Table 1. (Continued)

What isn't in this news story is a controversy over the effect of nearby freeway traffic on the parking structure. Highway 17 was not damaged by the earthquake, and was a primary alternative route for all traffic traveling from the south into downtown Los Angeles. Consequently, the highway was carrying much more traffic than usual. The highway passes directly adjacent to the parking garage, and many engineers were concerned that vibrations from the traffic on the highway could cause more damage to the parking garage, further endangering the trapped victim. These engineers suggested shutting down the highway until the victim could be extracted from the collapsed garage. However, the highway was estimated to be carrying about 230,000 cars per day, all of which would be diverted onto surface streets if it were shut down. This would add an average of an hour an a half to commuting time into downtown. Keeping the highway open would not endanger the rescuers, but could produce further structural shifting, with risks to the trapped victim. If you had been in the position of having to make a decision about the freeway, how strongly would you have supported closing the freeway?

been applied. In the *ex post* case the individual had been exposed and had to be located; in the *ex ante* case the individual was about to be exposed, unless she could be located first. The *ex post/ex ante* distinction suggests that the former scenario will be judged more important.

Table 2. Scenarios testing the effect of certainty and uncertainty.

Study 1

[Uncertain] A major food distributor has just discovered that its newly introduced yogurt can cause death to individuals who are allergic to its new ingredient. Approximately 1% of the general population is allergic to this particular ingredient, but the existence of the allergy is not well known. The yogurt has been distributed to a large number of retailers, and sold to about 1000 different consumers. Each consumer therefore has a 1% chance of becoming ill and dying from the yogurt, and the best estimate is that 10 people will die, but more or fewer may die depending on the prevalence of the allergy. These people can be saved if all the consumers are located and treated.

[Certain] A major food distributor has just discovered that a small number (10 containers) of the yogurts it distributed yesterday were contaminated, and that the contamination will result in the death of anyone who has eaten the yogurt, unless an antidote drug is administered. The yogurt was distributed to a large number of retailers, and has since been sold to approximately 1000 consumers. 10 deaths will result unless the consumers are located and the antidote drug administered. If all the consumers are located and the antidote is administered, no one will be harmed.

Study 2

On average, about 100 children under the age of 4 die each year from suffocation associated with thin-layer plastic (bags and wrappings) in the United States. Over the past 10 years, annual deaths have ranged from [92 to 110] [34 to 168]. Most of these deaths are associated with plastic bags used by dry cleaners and with plastic wrapping from toy packages. Some scientists have suggested that replacing plastic with paper wrappings for these purposes would virtually eliminate the problem of children suffocating on plastic wrap. Legislation has been introduced that will require all dry cleaners and toy manufacturers in the U.S. to begin packaging with paper rather than plastic in 1996, with complete phase-out of plastic by the year 2000. Think about other legislation concerned with safety that is being, or could be, considered, from legislation you don't care at all about to legislation you care very much about. Relative to other legislation, what priority would you place on having this legislation passed and implemented?

Table 3. Scenarios testing the effect of the proportion of the reference group that can be saved.

Study 1
[Large reference group] Approximately 50,000 people die every year in traffic accidents in the United States. A new program has been proposed that will save exactly 25 of these 50,000 lives every year.
[Small reference group] 25 people die every year in traffic accidents on a specific highway interchange. A new program has been proposed that will eliminate the risks at this interchange. If the program is undertaken, it is expected that there will be no further fatalities at this interchange.

Study 2
At an intersection in downtown Pittsburgh, there are several automobile-pedestrian accidents every year, and in each of the past three years 2 pedestrians have been killed at that intersection. These pedestrian accidents account for [2 of 4 people who died in accidents at that intersection] [2 of 112 people who died in auto-related accidents in southwestern Pennsylvania] [2 of 1700 people who died in auto-related accidents in Pennsylvania] last year. To reduce the risks to pedestrians, city engineers have proposed installing automobile barriers between the sidewalks and the streets surrounding this intersection, and building a pedestrian overpass. Although expensive, they believe these measures will eliminate the possibility of future pedestrian accidents at the intersection. At the same time, there are many other useful traffic safety and improvement projects proposed both for the city and for the state, and there is not enough funding to implement them all. Relative to other automobile and traffic safety projects you know about or can imagine, what priority do you think should be given to funding this project?

These scenarios may seem, in isolation, to be artificial and unrealistic. This is in part because real-world identifiable victims are often characterized by several of these distinctions, so it is extremely difficult to manipulate them independently in a complete factorial design.

The existence of any one of the four factors implies the existance of at least one other factor. For example, if a victim is certain, that victim also composes a large proportion of the reference group (in this case, certain victims automatically become their own reference group, and in fact, compose 100% of the reference group). However, when a large portion of the reference group is at risk, those victims do not have to be certain victims. For example, everyone in a population could be susceptible to a specific disease, but the probability that the disease will kill a susceptible individual might be quite low.

Figure 1 illustrates the relationships between the four factors, where arrows represent logical implication. For example, the arrow from *certain* to *high proportion of reference group* indicates that a certain victim also represents a high proportion of the reference group. However, there is no arrow from *high proportion* to *certain*, so victims who comprise a high proportion of the reference group are not necessarily certain victims.

The complex relationships between these four possible causes make it impossible to develop scenarios in which all four causes are varied independently. For example, if factor A is necessary for factor B, the combination of B, not A, is logically impossible. However, no one factor is both necessary and sufficient for any other factor, and thus no two of these factors are perfectly confounded. This makes it possible to examine the effect of each cause independently, with the other three held constant, as we did in these two studies.

Table 4. Scenarios testing the effect of *ex post* and *ex ante* evaluation.

Study 1
[*Ex post*] The EPA has approved a field test of a new pesticide and it has been applied to a wheat field. It has just been discovered that someone from a nearby community was exposed to toxic levels of the pesticide during the application and that if they are not treated quickly, they will die. Locating this individual will require immediate door-to-door search of the local community. [*Ex ante*] The EPA has approved a field test of a new pesticide and is about to apply it to a wheat field. It has just been discovered that someone from a nearby community is camping near the field and will soon be exposed to toxic levels of the pesticide, such that they will die from the exposure. To prevent this exposure will require conducting a thorough search of the nearby area.

Study 2
Park rangers for the California Department of Parks have just closed a small area in the remote Sierra Nevada to camping and hiking, due to the discovery of strong toxic chemicals in a fresh-water spring located near an abandoned mine. Campers in that region are required to sign in and sign out with park officials, so all campers are now being warned to steer clear of this abandoned mine. However, in checking the filed hiking plans of visitors currently in the general area, they discover that a hiker already on the trail has plans to camp in the now-closed area near the abandoned mine. They suspect he intends to use water from the springs for cooking and drinking. According to the hiker's plans, he [will enter the contaminated area tomorrow] [entered the contaminated area yesterday]. Rangers have the option of asking the local search and rescue team to go after the hiker to [prevent him from drinking the contaminated water and send him to camp elsewhere] [see if he used the contaminated water and if so, bring him out to seek medical attention]. However, if they send the search and rescue team after the hiker, they will be unavailable for other emergencies which may arise. Consider the seriousness of other problems you know about or can imagine that the search and rescue team may be called on to handle. Relative to these other emergencies, what priority would you place on sending the search and rescue team after the hiker?

Subjects. The questionnaire was administered to 70 undergraduates at Carnegie Mellon University, 30 visitors to a mall in south suburban Boston, and 27 visitors (mainly students) to the University of Pittsburgh and Carnegie Mellon University student centers. Forty-one respondents received the direct comparison questionnaire, and 86 received the rating version. We tested approximately twice as many subjects in the rating condition because the statistical power of the planned between-subjects comparisons is lower than

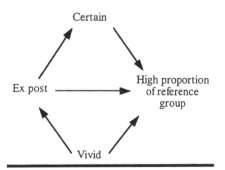

Figure 1. Logical relationships between the four possible causes. Arrows represent implication.

the within-subject comparisons of the direct comparison condition. All subjects received all versions of each scenario, with scenarios designed to test the same cause separated by other questions.

Results. Despite the heterogeneity of the three sample populations, there were no significant differences in their responses, and no order effects, so the data were aggregated. The results for both the rating and the direct comparison conditions are summarized in Table 5. This table lists the number of respondents rating or choosing each scenario as more important. For each of the four possible causes, the first column of data shows the number (fraction in parentheses) of subjects whose responses are consistent with the explanation being tested. For example, if the vividness of the victim is a cause of the identifiable victim effect, subjects should say it is more important to take action when the victim is vividly described. The first column of data shows the number of subjects who ranked the scenarios in an order consistent with this explanation. The second column of data shows the number answering in the direction inconsistent with the explanation, and the third column shows the number who rated the two programs as equally important, or who chose "equally important" in the direct comparison version. The final column indicates whether there is a significant difference between the number of subjects responding in the pre-

Table 5. Number of subjects rating each scenario as more important: Study 1.

	Vivid	Anonymous	Equally important	Significance
Vividness				
Ratings	8 (.06)	13 (.15)	64 (.79)	NS
Direct Comparison	4 (.10)	1 (.03)	35 (.88)	NS

	Certain	Uncertain	Equally important	Significance
Certainty and uncertainty				
Ratings	26 (.30)	6 (.07)	54 (.63)	<0.005
Direct Comparison	11 (.29)	8 (.21)	19 (.50)	NS

	Smaller reference group	Larger reference group	Equally important	Significance
Proportion of the reference group				
Ratings	44 (.51)	13 (.15)	29 (.34)	<0.001
Direct Comparison	21 (.51)	3 (.07)	17 (.41)	<0.001

	Ex post	Ex ante	Equally important	Significance
Ex post/ex ante				
Ratings	12 (.14)	24 (.28)	50 (.58)	(1)
Direct Comparison	7 (.17)	9 (.22)	25 (.61)	NS

Numbers in parentheses show the fraction of respondents answering in each order.
(1) $p < 0.05$, significant in opposite direction from prediction.

dicted direction and the number responding in the opposite direction. To determine significance, the number of subjects responding in the predicted direction was compared with the number responding in the opposite direction using a sign test.

The modal response to most of the scenarios was to rate the two situations as equivalent. That is, for questions testing each possible explanation, subjects felt it was equally important to save lives in the two scenarios. However, the responses of those subjects expressing a preference are quite interesting.

Subjects did not rate the familiar victim as more important than the anonymous victim, either in rating or direct comparison, contrary to the result that might be expected if vividness is a primary determinant of the effect. There is no significant difference between the responses in the rating and direct comparison conditions ($\chi^2(2) = 4.49$, $p \approx 0.11$).

The rating task showed people to be significantly more concerned about certain than about uncertain deaths, but the direct comparison task did not. In this case, the difference between respondents in the direct comparison and the rating versions is marginally significant ($\chi^2(2) = 5.47$, $p < 0.1$).

Subjects are significantly more concerned with saving lives when they represent a large portion of the reference group. In fact, for the proportion-of-the-reference-group questions, the modal response was to rate saving 25 out of 25 casualties as more important than saving 25 out of 50,000. This was the case in both the rating and the direct comparison versions, and further, there is no significant difference in the responses from the two conditions ($\chi^2(2) = 1.8$, $p \approx 0.4$).

Finally, subjects in the rating condition felt it was more important to take action *ex ante* (preventative measures) than to take action *ex post* (remedial measures). This is the opposite of the result that is expected if the *ex post/ex ante* distinction is a cause of the identifiable victim effect. However, the effect of this distinction was not significant in the direct comparison condition. Note, however, that there is no significant difference between the responses in the rating and direct comparison conditions ($\chi^2(2) = 0.60$, $p \approx 0.7$).

Discussion. The results of this experiment provide support for two possible causes of the identifiable victim effect: the certainty effect and the proportion-of-the-reference group hypothesis. Furthermore, the differences between responses in the rating and direct comparison conditions indicate that the effect of certainty appears unintended, whereas the percentage reduction in risk is something that subjects consciously take into account.

We found no support for the hypothesis that the vividness with which a victim is described increases subjects' desire to save that victim. Apparently simply knowing that "a person" is definitely at risk and can be saved by taking action is enough to engender our concern.

Finally, the hypothesis that the distinction between *ex post* and *ex ante* action is critical was not supported by our results. To the degree that subjects care about this distinction, they appear to believe that preventative actions are more important than remedial actions.

The lack of response to the vividness manipulation is not easily explained, unless there was something specific about the "vivid" victim that made her unsympathetic. However, in retrospect, there may be alternative explanations for some of our other results. The questions testing the certainty hypothesis are acknowledged to be highly unlikely, although the two scenarios are similarly implausibile, so this alone would not be enough to produce the effect found. However, a food distributor can be blamed for a contamination problem much more easily than for allergic reactions. The saliency of blame may have contributed to the perceived importance of saving the more certain victims. The scenarios testing the proportion of the reference group hypothesis describe two programs, each of which is estimated to save 25 lives. The program saving 25 out of 25 might naturally be seen as more effective than that saving 25 out of 50,000, or more believable, or more cost-effective. These reactions would result in subjects rating saving 25 out of 25 lives as more important than saving 25 out of 50,000 lives. Finally, in the scenarios testing the difference between *ex post* and *ex ante* action, the *ex ante* decision could be simply not to apply the pesticide to the field. The existence of an easy and costless solution to prevent the risk *ex ante* may account for the direction of the effect.

3.2. Study 2

Given the somewhat surprising results obtained from the first study—the failure to find a vividness effect and the strong effect of reference group size—we designed a second study to test further the same four possible causes of the identifiable victim effect. Again we used a variety of different scenarios, manipulating the vividness of the victim description, the degree of uncertainty about the risks, the proportion of the reference group at risk, and whether the proposed action takes place before or after the risks are realized.

Method. Given the weak response to the various manipulations in Study 1, our first goal was to validate the identifiable victim effect itself by comparing subjects' reactions to an obvious example of an identifiable versus statistical fatality, where the identifiable case demonstrates most or all of the four characteristics and the statistical case demonstrates none. We developed two scenarios involving lead poisoning in children, presented in Table 6. In both cases action could be taken that had a 0.1% chance of saving a life. In the identifiable case the victim was a child who was hospitalized with acute lead poisoning,

Table 6. Scenarios testing the effect of identifiable and statistical victims.

Study 2
[Identifiable] Suppose that you are a hospital administrator running a large metropolitan hospital under tight budget constraints. A young child has been brought in with acute lead poisoning, and is unlikely to live. His physician has suggested trying new, untested treatment that might help. However, the treatment is experimental, very expensive, and is estimated to have only a 0.1% chance of saving the child's life. Assume that you decide not to approve the treatment, and that the child dies. How personally responsible would you feel?
[Statistical] Suppose that you are a hospital administrator running a large metropolitan hospital under tight budget constraints. A local community group has requested that the hospital provide free lead level screening tests to all children in the community. Comprehensive lead screening of all children would be very expensive, the experience with lead levels in the community suggest there is only a 0.1% chance any child will be exposed to fatal levels of lead under current circumstances. Assume that you decide not to institute the lead-level screening program, and later in the year a child dies from acute lead poisoning. How personally responsible would you feel?

and certain to die unless a new, experimental treatment is used (and likely to die even with the treatment). So the victim is described (vivid), comprises 100% of the reference group, is certain die without treatment, and has already experienced the risk. In the statistical case the proposed action is preventative (community-wide lead screening tests), and the victim is an anonymous child, comprising a small proportion of the reference group (all children in the community), who is not certain to be exposed or die from the risk, and who has not yet experienced the risk. In both scenarios subjects were asked to assume that they did not take action (did not approve the treatment or did not fund a testing program) and a child died. They were asked to rate how responsible they would feel, on a one to seven scale. Since the victim in the identifiable scenario possesses all of the characteristics we hypothsize may cause the identifiable victim effect, we predicted that subjects will feel more responsible for that death than for the death of one anonymous child in the community.

To test the vividness hypothesis more thoroughly we developed a set of scenarios which include a variety of specific victims, and different levels of description. In this scenario a victim is trapped in a collapsed structure after an earthquake and rescue efforts are underway. Subjects read a realistic news story describing the situation, where the victim is presented either (1) generically, as "a man" or "a woman," (2) with a description including the sex, age, occupation, marital status, and quotes about the victim from friends or relatives, or (3) with the same description and a picture. After reading about the victim, subjects were asked how strongly they would support (on a one to seven scale) a very expensive action (closing a nearby freeway) to reduce risks marginally to the trapped victim. Two generic and eight specific victims were created, half male and half female. The ages and occupations of the victims were randomly selected using the base rates of the ages and occupations of U.S. citizens. Using a variety of victims should reduce the possibility that subjects are simply responding to a very sympathetic (or unsympathetic) victim. The second panel of Table 1 presents the scenario and an example of one of the victim descriptions. If the vividness of the description matters, subjects should be more willing to close the freeway for the victims who are described, or described and pictured, than for generic victims. Subjects were also asked to indicate how much they cared about what happened to the trapped victim.

Uncertainty about expected fatalities can come from two sources: uncertainty about who will be a victim, and uncertainty about how likely any given victim is to die. In Study 1, we attempted to manipulate only the second type of uncertainty. In Study 2, we combined these two types of uncertainty and presented a range of possible fatalities. The uncertainty scenarios involved young children suffocating on thin-layer plastic wrap and bags. The scenarios are shown in Table 2. Subjects were told that the average number of deaths from suffocation for children under the age of 4 is 100 per year, with a range of 92 to 110 (low variance case) or 34 to 168 (high variance case). They were asked to indicate how strongly they would support legislation requiring the phasing out of thin-layer plastic in packaging and drycleaning. While in neither of these scenarios are fatalities certain, if people are more concerned about "certain" fatalities, they should be more concerned about the fatalities in the low variance case, which are "less uncertain," than in the high variance case. To test whether the possibility of zero fatalities carries any special significance, we ran a second uncertainty study where the expected number of deaths was 20, and the uncertainty ranged from 15 to 25, or from 0 to 40.

To test the effect of the proportion of the reference group that can be saved, we again used a scenario involving traffic fatalities. These scenarios are presented in Table 3. To reduce any ambiguity about the locations of the fatalities, and the type and efficacy of the risk-reducing actions, we described a specific type and location of accident (pedestrian fatalities at a single intersection in downtown Pittsburgh), as well as the proposed actions to eliminate those risks (installing auto barriers and a pedestrian overpass). Only the size of the reference group was varied (2 of 4, 112, or 1700), and subjects were asked to indicate what priority they would assign to the proposed project on a one–to–ten scale.

Finally, the *ex post/ex ante* distinction was tested with a more believable scenario than in the earlier study (see Table 4). A camper in the remote mountains either has been exposed to dangerously contaminated water and is in need of immediate help (*ex post*), or is about to be exposed and in need of warning (*ex ante*)[3]. Subjects were asked to rate the importance of rescuing this victim.

Subjects. The questionnaire was administered to 121 adult visitors to the Pittsburgh International Airport. All subjects answered only one question from each set of scenarios: that is, one question designed to test each of the hypothesized causes. Questions related to each hypothesis were randomized over 24 different versions of the survey. The second question involving uncertainty was answered by 100 adult visitors to the airport.

Results. To reduce variance caused by inter-subject heterogeneity in average concern for victims and in use of the scales, we normalized each subject's responses by subtracting from each concern rating the weighted average of all that subject's concern ratings. Table 7 shows the mean normalized rating for each question. The last column indicates whether the difference in mean ratings reaches statistical significance, by either a t-test or an F-test, as appropriate. As shown in the table, most of the questions did not yield significantly different mean ratings.

Subjects feel significantly more responsible for the specific, identifiable victim in the medical (lead-level) questions who dies because s/he doesn't get treatment than for the anonymous victim who dies because the county-wide lead screening program is not approved. This is simply the identifiable victim effect itself, demonstrated in an experimental setting.

We again observed an unexpected effect of vividness, even though we stengthened the vividness manipulation and took pains to ensure that victim described was statistically representative. Although in Study 1 subjects were more concerned about the anonymous victim, in this study subjects stated that they cared the most when a verbal description of the victim was provided and slightly less when the victim was described simply as "a man" or "a woman," although the difference did not approach statistical significance. However, surprisingly, subjects cared least when the a picture of the victim was included along with the description. No consistent effect was observed of vividness on willingness to support the risk-reduction project.

Table 7. Mean rating for each scenario in Study 2.

	n	Mean rating	Significance
Identifiable/Statistical			
Identifiable	54	−1.61	p < .005
Statistical	60	−2.40	[t(112)]
Vividness–support project			
no description	38	1.12	NS
description	41	.61	[F(2,111)]
description with picture	35	1.03	
Vividness–care about victim			
no description	38	.44	NS
description	41	.64	[F(2,111)]
description with picture	35	.17	
Certainty and uncertainty			
low variance (92–110)	58	.70	NS
high variance (34–168)	55	1.12	[t(112)]
low variance (15–25)	49	5.90	NS
high variance (0–40)	51	5.23	[t(98)]
Proportion of the reference group			
large (2 of 4)	39	.66	p < .06
medium (2 of 112)	35	.19	[F(2,111)]
small (2 of 1700)	40	−.25	
Ex ante/ex post			
ex ante	59	.74	NS
ex post	55	1.09	[t(112)]

In a slight departure from our earlier results, Study 2 failed to find significant differ-ences in the importance ratings for the questions testing the effect of different levels of uncertainty.

Consistent with the results of Study 1, however, subjects place significantly higher priority on a project that is estimated to save two lives if those lives represent a high proportion of the reference group (2 out of 4), than on that identical project if those same two lives represent only a small proportion of the reference group (2 out of 1700). Although this effect is significant only at the .06 level (two-tailed test), the ANOVA is conservative because it does not take account of the ordering of means, which is as-predicted.

Finally, we did not find a significant effect for the *ex post/ex ante* distinction.

Discussion. The results of this experiment provide additional support for one possible cause of the identifiable victim effect: the proportion of the reference group at risk appears to be an important factor affecting subjects' support for risk-reducing actions.

As in Study 1, these results do not support the hypotheses that more vivid descriptions increase subjects' concern for, or desire to save, that victim, that people care more about more certain than less certain fatalities, or that *ex post* victims are more important than *ex ante* victims. The uncertainty finding is a slight departure from the results of Study 1, where certain risks were judged more important than uncertain risks, although only in the rating condition.

4. General discussion

Although there have been numerous references to the identifiable victim effect, this study is, to the best of our knowledge, the first to examine the effect systematically. Despite the superficial simplicity of the distinction between identifiable and statistical lives, we noted that there are actually several differences between them that could account for their differential treatment.

One major surprise to emerge from the studies is that vividness does not appear to have an effect on subjects' willingness to support risk–reducing actions. When we have spoken to friends and colleagues about this project, many propose vividness as the explanation for the identifiable victim effect. We should note, however, that our research is not the first to obtain weak vividness effects (Taylor and Thompson, 1982).

Based on our research, of course, we cannot conclude that all vividly described victims will be seen as no more important than anonymous victims in terms of decision making. Certainly it would be possible to create scenarios with a particularly compelling or sympathetic victim, or a vivid scenario, in which subjects would express a preference for saving the "familiar" victim. Our experiment attempted to see if more detailed information about the victim would, by itself, cause the identifiable victim effect. The questions of what information about a victim increases our sympathy, and of what, if any, information will make us care more about one identified victim than about another identified victim are interesting issues discussed in the literature on helping behavior (see, e.g., Piliavin, Rodin and Piliavin, 1969), but not addressed by our study.

When victims are identified it is clear exactly how many people will die, but when victims are statistical it is always possible that more or fewer will die. In our first study, subjects felt avoiding certain fatalities was more important than avoiding uncertain fatalities when they were not able to compare scenarios directly. However, subjects judged certain and probabilistic deaths as equally important when they compared the two situations directly. Thus, the judgment that it is more important to address certain risks than to address probabilistic risks appears to be an unconscious one. Our second study found no significant difference between the reaction to high or low variance distributions when the expected number of deaths is held constant.

Our findings suggest that the major cause of the identifiable victim effect is the relative size of the reference group compared to the number of people at risk. Identified victims constitute their own reference group, 100% of whom will die if steps are not taken to save them. Further, the response to the relative size of the reference group is consistent even under conditions where subjects explicitly contrasted scenarios which clearly differed only in the fraction of those at risk who can be saved. Thus consideration of the proportion of those at risk who can be saved appears to be a factor subjects would endorse for making decisions about risk-reducing activities.

The *ex post/ex ante* results are somewhat less surprising on reflection. It appears that once we know an individual is definitely at risk, there is no difference in the importance of taking action after the risk is realized or before the risk has occurred: in fact, there is a slight preference for preventative action. Conventional wisdom suggests this result, as we often hear "an ounce of prevention is worth a pound of cure." Perhaps the *ex post/ex ante* distinction is simply a short-hand way for referring to the multitude of emotional and ethical issues that come into play once a victim has been identified; isolated from those issues, it does not appear to produce the identifiable victim effect.

In combination, these results point to the somewhat surprising conclusion that the identifiable victim effect, per se, may be wholly attributable to the effect of the relative size of the reference group. We wonder whether the identifiable victim effect could more accurately (but less elegantly) be labeled the "percentage of reference group saved effect."

If the identifiable victim effect is, in fact, largely due to the relationship between identifiability and the size of the reference group, this raises significant questions about the normative status of the effect and the role it should play in policy decisions, because the normative arguments for a reference group effect are tenuous. The reference group is often largely a matter of framing, and it is difficult to defend a distinction between a situation where there is a group of 10 randomly distributed "vaccine sensitive" people who are at risk of death from a flu vaccine, but who cannot be identified beforehand, and a situation in which 10 random people will be killed by the same vaccine.

Most policy decisions about risk involve statistical fatalities, while most private decisions involve identifiable fatalities. The normative status of the effect is not necessarily relevant to private decisions—no one would declare it irrational for parents to go to all extremes to save the life of their child. However, it is relevant to public policy decisions—we can legitimately ask whether it makes sense for society to go to extremes to save one identified life when those resources could be spent more productively to save a larger number of statistical lives. As Keeney (1995) notes, there is no right or wrong answer. He suggests that we may want to assign different economic values to identified and statistical lives. But which of these values should form the basis for policy decisions? Allowing risk policies to vary depending on whether the victims are identified or statistical may create incentives for advocates of one policy to play up the identifiable victims that could be saved under that policy, while pointing out that we don't know who will be saved under another. However, Viscusi (1992) points out that if we assign a higher value to saving any identified victim than to saving a statistical victim, then perhaps we need to rethink how we value statistical victims, since at some point all victims are identified.

Questions about whether and how identifiable and statistical victims should be considered differently in policy decisions are not easily answered. However, given the arbitrariness of the reference group that applies to a specific risk, it seems inadvisable to recommend reference group size as an input into public policy except, perhaps, when the group is defined geographically or by a sensitive demographic characteristic.

Why did the plight of young Jessica McClure engender such sympathies and such a strong response? Certainly she represented a very sympathetic victim, and the media coverage of the event ensured that we knew a great deal about her. It would seem heartless to suggest that she not be saved, or that a cost-benefit analysis be conducted before rescue efforts could commence. However, our study points to two other factors that may have been the most important in producing the powerful response: she was certain to die if not removed from the well, and she comprised 100% of the risk group.

Acknowledgements

We thank Jonathan Baron, Graham Loomes, Keith Murnighan, Daniel Read, and Peter Ubel for helpful comments. This work was supported under a National Science Foundation Graduate Research Fellowship, and by the Center for Integrated Study of the Human Dimensions of Global Change (NSF Grant #SBR 95-21914). Any opinions, findings, conclusions, or recommendations expressed in this paper are those of the authors and do not necessarily reflect the views of the National Science Foundation.

Notes

1. Although the identifiable victim effect may apply to many less severe, impacts, our focus in this paper is on fatal victims.
2. Scenario studies of this type have several limitations. First, the manipulated factors will almost inevitably interact with the specific content of the scenarios, raising questions about external validity (see Shotland, 1983). Second, subjects rate their own level of concern, raising the issue of self-presentation and the accuracy of introspection.
3. We thank an anonymous reviewer for suggesting this scenario.

References

Batson, C. Daniel, et al. (1991). "Empathic joy and the empathy-altruism hypothesis." *Journal of Personality and Social Psychology* 62, 413–26.
Bullard, Robert D. (1993). *Confronting Environmental Racism: Voices from the Grassroots*. Boston: South End Press.
Calabresi, Guido, and Philip Bobbitt (1978). *Tragic Choices*. New York: W.W. Norton and Co.
Cialdini, Robert B., et al. (1987). "Empathy-based helping: is it selflessly or selfishly motivated?" *Journal of Personality and Social Psychology* 52, 749–58.
Cohen, M, J. Y. Jaffray, and T. Said (1987). "Experimental comparison of individual behavior under risk and under uncertainty for gains and for losses," *Organizational Behavior and Human Decision Processes* 39, 1–22.
Cushman, John H. Jr. (1994). "Clinton to Order Effort to Make Pollution Fairer," The New York Times, February 10, page A1.
Douglas, Mary (1992). *Risk and Blame: Essays in Cultural Theory*. New York: Routledge.
Egan, Timothy (1994). "A 3-Strike Law Shows It's Not as Simple as it Seems," The New York Times, February 15, p. A1.
Gibbard, Allan (1986). "Risk and Value," in Douglas MacLean (Ed.), *Values at Risk*. New Jersey: Rowan and Allanheld.
Gillette, Clayton P., and Thomas D. Hopkins (1988). Federal Agency Valuations of Human Life. Administrative Conference of the United States, Report for Recommendation 88–7.
Glover, Jonathan (1977). *Causing Death and Saving Lives*. New York: Penguin Books.

Goodman, Walter (1993). "TV, by its very nature, can stack the deck," The New York Times, September 13, p. C20.

Gore, Al (1992). *Earth in the Balance: Ecology and the Human Spirit*. New York: Plume.

Horowitz, John K. and Richard T. Carson (1993). "Baseline risk and Preference for Reductions in Risk to Life." *Risk Analysis* 13 (2), 457–462.

Keeney, Ralph L. (1995). "Understanding Life-Threatening Risks," *Risk Analysis* 15 (6).

Kahneman, Daniel and Amos Tversky (1979). "Prospect Theory: An Analysis of Decision Under Risk." *Econometrica* 47(2).

Latané, Bibb, and John M. Darley (1970). *The Unresponsive Bystander: Why doesn't he help?*. New York: Appleton-Century-Crofts.

Linden, Eugene (1988). "Helping Out Putu, Siku and Kanik," *Time Magazine*, pp. 76–77. October 31.

MacLean, Douglas (1986). "Social Values and the Distribution of Risk," in Douglas MacLean (Ed.), *Values at Risk*. New Jersey: Rowan and Allanheld.

National Research Council (1989). *Improving Risk Communication*. Washington DC: National Academy Press.

Nisbett, Richard and Lee Ross (1980). *Human Inference: Strategies and Shortcomings of Social Judgment*. New Jersey: Prentice-Hall, Inc.

People Weekly (1987). "America's heart goes out to Baby Jessica." Volume 28:18. November 2.

People Weekly (1990). Volume 33:15. April 16.

Piliavin, Jane A., et al. (1981). *Emergency Intervention*. New York: Academic Press.

Piliavin, Irving M., Judith Rodin, and Jane A. Piliavin (1969). "Good samaritanism: an underground phenomenon?" *Journal of Personality and Social Psychology* 13, 289–299.

Rawls, John (1971). *A Theory of Justice*. Cambridge, Massachussetts: Harvard University Press.

Rawls, John (1993). *Political Liberalism*. New York: Columbia University Press.

Raynor, Steve (1992). "Cultural Theory and Risk Analysis," In Seldon Krimsky and Dominic Golding (Eds.), *Social Theories of Risk*. Connecticut: Praeger Press.

Redelmeier, Donald A. and Amos Tversky (1990). "Occasional Note: Discrepancy Between Medical Decisions for Individual Patients and for Groups," *The New England Journal of Medicine*, April 19.

Ritov, Ilana, and Jonathan Baron (1990). "Reluctance to Vaccinate: Omission Bias and Ambiguity," *Journal of Behavioral Decision Making* 3, 263–277.

Schelling, T. C. (1968). "The Life You Save May Be Your Own," in Samuel Chase (Ed.), *Problems in Public Expenditure Analysis*. Washington DC: The Brookings Institute.

Shotland, R. Lance (1983). "What's wrong with helping behavior research? Only the independent and dependent variables." *Academic Psychology Bulletin* 5, 339–350.

Shrader-Frechette, K. S. (1991). *Risk and Rationality: Philosophical Foundations for Populist Reforms*. Berkeley: University of California Press.

Skelton, George (1993). "A Father's Crusade Born From Pain," The Los Angeles Times, December 9, p. A3.

Slovic, P., B. Fischhoff, and S. Lichtenstein. (1980). "Facts and Fears: Understanding Perceived Risk," In Richard C. Schwing and Walther A. Albers, Jr. (Eds.), *Societal Risk Assessment: How Safe is Safe Enough?* New York: Plenum Press.

Taylor, S. E. and S. C. Thompson (1982). "Stalking the elusive 'vividness' effect." *Psychological Review* 89, 155–181.

Toufexis, Anastasia (1993). "The Ultimate Choice." *Time Magazine*, pp. 43–44. August 31.

Tversky, Amos, and Daniel Kahneman (1981). "The Framing of Decisions and the Psychology of Choice," *Science* 211, 243–258.

Tversky, Amos, and Daniel Kahneman (1986). "Rational Choice and the Framing of Decisions," *Journal of Business* 59 (4), part 2.

Variety (1989). "TV Reviews—Network: Everybody's Baby," Volume 335:7, May 31.

Viscusi, W. Kip and William N. Evans (1990). "Utility Functions That Depend on Health Status: Estimates and Economic Implications," *The American Economic Review* 80 (3), 353–374.

Viscusi, W. Kip (1992). *Fatal Tradeoffs: Public and Private Responsibilities for Risk*. New York: Oxford University Press.

Weinstein, Milton C., Donald S. Shepard, and Joseph S. Pliskin (1980). "The Economic Value of Changing Mortality Probabilities: A Decision-Theoretic Approach," *Quarterly Journal of Economics* 94, 373–396.

Whipple, Chris (1992). "Inconsistent Values in Risk Management" in Seldon Krimsky and Dominic Golding (Eds.), *Social Theories of Risk*. Connecticut: Praeger Press.

Part II
The Value of Life: Labor Market Studies

[10]

The Value of Saving a Life:

Evidence from the Labor Market *

RICHARD THALER

UNIVERSITY OF ROCHESTER

AND

SHERWIN ROSEN

UNIVERSITY OF ROCHESTER

INTRODUCTION

LIVELY controversy has centered in recent years on the methodology for evaluating life-saving on government projects and in public policy. It is now well understood that valuation should be carried out in terms of a proper set of compensating variations, on a par with benefit measures used in other areas of project evaluation. To put it plainly, the value of a life is the amount members of society are willing to pay to save one. It is clear that most previously devised measures relate in a very imperfect way, if at all, to the conceptually appropriate measure.[1] However, in view of recent and prospective legislation on product and industrial safety standards, some new estimates are sorely needed.

This paper presents a range of rather conservative estimates for one important component of life value: the demand price for a person's own safety. Estimates are obtained by answering the question, "How much will a person pay to reduce the probability of his own death by a 'small' amount?" Another component of life value is the amount other people (family and friends) are willing to pay to save the life

* This research was partially funded by a grant from the National Institute of Education. Martin J. Bailey, Victor Fuchs, Jack Hirshleifer, and Paul Taubman provided helpful comments on an initial draft.

[1] See Schelling (1968), Usher (1972) and especially Mishan (1971) and the references therein.

266 *Market and Nonmarket Aspects of Real Earnings*

of a particular individual. This second component is ignored. As a matter of course, a new conceptual framework for analyzing this problem is offered. We believe our model will be valuable for other investigations in this and related areas.

The usual methodology of preference revelation from observed behavior in demand theory is the most natural way of approaching the problem. Two types of behavior are relevant in this connection. First, individuals voluntarily undertake many risks of death and injury that are not inherent in their everyday situation, and which could be avoided through expenditure of their own resources.[2] Suppose a person is observed taking a known incremental risk that could be removed by spending one dollar. Then the implicit value of avoiding the additional risk must be something less than one dollar or else it would not have been observed. For example, many people would not purchase automobile seat belts if they were not mandatory. Further, when installation was required, many individuals did not use them, or at least that was so prior to the tied installation of ignition locks and warning buzzers. Some people make a point of crossing streets in the middle of the block rather than at corners, most do not completely fireproof their homes, and so forth. While these and other examples provide scattered evidence on death and injury risk evaluation, it appears doubtful whether they can be systematized enough to yield very convincing evidence on the matter. The second kind of behavior is observed in the labor market in conjunction with risky jobs. Analysis of those data is pursued here.

Our method follows up Adam Smith's ancient suggestion that individuals must be induced to take risky jobs through a set of compensating differences in wage rates. Here the evidence is highly systematic and the data are good. Different work situations exhibit vastly different work-related probabilities of death and injury. Moreover, lots of data are available on wages in these jobs, on the personal characteristics of people who work at them, and on the industrial and technical characteristics of firms who offer them. Further, parties who voluntarily face such risks daily and as a major part of their lives, or production processes, have a special interest in obtaining reliable and objective information about the nature of the risks involved. This is especially true of very risky jobs. Finally, we have uncovered a new source of genuine actuarial data on death rates in risky occupations that is superior to other existing data sources and that until now has not been used for estimation.

---

[2] Such an approach is suggested by Bailey (1968) and Fromm (1968).

The Value of Saving a Life 267

Smith's theory has been familiar to economists for almost two hundred years and, in fact, forms the basis for the best recent inquiries into the economics of safety.[3] Yet very little effort has gone into empirical implementation of the idea. Some people have been hostile to it, asserting — without proof — that forces producing observed wage variation are so varied and complex as to preclude isolating the effect of risk. As will be demonstrated below, Smith's logic suggests that the labor market can be viewed as providing a mechanism for implicit trading in risk (and in other aspects of on-the-job consumption) with the degree of risk (and other job attributes) varying from one job to another. It certainly is not clear why price determination in such markets should be more complex than in any other markets where tied sales occur, such as the housing market. Indeed, the hedonic reconstruction of demand theory suggests that tied sales and package deals of product "characteristics" are the rule and not the exception in virtually all market exchange. Moreover, estimates presented below belie the assertion that partial effects of job risk on wage rates cannot be observed.

Given that risk-wage differentials can be estimated, How are the estimates to be interpreted, and How do they relate to the demand price for safety? Existence of a systematic, observable relationship between job risk and wage rates means that it is possible to impute a set of implicit marginal prices for various levels of risk. Like other prices, the imputations result from intersections of demand and supply functions. In the present case, there are supplies of people willing to work at risky jobs and demands for people to fill them. Alternatively, workers can be viewed as demanding on-the-job safety and firms can be regarded as supplying it.

Difficulties of interpretation arise from two sources. Individuals have different attitudes toward risk bearing and/or different physical capacities to cope with risky situations. In addition, it is not necessarily true that observed risks are completely and technologically fixed in various occupations and production processes. For example, changing TV tower light bulbs on top of the World Trade Building in New York is inherently more risky than changing light bulbs inside the offices of that building. However, it is conceivable to think of ways in which the first job could be made safer, though at some real cost. Whether, in general, firms find it in their interest to make safety-enhancing expenditures, and in what amounts, depends on weighing the costs of providing additional safety to workers against prospective

[3] For example, see Calabresi (1972).

268 *Market and Nonmarket Aspects of Real Earnings*

returns. Costs are incurred from installing and maintaining safety devices and returns come in the form of lower wage payments and a smaller wage bill. How can it be known whether observed risk-wage relationships reflect mainly marginal costs of producing safety—the supply of job safety—rather than the demand for it?

This question raises fundamental and familiar issues of identification. Its resolution in terms of job attributes (or in terms of goods attributes in the hedonic view of demand, for that matter) requires a framework of analysis slightly altered from the usual one. The identification problem is resolved on a conceptual level in the following sections, where the nature of equilibrium in the implicit market for job risk is examined in some detail.[4] We show how the observations relate to underlying distributions of worker attitudes toward risk and to the structure of safety technology and particular production processes. The extent to which inferences about the demand for safety can be unscrambled from wage and risk observations quite naturally follows from this exercise. Data, estimates and interpretation of the results are presented subsequently.

THE MARKET FOR JOB SAFETY

As noted above, the theory of equalizing differences suggests labor market transactions can be treated as tied sales. Workers sell their labor, but at the same time purchase nonmonetary and psychic aspects of their jobs. Firms purchase labor, but also sell nonmonetary aspects of work. Thus, firms are joint producers: some output is sold on products markets and other output is sold to workers in conjunction with labor-service rentals. For purposes of exposition, we concentrate on one nonmonetary aspect of jobs, namely the risks of injury and death to which they give rise. The model can easily be extended to several attributes such as free lunches, good labor relations, prospects for on-the-job learning and the like, but the resulting complexity would detract from the main point.

For purposes of analyzing demand for job safety, it is sufficient to consider a market for productively and personally homogeneous workers. Assume worker attitudes toward death and injury risk are independent of their exogenously acquired skills. Workers in this market all have the same skill and personal characteristics, though tastes for job risk bearing generally differ among them. Workers are productively homogeneous, and the only distinguishing characteristic of jobs is the amount of death and injury risk associated with

---

[4] In fact, the model is an empirical application of a general model suggested by Rosen (1974).

The Value of Saving a Life 269

each of them.[5] Jobs exhibiting the same risks are identical, and, by assumption, the personal identity of particular employers and employees is irrelevant to the problem. Job risk itself is a multidimensional concept and requires, at least, a distinction between deaths and injury probabilities, on one hand, and various levels of injury severity, on the other. Again, in line with our aim at simplification, represent job risk by a univariate index p. Further, let p denote the probability of a "standard accident." Then, each job is perfectly described by a particular value of p on the unit interval.

Equilibrium in the job market is characterized by a *function* $W(p)$, yielding the wage rate associated with each value of p. In fact $W(p)$ is a functional generalization of Smith's equalizing differences concept. Given an equilibrium function $W(p)$, each worker chooses an optimal value of p by comparing psychic costs of increased risk with monetary returns in the form of higher wages. This assumes, of course, that workers are risk averse and $W(p)$ is increasing in p. Operationally, optimal choice is achieved through each worker applying for a job offering the desired degree of risk (p). Firms decide what risks their jobs contain by comparing costs of providing additional safety with returns in the form of lower wage payments, and are constrained by their basic underlying technologies. $W(p)$ is an equilibrium function when the number of workers applying for jobs at each value of risk equals the number of jobs offered at each risk. Therefore, $W(p)$ serves as an equilibrating device for matching or marrying off workers and firms, the same role that prices play in standard markets.

Analysis of optimal choices of workers and firms gives an intuitive picture of the mechanism generating the observations on risk and prices (the function $W(p)$). Both decisions are considred in turn. We have sometimes found it convenient to think in terms of supply of workers to risky jobs and firms' demands for job risk, rather than the obverse concepts of workers' demand for job safety and firms' supply of it: safety is the negative of risk.

---

[5] The reader should note that analysis of worker job choice is confined to people with identical personal characteristics. The point is tricky and will be considered again below. For now, the following example will have to do. Suppose clumsy and careless persons have large negative externalities in risky settings involving groups of workers. Then a set of equalizing differences must arise on worker characteristics (one of which is "carelessness") that are not independent of risk. Costs of employing a careless worker exceed the costs of employing a careful one, and the latter must be paid less than the former. Employers attempt to internalize these externalities by choosing employees with the optimal packages of personal characteristics. It is as if there are separate risk markets for workers with each bundle of personal characteristics, and the present analysis of worker choice is confined to only one of those markets.

270 *Market and Nonmarket Aspects of Real Earnings*

AN EXAMPLE

A good starting point for our analysis is the essay by Walter Oi (1973). Some fundamental aspects of the problem and our basic methodology are well illustrated by proving a variant of Oi's main result in very simple fashion and going on from there.

Again, suppose all job risk involves standard injuries and can be represented by work time lost and, consequently, by earnings lost. Deaths and "pain and suffering" due to injuries are ignored for the time being. Adopting this simplification, injuries can be measured in monetary equivalents: a proportion of the wage permanently lost, say, kW, where k is an exogenously determined constant and $0 < k < 1$. Workers choose jobs offering injury probability p, basing decisions on maximization of expected utility. Let $U(Y)$ represent some worker's utility function, where Y is the prospect of certain income. Assume risk aversion: $U' > 0$ and $U'' < 0$. Assume a perfect insurance market: the cost of insurance equals its actuarial value, with no additional load factor, and workers choosing jobs offering injury probability p can purchase insurance at price $p/(1 - p)$ per dollar coverage. Both workers and insurance companies know the true probabilities and there is no moral hazard. Let I denote the amount of insurance purchased. Expected utility is given by

$$E = (1 - p)U[W(p) - \frac{p}{1 - p} I] + pU[(1 - k)W(p) + I] \qquad (1)$$

where $W - [p/(1 - p)]I$ is net income if an accident does not occur, and $W(1 - k) + I$ is income if it does. The worker chooses p and I to maximize E.

Consider optimal amounts of insurance coverage first, conditional on an arbitrary value of p. Differentiate E with respect to I, set the result equal to zero and simplify to obtain

$$U'(W - \frac{p}{1 - p} I) = U'[W(1 - k) + I] \qquad (2)$$

or equalization of marginal utility in both states of the world. In that losses are converted into monetary equivalents and U is strictly increasing in its argument, condition (2) can be realized only if incomes in both states of the world are equated. That is, (2) implies $I = (1 - p)kW$. Substituting this result into equation 1 and simplifying gives

$$E = U[(I - pk)W(p)] \qquad (3)$$

The Value of Saving a Life 271

The problem has been converted to optimal choice of p, conditional on prior optimization of insurance coverage.

Define an *acceptance wage* θ as the payment necessary to make the worker indifferent to jobs offering alternative risks, again conditioned on purchasing optimal insurance coverage for each risk. The acceptance wage is defined for a constant expected utility index E, and with recourse to (3) implicitly is defined by

$$E = U[\theta(p, E; k)(1 - pk)] \qquad (4)$$

Invert equation (4)

$$\theta(p, E; k) = U^{-1}(E)/(1 - pk) \equiv f(E)/(1 - pk) \qquad (5)$$

Equation 5 defines a family of indifference curves in the earnings/risk (θ,p) plane such that the compensated (utility held constant) acceptance wage is increasing in risk at an increasing rate: The marginal rate of substitution between job risk and money is positive and increasing. Differentiating the log of (5) with respect to p shows that the relative marginal acceptance wage, $\dfrac{1}{\theta}\dfrac{\partial\theta}{\partial p} = k/(1 - pk)$, depends only on risk, and k is independent of E. In other words, relative marginal acceptance wages are the same for all workers, independently of workers' degrees of risk aversion. This is due to the presence of perfect insurance so that full coverage is rational.

The fact that the function $\dfrac{1}{\theta}\dfrac{\partial\theta}{\partial p}$ is equal for all workers yields some arbitrage restrictions on observable wage/risk relationships in the market. Arbitrage mandates the restriction $W'(p)/W(p) = \dfrac{1}{\theta(p,E)}$. $\dfrac{\partial\theta(p,E)}{\partial p}$ for every possible value of p. For proof, assume to the contrary that at some value of p, say p^*, $W'(p^*)/W(p^*) > \dfrac{1}{\theta(p^*,E)}$. $\dfrac{\partial\theta(p^*,E)}{\partial p}$. Then, everybody currently working at a job with risk p^* could improve themselves by applying for jobs involving slightly higher risk. Additional wages on higher-risk jobs exceed relative marginal valuations of them and expected utility must rise from taking slightly larger risks. Jobs such as p^* are unfilled, and relative wages have to change in an obvious way to induce people to apply for them. Exactly the opposite logic applies when the inequality goes in the other direc-

272 *Market and Nonmarket Aspects of Real Earnings*

tion. In that case, it is also not rational for anyone to apply for any job offering risk p^*. Jobs offering smaller risks yield larger expected utility and $W'(p^*)/W(p^*)$ must increase if p^* type jobs are to be filled. Therefore $W'(p)/W(p) = \dfrac{1}{\theta}\dfrac{\partial\theta}{\partial p}$ must hold for all p, and the observed market wage-risk function must satisfy $W'(p)/W(p) = k/(1 - pk)$. This market equilibrium condition can be integrated to yield

$$W(p) = C/(1 - pk) \tag{6}$$

In (6), C is a constant of integration, determined by the side condition that total quantity of labor supplied to the market equals total demand for it. Only if market observations lie along an approximately semi-log function such as (6) can the labor market be in equilibrium in this simple example.

The problem considered above reveals the basic essentials of Smith's theory. In this case, wage differentials are exactly equalizing everywhere, at both the margin and on the average, and wage differences only reflect actuarial differences in risk between jobs. To see this, note that expected earning is $(1 - p)W(p) + p(1 - k)W(p)$, which, from (6), equals C: Expected earning is constant across all jobs, independent of job risk and the distribution of risk aversion in the labor force. Following the general "free lunch theorem," such a distinct and strong result comes from strong assumptions. Perfect insurance implies all risk-averse workers act as expected income maximizers and induces them to act alike, independently of their degree of risk aversion. The result would not have been true had we allowed for pain and suffering, imperfect insurance (nonzero load and hence incomplete coverage), or interpersonal differences in physical capacities to cope with job risk.[6] Equalizing wage-risk relationships depends on the demand for workers, as well as on the supply of them, in those cases, as will be spelled out below.

It is important to note differences between compensation and earnings before turning to a more general formulation of the problem. The

---

[6] Suppose realized risks in a given situation differ from person to person for exogenous reasons and that personal characteristics (e.g., sense of balance) involve no externalities. Also, in line with footnote 5, assume equalizing difference functions for job risk $W(p)$ and personal characteristics are independent of each other in the relevant sense. Differences in real risks can be handled in the example by specifying a distribution on k across workers. Then the arbitrage-everywhere argument breaks down because all workers cannot be indifferent to all jobs. Even in the presence of perfect insurance, relative marginal acceptance wages depend on k and are not equal for everyone. Obviously those individuals for whom k is small apply for the riskier jobs.

The Value of Saving a Life   273

two are related by an identity: Compensation ≡ earnings + fringe benefits. Fringe benefits were ignored above. Had they been included (employers "pay" insurance premiums), no systematic relationship between earnings and risk would have occurred. However, the relationship between compensation and risk would have been described by (6). Insurance fringes act like a tax that is completely "backward shifted" and nominal earnings fall by the amount of the benefit. Workers always pay these costs, whether or not they nominally do so. Therefore, since earnings before fringe benefits and insurance premiums stand in a fixed relationship to each other (the insurance premium is pkW), differences in compensation serve to equalize the market, not differences in net earnings. For example, workmen's compensation is a force making for uniformity in net wage rates across jobs with alternative risks, so long as benefit schedules reflect true monetary (and psychic) losses and the amount of insurance is no more than workers would buy voluntarily. Henceforth the words wage and compensation will be used interchangeably.

SUPPLY PRICE OF JOB RISK

Now the assumptions of perfect insurance and the absence of pain and suffering are relaxed. Only two states of the world were distinguished in the example above, accident-no accident. Taking account of alternative levels of injury severity requires introducing N possible states. For example, N might be 4, a value of 1 indexing no accident, 2 indexing "minor" accidents, 3 "nonminor," nondeath accidents, and 4 indexing death. Demarcation between states 2 and 3 or any other boundaries along the injury-severity continuum are achieved through the use of dummy variable splits on an index such as work days lost. For instance days lost greater than zero but less than some number D_1 correspond to state 2, days lost between D_1 and D_2 correspond to state 3, and so forth. Finer distinctions (and more states) can be made by combining work-days-lost severity indexes and the physical nature of accidents, such as loss of limb, impairment of hearing, and so on.

Conceptually, pain and suffering are represented by different-state utility functions depending on the states themselves. For example, suppose losses for states n through $n + m$ can be converted into monetary equivalents. Then the n through $n + m$ state utility functions are of the same functional form as utility associated with the no-accident state. All other states have utility functions specific to themselves

274 *Market and Nonmarket Aspects of Real Earnings*

measured in such a way as to be conformable with expected utility axioms.[7]

In general, each possible job is described by an $N - 1$ component vector of probabilities $(p_2, p_3, \ldots, p_N)$ with p_i indexing the probability of state i. [The no-accident probability is ignored because it can be inferred from all the other probabilities: $p_1 = 1 - \prod_{j=2}^{N} p_j$, assuming independence.] In other words, each job is perfectly described by a bundle of different accident probabilities, with the package varying from one job to another. Jobs are associated with a multivariate function, $W(p_2, \ldots, p_N)$, giving the market wage for alternative bundles of job risk. Workers maximize expected utility over all states subject to the equalizing difference function $W(p_2, \ldots, p_N)$. Each worker chooses an optimal p-vector and applies for the job offering those probabilities.

We shall not attempt to present a completely general treatment of the problem. Discussion is specialized to two states for purposes of illustration. State 1 represents no-accident; and state 2, accidents resulting in death. Workers either survive their jobs or they don't, certainly two mutually exclusive events! Each job is associated with a number p, now indexing the probability of death. The market reveals an equalizing difference function $W(p)$ giving compensation as a function of death risk. $W'(p)$ is positive, and other restrictions will be put on it later. Insurance is available at market price $\lambda p/(1 - p)$ per dollar of coverage, with $\lambda \geq 1$. The load factor is $(\lambda - 1)$.

Assume a concave utility function $U(Y)$ for the life state as before, choosing the origin so that $U(0) = 0$. The utility (bequest) function for the death state is $\psi(Y)$, also concave with $\psi(0) = 0$. For obvious reasons, U and ψ are restricted to obey the inequality $U(Y) > \psi(Y)$ for all common values of Y. The worker chooses p and I to maximize

$$E = (1 - p)U[W(p) + y - \frac{\lambda p}{1 - p} I] + p\psi(y + I) \qquad (7)$$

where y is nonlabor income. $W + y - [\lambda p/(1 - p)]I$ is income if the worker lives and $y + I$ is beneficiaries' income if he dies. Assuming E is strictly concave in p and I, necessary and sufficient conditions for a maximum are

$$E_I = -p(\lambda U' - \psi') = 0$$

$$E_p = -U + \psi + (1 - p)U'[W' - \lambda I/(1 - p)^2] = 0 \qquad (8)$$

---

[7] See Hirshleifer (1965).

The Value of Saving a Life 275

Equations (8) jointly determine optimal values of p and I. Notice that it is no longer true that marginal utilities in both states are equal. Even if they were (i.e., if $\lambda = 1$), equality would not imply equal incomes in both states, because U' and ψ' are not identical functions. Hence the arbitrage argument used in the example above no longer applies because people with alternative utility functions behave differently.

Conditions (8) are not very informative in and of themselves unless functional forms are specified for U and ψ. In the absence of that, a very general picture of equilibrium is obtained by going the route described in the section above. Again define an acceptance wage θ as the amount of money the worker would willingly accept to work on jobs of different risks at a constant utility index, conditioned on optimal purchase of insurance. Then $\theta(p, E; y, \lambda)$ is defined implicitly by solving for θ and I in terms of E, y and λ from

$$E = (1 - p)U[\theta + y - \frac{\lambda p}{1 - p} I] + p\psi(y + 1)$$

$$0 = \lambda U'\{\theta + y - [\lambda p/(1 - p)]I\} - \psi'(y + I) \qquad (9)$$

The following properties of θ can be derived from the implicit function theorem [8]

$$\theta_p > 0, \ \theta_{pp} > 0 \qquad (i)$$

The marginal acceptance wage is positive and increasing in risk. θ_p is the expected-utility compensated supply price to risky jobs and is rising because of risk aversion, imperfect insurance, and pain and suffering (U is not the same as ψ). Property (i) is crucial to what follows.[9]

$$\theta_E > 0, \ \theta_y < -1 \qquad (ii)$$

The acceptance wage is increasing in expected utility and decreasing in nonlabor income at any given risk. Moreover, an additional dollar of nonlabor income lowers the acceptance wage (utility held constant) by more than a dollar. The reason for the latter is that additional dollars of nonlabor income increase utility in both states, thereby reducing

---

[8] These results can easily be checked by the reader. Take care always to treat θ *and I* as dependent variables and p, E, y, and λ as independent variables in the differentiation.

[9] It is conceivable that no insurance is purchased if strict concavity in (7) is not assumed. Suppose marginal utility of bequests rapidly approach zero after some dollar value. A husband might want to leave his wife with at least $100,000 if he dies, but bequest dollars in excess of 100,000 do not yield much additional utility. It may be rational for him not to purchase insurance if his nonlabor wealth is in the neighborhood of $100,000. Even in such cases, the fundamental convexity property of indifference curves in Figure 1 still applies.

276 *Market and Nonmarket Aspects of Real Earnings*

optimal amounts of insurance and payments of insurance premiums in the life state.

$$\theta_{pE} > 0, \; \theta_{py} < 0, \; \theta_{p\lambda} > 0 \tag{iii}$$

The marginal acceptance wage increases at higher levels of welfare: the better off a person is, the larger the monetary inducement necessary to coax him into a higher risk job. On the other hand, marginal acceptance wages decrease as nonlabor income rises (utility "held constant") for reasons stated under property (ii). Finally, increasing λ renders risk bearing more expensive and increases its reservation price.

Risk/earnings indifference curves $\theta(p; E, y)$ for a worker with some fixed amount of nonlabor income are shown in Figure 1. Labels E_1, $E_2, \ldots$, are in ascending order of expected utility, from property (ii). Convexity follows from property (i). Notice that the slopes of the indifference curves rise along a vertical line, a result of property (iii).

The heavy line labeled $W(p)$ represents risk/earnings opportunities or the market equalizing-difference wage function.[10] As usual, optimum choice of p (represented by p^* in the figure) occurs where the budget line and an adjoining indifference curve have a common tangent. Clearly, the curvature of $\theta(p)$ and $W(p)$ must stand in a proper relationship to each other if the solution is to be unique and interior, as is true in the assumption of strict concavity of (7).

Three empirically meaningful propositions emerge from properties (i)–(iii) and the equilibrium condition in Figure 1.[11]

Proposition I: Job safety is a normal good.

This statement needs careful interpretation and qualification. Consider the following parameterization of the budget: $W(p) = A + BV(p)$, where $V(p)$ is an increasing function of p and A and B are parameters. The statement holds true for changes in A. For example, let A increase. The budget line rises parallel to its initial position and expected utility also rises. But property (iiia) implies marginal acceptance wages rise too. Hence risk falls and the worker chooses a safer job.[12] Changes in A are analogous to pure income effects in demand

---

[10] As shown by example in the preceding section, there is no reason for $W(p)$ to be linear in p. The budget constraint can be distinctly nonlinear.

[11] These statements are easy to prove analytically. Differentiate equations (8) and exploit second-order conditions for a maximum, as usual.

[12] Some casual evidence is relevant here. Secularly increasing job safety in the U.S. has been accompanied by a trend of rising real wages. No doubt improvements in safety technology have decreased the price of safety as well.

The Value of Saving a Life   277

FIGURE 1

Worker Equilibrium

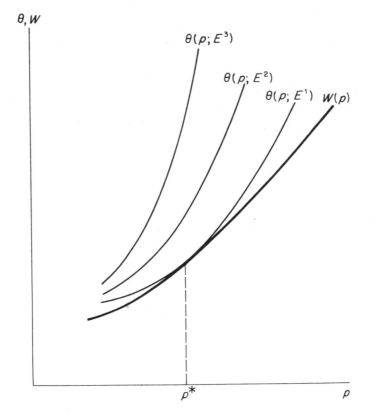

theory. The statement does not hold for changes in B. An increase in B results in a negative income effect (on risk), but a positive substitution effect (on risk) in that increasing marginal earnings on riskier jobs makes risk bearing more attractive. The net outcome is unpredictable without further specification.

Proposition II: Job safety is positively related to the price of insurance.

This is an immediate consequence of (iiic). Decreasing the insurance load factor makes risk bearing cheaper, everywhere decreasing marginal rates of substitution between money and risk. More risk necessarily is purchased.

278 *Market and Nonmarket Aspects of Real Earnings*

Proposition III: Job safety is not necessarily normal with respect to property income.

This nonintuitive result can be motivated in part as follows: Increasing nonlabor income provides a kind of self-insurance against the death state, since nonlabor income (willed to one's heirs) is not at risk in the labor market. This reduces needs for market insurance and makes risk bearing less expensive, a kind of substitution effect. However, increasing y also increases expected utility and has the effect of increasing the marginal acceptance wage for any incremental risk, a kind of income effect. The two effects work against each other. Mechanically, the result comes from properties (iib), (iiia) and (iiib). An additional dollar of nonlabor income shifts the entire indifference map downward by more than a dollar (iib) and also reduces marginal rates of substitution for given expected utility measures (iiib). However, marginal valuation of risk is increasing in expected utility (iiia) and marginal rates of substitution still increase along any vertical line in Figure 1. The first effect is a force making for increased risk, while the second works in the opposite direction. Curiously, it can be shown analytically that risk is necessarily inferior in nonlabor income when the insurance load is zero (i.e., $\lambda = 1$). Evidently, when the price of insurance exceeds its actuarial value there is a possibility for the kind of substitution effect described above to dominate the real income effect, tantamount to a type of risk preference.

EQUALIZING DIFFERENCES AND SUPPLY PRICES

The discussion above shows that worker choice is characterized by two equilibrium conditions: $W(p) = \theta(p, E)$ and $W'(p) = \partial\theta/\partial p$, two equations in two unknowns, p and E. Workers differ in their attitudes toward risk, bequest motives, and nonlabor income. Consequently there is a distribution of acceptance wage functions in the market. Those with less risk aversion have smaller marginal acceptance wages (i.e., smaller values of $\partial\theta/\partial p$) and lower reservation prices to risky jobs. The opposite might be true of people with many dependents or with high degrees of risk aversion in the accident state. Whatever the source of interpersonal differences, workers with lower marginal acceptance wages work on riskier jobs.

A picture of market equilibrium on the supply side of the market is shown in Figure 2. Ignore the curves labeled ϕ^j for the moment. $W(p)$ is the equalizing difference function as in Figure 1. Two workers are shown in Figure 2, one with acceptance wage θ^1 and the other with θ^2. $(\partial\theta^1/\partial p) > (\partial\theta^2/\partial p)$ and worker 2 is employed on a riskier job, since

The Value of Saving a Life 279

FIGURE 2

Market Equilibrium

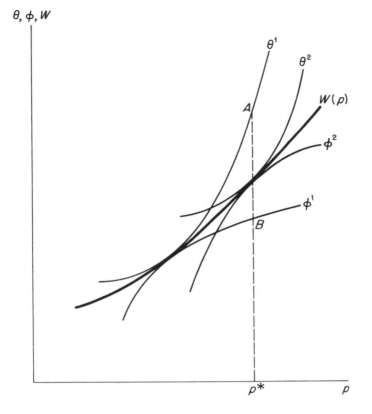

safety is not as valuable to him. The picture may be generalized. Add more workers and fill in all points on the $W(p)$ line. It is apparent that $W(p)$ is the lower envelope of a family of acceptance wage functions depending on the joint distribution of y, U and ψ across workers. $W(p)$ is observed, while the functions θ^i are not. However, evaluate the derivative of the equalizing wage difference function at some value of p, say p^*. Then, from the equilibrium conditions, $W'(p^*) = \partial\theta^i(p^*, E^*)/\partial p$ for workers finding p^* optimal, and $W'(p^*)$ identifies the marginal acceptance wage for such workers. Therefore, $W'(p^*)$ identifies $\partial\theta^i/\partial p$. $W'(p^*)$ estimates how much money is necessary to induce a person into accepting a small incremental risk. Alternatively, it esti-

280 *Market and Nonmarket Aspects of Real Earnings*

mates how much the person will pay to reduce risk by a small amount, exactly the number we seek.

The empirical work reported below uses data from very risky jobs, on the average perhaps as much as five times more risky than most jobs in the U.S. economy. It must be true that individuals working on such jobs have lower reservation supply prices and consequently smaller demand prices for safety than the average worker. The point is illustrated in Figure 2. Evaluating W' at p^* provides the correct estimate for person 2, but is an underestimate for person 1. The price the latter is willing to pay for safety at p^* is given by the slope of his acceptance wage function evaluated at p^*, the slope of θ^1 at the point marked A in Figure 2. It follows from the fact that compensated supply functions to risky jobs are rising (i.e., acceptance wage functions are convex) that $\partial\theta^1(p^*, E^*)/\partial p$ exceeds $W'(p^*)$. Most people in the labor force do not work on risky jobs. Therefore, use of data on very risky jobs understates average demand prices for safety at the observed risk levels in our sample. This justifies our initial assertion that the estimates below are conservative and probably biased downward when extrapolated to the population as a whole.

DEMAND PRICE FOR JOB RISK

It was demonstrated above that $W'(p)$ identifies supply price of risk at the relevant margin. That conclusion was reached independently of demand considerations. We now consider a very simple model of demand prices and firm decisions in order to complete the model. It will hardly be shocking to discover that $W'(p)$ also identifies demand price for risk at some margin.

Accidents are an unpleasant, though in part avoidable, by-product of production. This fact of life (or of death!) can be represented analytically by a joint production function $F(x, p, L) = 0$ for some firm, where x is marketable output, p is the accident rate, and L is labor input. Inputs other than labor are ignored. p can be a vector of state accident probabilities as mentioned above. However, to simplify, collapse it into a univariate index denoting the probability of death. Invert F and assume the following properties for $x = g(p, L)$: (i) $g_L > 0$ and $g_{LL} < 0$. Labor has positive and diminishing marginal product. (ii) $g_{Lp} < 0$. Safety increases the marginal product of labor. (iii) $g_p > 0$ for $0 \leqslant p < \bar{p}$, $g_p \gtrless 0$ for $p \geqslant \bar{p}$, where $\bar{p}$ is some "large," technically determined constant, and $g_{pp} < 0$. The assumptions on

The Value of Saving a Life   281

g_p are best explained by noting that they imply that the transformation locus between output (x) and safety ($1 - p$) is negatively inclined, except possibly at very low levels of safety. Accidents are "productive," at least up to a certain point, and can be avoided only by changing the organization of production within the firm away from marketable output and toward accident prevention. The assumption on g_{pp} means the transformation function is concave.

The production function $g(p, L)$ has been written so that safety is, in effect, produced internally by the firm. Safety devices (such as guard rails and hard hats) can also be purchased and installed externally. Let $G(1 - p)$ represent the cost of externally provided safety (converted to an annual flow), with G' and $G'' > 0$. The latter means installation activities are subject to increasing costs, though that is not strictly necessary to what follows.

The firm maximizes profit Π with respect to L and p

$$\Pi = g(p, L) - W(p)L - G(1 - p) \tag{10}$$

where the price of x has been normalized at unity. Again $W(p)$ represents the competitive wage that must be paid for alternative levels of risk. Necessary conditions for a maximum are

$$g_p + G' = W'(p)L$$

$$g_L = W(p) \tag{11}$$

Labor is hired up to the point where its wage and marginal product are equal. Marginal costs of risk are the additional market wage payments necessary to attract workers to riskier jobs. Marginal benefits come in the form of additional market output and cost savings from installing fewer safety devices. Second-order conditions require certain curvature restrictions on $W(p)$ as will be shown.

Symmetrically with the treatment above, define an *offer* function ϕ as the amount the firm willingly pays the optimal number of workers at alternative levels of risk and constant profit. With recourse to the definition of profit and the marginal condition on labor, $\phi(p, \Pi)$ is defined implicitly by

$$\phi = [g(p, L) - G(1 - p) - \Pi]/L$$

$$\phi = g_L(p, L) \tag{12}$$

Clearly $\partial\phi/\partial p$ is the compensated demand price for risk. Differentiating (12) [again, always treat ϕ and L as dependent variables, and Π and p as independent variables]

282 *Market and Nonmarket Aspects of Real Earnings*

$$\partial\phi/\partial\Pi = -1/L$$

$$\partial\phi/\partial p = (g_p + G')/L$$

$$\frac{\partial^2\phi}{\partial p^2} = [(g_{pp} - G'')g_{LL} - (\phi_p - g_{Lp})^2]/Lg_{LL} \gtreqless 0$$

The marginal demand price for risk is positive. However, even the common assumption of concavity of the production function does not guarantee that the compensated demand schedule is negatively inclined: $\partial^2\phi/\partial p^2$ can be positive.

The offer function $\phi(p, \Pi)$ defines a family of indifference curves in money and risk, one member of which is shown in Figure 2. ϕ^1 refers to one firm and ϕ^2 refers to another firm, possibly in a different industry and in any case, with a different technology than firm 1. The diagram assumes $\partial^2\phi/\partial p^2 < 0$, which is not necessarily true. Equilibrium of each firm is characterized by tangency between the market availabilities function $W(p)$ and the lowest possible constant-profit indifference curve (profit increases as ϕ decreases at any level of risk, since $\partial\phi/\partial\Pi < 0$). W'' must exceed $\partial^2\phi/\partial p^2$ at the point of tangency for an interior maximum.

Similarly to the case of worker choice, $W'(p) = \partial\phi/\partial p$ at equilibrium, and $W(p)$ represents an upper envelope of the distribution of offer functions in the market. The family of offer functions depends on the nature of production functions in various firms and industries and on corresponding distributions of industrial safety technology. In any event $W'(p^*)$ also identifies $\partial\phi^i(p^*, \Pi^*)/\partial p$, where firm i is one that has chosen p^* optimally. Using the same logic as above, $W'(p^*)$ overestimates the average supply price of safety (again, at p^*) if p^* is a very risky job. This is easily seen in Figure 2, since the slope of $\partial\phi^1/\partial p$ at point B necessarily is smaller than the slope of $\partial\phi^2/\partial p$ evaluated at the same level of job risk.[13]

MARKET EQUILIBRIUM: SUMMARY

It will be useful to summarize results of the model so far.

(a) The observable wage-risk relation represents a double envelope

---

[13] Suppose L is exogenous. Then, the offer function is defined by the first equation in (12), and it is easy to show that increased values of L reduce demand price for risk ($\phi_{pL} < 0$), providing incentives to offer safer jobs. Increasing incentives toward job safety vary directly with establishment size because of larger cost savings from lower wage rates. It is well known that accident rates decline with establishment size, at least after some minimum size. Accident rates also tend to be low in very small establishments as well, so this cannot be the entire story.

The Value of Saving a Life   283

function: It is the lower boundary of a set of acceptance wage functions and the upper boundary of a set of offer wage functions. Marriages between jobs and applicants at each level of risk are represented by common tangents of appropriate acceptance wage and offer wage functions.

(b) The envelope property in (a) implies that the derivatives of observed risk-wage differentials (evaluated at each level of risk) identify *marginal* supply and demand prices of workers and firms choosing those particular job risks.

(c) Supply price of risk (equivalently, demand price for safety) identified in (b) from very risky jobs underestimates the average supply price in the labor force for those risks, since people choosing risky jobs have a comparative advantage at job risk bearing. Similarly, demand price for risk (supply price of safety) identified from very risky jobs overestimates the average demand price for most firms in the economy, since firms offering risky jobs have a comparative disadvantage at producing safety.

(d) The numbers identified in (b) represent single points on compensated supply and demand functions, not the functions themselves. Use of such numbers for evaluation overestimates consumer surplus of finite increases in safety because workers' compensated demand schedules for safety are negatively inclined.

EQUILIBRIUM AND WORKER CHARACTERISTICS

A very simple demand model has been specified above, and it may be too simple. Recall the production function has been written $x = g(p, L)$, where L is labor and p is risk. But what is labor? [14] Our data contain indicators of personal productivity such as education and work experience. Suppose there are m such indicators, denoted by a vector $c = (c_1, \ldots, c_m)$. Of course, sample wages vary with worker characteristics as well as with job risk. Let $W(p, c)$ represent the market wage-risk–characteristics equalizing difference function. Writing the production function for a firm as we did implies that firms act as if there exists a single index of labor input, $L = f(c_1, \ldots, c_m)$ defined independently of job risk. If so, the production function must be separable in c and p. This is also a sufficient condition for separability of $W(p, c)$ as well. Suppose $W(p, c)$ is additive in p and c: $W(p, c) = V(p) + T(c)$. Hence, firms care only about total amounts of "skill" they employ (i.e., L) independently of how skills come packaged in

[14] The reader may be thinking, "What is risk?" The two questions are very much related. See below.

284 *Market and Nonmarket Aspects of Real Earnings*

people and also independently of job risks to which their employees are subjected. In effect, it means that packages of worker characteristics can be untied. For example, firms might be indifferent between a worker with 8 years of schooling and 10 years of experience and another with 12 years of school and 3 years of experience, or between workers with other combinations of these characteristics.

The real issue under discussion here involves how many interactions to allow in the risk and characteristics wage-explaining regression. At one extreme is the possibility for a universal implicit market for risk, independent of worker personal productivities (no interactions). At the other extreme are separate implicit markets for all possible combinations of personal characteristics (complete interactions). The former case corresponds to the firm choice model sketched above. Yet there is a distinct possibility that risk affects productivity in a nonhomogeneous manner with respect to various productivity indicators. Then some interactions are required. In general, the market reveals implicit prices for both risk and worker characteristics. All prices are determined simultaneously and cannot be separated,[15] and the firm choice model sketched above must refer to a single type of worker (c held constant).

If there is no interaction in production between worker characteristics and safety, only one risk premium for each value of risk appears in the market. Furthermore, the risk-wage function is independent of any further interaction between worker characteristics and attitudes toward risk. Differences in worker characteristics (age, marital status, and so on) that result in different acceptance wage functions simply help identify which workers accept riskier jobs. On the other hand, if there are interactions in production, differential risk premiums according to personal characteristics generally appear, so long as the preferred characteristics are in sufficiently scarce supply. If these characteristics are not in short supply, only those workers with preferred attributes work on risky jobs and no differential risk premium need arise in the market. Finally, if differential risk premiums exist, $W(p)$ in Figures 1 and 2 becomes a family of curves $W(p, c)$, one for each value of c, as was noted above (see footnote 5).

[15] In part, firm decisions can be handled formally as follows. The production function is $x = h(p, c_1, \ldots, c_m) = h(p, c)$. Profit is $h(p, c) - W(p, c)$, maximized over p and c. The firm organizes production taking account of factor supplies (i.e., $W(p, c)$), designing jobs and their risks and determining a set of worker-characteristics requirements. Workers not meeting requirements are not hired by the firm. Now define a joint offer-requirements function $\zeta(p, c, \Pi)$, indicating offer prices for alternative risk-characteristics requirements at constant profit, and compare the resulting indifference surfaces in (money, p, c) space with market availabilities $W(p, c)$.

The Value of Saving a Life   285

The issue is rather thorny, but an example will clarify it. Consider the regression model

$$W = a_0 + a_1 p + a_2(pz) + \text{random error} \qquad (13)$$

where W is observed wages, p is risk, z is worker age, and the a's are regression coefficients. The pure effect of age, higher order terms in p, and all other explanatory variables are impounded in the constant term a_0 for purposes of this discussion.

Age presumably affects worker's acceptance wages. Young workers risk entire lifetimes of future consumption in taking high risk jobs and have far more to lose than their older counterparts. Supply price to risky jobs should fall with age on that account. Further, a typical individual may become more or less risk averse over his lifetime, inducing shifts in acceptance wage functions over the life cycle. Job risk should be systematically related to age for both reasons. However, variations of this variety are completely captured by movements along the observed risk-wage function (taking account of possible effects of age on a_0) and there is no role here for extra marginal effects of age on risk premiums per se. Look at Figure 1. The changes under consideration are represented by systematic variations in money-risk preferences, resulting in moving points of tangency between a life-cycle shifting acceptance wage function and a fixed risk, market opportunities function. Movements along $W(p)$ should not be confused with shifts in it, and all such changes are already counted in the pure risk coefficient a_1.

Age can affect market risk premiums only insofar as it reflects unmeasured characteristics whose productivities are affected by differential risk. Exposure to risky situations makes some people far less effective agents of production than others. They not only accomplish less work of their own, but also impose extra costs on others. Both effects have to reduce wage rates of these persons if they are observed working at risky jobs. Such wage differentials serve as compensation for additional costs firms incur in employing them. For example, "nerves of steel" is a scarce factor, but steely nerves capture rents only in risky situations. Good balance is valuable to iron workers on building sites but not to desk clerks, and so forth. In the present case, young workers on the average have speedier reflexes than older ones and have faster reactions to potential accidents. But older workers have had more exposure and experience with job risk, and experience and quick reflexes probably are substitutes. Hence the effect of age on productivity in the presence of risk is uncertain, though we might ex-

286 *Market and Nonmarket Aspects of Real Earnings*

pect the reflex effect to dominate, by and large, for workers past some age that varies across occupations.

Whatever the interactions between risk differentials and personal characteristics, the analysis underlying Figure 1 still applies. The marginal effect of risk on wages evaluated at the person's exogenously determined characteristics estimates supply price for risk or demand price for safety. It also estimates firms' supply price of safety to workers with those characteristics. It is certainly possible, however, that observed risk differentials vary with worker attributes.

THE DATA

Empirical implementation of the model requires information on earnings of individuals, job risks they face, and their personal and job-related characteristics. It involves augmenting standard wage equations with job-risk measures. Many cross-sectional sources of earnings data are available and we have chosen one of them, the 1967 Survey of Economic Opportunity (SEO). The SEO survey was designed to heavily represent low-income populations and our sample is restricted to an extract of the data, consisting of a random sample of 9,488 representative households in the U.S. population. Of these observations, the sample was further reduced to adult male heads of households. The SEO data provides information on personal and industrial characteristics and labor force activities of individuals. It also lists individuals' industry of employment and occupation.

The standard source of data on industrial hazards is published by the Bureau of Labor Statistics (BLS) in conjunction with compliance and experience surveys under the Workmen's Compensation Act. These data give accidental death and injury rates for 4-digit SIC industry codes on an annual basis. Unfortunately, the BLS death and injury data cannot be adequately matched to individuals and is unsuitable for the purposes of this study. For example, it is possible to assign the BLS average death and injury indexes (by industry) to individuals in the SEO tape because the individual's industrial attachment is known. However, using the death and injury statistics in that manner implies introducing a huge component of measurement error for individuals, because job risks in each industry are not uniform across occupations. Hence, any estimates of the risk premium obtained in this way will probably be biased.

Luckily, another data source was discovered which does not suffer from the aggregation problems inherent in published BLS sources. The data used here come from the 1967 Occupation Study of the

The Value of Saving a Life 287

Society of Actuaries. The purpose of the 1967 study was to measure *extra* risks associated with some very hazardous occupations and the study was based on a sample of insurance company records covering 3,252,262 policy years of workers' experience over the period 1955–1964. The data were tabulated on a combined industry and occupational basis, and can be matched directly to individuals on the SEO sample, using Census categories contained in the latter. The matching procedure yielded 37 occupations on about 900 individuals. The occupations and their sample actuarial risks are listed in Table 1. Of course, it would be quite rash to assert that the actuarial data overcome all matching difficulties, because Table 1 shows that the actuarial classifications are rather broad. However, they are far more narrowly defined than the BLS data. We are extremely confident that the degree of measurement error in attributing risks to SEO individuals using the actuarial data is perhaps as much as an order of magnitude smaller than would be true had we matched with BLS risk data—especially for individuals working on very risky jobs, such as most of those in Table 1. In other words, the actuarial study simply provides the best data that are available for estimating risk premiums in the labor market.[16]

The actuarial data have one other very good feature. An expected number of deaths was estimated in each occupation, based on the age distribution of persons in the sample records and standard life tables. Expected deaths were then subtracted from actual deaths and the result normalized to yield an *extra* deaths per thousand policy years statistic (those numbers are multiplied by 100 in Table 1). Hence the numbers in Table 1 are net of normal age-specific death experience and measure extra death risk associated with occupations. These statistics reflect genuine occupational hazards that may cumulate with time spent in the profession. To see how risky these jobs are, note that the mean value in Table 1 is approximately 100. In probability terms, this amounts to an extra 1 in 1,000 probability of death. The probability of death from the 1967 life table for white males 35 years of age was 2 in 1,000. Thus, though the probabilities are small in absolute terms, they are very large relative to the risks most people incur in the ordinary course of their lives.

[16] After this study was completed, we discovered a paper by R. Smith (1973), who used the BLS hazard data. At an earlier stage of our research, and before discovering the Actuaries Study, we too experimented with BLS data. Our results were very similar to Smith's. However, in view of the measurement error, we believe that Smith's very strong conclusions about the workings of the labor market are totally unwarranted and that his estimates must surely be seriously biased.

288 *Market and Nonmarket Aspects of Real Earnings*

TABLE 1

Sample Occupations and Risks

Occupation	Risk [a]	Occupation	Risk [a]
Fishermen	19	Truck drivers	98
Foresters	22	Bartenders	176
Teamsters	114	Cooks	132
Lumbermen	256	Firemen	44
Mine operatives	176	Guards, watchmen, and	
Metal filers, grinders and		doorkeepers	267
polishers	41	Marshals, constables,	
Boilermakers	230	sheriffs and bailiffs	181
Cranemen and derrickmen	147	Police and detectives	78
Factory painters	81	Longshoremen and steve-	
Other painters	46	dores	101
Electricians	93	Actors	73
Railroad brakemen	88	Railroad conductors	203
Structural iron workers	204	Ships' officers	156
Locomotive firemen	186	Hucksters and peddlers	76
Power plant operatives	6	Linemen and servicemen	2
Sailors and deckhands	163	Road machine operators	103
Sawyers	133	Elevator operators	188
Switchmen	152	Laundry operatives	126
Taxicab drivers	182	Waiters	134

SOURCE: Society of Actuaries.

[a] Units of measure are extra deaths per 100,000 policy years. To convert to the probability of an extra death per year on each job multiply by 0.00001.

A less attractive feature of the actuarial risk data is that they only include death rates. Separate indexes for death and nondeath accidents would be preferable, but nondeath accident statistics comparable to those in Table 1 are not available. We must rest content with the knowledge that death rates and injury rates in the BLS industry data are highly correlated, and there is no reason for that not to be true in our data as well.

Several earnings measures are available from SEO data. We have experimented with all of them and settled on the weekly wage, because it probably is measured most accurately. We would prefer to use a measure of total compensation, but the value of fringe benefits are not available on the SEO tape or any other data set on individuals known to us. This omission must reduce the observed risk differential, again

The Value of Saving a Life   289

pointing toward conservative estimates. The extent of bias depends on the size of the load factor and the importance of pain and suffering, as well as on the precise differences between life (U) and bequest (ψ) utility functions. In any event, the average amount of life insurance provided in fringe benefits is not very large, and this source of bias must be rather small.

ESTIMATION

Our goal is to estimate the equalizing difference function $W(p, c)$. Four types of independent variables are used to control for factors determining wage rates other than job risk. These are the content of the c variables. The first set controls for regional and urban-nonurban wage differentials. The second set measures individuals' personal characteristics, including age, education, family size (or marital status), and race. The square of age and education can be included to allow for nonlinearities. The third set controls for other characteristics of the job, including unionization, dummy variables for manufacturing and service industries, and three major occupational dummy variables, one for operatives (OC1), another for service workers (OC2), and a third for laborers (OC3). Socioeconomic status (SES) was used at one stage instead of the occupational dummies as a crude measure of other nonpecuniary aspects of work. SES is an index number based on occupation, education, and income, and it might capture some other types of equalizing differences, though it was not constructed for that purpose.

Means and standard deviations of all variables are shown in Table 2. Note that the sample includes a much higher proportion of union members than obtains in the labor force generally. Sample mean earnings on an annual basis is about $6,600 ($= 132 \times 50$), which is a bit less than average earnings among male manufacturing workers during this period.

Regression planes have been fitted by least squares, using arithmetic values of earnings as the dependent variable; and alternatively, using the log of earnings as the dependent variable. The arithmetic results are shown in Table 3. Results using the log of earnings are reported in Table 4 and are very similar to the arithmetic results when evaluated at sample means.

The first two columns in Table 3 give alternative estimates of $W(p, c)$ on the strong assumption of no interactions. All the nonrisk variables are assumed to simply shift the wage-risk relationship, leaving its slope intact. Regression coefficients of almost all characteristics

290 *Market and Nonmarket Aspects of Real Earnings*

TABLE 2

Summary Statistics

Variable	Mean	Standard Deviation
Dummy variables [a]		
Urban	.69	.46
Northeast	.28	.45
South	.29	.45
West	.17	.38
Family size exceeds 2	.76	.42
Manufacturing industry	.24	.42
Service industry	.58	.49
Worker is white	.90	.30
Worker is employed full time	.98	.10
Worker belongs to union	.45	.49
Worker is married	.92	.26
Occupation is operative	.27	.44
Occupation is service	.45	.49
Occupation is laborer	.22	.42
Continuous variables		
Age (years)	41.8	11.3
Education (years)	10.11	2.73
Weeks worked in 1966	49.4	5.4
Hours worked last week	44.9	11.6
Risk (probability $\times 10^5$)	109.8	67.6
Weekly wage (week prior to survey)	$132.65	50.80

[a] Mean is proportion in sample with designated characteristic. The number of observations is 907.

variables have the expected signs found in most other studies, and most are statistically significant. Further discussion is unwarranted here.

The theory requires the wage-risk function to be positively inclined, and that is certainly the case on the appropriate one-tailed test of significance (see equations 1 and 2 in Table 3). [It is interesting to note that the simple correlation between risk and wage (not shown) is negative in these data.] $(Risk)^2$ was also entered in the regression but was not significant. We are not trying to argue here that $W(p, c)$ is linear in p, since most of the results using log W as dependent variable in Table 4 are at least as good as those in Table 3. The data simply do

The Value of Saving a Life 291

TABLE 3

Regression Estimates of $W(p, c)$ — Linear Form

Independent Variable	Equation 1	Equation 2	Equation 3	Equation 4
Risk	.0352	.0520	.100	.0410
	(.0210)	(.0219)	(.108)	(.102)
Risk × age	–	–	−.0019	−.0030
			(.0018)	(.0019)
Risk × married	–	–	.0791	.0701
			(.0380)	(.0412)
Risk × union	–	–	.0808	.0869
			(.040)	(.042)
Risk × white	–	–	−.118	–
			(.072)	
Urban	13.80	15.71	17.0	17.0
	(4.2)	(2.95)	(3.0)	(3.2)
Northeast	−3.71	−4.29	−4.27	−4.92
	(3.65)	(3.67)	(3.63)	(3.83)
South	−8.86	−8.90	−10.5	−8.18
	(3.70)	(3.74)	(3.72)	(3.97)
West	9.13	10.30	9.57	9.50
	(4.13)	(4.18)	(4.12)	(4.37)
Age	3.89	3.81	3.83	3.78
	(0.80)	(0.83)	(0.82)	(0.87)
$(Age)^2$	−.0479	−.0468	−.0442	−.0415
	(.0092)	(.0097)	(.010)	(.011)
Education	3.40	3.27	4.13	4.81
	(0.55)	(2.40)	(2.39)	(2.80)
$(Education)^2$	–	−.021	−.0237	−.042
		(.128)	(.128)	(.148)
Manufacturing industry	–	–	−13.0	−14.7
			(4.3)	(4.62)
Service industry	–	–	−9.45	−10.9
			(3.95)	(4.24)
White	22.92	22.93	37.7	–
	(4.53)	(4.50)	(9.6)	
Family size > 2	–	–	.400	2.10
			(3.57)	(3.89)
Union	25.5	27.16	15.9	15.39
	(3.25)	(3.23)	(5.4)	(5.72)
Full-time	−1.63	−.86	−1.16	.45
	(12.9)	(12.6)	(12.6)	(15.0)
Hours worked	1.50	1.41	1.47	1.44
	(.12)	(.12)	(.123)	(.129)
Occupation 1: operative	−18.7	–	−13.9	−13.5
	(9.2)		(3.24)	(3.51)

continued overleaf

292 *Market and Nonmarket Aspects of Real Earnings*

TABLE 3 (concluded)

Independent Variable	Equation 1	Equation 2	Equation 3	Equation 4
Occupation 2: service worker	−24.6 (9.5)	−	−18.1 (4.66)	−19.9 (5.05)
Occupation 3: laborer	−25.0 (13.4)	−	−	−
SES 1	−	4.68 (5.17)	−	−
SES 2	−	−17.17 (3.34)	−	−
SES 3	−	−20.69 (5.53)	−	−
R^2	.41	.41	.42	.39
Number of observations	907	907	907	813
Sample	All	All	All	White only

NOTE: The dependent variable is the weekly wage rate. The SES index has been converted to dummy variables. Standard errors are in parentheses.

not provide enough resolution on functional form to make a choice. The implied t statistic on risk is larger when SES is used in place of occupation (equation 2, Table 3), though the point estimates are not very different. First, consider the point estimate 0.0352 obtained from equation 1 of Table 3. The risk variable has been scaled by 10^5 for computational purposes and the estimate 0.0352 implies that jobs with extra risks of 0.001 (a value near the sample mean) pay $3.52 per week more than jobs with no risk. This amounts to about $176 per year, and the slope of the regression on a yearly basis is $176,000 (= .0352 × 50 × 10^5). Recall that the slope of the wage-risk relation $W'(p)$ estimates the implicit supply and demand price to risky jobs. To interpret the result, think in terms of the following conceptual experiment. Suppose 1,000 men are employed on a job entailing an extra death risk of .001 per year. Then, on average, one man out of the 1,000 will die during the year. The regression indicates that each man would be willing to work for $176 per year less if the extra death probability were reduced from .001 to .0. Hence, they would together pay $176,000 to eliminate that death: the value of the life saved must be $176,000. Furthermore, it must also be true that those firms actually offering jobs involving .001 extra death probabilities must have to spend more than $176,000 to reduce the death probability to zero, be-

The Value of Saving a Life   293

TABLE 4

Regression Estimates of $W(p, c)$ – Semilog Linear Form

Independent Variable	Equation 1	Equation 2	Equation 3	Equation 4
Risk	.000206	.000286	.000943	.000108
	(.000167)	(.000174)	(.000856)	(.000782)
Age × risk	–	–	−.000022	−.000032
			(.000014)	(.000015)
Married × risk	–	–	.000969	.000907
			(.000301)	(.000316)
Union × risk	–	–	.000823	.000895
			(.000315)	(.000320)
Race × risk	–	–	−.001312	–
			(.000572)	
Urban	.114	.132	.144	.135
	(.033)	(.024)	(.023)	(.024)
Northeast	−.00357	−.00573	−.00904	−.0131
	(.00289)	(.0291)	(.0288)	(.0293)
South	−.0632	−.0568	−.0729	−.0459
	(.0293)	(.0298)	(.0295)	(.0304)
West	.0857	.0974	.0933	.0855
	(.0327)	(.0332)	(.0327)	(.0334)
Age	.0381	.0385	.0390	.0380
	(.0063)	(.0065)	(.0065)	(.0067)
$(Age)^2$	−.000469	−.000475	−.000450	−.000419
	(.000073)	(.000077)	(.000078)	(.000081)
Manufacturing industry	–	–	−.0790	−.0888
			(.0340)	(.0353)
Service industry	–	–	−.0758	−.0922
			(.0314)	(.0324)
Education	.0332	.0531	.0623	.0613
	(.00436)	(.0190)	(.0189)	(.0215)
$(Education)^2$	–	−.00129	−.00147	−.00133
		(.00101)	(.00102)	(.00113)
White	.228	.228	.389	–
	(.036)	(.036)	(.076)	
Family size > 2	–	−.00204	−.0194	−.00220
		(.0274)	(.0283)	(.0297)
Union	.203	.214	.108	.0997
	(.026)	(.025)	(.043)	(.0437)
Full-time	.275	.303	.284	.340
	(.103)	(.101)	(.100)	(.115)
Hours worked	.0113	.0105	.0109	.0101
	(.00096)	(.00095)	(.00098)	(.00099)
Occupation 1: operative	−.0885	–	−.105	−.101
	(.0728)		(.026)	(.027)

continued overleaf

294 *Market and Nonmarket Aspects of Real Earnings*

TABLE 4 (concluded)

Independent Variable	Equation 1	Equation 2	Equation 3	Equation 4
Occupation 2: service worker	−.126 (.075)	–	−.110 (.037)	−.124 (.039)
Occupation 3: laborer	−.218 (.106)	–	–	–
SES 1	–	.0152 (.0411)	–	–
SES 2	–	−.128 (.026)	–	–
SES 3	–	−.194 (.042)	–	–
R^2	.47	.46	.48	.43
Number of observations	907	907	907	813

NOTE: The dependent variable is the log of the weekly wage rate. The SES index has been converted to dummy variables. Standard errors are in parentheses.

cause there is a clear-cut gain from risk reduction if costs were less than that amount.

Use of SES dummies instead of occupational dummies increases the point estimate of the risk variable to .0520, with virtually no change in its standard error. Going through the same argument as above implies a value of life of $260,000. Though the *t* statistic is larger in equation 2 than in equation 1 of Table 3, we are not prepared to accept equation 2 as a necessarily better specification because of some reservations on the meaning of the SES variable. Corresponding estimates in Table 4 evaluated at the sample mean wage range somewhat smaller than those in Table 3. Equation 1 of Table 4 implies a point estimate of $136,000 (= .000206 × 132 × 50 × 10^5), while equation 2 implies an estimate of $189,000 (= .000286 × 50 × 132 × 10^5). Further, standard errors of risk coefficients are slightly larger in Table 4. Nevertheless, the estimates lie in a reasonably narrow range of about $200,000 ± $60,000.

Equation 3 in Tables 3 and 4 shows the results of limited interactions between risk and some of the other characteristics. Limitations on sample size forced a simple cross-product specification, rather than separate regressions on corresponding data cells. Risk is crossed with age, union membership, marital status and race in equation 3. As explained earlier, cross-product terms do not reflect differences in indi-

The Value of Saving a Life 295

vidual's utility functions. Instead, they represent differences in the locus of opportunities available to them, due to differential ability to work in risky situations.

A. Age

To reiterate our example above, age is likely to cut two ways on risky jobs. Young workers lack caution and experience, but have superior reflexes and recuperative ability. Our hypothesis was that physical deterioration of skills would eventually dominate and the results seem to be consistent with it. The age-risk cross-product term is negative though not significant, and firms offer older workers smaller risk premiums than younger workers. Evidently younger workers are more productive in risky situations. However, the estimate may also reflect measurement error.[17]

B. Marital Status

There is also some evidence that marital status affects risk premiums. Of course, we expect married workers to have a higher supply price to risky jobs than nonmarried workers, because they have more dependents. Again, this should induce married workers to apply for less risky jobs, other things being equal, and not change the observed risk premium. The fact that marital status increases the risk premium must mean that when married workers do in fact take risky jobs they are more productive at working on them. Exactly how such differential productivity arises is difficult to say, though we conjecture that married workers might on the average be more careful and cautious than the nonmarried.

C. Unionism

Unionism also increases the risk premium. Here the market is restricted, and unions might collect their rents through higher risk premiums rather than by other means. It is possible that lack of free entry into these markets renders the typical union member more risk averse than would be true in free markets, forcing firms to pay higher risk premiums in order to entice unwilling union members to work on

[17] There is a possibility that the negative regression coefficient reflects measurement error. Older workers may be heavily weighted in the low risk end of each occupation and our risk measures may overstate the real risks they face. If $W(p)$ is truly increasing, earnings are lower for older workers appearing to work on riskier jobs in our data than they really do. We know age-specific extra-risk data must be available on the work sheets of the actuarial study because the published statistics have been age adjusted in the manner described above. Unfortunately, we were unable to obtain the raw data.

296 *Market and Nonmarket Aspects of Real Earnings*

the riskier jobs. Again, we cannot rule out the hypothesis that unionism and its resulting "industrial discipline" make workers more productive on risky jobs.

D. Race

The relationship between race and risk premiums is very complex. The white-risk cross-product term is negative (and not significant at conventional levels), but the results are not easy to interpret. For one thing, we know from other studies that nonwhites tend to be loaded in the low wage end of occupational job classifications. Notice again that the occupations in Table 1 may be too broadly defined for detecting racial differences. If nonwhites tend to be highly represented in the riskier subcategories of each classification, our risk index is measured erroneously for them. This in itself would tend to produce the result found in Tables 3 and 4 and cross-terms would reflect measurement error in the data. The coefficient suggests that nonwhites receive higher risk premiums than whites, but it may simply be the case that they work at even more risky jobs than our data say they do (again, assuming $W'(p) > 0$). Alternative hypotheses are also available. (1) Nonwhites may be better workers in risky situations than whites. For example, we know that a large fraction of structural iron workers are nonwhite, and it is said that these individuals have an unusual sense of balance compared to most people in the population. (2) There may be less discrimination against nonwhites in risky jobs than in less risky ones.

To get around possible measurement errors, we reran the regression excluding nonwhites from the sample. The result is shown by equation 4 in Table 3, and previous conclusions regarding other variables are hardly affected.[18]

CONCLUSION

We have estimated marginal valuations of safety for a select group of individuals in 1967. All qualifications surrounding our estimates have

---

[18] Computation of the marginal risk premium under the cross-product specification must be made at specific values of the interactive variables (age, race, and so on) because $W'(p)$ is then a function of those variables. A little experimentation with equations (3) and (4) of Tables 3 and 4 shows that the imputations vary a great deal, depending on the point in the sample at which they are made. Indeed, some of these imputations are actually negative (e.g., older white nonunion, nonmarried individuals), which may indicate an undesirable restriction of the functional form or measurement error and not necessarily a model defect. We have not imposed any nonnegative restrictions on the estimates. Further, the possibilities of measurement error extensively pointed out at several points in the text preclude too much massaging of the data. Hence, we regard the cross-product results as suggestive only.

The Value of Saving a Life   297

been given in the text and there is no need to repeat them here.[19] Certainly this study indicates feasibility of the method, the usual caveats about data quality notwithstanding. Are the estimates reasonable? We are unaware of similar studies with which to compare our results. However an example suggested by Bailey (1968) may be informative in this regard, and also illustrates how the estimates can be used.

The National Safety Council estimates that highway deaths would be reduced by about 10,000 per year if all automobile users wore lap safety belts. Assuming that the estimate is correct, seat belts reduce the probability of dying in an automobile accident from about 25 per hundred thousand (25×10^{-5}) per year to about 20 per hundred thousand per year (20×10^{-5}). Using the risk coefficient in equation 1 of Table 3 we estimate that the *average person in our sample* would be willing to pay *at least* \$8.80 per year (in 1967 dollars) for a seat belt for himself. The cost of seat belts includes not only the purchase price and installation costs, but also costs associated with use, including bother and time spent buckling and unbuckling, so that it is easily within the realm of possibility that decisions not to purchase seat belts prior to the law were rational. We can make some more back-of-the-envelope calculations. How much would the time and bother costs (of individuals in our sample) have to be to justify not using seat belts even after they are mandatory? The sample mean hourly wage was about \$3.50. Using that as an estimate of the value of time, time spent buckling and unbuckling would have to be about 2.5 hours per year to cost as much as \$8.80. Assuming 500 trips per year, this amounts to about 18 seconds per trip in time-equivalent costs of using seat belts, a much smaller number than Bailey assumed. We leave it to the reader to experiment with other possibilities.

REFERENCES

Bailey, M. J. "Comment on T. C. Schelling's Paper." In S. B. Chase, ed., *Problems in Public Expenditure*. Washington, D.C.: Brookings Institution, 1968.

Calabresi, G. *The Costs of Accidents: A Legal and Economic Analysis*. New Haven: Yale University Press, 1970.

Fromm, G. "Civil Aviation Expenditures." In R. Dorfman, ed., *Measuring Benefits of Government Investments*. Washington, D.C.: Brookings Institution, 1965.

Hirshleifer, J. "Investment Decision Under Uncertainty: Choice Theoretic Approaches." *Quarterly Journal of Economics* 79 (November 1965): 509–536.

Mishan, E. "Evaluation of Life and Limb: A Theoretical Approach." *Journal of Political Economy* 79 (July/August 1970): 687–705.

Oi, W. "An Essay on Workmen's Compensation and Industrial Safety." In *Supplemental Studies for the National Commission on State Workmen's Compensation Laws*, Vol. I, pp. 41–106, 1973.

[19] These issues are discussed in greater depth in Chapter 1 of Thaler (1974).

298   *Market and Nonmarket Aspects of Real Earnings*

Rosen, S. "Hedonic Prices and Implicit Markets: Product Differentiation in Pure Competition." *Journal of Political Economy* 82 (January/February 1974): 34–55.

Schelling, T. C. "The Life You Save May Be Your Own." In S. B. Chase, ed., *Problems in Public Expenditure*. Washington, D.C.: Brookings Institution, 1968.

Smith, R. S. "Compensating Wage Differentials and Hazardous Work," Technical Analysis Paper No. 5, Office of Evaluation, Department of Labor, August, 1973.

Thaler, R. "The Value of Saving a Life: A Market Estimate." Ph.D. dissertation, University of Rochester, 1974.

Usher, D. "An Imputation to the Measure of Economic Growth for Changes in Life Expectancy." In Milton Moss, ed., *The Measurement of Economic and Social Performance*. New York: NBER, 1973.

[11]

WEALTH EFFECTS AND EARNINGS PREMIUMS FOR JOB HAZARDS

W. Kip Viscusi*

I. Introduction

ADAM Smith (1937) observed that "the whole of the advantages and disadvantages of the different employments of labor and stock must, in the same neighborhood, be either perfectly equal or continually tending to equality." If a job poses health and safety risks that are especially great, a worker will require higher levels of compensation or greater non-pecuniary benefits in order for him to accept the risky job. Despite the fact that the theory of compensating differentials is almost two centuries old, it has been only recently that this theory has been subjected to successful empirical tests.[1]

The purposes of this essay are twofold. First, in section II, I will formalize the theory of individual choice among potentially hazardous jobs for the general situation in which worker preferences are contingent on the health state outcome. An important implication of this analysis is that the job risk that a worker selects will be negatively related to his wealth. The second purpose of the investigation is to test the two principal conceptual hypotheses. The characteristics of the principal data source to be used are summarized in section III. The University of Michigan Survey of Working Conditions, which is the data set used in the compensating differentials analysis, provides very extensive information concerning the nature of the worker's particular job and his personal characteristics. Section IV presents the analysis of the earnings differentials generated by job hazards and other job attributes. In section V, I consider the responsiveness of the job risk to a worker's wealth. The empirical findings, which are consistent with the theoretical predictions, are summarized in section VI.

II. Optimal Choice among Hazardous Job Alternatives

Recent economic analyses of choices among potentially hazardous jobs have generalized Adam Smith's notion of compensating wage differentials to probabilistic contexts. The study by Oi (1973) views adverse job consequences as being tantamount to a drop in income. He concludes that jobs posing greater risks will command compensating wage differentials. A more detailed analysis along similar lines is presented by Thaler and Rosen (1976), who develop Oi's approach and also consider the situation in which individuals face lotteries on life and death.[2] The payoff after an adverse outcome (death) is represented by a bequest function. The approach taken here also can be viewed as a probabilistic generalization of the compensating differential analysis. It differs in that individuals' utility functions are assumed to be dependent on one's health state. The static model in this section illustrates the properties of the optimal job choice of a worker who is choosing from a set of job opportunities that involve the same number of work hours but have differing probabilities of an adverse consequence.[3] This approach does not impose assumptions that are unduly restrictive since most job opportunities offer little individual leeway in the choice of hours.

Received for publication November 29, 1976. Revision accepted for publication May 20, 1977.

*Northwestern University.

Professors Kenneth Arrow, Richard Freeman, Richard Zeckhauser, and an anonymous referee provided helpful comments. The U.S. Department of Labor provided financial support. This essay is adapted from Viscusi (1976).

[1] The recent investigations by Smith (1976) and by Thaler and Rosen (1976) consider wage premiums for death risks faced by workers. An earlier study of skill differentials is that of Reder (1962).

[2] Thaler and Rosen (1976) also set up, but do not fully develop, a more general model in which there are N possible outcomes.

[3] Theoretically, there is little that can be said about a fully generalized multi-attribute case that does not represent a straightforward extension of this simple model. Perhaps the most important implication of a generalized model is that a worker should be cognizant of the entire portfolio of risky actions and should not make piecemeal decisions when strong interdependencies are involved.

WEALTH AND EARNINGS PREMIUMS FOR JOB HAZARDS   409

For simplicity, assume that there is no income uncertainty associated with any particular job. Although the wage rate is known, the health state resulting from one's activities is determined probabilistically. In this simple model, one's health does not affect one's earnings. Two health states will be considered. State 1 refers to good health, while state 2 refers to ill health, such as being injured. The individual's objective is to select the job that maximizes his expected utility.

This formulation of worker preferences permits the marginal utility of consumption (or alternatively of wealth) to differ according to one's health status. An alternative approach of using a conventional utility function that depends on wealth alone could be employed in the job injury context by viewing an injury as being tantamount to a drop in wealth. However, if utility functions are assumed to be of the usual concave form, this formulation would imply that the marginal utility of income is less when a person is healthy than when he is not.

The shortcomings of this approach become particularly apparent if actuarially fair income insurance is available. Workers will, of course, equate the marginal utility of income in the two possible states. In a model in which health and safety impacts have monetary equivalents, the absolute level of the individual's welfare will be identical irrespective of the job outcome. If, however, worker utility functions are allowed to vary according to the worker's health, such a result need not occur, as lower welfare levels for the unhealthy state may result.[4]

The notation to be used in analyzing the worker's choice problem is summarized below:

u^j = the utility function in health state j, where $j = 1, 2$;

x = the composite consumption good whose price equals one;

p = the probability of the unattractive state 2 occurring;

$w(p)$ = the wage for a job offering probability p of state 2 occurring;

A = initial assets;

λ = the shadow price of the goods constraint.

Letter subscripts on the u^j and w terms indicate partial derivatives. The u^j's and $w(p)$ functions are assumed to be continuous and twice differentiable. The wage schedule $w(p)$ represents the highest wage available for a job with probability p of injury.[5] The worker receives the same wage for his job irrespective of the actual health impact. The possibility of purchasing insurance has been excluded in the interest of analytic implicity.[6] It should be noted, however, that non-discretionary insurance benefits, such as workmen's compensation, are not omitted since the state-dependent utility functions encompass influences such as these.

Suppose that workers must select from a range of job alternatives that are equally attractive in terms of their time allocations but which offer different probabilities of unfavorable state 2 occurring. This range is assumed to be continuous and to span all values of p. The set of alternatives that must be considered can be restricted to the efficient set of jobs that offer the highest value of w for any value of p. The worker's optimal choice from among the market alternatives is determined by maximizing the Lagrangian given by

$$L = (1-p)u^1(x) + pu^2(x) + \lambda[x - A - w(p)].$$

The job with the optimal risk p is determined by solving the following first-order conditions for a maximum (as well as the budget constraint):

$$L_x = 0 = (1-p)u_x^1 + pu_x^2 + \lambda, \tag{1}$$

and

$$L_p = 0 = -u^1 + u^2 - \lambda w_p. \tag{2}$$

Solving for w_p produces the result

$$w_p = \frac{u^1 - u^2}{(1-p)u_x^1 + pu_x^2} > 0. \tag{3}$$

---

[4] If the marginal utility of consumption is lower in the injured state, as is plausible, workers faced with actuarially fair insurance possibilities will have a lower absolute welfare level in the injured state when the marginal utility of consumption is equated for the two states.

[5] For this static formulation, it does not matter whether p is uncertain or known with precision. The compensating differential results generalize with some modification to multiple periods and instances in which there is worker learning. See Viscusi (forthcoming).

[6] The analysis of the role of insurance is presented in Viscusi (1976).

410   THE REVIEW OF ECONOMICS AND STATISTICS

The necessary condition for an interior maximum is that a marginal increase in the wage as a result of the increased job risk be positive and equal to the difference in the two states' utilities divided by the expected marginal utility of consumption.[7] Thus the job market equilibrium function $w(p)$ is necessarily an increasing function of p if workers are employed at each level of p. Jobs with identical stochastic properties will be rewarded equally in equilibrium.[8] The positive sign of w_p is a result of the nature of the job choice problem. It is not an assumption. The derivation of this result did not require that workers be risk averters. The only key assumption required was that the good health state be more desirable than the ill health state.[9]

To assure that a solution to equation (3) is indeed a maximum, the second-order condition also must be fulfilled. In mathematical terms, the marginal rate of change of w_p with respect to further increases in p must be either negative

of consumption is diminishing (i.e., $u_{xx}^1 < 0$ and $u_{xx}^2 < 0$) and that the marginal utility of consumption is greater in the healthy state than in the injured state (i.e., $u_x^1 > u_x^2 > 0$).

This model can also be profitably applied to ascertain the influence of one's initial wealth on the level of job hazards one will select. The positive relationship between individual wealth and the attractiveness of the nonmonetary attributes of one's job has long been noted by labor market analysts, such as Reder (1962). This relationship was recently analyzed by Weiss (1976)' and Thaler and Rosen (1976). Results in a similar vein can be obtained under somewhat different assumptions within the context of the health state model of job choice.

To determine the relationship of one's assets to the optimal probability of injury, one can totally differentiate the first-order conditions (equations (1) and (2) and the budget constraint), and solve for dp/dA using Cramer's rule, producing the result that

$$\frac{dp}{dA} = \frac{-\left[(1-p)u_{xx}^1 + pu_{xx}^2\right]w_p - \left[u_x^2 - u_x^1\right]}{w_p^2\left[(1-p)u_{xx}^1 + pu_{xx}^2\right] + 2w_p\left[u_x^2 - u_x^1\right] + w_{pp}\left[pu_x^2 + (1-p)u_x^1\right]} \tag{5}$$

or positive, but not too large:

$$w_{pp} < \left\{ -(w_p)^2\left[(1-p)u_{xx}^1 + pu_{xx}^2\right] \right.$$
$$\left. -2w_p\left[u_x^2 - u_x^1\right]\right\}\left\{ pu_x^2 + (1-p)u_x^1\right\}^{-1}. \tag{4}$$

The right hand side of equation (4) is positive, assuming plausible restrictions on the utility function. In particular, I will assume throughout this section that the marginal utility

[7] Throughout the rest of this section, I will consider interior solutions only. The corner solutions are neither realistic nor analytically interesting.

[8] No attempt is made here to provide a detailed discussion of market equilibrium since doing so would duplicate Thaler and Rosen's (1976) analysis.

[9] If one uses a model with a single utility function (not conditional on one's health) in which job risk outcomes are viewed as monetary equivalents, w_p is positive so long as $u' > 0$ and the argument of u is greater when the worker is not injured on the job. This property is quite unrestrictive and implies nothing whatsoever about the risk aversion, or lack thereof, on the part of the worker. For this single-argument case, the worker is said to be risk-averse if $u'' < 0$. The second-order conditions for a maximum impose other restrictions, but do not require risk aversion. For simplicity, I will assume that the marginal utility of consumption is diminishing.

Since the numerator is clearly positive, the sign of dp/dA is the same as that of the denominator. Hazardous jobs will be an inferior occupational pursuit, as is plausible, if

$$w_p^2\left[(1-p)u_{xx}^1 + pu_{xx}^2\right] + 2w_p\left[u_x^2 - u_x^1\right]$$
$$+ w_{pp}\left[pu_x^2 + (1-p)u_x^1\right] < 0. \tag{6}$$

But if this equation is solved for w_{pp}, the condition reduces to equation (4)—the second-order condition for a maximum. Consequently, the extent of the job hazard one chooses necessarily decreases with one's wealth. The problem features guaranteeing this result are the requirements that the worker be at an interior maximum and that the utility function satisfy the seemingly mild restrictions specified in the discussion of the second-order conditions.

III. The Sample and the Variables

The data source for my investigation of compensating differentials is the 1969–70 University of Michigan Survey of Working

WEALTH AND EARNINGS PREMIUMS FOR JOB HAZARDS   411

TABLE 1.—GEOGRAPHICAL, INDUSTRIAL, AND
OCCUPATIONAL CHARACTERISTICS OF THE SUBSAMPLE

Variable	Fraction in the Sample[a]
Location:	
Northeast	.32
Southeast and South-Central	.21
Urban	.15
Industry:	
Mining	.03
Construction	.11
Manufacturing Durables	.31
Manufacturing Nondurables	.14
Transportation, Communication and Other Utilities	.08
Wholesale and Retail Trade	.13
Miscellaneous Services	.15
Public Administration	.05
Occupation:	
Craftsmen, Foremen and Kindred Workers	.34
Service Workers	.17
Private Household Workers	.01
Laborers	.05
Operatives and Kindred	.43

[a] The standard deviations of these variables are given by $(m - m^2)^{.5}$, where m is the fraction in the sample.

TABLE 2.—MEANS AND STANDARD DEVIATIONS OF
SELECTED VARIABLES IN THE BLUE COLLAR
SUBSAMPLE OF THE MICHIGAN SURVEY OF WORKING
CONDITIONS

Variable	Mean or Function in Sample	Standard Deviation
Personal Background:		
AGE	39.71	13.71
FEMALE	0.234	[a]
BLACK	0.123	[a]
EDUC	10.30	3.03
HEALTH	0.266	0.918
TENURE	9.09	10.03
Enterprise Characteristics:		
SIZE	562.2	915.3
UNION	0.492	[a]
Job Characteristics:		
EARNG	6809.9	2870.7
DANGER	0.522	[a]
INJRATE	15.93	9.26
SUPER	0.359	[a]

[a] The standard deviations of the 0-1 dummy variables are omitted since they can be computed from their function m in the sample, where the standard deviation is $(m - m^2)^{.5}$.

Conditions (SWC). The SWC, which provides the most detailed information available concerning the nature of the individual's job, was a national survey of 1,533 workers that was undertaken from December 1969 to January 1970. Farmers and self-employed workers were excluded from the subsample that I considered since they did not respond to the job characteristic questions. In addition, white collar workers were also excluded from the analysis since the job characteristic questions asked were inappropriate for this group.[10] There were 496 full-time blue collar workers in the subsample that was analyzed.

As the data in table 1 indicate, the subsample being considered reflects substantial geographical and occupational diversity. The 3 locational categories listed comprise the 0-1 dummy variable list *LOCATE*. In terms of industrial distribution, the sample is also fairly representative, as large numbers of manufacturing and service workers were included in the survey. The industrial breakdown given is at an aggregative level. For the empirical analysis, a finer categorization by SIC code for the worker's industry was used to construct a list of

25 0-1 dummy variables that I will refer to as *INDUSTRY*. Over three-fourths of the workers were either operatives or craftsmen, foremen, and kindred workers. The first 4 of these occupational categories were used to construct the 0-1 dummy variable list *JOB*.

The characteristics of the key variables used in the subsequent analysis are summarized in table 2. The personal characteristic information available is comparable to that found in several other large data sets. There is information pertaining to the worker's age (*AGE*), sex (*FEMALE*), race (*BLACK*), years of schooling (*EDUC*), health limitations (*HEALTH*), marital status (*SINGLE*), and years of experience with the enterprise (*TENURE*). Since the survey did not include the worker's hourly wage rate, I will use the annual earnings from the worker's principal job (*EARNG*) and the natural logarithm of this variable (*LOGEARNG*) as the two dependent variables of interest.[11]

Close to half of the workers are members of

[10] Results for the pooled blue collar and white collar sample are reported in Viscusi (1976).

[11] Differences in worker hours are not of great importance since I focus on full-time workers and include an overtime work variable. The absence of a weeks worked variable prevents the construction of a wage variable.

a union (*UNION*). Although this fraction is double the nationwide average for the work force as a whole, it does not appear disproportionately large for the blue collar, non-farm population.

The most distinctive feature of the data set is the extensive information pertaining to the worker's job: number of employees at the enterprise (*SIZE*), union membership (*UNION*), whether the worker is a supervisor (*SUPER*), whether the job requires that the employee work fast (*FAST*), whether the worker is not allowed to make decisions (*NODEC*), whether the job requires that the worker not make mistakes (*MISTK*), job security (*SECURITY*), overtime work (*OVERT*), and training program availability (*TRAIN*). These variables pertain to the worker's particular job, not broadly defined industrial and occupational groups. The availability of these job characteristic variables enables one to obtain estimates of job risk premiums that are not subject to the severe omitted variables bias that might be present if one included no other job attributes in the analysis.

The self-assessed danger variable (*DANGER*) also pertains to the individual's particular job. This job risk measure is the dummy variable for whether or not the worker's job exposes him to dangerous or unhealthy conditions. As indicated in table 2, just over half of the workers considered their jobs to be hazardous—a result that casts doubt on the common assumption that workers systematically under-assess job risks. Detailed examination of the hazards cited revealed that the risks are consistent with the individual's particular job. For example, temperature and humidity extremes are cited by a truck driver for a canning company, inadequate shoring is listed by a construction worker, and slippery floors and footing are cited by a manufacturing worker in the plastic products industry. Experimentation with variables pertaining to the number or type of hazards cited by the worker did not yield results superior to the *DANGER* variable.

The principal advantage of this variable is that it is not an objective index but rather the subjective assessment of the risk, the magnitude that motivates individual behavior. To the

extent that *DANGER* pertains to the individual's particular job, it is likely to be subject to less measurement error than would an average risk figure for the worker's industry or occupation. The principal limitation of the variable is that it does not reflect the differing severities and likelihoods of the hazards faced. Ideally, one would like the subjective probability assessments for a variety of health state outcomes, not a 0-1 dummy variable pertaining to the presence of hazards.

An alternative job hazard measure *INJRATE* will also be employed. This variable is the number of disabling injuries per million hours worked in 1969 for the worker's 3-digit (SIC code) industry.[12] The industrial mix of the workers appears representative since the mean value of *INJRATE* is 15.93, which is slightly greater than the manufacturing average of 14.8 but is less than nonmanufacturing injury rate levels, such as the 18.4 average for transportation and public utilities.

The relationship between *DANGER* and *INJRATE* is summarized in table 3. The last column of the table lists the fraction of workers in each *INJRATE* interval who consider their jobs dangerous. As expected, there is a strong positive relationship between the industry injury rate and the self-assessed danger variable. The failure of the *DANGER* fraction to be a strictly increasing function of *INJRATE* throughout may be attributable to the fact that *INJRATE* pertains to the average hazard for the worker's industry group, not the risk posed by his particular job. Moreover, *INJRATE* reflects primarily safety hazards since health risks are not captured in the BLS

TABLE 3.—DANGER ASSESSMENTS AND THE INJURY RATE FOR THE WORKER'S INDUSTRY

		DANGER = 1	
INJRATE (IR)	Fraction	Fraction	Column 3 / Column 2
$0 < IR < 5$	.504	.120	.237
$5 < IR < 10$	.178	.076	.426
$10 < IR < 15$	.076	.036	.472
$15 < IR < 20$	.077	.041	.534
$20 < IR < 25$	.062	.042	.678
$25 < IR < 30$	.070	.046	.657
$30 < IR < 35$	.012	.007	.636
$35 < IR < 40$	.015	.009	.600
$40 < IR$	.005	.005	1.00

[12] The source of this variable is the U.S. Bureau of Labor Statistics (BLS) (1972).

WEALTH AND EARNINGS PREMIUMS FOR JOB HAZARDS   413

statistics. In contrast, the hazards included in *DANGER* are divided roughly evenly between health hazards (e.g., noise and noxious fumes) and safety hazards (e.g., slippery staircases).

IV. An Assessment of Compensating Earnings Differentials

Recent analyses by Thaler and Rosen (1976) and by Smith (1976) have indicated that workers in occupations and industries with higher death rates receive additional wage compensation.[13] The evidence in this section provides complementary findings for the two job risk variables *DANGER* and *INJRATE* in equations in which several other job characteristic variables are included in order to distinguish the influence of job risks per se, rather than job characteristics correlated with riskiness.

The two forms of equations to be estimated are

$$EARNG = \alpha + \sum_{k=1}^{m} \beta_k X_k + u,$$

and

$$LOGEARNG = \alpha' + \sum_{k=1}^{m} \beta_k' X_k + u',$$

where α and α' are constant terms, β_k and β_k' are coefficients, the X_k's are worker characteristics and job characteristics, and u and u' are error terms.[14] The linear form of the earnings equation implies a constant supply price per job characteristic unit, while the

[13] Smith (1976) utilized the death risk component of the *INJRATE* variable used here. His efforts to find positive and statistically significant wage effects for other variants of the BLS injury rate variable were unsuccessful. Thaler and Rosen (1976) employed the incremental death risk incurred by individuals in relatively hazardous occupations. As Lipsey (1976) noted, this variable compounds occupational risks and risks correlated with the personal characteristics of individuals in particular occupations. No job risk variable, including *DANGER* and *INJRATE*, is ideal. Each has its own relative strengths and weaknesses. What is clear is that the similarity in the compensating differential results for each of these variables lends strong support to Adam Smith's claim that more hazardous jobs will command premiums in the labor market.

[14] The earnings equation can be viewed as part of a larger recursive system. An attempt was made to estimate the simultaneous relationship between earnings and job hazards using two-stage least squares. The results were consistent with the recursive formulation. See Viscusi (1976).

semi-logarithmic form implies a rising supply price per characteristic unit. The procedure of viewing worker earnings as being dependent on the attributes of his job in effect involves the estimation of a hedonic earnings function, which is econometrically similar to the hedonic price index analysis.[15]

The regression results are reported in table 4. Equations (1) and (3) include *DANGER* in the *EARNG* and *LOGEARNG* regressions, respectively, while equations (2) and (4) include the objective hazard index *INJRATE*. Equations (2) and (4) omit the industry dummy variable list since *INJRATE* is the industry injury rate matched to the workers in the sample using their industry responses.

The coefficients for the first ten variables in the equations, which represent personal and enterprise characteristics, reflect familiar patterns of influence. Better educated workers earn more, as do those who belong to a union. Females and workers with health impairments earn less. The magnitudes of the effects often are less than are usually found since much of the impact of these exogenous variables is indirect via the job characteristic variables, such as whether the worker is a supervisor.[16]

The two job risk variables each reflect positive and statistically significant earnings premiums for hazardous work.[17] The results in equation (1) indicate that workers on jobs perceived as being dangerous earn an annual earnings premium of $375. Although this amount represents only 5.5% of workers' mean earnings of $6,810, the low level of compensation is not implausible in view of the large percentage of workers (52.2%) who claim that their jobs expose them to dangerous or unhealthy conditions.

An instructive check on the plausibility of the level of the job risk premium is to compare its magnitude with the average premium implied by *INJRATE*. Equation (2) indicates that workers receive an additional $26 for a one point increase in the frequency of disabling

[15] For a survey of the hedonic price index literature, see Griliches (1971).
[16] The reduced form estimates are more comparable to the results in the human capital literature.
[17] Throughout this analysis, references to statistical significance refer to tests at the 5% level. The value of $t_{.95}$ for a one-tailed t-test with an infinite sample size is 1.645.

THE REVIEW OF ECONOMICS AND STATISTICS

TABLE 4.—*EARNG* AND *LOGEARNG* REGRESSION RESULTS

Independent Variables	Coefficients and Standard Errors			
	EARNG		*LOGEARNG*	
	1	2	3	4
AGE	+138.22 (45.50)	+163.74 (44.40)	+.025 (.0072)	+.030 (.0070)
AGE × AGE	−1.63 (0.53)	−1.96 (0.51)	−.28E−3 (.083E−3)	−.34E−3 (.082E−3)
FEMALE	−2585.9 (278.9)	−2809.3 (244.8)	−.507 (.044)	−.534 (.039)
BLACK	−382.38 (276.19)	−429.00 (269.54)	−.063 (.044)	−.067 (.043)
EDUC	+128.84 (33.34)	+136.14 (32.76)	+.024 (.0053)	+.025 (.0052)
HEALTH	−194.91 (93.88)	−168.92 (93.14)	−.019 (.015)	−.017 (.015)
SINGLE	−1088.6 (343.9)	−981.16 (328.75)	−.231 (.054)	−.210 (.052)
SIZE	+0.233 (0.119)	+0.305 (0.104)	+.25E−4 (.19E−4)	+.38E−4 (.16E−4)
UNION	+543.07 (206.88)	+645.05 (196.53)	+.109 (.033)	+.113 (.031)
TENURE	+12.40 (11.28)	+6.25 (10.87)	−.13E−3 (1.78E−3)	−.0015 (.0017)
DANGER	+374.82 (177.67)	— —	+.055 (.028)	—
INJRATE	— —	+26.37 (10.14)	—	+.0040 (.0016)
SUPER	+372.24 (193.89)	+414.69 (191.43)	+.032 (.031)	+.043 (.030)
FAST	+519.54 (189.64)	+460.82 (184.22)	+.072 (.030)	+.063 (.029)
NODEC	−121.78 (83.85)	−146.67 (82.38)	−.016 (.013)	−.021 (.013)
MISTK	−127.91 (85.31)	−140.29 (82.79)	−.023 (.013)	−.027 (.013)
SECURITY	+521.27 (177.90)	+496.28 (172.06)	+.093 (.028)	+.097 (.027)
OVERT	+170.12 (67.41)	+191.76 (64.66)	+.032 (.011)	+.037 (.010)
TRAIN	+362.08 (201.14)	+519.59 (193.27)	+.059 (.032)	+.099 (.031)
Other Variables	LIST1	LIST2	LIST1	LIST2
R^2	.641	.611	.698	.669
S.E.E.	1813.5	1836.6	.286	.291

Note: Each equation also includes the variable lists *LOCATE* and *JOB*. Equations (1) and (3) also include industry dummy variable list *INDUSTRY*, which is omitted from the equations including *INJRATE* since this job risk index was constructed using information regarding the worker's industry.

WEALTH AND EARNINGS PREMIUMS FOR JOB HAZARDS   415

work injuries per million hours worked. Since the average value of *INJRATE* is 15.93, the mean level of annual earnings compensation for injuries is $420. This amount is only $45 more than was implied by the *DANGER* variable—a discrepancy that is well within the bounds of error. Both job hazard variables indicate an average level of compensation for risky jobs of about $400 annually in 1969.

The other job characteristic variables included in the regressions serve two functions. First, they control for a variety of job attributes, thus reducing the bias in the job hazard variables' coefficients. Second, they provide additional tests of the validity of the theory of compensating differentials.

The coefficients associated with these variables reflect the expected patterns of influence. Supervisors (*SUPER*) are paid more, as are employees whose jobs require them to work fast (*FAST*), who work overtime (*OVERT*), or who work for enterprises with training programs (*TRAIN*). Workers who do not make decisions (*NODEC*) and whose jobs require them not to make mistakes (*MISTK*) tend to be paid somewhat less, which is consistent with the lighter tasks and lower level assembly line work associated with these characteristics. The only variable with a sign opposite of what one might expect on the basis of the compensating differentials analysis is *SECURITY*. However, the higher earnings of individuals with job security is quite consistent with the greater security associated with upper level blue collar positions. This variable thus may be capturing primarily the relative ranking of the worker's job rather than any particular job attribute that is not appropriately compensated.

V. The Role of Worker Assets

The second major prediction of the conceptual analysis is that the optimal job risk will necessarily decrease with the worker's wealth, provided that certain mild restrictions on the worker's preferences and employment opportunities are imposed. The validity of this result cannot be tested using the SWC data since the survey did not include a worker wealth variable. One can, however, use the 1969 data from the National Longitudinal Survey of

Mature Men in conjunction with the 1969 BLS industry injury rates to ascertain whether there is any systematic relationship between the injury rate of the worker's industry and his wealth.

The sample to be considered consists of 1,932 males who were 45–59 years old when the survey began in 1966 and had a mean age of 53.7 in 1969. The dependent variable for the analysis is *INJRATE*. The independent variables used either have the same definitions as do the SWC variables (*AGE, EDUC*) or else are self-explanatory (*NONWHITE*). The explanatory variable of greatest interest is *ASSETS*, which is the worker's net asset position. *ASSETS* has a mean value of $21,717.

Table 5 reports the regression results. *ASSETS* has a statistically significant coefficient with the expected sign. The magnitude of the effect is rather small, however, since these results imply that the elasticity of the industry injury frequency rate with respect to worker wealth is only -0.011. This finding is likely to understate the wealth effect since it captures the influence of wealth only on the worker's choice of an industry. One might expect that much of the wealth effect would be reflected in the individual's occupation or particular job within the industry. It should be noted that the direction rather than the magnitude of the impact is of central concern since the negative elasticity estimate provides additional support of the validity of the overall conceptualization of individual choice.

TABLE 5.—REGRESSION OF *INJRATE* ON *ASSETS* AND OTHER PERTINENT VARIABLES

AGE	-0.018 (0.052)
NONWHITE	-1.38 (0.499)
EDUC	-0.629 (0.063)
ASSETS	$-0.81E-5$ (0.38E-5)
R^2	0.090
S.E.E.	8.91
F	15.83

Note: Other variables included were an area unemployment variable, 3 regional dummies, 1 SMSA dummy, union membership, and health status. The sample size was 1,932.

416   THE REVIEW OF ECONOMICS AND STATISTICS

VI. Conclusions

The conceptual analysis of individual choice among potentially hazardous jobs indicated that the optimal job risk for a worker should be negatively related to his wealth and that workers will demand earnings premiums for hazardous jobs—a result originally articulated by Adam Smith. The empirical analysis provided strong support for these conceptual results. The annual earnings premium for job hazards averaged $400 in 1969. This value is not particularly low in view of the large number of workers who viewed their jobs as being hazardous. The injury rate for an employee's industry also was negatively related to worker assets, although the effect was not as large as one would expect if more appropriate data were available to evaluate the magnitude of this relationship.

REFERENCES

Griliches, Zvi (ed.), *Price Indexes and Quality Change* (Cambridge: Harvard University Press, 1971).

Lipsey, Robert, "Comments on the Value of Saving a Life: Evidence from the Labor Market," in N. Terleckyz (ed.), *Household Production and Consumption*, NBER Studies in Income and Wealth no. 40 (New York: Columbia University Press, 1976), 301–302.

Oi, Walter, "An Essay on Workmen's Compensation and Industrial Safety," in *Supplemental Studies for the National Commission on State Workmen's Compensation Laws* (Washington, D.C.: U.S. Government Printing Office, 1973), 41–106.

Reder, Melvin, "Wage Differentials: Theory and Measurement," in *Aspects of Labor Economics* (Princeton: Princeton University Press, 1962), 257–311.

Smith, Adam, *The Wealth of Nations* (New York: Modern Library, 1937).

Smith, Robert, *The Occupational Safety and Health Act: Its Goals and Its Achievements* (Washington, D.C.: American Enterprise Institute, 1976).

Thaler, Richard, and Sherwin Rosen, "The Value of Saving a Life: Evidence from the Labor Market," in N. Terleckyz (ed.), *Household Production and Consumption*, NBER Studies in Income and Wealth no. 40 (New York: Columbia University Press, 1976), 265–298.

U.S. Bureau of Labor Statistics, *Handbook of Labor Statistics* (Washington, D.C.: U.S. Government Printing Office, 1972).

University of Michigan Institute for Social Research, *Survey of Working Conditions*, SRC Study no. 45369 (Ann Arbor: University of Michigan Social Science Archives, 1975).

Viscusi, W. Kip, *Employment Hazards: An Investigation of Market Performance*, Ph.D. dissertation, Harvard University, 1976.

———, "Job Hazards and Worker Quit Rates: An Analysis of Adaptive Worker Behavior," *International Economic Review* (forthcoming).

Weiss, Yoram, "The Wealth Effect in Occupational Choice," *International Economic Review* 17 (June 1976), 292–307.

[12]

Journal of Risk and Uncertainty 75-90 (1991)
© 1991 Kluwer Academic Publishers

Compensating Wage Differentials for Fatal Injury Risk in Australia, Japan, and the United States

THOMAS J. KNIESNER
Indiana University, Bloomington 47405, Department of Economics, Ballantine Hall (901)

JOHN D. LEETH
Bentley College, Department of Economics

Key words: hedonic equilibrium, compensating wage differentials, workers' compensation insurance

Abstract

Our research infers the effects of institutionalized wage setting and lengthy worker-firm attachment by comparing estimated compensating wage differentials for fatal injury risk in Japanese, Australian, and U.S. manufacturing. Hedonic labor market equilibrium regressions for Japan reveal a statistically fragile compensating wage differential of 0% to 1.4% for exposure to the average fatality risk compared to employment in a perfectly safe workplace. Australian workers receive a statistically robust 2.5% estimated wage premium. Using new data on work-related fatalities, we find a 1% compensating wage differential in U.S. manufacturing that becomes more positive and statistically less significant as data are aggregated.

Policymakers are reluctant to use estimated compensating wage differentials for health risks in designing programs to reduce environmental hazards or encourage workplace safety because the estimates vary widely (Viscusi, 1983, Chapter 6; Moore and Viscusi, 1988). Researchers have tried to understand the divergence across studies of compensating wage differentials and the implied value of a worker's life by focusing on parameter robustness to changes in functional form and risk measures using data for a single country's labor markets (Dillingham, 1985; Marin and Psacharopoulos, 1982; Leigh and Folsom, 1984; Moore and Viscusi, 1988; Olson, 1981). We take another tack and examine three countries' labor markets, each one having a feature likely to influence compensating wage differentials. In particular, by comparing estimated hedonic labor

The authors gratefully acknowledge the helpful comments of Richard J. Butler, Robert Gregory, Anthony D. Hall, Lawrence Kenny, Alan Kruger, Bruce Meyer, Haruo Shimada, W. Kip Viscusi, members of the Keio Economic Observatory, and an anonymous referee. Financial support has been provided by Keio University, where Professor Kniesner was Visiting Scholar, by The Australian National University, where Professor Kniesner was a Visiting Fellow, by The National Council of Compensation Insurance, and by The Institute for Research and Faculty Development, Bentley College. Thanks for expert typing assistance go to Dawn Holt. Research described here was present at the National Council on Compensation Insurance's Ninth Annual Seminar, "Economic Issues in Workers' Compensation," held at The Wharton School, University of Pennsylvania, November 1989.

market equilibrium equations for Australia, Japan, and United States, we clarify the effects of institutionalized wage setting, lengthy worker–firm attachment, and data aggregation on compensating wage differentials for fatal-injury risk.

Union workers in the United States earn a larger premium for exposure to workplace hazards than similar nonunion workerss (Thaler and Rosen, 1975). The effect of unionization on the compensating wage differential may reflect unions' concern with workplace safety or a larger proportion of union workers in high-risk industries. If unions negotiate contracts with workplace hazards in mind, then a highly unionized country, such as Australia, would have a higher estimated wage premium for injury risk than the United States. Alternatively, if union workers are just overrepresented in high-risk industries in the United States, then Australia, with its more equal unionization across industries, would have a lower wage premium for injury risk.

U.S. workers are rewarded for the type of job performed, and interfirm mobility and occupational identification contribute to a positive relationship between wages and the likelihood of a work-related injury or disease. The Japanese economy rewards workers for long-term attachment, since larger employers use internal labor markets and life-cycle measures, including age or years of service, to allocate training and promotion opportunities. Workers in the larger Japanese firms are also less tied to a particular occupation and more tied to a specific firm than workers in the United States, so a wage premium for workplace health hazards may not exist in Japan.

The extensive union and government involvement in wage setting in Australia and the relatively low interfirm worker mobility in Japan make us expect a higher compensating wage differential in Australia and a smaller compensating wage differential for injury risk in Japan than in the United States. Single-equation estimates of the hedonic equilibrium wage locus for two-digit manufacturing in Australia, Japan, and the United States yield the anticipated ranking of compensating wage differences.

The larger Japanese manufacturing firms pay higher wages and have safer workplaces; there is little econometric evidence of a positive relationship between wages and the rate of fatal injuries across two-digit manufacturing industries in Japan. The aggregate manufacturing data for Australia permit a more extensive list of independent variables including the ability to control for the effects of interstate differences in workers' compensation generosity and interindustry differences in firm size. We find that Australian manufacturing workers exposed to the mean fatality risk earn 2.5% higher wages than Australian workers will earn in a completely safe industrial setting. The 2.5% estimated compensating wage differential in Australia is robust to changes in the list of independent variables and estimation technique.

The U.S. Current Population Survey data are richer than the aggregate Australian and Japanese data in a number of ways—more independent variables and a larger sample size with potential for disaggregation—and can be matched to new measures of job-related injury risk produced by the National Institute for Occupational Safety and Health. We find a statistically significant 1% compensating wage differential for exposure to mean fatality risk in the individual manufacturing data. The estimated compensating wage differential in manufacturing rises, but loses statistical significance, with aggregation to states, regions, and the United States overall. A final benefit of the U.S.

data is the spacial variability of potential workers' compensation insurance payments. Our econometric results imply that the insurance for injuries implicit in compensating wage differentials trades off against formal insurance in the form of workers' compensation. We estimate that the U.S. workers' compensation system as it now exists lowers the compensation for exposure to the mean fatality risk in manufacturing from 11% to 1%.

1. Theoretical background

Our empirical research rests on the theory of compensating wage differentials in long-run labor market equilibrium. The eventual sorting of workers and firms in the labor market creates an equilibrium locus of joint wage–workplace safety outcomes conditioned by the characteristics of suppliers of labor, the characteristics of the demanders of labor, and elements of the institutional and legal environment. Although workers may not have enough information when initially accepting employment to establish compensating differentials for work-related health hazards, they eventually learn the true risks and create compensating differentials in a competitive environment through interfirm mobility (Viscusi, 1979). Worker mobility is not necessary for compensating wage differentials to exist, though, because the government or a union can formalize higher pay for workers with more hazardous jobs.

By reducing the monetary loss from a workplace injury, workers' compensation insurance lowers the pay premium necessary for workers to accept workplace health hazards. Interstate variation in available benefits creates additional variation in compensating wage differentials. The Japanese workers' compensation insurance system is a national program with uniform benefits across prefectures (Williams, 1985, 1988). In the cases of Australia and the United States, we emulate researchers who have accounted for differences in the workers' compensation system across states by including a potential generosity measure when estimating compensation for exposure to work-related health hazards (Viscusi and Moore, 1987; Moore and Viscusi, 1988).

For some issues, researchers must uncover the structural equations underlying hedonic equilibrium—employer cost curves and worker indifference curves. Recent research establishes the stringent identifying restrictions needed to estimate the supporting indifference and cost curves in hedonic equilibrium models (Brown and Rosen, 1982; Epple, 1987). Alternatively, a researcher can simulate the complete model over a set of structural equation parameter values, including parameters representing public policy influencing job safety (Kniesner and Leeth, 1988, 1989a, 1989b). The issues we address need only econometric estimates of the hedonic locus, which is a reduced-form equation estimable with single-equation methods.

Hedonic labor market equilibrium is described algebraically by

$$\ln W = f(I \mid S, D, WC, \epsilon), \tag{1}$$

where W is the wage rate and I is a vector of information concerning the likelihood of a work-related injury. The variables conditioning the equilibrium level of wages and the compensating wage differential, $\partial \ln W/\partial I$, include characteristics of the sellers of labor (S), characteristics of the buyers of labor (D), and characteristics of the workers' compensation system (WC). Note that we have included a stochastic error term (ϵ) to emphasize that the hedonic equilibrium relationship is inexact; we have also written the hedonic equilibrium in semilogarithmic form, the most popular specification in econometric research.

Estimates of the hedonic labor market equilibrium locus for the United States using the Bureau of Labor Statistics' fatality rate measures and micro-cross-section data on wages and worker–firm characteristics show a 2% to 4% annual wage premium on jobs with the mean risk of a fatal work-related injury compared to jobs with zero risk (Smith, 1979; Viscusi 1983, Chapter 6). The estimated compensating differential is reduced by potential workers' compensation payments (Viscusi and Moore, 1987). Our research uses manufacturing data to estimate compensating wage differentials and how they are affected by potential workers' compensation payments. We selected Australia and Japan to compare to the United States because they have labor market features that interest U.S. economists and policymakers.

The Japanese worker in a large firm gets more on-the-job training than the typical U.S. worker, which contributes to Japan's higher rate of economic growth (Mincer and Higuchi, 1988). A feature of the Japanese economy receiving less attention is the comparatively low worker interfirm mobility supporting the comparatively high on-the-job training accumulation. Postwar monthly worker separation rates are two to three times higher in U.S. manufacturing than in Japanese manufacturing (Mincer and Higuchi, 1988). Because worker mobility helps establish compensating differentials for workplace risks, we expect the estimated value of $\partial \ln W/\partial I$ to be smaller in Japan than in the United States.

The Australian labor market interests economist and policymakers because of its highly institutionalized wage-setting process involving both unions and government. There is a channel in Australia for establishing formal salary supplements, known as dirt pay, for exposure to unpleasant or dangerous working conditions (Brooks, 1988; Jones, 1988). Evidence from the United States indicates a larger premium for workplace hazards in the union sector, which can reflect unions' concerns with workplace health and safety issues or overrepresentation of union workers in riskier U.S. industries. The estimated hedonic wage locus for Australia, with its more uniform unionization and highly institutionalized wage setting across industries, should clarify the effect of unions on compensating wage differentials. Specifically, comparing the relative steepness of the estimated hedonic loci in Australia and the United States may help us distinguish between competing interpretations of the effect of unions on compensating wage differentials for injury risk.

The final step of our econometric work will be to estimate the hedonic locus for U.S. manufacturing. We produce our own estimates because we want to compute compensating wage differentials with a new fatality rate measure and to identify the effect of aggregation on compensating wage differences. Our Australian and Japanese data are aggregate two-digit manufacturing cross sections, whereas our U.S. data are a cross section of individuals from the Current Population Survey. Comparing the regression results using individual U.S. data with results from the U.S. data aggregated to mimic the Australian

COMPENSATING WAGE DIFFERENTIALS FOR FATAL INJURY RISK   79

and Japanese data should clarify the econometric effects of aggregation and suggest how estimated compensating wage differentials might change in Japan and Australia were they also estimated with individual data.

2. Empirical results—Japan

Because production levels affect injury rates and the equilibrium tradeoff between wages and injury risk, we have selected years for Australia, Japan, and the United States that are neither the troughs nor the peaks of business cycles. Regressions for Japan use public-use cross-section data, which cover firms with at least 30 employees in the 21 two-digit manufacturing industries in 1986 (*Yearbook of Labour Statistics, 1986*). Japan was experiencing a slight economic slowdown in 1986. Although the unemployment rate was unchanged from the year before, real GNP growth was lower, 2.4% in 1986 versus 4.9% in 1985. Inflation fell to 0.6% in 1986 from 2.0% in 1985, and the annual growth rate of nominal earnings in manufacturing fell to 2% in 1986 from 4% in 1985 (*Yearbook of Labour Statistics, 1986*).

Summary statistics for all regression variables appear in table 1. The dependent variable in all Japanese regressions is the logarithm of average monthly earnings, which averages about 300,000 yen or $1800.[1] The few independent variables available to represent the underlying conditioning characteristics of workers and firms in the two-digit industry public-use data for Japan are sex composition of the labor force, hiring and separation rates, and industry size. The *Yearbook of Labour Statistics* is richer in measures of workplace health hazards; it contains the rates of injuries overall, fatalities, permanent total disabilities, and temporary total disabilities. Work-related injuries are less frequent in Japan than in the United States. Based on Bureau of Labor Statistics data, the 1986 fatality rate in the United States is 1 per 10,000 manufacturing workers versus 0.3 per 10,000 manufacturing workers in Japan.

Table 2 reports weighted least squares estimates using the inverse of industry employment to adjust for heteroskedasticity.[2] The first two lines are bivarate regressions between injury rates and wages, which establish a baseline. Although wages vary inversely with both the overall injury rate and the fatality rate, only the coefficient of the injury rate is statistically significant at the 0.1 level. When independent variables are added to control the effects of sex composition, new hires, and separations on wages, the coefficient of the overall injury rate changes little. When both the overall injury rate and the fatality rate appear in the regression (table 2, line 4), the coefficient of the fatality rate is positive and significant at the 10% level using a one-tail test. The fatality rate regression coefficient indicates that workers exposed to the average Japanese manufacturing fatality rate receive 0% to 1.4% higher pay than they would in a perfectly safe Japanese manufacturing industry.

We conclude that the compensating wage differential is at most 1.4% in the two-digit Japanese manufacturing data because the coefficient of the fatality rate is fragile. The fatality-rate coefficient becomes negative and insignificant if we alter the measures of the hiring and separation rates, delete the overall injury rate from the regression, or use

Table 1. Summary statistics

Country/Variable	Mean	Standard deviation	Max.	Min.
Japan 1986, N = 20				
Injury rate				
(per 100 workers)	0.411	0.275	1.232	0.084
Fatality rate				
(per 100 workers)	0.0032	0.0046	0.018	0.0
Proportion female				
production workers	0.230	0.177	0.709	0.0
New hire rate (per 100 per mo.)	1.625	1.057	5.243	0.434
Separation rate	1.764	1.036	5.387	0.667
Earnings (yen/mo)	306993	72973	460355	165864
Australia 1984–1985 N = 44				
Injury rate				
(per 100 workers)	8.13	5.28	21.7	2.7
Fatality rate				
(per 100 workers)	0.014	0.022	0.12	0.0
WC benefit				
(death, $A)	49433	4265	52993	42390
Employees per firm	50.4	42.7	204.5	17.1
Proportion female	0.24	0.16	0.73	0.06
Change in inventories				
($A million)	82.1	117.1	559.3	− 47.3
Materials purchases				
($A million)	3773.6	4861.6	19955.9	448.2
Value added				
($A million)	2114.9	2087.1	9569.6	483.6
Investment	197.3	390.6	2532.5	18.6
Earnings ($A/year)	18467	2963	24630	12278
U.S.A. 1978, N = 8868				
Injury rate				
(lost workday accidents				
per 100 workers)	5.46	2.32	11.1	2.2
Fatality rate				
(per 100 workers)	0.0436	0.044	0.621	0
WC benefit				
(death, max. per				
week, spouse)	168.27	67.51	654	88
Limit				
(on death benefit)	0.51	—	—	—
WCbenefit*limit	82.58	94.11	330	0
Nonwhite	0.12	—	—	—
Female	0.32	—	—	—
Union	0.36	—	—	—
New hire rate				
(avg. per mo. per 100)	3.05	1.08	5.3	1.4
Separation rate	3.85	1.52	7.7	1.7
Age	37.10	12.59	74.0	15.0
Education				
(years completed)	11.65	2.73	18.0	0.0
Married	0.75	—	—	—
Earnings ($/week)	256.27	133.74	999.0	70.0

continued overleaf

COMPENSATING WAGE DIFFERENTIALS FOR FATAL INJURY RISK   81

Table 2. Compensating wage differentials in Japan and Australia

Country	Injury/Workers' comp. measures	Coefficient	P-value	Other independent variables	adj R^2
(1) Japan[a]	Injury rate	−0.520	0.0061	—	0.31
(2) Japan[a]	Fatality rate	−20.576	0.0556	—	0.14
(3) Japan[a]	Injury rate	−0.273[b]	0.0001	d	0.88
(4) Japan[a]	Injury rate	−0.325[b]	0.0001		
	Fatality rate	4.422[c]	0.1047	d	0.97
(5) Australia[e]	Injury rate	−0.0005	0.9112	—	−0.02
(6) Australia[e]	Fatality rate	2.1189	0.0611	—	0.06
(7) Australia[e]	Injury rate	−0.0058	0.0640		
	Fatality rate	1.8108	0.0290	f	0.65
(8) Australia[e]	Injury rate	0.0004	0.894		
	Fatality rate	1.729	0.0178		
	WC benefit	0.000014	0.0015	f	0.74
(9) Australia[e]	Injury rate	0.00063	0.8467		
	Fatality rate	10.6851	0.3373		
	WC benefit	0.000016	0.0031		
	Fatality rate * WC benefit	−0.00018	0.4194	f	0.73

[a]Dependent variable: log average monthly earnings in 1968, $N = 20$. Weighted least squares with (1/total employment) as weights.
[b]Changes little with alternative measures of separations and new hires or when estimated via ordinary least squares.
[c]Fatality rate coefficient goes to zero with changes in measures of separations and new hires or using ordinary least squares. Equals −8.199 with a P-value of 0.065 when injury rate is omitted and ordinary least squares used.
[d]Proportion of female production workers, new hire rate, and separation rate.
[e]Dependent variable: log annual earnings in 1984–1985, $N = 44$.
[f]Employees per firm, proportion women, change in inventories, materials purchased, value added, and investment.

ordinary least squares instead of weighted least squares as the estimation technique.[3] In addition, the coefficient of the overall injury rate is significantly negative in all regressions, which we interpret as indicating model misspecification. Specifically, the largest Japanese manufacturing firms have the lowest injury rates and pay the highest wages. Recent evidence from the United States emphasizes a firm-size effect on wages (Brown and Medoff, 1989). A defect in the regressions for Japan is our inability to hold firm size constant, which can create a negative omitted variable bias on the coefficients of the injury rates. We therefore caution against using public-use data on two-digit Japanese manufacturing industries in future research on wages.

3. Empirical results—Australia

In conjunction with the Australian Bureau of Statistics, each state publishes *Industrial Accidents* and *Manufacturing Establishments,* which provide the data for our Australian hedonic labor market equilibrium regressions. We study the 11 two-digit manufacturing industries in the four largest Australian states in 1984–1985. The states in our data—New South Wales, Victoria, Queensland, and South Australia—contain 90% of Australian manufacturing workers.[4]

Although the Australian economy was stagnating during the mid-1980s, there was an uptick during 1985. The unemployment rate declined to 7.9% from 8.3% in 1984, the inflation rate increased to 6% from 4.5% in 1984, and annual real GNP growth rate was the same in 1984 and 1985 (*Yearbook Australia 1988* and *Labour Statistics Australia 1986*).

Summary statistics of the variables in our Australian regressions also appear in table 1. The dependent variable is the logarithm of annual earnings, which averaged $A18,467 or $US14,774. Independent variables include average firm size, work-force sex mix, production levels, and nonlabor inputs. The set of conditioning variables is as complete as the aggregate Australian cross-section public-use data permit. Fatality rates in Australian manufacturing are closer to fatality rates in U.S. manufacturing than in Japanese manufacturing, averaging 1.4 per 10,000 workers. For comparison purposes, we discuss only regressions including the overall rate of injuries and diseases and the rate of fatal injuries and diseases, which are metered by Australian workers' compensation insurance claims.[5]

As in the United States, there is substantial interstate variation in available workers' compensation insurance benefits in Australia. To capture generosity differences simply and to use a generosity measure that is exogenous to individual worker behavior, we parameterize available workers' compensation benefits with each state's maximum benefits for a work-related death. The average maximum death benefit is $A49,400, or $US39,500, with the highest state benefit $A53,000 and the lowest state benefit $A43,000.

Baseline bivariate regressions for Australia appear in lines (5) and (6) of table 2. A similarity to Japan is that wages vary inversely with the overall injury rate, but the relationship is not significant statistically at conventional levels. In contrast to Japan, the fatality-rate coefficient is positive and significant ($p = .061$) in the baseline bivariate regressions for Australia.

One of the attractions of the Australian data is an ability to check whether workers' compensation benefits trade off against wages in hedonic equilibrium (to test whether the estimated value of $\partial \ln W / \partial WC$ is negative) and to check whether the compensating wage differential falls with workers' compensation benefit generosity (to test whether the estimated value of $\partial^2 \ln W / \partial I \partial WC$ is negative). In regression (8) of table 2, there is a positive partial relation between benefit generosity and wages, which we attribute to a simultaneous equations bias that we cannot remedy when using the aggregate cross-section data for Australia. Specifically, prosperous high-manufacturing-wage states also set up more generous workers' compensation systems.[6] Although statistically insignificant, the estimated interaction effect between the compensating wage differential for injury risk and potential workers' compensation benefits in Australia is negative in regression (9) of table 2.[7]

Finally, the regressions in table 2 say that manufacturing workers exposed to the mean Australian fatality risk receive a wage premium of about 2.5%. Unlike Japan, the 2.5% compensating differential in Australian manufacturing is robust to changing the list of control variables, including deleting the possibly endogenous measure of workers' compensation benefit generosity and replacing it with state dummy variables.

4. Empirical results—the United States

The Current Population Survey is the only micro cross section with enough individuals to examine the effects of data aggregation. We chose May 1978 because of its location in the business cycle and available ancillary data on worker union status and turnover. To elaborate, 1978 is at the middle of the 1975–1980 economic expansion. The unemployment rate was 6% in 1978 compared to 8.3% in 1975. Real GNP grew at a healthy 5.3% compared to 1.3% in the trough year. Inflation had also fallen to 7.6% in 1978 from 9.1% in 1975. Although later years have a similar position in the business cycle, only 1978 allows us both to identify union membership and to merge data on worker turnover rates (new hires, separations).

The Bureau of Labor Statistics no longer releases industry fatality rates at other than the one-digit level.[8] Our measures of workplace health hazards instead include average industry workdays lost to injuries and the fatality rates of the National Institute for Occupational Safety and Health, which are derived from a census of all occupational fatalities recorded on death certificates from 1980 to 1985.[9] Although the National Institute's fatality data are publicly available for only one-digit industries, they are disaggregated by state and provide an excellent picture of long-run interstate differences in fatality risk.[10] Moore and Viscusi (1988) prefer the National Institute's fatality data to those of the Bureau of Labor Statistics because the former are based on a census rather than a survey and are therefore freer of error. Moreover, the focus on interstate differences in the National Institute's data permits a more precise match of death risk with available workers' compensation benefits. Regression estimates of compensating wage differentials across one-digit industries using the National Institute's fatality data are larger than the typical regression estimates of compensating wage differentials using the Bureau of Labor Statistics' fatality data (Moore and Viscusi, 1988).

The dependent variable in our regressions with U.S. data is the logarithm of average weekly earnings of full-time manufacturing workers.[11] Independent varibles include race, sex, marital status, age, education, region, and the industry's average monthly new hire and separation rates. We again represent workers' compensation insurance generosity by a state's maximum weekly death benefits to the surviving spouse and include a dummy variable for whether the state had a maximum total spouse benefit.[12] We consider three levels of aggregation above the individual: states, regions, and two-digit manufacturing industries.[13]

The first block of regressions in table 3 illustrates the effect of aggregation on the estimated baseline compensating wage differentials. The fatality rate coefficient becomes more positive and less significant as the level of aggregation increases. The second block of four regressions in table 3 includes a set of control variables intended to mimic the Japanese regressions of table 2. Unlike Viscusi and Moore (1987), who find a weak tradeoff between potential workers' compensation insurance benefits and wage levels,

Table 3. Compensating wage differentials in the United States (see text for details)

Level of aggregation	Injury/workers' comp. measures	Coefficient	*P*-value	Other independent variables	adj R^2
Individuals[a]	Injury rate	0.0140	.0001	—	0.0047
Individuals	Fatality rate	−0.2748	.016	—	0.0005
Individuals	Injury rate	0.01412	.0001		
	Fatality rate	−0.2958	.0091	—	0.0054
States[b]	Injury rate	−0.00363	.503		
	Fatality rate	0.2572	.138	—	0.0009
Regions[c]	Injury rate	−0.00526	.665		
	Fatality rate	0.9340	.268	—	−0.0072
Nation[d]	Injury rate	0.00376	.862		
	Fatality rate	5.1219	.142	—	0.0214
Individuals	Injury rate	0.01905	.0001		
	Fatality rate	−0.03272	.735		
	WC benefit	0.0006	.0001		
	WC benefit * limit	0.0001	.0350	e	0.326
States	Injury rate	−0.00740	.153		
	Fatality rate	0.1812	.163		
	WC benefit	0.0009	.0001		
	WC benefit * limit	0.000008	.945	e	0.466
Regions	Injury rate	−0.01594	.114		
	Fatality rate	0.3387	.447		
	WC benefit	0.0014	.008		
	WC benefit * limit	0.00026	.506	e	0.789
Nation	Injury rate	−0.00107	.599		
	Fatality rate	0.0268	.232		
	WC benefit	0.0021	.466		
	WC benefit * limit	0.00055	.860	e	0.903
Individuals	Injury rate	0.0185	.0001		
	Fatality rate	0.1365	.1299		
	WC benefit	0.00037	.0001		
	WC benefit * limit	0.000014	.734	f	0.512
States	Injury rate	0.000331	.940		
	Fatality rate	0.0888	.456		
	WC benefit	0.00081	.0001		
	WC benefit * limit	0.000023	.827	f	0.623
Regions	Injury rate	0.00205	.784		
	Fatality rate	0.2920	.446		
	WC benefit	0.00019	.643		
	WC benefit * limit	0.00098	.042	f	0.906
Nation	Injury rate	−0.00772	.749		
	Fatality rate	0.5168	.850		
	WC benefit	0.00012	.645		
	WC benefit * limit	−0.0021	.647	f	0.961

COMPENSATING WAGE DIFFERENTIALS FOR FATAL INJURY RISK   85

Table 3. (continued)

Level of aggregation	Injury/workers' comp. measures	Coefficient	P-value	Other independent variables	adj R^2
Individuals	Injury rate	0.01782	.0001		
	Fatality rate	2.5141	.0001		
	WC benefit	0.00075	.0001		
	WC benefit * limit	0.00027	.0001		
	Fatality rate * WC benefit	−0.0121	.0001		
	Fatality rate * WC benefit · limit	−0.0056	.0001	f	0.514
States	Injury rate	0.0004231	.923		
	Fatality rate	3.4774	.0001		
	WC benefit	0.0013	.0001		
	WC benefit * limit	0.0003	.0254		
	Fatality rate * WC benefit	−0.0190	.0001		
	Fatality rate * WC benefit · limit	−0.0049	.0273	f	0.636
Regions	Injury rate	−0.000696	.923		
	Fatality rate	1.0490	.784		
	WC benefit	−0.00103	.342		
	WC benefit * limit	0.00281	.0006		
	Fatality rate * WC benefit	0.00034	.157		
	Fatality rate * WC benefit · limit	−0.00044	.005	f	0.915
Nation	Injury rate	0.01012	.631		
	Fatality rate	117.1689	.266		
	WC benefit	−0.0060	.674		
	WC benefit * limit	0.0778	.197		
	Fatality rate * WC benefit	0.1648	.601		
	Fatality rate * WC benefit · limit	−2.0370	.192	f	0.990

[a]Dependent variable: log average weekly earnings in 1978; N = 8868, ordinary least squares.
[b]N = 682, ordinary least squares.
[c]N = 80, ordinary least squares.
[d]Two-digit manufacturing industries, N = 20, ordinary least squares.
[e]Nonwhite, female, union, new-hire rate, separation rate.
[f]Age, age^2, nonwhite, female, union, education, region, marital status, new-hire rate, separation rate.

the coefficient of available insurance benefits is positive in all regressions in the second, parsimoniously specified, block of regressions in table 3.[14] Although the estimated fatality-rate coefficient again rises with the level of aggregation, the estimated compensating wage differential approaches statistical significance at conventional levels in only the state level regressions.

By comparing the second and third blocks of regressions in table 3, we see how the results change when an extensive set of independent variables replaces a list similar to the Japanese regressions of table 2. The effects of aggregation are now clarified. Because the averaging process removes noise from the data, adjusted R^2 rises espectedly with the level of aggregation. The coefficient of the fatality rate and its p-value also rise with aggregation. Reduced estimated coefficient precision with aggregation is the net result of two opposing forces: aggregation lowers both the regression's residual variance and the variances of the independent variables. In our case, the reduced variance of the independent variables dominates, lowering statistical significance with aggregation. Only the fatality-rate coefficient estimated with individual data is significant at the 0.1 level using a one-tail test, indicating a compensating wage differential for exposure to the mean fatality risk compared to employment in a completely safe manufacturing workplace of 1%.

Moore and Viscusi (1988) find a large reduction in the compensating wage differential with generosity of available workers' compensation benefits. The final group of regressions for the United States targets how potential insurance benefits affect the compensating wage differential for fatality risk in manufacturing. The coefficients of the regression using individual data indicate that if there were no workers' compensation insurance death benefits, then the estimated compensating wage difference in manufacturing would be 11%. At the means of the fatality rate and workers' compensation benefits–fatality interactions, the estimated compensating wage differential is 1%.[15]

Finally, the relatively small estimated compensating wage differential for death risk produced by the coefficients in table 3 is the result of our focus on manufacturing. By omitting other industries we exclude workers at the extremes of the risk spectrum. Specifically, in the Current Population Survey data the death rate in mining is 32 per 100,000 employees while the death rate in wholesale trade is 1 per 100,000 employees. When we include all workers in the eight nonagricultural one-digit industries in a hedonic wage regression, the estimated compensating wage differential for fatality risk rises to 3.4% (4.3% in the absence of available workers' compensation death benefits).[16] The 3% to 4% compensating wage differential across all industries is similar to other researchers' results using individual wage data and the National Institute's fatality rates (Moore and Viscusi, 1988).

5. Conclusion

Our research estimates the compensating wage differential for the risk of a work-related fatality in the manufacturing sectors of Australia, Japan, and the United States. The distinguishing features of the Australian and Japanese labor markets make us expect a lower wage differential in Japan and a higher wage differential in Australia than in the United States. Our econometric research produced three findings of note.

First, the relative ranking of estimated compensating wage differences is as expected. Because the estimated compensating wage difference is fragile in the regressions for Japan using aggregate two-digit manufacturing data, we conclude that the Japanese differential is not significantly different from zero. Using new data on work-related fatalities, we find a compensating wage differential in U.S. manufacturing of about 1%. Regressions for Australian manufacturing yield an estimated compensating wage differential of approximately 2.5%.

Second, we were able to aggregate workers in the U.S. manufacturing sector by state, region, and two-digit industry. The effects of aggregation are severe; estimated compensating wage differentials for fatality risk become more positive and statistically less significant as the level of aggregation increases.

Finally, researchers need to incorporate potential workers' compensation insurance benefits in hedonic labor market equilibrium regressions designed to estimate compensating wage differentials for workplace injury risks. We find that formal insurance for work-related fatalities substitutes for the insurance implicit in compensating wage differences in the U.S. manufacturing sector. Our estimates are that if there were no death benefits under workers' compensation insurance, the compensating wage differential would be 11% instead of 1%.

Notes

1. Separating earnings into contractual versus bonus components did not alter the empirical results.
2. A Goldfeld–Quandt test rejects the null hypothesis of homoskedasticity at the 10% level.
3. The fragility of the Japanese regression coefficients may also reflect small sample size. We therefore doubled the number of observations by combining data on the 20 manufacturing industries for 1984 and 1986. The results are similar to the coefficients reported in table 2. When we control for the proportion of women production workers, the new hire rate, and the worker separation rate in a weighted least squares regression, the fatality rate coefficient is significantly positive at the 10% level. However, the size of the estimated compensating wage differential for workers exposed to the mean fatality risk drops in half, to 0.73%. In a manner to our previously discussed results, the fatality rate coefficient is sensitive to the control variables used in the regression and to the use of weighted versus ordinary least squares. In no other specification, including ones incorporating time trends and industry (fixed) effects, is the fatality rate coefficient statistically significant; in many specification the fatality rate coefficient is negative.
4. The remaining 10% of manufacturing workers are in Tasmania, the Northern Territory, or in the Australian Capital Territory and are ignored because of missing data on work-related injuries.
5. See Kniesner and Leeth (1989a) for a numerical simulation of the difficulties with using workers' compensation claims data to study work-related injuries and compensating wage differentials.
6. Including a set of state indicators could potentially separate the effects of state-specific factors and workers' compensation benefits on wages. More than one year of data is needed because of the collinearity between state dummy variables and state workers' compensation benefits. We expanded our data set to include information on New South Wales, Queensland, and South Australia for 1986. (Data for Victoria are unavailable for 1986.) Additionally, because of limitations in the 1986 data, other conditioning variables are limited to industry work-force sex-mix and product turnover (essentially sales) per establishment. The coefficient estimates from pooled data for New South Wales, Queensland, and South Australia for 1984–1985 and 1985–1986 mirror the results of table 2 in both sign and significance when the state dummies (fixed effects) are excluded. When state dummy variables appear in the regression, the fatality rate coefficient remains positive and significant but the workers' compensation benefits coefficient turns negative and insignificant. Hence, the results of our ancillary regressions provide some evidence that workers' compensation benefits in the regressions of table 2 are, at least partly, reflecting unmeasured state-specific factors.
7. Workers' compensation death benefits should affect only the wages of workers exposed to potentially fatal workplace hazards, implying that only the interaction term between benefits and fatality rates need be included in regression (9) (Viscusi and Moore, 1987). When the workers' compensation variable is excluded, the fatality rate coefficient is insignificantly negative and the interaction term between benefits and fatality rates is insignificantly positive. Because workers' compensation benefits may be proxying for latent state-specific factors, we also ran regression (9) excluding workers' compensation generosity but including state dummy variables, and the results of table 2 were maintained.
8. The data from the Bureau of Labor Statistics are derived from a survey of establishments intended to measure injury risk, not fatality risk. The Bureau formerly released data at the two-digit and three-digit levels to researchers requesting it. After a study completed in 1985 by an outside consulting group, the

Bureau concluded that fatality rates derived from their establishment survey are misleading. The Bureau no longer releases two-digit or three-digit fatality data.

9. We thank Dr. Nancy A. Stout of the Division of Safety Research, Injury Surveillance Branch, Data Analysis Section, The National Institute for Occupational Safety and Health for providing us with the data, which are described in Moore and Viscusi (1988).

10. In states with less than six total deaths in the manufacturing sector, the National Institute did not calculate a fatality rate, and we coded it as zero.

11. Average weekly hours are 35 or more.

12. We also ran regressions where the spouse benefit was coded as zero if the worker was unmarried. This had no effect on our conclusion.

13. Fatality rates vary across national two-digit manufacturing industries because there is an unequal number of workers in each industry–state cell.

14. In a manner similar to Australia, the workers' compensation benefit variable may be capturing unmeasured state-specifc factors.

15. We also examined the impact of workers' compensation benefits on the compensating wage differential for fatal injury risk in regressions that exclude the level of benefits as a separate variable. (see note 7). At the individual level, and at every level of aggregation, the fatality rate coefficient is insignificantly negative and the interaction term between the fatality rate and available workers' compensation benefits is insignificantly positive. We interpret the lack of statistical significance as reflecting unmeasured state-specific factors that are indirectly controlled by including both the level of benefits and the interaction of workers' compensation benefits and fatality rates in the regression. Because, in the case of the United States, we use only data for 1978 for reasons discussed at the beginning of section 4, and because our fatal-injury risk measure varies only by state, we cannot try to separate workers' compensation insurance effects from state-specific (fixed) effects, as we did for Australia, by including a set of state indicator variables as regressors.

16. We include all independent variables listed in the last set of regressions of table 3 except overall injury rate, new hire rate, and separation rate. The worker turnover rates are unavailable for non-manufacturing industries, and omitting the overall injury rate does not affect the estimated fatality rate coefficient. For comparison purposes we reestimated the hedonic wage function with individual data for manufacturing workers, excluding the overall injury and worker turnover rates; the estimated compensating wage differential for fatality risk increased to 1.6% in manufacturing.

References

Brooks, Adrian. (1988). *Guidebook to Australian Occupational Health & Safety Laws*, 3rd edition. North Ryde, NSW, Australia: CCH Australia Limited.

Brown, Charles, and James Medoff. (1989). "The Employer Size-Wage Effect," *Journal of Political Economy* 97, 1027–1059.

Brown, James N., and Harvey S. Rosen. (1982). "On the Estimation of Structural Hedonic Price Models," *Econometrica* 50, 765–768.

Census of Manufacturing Establishments: Summary of Operations by Industry Class, New South Wales, 1984–85. (1987). Sydney, Australia: Australian Bureau of Statistics.

Dillingham, Alan E. (1985). "The Influence of Risk Variable Definition in Value-of-Life Estimates," *Economic Inquiry* 24, 277–294.

Employment Injuries New South Wales. 1985–86. (1987). Sydney, Australia: Australian Bureau of Statistics.

Epple, Dennis. (1987). "Hedonic Prices and Implicit Markets: Estimating Supply and Demand Functions for Differentiated Products," *Journal of Political Economy* 95, 59–80.

Gordon, Robert J. (1982). "Why U.S. Wage and Employment Behavior Differs from that in Britain and Japan," *Economic Journal* 92, 13–44.

Industrial Accidents, South Australia, 1985–86. (1987). Adelaide, Australia: Australian Bureau of Statistics.

Industrial Accidents, Queensland, 1985–86. (1987). Brisbane, Australia: Australian Bureau of Statistics.

Industrial Accidents and Diseases, Victoria. 1984–85. (1986). Melbourne, Australia: Australian Bureau of Statistics.

Jones, Gregory P. (1988). *A Guide to Sources of Information on Australian Industrial Relations.* Rushcutters Bay, NSW, Australia: Pergamon Press.

Kniesner, Thomas J., and John D. Leeth. (1988). "Simulating Hedonic Labor Market Models," *International Economic Review* 29, 827–854.

Kniesner, Thomas J., and John D. Leeth. (1989). "Separating the Reporting Effects from the Injury Rate Effects of Workers' Compensating Insurance," *Industrial and Labor Relations Review* 42, 280–293.

Kniesner, Thomas J., and John D. Leeth. (1989). "Can We Make OSHA and Workers' Compensation Insurance Interact More Effectively in Promoting Workplace Safety?" *Research in Labor Economics* 10, 1–51.

Labour Statistics Australia, 1986. (1987). Canberra, ACT, Australia: Australian Government Publishing Service, for the Australian Bureau of Statistics.

Labour Statistics Australia, 1986. (1987). Canberra, ACT, Australia: Australian Bureau of Statistics, Catalogue No. 6101.0.

Leigh, J. Paul, and Roger N. Folsom. (1984). "Estimates of the Value of Accident Avoidance at the Job Depend on the Concavity of the Equalizing Differences Curve," *Quarterly Review of Economics and Business* 24, 56–66.

Manufacturing Establishments: Details of Operations by Industry, South Australia, 1984–85. (1986). Adelaide, Australia: Australian Bureau of Statistics.

Manufacturing Establishments: Summary of Operations, Queensland, 1984–85. (1986). Queensland, Australia: Australian Bureau of Statistics.

Manufacturing Establishments: Details of Operations, Victoria, 1984–85. (1986). Melbourne, Australia: Australian Bureau of Statistics.

Marin, Alan, and George Psacharopoulos. (1982). "The Rewards for Risk in the Labor Market: Evidence from the United Kingdom and a Reconciliation with Other Studies," *Journal of Political Economy* 90, 827–854.

Mincer, Jacob, and Yoshio Higuchi. (1988). "Wage Structure and Labor Turnover in the United States and Japan," *Journal of the Japanese and International Economies* 2, 1–37.

Moore, Michael J., and W. Kip Viscusi. (1988). "Doubling the Estimated Value of Life: Results Using New Occupational Fatality Data," *Journal of Policy Analysis and Management* 7, 476–490.

Olson, Craig A. (1981). "An Analysis of Wage Differentials Received by Workers on Dangerous Jobs," *Journal of Human Resources* 16, 167–185.

Rosen, Sherwin. (1986). "The Theory of Equalizing Differences." In Orley Ashenfelter and Richard Layard (eds.), *The Handbook of Labor Economics.* Amsterdam: North-Holland.

Skully, Michael J. (1988). "Australia—Worker's Compensation in Transition," *NCCI Digest* 3, 1–12.

Smith, Robert S. (1979). "Compensating Wage Differentials and Public Policy: A Review," *Industrial and Labor Relations Review* 32, 339–352.

Thaler, Richard, and Sherwin Rosen. (1975). "The Value of Saving a Life: Evidence from the Labor Market." In Nester Terleckyj (ed.), *Household Production and Consumption.* New York: Columbia University Press.

The Current Population Survey, Design and Methodology. (1978). Technical Paper 40, U.S. Department of Commerce, Bureau of the Census.

Viscusi, W. Kip. (1979). *Employment Hazards: An Investigation of Market Performance.* Cambridge, MA: Harvard University Press.

Viscusi, W. Kip. (1983). *Risk by Choice, Regulating Health and Safety in the Workplace.* Cambridge, MA: Harvard University Press.

Viscusi, W. Kip, and Michael J. Moore. (1987). "Workers' Compensation: Wage Effects, Benefit Inadequacies, and the Value of Health Losses," *Review of Economics and Statistics* 64, 249–261.

Williams, C. Arthur Jr. (1985). "Workmen's Accident Compensation Insurance: Japan's Lesser Known Social Insurance Scheme," *Keio Business Review* 22, 67–89.

Williams, C. Arthur Jr. (1988). "How the Japanese Workers' Compensation System Differs from Ours," *NCCI Digest* 3, 13–22.

Workers' Compensation in Australia, 1984. (1985). Canberra, ACT, Australia: Australian Government Publishing Service, for the Australian Department of Social Security.

Yearbook Australia, 1988. (1988). Canberra, ACT, Australia: Australian Bureau of Statistics.

Yearbook of Labour Statistics, 1986. (1987). Tokyo, Japan: Policy Planning and Research Department, Minister's Secretariat, Japan Ministry of Labour.

[13]

Compensating Differentials for Gender-Specific Job Injury Risks

By Joni Hersch*

The theory of compensating differentials holds a prominent place in the analysis of wage determination, and a large empirical literature documents substantial wage-risk trade-offs.[1] Although women comprise over 45 percent of the labor force, job risks have been viewed as primarily a male province, and studies have largely excluded female workers from the analyses. Since most of the occupational injury data are available only at the industry level, if women are in safer jobs within industries, matching industry injury rates to female workers may lead to large measurement problems and misleading estimates.

In this paper I use new national data to construct gender-specific estimates of injury and illness incidence rates by both industry and occupation. These rates are the first gender-specific injury incidence rates in the literature, as well as the first occupational incidence rates. Although women are less likely than men to be injured on their jobs, their injury experience is considerable, as one-third of all injuries and illnesses with days away from work are to women. Adjusted for gender differences in employment, women face a job risk that is 71 percent of men's. Further, the gender-specific injury rates reveal substantial and statistically significant wage-risk trade-offs for female workers. All female workers, not only those employed in blue-collar occupations, receive a significant compensating differential for job risks. Female workers at the average level of risk receive a wage premium of 2–3 percent, equal to an ad-ditional \$400–\$563 per year as compensation for nonfatal job risks.

The results using the gender-specific injury measures are in stark contrast to those obtained for women using the standard industry risk measures. Estimates based on the U.S. Department of Labor, Bureau of Labor Statistics (BLS), industry injury and illness incidence rates do not indicate a significant wage-risk trade-off. These findings suggest that assigning industry risk measures to female workers without adjusting for gender differences in injury experience may lead to biased estimates of the returns to job risk and a misleading view of who bears injury risks in the workplace.

I use these estimates of the wage-risk trade-off based on the gender-specific incidence rates to calculate the first estimates in the literature of the implicit value of an injury or illness for women workers. The values, which range from \$20,000 using the female-specific industry rate, to \$30,000 using the female-specific occupation rate, are similar to those I find for male blue-collar workers.

Similar concerns about measurement error have led to the exclusion of white-collar male workers from most studies. The industry- and occupation-specific risk measures calculated here certainly reduce this measurement error. In contrast to the findings for female workers, however, in many cases there is an inverse relation between wages and risk for white-collar males, whether the risk measure pertains to the individual's three-digit industry or three-digit occupation.

The estimating procedure used in this paper follows the standard approach in the literature of matching average risk measures to individuals by industry or occupation. Because all workers within an industry or occupation are assigned the same injury rate, the residuals in the regression for workers in a given industry or occupation group are likely to be correlated. The robust standard errors calculated in this paper are generally 2–3 times the size of those calculated without recognizing this source of correlation.

* Department of Economics and Finance, University of Wyoming, Laramie, WY 82071. I thank Kathryn Anderson, Stephen Cosslett, Jahn Hakes, Daniel Hamermesh, Leslie Stratton, and the anonymous referee for their very helpful suggestions, and Linda Garris and Larry Jones of the Office of Safety, Health, and Working Conditions, Bureau of Labor Statistics, for providing tables of injury statistics prior to their public release.

[1] A recent survey of the literature is by W. Kip Viscusi, 1993.

I. Industry Job Risks and the Treatment of Female Workers in the Literature

Before discussing the construction of gender-specific injury incidence rates, it is useful to consider the method used by the Bureau of Labor Statistics. For each industry, the incidence rate is calculated as

(1)   BLS Industry Rate $= (N/H) \times 200{,}000$,

where N = number of injuries and illnesses, H = total hours worked by all employees during the calendar year, and $200{,}000$ = base for 100 full-time equivalent workers (40 hours per week, 50 weeks per year.) These values are reported annually in the *Survey of Occupational Injuries and Illnesses in the United States, 1993* (BLS, 1995a).

These incidence rates pertain to all workers within an industry, so that, for instance, secretaries and miners within the mining industry are assigned the same risk measure. Since data on occupational injuries and on the gender distribution of injury cases were not available until recently, the standard practice in the literature has been to impute these industry risk values to all individuals in the wage sample by three-digit industry code. If workers with certain characteristics are in riskier or less risky jobs within their industry, however, the estimated returns to risk may be biased.[2] In

---

[2] In the hedonic wage model, an individual worker i is compensated for market beliefs about the objective riskiness R_i^* of his or her job. The wage equation for the ith individual can be written as

(i) $y_i = \beta R_i^* + \mu_i$,

where y_i is the log of wage and μ_i is a random error term. In general, R_i^* is not observed, but is related to the observed average industry risk R_i as

(ii) $R_i^* = R_i + \varepsilon_i$,

where ε_i is an unobserved risk component associated with the specific type of job held by the individual within the industry. The wage equation to be estimated is

(iii) $y_i = \beta R_i + v_i$,

where $v_i = \beta \varepsilon_i + \mu_i$. If ε_i and μ_i are uncorrelated with R_i, then by solving for the OLS estimator of β and taking

order to reduce this potential source of bias, many authors limit their sample to male blue-collar workers or to workers in manufacturing. In addition, other restrictions are typically imposed, such as restrictions to household heads, hourly workers, or to full-time employees. Even among samples which do not explicitly exclude women, such restrictions severely limit the number of women eligible for inclusion in the analyses.

Given the small samples of female workers remaining after such restrictions have been imposed, most authors either exclude women entirely from the analysis, or include them by allowing gender to affect wages only through an intercept. While these approaches are reasonable in the absence of data on gender-specific injury experience, they do not allow tests of whether women receive a compensating differential for the job risks they face. Furthermore, since women are disproportionately employed in white-collar occupations, estimates of compensating differentials for blue-collar workers would not be representative of the population of women workers overall.

II. Gender-Specific Injury and Illness Incidence Rates

In this section, I calculate gender-specific injury and illness incidence rates for both industry and occupation. Recently, the BLS began collecting more extensive information on the worker and case characteristics of injury and illness cases involving days away from work. The restriction of the survey coverage to injuries and illnesses involving at least one day away from work provides a lower bound on the severity of the incidence, and increases the homogeneity of the definition of injury and

---

the expected value, one can show that the OLS estimator of β is unbiased. The variance of the error term in equation (iii) is larger than in equation (i), so the estimated standard errors of the coefficients in the wage regression will tend to be larger using group means. If ε_i is correlated with R_i (for instance if women tend to be in less risky jobs within industries), then using industry average risk can lead to biased and inconsistent estimates. This is a kind of omitted variable bias and can be either positive or negative.

illness.[3] These data reveal that female workers experience a surprising number of job injuries and illnesses. Of 2.25 million BLS-reported nonfatal occupational injuries and illnesses with days away from work in 1993, one-third occurred to women. It is notable that, at least in terms of duration, men and women suffer injuries of similar severity. The median days away from work for those experiencing such an injury or illness is five days for both male and female workers (BLS, 1995b). Furthermore, the same five injury types account for 68–69 percent of the injuries for both male and female workers.[4]

Although women's share of injuries of 32.7 percent is less than their employment share of 46 percent of private industry employees, the magnitude of their injury experience is quite surprising since women are largely concentrated in the safer white-collar occupations. Taking into account the different levels of employment by gender, women face a job risk that is 71 percent of men's. Only 20.8 percent of the cases with days away from work in 1993 occurred in white-collar occupations. Among private employees, 69 percent of the women, but only 43.5 percent of the men, are employed in white-collar occupations. Within white-collar occupations, the injury rate for women is 80 percent higher than for men.

To calculate gender-specific industry job risk rates, I use data from two BLS tables. These tables provide information on the number of cases with days away from work in 1993 by gender for three-digit or four-digit SIC code or three-digit occupation. The BLS does not calculate gender-specific incidence rates for either industry or occupation. Because of differences in the information available, I use different procedures, described below, to calculate these rates.

A. Industry Incidence Rates

In principle one could use equation (1) to calculate gender-specific incidence rates for each industry by replacing N and H with the corresponding gender-specific values. However, while the number of injuries and illnesses by gender are provided in the new BLS survey, total hours worked by industry and gender are not available. I therefore allocate the BLS average industry rate into gender-specific shares by weighing the BLS rate by the gender-specific share of cases relative to the gender-specific hours share for each industry i as follows:

(2)   Gender Industry Rate

$$= (N_g/N)/(H_g/H)$$

$$\times \text{ BLS Industry Rate,}$$

where N_g = total number of cases of gender g in industry i, and H_g = total hours worked by gender g in industry i. As in equation (1), N and H represent the total number of injury and illness cases and total hours worked by all employees.

To calculate gender-specific shares of total employment hours within three-digit industries, I use data from the *Census of Population and Housing, 1990* (U.S. Department of Commerce, Bureau of the Census, [1993]) 5-percent sample. Since government and self-employed workers are excluded from the BLS survey used to estimate injury incidence rates, I restrict the Census sample to paid employees in private industry who report working positive hours in the preceding week. This yields a sample of 4,149,478 observations.

Table 1 provides a comparison of the BLS industry incidence rate and the gender-specific rates for the major industry categories. For workers in private industry overall, the adjusted female incidence rate is 2.2 injury or illness cases with days away from work per 100 workers, considerably lower than the BLS average incidence rate of 2.9. Industries with larger shares of female employees, such as finance, insurance and real estate, and services, have lower than average risk. As the female/male incidence ratio in the last column indi-

---

[3] Injury and illness cases not involving days away from work are far more common. There were about 67 percent more cases without days away from work in 1993 than with days away from work.

[4] These injuries are sprains, strains and tears; bruises and contusions; fractures; cuts and lacerations; and soreness, pain, hurt, except the back.

TABLE 1—INJURY AND ILLNESS INCIDENCE RATES WITH DAYS AWAY FROM WORK BY MAJOR INDUSTRY, 1993[a]

Industry	Percent female in industry[b]	BLS rate[c]	Female rate[d]	Male rate[d]	Female/male ratio
Private industry	45.9	2.9	2.2	3.4	0.65
Goods-producing					
Agriculture, forestry, and fishing	22.9	4.2	3.5	4.6	0.76
Mining	13.5	3.3	0.8	4.1	0.19
Construction	10.4	4.9	1.1	5.3	0.21
Manufacturing	33.6	3.3	2.5	3.4	0.75
Service-producing					
Transportation and public utilities	30.4	4.3	2.5	4.6	0.55
Wholesale trade	31.0	2.8	1.3	3.7	0.35
Retail trade	53.1	2.7	2.3	3.1	0.74
Finance, insurance, and real estate	63.5	1.0	0.9	1.3	0.65
Services	64.7	2.3	2.4	2.4	1.00

[a] Per 100 full-time workers.
[b] Author's calculation from *Census of Population and Housing, 1990.* Sample restricted to private, paid employees employed in industries reporting injury and illness cases by gender.
[c] *Survey of Occupational Injuries and Illnesses, 1993.*
[d] Author's calculations. See text.

cates, on average women face considerably less risk than men in the high-risk industries such as mining and construction that employ relatively few women. This indicates that there is considerable occupational sorting by gender within these industries.

The correlation between the three-digit BLS industry rate and the female-specific industry rate is 0.67. The corresponding correlation between the BLS rate and the male-specific rate is 0.96. This suggests that estimates of wage-risk trade-offs for men are likely to be similar using either the BLS industry rate or the gender-specific rate, but this is less likely to be true for women.

B. *Occupational Incidence Rates*

The BLS does not provide occupational injury and illness incidence rates, so the procedure I use to estimate industry incidence rates

cannot be used. A modification of the BLS equation (1) leads to estimates of occupational risk for each occupation k:

$$(3) \qquad \text{Gender Occupation Rate}$$

$$= (O_g/H_{go}) \times 200{,}000,$$

where O_g = number of cases for gender g in occupation k, and H_{go} = total hours worked by gender g in occupation k. Since the BLS does not provide occupational employment values, I again use Census data to estimate employment within each occupation.

Table 2 lists representative incidence rates for occupations with a large number of cases for female workers. For comparison, the corresponding incidence rates for men in these occupations are also included. While women generally face less risk than men within occupations, in most the gap is fairly narrow.

602   THE AMERICAN ECONOMIC REVIEW   JUNE 1998

TABLE 2—SELECTED INJURY AND ILLNESS INCIDENCE RATES BY OCCUPATION, 1993

Occupation title	Percent female hours in occupation	Female rate	Male rate
Secretaries	98.9	0.46	1.03
Bank tellers	91.2	0.83	0.37
Cashiers	78.5	1.50	1.77
Registered nurses	94.5	2.12	3.30
Health aides, except nursing	81.2	7.80	9.04
Nursing aides, orderlies, and attendants	89.2	8.05	7.85
Miscellaneous food preparation	45.8	8.33	8.09
Truck drivers	4.3	9.63	6.62
Laborers, except construction	21.5	9.71	15.74
Public transportation attendants	80.0	11.14	7.76

Source: Author's calculations. See text.

Furthermore, within many occupations, such as truck drivers and public transportation attendants, women actually face greater risk than men.

III. Empirical Specification and Data

In order to test for the presence of compensating differentials, I estimate wage equations for both female and male workers of the following form:

$$(4) \quad \ln(WAGE_i) = \alpha + \beta \, RISK_i$$

$$+ \Sigma_j \gamma_j X_{ij} + \varepsilon_i,$$

where $WAGE$ is the hourly wage rate; $RISK$ is a measure of job risk; X is a vector of explanatory variables such as years of work experience, education, union status, and occupation; α, β, and γ_j are parameters to be estimated; and ε is a random error term. The prediction of hedonic wage theory is that $\beta > 0$.

Equation (4) is the standard specification used in the hedonic wage literature. Since the ε_i may have different variances in different in-

dustries or occupations, many authors correct the standard errors for group heteroskedasticity. For comparability to the literature, I present these standard errors in Table 3 in parentheses.

However, since individuals within the same industry or occupation group are assigned the same risk rate, the residuals in the regression for workers in a given industry or occupation may be correlated. Standard errors not corrected for this correlation may be too small. I therefore use a procedure for robust estimation of the standard errors, which accounts for the within-group correlation by industry or occupation.[5] I present these in brackets below the standard errors corrected for group heteroskedasticity in Table 3.

To estimate the wage equations, I use data from the 1994 *Current Population Survey*

---

[5] Peter J. Huber (1967) and William H. Rogers (1993). The estimations are performed using *Stata Release 5.0* (StatCorp, 1997).

(CPS), U.S. Department of Commerce, Bureau of the Census. The wage equations include workers aged 18–65 whose hourly wage rate exceeds $2, and who provide complete information on all variables used in the analysis. Further restrictions corresponding to those made by the BLS in the scope of its job injury data collection are necessary in order to assign risk measures to the individuals in the study; that is, I exclude workers in public administration, self-employed workers, and private household workers. I also exclude workers employed in the agriculture, forestry, and fisheries industries. The resulting samples consist of 6,037 female and 5,960 male workers.

Hourly wage is the reported hourly wage for 64 percent of the women and 58 percent of the men, and is calculated from weekly pay and hours usually worked on this job for the remainder. Since information on actual work history is unavailable, I use years of potential experience, measured as age − education − 6. While this approximation is adequate for the purpose of this paper, comparisons by gender might lead to misleading conclusions, since potential experience overstates actual experience by a greater magnitude for women than for men.

Other variables in the wage equation include years of completed schooling and indicators of race and union status. Differences in cost of living that may affect wages are controlled for by indicators of region and city size. Industry and occupation characteristics other than job risk also have a direct effect on wage levels. To the extent that unobserved industry and occupation characteristics are correlated with job risk, the estimated returns to job risk may be biased. To reduce the likelihood of this source of bias, I include indicators of major occupation and industry categories.

Means and standard deviations for the risk measures are provided in the first column of Table 3. The BLS industry rate faced by women is lower than for private industry overall, and reflects the fact that women sort into safer industries. That women sort into safer jobs within industries in addition to sorting into safer industries can be seen by comparing the average BLS rate for women in the sample to the average female-specific rate, which is 16 percent lower than the average BLS rate.

IV. Wage Equation Estimates

A. Female Workers

Table 3, Panel A, presents coefficient estimates of the risk measures in the wage equations.[6] Equation (1) uses the customary BLS industry risk measure. Based on this measure, there is no evidence of a compensating differential for job risk for women workers. However, the estimates based on the gender-specific risk measures show strong evidence of compensating differentials. The results in column (2) using the female-specific industry risk measure indicates a wage-risk trade-off which is significant at the 1-percent level based on the heteroskedasticity-corrected standard errors, although it is no longer significant using the robust standard errors allowing for within-group correlation. However, the estimates in column (3) using the female-specific occupation risk measure reveals substantial and statistically significant effects (at the 5-percent level or better in 1-sided tests) based on either standard error. The magnitude of the estimated wage-risk trade-off is larger using the occupation risk measure than using the industry risk measure (0.014 and 0.009, respectively).

The results based on gender-specific injury and illness incidence rates strongly indicate that women do receive a compensating differential for their exposure to job risk. To determine whether the source of the job risk derives from the pervading riskiness of the industry, from the riskiness of the worker's specific job, or from both industry and occupation risk characteristics, I estimate wage equations including both industry and occupation risk. For instance, although secretarial jobs are quite safe, secretaries employed in textile mills may be exposed to various job hazards, such as cotton dust, that secretaries in insurance companies do not face.

Column (4) presents the estimates including the BLS rate as well as the occupational rate, followed by the estimates based on the female-specific industry and occupation rates in column

---

[6] Selectivity-corrected estimates of the wage equation for female workers are virtually identical and are available upon request.

604   THE AMERICAN ECONOMIC REVIEW   JUNE 1998

TABLE 3—WAGE EQUATION ESTIMATES[a]

	Mean (standard deviation)	Dependent variable: log of hourly wage[b]				
		(1)	(2)	(3)	(4)	(5)
Panel A: Female Workers (sample size = 6,037)						
BLS industry rate	2.48 (1.57) —	0.443 (0.360) [0.927]	—	—	−0.025 (0.388) [0.608]	—
Female industry rate	2.14 (1.56) —	—	0.897* (0.364) [0.953]	—	—	0.463 (0.387) [0.649]
Female occupation rate	1.94 (2.22) —	—	—	1.362* (0.374) [0.740]	1.369* (0.401) [0.739]	1.232* (0.395) [0.725]
Hourly wage	10.60 (7.39)	—	—	—	—	—
Adjusted R^2	—	0.45	0.45	0.45	0.45	0.45
Panel B: Male Workers (sample size = 5,960)						
BLS industry rate	3.05 (1.67) —	−1.959* (0.395) [0.646]	—	—	−1.894* (0.397) [0.643]	—
Male industry rate	3.35 (1.80) —	—	−2.042* (0.366) [0.573]	—	—	−1.982* (0.368) [0.570]
Male occupation rate	3.23 (3.58) —	—	—	−0.550 (0.262) [0.377]	−0.465 (0.260) [0.251]	−0.446 (0.260) [0.248]
Hourly wage	13.52 (8.80)	—	—	—	—	—
Adjusted R^2	—	0.45	0.45	0.45	0.45	0.45
Panel C: Male Blue-Collar Workers (sample size = 3,197)						
BLS industry rate	3.62 (1.56) —	1.360* (0.452) [1.073]	—	—	1.319* (0.454) [0.079]	—
Male industry rate	3.93 (1.65) —	—	1.280* (0.435) [1.032]	—	—	1.236* (0.438) [1.040]
Male occupation rate	5.24 (3.78) —	—	—	0.224 (0.236) [0.297]	0.158 (0.239) [0.272]	0.144 (0.239) [0.270]
Hourly wage	10.84 (6.50)	—	—	—	—	—
Adjusted R^2	—	0.34	0.34	0.34	0.34	0.34

TABLE 3—Continued.

	Mean (standard deviation)	Dependent variable: log of hourly wage[b]				
		(1)	(2)	(3)	(4)	(5)
Panel D: Male Hourly Blue-Collar Workers (sample size = 2,578)						
BLS industry rate	3.62 (1.52) —	1.578* (0.503) [1.133]	—	—	1.470* (0.503) [1.126]	—
Male industry rate	3.92 (1.61) —	—	1.472* (0.479) [1.085]	—	—	1.349* (0.480) [1.082]
Male occupation rate	5.42 (3.89) —	—	—	0.494** (0.252) [0.279]	0.431** (0.254) [0.275]	0.418** (0.255) [0.275]
Hourly wage	10.58 (6.61)	—	—	—	—	—
Adjusted R^2	—	0.37	0.37	0.37	0.37	0.37

* All coefficients are multiplied by 100. Data set is March 1994 *Current Population Survey*. Additional variables in each equation are a constant, potential experience, potential experience squared, education, and indicator variables for union, nonwhite, three regions, and five city sizes. The female equations and the equations for all male workers also include indicators for nine occupations and six industries. The blue-collar male equations also include indicator variables for two occupations and for manufacturing. See text for definitions of variables.
b Standard errors corrected for group heteroskedasticity in parentheses; standard errors corrected for within-group correlation in brackets.
* Indicates significance at the 1-percent level, and ** indicates significance at the 5-percent level (1-sided tests).

(5). As the results show, the coefficient of occupation risk is not affected by the inclusion of the industry rate. The industry rate is not significantly different from zero after controlling for occupation risk. Thus the source of the wage-risk trade-off for the female sample is predominantly due to the riskiness of the occupation.

B. Male Workers

Panels B, C, and D of Table 3 summarize the risk coefficients from the corresponding equations for men. Estimates pooling white- and blue-collar men are reported in Panel B and indicate a significantly negative wage-risk relation using either the BLS industry risk measure, the gender-specific industry risk measure, or the gender-specific occupation measure. Since the occupational risk measures calculated here should circumvent the large measurement error that may result from assigning industry average risk measures to men

in white-collar occupations, the negative wage-risk trade-off found for the full male sample is puzzling. It is possible that this results from pooling workers paid hourly with those on salary. For instance, salaried workers in risky jobs may be compensated by increased opportunities for promotion rather than directly for the riskiness of their jobs. However, the results restricted to hourly workers yield significantly negative effects of industry risk of about half the magnitude of that found for the full sample, while there is no significant effect of occupation risk. The results restricted to all white-collar workers are similar to those found for the full sample, with significant negative returns to both industry and occupation risk. Estimates restricted to white-collar males paid hourly indicate no significant wage-risk trade-off using any measure of risk.[7]

_____

[7] These results are available upon request.

606   THE AMERICAN ECONOMIC REVIEW   JUNE 1998

The results reported in Panel C, after making the customary restriction to blue-collar men, indicate the customary findings of a positive wage-risk trade-off using both measures of industry risk, which are significant based on the conventionally used standard errors. When corrected for within-group correlation, however, the large increase in the standard errors renders these coefficients insignificant. The coefficient of the BLS industry rate is slightly larger than that of the gender-specific rate (0.014 and 0.013, respectively). In contrast to the findings for women, the coefficient on the occupational risk measure, although positive, is not significantly different from zero in any specification.

Restricting the sample further to blue-collar men paid hourly, however, reveals a positive and significant effect (at the 5-percent level in 1-sided tests) of gender-specific occupational risk on wages, but the magnitude of the effect is about one-third that of industry risk for males as well as about one-third of the coefficient of occupation risk estimated for women. Based on the heteroskedasticity-corrected standard errors, the results indicate a significantly positive wage-risk trade-off for industry risk, but once again there is a large increase in the robust standard errors corrected for within-group correlation which renders these insignificant.

V. Implicit Value of an Injury or Illness

The preceding results demonstrate that women and blue-collar men receive a significant compensating differential for job risk. Table 4 provides estimates of the wage premia for bearing risk and the implicit value of an injury or illness based on the estimates presented in Table 3. The wage premium per unit of risk is $\partial w / \partial q$, where w is the hourly wage used in the estimation of the wage equations, and q represents the risk measure used. Evaluated at the sample means of risk and hourly wages, the compensation for female workers for average risk is 1.9–2.6 percent of hourly wages. Assuming 2,000 hours worked per year, female workers at the average risk level earn a wage premium of $408–$563 annually.

Since the injury and illness incidence rates are per 100 full-time workers, the implicit an-

nual value of an injury or illness is calculated as

$$(5) \qquad \partial w / \partial q \times 100 \times 2{,}000,$$

again assuming 2,000 hours worked per year for full-time employment. Based on the female-specific industry rate, the implicit value of an injury or illness is around $20,000, while the estimated value based on the occupation risk measure yields an implicit value around $30,000.

For comparison, Table 4 also presents corresponding values for blue-collar men. The values based on industry risk indicate that men's higher average risk level results in a larger annual compensation for risk. The values based on the occupational risk measures reveal similar values of annual compensation for female workers and for male hourly blue-collar workers. The implicit annual value of an injury or illness of about $30,000 is close to that obtained for women based on the occupational risk measure.

VI. Conclusion

Women have largely been excluded from analyses of compensating differentials for job risk since they are predominantly employed in safer, white-collar occupations. New data reveal that their injury experience is considerable. One-third of the total injury and illness cases with days away from work accrue to female workers. Adjusted for employment, women are 71 percent as likely as men to experience an injury or illness.

As one would predict on theoretical grounds, these risks generate compensating differentials. Based on gender-specific injury incidence rates for both industry and occupation, I find strong evidence of compensating wage differentials for the job risk faced by female workers. Furthermore, all women—not only women in the riskier blue-collar jobs—receive a substantial and statistically significant premium for bearing job risk. Occupational risk has a larger impact on the wage rate than industry risk, and when both risk measures are included in the wage equation, only occupational risk is significant. In contrast, there is a negative relation between risk and

TABLE 4—ANNUAL VALUES OF RISK COMPENSATION[a]

Risk measure:	All female		Male blue-collar		Male hourly blue-collar	
	Female industry rate	Female occupation rate	BLS industry rate	Male industry rate	Male industry rate	Male occupation rate
Annual compensation for average risk[b]	$408	$563	$1,067	$1,091	$1,221	$567
Risk differential as a percentage of average wage[c]	1.93	2.66	4.92	5.03	5.77	2.68
Implicit annual value of an injury or illness[d]	$19,631	$29,023	$29,485	$27,750	$31,148	$10,453

[a] Based on coefficient estimates in Table 3.
[b] Calculated as $q \times \partial w/\partial q \times 2,000$, where q denotes the risk measure.
[c] Calculated as $(q \times \partial w/\partial q)/w$.
[d] Calculated as $\partial w/\partial q \times 100 \times 2,000$.

earnings for white-collar men. This is a puzzling finding, since the use of occupation-specific incidence rates reduces the measurement error that may result from imputing industry risk averages to men in safer white-collar occupations.

In contrast to the estimates based on gender-specific risk measures, estimates based on the BLS industry rate fail to reveal evidence of a compensating differential for job risk faced by women. Imputing this measure of overall industry risk to female workers apparently results in measurement error too great to yield reliable estimates of the wage-risk trade-off for female workers.

The wage-risk trade-off and the implicit value of an injury or illness are of a magnitude similar to that found in this study for male blue-collar workers. Since women comprise over 45 percent of the labor force, it is comforting to discover that, at least with regard to job risk, women and blue-collar men face a wage-determination process yielding similar compensation for job risk.

REFERENCES

Huber, Peter J. "The Behavior of Maximum Likelihood Estimates Under Non-standard Conditions," in Lucien M. Le Cam and Jerzy Neyman, eds., *Proceedings of the fifth Berkeley symposium on mathematical statistics and probability*. Berkeley, CA: University of California Press, 1967, pp. 221–33.

Rogers, William H. "Regression Standard Errors in Clustered Samples." *Stata Technical Bulletin*, 1993, *13*, pp. 19–23.

StatCorp. *Stata statistical software: Release 5.0*. College Station, TX: Stata Corporation, 1997.

U.S. Department of Commerce, Bureau of the Census. *Census of population and housing, 1990*, [United States]: *Public use microdata sample: 5-percent sample* [computer file]. Washington, DC: U.S. Department of Commerce, Bureau of the Census [producer], 1993.

———. *Current population survey, March 1994: Annual Demographic Survey*. Washington, DC: U.S. Department of Commerce, Bureau of the Census, 1994.

U.S. Department of Labor, Bureau of Labor Statistics. *Survey of occupational injuries and illnesses in the United States, 1993*. Washington, DC: U.S. Government Printing Office, 1995a.

———. *News release USDL-95-142*. Washington, DC: U.S. Government Printing Office, 1995b.

Viscusi, W. Kip. "The Value of Risks to Life and Health." *Journal of Economic Literature*, December 1993, *31*(4), pp. 1912–46.

[14]

CIGARETTE SMOKERS AS JOB RISK TAKERS

W. Kip Viscusi and Joni Hersch*

Abstract—Using a large data set, the authors find that smokers select riskier jobs, but receive lower total wage compensation for risk than do nonsmokers. This finding is inconsistent with conventional models of compensating differentials. The authors develop a model in which worker risk preferences and job safety performance lead to smokers facing a flatter market offer curve than nonsmokers. The empirical results support the theoretical model. Smokers are injured more often controlling for their job's objective risk and are paid less for these risks of injury. Smokers and nonsmokers, in effect, are segmented labor market groups with different preferences and different market offer curves.

I. Introduction

THIS paper is motivated by our empirical observation that smokers face greater job risks than do nonsmokers but receive less hazard pay. This result is not consistent with existing models of compensating differentials. Workers may, of course, differ in their attitudes toward risk. Labor economists have long noted that workers who are more willing to bear risk will gravitate towards more hazardous jobs and their commensurately greater hazard pay. The empirical anomaly that we seek to explain is that smokers choosing very risky jobs actually receive less hazard pay than do nonsmokers in comparatively safer jobs. This outcome is seemingly irrational, because smokers presumably should also find jobs that pose lower risk but offer greater hazard pay more attractive than riskier, less remunerative jobs. Our explanation of this phenomenon will utilize a variant of the compensating differentials model in which worker risk preferences affect both the supply and demand sides of the market.

Studies of compensating differentials for job risk usually do not explicitly recognize individual heterogeneity in risk preferences in estimating average wage-risk tradeoffs. In practice, however, there are likely to be substantial differences in worker attitudes toward risk. These differences in preferences may affect both the risks that workers select as well as their associated wage-risk tradeoff. Moreover, in situations in which workers' safety behavior is an important contributor to the riskiness of the job, the nature of the labor market opportunities may differ as well.

The standard hedonic wage model hypothesizes that worker preferences affect the worker's choice of the job from the offer curve, but they do not generally influence the offer curve itself. To the extent that there is an effect, it is indirect. If, for example, too few workers select jobs at high risk firms, firms will close such operations, leading to a reallocation of capital to lower risk enterprises. This paper examines heterogeneous worker attitudes toward health risks, which will affect their job safety performance as well as their job choice. Firms will alter their offer curves in response to differences in riskiness. Differences in worker attitudes toward risk consequently affect the shape of worker indifference curves as well as the market opportunities from which they choose.

Although it is not possible to observe worker health risk preferences directly, these preferences are likely to be revealed through other risk-taking behavior. The measure that we use as a proxy for these risk attitudes is cigarette smoking.[1] Because cigarette smoking poses a lifetime mortality risk of 0.18 to 0.36, this risk is usually several orders of magnitude greater than almost any other personal risk.[2] Further, controlling for observable characteristics, smokers earn less than nonsmokers do overall.[3]

Our model predicts unambiguously that, if all workers face the same offer curve, smokers will select a greater job-risk level than will nonsmokers. At a higher risk level, smokers should necessarily receive greater total risk premia than nonsmokers. However, this result is not borne out in our empirical analysis. Smokers choose jobs in higher risk industries but have a sufficiently lower wage-risk tradeoff that their total risk compensation is less. The implicit value that smokers attach to a statistical job injury is one-half that of nonsmokers. Such a finding is inconsistent with smokers and nonsmokers facing the same wage offer curve. The observed result could arise if smokers were more hazard-prone and, as a result, faced a wage offer curve that was flatter. Indeed, we find that smokers are more hazard-prone on the job, controlling for the industry risk level. They are also more hazardous in their personal actions.

It should be emphasized that concave offer curves alone, coupled with smokers picking higher risk jobs, cannot account for our results. Smokers face higher risk and have lower wage-risk tradeoffs. These results could be consistent with being on the same offer curve. However, they also receive less hazard pay for more total risk, which is not consistent with smokers being on the same offer curve as nonsmokers. Their offer curve must be flatter. Moreover, smokers are paid less than nonsmokers for a zero risk job, which also indicates that their offer curve is lower as well as flatter than that for nonsmokers.

Received for publication March 25, 1998. Revision accepted for publication June 23, 2000.

* Harvard Law School.

A preliminary version of this paper was presented at the 1998 American Economic Association meetings. Two anonymous referees made valuable suggestions. The authors' research was supported by the John M. Olin Center for Law, Economics and Business and the Sheldon Seevak Research Fund.

[1] Ippolito and Ippolito (1984) present related evidence on the implications of smoking behavior for smokers' value of life. See Fuchs (1986), Manning et al. (1991), and O'Conor, Blomquist, and Miller (1996) for a broader analysis of the effect of smoking status on health-related decisions. Also see Hersch and Viscusi (1990) and Hersch and Pickton (1995) for analyses of wage-risk tradeoff effects of smoking status.
[2] Supporting statistics appear in Viscusi (1992), especially p. 70.
[3] See Levine, Gustafson and Velenchik (1997) for an analysis of the wage effects of smoking status.

The Review of Economics and Statistics, May 2001, 83(2): 269–280
© 2001 by the President and Fellows of Harvard College and the Massachusetts Institute of Technology

After developing the model in section II, we describe the data used in the empirical analysis in section III. Section IV presents estimates of wage equations. Section V documents the higher industry risks of the jobs selected by smokers, and section VI explores smokers' injury performance. We conclude that the combined implications of these results are that smokers and nonsmokers differ both in terms of their preferences and their market offer curves.

II. Smoking Status and Compensating Differential Theory

A. Optimal Job Risks

The standard formulation of compensating differentials models the choices made by a representative worker.[4] Choices by a variety of such individuals give rise to the supply side of the market. Although past studies do not assume that all workers are homogeneous, they typically do not explore the explicit economic factors that lead to heterogeneous preferences. This paper extends these approaches by incorporating the role of smoking status into both sides of the market. We develop our model of the role of workers' risk preferences using smoker status as an indicator of risk attitudes, because this approach allows a direct empirical test. However, the theory applies generally to any stratification of workers by their risk preferences.

Both the supply and demand components of the hedonic wage model vary depending on smoking status. Firms' offer curves define the market opportunities facing workers, in which the envelope of these individual offer curves is the nondominated choice set. The variable s is a measure of smoking intensity, where higher values of s reflect greater intensity. The value of s is 0 for nonsmokers.

Let the job risk be denoted by p, where $0 \le p \le 1$, and let w denote the wage rate. The market opportunities locus is denoted by $w(p, s)$. Market wage premia for risk, w_p, are positive, reflecting the positive marginal cost of safety to the firm, which results in greater willingness to pay higher wages for increased risk levels. Because the marginal costs to the firm of safety improvements are increasing, the cost savings to the firm from higher levels of risk are diminishing, or $w_{pp} < 0$. If smoking intensity does not affect worker productivity, then $w_s = 0$. For situations in which this equality always holds, $w_{ps} = 0$ as well. However, if smokers are less productive—perhaps in part because they are riskier workers—w_s will be negative. To summarize, the overall shape of $w(p, s)$ has the properties that $w_p > 0$, $w_{pp} < 0$, and $w_s \le 0$. If smokers are

more productive, then $w_s > 0$, but this possibility is not consistent with subsequent empirical results.

Monitoring smoking-related differences must be feasible for firms to be able to link wages to smoking status. For firms' offer curves to vary with smoking status in this model, firms must either observe smoking status directly or observe other characteristics correlated with smoking status, and they must be able to ascertain how these attributes are correlated with productivity or greater riskiness. In the extreme case in which neither smoking status nor attributes correlated with smoking are observable, all influences discussed below will be through worker preferences on the supply side of the market rather than through differences in labor demand.

Workers have state-dependent utility functions for two states of nature: no injury and injury. If the injury is fatal, the utility function is a bequest function. The main role of smoking intensity in the model is to serve as an index of the unobservable utility function parameter $h(s)$ that indicates a greater willingness to bear health risks. People who smoke more have revealed that they are more willing to incur risks of ill health. Smoking intensity could potentially reflect differences in tastes that affect preferences in both health states. However, it is sufficient and more tractable to assume that only the injury (or ill-health) state is affected. The final assumption governing the utility function formulation is that, with no loss of generality, the role of nonwage income such as assets or workers' compensation will be subsumed in the functional form of the utility functions.

Although smokers endanger their health more than nonsmokers, whether these differences in risky behavior arise from preferences or perceptions has not been fully resolved. Three possibilities for how smoking status may affect job risk decisions are most salient.[5] First, smokers may not value their health as much as do nonsmokers. This case stems from an underlying difference in preference structures and will be the focus of the analysis here. Second, smokers may value ill health less if they undervalue the losses they will suffer.[6] A high discount rate with respect to future health losses likewise could account for this effect. These examples of undervalued health losses simply involve a different interpretation of the reason why smokers have a different utility function in the ill-health state. Our model also pertains to this case. Third, one could hypothesize that smokers underperceive health risks of all kinds. However, this possibility is not borne out by our evidence on workers' own subjective job-risk perceptions and the associated compensating differentials by smoking status reported in Hersch and Viscusi (1990). As a result, the model below focuses on preference-related differences, recognizing that one cannot

---

[4] The first wage-risk estimates in the modern literature appear in Smith (1974). See, among many others, Thaler and Rosen (1976), Rosen (1986), and the surveys by Viscusi (1983, 1993), Jones-Lee (1976, 1989), Kniesner and Leeth (1995), Smith (1979), and Brown (1980). For international evidence, see Kniesner and Leeth (1991). The model here extends the formulation in Viscusi (1979). See Viscusi and Evans (1990) for empirical estimation of utility functions for workers that yield results consistent with this formulation.

[5] Fuchs (1986) provides an early discussion of many of these issues.

[6] The rationality of smoking decisions is of particular concern with respect to youth smoking. Chaloupka (1991) examines whether younger and less educated individuals are more likely to be myopic in their smoking behavior.

TABLE 1.—SUMMARY OF DIFFERENCES IN RISK OUTCOMES

Effect of Smoking Status on Wages	Offer Curve	Effect on Smokers' Outcomes Relative to Nonsmokers		
		Risk p	Total Risk Premium	Wage Rate
1. $w_s = 0$, $w_{ps} = 0$	Same for both groups.	↑	↑	↑
2. $w_s < 0$, $w_{ps} = 0$	Smokers have offer curve that is a downward parallel shift of nonsmokers' curve.	↑	↑	?
3. $w_s < 0$, $w_{ps} > 0$	Smokers face steeper wage offer curve that starts below nonsmokers' curve.	↑	↑	?
4. $w_s < 0$, $w_{ps} < 0$	Smokers face flatter wage offer curve that lies below nonsmokers' curve.	?	?	?

The ↑ indicates higher effects, and the ? denotes effects of uncertain direction.

necessarily impute complete rationality to the observed choices, only consistency across risk-taking domains.

Our specification of the nature of preferences is consequently quite general. The utility of good health is $U^1(w(p, s))$ and the utility in the injured state is $U^2(w(p, s), h(s))$.[7] In the good-health state, utility is a function of the wage only. In the post-injury state, utility is also a function of $h(s)$, which relates smoking to unobservable taste characteristics. We assume that smokers suffer less of a drop in utility with injury than do nonsmokers and that people are either risk-averse or risk-neutral (U^1_w, $U^2_w >$ 0, and U^1_{ww}, $U^2_{ww} \leq 0$). The key assumption driving compensating differentials is not risk aversion with respect to financial losses but an assumed preference for being healthy rather than not, or $U^1(w) > U^2(w, h)$ for any given wage value w. The marginal utility of income is higher in the good-health state for any given level of w, or $U^1_w > U^2_w$. We also assume that smoking intensity has a nonnegative effect on the utility of ill health, or $U^2_h h_s \geq 0$, and that smoking intensity has a nonnegative effect on the marginal utility of income in the injury state, or $U^2_{wh} h_s \geq 0$.

The worker selects the optimal job risk p from the available wage offer schedule to maximize expected utility V, or

$$\text{Max}_p \; V = (1 - p)U^1(w(p, s)) \tag{1}$$
$$+ pU^2(w(p, s), h(s)),$$

leading to the first-order condition

$$w_p = \frac{U^1 - U^2}{(1 - p)U^1_w + pU^2_w}. \tag{2}$$

At the optimal job risk, the worker equates the marginal compensating differential w_p to the difference in utility in the two health states normalized by the expected marginal utility of income. The second-order condition is also satisfied given the assumptions above. We label the second-order condition expression D, where $D < 0$.[8]

[7] If there is a lag before the injury occurs, the value of U^2 could subsume the role of discounting.
[8] In particular,

B. The Effect of Smoking Status

The choices implied by equation (2) vary with the structure of utility functions and wage offer curves, each of which may vary with smoking status. To assess the effect of smoking intensity on the optimal job risk selected, we totally differentiate equation (2) and solve for dp/ds, yielding

$$\frac{dp}{ds} = \{-(U^1_w - U^2_w)w_s + (1 - p)U^1_{ww}w_s w_p$$
$$+ (1 - p)U^1_w w_{ps} + U^2_h h_s + pU^2_{ww}w_s w_p \tag{3}$$
$$+ pU^2_{wh}w_p h_s + pU^2_w w_{ps}\}/(-D).$$

Because $U^1_w > U^2_w$, all terms in the bracketed expression in the numerator of equation (3) are nonnegative with the possible exception of the two terms involving w_{ps}, which represents the effect of smoking intensity on the marginal wage-risk tradeoff offered to workers. If w_{ps} is positive, smokers face a steeper wage-risk curve than do nonsmokers. The sign of w_{ps} also influences the relation between smoking status and optimal job risks. If w_{ps} is not negative, dp/ds will be positive: the optimal job risk increases with smoking intensity. However, if w_{ps} is negative, dp/ds could be negative as well if this influence is dominant.

Because of this indeterminacy, there are a variety of different possible effects of smoking status on the slope of the wage-risk tradeoffs.[9] Table 1 summarizes the four dif-

_____

$$D = -2w_p(U^1_w - U^2_w) + (1 - p)U^1_{ww}(w_p)^2 + pU^2_{ww}(w_p)^2$$
$$+ (1 - p)U^1_w w_{pp} + pU^2_w w_{pp} < 0.$$

[9] The indeterminacy of the slope of the tradeoff rate selected is attributable to the absence of a clearcut relationship between

$$w_p(p_0, 0) = \frac{U^1(w(p_0, 0)) - U^2(0, w(p_0, 0))}{(1 - p)U^1_w(w(p_0, 0)) + pU^2_w(w(p_0, 0))} \quad \text{and}$$

$$w_p(p_s, s) = \frac{U^1(w(p_s, s)) - U^2(w(p_s, s), h(s))}{(1 - p)U^1_w(w(p_s, s)) + p_s U^2_w(w(p_s, s), h(s))},$$

where p_s is the risk selected by smokers and $h(0)$ is assumed to be zero, without loss of generality.

FIGURE 1.—SUMMARY OF SMOKER WAGE-RISK CASES

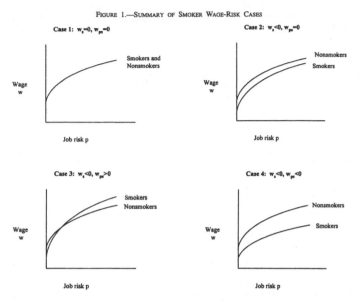

ferent situations based on possible signs of w_s and w_{ps}. Figure 1 illustrates these four cases.

Whether the total risk premium received by smokers is greater than that of nonsmokers depends on whether all workers face the same wage offer curve. For each of the four cases shown in table 1 and figure 1, smokers and nonsmokers will have constant expected utility loci that are upward sloping with a positive second derivative with respect to job risks. The character of the labor market outcome is similar for three of the cases and is ambiguous for one.

In case 1, in which smokers and nonsmokers face the same offer curve, smokers will select a greater job risk and consequently receive a greater risk premium, as well as a higher total wage rate. If smokers' market offer curve involves a downward parallel shift as in case 2, these results for the risk level and risk premium continue to hold except that the wage rate received by smokers may be less. In case 3, for which $w_{ps} > 0$, the greater steepness of the wage offer curve for smokers makes risky jobs more attractive to smokers than in the counterpart case 2. The general spirit of the results in terms of the effects on risk, compensating differentials, and wages follows the identical pattern as in case 2. Increasing the steepness of smokers' offer curves in case 3 does not alter the general character of the results found for case 2. The same is not true if the wage offer curve for smokers is flatter. Case 4 permits the wage offer curve to be flatter for smokers, leading smokers to possibly select higher or

lower job risk levels, with ambiguous effects on compensating risk differentials and wage levels.

The strategy for the empirical work is to ascertain the various effects of smoking status on job risks and compensating differentials for risk. These influences will make it possible to distinguish which market offer curves could be consistent with the market outcome. If, as we will find below, smokers incur greater job risks but are paid less in total risk compensation, cases 1 through 3 can be ruled out.

The reasoning is the following. Let p_2 be the risk chosen by smokers and p_1 be the risk chosen by non-smokers. Suppose that empirically we observe that $p_2 > p_1$ after controlling for other personal characteristics. Then suppose that we observe empirically that the wage premium for risk received by smokers is less than for nonsmokers, or

$$w(p_2, s) - w(0, s) < w(p_1, 0) - w(0, 0). \qquad (4)$$

However, if smokers and nonsmokers faced the same offer curves, then

$$w(0, s) = w(0, 0), \qquad (5)$$

so that equation (4) reduces to

$$w(p_2, s) < w(p_1, 0). \qquad (6)$$

An assumption of identical offer curves for smokers and nonsmokers implies that

$$w(p_2, s) = w(p_2, 0). \qquad (7)$$

But, because $p_2 > p_1$, $w(p_2, 0)$ should exceed $w(p_1, 0)$ if $w_p > 0$ for firms' offer curves, leading to a contradiction of the implications of equation (6) and (7). Moreover, workers will never locate on a segment of the wage-offer curve for which $w_p \le 0$.[10]

III. The Risk and Employment Data

To explore the implications of smoking status for job-safety decisions, we need data on wages, individual smoking behavior, a measure of the objective riskiness of the worker's job, and a measure of the worker's own job-risk behavior. The data set we use is the 1987 National Medical Expenditure Survey (NMES), which is a national probability sample of the noninstitutionalized population of the United States. These data uniquely offer the advantage of including comprehensive labor market variables as well as information pertaining to the worker's on-the-job injury experience and smoking behavior. Thus, it is possible to investigate not only whether smoking affects compensating differentials for risk but also whether smokers are more accident-prone in their jobs. The NMES does not, however, include a state identifier so that an expected workers' compensation variable could not be included in this analysis. Similarly, the absence of state information does not permit us to use state tax rates to create an instrument for smoking status.

We restrict the sample to male employees, age 18 to 65, with hourly wages of $2 to $100 per hour, and with complete information on the variables used in the analyses. In order to match individuals to the U.S. Bureau of Labor Statistics (BLS) risk measures, we exclude agricultural workers, the self-employed, and private household workers. This results in a sample of 4,821 individuals, with 3,273 nonsmokers and 1,548 smokers.

Table 2 summarizes the sample characteristics by smoking status. The smoking rate for this sample is 32%, which is just above the U.S. average for adults. The corresponding national rate for males in 1987 is 31.2% (U.S. Department of Commerce, 1995).

Smokers and nonsmokers in this sample are largely similar in their demographic characteristics. Although there are statistically significant differences in residence in an SMSA and whether physical conditions limit work, the differences are minor. There are no statistically significant differences by smoking status in race and union status. However, there is a large difference in years of education, with nonsmokers averaging over one year of college and smokers averaging less than twelve years of education.

[10] This result is derived by Viscusi (1979) for an analogous model without heterogeneity.

TABLE 2.—SAMPLE CHARACTERISTICS

Variable	Mean (Standard Deviation)		Absolute Value of t-Statistic of Difference in Means or Proportions
	Nonsmoker	Smoker	
Job and Personal Characteristics			
Hourly wage (1987$)	10.44	9.34	5.84
	(6.32)	(5.49)	
Age	36.00	36.81	2.21
	(12.22)	(11.15)	
White	0.76	0.77	1.01
	(0.43)	(0.42)	
Education	13.12	11.89	14.44
	(2.83)	(2.61)	
Experience	16.58	18.60	5.35
	(12.49)	(11.70)	
Tenure	7.14	6.20	3.41
	(8.50)	(7.69)	
Married	0.63	0.64	0.03
	(0.48)	(0.48)	
Physical condition limits work	0.06	0.08	2.75
	(0.23)	(0.27)	
Union member	0.20	0.22	1.51
	(0.40)	(0.41)	
White-collar	0.46	0.28	12.53
	(0.50)	(0.45)	
SMSA	0.77	0.73	3.46
	(0.42)	(0.45)	
Risk Characteristics[a]			
BLS Lost Workdays Rate	77.90	91.98	8.22
	(54.67)	(57.38)	
BLS Injury Rate	4.20	4.87	8.55
	(2.56)	(2.59)	
Worker injury (percentage)	3.33	5.81	4.05
Accident at home (percentage)	1.50	2.71	2.90
Individual injury (percentage)	7.03	10.01	3.59
Sample size	3,273	1,548	

Data are drawn from the 1987 National Medical Expenditure Survey.
[a] BLS injury rates are taken from *Occupational Injuries and Illnesses in the United States by Industry, 1987*, Table 1, Bureau of Labor Statistics (Bulletin 2328, May 1989). All injury statistics are per 100 workers.

Nonsmokers have more years of experience with their current employer (*Tenure*). Smokers are much less likely to be employed in a white-collar job (28% versus 46%). Given these differences in human-capital characteristics, it is not surprising that smokers earn less, with nonsmokers earning $1.10 more per hour.

Following the conventional practice in the compensating differentials literature, we match each worker to BLS risk measures based on the worker's reported three-digit industry code. We use two such measures to capture both injury frequency and duration-weighted frequency. The first measure is the annual number of lost workdays due to injury and illness per 100 full-time employees (*BLS Lost Workdays Rate*), and the second variable is the annual lost workday injury and illness incidence rate per 100 full-time workers (*BLS Injury Rate*).

To measure individual-specific injury experience, we use additional data requested in the survey. The NMES survey asked all respondents to report the location of any accidents that caused an injury in 1987 leading to a period of disability or use of medical services or goods. If the reported accident occurred at a work location-and caused the worker to lose work, we coded the accident as a work-related injury (*Worker Injury*).[11] We emphasize that survey respondents were instructed to report only those injuries that resulted directly from an accident. Other lost workday injuries and illnesses that do not result from an accident will be under-reported. For example, lost workdays that result from repetitive-motion disorders will not be included.[12]

The own injury variable captures two types of effects. First, this variable may be a more accurate index of the riskiness of the worker's particular job than the BLS risk variable, which reflects the average risk for the industry. Second, for any given level of objective riskiness of the job, workers may differ in their degree of care and propensity to injury. Past injury experiences consequently may indicate that the workers themselves are riskier, not that the job itself poses higher objective risks. We recognize that, although the own injury variable has the advantage of being job specific, it is not a better job risk measure than objective industry risk data based on large samples of injury experiences. Seriously injured workers also may switch jobs, starting a new injury history record for their job.

The risk characteristics of the sample differ considerably by smoking status. The BLS industry average risk measures indicate that smokers sort themselves into riskier industries on average. Smokers are also more likely to get injured. Although smokers' higher work injury rate is due in part to employment in higher-risk industries, it is noteworthy that smokers are significantly more likely than nonsmokers to have an accident at home (*Accident at Home*) or an accident of any kind (*Individual Injury*). The Individual Injury variable exceeds the sum of Worker Injury and Accident at Home because it also includes other classes of accidents, such as those due to motor vehicles and recreational activities.

IV. Wage-Risk Tradeoff Rates

A. Compensating Differentials Estimates

The empirical analysis begins with a conventional compensating differentials equation to capture the equilibrium labor market tradeoffs that reflect the joint influence of supply and demand factors.

To explore the effect of smoking, we estimate an equation of the following form:

$$\ln wage = \beta_0 + X\beta_1 + \beta_2 BLS\ Rate \tag{8}$$
$$+ \beta_3 Worker\ Injury + \varepsilon,$$

where X is a vector of personal and job characteristics, such as education, experience, union status, and handicapped status. The variable *BLS Rate* measures the industry's risk level and *Worker Injury* is a dummy variable indicating whether the worker had an on-the-job injury in the preceding year. The term ε is a random-error term that we assume is normally distributed. The semilogarithmic form in equation (8) is the norm in the compensating differential literature and the labor economics literature more generally. Although the offer curve is concave, worker indifference curves are convex. What is being estimated is the locus of tangencies for observed wage-risk combinations rather than the wage offer curve itself.[13] Because both the offer curve and the constant expected utility loci could differ by smoking status, we estimate separate equations for smokers and nonsmokers. Tests for whether smoking status enters simply by altering the intercept rather than the entire equation structure indicated that one could reject the hypothesis that the effect of smoking was restricted in such a manner.[14]

If nonsmokers and smokers face wage offer curves that are similarly shaped but with possibly different intercepts, as in the case 1 or 2 models, the value of β_2 is larger for nonsmokers than it is for smokers. Nonsmokers should select a lower risk job on the steeper section of the wage offer curve. For case 3 as well, smokers will select greater risks than will nonsmokers. As a consequence, they will also receive greater total risk premia due to their higher wage-risk tradeoff. For the case 4 model, there is ambiguity regarding relative risk levels, risk premia, and wage-risk tradeoffs.

The expected sign of the coefficient β_3 on the own worker injury variable is ambiguous. If the own worker injury risk variable better reflects the objective riskiness of the job that drives market risk premia, then β_3 should be positive. If, however, the role of the variable is to reflect differences in worker riskiness, then β_3 will be negative.

A longstanding issue in the literature has been the joint determination of wages and risk levels. Thus, the risk level is correlated with the error term in the wage equation. The standard compensating differential model

---

[11] We coded an accident as a workplace accident if the respondent reported the location was at an industrial place, at work, at business, or adjacent to business. The survey asked if the worker had lost at least one-half of day of work due to the accident.

[12] The injury rate calculated using the NMES will not correspond exactly to the BLS injury rate. The BLS injury rate is derived from a survey of employers and includes lost workdays resulting from any occupational injury or illness. The injury rate calculated in the NMES is based on workers' self-reported accidents, and excludes other occupational illnesses and injuries. Further, individuals whose injuries prevent them from returning to work are not represented in the sample.

[13] Explorations of alternative functional forms, such as the inclusion of quadratic risk variables, failed to yield significant effects for the quadratic form. Other specifications, such as log wage-log risk yielded significant job risk effects for nonsmokers only. Although there is no theoretical basis for selecting the semilogarithmic form as there is for models linking wages to education, this specification is in line with that used in the literature.

[14] We rejected the hypothesis that the coefficients on job risk, own injury, tenure, union, and professional occupation are the same for smokers and nonsmokers (p-values are 0.02 and 0.03) based on equations including *BLS Lost Workdays Rate* and *BLS Injury Rate*, respectively.

CIGARETTE SMOKERS AS JOB RISK TAKERS   275

TABLE 3.—LOG WAGE EQUATION ESTIMATES

Independent Variables	Nonsmokers	Smokers	Nonsmokers	Smokers
BLS Lost Workdays Rate	0.101	0.058		
	(0.016)**	(0.020)**		
	[0.027]**	[0.021]**		
BLS Injury Rate/100			1.500	0.733
			(0.340)**	(0.434)*
			[0.606]**	[0.491]
Worker Injury	−0.008	−0.086	−0.009	−0.083
	(0.037)	(0.038)**	(0.037)	(0.038)*
	[0.032]	[0.037]**	[0.032]	[0.037]**
Experience	0.010	0.010	0.010	0.010
	(0.001)**	(0.001)**	(0.001)**	(0.001)**
	[0.001]**	[0.001]**	[0.001]**	[0.001]**
Tenure	0.034	0.026	0.034	0.025
	(0.003)**	(0.004)**	(0.003)**	(0.004)**
	[0.004]**	[0.005]**	[0.004]**	[0.005]**
Tenure squared × 100	−0.083	−0.064	−0.083	−0.064
	(0.010)**	(0.013)**	(0.010)**	(0.013)**
	[0.011]**	[0.014]**	[0.011]**	[0.014]**
Education	0.054	0.047	0.054	0.047
	(0.004)**	(0.005)**	(0.004)**	(0.005)**
	[0.005]**	[0.006]**	[0.005]**	[0.006]**
White	0.115	0.119	0.114	0.119
	(0.018)**	(0.026)**	(0.019)**	(0.026)**
	[0.021]**	[0.022]**	[0.021]**	[0.022]**
Handicapped	−0.132	−0.078	−0.132	−0.080
	(0.038)**	(0.043)*	(0.038)**	(0.043)*
	[0.037]**	[0.050]*	[0.037]**	[0.045]*
Union	0.146	0.216	0.152	0.220
	(0.021)**	(0.027)**	(0.021)**	(0.027)**
	[0.029]**	[0.036]**	[0.030]**	[0.036]**
R^2	0.39	0.39	0.39	0.38

Dependent variable: log of hourly wage. Additional variables in each equation are a constant, and indicator variables for eight census divisions, SMSA, and eight occupations.
Standard errors corrected for heteroskedasticity in parentheses; standard errors corrected for within-group correlation in brackets. ** (*) by the standard error indicates that the coefficient is significant at the 1% (5%) level based on that standard error (one-sided tests).

does not seek to estimate the underlying economic structure but focuses only on the observed market equilibrium tradeoffs.

However, the data set afforded a number of potential instruments, so we explored the endogeneity issue using IV estimation. The potential instruments included self-reported risk taking, height, weight, seatbelt use, checking blood pressure, exercising, flossing teeth, and limitations on walking, climbing stairs, and lifting heavy objects. Jointly, these variables were only marginally significant (10% level) in determining the individual's choice of industry level risk. In addition, subsets of these variables yielded even weaker explanatory power. Nonetheless, using these admittedly weak instruments in a wage equation, a Hausman test indicated that we could not reject the hypothesis that the job risk variable was exogenous. This result is not unexpected because of the weak nature of available instruments. As a result, our empirical model uses a standard OLS regression equation.

Table 3 summarizes the key coefficients for the estimated wage equations by smoking status. Selection-corrected estimates for the probability that an individual is a smoker yields essentially identical results, for example, *BLS Injury Rate* coefficients of 1.416 for nonsmokers and 0.742 for

smokers.[15] The first set of equations uses *BLS Lost Workdays Rate* to indicate industry risk, and the second set uses the *BLS Injury Rate*. We present two sets of standard errors. The first set indicated in parentheses are the White (1980) heteroskedasticity-adjusted standard errors. However, because we assign the same BLS risk measure to all individuals within the same industry, the residuals in the regression for workers in the same industry may be correlated. Standard errors that do not account for this correlation may be too small. As a result, we also present, in brackets, robust standard errors that account for this within-group correlation.[16]

The demographic variables follow the usual patterns, with better educated and more experienced workers earning more. The difference in the rates of return to education is not significant, so that, even though smokers have less education, it does not offer a higher rate of return. Smokers' different risk choices consequently are not attributable to

[15] The instruments used in the IV equation are also used here in the selection equation.
[16] See Huber (1967) and Rogers (1993). This correction appears in Hersch (1998) but not elsewhere in the compensating differentials literature.

differences in rates of time preferences with respect to income.[17]

The results in table 3 indicate that all workers receive positive compensation for bearing job risks. The estimated job risk premia per unit risk for smokers are consistently below those of nonsmokers, with the difference significant at the 5% level based on the *BLS Lost Workdays Rate* and at the 9% level based on *BLS Injury Rate* (one-sided tests). The magnitude of the coefficients differs considerably by smoking status, with the job-risk coefficient for nonsmokers being twice that of smokers using either measure of industry risk. The estimated compensating differentials suggest that smokers have lower wage-risk tradeoff rates than do nonsmokers. However, these results alone do not identify which of the possible wage-offer curves pertain to smokers and nonsmokers.

The own worker injury variable adds information on the effect of personal job safety on wages. Wages of nonsmokers are not affected by whether the worker had been injured on the job in the preceding year. However, there is a negative effect of own injury on the wages of smokers. This result would occur if smokers are more careless for a given industry risk level and consequently less productive in promoting workplace safety.[18] Nonsmoking careless workers also should be paid less.[19] Because nonsmokers who suffer injuries do not incur any wage penalty, it may be that the character of their injuries is different. For example, nonsmokers' accidents may be more attributable to workplace characteristics than dysfunctional worker behavior. Although we do not have data to distinguish all such influences, we will examine the hypothesis that smokers are riskier workers and riskier people more generally.

B. Risk Compensation and the Implicit Value of Job Injuries

Table 4 summarizes the implicit injury values and total wage compensation for risk implied by the wage equation estimates in table 3.[20] A measure of the tradeoff rate is the implicit value of a statistical workplace injury. For any injury-frequency risk measure *Risk*, this value is simply $\partial w/\partial Risk$, with appropriate adjustment for the annual units of wages (assuming 2,000 hours per year) and risk. Panel A of table 4 summarizes these implicit value results. Based on

[17] One might hypothesize, of course, that rates of time preference for different health states over time could differ from rates of time preference for money, but if what is being discounted is utility in different time periods, both income and health would be treated symmetrically.
[18] This result could also occur if smokers picked safer jobs for any given industry risk level, although this interpretation appears less plausible because smokers tend to work in higher risk industries.
[19] It is difficult to develop a long list of occupations in which recklessness is valued. For high rise construction work and race-car driving, boldness is desirable, but carelessness that leads to work accidents is not generally desirable even in those risky pursuits.
[20] For a survey of the value of worker injuries, see Viscusi (1993). Our findings are consistent with the estimated range in past studies for combined samples of smokers and nonsmokers.

TABLE 4.—WAGE-RISK TRADEOFFS IMPLIED BY REGRESSION RESULTS

Panel A: Implicit Values of Injury Days and Injuries		
	Nonsmokers	Smokers
BLS Injury Rate		
Implicit value per injury	$31,320	$13,692
BLS Lost Workdays Rate		
Implicit value per injury day	$2,109	$1,083
Implicit value per injury	$39,017	$20,469

Panel B: Total Wage Compensation Compared to Zero Risk Level[a]		
Initial Risk Level	Nonsmokers	Smokers
BLS Injury Rate (mean)		
Nonsmoker risk (4.20)	$1,122	$516
Sample average risk (4.41)	$1,214	$542
Smokers' risk (4.87)	$1,346	$594
BLS Lost Workdays Rate (mean)		
Nonsmoker risk (77.90)	$1,394	$756
Sample average risk (82.42)	$1,512	$798
Smokers' risk (91.98)	$1,696	$888

[a] These amounts pertain to $w(p, s) - w(0, s)$ for different risk-level p values specified in the table. Estimates were obtained using the wage equations for the different smoking groups, where all calculations are done on an individual worker basis. If the individual belongs to the particular risk level group, then the own risk level is used. Otherwise, the sample average risk is used.

the discrete injury frequency rate results, nonsmokers receive $31,320 per expected job injury and smokers receive just under half this amount ($13,692 per injury). The estimates taking into account injury duration yield a similar pattern. Nonsmokers receive $2,109 compensation per expected day lost due to injury as compared to $1,083 for smokers. The duration of smokers' injuries is somewhat greater than for nonsmokers so that there is a narrower relative spread between the implicit value of an expected injury spell than the value per injury day: $39,017 for nonsmokers and $20,469 for smokers.

Another measure of the difference in wage compensation for risk is the total value of compensation that workers receive relative to what the earnings equations would predict. For zero risk, this value is $w(p, s) - w(0, s)$, which we calculate on an individual worker basis using the particular group's log wage equation. At the individual's own risk level, nonsmokers average $1,122 in risk compensation compared to $594 for smokers based on the injury-rate regressions, and $1,394 for nonsmokers and $888 for smokers based on the lost-workday rate regressions. These differences are surprising because smokers face higher job risks yet receive less total job risk compensation. The estimates imply that the wage difference between smokers and nonsmokers stemming from hazard pay alone is $528 based on the injury rate estimates and $506 based on the lost-workday risk estimates. Note that the overall wage gap between smokers and nonsmokers is $2,200 annually, so that risk premiums account for about one-fourth of the difference. The differences in compensation due to job risks would be even greater if smokers and nonsmokers faced the same risk level.

Smokers and nonsmokers receive different wages for reasons other than risk. Three of the cases illustrated in figure 1 indicate that smokers and nonsmokers wages may differ due to factors other than risk. Indeed, our estimates suggest that approximately three-fourths of the earnings difference would remain at a zero risk level.

Panel B of table 4 also indicates the total wage risk premiums for different base risk levels, as compared to the zero risk level. If both smokers and nonsmokers were at the smokers' risk level, the earnings difference would widen by $224 to $302 beyond their observed amount. Earnings differences if all workers were at the average sample risk or at the nonsmokers' risk level would be less. These results illustrate how the higher risk level faced by smokers narrows the nonsmoker-smoker relative risk-compensation gap, but not by enough to generate higher wage-risk premia for smokers.

V.   Industry Risk Differences of Smokers and Nonsmokers

A principal theoretical prediction in section II is that, if smokers face a wage offer curve with the same or steeper slope than do nonsmokers, they will choose jobs with greater objective risk. Only a flatter market offer curve for smokers could potentially lead to the result that smokers are on jobs with lower objective riskiness. Results in section IV indicate that smokers have a lower wage-risk tradeoff and receive lower compensation for risk. If we also can assess the risk level selected by smokers after controlling for personal characteristics, we can potentially distinguish which offer curve smokers are on and where they are situated.

Based on both risk measures, smokers incur greater job risks but receive lower total risk premia.[21] If smokers faced the same market opportunities locus as nonsmokers, such behavior would be irrational. Such an outcome could occur under case 4. Moreover, case 4 assumes that smokers receive a lower wage when $p = 0$, which is also the case. This discussion of the possible cases presupposes, however, that the reason why smokers are located at higher job risk levels along the market offer curve is due to their smoking status, not variables correlated with smoking. If, for example, differences in educational background accounted for the job risk difference rather than smoking status, then the interpretation of the compensating differential results could differ. Thus, a fundamental empirical concern is whether smoking status per se leads smokers to select a higher job-risk level.

Consistent with the theory, the empirical analysis of job risk choice utilizes a reduced form model in which only exogenous personal characteristic variables are included. Variables such as job tenure and worker injury experience consequently do not appear in the model. Let

$$Risk = \gamma_0 + Y\gamma_1 + \gamma_2 Smoker + \varepsilon, \tag{9}$$

[21] Recall the descriptive statistics in table 2 and see the regression results in table 5.

TABLE 5.—REGRESSION ESTIMATES OF BLS INDUSTRY RISK EQUATIONS

	Dependent Variable	
	BLS Lost Workdays	BLS Injury Rate
Smoker	6.422**	0.304**
	(1.760)	(0.080)
Age	1.729**	0.069**
	(0.450)	(0.021)
Age Squared × 100	−2.199**	−0.092**
	(0.558)	(0.026)
White	−2.694	−0.168*
	(1.891)	(0.087)
Education	−5.299**	−0.265**
	(0.307)	(0.014)
Married	4.245**	0.157
	(1.822)	(0.084)
Handicapped	−4.248	−0.152
	(3.439)	(0.157)
SMSA	−5.552**	−0.247**
	(1.906)	(0.088)
R^2	0.10	0.11

Equations also include a constant and indicators for eight census divisions.
Standard errors are in parentheses. ** (*) indicates significance at the 1% (5%) level (one-sided tests).

so that the risk level chosen by the worker is a function of a vector of demographic and regional variables Y with the coefficient vector γ_1, and smoking status with coefficient γ_2. The *Risk* variable pertains to each of the two BLS measures. *Smoker* is a 0-1 indicator variable. The expected sign of γ_2 predicted by the theory is positive in cases 1 through 3 and is ambiguous in case 4.

Table 5 reports the estimated risk equations for both BLS risk measures. The key finding is that, controlling for individual characteristics, workers who smoke select jobs in higher-risk industries. Education and age also affect the chosen risk level, with better educated workers choosing less risky industries. Job risk levels rise with age but at a diminishing rate.

Controlling for other personal characteristics, the magnitude of the coefficient on smoking status is substantial. Smokers select jobs in industries with a *Lost Workdays Rate* that is 6.4 per 100 workers higher—or more than 8% greater—than the average *Lost Workdays Rate* of 77.9 for nonsmokers. However, the total average gap between smokers' and nonsmokers' *Lost Workdays Rate* is 14.1, so that more than half of the smoker-nonsmoker difference is attributable to demographic characteristics of smokers other than smoking status alone.

The results for the *BLS Injury Rate* variable are similar in that smokers' industries have a significantly higher injury rate that is 7% greater than that of nonsmokers after taking into account other personal characteristics. However, the total unadjusted smoker-nonsmoker *BLS Injury Rate* difference is 16%, so that just under half of the unadjusted smoker-nonsmoker risk difference is attributable to smoking status per se.

The finding here using both risk measures is that smokers face greater industry risks controlling for other personal characteristics. As we found in section IV, smokers also have lower wage-risk tradeoffs and receive less total risk compensation. For the wage-offer curve facing smokers to be flatter, there must be some demand-side influence that would account for such an effect. One such possibility is that smokers are less effective in producing safety (that is, they are more injury-prone), so that their productivity in unsafe jobs is comparatively low. We examine this possibility below.

VI. Workers' Own Injury Experiences

If smokers are less averse to being injured, they should be less careful than nonsmokers within jobs of given riskiness. Smokers consequently should experience more work injuries controlling for the industry risk level and other measures of the objective job characteristics. Measurement error could also be a contributing influence. Smokers could be more injury-prone if the actual risks of their jobs are greater than the industry risk average. Although such a relationship is possible, it is not supported by the evidence on wage premia for higher personal injury risks, which were found to be negative for smokers and insignificant for nonsmokers.

To explore whether smokers are riskier workers, we estimate the relationship

$$Injury = \delta_0 + Z\delta_1 + \delta_2 BLS\ Rate$$
$$+ \delta_3 Smoker + \varepsilon, \tag{10}$$

where Z is a vector of personal and job characteristic variables. We expect the coefficient δ_2 for *BLS Rate* and δ_3 for *Smoker* to be positive.

We consider three measures of worker riskiness. The first measure is whether the worker has had a lost-workday accident in the past year on the worker's current job (*Worker Injury*). This variable is the own injury variable that entered the wage equations above. The second risk measure is whether the worker has experienced any accident in the past year—whether at work or elsewhere—that has caused the worker to miss at least one-half day of work (*Individual Injury*). The final personal risk variable is whether the worker has experienced a home accident in the past year (*Accident at Home*). This variable captures riskiness of behavior in contexts other than the job, which should be instructive in indicating the degree of risks and precautions the person selects. Because job risks are not a measure of home accident conditions, the *BLS Rate* variable does not enter this equation.

Because the injury experience variable is discrete, we use probit to estimate the marginal probability of an injury based on a one-unit change in each of the independent variables. The BLS risk measure used in the two equations with dependent variables encompassing job safety is the *BLS Injury Rate*. Results were similar using the *BLS Lost Workdays Rate*. Once again, we report robust standard errors corrected for heteroskedasticity (errors in parentheses) for all equations and standard errors corrected for

TABLE 6.—PROBIT ESTIMATES OF THE PROBABILITY OF INJURY EXPERIENCE

	Dependent Variable		
	Worker Injury	Individual Injury	Accident at Home
Smoker	0.011	0.015	0.008
	(0.005)*	(0.008)*	(0.004)*
	[0.005]*	[0.008]*	—
BLS Injury Rate/100	0.269	0.537	—
	(0.099)**	(0.153)**	—
	[0.105]**	[0.132]**	—
Age × 100	−0.037	−0.203	0.115
	(0.128)	(0.235)	(0.116)
	[0.120]	[0.214]	—
Age Squared × 10,000	−0.066	−0.046	−0.002
	(0.163)	(0.302)	(0.001)
	[0.150]	[0.274]	—
White	0.007	0.015	0.008
	(0.005)	(0.008)	(0.004)*
	[0.006]	[0.008]	—
Education	−0.003	−0.006	−0.002
	(0.001)**	(0.002)**	(0.001)*
	[0.001]**	[0.002]**	—
Married	0.010	0.014	0.004
	(0.005)*	(0.008)	(0.004)
	[0.004]*	[0.008]	—
Handicapped	0.011	0.043	0.006
	(0.011)	(0.019)**	(0.008)
	[0.011]	[0.020]*	—
Tenure	−0.002	−0.002	—
	(0.001)**	(0.001)	—
	[0.001]*	[0.002]	—
Tenure Squared × 100	0.006	0.005	—
	(0.003)*	(0.005)	—
	[0.003]*	[0.005]	—
Log-Likelihood	−758.64	−1267.33	−437.79

Additional variables in Worker Injury and Individual Injury equations are a constant and indicators for SMSA, eight census divisions, and eight occupations. Additional variables in the Accident at Home equation are a constant and indicators for SMSA and eight census divisions.
Standard errors corrected for heteroskedasticity in parentheses; standard errors corrected for within-group correlation in brackets. ** (*) by the standard error indicates that the coefficient is significant at the 1% (5%) level based on that standard error.

within-group correlation (errors in brackets) for the two equations including the *BLS Injury Rate*.

As the results presented in table 6 indicate, workers in risky industries based on BLS measures are more likely to experience an on-the-job injury, as expected. Better educated workers are injured less often, which is consistent with a lifetime wealth effect. Also, injuries diminish at a decreasing rate with job tenure, reflecting the role of workers learning about job risks and the effect of experience on work accidents.[22]

The main variable of interest is smoking status, which is consistently positive and statistically significant for all three personal risk measures. Smokers have significantly higher accident rates on the job than do nonsmokers, controlling for the average industry risk level and personal characteristics. Smoking status increases the annual job injury probability by 0.011 above that for nonsmokers. As noted in table 2, nonsmokers have a work injury probability of 0.033,

---

[22] As is shown in Viscusi (1979), if workers experiment with risky jobs and quit if their experiences are sufficiently unfavorable, there will be a negative relationship between tenure and job riskiness apart from any safety productivity effect.

TABLE 7.—ALTERNATIVE PROBIT ESTIMATES OF THE EFFECT OF SMOKING STATUS ON INJURY EXPERIENCE

	Dependent Variable			
	Worker Injury		Individual Injury	
	(1)	(2)	(3)	(4)
Smoker	0.009	0.011	0.017	0.016
	(0.012)	(0.005)*	(0.017)	(0.008)*
	[0.011]	—	[0.016]	—
BLS Injury Rate/100	0.261		0.547	
	(0.125)*		(0.188)**	
	[0.133]*		(0.175)**	
BLS Injury Rate × Smoker	0.019		−0.025	
	(0.176)		(0.281)	
	[0.156]		[0.245]	
Log-Likelihood	−758.64	−762.70	−1267.32	−1273.45

Additional variables in each equation are a constant, age, age squared, education, tenure, tenure squared, and indicators for race, married, handicapped, SMSA, eight census divisions, and eight occupations.
Standard errors corrected for heteroskedasticity in parentheses; standard errors corrected for within-group correlation in brackets. ** (*) by the standard error indicates that the coefficient is significant at the 1% (5%) level based on that standard error.

and smokers have an average probability of 0.058. Smoking status per se accounts for 0.011 of the 0.025 overall average smoker-nonsmoker job injury probability difference between smokers and nonsmokers. Background variables correlated with smoking status also account for much of the propensity toward job risks. Smoking status consequently may be a signal of being risky in other ways.

Smokers' greater riskiness on the job is consistent with the other two risk-behavior equations. Smokers have an annual probability of any injury—on or off the job—that will lead to a loss of work that is 0.015 greater than for nonsmokers. The overall individual accident rate difference averages 0.03 (from table 2), so that smoking status alone accounts for half of the difference without controlling for other demographic factors. Smoking status increases the annual probability of an injury at home by 0.01, as compared to the nonsmokers' average home accident rate of 0.02 per year. Smokers are thus one-and-a-half times as likely to experience home accidents as are nonsmokers. Smokers are consequently riskier people in a variety of pursuits, an effect that will make it desirable for firms' offer curves to be flatter for smokers than nonsmokers.

Table 7 examines the robustness of these estimates using different specifications to examine the influence of the smoking and risk variables. Equation (1) and (3) in table 7 add an interaction term between the *BLS Injury Rate* and *Smoker*, but this effect is not statistically significant in either the work-injury or overall individual-injury equation. *Smoker* and the interaction term are highly correlated ($r = 0.84$), so it is difficult to distinguish these effects.[23] Because smoking status is reflected in part in the objective job risk selected by the worker, equation (2) and (4) omit this objective risk measure. The magnitudes of the smoking coefficients are almost identical to those in table 6.

[23] The two smoking variables remain jointly significant at the 10% level (p-value = 0.09).

VII. Conclusion

Smoking status influences the character of the compensating risk differential mechanism. Somewhat paradoxically, smokers incur greater job risks but receive lower total wage compensation for risk than do nonsmokers. A difference in wage-risk tradeoffs arising from different risk preferences of smokers cannot account for this result. The evidence suggests that smokers differ not only in their preferences but also in their market opportunities. Smokers face a lower and flatter wage offer curve.

The only situation in which these results could occur is case 4 in table 1. Because smokers also would receive a lower wage rate even for jobs with zero risk (at the 90% significance level), case 4 is also consistent with the specified level of the intercept. Smokers are more willing to incur risks, and they face market offer curves that are lower and flatter than those of nonsmokers. The underlying economic rationale for this difference is that smokers are less efficient in the production of safety. Smokers are more prone to accidents at work. They are also more likely to be injured at home and, given the substantial health risks posed by smoking, are more likely to incur risks of other kinds as well. An economically interesting aspect of this heterogeneity is that the pattern of influences suggests that both the supply and demand components of the hedonic market equilibrium vary with smoking status.

Smokers value an expected lost workday injury from $14,000 (*Injury Rate*) to $20,000 (*Lost Workdays Rate*), whereas nonsmokers value an expected injury as $31,000 (*Injury Rate*) to $35,000 (*Lost Workdays Rate*). The extent of the risk-money tradeoff discrepancy between smokers and nonsmokers is roughly 100% for results using comparable risk measures. Overall, differences in job risk premia account for about one-fourth of the smoker-nonsmoker wage gap. If smokers faced the same job risk levels as do nonsmokers, the wage gap would even be greater because smokers have much higher risk jobs.

These findings do not necessarily imply that smokers are making fully rational decisions. However, they do suggest that smokers are exhibiting a consistent pattern of risk-taking behavior. More importantly, they illuminate the role of heterogeneity in the compensating differential process, which responds in quite reasonable ways to the greater riskiness of smokers.

REFERENCES

Brown, Charles, "Equalizing Differences in the Labor Market," *Quarterly Journal of Economics* 94:1 (1980), 113–134.

Chaloupka, Frank, "Rational Addictive Behavior and Cigarette Smoking," *Journal of Political Economy* 99:4 (1991), 722–742.

Fuchs, Victor, *The Health Economy* (Cambridge, MA: Harvard University Press, 1986).

Hersch, Joni, "Compensating Differentials for Gender-Specific Job Injury Risks," *American Economic Review* 88:3 (1998), 598–607.

Hersch, Joni, and Todd S. Pickton, "Risk-Taking Activities and Heterogeneity of Job-Risk Tradeoffs," *Journal of Risk and Uncertainty* 11:3 (1995), 205–217.

Hersch, Joni, and W. Kip Viscusi, "Cigarette Smoking, Seatbelt Use, and Differences in Wage-Risk Trade-offs," *The Journal of Human Resources* 25:2 (1990), 202–227.

Huber, Peter J., "The Behavior of Maximum Likelihood Estimates under Nonstandard Conditions," *Proceedings of the Fifth Berkeley Symposium in Mathematical Statistics and Probability* 1 (1967), 221–233.

Ippolito, Pauline, and Richard Ippolito, "Measuring the Value of Life Saving from Consumer Reactions to New Information," *Journal of Public Economics* 25:1–2 (1984), 53–81.

Jones-Lee, Michael, *The Value of Life: An Economic Analysis* (Chicago: University of Chicago Press, 1976).

——— ,*The Economics of Safety and Physical Risk* (Oxford: Basil Blackwell, 1989).

Kniesner, Thomas, and John Leeth, "Compensating Differentials for Fatal Injury Risk in Australia, Japan, and the United States," *Journal of Risk and Uncertainty* 4:1 (1991), 75–90.

——— , *Simulating Workplace Safety Policy* (Boston: Kluwer Academic Publishers, 1995).

Levine, Phillip B., Tara Gustafson, and Ann Velenchik, "More Bad News for Smokers? The Effects of Cigarette Smoking on Wages," *Industrial and Labor Relations Review* 50:3 (1997), 493–509.

Manning, Willard G., E. B. Keeler, J. P. Newhouse, E. M. Sloss, and J. Wasserman, *The Costs of Poor Health Habits* (Cambridge, MA: Harvard University Press, 1991).

O'Conor, Richard, Glenn Blomquist, and Ted Miller, "Healthy Lifestyle and Safety: An Expected Net Benefit Approach to Seat Belt Use," *Managerial and Decision Economics* 17:5 (1996), 483–492.

Rogers, William H., "Regression Standard Errors in Clustered Samples," *Stata Technical Bulletin* 13 (1993), 19–23. (Reprinted in *Stata Technical Bulletin Reprints*, 3 (1994) 88–94.)

Rosen, Sherwin, "The Theory of Equalizing Differences" (pp. 641–692), in Orley Ashenfelter and Richard Layard (Eds.), *Handbook of Labor Economics* (Amsterdam: North-Holland, 1986).

Smith, Robert S., "The Feasibility of an 'Injury Tax' Approach to Occupational Safety," *Law and Contemporary Problems* 38:4 (1974), 730–744.

——— , "Compensating Differentials and Public Policy: A Review," *Industrial and Labor Relations Review* 32:3 (1979), 339–352.

Thaler, Richard, and Sherwin Rosen, "The Value of Saving a Life: Evidence from the Labor Market" (pp. 265–298), in N. Terleckyz (Ed.), *Household Production and Consumption* (New York: Columbia University Press, 1976).

U.S. Department of Commerce, *Statistical Abstract of the U.S.* (Washington, D.C.: Government Printing Office, 1995).

Viscusi, W. Kip, *Employment Hazards: An Investigation of Market Performance* (Cambridge, MA: Harvard University Press, 1979).

——— , *Risk by Choice: Regulating Health and Safety in the Workplace* (Cambridge, MA: Harvard University Press, 1983).

——— , *Smoking: Making the Risky Decision* (New York: Oxford University Press, 1992).

——— , "The Value of Risks to Life and Health," *Journal of Economic Literature* 31:4 (1993), 1912–1946.

Viscusi, W. Kip, and William Evans, "Utility Functions that Depend on Health Status: Estimates and Economic Implications," *American Economic Review* 80:3 (1990), 353–374.

White, Hal, "A Heteroskedasticity-Consistent Covariance Matrix Estimator and a Direct Test for Heteroskedasticity," *Econometrica* 48:3 (1980), 817–830.

Part III
The Value of Life: Product and Housing Market Studies

[15]

Value of Life Saving: Implications of Consumption Activity

Glenn Blomquist

Illinois State University

This paper focuses on the typical individual's value of a small change in the probability of his survival. With a simple life-cycle model, the value is shown to be implied by consumption activity which affects risk. The premium an individual is willing to pay to reduce risk is estimated using probit analysis of automobile seat-belt use. The "value of life" is found to be about $370,000. This estimate is contrasted with the foregone-earnings approach by showing that a surplus value above earnings exists and the elasticity of the value with respect to earnings is less than one.

Society must inescapably place a value on life saving if it is to allocate its resources efficiently. The measure most frequently recommended by economists has been foregone earnings, which has been used in many variants (e.g., see Dowie 1970, Weisbrod 1971, and Faigin 1975). However, the relevance of the foregone-earnings measure has been increasingly questioned. Despite its numerical manageability, foregone earnings is unsatisfactory because there is little theoretical basis for its use. Foregone earnings neglect the value of nonmarket activity as well as the surplus value of living and unreasonably imply that the value of life saving for self-sufficient persons, housewives, and retirees is zero.

Schelling (1968) and Mishan (1971b) argue that the relevant benefit measure of an endeavor which affects human life is one based on an individual's willingness to pay for a marginal change in the probability of his survival. Empirical estimates of the value of life saving based

For helpful comments I am grateful to D. Gale Johnson, Sam Peltzman, Rati Ram, and Charles Upton. I am especially indebted to Sherwin Rosen and George Tolley for their valuable criticism and suggestions. Remaining errors are my responsibility.

[*Journal of Political Economy*, 1979, vol. 87, no. 3]

VALUE OF LIFE SAVING   541

on individual willingness to pay are nearly nonexistent. The notable exception is the work of Thaler and Rosen (1975), who analyze
a sample of 900 individuals in 37 occupations and estimate risk-
compensating wage differentials. When, for ease of reference only,
the risk premiums are extrapolated to unit (0–1) changes in the
probability of death, they imply what is conveniently referred to as
a value of life of about $390,000 in 1978 dollars.[1] A possible source
of upward bias in the Thaler and Rosen estimate is the neglect of
disamenities associated with risky occupations. A possible source of
downward bias is that those employed in risky occupations either cope
with risk more efficiently or like risk more than the representative individual. It is desirable to try other approaches free from these
biases.[2]

The purposes of the present paper are (a) to develop a simple
model of individual life-saving activity and to show how the value of
life saving is implied by observable behavior,[3] and (b) to estimate a
value of life based on the premium individuals are willing to pay in
the consumption activity automobile seat-belt use to reduce the risk of
accidental death.[4]

Section I presents a life-cycle framework with risk of death in which
an individual maximizes expected lifetime utility. The framework
explains the derived demand for life-saving activity and implies a
necessary relation among the productivity of life-saving activity, the
costs of life-saving activity, and the value of life. This relation provides
a basis for estimating the value of life. Section II gives empirical
results and a brief description of the seat-belt survey data and the
variables used along with the rationale for each. It is found that
multivariate probit analysis, using the economic and traffic safety
variables suggested by the model, provides a statistically highly
significant explanation of the variation in seat-belt use among drivers. Value-of-life estimates are presented in Section III. The probit

[1] "Value of life," as the term is used in this paper and in Thaler and Rosen (1975), is
based on changing the probability of survival by a small amount. For easy comparison
among situations where the changes are small but unequal and lack of an accepted unit
of account only, the value of a marginal change is extrapolated to a unit (0–1) change.
Clearly, it is inappropriate to apply any such value of life to a situation where an
identifiable person faces certain death. All conversions to 1978 dollars are made using
the average annual Consumer Price Index, except for 1978 when the June figure is
used.

[2] Dillingham (1979) estimates risk-compensating wage differentials for male blue-
collar workers in manufacturing and construction and finds a value of life of $290,000
in 1978 dollars. Jones-Lee (1976) summarizes existing empirical studies, few of which
are based on willingness to pay.

[3] Independently of the work of this paper, Conley (1976) developed a theoretical
model of the demand for safety based on the willingness-to-pay concept.

[4] Analysis of seat-belt use is suggested by Bailey (1968) in his discussion of Schelling's
paper.

results are combined with estimates of average seat-belt productivity and average seat-belt use cost to estimate a value of life. Information from outside the sample is used to convert the standardized probit results to actual values. Disutility costs are estimated from the parameterized probit equation. The probit results are further used to establish a relationship between the estimated value of life and foregone earnings. Section IV contains the conclusions.

I. Theory of Life-saving Activity and the Value of Life

Life-Cycle Model with Risk of Death

For an individual concerned with the present period, which he is certain to survive, and one future period, which he will survive with some probability, the expected utility is

$$E(U) = U(C_1, S) + PU(C_2), \tag{1}$$

where $E(U)$ is expected lifetime utility and $U(C_1, S)$ is period 1 utility, which depends on period 1 consumption (C_1) and life-saving activity (S). The appearance of S in $U(C_1, S)$ allows for a disutility (it could be utility) of life-saving activity over and above the resource cost of life-saving activity which appears in the budget constraint. The variable P is the probability of survival to the end of period 2, and $U(C_2)$ is the utility of period 2 consumption (C_2).

Life-saving activity is a choice variable which for the individual affects the probability of survival (P) and the probability of (nonfatal) injury (R). The production function for P is $P = P(S), P' > 0$; and the production function for R is $R = R(S), R' < 0$, reflecting the gain in avoiding injury costs.

Life-saving activity (S) affects expected lifetime utility in three ways: (a) an effect on period 1 disutility via S which enters directly in equation (1), (b) an effect on the probability, P, that the individual will experience period 2 utility, and (c) the budget constraint, which brings in the resource costs of life-saving activity as well as avoidable injury costs. Assuming individuals possess some nonhuman assets, the budget constraint is

$$C + qS + RI + [C/(1 + i)] = WT + [WT/(1 + i)] + A, \tag{2}$$

where the left-hand side (LHS) is the present value of expenditures on consumption and life-saving activity less the expected cost of morbidity, that is, nonfatal injury; and the right-hand side (RHS) is the present value of labor earnings plus nonhuman assets. In equation (2), q is the cost of life-saving activity in terms of consumption, I is the present value of the morbidity loss in period 2, i is the rate of return on nonhuman capital, W is the individual's value of time, T is total time in a period, and A is the present value of nonlabor income.

The individual chooses period 1 consumption, period 2 consumption, and life-saving activity to maximize expected lifetime utility subject to the budget constraint. The first-order conditions are obtained by differentiating the Lagrangian with respect to C_1, C_2, and S. The condition of interest in this paper is that for life-saving activity, one form of which yields the statement that the value of marginal product in reducing mortality plus the value of marginal product in reducing injury loss equals marginal cost.

$$P'V - R'I = K, \tag{3}$$

where $V = U(C_2)/\lambda$, $K = q - U_s/\lambda$, and $R' < 0$. On the LHS of equation (3), P' is the change in the probability of survival due to a change in life-saving activity and is the marginal physical product in reducing mortality. The value of life (V) is the value of a unit change in the probability of survival[5] and is equal to the monetary worth to the individual of his future utility from period 2 consumption; λ is the marginal utility of income; R' is the (negative) change in the probability of nonfatal injury due to a change in life-saving activity and is the marginal physical product in reducing injury; I is the present value of the avoided morbidity loss. On the RHS of equation (3), K is the cost of life-saving activity, which is the dollar marginal cost (q) plus the monetary worth of the disutility cost (U_s/λ); U_s is the marginal disutility of S.

The equilibrium condition depicts the determination of the optimal amount of life-saving activity, S. Holding constant the value of the marginal product curve, anything which increases the cost of life-saving activity shifts the marginal cost curve up and reduces S. Thus, an increase in either the dollar cost (q) or the disutility cost (U_s/λ) will cause a decrease in S. Holding the marginal cost curve constant, anything which increases the value of marginal product of life-saving activity shifts the value of the marginal product curve up and increases S. Thus, an increase in the marginal product (P'), the value of life (V), the marginal product (R'), or the value of avoided morbidity loss (I) will increase S. The value of life can be expected to increase as there are increases in the present values of labor and nonlabor income and the amount of time available (T); T may be influenced by health.[6]

---

[5] See n. 1.

[6] In Blomquist (1977) where the model of life-saving activity is presented in detail, the first- and second-order conditions are derived for both borrowers and nonborrowers against future labor income. For both, it is shown that the value of life can be expected to vary directly with the present values of labor and nonlabor income. The partial effects of other variables, like P', are also considered.

Implied Value of Life

Taking equation (3), if life-saving productivities (P' and R'), morbidity loss (I), and cost (K) are known, the individual's value of life can be solved for and is $(K + R'I)/P'$. The value of life equals the costs less the morbidity benefits, all divided by the change in the probability of survival.[7]

The starting point for the empirical work of this paper is the observation that some information can be obtained on the optimal amount of life-saving activity. Observing that S varies among individuals means that the comparison in equation (3) is not identical for all individuals. The theory suggests reasons for such differences, including differences in characteristics of value of life (V), morbidity loss (I), productivities (P' and R'), and cost (K). Because it is not possible to measure all differences among individuals with the same values for each measurable characteristic, some individuals engage in some life-saving activity and others will not. If the myriad of unobservable characteristics upon which value of life depends (i.e., basically characteristics other than income) are more important than those for I, P', R', and K, then the problem is to find the value of life for the average individual rather than the value for those (possibly atypical) individuals who engage in some life-saving activity.

The seat-belt-use decision is based on the net benefit of seat belts such that if the net benefit is positive seat belts are used, and if it is nonpositive seat belts are not used. In terms of the preceding paragraph, the decision can be viewed in terms of an index, $s = \beta x + u$, where β is a vector of fixed parameters, x is a vector of measurable benefit and costs variables, and u is a random term for unobservable differences among individuals with $E(u) = 0$ and $E(u^2) = \sigma^2$. If $s > 0$, seat belts are used; and if $s \leq 0$, they are not used. For probit analysis of the life-saving activity, automobile seat-belt use, where additivity of both benefits and costs is retained, a standardized index is used. The index is $s^* = \beta^* x + u^*$, where $s^* = s/\sigma$, $\beta^* = \beta/\sigma$, $u^* = u/\sigma$, $E(u^*) = 0$, and $E(u^{*2}) = 1$. Since the probit coefficients are estimates of β^* and $E(u^*) = 0$, it follows that

$$E(s/\sigma) = \beta^* \bar{x}, \qquad (4)$$

---

[7] A caveat about the implied value of life concerns the correctness of an individual's perceptions. When changes in risks and costs are small, one can reasonably doubt the accuracy of perceptions (and the implied value of life), for they may be beyond some threshold where changes go unnoticed. The problem is fairly widespread in economics, and Mishan (1971a, p. 163) offers this cogent thought: "People's imperfect knowledge of economic opportunities, their impudence and unworldliness, has never prevented economists from accepting as basic data the amounts people freely choose at given prices. Such imperfections therefore cannot be consistently invoked to qualify people's choices when, instead, their preferences are exercised in placing a price on some increment of a good or 'bad.'"

VALUE OF LIFE SAVING   545

where $\bar{x}$ are the observed independent variables evaluated at the sample mean. From the data, we will know the value taken by $\beta^*\bar{x}$; call it $\bar{B}$, which is defined by $Pr(\bar{s} > 0) = \int_{-\infty}^{\bar{B}} n(s)ds$, where n is the standard unit normal density function. Variable B is the value along the abscissa in a graph of the function, and variable $\bar{B}$ is the standardized net benefit for the average driver.

The average value of life is obtained by using equation (4), the theory of life saving, and information from outside the sample of drivers statistically analyzed. According to the theory, the net benefit of seat-belt use (s) is $P'V - R'I - K$. When estimates of P', R', I, and K for the typical driver are substituted for s in equation (4), the result is

$$(\bar{P}'V - \bar{R}'I - \bar{K})/\sigma = \beta^*\bar{x} = \bar{B}, \tag{5}$$

where the bar over each variable indicates its average value. The LHS of equation (5) is the standardized net benefit, and the RHS is the value of the probit equation evaluated at the sample mean. While estimates of $\bar{P}', \bar{R}'$, and $\bar{I}$ are available and the value of $\bar{B}$ is easily found, the value of life cannot be determined because $\bar{K}$ and σ as well as $\bar{V}$ itself are unknown, that is, equation (5) solved for $\bar{V}$ is $\bar{V} = (\bar{B}\sigma + \bar{R}'I + \bar{K})/\bar{P}'$, where σ and $\bar{K}$ are unknown.

An estimate of σ is made by using β^* from the probit equation and information about $\bar{K}$. Seat-belt-use costs consist of money costs (q) and disutility costs (U_s/λ). If, ignoring installation costs, the cost consisted entirely of time cost, K would in fact be observable as it would consist of the value of time multiplied by the time required to use seat belts (t) or

$$q = awt, \tag{6}$$

where w is the driver's wage rate and a is a constant which allows the value of time to differ from the wage. With information on a and t, the way in which cost varies with wage is known, $\partial q/\partial w = at$. This same relationship is estimated by the probit coefficient of the wage rate, β_w^* $= \beta_w/\sigma$. By substitution, it follows that $\beta_w^* = at/\sigma$, and the estimate of the standard deviation of s is $\sigma = at/\beta_w^*$. With this estimate of σ and with cost broken down into its components, equation (5) for the net benefit of seat-belt use becomes

$$(\bar{P}'\bar{V} - \bar{R}'\bar{I} - \overline{awt} + \overline{U_s/\lambda})/(\overline{at}/\beta_w^*) = \bar{B}, \tag{7}$$

which is one equation with two unknowns, the value of life $(\bar{V})$ and disutility cost (U_s/λ).

The disutility of seat-belt use can result from disutility in the common usage of the word, as due to discomfort of using belts or the distastefulness. These include a resistance to use due to habit. The distastefulness of the activity of buckling and unbuckling. Other influences can have the same effect on behavior as discomfort and payment that would be necessary to overcome habit is a fixed cost that would have to be paid to induce seat-belt use and is indistinguishable in observed behavior from discomfort. Another influence is knowledge. People lacking knowledge of the beneficial effects of seat belts will fail to use them even when warranted and in observed behavior will act as if there were a discomfort. Indeed, people conceivably could act as if there were positive consumption value if, as a result of propaganda, they were led to believe that seat belts are more effective than they really are. If disutility costs depend on the time involved, then it is reasonable that the disutility associated with the discomfort of restricted movement, wrinkled clothing, and chaffing from minutes and hours of driving with the seat belt fastened will be greater than the disutility associated with the bother of a few seconds or minutes of buckling and unbuckling or the value of that time. In this case, the majority of drivers will not use seat belts even if the time cost (*awt*) is negligible.

While these disutility costs (U_s/λ) prevent estimation of an average value of life, we can obtain information on a lower bound. If time and disutility costs were zero, this would be sufficient inducement to get all drivers to use seat belts because there clearly are benefits of using the belts. In terms of the probit equations, since B_{all} is the B which satisfies $Pr\,(s > 0) = \int_{-\infty}^{B} n(s)ds = 1.0$, B_{all} would have to be infinitely large if literally all drivers were to use belts. However, if 99 percent, which is virtually all drivers, is a good approximation, then $B_{all} = +2.326$, and a value of life can be found. The net benefit equation (7), using $\hat{\sigma}$ for $\overline{at}/\beta_w^*$, becomes $(\overline{P}'V - \overline{R}'\overline{I})/\hat{\sigma} = B_{all}$, which when solved for the implied value of life yields

$$V = (B_{all}\hat{\sigma} + \overline{R}'\overline{I})/\overline{P}', \tag{8}$$

where B_{all} is the value of the probit equation when all individuals use seat belts. Everything on the RHS is known. In the sense that zero cost is sufficient inducement to get all drivers to use seat belts but it is necessary only that net benefits be positive for universal usage, the estimate is a lower bound on the value of life.

Thus, following the theory of life-saving activity and using available information on several parameters, the probit analysis yields an estimate which is a lower bound on the value of life vis à vis a rudimentary calculation for an atypical person who finds it just worthwhile to use seat belts. The value of life can be conveniently thought of as time cost plus disutility costs less morbidity benefits, all divided by the change in the probability of survival.

II. Probit Results

Seat-Belt-Use Data

A data set particularly well suited to explaining seat-belt use in conjunction with estimating the value of life is *A Panel Study of Income
Dynamics, 1968–1974* (Survey Research Center 1972, 1973, 1974).
The *Panel Study,* which is used in this paper, gives detailed information on user characteristics not available in other surveys. It is a
nationwide survey of 5,517 households followed through the 7-year
period, with approximately 500 variables for each household. The
seat-belt-use variable is for 1972 and takes on a value of 1 if the driver
claims to use seat belts all of the time and 0 if he claims to use them
none of the time. Passenger use of seat belts, part-time use of seat
belts, and use in other years are not considered due to various data
limitations. The sample is limited to drivers whose cars have seat belts
already installed in them to avoid the problem associated with the
costs of purchasing a car with seat belts or with having seat belts
installed. Also, since a crucial variable in estimating $\bar{V}$ is the driver's
wage rate, the sample is limited to drivers who worked in 1972 so as to
avoid the problem associated with estimating the driver's shadow
wage. Seat-belt use is analyzed statistically with measurable seat-belt
productivity, cost of seat-belt use, and value-of-life variables, as the
model suggests.

Probit Analysis

Estimation of the value of life depends on probit analysis of seat-belt
use, the results of which are presented in table 1, with definitions and
means of the variables given in table 2. The calculated statistic, $-2 \times$
the likelihood ratio, is 261, which is significant at the 99.5 percent
level. The ratio of the homogeneity χ^2 divided by degrees of freedom
is 1.03.[8] While an extended discussion of the rationale for each variable based on the traffic safety literature can be found elsewhere, we
now briefly consider the results for each variable.[9] The use of seat
belts can be expected to be greater, the greater their productivity in
preventing injury. Seat-belt-productivity variables found to be important are age of driver (because older drivers are more likely to be
involved in an injury accident), male sex (because women tend to

---

[8] Assuming a lognormal distribution does not yield improved results, as is indicated
by ordinary least squares regressions of seat-belt use on the same variables used in
probit analysis.

[9] For a discussion of the seat-belt-use results including alternative explanations as well
as, looking ahead, a detailed justification of the most reasonable values used in estimation of the value of life, see Blomquist (1977).

TABLE 1

PROBIT RESULTS FOR SEAT-BELT USE AND NONUSE

Variable	Coefficient	*t*-Value	Significance Level
RSPEED	.00664	1.15	75
SEXF	−.525	−3.16	99
AGE	.0211	3.94	99
EDUC	.309	8.01	99
WAGE	−.0796	−1.89	94
EARN	.00706	2.95	99
WORKLN	.00621	2.06	96
VACLN	.0288	2.56	99
PROPY	−.0440	−2.08	96
HEALTH	.992	3.12	99
KIDS	−.0650	−3.18	99
MARR	−.292	−2.15	97
CHURCH	.00523	3.57	99
CONSTANT	−7.217	−4.86	99

NOTE.—The value of the log-likelihood ratio × −2 is 261 with 13 degrees of freedom. The number of observations is 1,854. The percentage of correct predictions is 77. The definitions of the variables are given in table 2.

drive under safer conditions than men), and rural speed limit (because high-speed driving is relatively dangerous).[10]

Higher costs of using seat belts can be expected to reduce seat-belt use, for example, Hix and Ziegler (1974) find a perfect correlation (+1) between seat-belt-usage rate by car manufacturer and the comfort-convenience rating given to the seat-belt configuration of that manufacturer. Cost variables found to be important are driver's wage rate (because high-wage users face greater time costs),[11] length of work-commutation trip and length of vacation (because longer trips entail less fastening and unfastening), married driver and number of children (because each implies greater time and disutility costs due to extra adjustment and fastening associated with the spouse's different dimensions and tending to youngsters), and education (primarily because more-educated drivers gather information more easily [indistinguishable from low U_s/λ]).[12]

[10] One suspects that the age–seat-belt-productivity relationship is nonlinear. While a quadratic relationship with AGE and AGE^2 produced a negative sign on AGE^2 with a *t*-value near −1, stratification of drivers into 17–34, 35–55, and 56–69 groups was significant according to a restriction *F*-test and showed seat-belt use was indeed most sensitive to changes in age for the oldest group.

[11] The negative sign of the WAGE coefficient could reflect that drivers with high wages drive newer, safer cars and hence use seat belts less. However, when value of car was tried as a variable, it was statistically insignificant.

[12] Since EDUC is based on Welch's (1966) weights (derived by finding the rates of return of education levels), one wonders if those weights are better than giving each additional year of schooling an equal weight. Using ordinary least squared regressions

TABLE 2

MEANS OF PROBIT VARIABLES, 1972

Variable	Definition	Mean Value	Units
SBU	Seat-belt use–nonuse	.23	Belt users/all drivers
RSPEED	Rural speed limit	60.0	Miles per hour
SEXF	Sex	.119	Female drivers/all drivers
AGE	Driver age	39.2	Years
EDUC	Education	2.30*	Welch index
WAGE	Wage rate	4.66	Dollars per hour
EARN	Labor wealth	94.19	Thousands of dollars
WORKLN	Length of work trip	7.98	Miles
VACLN	Length of vacation	2.02	Weeks
PROPY	Nonlabor income	1.19	Thousands of dollars
HEALTH	Health	4.515	Thousands of healthy hours
KIDS	Children	1.83	Number of children
MARR	Marital status	.823	Married drivers/all drivers
CHURCH	Religious attendance	23.2	Services per year

* The average driver has just a bit more than a high school education.

Finally, we turn to the value-of-life variables (V), expecting that drivers with high V will use seat belts more. Wealth increases the amount of life-saving activity in which a person will engage. Human wealth, which typically is most of a driver's wealth, is measured by EARN, the present value of expected future labor earnings. The value of EARN is based on the concept of the age-earnings profile, and by utilizing these earnings patterns some of the obvious errors in measuring income by observing people at different stages of the life cycle are avoided. In generating EARN, we parameterize the age-earnings profile for each of the seven education levels for which Mincer (1974) gives data. The information available for each driver from the *Panel Study* is utilized, for while each individual is assumed to have a typically shaped (sloped) profile for his respective education level, the intercept of the equation which describes the profile is allowed to vary by individual. Each year's earnings is predicted and

for comparison, one finds that the regression with EDUC has a higher R^2 and larger t on education than a similar regression with an education variable which has equal weights. To explore the usefulness of the EDUC weighting scheme further, the drivers were stratified by grade of school completed. Several stratification schemes were tried among the eight education levels. Using restriction F-tests for similarity of coefficients, it was found that the first four levels could be lumped together, grades 1–12, but the remaining four could only be grouped in twos, grades 13–15 and 16 or more grades. The larger group at moderate education levels and the small groups at high education levels are consistent with the increasing weights used in EDUC.

multiplied by a factor which accounts for time preference and probability of survival.[13] The positive sign of the EARN coefficient is evidence of the higher value of life for drivers with greater human wealth. However, as will be shown later, the value of the life–foregone-earnings relationship is not dollar for dollar.

Other value-of-life variables found to be important are healthy hours (because of their wealth effect), church attendance (because of life-style effects or possibly the tendency of these drivers to overstate both church attendance and seat-belt use), and nonlabor income. The negative sign of PROPY is not so much to be considered evidence that drivers with much nonlabor income have low V but, rather, that there is a data problem. Unfortunately, the definition of PROPY is based on net taxable asset income, which is conceivably (and in some observations actually) negative—a not surprising result, especially for wealthy people, in view of rapid allowable depreciation and other tax provisions. Consideration of the driver's desire to leave an estate could shed light on PROPY, as shown by Blomquist and Tolley (1977). The PROPY variable does not affect the coefficients of WAGE, EARN, or other variables except AGE, the coefficient of which falls by 10 percent if PROPY is deleted from the probit equation. The negative signs of MARR and KIDS are taken as evidence that the negative cost effect outweighs any positive effect of dependents of the value of life due to interdependent utility functions or household production advantages.

III. Estimation of the Value of Life

Most Reasonable Case

Upon establishing reasonable values for the parameters $\bar{a}$ and l, the probit coefficient of WAGE is used to determine the standard deviation of net benefits, σ. Using the means of sample drivers for $\bar{w}$ and $\bar{B}$ and establishing reasonable values for $\bar{P}'$, $\bar{R}'$, and $\bar{I}$, the implied value of life ($\bar{V}$) can be written as a function of disutility costs (U_s/λ) in accordance with equation (7). Using the value of B, which induces

---

[13] To test the sensitivity of the EARN finding to the definition of foregone earnings, several definitions of the earnings variable were investigated. Four different intercepts of the age-earnings profile were considered, including actual 1972 labor earnings and a 7-year average of actual labor earnings and three different discount rates—5, 10, and 15 percent. In addition, the age-earnings profile was constrained never to fall once a peak is reached, in accordance with the idea that it is a decline in labor force participation, not the wage rate, which causes earnings to fall as a worker ages. Using ordinary least squares regressions, it was found that EARN (1972 wage times 2,000, 10 percent and unconstrained) produced the best results, i.e., the highest t-value for an earnings variable and the highest R^2.

virtually all drivers to use seat belts, disutility costs can be estimated and V imputed from equation (8).

First, let us estimate σ. For $\bar{a}$, there exists considerable evidence that the value of time in a vehicle which is relevant to the valuation of benefits of time-saving projects is less than the average wage rate. The most reliable work (e.g., Lisco 1967 and Domencich and McFadden 1975) indicates that a is about 0.40. For $\bar{t}$, no formal studies have been done of the time required per trip to find, perhaps untangle, fasten, perhaps adjust, and unfasten seat belts. Several highway safety people contacted during the course of this work suggest that a simple time and motion study will give a sufficiently good estimate of the time expenditure per trip. I carried out such a study and found that on pre-1973 cars it takes 4–6 seconds to find and fasten seat belts if there is no entanglement or adjustment and about 2 seconds to unfasten the belt. Entanglement and adjustment caused an additional 3–8 seconds to be spent fastening the belt, with the median time added being about 4 seconds. The average time per one-way trip spent to use seat belts is the sum of 5 seconds for finding and fastening, 1 for adjustment, and 2 for unfastening. Total time per trip is about 8 seconds. The 8 seconds must be multiplied by the number of one-way trips per year to get average annual time expenditure (t) on seat-belt use. The estimate of the number of annual trips the driver takes is based upon the average annual miles driven by the driver and his family and the length of the trip to work. The estimate, 1,504, comes out to a little more than two round trips per day. The average annual time expenditure ($\bar{t}$) on seat-belt use is about 3.342 hours. Using the coefficient of WAGE from table 1 and recalling that $\sigma = a\bar{t}/\beta_w^*$, the estimate of σ is $(0.40)(3.342)/(0.0796) = 16.79$. The value of σ may seem a bit small, but note that u is the difference between two random effects (those for interpersonal differences in costs) and that the covariance term may make σ small.

Second, let us determine the relationship between $\bar{V}$ and U_s/λ. The increase in probability of survival (P') and probability of avoiding morbidity loss (R') is due to the effectiveness of seat belts in the reduction of injury. Weighing the results from different studies, effectiveness with respect to fatalities is taken to be 0.50, while effectiveness with respect to nonfatal injuries is 0.25.[14] While seat belts can help save a driver's life, their effectiveness matters only if the driver has a potentially injurious accident. Based on 1972 accident and driver data, the estimate of the probability of a driver being killed in an accident is 3.027×10^{-4}. Thus, $\bar{P}'$ is 1.514×10^{-4}. In a similar

---

[14] The estimates of seat-belt effectiveness made by Levine and Campbell (1971), Campbell, O'Neill, and Tingley (1974), and Council and Hunter (1974) range from 0.40 to 0.60, while for R' they range from 0.20 to 0.35.

manner, the probability of a driver incurring a nonfatal injury acci-
dent is calculated to be 1.392×10^{-2}. Thus, $\bar{R}'$ is -3.481×10^{-3}.[15]
While one might expect a reduction in the severity of injury given that
an accident occurs, the traffic safety literature gives no evidence that
such a reduction occurs.

For $\bar{I}$, judging from the traffic safety literature (esp. U.S. Department of Transportation 1975), the average nonfatal injury loss which
can be avoided by seat-belt use is $950. Included are $850 of labor
productivity loss and a small, admittedly arbitrary, amount of $100
for pain and suffering. Excluded are costs, such as property damage
and insurance administration, which the individual cannot avoid
through seat-belt use.

Substituting into equation (7) the values for $\bar{P}', \bar{R}', \bar{I}, \bar{a}, \bar{w}, \bar{t}, \sigma$, and
$\bar{B}$ gives an equation with $\bar{V}$ and U_s/λ as variables:

$$[(1.514 \times 10^{-4})\bar{V} - (-3.481 \times 10^{-3})(950) \quad (9)$$
$$- (0.40)(4.66)(3.342) + U_s/\lambda]/16.79 =. -0.748,$$

where $4.66 is the sample mean of WAGE from table 2. The value for
$\bar{B}$ is $\beta*\bar{x}$, which can be computed from tables 1 and 2 and is the value
corresponding to about 23 percent of drivers using seat belts, that is,
$Pr(s > 0) = \int_{-\infty}^{-0.748} n(s)ds \doteq 0.23$. For the average driver, net benefit is
negative, -0.748, and seat belts are not worth using. Solving equation
(9) for the value of life in terms of disutility cost gives

$$\bar{V} = -63,653 - 6605U_s/\lambda. \quad (10)$$

This equation illustrates that the utility component of seat-belt use,
U_s/λ, must indeed be negative (algebraically less than -9.64), that is, a
disutility cost, if the value of life is positive. An indication that disutility costs are important is that when time costs are assumed to be zero
($t = 0$), the probit equation predicts that the majority (65 percent) of
drivers do not use seat belts.

Now, let us estimate the value of life, taking as given that all drivers
will use seat belts if all costs, disutility, and time are zero. Taking 99
percent of the drivers to be virtually all means that B_{all} is 2.326.
Substituting this and values for $\sigma, \bar{R}', \bar{I}$, and $\bar{P}'$ into equation (8) gives
an implied average value of life of

$$V = [(2.326)(16.79) + (-3.307)]/(1.514 \times 10^{-4}) = \$236,107 \quad (11)$$

in 1972 dollars (or about $370,000 in 1978 dollars).

The estimate of V when substituted into the relationship between V
and U_s/λ means that disutility costs are $45.38 per year, that is,

---

[15] Calculations are based on data from the National Safety Council (1973), the U.S.
Dept. of Transportation (1973), and the Illinois Dept. of Transportation (1975). Detailed calculations are available from the author upon request.

solving equation (10) gives $U_s/\lambda = -45.38$. The amount is the annual subsidy (bribe) which must be paid to the average driver to offset disutility costs. Since the important disutility cost is that which is associated with wearing (vis à vis fastening) the seat belt, the disutility cost per trip hour might lend some perspective. In determining fastening time (t), it was found that the typical driver would make 1,504 one-way trips per year. For the sample of drivers, the average trip length was about 9 miles, which implies 13,536 miles are driven each year. Recognizing that high average speeds are unlikely for short trips, it is assumed that the average speed for these miles was 40 miles per hour. For the 338 hours of travel per year, the $45.38 annual disutility cost reduces to about 13¢ per trip hour, which does not seem unreasonable. That the disutility cost is reasonable is pertinent since, in contrast to the relationship between the value of life and disutility which is based on the probit equation evaluated at the sample mean, the value-of-life estimate is based on B_{all} (+2.326), which is far from the sample mean (−0.748). As such, the estimate could be sensitive to the specific functional form and has a wide confidence band around it in any case.

The implied value of life depends on the point estimate of several terms as well as on the value chosen for B_{all}, which determines disutility costs. Table 3 shows the sensitivity of the most reasonable estimate of V ($368,000) to each of these parameters.

Value of Life and Foregone Earnings

The positive coefficient on EARN indicates that drivers with high earnings place a high value on their lives and in turn are more likely to use seat belts. The foregone-earnings approach to value of life holds that the value of life (V) and EARN are equal and should change on a dollar-for-dollar basis, implying that the elasticity of V with respect to EARN is one. For the 1972 sample of individuals, the mean of EARN is $94,188, which is only 40 percent of V instead of equal to it. It should be noted that a value of life greater than foregone earnings is possible because, as defined above, the value of life is merely a convenient way of expressing the value-of-life saving for a small change where that change is extrapolated to unit change. Since only marginal changes are considered, there is no violation of the budget constraint.

An elasticity of V with respect to EARN can be calculated by performing the following hypothetical experiment. For average drivers, the net benefit of seat-belt use is negative and seat-belt use is only 23 percent, that is, $Pr(\bar{s} > 0) = \int_{-\infty}^{-0.748} n(s)ds = 0.23$. The benefits of seat-belt use are small relative to the costs, including time costs which

TABLE 3

Sensitivity of V

	V	
VALUE OF TERM	1972\$	1978\$
B_{all}:		
1.645 (95%)	160,585	250,000
2.326 (99%)	236,107*	368,000*
3.090 (99.9%)	320,833	500,000
Seat-belt effectiveness (part of P'):		
.60	196,842	307,000
.50	236,107*	368,000*
.40	295,182	460,000
I:		
1972\$ = 1,500; 1978\$ = 2,339	223,461	348,000
1972\$ = 950; 1978\$ = 1,481	236,107*	368,000*
1972\$ = 500; 1978\$ = 780	246,456	384,000
β_{WAGE}^*:		
$-.1217$ (SD = -1.0)	146,907	229,000
$-.0796$ (SD = .0)	236,107*	368,000*
$-.0375$ (SD = 1.0)	525,827	820,000
a:		
.30	171,734	268,000
.40	236,107*	368,000*
.50	300,632	469,000
t:		
2.500	170,751	266,000
3.342	236,107*	368,000*
4.000	286,959	447,000

Note.—V = value of life; B_{all} = value of the probit equation when all individuals use seat belts; P' = the change in the probability of survival due to a change in life-saving activity and is the marginal physical product in reducing mortality; I = the present value of the morbidity loss in period 2; β_{WAGE}^* = the vector of the fixed parameters of the wage rate; a = a constant which allows the value of time to differ from the wage; and t = the time required to use seat belts.

* For the most reasonable case, V is approximately \$236,000 in 1972 dollars or \$368,000 in 1978 dollars. The Consumer Price Index is used to convert 1972 to 1978 dollars.

depend on the value of time. When EARN increases, the net benefit increases, and seat-belt use increases if costs remain constant. (Although EARN and WAGE would usually vary together, EARN could increase with WAGE unchanged through an increase in the annual probabilities of survival or a decrease in the discount rate.) The experiment consists of hypothetically increasing EARN, in this way keeping all other variables at their mean values, finding the new higher level of seat-belt use with the estimated probit equation, finding the new higher level of WAGE which will increase costs by an amount enough to offset the increase in benefits exactly, and calculating the implied value of life using the parameterized equation (9) for the net benefit of seat-belt use.

If EARN for the average driver is increased 10 percent from the mean of \$94,188 to \$103,607, seat-belt use would increase from 23 to

25 percent, that is, $Pr(s > 0) = \int_{-\infty}^{-0.682} n(s)ds \doteq 0.25$. If concurrently WAGE is increased from the mean, \$4.660, to \$5.495, cost increases enough to make standardized net benefit again equal -0.748 and seat-belt use $\overline{23}$ percent. Using equation (9) with WAGE equal to \$5.495 and $\overline{U_s}/\lambda$ equal to $-\$45.38$ and solving for V, we get $V = [(-0.748)(16.79) + (-3.481 \times 10^{-3})(950) + (0.40)(3.342)(5.495) - (-45.38)]/(1.514 \times 10^{-4}) = \$243,461$ in 1972 dollars. Therefore, V for the average driver is \$236,107, meaning that V increased \$7,354 or 3.1 percent. Since the 10 percent increase in EARN produced a 3.1 percent in V, the elasticity of the average value of life with respect to foregone earnings is about $+0.3$. Contrary to the foregone-earnings approach, the elasticity is 0.3, not 1.0.

The above elasticity and value-of-life estimate are consistent with the theoretical work of Usher (1973) and Conley (1976). Although the connection between the expected present value of future labor earnings and consumption is not direct, the finding that the elasticity of value of life with respect to earnings is about 0.3 is consistent with the notion that people get more from life than what they derive from market consumption.

IV. Conclusions

The value of life saving is derived from a simple life-cycle model with a partly endogenous risk of death and estimated through analysis of the consumption activity, automobile seat-belt use. The life-cycle model is developed to yield a method of estimating the value of life saving. The time cost of seat-belt use is estimated from estimates of the time required and the wage rate of the driver. The life-saving benefit of seat-belt use is the reduction in probability of death multiplied by the value of life, as that term has been used in this paper. Thus, with no benefits other than mortality benefits and no costs other than time costs, the value of life is the time cost divided by the reduction in the probability of death. The method accommodates morbidity benefits as well as disutility costs, broadly defined to include discomfort, inconvenience, and lack of knowledge, and these benefits and costs are included. Since only 23 percent of drivers use seat belts, probit analysis is used to find the implied value of life for the typical driver who does not use seat belts. The value is imputed using the theory about seat-belt-use time costs, information on these costs, and the probit coefficient of WAGE to convert standardized to actual costs.

Probit analysis of seat-belt use produces statistically extremely significant and reasonable results. Use of seat belts is found to be greater, the greater their productivity in preventing injury. Higher costs of using seat belts are found to reduce seat-belt use. Seat-belt use is found to be greater, the greater the value the driver places on his life. The future-earnings variable, an important value-of-life variable, was based on age-earnings profiles by education level, positioned to an individual's actual earnings, discounted and reduced to allow for the probability of survival.

Following the approach just outlined, this paper adds further evidence that people are willing to pay (accept) a determinable, finite amount for an increase (a decrease) in the probability that they will continue living. Using a different theory and a different body of evidence, the value of life estimated in this paper is of the same general order of magnitude as that of the other existing study based on a willingness-to-pay approach. By choosing a sample from the population at large (automobile drivers), the problem has been avoided of basing inferences about the willingness to pay on categories of persons, such as those in hazardous occupations, who may by self-selection have atypical risk attitudes. Morbidity, as well as mortality, has been systematically included. Disutility, the counterpart to occupational disamenity, has been allowed. Indications of the importance of disutility are that a subsidy would be required to induce the average driver to use seat belts and that an individual's education affects seat-belt use more than can be accounted for by its wealth effect.

The estimate of the value of life in 1978 dollars for the most reasonable case is approximately $370,000. It is to be contrasted with what would be obtained with a foregone-earnings approach in that the estimate is more than twice the average foregone earnings of the drivers studied. Moreover, the elasticity of the value of life with respect to future labor earnings is about 0.3, far less than the 1.0 which is inherent in the foregone-earnings approach to value of life. For benefit-cost analysis, the estimate, which is for the entire population of drivers, is of interest as it is usually impractical to place different values on different lives for decisions concerning public expenditures. The estimate is based on individual willingness to pay. Any adjustment for the value of life of the individual to others not internalized by him, an externality not considered herein, would raise the estimated value of life.

References

Bailey, Martin J. "Comment on T. C. Schelling's Paper." In *Problems in Public Expenditure Analysis*, edited by Samuel B. Chase, Jr. Washington: Brookings Inst., 1968.
Blomquist, Glenn. "Value of Life: Implications of Automobile Seat Belt Use." Ph.D. dissertation, Univ. Chicago, 1977.

Blomquist, Glenn, and Tolley, George S. "The Value of Life as Influenced by Bequest, Insurance, Annuities and Age." Paper presented at the Conference on Environmental Benefit Estimation, Chicago, June 8–9, 1977.

Campbell, B. J.; O'Neill, Brian; and Tingley, Beth. "Comparative Injuries to Belted and Unbelted Drivers of Subcompact, Compact, Intermediate and Standard Cars." Paper presented at the Third International Congress on Auto Safety, San Francisco, July 15–17, 1974.

Conley, Bryan C. "The Value of Life in the Demand for Safety." *A.E.R.* 66 (March 1976): 45–55.

Council, Forrest M., and Hunter, William W. *Seat Belt Usage and Benefits in North Carolina Accidents.* Chapel Hill, N.C.: Highway Safety Res. Center, 1974.

Dillingham, Alan E. "The Injury Risk Structure of Occupations and Wages." Ph.D. dissertation, Cornell Univ., 1979.

Domencich, Thomas A., and McFadden, Daniel. *Urban Travel Demand.* New York: American Elsevier, 1975.

Dowie, J. A. "Valuing the Benefits of Health Improvement." *Australian Econ. Papers* 9 (June 1970): 21–41.

Faigin, Barbara M. "Societal Costs of Motor Vehicle Accidents for Benefit-Cost Analysis." In *Proceedings of the Fourth International Congress on Automotive Safety.* Washington: Dept. Transportation, Nat. Highway Traffic Safety Admin., 1975.

Hix, R. L., and Ziegler, P. N. *1974 Safety Belt Survey NHTSA/CU Research Project.* Falls Church, Va.: McDonnell Douglas Automation Co., August 1974. Report DOT HS-801 224 prepared for Dept. Transportation, Nat. Highway Traffic Safety Admin.

Illinois Department of Transportation. *1974 Accident Facts.* Springfield, Ill., 1975.

Jones-Lee, M. W. *The Value of Life.* Chicago: Univ. Chicago Press, 1976.

Levine, Donald M., and Campbell, B. J. *Effectiveness of Lap Seat Belts and the Energy Absorbing Steering System in the Reduction of Injuries.* Chapel Hill, N.C.: Highway Safety Res. Center, 1971.

Lisco, Thomas. "The Value of Commuter's Travel Time: A Study in Urban Transportation." Ph.D. dissertation, Univ. Chicago, 1967.

Mincer, Jacob. *Schooling, Experience, and Earnings.* New York: Nat. Bur. Econ. Res., 1974.

Mishan, E. J. *Cost Benefit Analysis: An Informal Introduction.* New York: Praeger, 1971. (a)

———. "Evaluation of Life and Limb: A Theoretical Approach." *J.P.E.* 79, no. 4 (July/August 1971): 687–705. (b)

National Safety Council. *Accident Facts.* Chicago: Nat. Safety Council, 1973.

Schelling, T. C. "The Life You Save May Be Your Own." In *Problems in Public Expenditure Analysis,* edited by Samuel B. Chase, Jr. Washington: Brookings Inst., 1968.

Survey Research Center. *A Panel Study of Income Dynamics, 1968–1974.* Ann Arbor: Univ. Michigan, Inst. Soc. Res., 1972, 1973, and 1974.

Thaler, Richard, and Rosen, Sherwin. "The Value of Saving a Life." In *Household Production and Consumption,* edited by Nestor E. Terleckyj. New York: Nat. Bur. Econ. Res., 1975.

U.S. Department of Transportation. Federal Highway Administration. *Fatal and Injury Accident Rates.* Washington: Government Printing Office, 1973.

———. National Highway Traffic Safety Administration. *Proceedings of the*

Fourth International Congress on Automotive Safety. Washington: Government Printing Office, 1975.

Usher, Dan. "An Imputation to the Measure of Economic Growth for Changes in Life Expectancy." In *The Measurement of Economic and Social Performance,* edited by Milton Moss. New York: Nat. Bur. Econ. Res., 1973.

Weisbrod, Burton A. "Costs and Benefits of Medical Research: A Case Study of Poliomyelitis." *J.P.E.* 79, no. 3 (May/June 1971): 527–44.

Welch, Finis. "The Determinants of the Return to Schooling in Rural Farm Areas, 1959." Ph.D. dissertation, Univ. Chicago, 1966.

[16]

JOURNAL OF ENVIRONMENTAL ECONOMICS AND MANAGEMENT 8, 72–78 (1981)

Housing Prices, Health Effects, and Valuing Reductions in Risk of Death[1]

PAUL R. PORTNEY

Resources for the Future, Washington, D.C. 20036

Received March 3,1980

By combining estimates of the effect of air pollution on both property values and human health risks, it may be possible to draw inferences about individuals' valuations of risk. Although valuations thus derived must be interpreted carefully, they may be of use in determining the welfare effects of environmental and other regulatory policies.

INTRODUCTION

Many of the programs undertaken by government have as an objective reducing individuals' risk of death from various causes. The welfare effects of such programs are often difficult to determine, in part because we lack information on individuals' valuations of reduced risks, valuations which Mishan and others have pointed out are the proper measure of the benefits of such programs.

Recently, Thaler and Rosen [12] provided the first estimates of individuals' revealed willingness to trade off dollars for safety. Using data on occupational risks and pay differentials, they found that workers were willing to accept an additional $390 per year to work jobs that would increase their annual risk of death by one in one thousand.[2] From this Thaler and Rosen observed that a "statistical life" was implicitly valued at $390,000 since a thousand such individuals would be willing to pay the appropriate premium to reduce the annual risk of death to each by 0.001.

While ingenious, Thaler and Rosen's estimates are open to at least two criticisms. First, as a number of people have noted, the occupations on which their estimates are based are relatively dangerous and are likely to attract individuals with abnormally low risk aversion.[3] Therefore, while Thaler and Rosen's estimates may accurately reflect the rate at which "risk-lovers" will trade dollars for job safety, they may give us little information about the amount that other individuals must be offered to accept added risk (or would be willing to pay to avoid it).

A second difficulty concerns the applicability of Thaler and Rosen's premiums to the valuation of other, non-occupational risks. Even if all individuals were willing to voluntarily accept $390 for an additional 0.001 chance of occupational death, it does not follow automatically that such a sum would compensate them for identical increases in other kinds of risk. Individuals may require more compensation for added risks over which they have little or no control, those resulting from

---

[1] This paper was written while I was a Visiting Professor at the Graduate School of Public Policy, University of California at Berkeley. It has benefitted from the comments of a number of people. They include Martin Bailey, William Baumol, Judith Bruser, William Fischel, Anthony Fisher, Rick Freeman, Lee Friedman, David Harrison, Allen Kneese, Jon Nelsen, Fritzie Reisner, Clifford Russell, Eugene Seskin, Kerry Smith, and Jon Sonstelie. The usual disclaimer applies.

[2] For ease of comparability, all estimates presented here are expressed in 1978 dollars.

[3] See Rhoads [8], Viscusi [13], and Blomquist [2], for example.

0095-0696/81/010072-07$02.00/0

certain environmental conditions, for example. Thus, the wider the range of implicit risk valuations we have, the more likely it is that we will have accurate estimates of the value society attaches to certain risks and their reduction. For instance, Blomquist [2] recently estimated in clever fashion individuals' implicit valuations of the risk of accidental traffic death.

There is another market in which individuals with widely varying risk preferences participate and in which they may reveal some information about their valuation of still another important kind of risk. I refer to the market for single-family dwellings, the air quality surrounding which may significantly affect the occupants' likelihood of death from tuberculosis, other respiratory diseases, and cancer.

It is my purpose here to indicate a way in which conventional property-value studies might be combined with epidemiological or mortality studies to reveal valuations of risk by individuals considerably more risk-averse than those studied by Thaler and Rosen. My primary purpose is to suggest a methodology for evaluating certain environmental risks. I do illustrate it, however, using evidence from two different kinds of studies of Allegheny County, Pennsylvania, the center of the Pittsburgh SMSA. These studies are combined to derive very preliminary estimates of the value of risk reduction as revealed by residents there.

AIR POLLUTION, PROPERTY VALUES, AND HUMAN HEALTH

Using hedonic estimation, the determinants of residential property values have been well explored.[4] These determinants include the physical characteristics of a dwelling (its size and that of its lot, its age and the quality of its construction, special features like a swimming pool or an attractive view, etc.), as well as the quality and cost of the public services provided by the community in which it is located. These latter include schools, police and fire protection, recreation and public works, and so on. Accessibility to major employment centers has generally been a significant determinant of property values as have been certain of the environmental amenities that a dwelling and neighborhood provide.[5]

Air quality is the environmental amenity most often included in such studies although the reasons for its inclusion are seldom stated. Presumably, those purchasing houses in "clean air neighborhoods" find them esthetically more pleasing, are forced to repaint their homes and cars less frequently, enjoy lower cleaning bills, and, perhaps most importantly, enjoy longer and healthier lives on account of the reduced pollution to which they are exposed.

Taking account of this latter point, the usual hedonic relationship between property values and their determinants can be expressed in the following modified fashion: Let

$$V^i = V(x^i, y^i, A^i, R^i), \qquad (1)$$

where V^i is the value of the ith dwelling; x^i is a vector of the dwelling's structural characteristics; y^i is a vector capturing both the quality and cost of the public

---

[4] The standard reference is Oates [7]. More recently see Sonstelie and Portney [10]. These property value studies are reviewed in Denne [4] and Ball [1].

[5] Smith [9] has surveyed the studies linking environmental amenities to property values.

services provided by the community in which the dwelling is located (including its accessibility to downtown); A^i is a measure of the environmental amenities the dwelling provides (which depend primarily on the surrounding air quality, Q); and R^i is the risk of death from air pollution-related illness to which residence in the ith dwelling gives rise.[6] Both $\partial V/\partial A$ and $\partial A/\partial Q$ are assumed to be positive.

Dropping the superscript and differentiating (1) totally with respect to air quality, Q, gives

$$\frac{dV}{dQ} = V_x\frac{dx}{dQ} + V_y\frac{dy}{dQ} + V_A\frac{dA}{dQ} + V_R\frac{dR}{DQ},\qquad(2)$$

where subscripts indicate partial derivatives. Assuming x and y are invariant with respect to Q, we can rearrange terms and solve V_R to get

$$V_R = \frac{\dfrac{dV}{dQ} - V_A\dfrac{dA}{dQ}}{\dfrac{dR}{dQ}}.\qquad(3)$$

It is V_R in which we are interested because it is interpreted as the additional amount people reveal themselves willing to pay in higher property values for dwellings that expose them to a lesser risk of death from illnesses related to air pollution. Then,

$$V_R = \frac{dV/dQ}{dR/dQ} - M,\qquad(4)$$

where

$$M = \left[V_A\frac{dA}{dQ}\right]\bigg/\frac{dR}{dQ}.$$

We probably overestimate V_R in (4) by ignoring M, the interpretation of which we return to below. Nevertheless, the first term on the right-hand side of (4) can serve as an approximation to the implicitly revealed equilibrium valuation of reduced risk.

Fortunately data exist which allow us to calculate this approximation of V_R from dV/dQ and dR/dq. These data come from a study of the effect of air pollution on the value of single family dwellings in Allegheny County, Pennsylvania (Spore [11]); and an EPA study of the effect of air pollution on age- and sex-specific annual mortality rates in the same county during the same period (Gregor [5]).

Among the independent variables in the property value study are two measures of air pollution—total dustfall (measured in tons/ square mile/ month) and sulfur dioxide (SO_2) concentration (measured in parts-per-million/day)—as well as many

---

[6] We assume that this dwelling is one of many in a large metropolitan area made up of a number of distinct political jurisdictions.

TABLE 1

Pollution Related Mortality Rate[a] (Deaths/100,000)

Variable	45 years of age		45–64		65 and over	
	Male	Female	Male	Female	Male	Female
SO_2 (ppm/day)	0.00004	0.00003	0.00163	0.00027	0.00101	0.00268
	(0.1)	(0.1)	(0.6)	(0.3)	(0.1)	(0.4)
Total particulates ($\mu g/m^3$)	0.500	0.349	4.014	1.570	10.291	9.514
	(1.9)	(2.0)	(2.7)	(2.6)	(1.9)	(2.1)

Note: t ratio in parentheses.

[a]Adapted from Gregor [5, p. 30]. Independent variables not shown are percent of adult white population with high school education, number of days on which maximum temperature was below 32°F, number of days on which precipitation exceeded one-tenth of an inch, and residential population per 0.01 square mile.

of the more conventional determinants discussed above.[7] In the EPA study, age- and sex-specific mortality rates at the census tract level are explained by concentrations of SO_2 and total particulate matter (measured by micrograms per cubic meter, $\mu g/m^3$), as well as by percent of population with high school education, number of days per year in which rainfall exceeded 0.1 inch, number of days per year in which the maximum temperature was less than 32°, and residential population per square mile.

Consider first the effect of an improvement in air quality on property value, dV/dQ in Eq. (4). According to Spore's estimates, when evaluated at the mean a reduction in total dustfall of, say, 5 tons/sq. mi./month coupled with a reduction in daily SO_2 concentrations of 0.005 parts per million (ppm) increased the value of the average dwelling by as much as $335.[8] All other things being equal, this is the amount a household would have to pay to enjoy these air quality improvements.

Before we can determine the reduction in pollution-related mortality that such an improvement in air quality would produce, one problem must be addressed. While SO_2 is used as one measure of air pollution in both studies, total dustfall is used as a second measure of pollution in the property value study and total particulate concentration is used as the second measure in the mortality study. Dustfall is defined as "the particulates in the atmosphere which are larger than 10 but less than 500 μg in diameter,"[9] and hence comprises a fraction of total particulates. Therefore, I have assumed that the 5 tons/sq. mi./mo. reduction in dustfall, a reduction of 15% from the mean, results from a 15% reduction in total particulates of all sizes. This implies a reduction in total particulates of 18 $\mu g/m^3$ which is used to calculate reduced risk.

Using the results from the mortality study (the air pollution coefficients of which are reproduced as Table 1), it is possible to translate the dustfall and SO_2 reductions into reduced risk (dR/dQ in eq. (4)). To do so, we must recognize that this reduction in air pollution benefits all the members of a household, here

[7]These other determinants are median family income, household size, house size, lot size, distance to the central business district, the property tax rate, a measure of the age of the dwellings, percent nonwhite in the census tract, percent of dwellings that are substandard, and percent of nearby land devoted to open space.

[8]See Spore [11, p. 99].

[9]Spore [11, p. 67].

TABLE 2
Implicit Valuation of a Statistical Life ($1978)[a]

	Age				
Less than 45		45–64		Over 65	
Male	Female	Male	Female	Male	Female
377,780	566,667	47,222	121,428	18,400	19,883

[a]As revealed by a single individual purchasing the stated air quality improvement
in Allegheny County, Pennsylvania.

assumed to consist of a 40-year-old couple with one child. Table 1 indicates that
each ppm reduction in SO_2 reduces the number of deaths per year from pollution
related illness by only 0.00004 for a male less than 45 years of age. Hence, a 0.005
ppm reduction in SO_2 will have virtually no effect on the risk of death for any
member of such a household.[10]

A reduction of one $\mu g/m^3$ in total particulate concentration, however, reduces
the annual mortality rate for males under 45 by 0.5 per hundred thousand, and that
for females by 0.35. Therefore, the 18 $\mu g/m^3$ reduction in total suspended particulates reduces the annual risk of death for the husband by 0.00009 (equal to
18 × 0.5 divided by 100,000) and for the wife by 0.00006. Assuming the child is
male, and that the household values equally reductions in risk to each of its
members, we can add the individual risk reductions to obtain the total reduction
for the household. For the typical household, this is 0.00024 per year.

Placing a dollar value on this risk reduction follows directly. At an interest rate
of 10% the $335 housing price differential necessary to "purchase" the air quality
improvement in question implies an annual cost of $34. Therefore, subject to the
caveats discussed below, a household paying this annual premium to reduce its
total annual risk exposure by 0.00024 is implicitly valuing a statistical life at about
$142,000.

We can also use this method to examine the implicit valuation of risk revealed by
single individuals, of course. Suppose a 42-year-old male, the typical worker in
Thaler and Rosen's sample, was willing to pay $34 more per year for the stated air
quality improvements? What implicit valuation would he be revealing? This is
easily obtained by dividing $34 by 0.00009. The resulting valuation is about
$378,000, extremely close to the implicit valuation obtained by Thaler and Rosen
using data on occupational risk. The corresponding valuation for a single woman
less than 45 years old is $576,000, higher than but still consistent with Thaler and
Rosen's estimate using comparably aged individuals.

Note that older individuals, who are more vulnerable to air pollution related
illness, purchase greater risk reductions for the same housing price differential;
hence, their revealed implicit valuation of a statistical life will be lower than that of
younger individuals. For example, a male over 65 years who is willing to pay $34
annually for the stated air quality improvement is implicitly placing a minimum
value on a statistical life of $18,400 (a minimum value because he might be willing
to pay more for the risk reduction but does not have to). Table 2 presents the

[10]Since the 0.005 ppm reduction in SO_2 concentration has a negligible effect on the risk of death for
all age and sex groups, we henceforth ignore it in calculating valuations of risk reductions.

implicit valuations of men and women in the three age groups used in the mortality study, based on an annual premium of $34.00. Of course, these valuations are based on the assumption that the individual in question "purchases" the risk reduction for him- or herself alone, rather than as part of a household unit.

REMARKS

My primary purpose here has been to suggest a methodology for the derivation of risk valuations. Hence, it is extremely important to point out the many respects in which the illustrative valuations derived above must be qualified. First, it should go without saying that neither the typical household discussed above nor any other would be indifferent to $142,000 and the certain death of one of its members. Like Thaler and Rosen's estimates, those presented here only concern the valuation of low-level, marginal risks.

Second, it is improbable that the households in the sample were fully aware of the specific effects on human health of the pollutants included in the property value and mortality studies. This is to be contrasted with the Thaler and Rosen study where it is more reasonable to assume that the workers had an understanding of the added risks borne in different occupations. However, given the long history of air pollution and its related problems in the Pittsburgh area, I do believe it fair to presume that households there had at least some idea that cleaner neighborhoods were better for them than polluted ones. This raises the further question whether households had good information about the air quality differentials between neighborhoods, although the significance of the combined air pollution variables in the property value study suggests they did.

Third, both the mortality and property value studies used to generate these estimates are somewhat primitive. For example, the mortality study does not contain the detailed measures of socioeconomic characteristics found in Lave and Seskin [6] nor the data on smoking, dietary habits, or access to medical care found in Crocker, *et al.* [3]. Similarly, the property value study could be improved by the inclusion of variables measuring public service quality and by experimentation with alternative functional forms of the estimating equation (see Sonstelie and Portney [10]). Future replications of the exercise carried out above using more recent data on the determinants of both mortality and property values is desirable.

The estimates presented above can be presumed to overstate valuations of reduced risk and hence statistical lives to the extent that they ignore the term, M, in Eq. (4). In order to derive the estimates above, the entire premium paid for improved air quality was attributed to reduced risk of death. As pointed out, clean air also means lower cleaning, painting, and repair bills as well as enhanced aesthetic appeal; these we would expect to be capitalized into property values and, hence, reflected in the differential we observe when air quality is improved. If these effects are significant, the estimates above may overstate the value of risk reductions.

On the other hand, if people underestimate or are unaware of the health risks of air pollution, the estimates presented above may underestimate individuals' valuations of risk. While beyond the scope of this study, it will be interesting to see how property value differentials change over time as the health risks associated with air pollution come to be better understood. Finally, it should be pointed out that individuals protect themselves against sickness and death in ways other than

residential location. They may spend money on visits to the doctor, health insurance, good food, exercise and the like. But if we are observing individuals in
consumption equilibrium, a dollar spent on clean air ought to buy the same
reduction in risk as dollars spent elsewhere. Therefore, we should be able to make
valid inferences about their marginal evaluations of risk reductions from their
behavior in the housing market.

While extremely tentative, the results presented here point toward an interesting
conclusion. Namely, the valuations of risk (and, by extension, of human life)
revealed by individual choice in the housing market may be similar to those
derived from labor market data. This is in spite of the fact that the households we
observe in the housing market can be presumed to be much more risk-averse than
the individuals Thaler and Rosen studied.

REFERENCES

1. M. Ball, Recent empirical work on the determinants of relative house prices, *Urban Studies* **10**, 213–233 (1973).
2. G. Blomquist, Value of life saving: Implications of consumption activity, *J. Pol. Econ.* **87**, 540–558 (1979).
3. T. Crocker, W. Schulze, S. Ben-David, and A. Kneese, "Methods Development for Assessing Air Pollution Control Benefits, Vol. I, Experiments in the Economics of Epidemiology," Environmental Protection Agency, Washington D.C. (1979).
4. R. Denne, "The Determinants of Value: An Annotated Bibliography," HUD Bibliographic Series, No. 6 (1976).
5. J. Gregor, "Intra-Urban Mortality and Air Quality: An Economic Analysis of the Costs of Pollution Induced Mortality," EPA Research Report #EPA-600/5-77-009 (1977).
6. L. Lave, and E. Seskin, "Air Pollution and Human Health," Johns Hopkins Press for Resources for the Future, Baltimore (1977).
7. W. Oates, The effects of property taxes and local public spending on property values, *J. Pol. Econ.* **77**, 951–971 (1969).
8. S. Rhoads, How much should we spend to save a life?, *The Public Interest* **51**, 74–92 (1978).
9. V. K. Smith, Residential location and environmental amenities: A review of the evidence, *Reg. Studies* **11**, 47–62 (1977).
10. J. Sonstelie, and P. Portney, Gross rents and market values: Testing the implications of Tiebout's hypothesis, *J. Urban Econ.* **11**, 102–118 (1980).
11. R. Spore, "Property Value Differentials as a Measure of the Economic Costs of Air Pollution," Ph. D. dissertation, Pennsylvania State University (1972).
12. R. Thaler, and S. Rosen, The value of saving a life: Evidence from the labor market, *in* "Household Production and Consumption" (Nelson Terleckyj, Ed.), NBER, Vol. 40, pp. 265–298, Nat. Bur. Econ. Res., Washington, D. C. (1976).
13. W. K. Viscusi, Labor market valuations of life and limb, *Public Policy* **26**, 359–386 (1978).

[17]

Journal of Public Economics 25 (1984) 53–81. North-Holland

MEASURING THE VALUE OF LIFE SAVING FROM CONSUMER REACTIONS TO NEW INFORMATION

Pauline M. IPPOLITO

Federal Trade Commission, Washington, DC 20580, USA

Richard A. IPPOLITO*

U.S. Department of Labor, Washington, DC 20210, USA

Received July 1983, revised version received April 1984

Past studies have relied on cross-section patterns of risky behavior to generate estimates of the value of life saving. This approach is colored by several problems that affect the reliability of the results in potentially serious ways. It is difficult to separate the risk components from the (dis)utility attributes of work or consumption; to avoid selectivity biases; and to disentangle user costs (e.g. wearing a face mask) from the risk premium paid for accepting risk. To circumvent some of these difficulties, this paper uses a different approach, one which exploits the information about the value of risk reduction that is provided by changing consumption patterns over time brought about by changes in available information about risks. This approach makes it possible to more reliably estimate the pure effects of risks on behavior and to generate unbiased distributions of the value of life saving. The case of cigarette consumption over time provides an ideal setting to illustrate this methodology.

1. Introduction

It is now generally accepted that the value of reducing risks to life can in principle be estimated by observing individuals' behavior in dealing with life-threatening risks in market transactions. Numerous studies have adopted this approach by comparing either wage or consumption patterns against various measures of risk.[1] Though substantial progress has been made in overcoming many measurement and technical problems with the estimates, several methodological difficulties remain that hinder attempts to develop more refined and reliable measures of the amount individuals are willing to pay to reduce small risks of death.

---

*The views expressed in this paper are those of the authors and therefore do not necessarily reflect the position of any agency of the U.S. Government. We are indebted to Gerry Butters, Alan Gustman, John Turner and participants of the law and economics workshop at the University of Chicago and of the Federal Trade Commission seminar for helpful comments at various stages of the project. We owe a special debt of gratitude to two anonymous referees at this journal for the extensive and valuable comments they provided. Pauline Ippolito, Bureau of Economics, Federal Trade Commission, Washington, D.C. 20580, U.S.A.

[1]For instance, see the classic papers by Mishan (1971) and Thaler and Rosen (1975) as well as the recent review by Blomquist and other papers in Jones-Lee (1982).

These problems include self-selection issues and the difficulties of separating the risk components from the utility attributes of risky activities. Coal miners receive wage premiums for (unmeasured) job attributes other than risk. High-rise construction workers are not randomly chosen from the population. For the most part, these problems are inherent in methods that extract value of life estimates[2] from cross-section observations on risky activities.[3] It is extremely difficult to measure risk premiums or to avoid selection bias once markets have internalized the presence of unusual risk.

In this paper, an attempt is made to derive estimates of the value of reducing the risk of early death that are free from these biases and to accommodate a number of the criticisms that have been made about previous work. As a first step, the study deliberately avoids reliance on existing patterns of risky behavior to generate information on the value of life saving. Instead, advantage is taken of changing consumption patterns over time brought about by changes in available information about risks.

In particular, consumer reactions to cigarette health information are considered. The analysis is performed over a period in which cigarette smoking changed from being considered relatively safe to being considered quite risky. The well-publicized campaign to inform consumers of the dangers of smoking cigarettes has no serious competition as an explanation for the dramatic switch toward safer smoking habits over the last 30 years. As such, the risk component of cigarette demand can be more reliably separated from its utility component. Moreover, by utilizing data that describes market behavior before and after the period of adjustment to the new information, the reactions of a representative population of consumers can be measured.

The approach presented here is designed to go further than providing an arguably unbiased estimate of the average value of life saving. An attempt is also made to estimate the distribution of values across the population. Critics who have suspected that the variance of values of life saving held by the population is too large to be represented by average back-of-the-envelope calculations will not be disappointed by the results reported below. For example, consumers who continue to smoke, despite health warnings, are estimated to hold values of life saving that are approximately one-half those held by non-smokers.

Three additional novelties considered below are worth highlighting. First, the paper accounts for product quality adjustments to risks. If risk exposure

---

[2]Throughout the paper, the terms 'value of risk reduction', 'value of life saving' and 'value of life' will be used interchangeably to refer to that amount which when multiplied by a small risk of death gives the (approximate) amount an individual is willing to pay to reduce the risk of death by the specified amount. This willingness-to-pay amount is very close to the Hicks compensating variation measure of consumer surplus associated with the change in risk.

[3]Conceptually, the self-selection issue could be dealt with by estimating the entire wage–risk hedonic function, but in practice this is a very difficult exercise. See Marin and Psacharopoulos (1982) for an interesting effort in this direction.

is partly reduced by a user cost of sorts (e.g. wearing a face mask), observed risk premiums partly represent compensation for accepting remaining risks and partly represent compensation for the user cost. A primary reaction to risk disclosures has been the switch to cigarettes with less taste (and less nicotine). The reduction in cigarette demand is presumably smaller than it would be if low nicotine cigarettes were not available and is made up of two parts: the reduction in value directly attributable to the now-known hazards of smoking (low nicotine) cigarettes and the reduction due to the inferior taste of the new cigarettes. By disentangling these effects, it is discovered that approximately one-fourth of the information-related reduction in demand is attributable to the quality effect. It is also found that the estimate could have been misstated by as much as 50 percent had this aspect been ignored.

Second, the study evaluates consumer reactions to a health hazard. Compared to, say, highway or occupational accidents, cigarette smoking causes reductions of life in later years with a much higher degree of certainty (as in the development of lung cancer or heart disease after 20–30 years of smoking). As such, individuals' time preference rates and the time pattern of the risk over life become central features in the value of life calculation.

Finally, attention is given to a recurring complaint about previous studies, namely that consumer perceptions of risks may differ significantly from scientific measures of risk. Individuals who accept relatively high risks may attach relatively low values to incremental probabilities of living longer; alternatively, they may hold unrealistic perceptions about the magnitude of the risks they face. Using survey data that describe consumer beliefs about the health hazards of smoking, the implications of varied subjective beliefs are systematically considered. In the case of cigarettes, it turns out that these considerations do not substantially alter the conclusions of a model that excludes the issue of subjective beliefs, but their potential for significantly changing the results is aptly demonstrated.

Imperfect consumer knowledge and selection bias problems are often used to dismiss estimates of the value of life saving as being too low to be even a broad guide for safety policy. The results of this study clearly contradict this view. Having accommodated the selection and belief issues, this study decidedly supports use of value of life saving estimates that are in the lower half of the range previously reported in the literature. Our best estimates of the mean value fall in the $300 000–$600 000 range (1980 dollars), and under a wide range of sensitivity tests our high estimates remain under $1 million.

2. A brief outline of the approach

The basic approach used below to measure the value of risk reduction can be easily demonstrated with the aid of fig. 1. Suppose there are two types of cigarettes and suppose the individual will smoke one type or the other at a

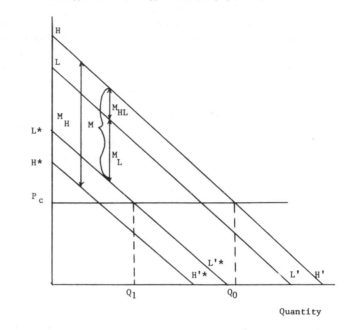

Fig. 1. Pre- and post-information demand when the optimal quality of cigarette changes.

constant rate over life. Both sell for the price P_c but one is a high nicotine and high taste (H) cigarette and the other is a low nicotine and therefore low taste (L) cigarette. In fig. 1 the underlying demand curves for the two types of cigarettes are shown as HH' and LL'. If an individual is unaware of the health cost of smoking, he naturally chooses the higher taste cigarette because there is no price premium for the additional taste; at price P_c, the individual smokes Q_0 high taste cigarettes per period.

After receiving information about the risks of smoking, the demand curves for high taste and low taste cigarettes fall to reflect the health costs of smoking. In fig. 1, these revised demand curves are depicted by the schedules $H^*H'^*$ and $L^*L'^*$. The vertical shifts M_L and M_H in these demand curves reflect the individual's assessment of the health cost of smoking each type of cigarette. Because of the higher health price associated with high taste cigarettes, the high taste demand falls by more than the low taste demand ($M_H > M_L$). In the case illustrated in fig. 1, the individual now finds it optimal to switch to low taste cigarettes.

If either the two high taste or the two low taste curves could be observed, the individual's valuation of this risk could be measured directly from the observed shift. If the reduced life expectancy per cigarette is b_L and b_H for low and high taste cigarettes, the individual's value of life saving is M_L/b_L or equivalently M_H/b_H. If, however, the individual reacts to the health risk by reducing the quality of cigarette smoked, it is possible to observe only the no-information demand for high taste cigarettes (HH' in fig. 1) and the post-information demand for low taste cigarettes ($L*L'*$ in fig. 1).

The observed shift in demand M in this case is comprised of two parts. M_L reflects the health cost of smoking the low taste cigarettes. M_{HL} reflects the utility cost to the individual of switching to low taste (low risk) cigarettes. While the latter shift component reflects a safety decision, it does not readily yield information on the value of risk reduction.[4] This value can be calculated only by disentangling the product quality effect M_{HL} from the direct risk effect M_L; so that the individual's value of saving life can be computed as M_L/b_L.

Even if aggregate demand shifts could be decomposed to account for the quality component of the reaction, the classic selectivity problem in value of life studies remains — though in a somewhat different form. For some smokers, the information causes their demand curves to fall so much that no cigarette is worth smoking. In fig. 1, the post-information demand curves for these individuals would fall completely below the price line P_c. In these cases, the observed demand curve shift M is truncated at the price P_c, and therefore these individuals' valuations of the risk are not fully reflected in shifts in aggregate demand. The truncation problem is accompanied by a selectivity bias because individuals who value life most highly are more likely to quit smoking when health costs become known.

As a result of these difficulties, the model of individual behavior outlined in fig. 1 was developed to explicitly recognize that individuals are different and that as a result they react to health information in different ways. Towards this end, individuals in the model are allowed to have different tastes for smoking, different values of risk reduction and, in some parts of the analysis, different beliefs about the health effects of smoking. The aggregate behavior predicted by the summation of individuals' choices can then be compared to actual market data in a way that accommodates truncation, self-selection, and product quality issues. The value of life saving distribution fitted to this data reflects unbiased measures of the values held by the population.

---

[4]The shift M_{HL} reflects the savings in life generated by the switch to less harmful cigarettes, measured by $b_H - b_L$. However, $M_{HL}/(b_H - b_L)$ understates the true value of life. In an n-quality model, the individual can be thought of as making a series of switches to lower nicotine cigarettes. At first, the reductions in tastes are outweighed by increases in life expectancy; and so, the individual continues to switch to ever poorer tasting cigarettes until these factors exactly balance. Thus, the sum of life expectancy gains from the infra-marginal switches exceeds the sum of the utility costs of smoking lower taste cigarettes.

3. A model of smoking behavior

In this section the model of cigarette consumption and the functional form assumptions used as a basis for the empirical estimates are developed. The presentation is designed to highlight several distinguishing features of the approach used here to calculate the revealed values of risk reduction:[5] in particular, treatment of the quality/quantity aspects of cigarette consumption; allowance for individual differences in beliefs, tastes and the value of life saving; and incorporation of the lifetime nature of the decision and its effects on the risk of death.

Individuals are assumed to choose a single nicotine type cigarette n and a (fixed) rate of consumption Q to maximize expected lifetime utility specified as

$$E(U) = \sum_{i=0}^{N} a^i p(i) q(i, Q, n) U(x, Q, n; r), \tag{1}$$

where i is age, a is a time preference factor, p is the probability of being alive at age i if the individual does not smoke, q is the individual's belief about the probability of not dying at age i from smoking-related causes,[6] Q is the quantity of cigarettes, n is the nicotine content of the cigarettes,[7] r is the taste parameter which may vary by individual and x is the quantity of other goods consumed. Thus, for our purposes, the primary health cost of smoking is modeled as an increase in the likelihood of early death.[8]

Normalizing so that the price of the representative good is unity, the per period budget constraint is $x + PQ = I$, where P is the price of cigarettes and I is income per period (both assumed constant over life).[9] The money cost of

---

[5]Conceptually, our model of cigarette smoking is quite similar to Atkinson and Skegg's (1973) model except in these respects.

[6]Replacing this assumption with a weaker one — that the individual has a perception of the effects of smoking on expected lifespan — does not affect the no-discount results generated below.

[7]Nicotine is highly correlated with other determinants of the smoking risk, e.g., tar and carbon monoxide.

[8]The money cost and the disutility cost of a smoking-related fatal illness are not necessarily higher than those that would otherwise be incurred for an unrelated fatal illness. Lower health levels that may be caused by smoking during life (shortness of breath, coughing, etc.) were presumably more widely known, and therefore internalized, prior to disclosures. For these reasons, the primary newly disclosed health cost of smoking is taken to be a reduction in life expectancy. To the extent that these assumptions are invalid, our estimated value of life saving is biased high.

[9]This simplifying assumption could be relaxed to include an overall wealth constraint with variable income over life and savings possibilities. However, these generalities are superfluous for the consideration of smoking behavior.

smoking is assumed to depend only on the quantity and not on the type of cigarette.[10]

To capture the essence of the argument in fig. 1 as simply as possible, utility in (1) is assumed to have the form:

$$U(x, Q, n; r) = U_0(x) + k'Q(r^2 - rQ/2) - k(n^* - n)^s Q, \qquad (2)$$

where k', k and s are positive constants.

This specification incorporates two basic assumptions about the individual's demand for cigarettes: that quality acts as a vertical shift parameter in the individual's demand curve, and that for each nicotine type, the demand is linear.[11] Nicotine is assumed to be a positively valued quality up to the intensity level n^*; beyond this level, the cigarette becomes so harsh that incremental units of nicotine are negatively valued.[12] The specification of the role of the taste parameter r is dictated by empirical facts: the observable market reaction to health information requires that high-taste individuals react more reluctantly to health announcements than low-taste individuals.[13] In the specification in (2), low-taste individuals buy fewer cigarettes at any given price P *and* are more sensitive to price changes than high-taste individuals. Finally, $U_0(x)$ reflects the overall utility of living and consuming all other things, which may vary by individual.

If a consumer has no health information about smoking (that is, $q = 1$), he smokes n^*-type cigarettes and his demand is[14]

$$Q = r - cP/r, \qquad (3)$$

where $c = \lambda/k'$.

[10]The price of same-sized cigarettes is generally insensitive to the tar and nicotine content per cigarette.

[11]We did not model smoking as an addiction in the sense that quitting imposes a physical withdrawal cost on the individual. If the addictive characteristics of smoking were important in the aggregate, it would follow that after 1964 (the date of the first Surgeon General's Report), the reduction in start rates would have been proportionally larger than the corresponding reduction in overall participation rates; that adjusting for other factors, pre-1964 starters would smoke either more cigarettes or higher nicotine content cigarettes than post-1964 starters; and that post-1964 quit rates would be lower for older smokers than for younger smokers. Available empirical evidence rejects these hypotheses. See Ippolito et al. (1979). If there is a one-time cost of changing smoking behavior, our estimated value of life saving is biased low by that amount.

[12]Note that the model is not based on the simpler approach of describing utility as a function of total nicotine consumption. Empirical evidence clearly shows that consumers are not indifferent to the number of cigarettes they smoke; consumers voluntarily smoke low nicotine cigarettes rather than a smaller number of same-priced, high nicotine cigarettes.

[13]A simpler specification of demand, one where taste affects only the position, not the slope of demand, was inconsistent with aggregate response data. A more general form of the demand curve was investigated where price P was raised to a power, but values of the power different from unity did not generate better fits to the data.

[14]In this sense, the model is consistent with historical evidence. During the 30-year period preceding the appearance of disclosures, a few very similar nicotine-content brands dominated the cigarette market (see appendix).

If the consumer now receives information on the hazards of smoking, he is assumed to adjust his beliefs (possibly imperfectly) about the risks of early death and to (costlessly) reassess his rate and type of cigarette consumption. For our estimate, it is assumed that if a person is age j when he receives the information, these new beliefs can be parameterized as

$$q(i, Q, n) = e^{-bnQ}, \quad \text{for all } i \geq j. \tag{4}$$

This specification implies that if an individual quits at age j, his life expectancy will increase in proportion to his remaining expected lifespan. Thus, a person who quits half way through his adult life expects to gain half the increased lifespan as a young adult who never starts.[15]

If the individual incorporates the health information, he smokes n-type cigarettes and his demand for these cigarettes is

$$Q = r - c(P + M)/r, \tag{5}$$

where the demand shift M is[16]

$$M = M_L + M_{HL} \cong bnU_0(x)/\lambda + k(n^* - n)^s/\lambda \tag{6}$$

and the type of cigarette is

$$n \cong n^* - [bU_0(x)/ks]^{1/s-1}. \tag{7}$$

The two components of the demand shift correspond to those in fig. 1; M_L is the per-pack health cost of smoking the lower nicotine cigarette and M_{HL} is the per-pack cost of switching to an inferior tasting cigarette.

The measure of the value of life saving the individual uses for small risk changes is apparent from these relationships. In particular, since each pack of low nicotine cigarettes is believed to cost bn years of expected lifespan, the individual's annualized value of lifesaving v can be directly computed as in

---

[15]This specification is consistent with the evidence suggesting diminishing mortality effects from higher rates of smoking and a lagged health response to reduced consumption [U.S. Department of Health, Education and Welfare (1979)]. The results are not changed substantially if a linear relationship between nicotine and life expectancy is assumed.

[16]Note that eq. (6) is an approximation because the precise measure of the health component of the demand shift $bnU(x, Q, n; r)/\lambda$ is replaced by $bnU_0(x)/\lambda$. This approximation, which permits us to ignore a small non-linearity in the shifted demand curve, requires only that the utility of living and consuming all other things is large relative to the utility of smoking, a quite plausible assumption even for smokers (who are trading a small probability of losing this lifetime stream of utility early for the gains from smoking). Similarly, this approximation predicts a single nicotine choice rather than the (small) range of nicotine choices the model would predict precisely. Empirically, this seems to be a good approximation because most smokers appear to smoke a single type of cigarette.

fig. 1 as $v = M_L/bn$. The demand shift M can therefore be related to this valuation through eqs. (6) and (7) as

$$M = M_L + M_{HL} \cong bv[n^* - [(s-1)/s](bv/sc')^{1/s-1}], \tag{8}$$

where $c' = k/\lambda$. Thus, once the individual's full demand shift M is measured, his annualized value of risk reduction v can be directly computed under the assumptions of our model.

For empirical purposes, then, individuals are allowed to differ in three ways: in their taste for cigarettes r, in their implicit valuation of life v, and in some of our estimates below, in their beliefs about the risk of smoking b. To determine aggregate behavior in our model, individual behavior is simply summed across the (as yet unspecified) distributions of these individual characteristics as appropriate.

4. Estimate of the distribution of individuals' values of life saving

4.1. Methodology

Since there are no longitudinal micro data sets that track individual smoking patterns and beliefs over time, traditional statistical techniques based on individual data cannot be used to fit the underlying taste and value of life distributions in the model.[17] Moreover, there is little evidence about consumer beliefs through the adjustment period, making direct estimation of taste and value of life distributions using (aggregate) time series data infeasible.

As a result of these problems, a somewhat different approach to the estimation is taken, an approach more akin to a before and after analysis. Traditional estimation techniques were used to predict what the (aggregate) market for cigarettes would have looked like in 1980 had no disclosures ever appeared about the hazards of smoking (the before market). Data is also available that describes what the market actually looked like in 1980 (the after market). Finally, survey data permits reasonable inferences about the state of consumer knowledge about smoking risks in 1980. Our estimates of the distribution of individuals' values of life saving are based on the simple idea that with minimal assumptions on the functional forms of the underlying distributions, a comparison between actual smoking behavior in 1980 and the counterfactual no-information cigarette market in 1980 can be used

---

[17]Occasional snapshots of cross-section behavior have been taken. These data sets are generally not comparable, and the data that supports the principal pre-1964 survey (the 1955 Consumer Population Survey) is no longer available in its raw form. In addition, it is widely known that the distribution of reported quantities in these samples is inconsistent with verifiable aggregate data. Thus, available cross-section quantity data is less abundant and less reliable than aggregate quantity data.

with evidence on 1980 beliefs to reliably infer the value of life saving distribution that accounts for the difference in the before and after snap-shots.[18] The reliability of the estimates will be explored by considering their sensitivity to a number of underlying assumptions.

The various parameters that characterize the cigarette market in 1980 with and without information on the hazards of smoking are estimated in the appendix and summarized in table 1. We know that in 1980 (the after market) 32.5 percent of the population smoked, per capita cigarette consumption was 195 packs per year and the average cigarette contained 0.996 milligrams of nicotine with a standard deviation of 0.34 milligrams. Our estimates also suggest that had there been no health information in 1980 (the before market), 54.2 percent of the population would have smoked, per capita consumption would have been 386 packs per year, and a single cigarette type that contained 1.49 milligrams of nicotine would have been available. The price elasticity in either scenario is estimated to be -0.48. The problem before us is to extract the distribution of individuals' values of risk reduction implicit in this description of the 1980 cigarette market with and without information.

Table 1

Available evidence about smoking behavior with and without disclosures, 1980.

Smoking behavior	Without information	With information
Per capita cigarette consumption (packs per year; 18 years old and over)	386*	195
Percent of population smoking (18 years old and over)	54.2*	32.5
Elasticity of cigarette demand	-0.48*	-0.48*
Nicotine content per cigarette smoked (milligrams)		
Mean	1.49*	0.996
Standard deviation	0	0.34

Note: The numbers *not* marked by an asterisk are data reported by or calculated from published sources in 1980. The numbers marked by an asterisk are estimates of what smoking behavior would have been in 1980 if cigarette–health disclosures had never been made available. For purposes of application, the nicotine content distribution that existed in 1980 was fit by a logistic equation. All data sources and estimations are provided in the appendix.

[18]This calculation thus assumes that the counterfactual cigarette market is one in which consumers do not believe that smoking affects life expectancy. This is a potentially limiting assumption. If life expectancy effects were widely believed and of substantial magnitude prior to 1953, the belief estimates of the number of years lost due to smoking should actually be regarded as the *difference* between the pre-1953 beliefs and the 1980 beliefs. Sensitivity analysis presented below permits evaluation of the potential importance of this characterization of pre-1953 beliefs.

4.2. Individuals' tastes for cigarettes

The first step in the estimation is to use the market without information in 1980 to estimate the underlying taste distribution that determines smoking behavior in this case. To do this, the taste parameter r is assumed to be positive and distributed across the population in such a way that at the 1980 price P_0, the corresponding quantities Q_0 have a beta distribution.[19] This beta specification is consistent with survey evidence on individual quantities that shows a strong right skewness to the density.[20] The distribution also allows for negative quantities to accommodate the possibility that, even without the health risk, some individuals would require a subsidy to smoke at price P_0.

The taste parameter distribution is determined by finding the unknown demand parameter c in (3) and the unknown beta distribution parameters that make the model's aggregate characteristics precisely match the per capita consumption and participation characteristics of the 1980 market without information (see table 1).[21] The solution is characterized by $c = 505\,000$ with the taste distribution such that approximately 26, 28, 25, 16 and 4 percent of smokers consume between 0–1, 1–2, 2–3, 3–4, 4–5 packs per day.[22]

Besides precisely fitting the 1980 market without information, several characteristics of this taste solution are worth noting as additional checks on the reliability of the model. First, the no-information demand curve generated by the model solution is virtually identical to the estimated demand curve in the appendix. Also, the fitted distribution of individual quantities smoked is generally consistent with the limited information available on cigarette consumption by smokers.[23]

[19]Specifically, no-information quantities Q_0 are distributed according to

$$h(Q_0) = (A_0 + L)^{x-1} (T - Q_0)^{y-1} / B(x, y)(T + L)^{x+y-1},$$

where B is the beta function. The shape parameters x and y and the right endpoint T are positive. The left endpoint $-L$ of the distribution is allowed to be negative to reflect the possibility that some individuals would require a subsidy to smoke at price P_0.

[20]This is a common characteristic of all smoking surveys. See U.S. Department of Health, Education and Welfare (1956, 1968, 1975).

[21]For more detail on the solution algorithms, see Ippolito and Ippolito (1982).

[22]The solution to the model is not unique in a technical sense; in fact, there is an infinity of parameters which fit the prescribed data. However, all of these solutions are essentially the same in the range where individuals smoke (at the price P_0). In an exhaustive computer search, no solution deviated by more than two percentage points in any of the described consumption categories. For these reasons, we will speak of the solution (c, h) as *the* taste solution to the model. The results which follow are virtually unchanged if any of the other solutions are adopted. For the reported estimates, the distribution parameters are $x = 9$, $y = 2.6$, $T = 1825$ and $L = 6300$.

[23]Such comparisons are somewhat subjective and qualitative in nature. However, if the estimated distribution is compared to the 1955 Consumer Population Survey distribution (which is presumably free of most of the effects of information), it is apparent that the basic shapes of the distributions are the same. Both distributions are skewed right and contain approximately 50 percent of their weight to either side of their mean values.

4.3. The distribution of individuals' reactions to information

The next step in our estimation is to use the description of the 1980 market with information to estimate the distribution of individuals' demand reductions M. These demand reductions are assumed to be positive (everyone treats the hazards of smoking as a cost) and to have a beta distribution (thereby allowing for an asymmetric reaction across the population). The estimated distribution is taken to be the M-distribution which, together with the estimated taste distribution, dictates aggregate behavior that precisely matches the per capita consumption, demand elasticity and participation characteristics of the 1980 market with information (see table 1).

The mean of the M-distribution that satisfies these criteria is \$1.15; the standard deviation is \$0.99.[24] The estimates suggest that in 1980 if cigarettes could have been purged of risks, former (and would be) smokers would have been willing to pay an additional \$1.15 on average beyond the out-of-pocket costs of \$0.656 for a pack of their favorite (pre-information) cigarette.

There are two notable features of the fitted reaction distribution: it is skewed right and it has a non-trivial variance. In the solution, almost 20 percent of the population exhibits demand shifts exceeding \$2, while 54 percent had shifts of less than \$0.50. In short, in order to explain the facts in the aggregate data, it must be true that individuals reacted in very different ways to the same announced health disclosures.

The standard errors that underlie the aggregate estimates were used to test the sensitivity of the estimated shift distribution. Using the 95 percent confidence interval around these estimates the mean of the shift distribution was found to vary from \$0.91 to \$1.28 with correpsonding variation on other features of the distribution. The qualitative features of the solution remain the same.

4.4. The value of life saving

One of the clear results of the estimation to this point is that individuals have reacted in very different ways to the health information on smoking. To estimate a value of life from these reactions it is necessary to make some assumption (or gather some evidence) about the *perceived* risks that individuals are reacting to. The approach taken in the literature to date has been to assume that individuals know the best scientific estimate of the risk. For

---

[24]The shift distribution g which fits this data is characterized by the shape parameters $xx = 1.00008$, $yy = 5.957$ and the endpoint $TT = 8$ for the distribution

$$g(M) = M^{xx-1}(TT-M)^{yy-1}/B(xx, yy)TT^{xx+yy-1}.$$

The solution is relatively insensitive to changes in the right endpoint TT. Such changes leave the mass of the distribution virtually unchanged.

our initial estimate, this approach is also taken. That is, it is assumed that *all* consumers believe that smoking a pack of cigarettes a day costs 3.5 years of expected lifespan.[25] Below, the sensitivity of the results to alternative belief assumptions is considered.

This belief assumption implies that all consumers have the same belief parameter b in eq. (4). As such, different reactions to the same information are directly attributable to different values of life [from eq. (8)]. Similarly, the observed distribution of different type cigarettes chosen in 1980 also reflects these different values of life [from eq. (7)].

The value of life distribution generated by the estimated demand reaction distribution that is in some sense most consistent with the observed 1980 nicotine distribution is the ultimate solution to the model. More specifically, each pair of nicotine taste parameters s and c' implies a value of life distribution directly from the shift distribution [by eq. (8)].[26] This value of life distribution in turn implies a nicotine distribution [through eq. (7)].[27] The solution of the model is taken as the particular values of the parameters s and c' that minimize the sum of squares difference between the model-generated nicotine distribution and the nicotine distribution actually observed in 1980.[28]

Using the best demand estimates above (characterized by the $1.15 mean demand shift), the model solution is found to have parameter values $s = 3.0$ and $c' = 1.2$ with the sum of the squared error equal to 0.029 after minimization.[29]

[25]Based on smoking surveys and subsequent follow-ups upon the death of respondents, several studies have estimated the effects of smoking on life expectancy. The estimates are generally based on the consumption of pre-information nicotine content cigarettes. Standardizing to the same intensity levels, the results range from 2.3 to 4.8 years of expected life lost for lifetime pack-a-day smokers [see Ippolito et al. (1979), Hammond (1967) and U.S. Department of Health, Education and Welfare (1979)]. Consumers' perception of mortality warnings appear to be consistent with these estimates on average. Hamermesh (1983) conducted a survey of 26–39-year-old academics. Other things constant, smokers in his sample estimated their life expectancies to be 3.5 years shorter than non-smokers. In a Roper survey conducted for the Federal Trade Commission in 1980, respondents estimated that a lifetime pack-a-day habit would result in a reduction of life expectancy of about 4 years.

[26]In particular, the density for the values of life is $h(v) = g(M(v))[b[n^* - (bv/sc')]^{1/(s-1)}]$, where $g(M)$ is the density function for M determined above and $M(v)$ is the demand shift corresponding to the value of life saving v [from (8)].

[27]The density for the nicotine choices generated by the model is $J_{c',s}(n) = h(v(n))c's(s-1)(n^* - n)^{s-2}/b$, where h is defined in the preceding footnote and $v(n)$ is the value of life corresponding to a particular nicotine choice [from (7)].

[28]That is, if $j(n)$ is the observed 1980 distribution of nicotine choice and $J_{c',s}(n)$ is the corresponding distribution generated by the model for parameters c' and s, the solution is determined by the criterion

$$\min_{c',s} \int_0^{n^*} [J_{c',s}(n) - j(n)]^2 dn.$$

[29]This compares favorably with a total sum of squares of 0.927 for the nicotine distribution; that is:

$$\int_0^{n^*} j(n)^2 dn = 0.927.$$

The estimated value of life distribution is shown by the very skewed density function in fig. 2. The mean value of the distribution is $8622 (1980 dollars); the standard deviation is $9170. To explore the sensitivity of the estimate, the value of life distribution was also computed using the 95 percent confidence intervals around the empirical estimates (recall that these bounds generated M-shift distributions with means ranging from $0.91 to $1.28). The uniform belief assumption was also varied from two years to five years. The mean values of the estimated distributions varied from $5142 to $16008 per year; the results are shown in table 2.

These results are not directly comparable to other estimates in the literature because they are annualized values. When converted to the usual measure,[30] the mean value of life saving is estimated to be between $179970 and $560280.[31] These estimates are presented in the first row of table 3.

The spread of the estimated distributions is an important feature of the results and one which survived various sensitivity analyses. The variation across the population suggests that the value of life saving is substantially different for different segments of the population. As such, concern about selectivity problems that color estimates of the value of life could be significant depending on the sample basis for the estimate. For example, if comparably risky jobs attract individuals from the lower 25 percent of the population in fig. 2, the estimated value determined from wage premiums attached to those risky jobs should yield a value of life saving of less than $3200 per year. In contrast, if certain types of safety items are purchased by those in the upper 25 percent of the distribution, the value of life reflected by the market would be approximately $12000 per year.

This point is also forcefully made by a comparison of smokers with non-smokers. It is apparent from the model that individuals with relatively high values of life saving will tend to select themselves out of the cigarette market after disclosures. As such, it is not surprising that while the overall valuation for the population is $8622 in the distribution in fig. 2, the average value for post-disclosure smokers turns out to be $5700, and for non-smokers, $10500. These estimates clearly illustrate the potential bias inherent in methodologies that estimate values of life saving based on observed premiums received by risk-takers alone (in this case, persistent smokers after disclosures).

The estimated distribution is not only dispersed, but it also exhibits its highest density near zero, falling monotonically over higher values of life.

---

[30]Previous measures in the literature reflect the value attached to small risks of saving the entire remaining life of a typical consumer or worker, not just one year. Recalling the initial assumption, however, that the time preference rate is zero, the single-year values can be converted to the usual measure by taking the expected present value of the single-year measure at the average age of the population used in other studies.

[31]In most wage studies, for instance, the value of life calculation refers to the average male worker who is approximately 37 years old. Expected lifespan at this point is approximately 35 years. Therefore, without time preference, our best estimate of the comparable average value of life derived from our measure is equal to 35 times the single-year measure.

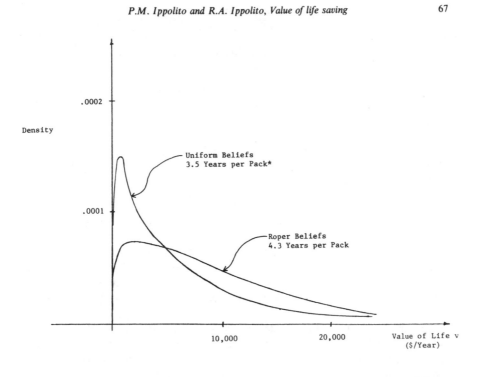

* The density function for uniform beliefs of 4.3 years is very similar to the 3.5 year function.

Fig. 2. Value of life density functions.

Table 2

Estimated values of one year of life saved.

Mean demand shift[a]	Years lost per pack[b]		
	2.0	3.5	5.0
$0.91	$12 649	7327	5142
$1.15	14 855	8622	6050
$1.28	16 008	9237	6507

[a]The range of demand shifts is determined by the 95 percent confidence intervals of underlying statistical estimates of quantity and smoking participation reactions to disclosures. In cases where several estimates were made, the largest standard errors found in any estimate were used.
[b]The estimates of the reduction is expected life caused by smoking assumes daily lifetime consumption of a typical 1952-equivalent nicotine content cigarette. They also assume that all consumers hold the same uniform belief about these effects.

Table 3

Estimates of the value of life saving.

Discount rate	Lower bound estimate	Best estimate	Higher bound estimate
0	$179 970	$301 770	$560 280
0.0125	196 678	331 465	618 220
0.025	217 613	368 495	690 351
0.050	294 502	503 132	950 426
Demand shift	$0.91	$1.15	$1.28
Years lost from smoking	5.0	3.5	2.0

While this result may violate prior expectations about nicely humped distributions, it is in some sense inevitable in light of the empirical finding that a substantial portion of the population exhibited a small reaction to the cigarette–health information. Under an assumption that all consumers hold the same belief about the health cost of smoking, this finding translates directly to an inference that many individuals place relatively low values on life saving.

The shape of the value of life distribution raises the issue of consumer beliefs in a striking way. If consumers do not share the same belief about the life-threatening effects of smoking, the unexpectedly high density of small values of life might be simply a symptom of the misspecified belief assumption. This issue is explored more fully below.

Before accommodating this complication, it is worth considering the magnitude of the mean value of life in more detail. In particular, for the case in fig. 2, the means of the estimated direct risk and the quality components of the M-shifts are $M_L = \$0.86$ and $M_{HL} = \$0.29$. Thus, approximately 75 percent of the mean demand shift of $1.15 is attributable to the life cost of smoking the relatively safe (low taste) cigarettes that were consumed in 1980. The remaining 25 percent of the reduction is attributable to smokers' switching from higher to lower quality cigarettes.

These estimates provide a basis for determining the degree of bias inherent in methodologies that ignore quality reactions to the announcement of risk. If the position were adopted in this study that a cigarette is a cigarette, the value of life saving would be estimated as M/b_H, where b_H is the life loss per pack of high taste cigarettes. This approach would underestimate the mean value of life by approximately 10 percent.[32] Alternatively, one could argue that the reduction in demand would more appropriately be matched to the

---

[32]That is, since tar is assumed to be exponentially related to life expectancy and since average nicotine per cigarette fell from 1.49 milligrams to 0.99 milligrams, the life loss for the low tar cigarette b_L is about two-thirds that of the high tar cigarette b_H. Thus, the average value of life M_L/b_L is $0.86/b_L$ and the alternative measure is $M/b_H = \$1.15/(3/2 \times b_L) = \$0.77/b_L$.

risk b_L remaining in the average low tar cigarette. In this case, the measure would be approximately 50 percent higher than it should be. If the value attached to the quality switch had been higher than the direct risk effect, the relative magnitudes of the errors would have been reversed. These simple computations demonstrate the potential importance of explicitly treating the quality reaction to risk.

5. Value of life estimates with subjective discounting

The value of life estimates to this point have been based on an assumption that consumers do not exhibit time preference (beyond that induced by the uncertainty of survival). However, assumptions about consumer time preference play a potentially important role in estimating the value of risk reduction.

A hazard like smoking is characterized by significant lags between consumption and its ultimate health effects. When new information about the hazard is released, the individual considering a reduction in consumption incurs a utility cost throughout his life for the sake of benefits that are concentrated later in life. If the individual is discounting these future benefits, a methodology that matches his observed reduction in demand to undiscounted life saving benefits will lead to underestimates of the value of life.[33]

Mortality data is available to estimate the timing of deaths for smokers relative to non-smokers. In particular, a function of the form $P_e = A \exp(K/\text{Age}^2)$, where P_e is the difference in the probability of death for smokers relative to non-smokers was fit to data available from a study of mortality patterns of smoking and non-smoking U.S. Veterans [U.S. Department of Health, Education and Welfare (1979)]; the coefficients $A=0.55$ and $K=-6316$ provided the best fit ($R^2=0.98$). For purposes of estimation, individuals are assumed to know the basic shape of this excess death function. A multiplicative scaling factor is used to generate different beliefs about the number of years of expected life lost through smoking.[34] As in the case of no discounting, the scaling parameter was set to reflect a range of assumptions about life expectancy beliefs (see table 2).

---

[33]Previous studies estimate the expected present value of future losses in utility if the individual does not die from an instantaneous risk (long-term health hazards have not been considered). These estimates reflect consumer discounting, if it exists. The same approach could be used for the cigarette measure, but the resulting value of life saving calculation would be applicable only to other hazards with the *same pattern of risk* over life; that is with the same lagged structure of mortality. In order to make the cigarette measure comparable to previous estimates in the literature (and therefore relevant to instantaneous risks), it must be converted to represent the expected present value of living if the hazard is not consumed.

[34]That is to say, consumers are assumed to estimate the excess probability of death due to smoking at any age to be $P_e = dA \exp(K/\text{Age}^2)$, where d is a scaling factor that reflects beliefs about the magnitude of the harm from smoking.

Arguably, the appropriate time preference rate for this context is bounded by the real interest rate. Fisher and Lorie (1977) have put this rate at no more than 2.5 percent over the last 50 years. To allow for the possibility that imperfections in the capital market inhibit time preference from being fully reflected in the observed interest rate, time preference rates up to 5 percent were also considered. By incorporating these discount rates and the associated excess death function P_e into the algorithms discussed above, revised value of life distributions were fitted. The results are presented in rows 2–4 in table 3.

When the time preference rate is set equal to the interest rate 0.025, the best no-discount estimate of $301 770 increases to $368 495. Doubling the time preference rate to 0.05 increases the estimate to $503 132. The lower and higher bound estimates under the no-discount assumption increase by similar amounts. In short, while the introduction of discounting does increase the measured values of life, these increases are not large enough to change the order of magnitude of the results.

The results in table 3 are relatively low when compared to previous estimates of the value of life saving. Blomquist (1979) and Thaler and Rosen (1975) generate results that are in the $450 000–$500 000 range (1980 dollars). Our best estimates are approximately two-thirds as large as these estimates without discounting, and just as large with discounting at a rate of 5 percent. Similarly, the estimates are considerably below other estimates in the literature that range from $1 million (1980 dollars) to almost $3 million per life saved [Blomquist in Jones-Lee (1982)]. Thus, when compared to previous studies, our results to this point support the use of generally lower values of life.

6. Value of life estimates when consumer beliefs are not identical

The estimates presented above are based on the assumption that all consumers have the same assessment of the life loss due to smoking. While this assumption has been widely used in the literature, it is troublesome on theoretical and empirical grounds. To the extent that individuals with weak responses believe that the longevity effects of smoking are relatively small, their computed values of life saving should be higher than those reflected in fig. 2. Similarly, consumers who reacted strongly to the hazard information but who hold higher estimates of the life-shortening effect of smoking should be computed to exhibit lower values of life saving. The net effect of these competing adjustments on the mean value of life depends on the particular belief distribution held by the population.

Reliable belief information is not easily obtained. The best evidence available in the case of cigarettes is a nationally projectable U.S. survey conducted by the Roper Organization for the Federal Trade Commission in

November 1980. Individuals were asked to judge the truthfulness of an assertion that a 30-year-old pack-a-day smoker had a lower life expectancy than a comparable non-smoker.[35] Those who answered in the affirmative were then asked how many years of life were lost on average. The survey results are shown in table 4.

Table 4

Results of the Roper survey of consumer beliefs about the life expectancy cost of smoking, 1980.[a]

Estimated life expectancy loss from smoking[b] (Years)	Respondent distributions (percent)		
	Total	Smokers	Non-smokers
Zero	30.4	40.9	24.7
Less than 2	5.2	5.6	5.0
2–4	11.9	13.3	11.3
4–6	15.5	14.2	16.2
6–8	10.0	8.0	11.0
8–10	10.7	6.2	13.1
More than 10	4.6	2.7	5.6
Don't know how much[c]	11.7	9.1	13.1
Total	100.0	100.0	100.0

[a]In 1980, the Federal Trade Commission asked the Roper Organization to include a number of smoking questions in their 1980 random survey. The survey included 1005 individuals, including 339 smokers, reflecting the national smoking participation rate (see appendix).

[b]Individuals were asked whether a 30-year-old person reduces his life expectancy if he smokes at least one pack a day for life. If he answered in the affirmative, the respondent was then asked to estimate the life expectancy cost.

[c]These individuals said they thought that smoking reduced life expectancy but were unable to assign a particular number of years to this loss.

While these results are suggestive of consumer knowledge of smoking risks, some problems are evident. For instance, 30 percent of the population (and 40 percent of smokers) deny that smoking affects life expectancy. Yet, these responses are directly contradicted by the individuals themselves in other parts of the survey and by overall market response behavior.[36] Notwithstanding these shortcomings, the survey results suggest several qualitative features of current consumer knowledge of smoking.

[35]More precisely, individuals were asked to categorize the statement: a 30-year-old person reduces his life expectancy if he smokes at least one pack a day. Responses were Know it's true, Think it's true, Don't know if it's true, Think it's not true, and Know it's not true. Responses in the first two categories were considered affirmative. Those in the last two categories were considered negative.

[36]For instance, in the same survey, only 2.9 percent of the population and 5.1 percent of smokers denied that smoking causes lung cancer, a widely acknowledged fatal disease. Moreover, aggregate data shows that while 40 percent of smokers may say that smoking does not cause early death, only seven percent of smokers persist in smoking non-filtered cigarettes (see Maxwell (1981)].

First, on average, individuals do not appear to underestimate the risk of smoking. Taking the survey results at face value, and ignoring the non-responses, the mean life loss is approximately 3.5 years, which closely corresponds to epidemiological results (see footnote 25).

Second, the belief distribution is not symmetric; even if zero-cost responses are eliminated, the distribution is skewed to the right. While a greater number of consumers apparently underestimate the life loss of smoking, those who do overestimate, do so by a greater margin on average.

Third, and finally, the distribution exhibits a high variance. For instance, including the zero-cost respondents in the lowest cost group, the standard deviation of the Roper distribution is 4.7 years, thereby suggesting that the dispersion of beliefs about the mean life loss could be quite high.

The deviations in reported beliefs are large enough to introduce the possibility that the estimated values of life saving reflected in table 4 and the corresponding distributions are largely an artifact of the uniform belief assumption. To investigate this issue, the value of life distribution was re-estimated incorporating the Roper survey data. For our primary Roper estimate, consumers who responded that smoking had no life expectancy effects were placed in the lowest Roper category of 0–2 years lost per pack;[37] those who could not quantify the loss were assumed to be distributed like the rest of the population. Consumers in each category are assumed to be uniformly distributed across the category. This belief distribution has a mean of 4.67 years. It is also assumed that an individual's reported belief about the longevity effect of smoking is independent of his underlying taste for cigarettes r and his value of life saving v.

With appropriate adjustments to the solution algorithm, the model can be solved under the Roper belief assumption.[38] The solution is characterized by

[37]The assignment of these individuals to the lowest Roper category is arbitrary. As a technical matter, however, some assignment must be made for estimation purposes in light of the empirical fact that virtually no smokers continue to smoke the same quantity or the same type of pre-1953 cigarettes. To test the sensitivity and fit of this assignment, estimates were also made under the assumptions that these individuals had beliefs between 0 and 1 year of expected life lost and between 0 and 0.5 years of life lost. The mean value of life increased as expected, but the sum of squared error also increased substantially. For instance, in moving from the initial assumption to the 0–1 year assumption, the mean value of life increased from \$10 250 to \$15 050, but the sum of squared error doubled from 0.035 to 0.077. The fit when these individuals were assigned to the 0–0.5 interval was still worse.

[38]In particular, the density function for the shift M is now

$$h(M) = \int_0^{\max b} f(v(M,b))R(b)/[n^* - (bv/sk')^{1/(s-1)}]b\, db$$

where f is the density of individual values of life, $v(M,b)$ is the value of life corresponding to M and b, and R is the Roper density for the belief parameter b. The corresponding density function for nicotine choices is:

$$J(n) = \int_0^{\max b} f(v(n,b))R(b)[s(s-1)k'(n^* - n)^{s-2}b]db.$$

parameters $s = 3.1$ and $c' = 1.3$ and a value of life distribution with a mean of $10\,250 per year of life saved, a standard deviation equal to $7\,850, and a sum of squared errors of 0.035. The 'best' uniform belief assumption of 3.5 years yielded a mean value of life saving of $8622 and a standard deviation of $9170 with a sum of squared error of 0.029. Thus, the use of the Roper beliefs increases the estimated mean value of life saving by 19 percent.

It is important to note, however, that this increase is a composite of two competing effects which masks the potential impact of introducing actual beliefs. The higher mean belief in the Roper survey (4.67 years) compared with the mean of the best technical estimates upon which the uniform belief model is based (3.5 years) leads to lower estimates of the value of risk reduction. Holding the mean belief constant, however, the introduction of the dispersion in beliefs alone, leads to higher estimates. When the distribution is computed for a uniform belief of 4.67 years, the mean value of life saving is found to be $6282 with a standard deviation equal to $6777, and a sum of squared errors of 0.029. Thus, holding the mean belief constant at 4.67 years, the introduction of the Roper *distribution* of beliefs alone increases the mean by 63 percent.

The value of life saving distribution for the Roper belief distribution is shown by the humped density function in fig. 2. The corresponding uniform belief case (4.67 years) is very similar to and slightly to the left of the uniform belief case of 3.5 years also shown in fig. 2. As expected, the introduction of differing consumer beliefs acts to push the mass of the distribution away from zero. More importantly, perhaps, the Roper belief assumption increases the mean value of life saving by approximately 19 percent when compared to the 3.5 year uniform belief assumption and by 63 percent when compared to the 4.67 year assumption. These increases are primarily attributable to the net reduction in the density of individuals near zero. It is interesting to note, however, that despite the decidedly skewed nature of the Roper survey responses, the fitted value of life distribution continues to have a clear non-symmetric character with a concentration of density at lower values. Moreover, our previous findings of a substantial variation in individual values of life remains.

7. Conclusion

This study used evidence of consumer reaction to health information about cigarettes to derive a measure of consumers' valuations of life saving. The

---

The solution algorithm again requires iteration on the parameters of the value of life distribution as well as the nicotine taste parameters s and k'. However, because of the joint determination of the shift M, the model-generated densities for both M and n must be compared against the market-generated densities. The minimum sum of squared differences is again used as a solution criterion.

study found that cigarette–health disclosures led to a reduction in the demand for cigarettes of $1.15 on average. This shift can be compared to the 1980 price per pack of cigarettes of $0.656. From these reactions, the best estimates of the average value of life saving held by the population were in the range of $300 000–$600 000. Sensitivity tests allowed the estimates to increase to a high of $1 million. These estimates differ from those in the literature because they consider the implications of the quality adjustments to risk for the value of life saving calculations as well as the implications of the time pattern of the risk. Considerable care also went towards addressing the issue of consumer perceptions about smoking risks.

The primary estimates of the value of risk reduction were performed under the usual assumption that all consumers hold the best technical estimate of the loss in expected life for a pack-a-day smoker (3.5 years). Estimates were also made under the alternative assumptions that consumers uniformly believed this loss to be as little as 2 years or as much as 5 years. More significantly, estimates were also made using survey data that showed a wide variation in consumer beliefs. Use of these survey results caused the estimated mean value of life saving to increase compared to the equivalent uniform belief assumption. Still, while the potential for varied beliefs to substantially alter the results was demonstrated, the order of magnitude of the primary quantitative results did not change.

A clear lesson of this study is that if time series studies are performed to circumvent biases inherent in cross-section data, it is inevitable that the emphasis of value of life studies must move towards health hazards and away from accidental risks. In the case of accidents, risks are more apparent and therefore offer little chance to observe market reactions to new information about risks. The study of health hazards, however, inevitably requires an explicit treatment of time preference rates as well as estimates of the time profile of the mortality effects over individual lifetimes.[39] Moreover, because individuals may assimilate new information slowly, the practice of assuming accurate consumer/worker risk perceptions becomes more questionable. Progress on the thorny problem of measuring consumer beliefs about hazards thus becomes a more important research priority.

Future studies could significantly benefit from access to longitudinal micro data sets which include behavioral and belief information. In this paper, various distributions were inferred from available information describing aggregate behavior. More reliable results and better error measurements could be made by studying a cross-section of individuals' reactions (and beliefs) over a similarly critical time period. While such data bases are rare, they could significantly improve our knowledge of the way individuals react to risk and the role consumers' own estimates of health cost play in determining their behavior.

[39]For a theoretical treatment of the reactions to long term health hazards, see Ippolito (1981).

Finally, for policy purposes, there are clear expositional advantages to measuring the value of life from a reaction to information about hidden hazards of consumption. The case of cigarettes is typical in allowing us to overcome questions about the affordability of risk avoidance and the limited options of low income individuals; once informed of the hazard potential, individuals must pay an out-of-pocket cost for the opportunity to expose themselves to risks. A basic point of value of life studies — that individuals are not willing to spend unlimited amounts for safety — may be more convincing to skeptics when drawn from behavior that is less directly influenced by a person's initial wealth position.

Appendix: Effects of health disclosures on cigarette smoking habits in the United States

The history of cigarette health disclosures in the United States has been given elsewhere [see, for example, Ippolito et al. (1979)]. In essence, the health hazards of smoking were widely publicized in the United States beginning in about 1952, culminating in the now-famous Surgeon General's Report in 1964. Additional reports and much additional publicity have ensued. In this appendix, estimates are made of what per capita cigarette consumption, nicotine content per cigarette smoked and the overall smoking participation rate would have been in 1980 if no health disclosures had ever appeared.

Per capita cigarette consumption

In 1980, per capita cigarette consumption was 195 packs per year [U.S. Department of Agriculture (1981)]. The per capita consumption that would have occurred without disclosures is estimated by analyzing aggregate cigarette consumption in the United States over time.

In generating these estimates, the demand curve was assumed to have the functional form

$$\log C = b_0 + b_1 \log T + b_2 D53 + b_3 D64\ T64 + b_4 P + b_5 \log Y + \text{error},$$

where C is per capita consumption by adults in the United States, P is a real cigarette price index, Y is deflated per capita income, T is a trend term, $D53$ is a dummy variable that denotes the appearance of initial health disclosures and subsequent publicity and equals one during the period 1953–1980 and zero otherwise, $D64$ denotes the appearance of the Surgeon General's Report and subsequent publicity and equals one during the period 1964–1980 and zero otherwise, and $T64$ is a counter beginning at one in 1964.

The general nature of the functional form specified above, including the non-linear nature of the post-1964 disclosure response, has been discussed in considerable detail elsewhere [see Hamilton (1972), Ippolito et al. (1979), and Klein et al. (1981)]. A similar discussion pertaining to the English experience is found in Atkinson and Skegg (1973). For present purposes, it is important to note that the empirical specification is consistent with the theoretical demand curve used in the text.[40] It is also noted that various alternative demand specifications were tried that included different time trends, various lag structures, additional variables (e.g. dummy variables that denoted the TV advertising ban and the Fairness Doctrine[41]) and different functional forms. The results remained robust in the face of these alternatives.

The estimates using ordinary least squares are presented in eq. (1) in table 5.[42] The estimates suggest that the 1953 health disclosures and subsequent publicity led to an almost immediate reduction in per capita consumption in the vicinity of 17 percent. Through other experiments, it was found that the data lends no support to the notion that this response either waned or intensified over the post-1953 period.[43] In contrast, the results are consistent with the notion that the Surgeon General's Report and subsequent publicity led to a gradual and persistent reduction in per capita consumption on the order of 3.17 percent per year throughout the period 1964–1980. The price elasticity, which also remained stable in the face of many experiments, is put at −0.48. These results are consistent with other estimates in the literature based on somewhat different time periods and methodologies.[44]

Together, these measures suggest that per capita cigarette consumption in 1980 was 50.4 percent of what it would have been in the absence of

[40]In particular, it is noted that changes in cigarette types as a result of information are completely captured by the information variables (they are part of the demand shift M). It is also noted that the model permits the price elasticity to change with information [health information makes individuals' demand curves more elastic, but low-taste smokers (who have the higher demand elasticities in the model) tend to quit with a greater frequency]. But the time series could not accommodate additional price-information interaction terms to test this notion.

[41]When dummy variables were introduced to represent the Fairness Doctrine period (1968–1970) and the TV advertising ban period (1971 to end-of-sample), their coefficients were not significantly different from zero; the information coefficients increased slightly. To the extent that the advertising policy effects are commingled with the information response, and hence are embodied in the coefficient b_3, the estimated information response is biased in an upward direction.

[42]These results remained virtually unchanged when estimated using the Cochrane–Orcutt technique to correct for serial correlation.

[43]An alternative specification that permitted the post-1953 effects to be non-linear over time was tried. In particular, the term D_{53} was replaced by $D_{53}/T_{53}{}^b$, where T_{53} is a time counter starting at one in 1953. If the disclosure effect is linear, the estimate on b should be small and insignificantly different from zero. Solving the equation by non-linear least squares, the estimate for b was 0.043 with a t-statistic equal to 0.57. The remaining coefficients were virtually unchanged.

[44]Hamilton (1972), Ippolito et al. (1979) and Klein et al. (1981) have estimated the effects of information disclosure on per capita cigarette consumption in the United States. While these studies have used different methodologies and covered somewhat different time periods, the estimates of consumer response, when extrapolated to common years, have been remarkably similar. The price elasticity estimated above is also similar to results found in other studies.

Table 5

Effects of health information on cigarette consumption.

Dependent variable	Constant	Log of time trend	D53	Post-1964 reaction variable[a]	Price variable[b]	log Y	R^2	D.W.
(1) Log of per capita consumption	3.50 (18.73)	0.557 (8.97)	-0.171 (7.33)	-0.0317 (20.35)	-0.733 (7.64) (-0.48)[c]	0.627 (7.29)	0.988	1.26
(2) Log of smoking participation rate	-0.73 (1.82)	0.049 (5.02)	0.028 (2.64)	-0.0018 (8.40)	-0.059 (0.83)	-0.066 (0.86)	0.974	2.14
(3) Log of smoking participation rate	-1.12 (114.6)	0.023 (3.33)	0.033 (2.54)	-0.0022 (21.57)			0.960	1.38

Note: Numbers in parenthesis are *t*-statistics. The equations were estimated using ordinary least squares; the results remained virtually unchanged when estimated by the Cochrane–Orcutt method to reduce serial correlation. For purposes of calculating the bounds for estimates of the value of risk reduction, the larger standard errors found in either eq. (2) or eq. (3) or using OLS or Cochrane–Orcutt estimates were used.
    The per capita consumption regression includes annual data for the years 1934–1980. The participation rate regressions include data for the years 1947–1975.

[a]The reaction variable in eq. (1) is $D64 \cdot T64$; the variable in eqs. (2) and (3) is $D64 \cdot T64^2$ (see text).
[b]The price variable in eq. (1) is price itself; the variable in eq. (2) is log of price.
[c]Number in parentheses is the price elasticity of demand evaluated at the 1980 price per pack of cigarettes.

smoking–health publicity. Thus, without the appearance of disclosures, the estimates suggest that per capita consumption would have been 386 packs per year in 1980 compared to actual consumption of 195 packs per year.

While our use of cumulative responses as of 1980 may understate true long-term response, it is not apparent that the estimated values of risk reduction based on this measure are underestimated. The issue revolves critically around the reason why a gradual (and not a sudden) response occurred after 1964. For example, consider the plausible case where the delayed reaction to disclosures is related to the time it takes consumers to formulate correct estimates of the true health harm.[45] In this case, the estimates of the value of saving a life derived in the text are not biased if the survey data used to estimate beliefs accurately measures actual consumer perceptions held by the population in 1980. If the perceived health costs continue to increase with time, so will the intensity of response. Since higher beliefs and higher responses enter the calculations of the value of life saving in exactly offsetting ways, the net results are not affected. Ultimately, the results can only be verified by applying the same methodology to updated response *and* belief data that becomes available in future years.

Nicotine content

The relative harm associated with smoking a particular type of cigarette can be indexed by its nicotine content.[46] Nicotine content by brand and variety and corresponding market share data are available [Federal Trade Commission (semi-annual) and Maxwell (1975, 1981)].[47] Thus, it is straight-forward to fit the 1980 nicotine market share distribution with the following logistic equation:

$$\log(Z/(1-Z)) = -5.11 + 5.66n, \qquad R^2 = 0.99,$$
$$(49.09)(50.47)$$

where n is nicotine content, Z is the proportion of cigarettes sold whose nicotine content is less than or equal to n, and the numbers in parentheses are t-statistics. This distribution is characterized by a mean nicotine content of approximately one milligram per cigarette.

[45]Evidence has already been cited that disputes the hypothesis that cigarette smokers are plagued by habit or addiction and that this is the reason that reaction to disclosures proceeded slowly. See footnote 11.

[46]The correlation between nicotine and tar (the other major index of harm) is very high (0.92 using 1975 Federal Trade Commission data).

[47]While the calculations in the text require the distribution of smokers across nicotine types, it is well documented that smoking intensity is invariant to cigarette-type [see Ippolito et al. (1979) and Health Consequences of Smoking (1981)]. Hence, the distribution of market shares across nicotine-type cigarettes is equivalent to the distribution of smokers across nicotine-type cigarettes.

What types of cigarettes would individuals have smoked in 1980 if disclosures had not appeared? Arguably, the best answer to this counter-factual question is provided by historical evidence. Prior to 1952, a few non-filter cigarettes with very similar nicotine contents dominated sales for over twenty-five years [Maxwell (1975)].[48] If nicotine content within brands is assumed to be constant prior to 1952, the weighted nicotine content per cigarette smoked was virtually stable from 1926 to 1952. Therefore, it is reasonable to assume that in the absence of the intervening disclosures, nicotine content would have remained constant and that virtually all cigarettes would have had the same nicotine content.[49] Using the FTC and Maxwell data, the nicotine content of these no-information cigarettes is put at 1.49 milligrams.[50]

Smoking participation rate

The actual participation rate in 1979 is used as our best guess of the smoking participation rate in 1980. As of 1979, 32.5 percent of the adult population smoked cigarettes [Health Consequences of Smoking (1981)]. To determine the proportion of adults that would have smoked in the absence of the health disclosures, smoking participation rates over time were examined.

Participation rates for the age group 21–47 years old were available annually from 1947 to 1975 [U.S. Department of Health, Education, and Welfare (1975)].[51] The following specification provided the best fit to the data:

[48]For example, in 1926 three unfiltered regular-size brands (Camel, Chesterfield, and Lucky Strike) accounted for over 90 percent of the market; in 1935 they accounted for 88 percent of retail sales. By 1950, the big three still held a 70 percent market share; two additional unfiltered brands [Pall Mall (King) and Phillip Morris (regular)] held a combined 17 percent market share. Contemporary nicotine measurements (reported in *Reader's Digest* and *Consumer Reports*) show that all five of these brands contained similar nicotine content.

[49]It is arguable that the nicotine-type cigarette distribution would have naturally spread over time to include milder cigarettes either to attract a wider population of smokers or to satisfy the demands of (generally lower nicotine smoking) females who comprised a larger proportion of the smoking population over time. By assuming continuation of the point distribution to 1980, the entire reduction in the mean and the corresponding increase in the spread of the nicotine-type cigarette distribution is attributed to consumers' reaction to health information. Hence, estimates of the value of life saving are biased upward for this reason.

[50]Consistent nicotine measurements by brand have been available from the Federal Trade Commission since 1967. Since brand shares are also available from Maxwell, reductions in nicotine consumed per cigarette can be separated into within brand reductions and across brand switches for the post-1967 period. Using 1967 FTC nicotine measurements, the effects of brand switching on nicotine content over the period 1952 to 1967 can also be readily calculated. Assuming that within brand reductions in nicotine content over this period took place in the same proportion to brand switching as they did after 1967, the actual nicotine content per cigarette in 1952 (and prior years) is put at 1.49 milligrams.

[51]More particularly, the Center for Disease Control survey in 1975 described the smoking history of survey participants. Thus, adjusting the data to account for the higher death rate of smokers, it is straightforward to construct smoking participation rates by age and year for the ages 21–47 and the years 1947–1975.

$$\log A = c_0 + c_1 \log T + c_2 D53 + c_3 D64(T64)^2$$

$$+ c_4 \log P + c_5 \log Y + \text{error},$$

where A is the smoking participation rate (all other variables were described above). The equations were run with and without the price and income variables.[52]

As in the case of per capita cigarette consumption, many alternative formulations were tried. While the above specification fit the data best, the results remained robust in the face of various alternatives. The estimates based on this specification are presented in eqs. (2) and (3) in table 5.

The coefficient on the 1953 dummy variable is actually positive (but very small in magnitude). These results clearly reject the hypothesis that the 1953 disclosures and subsequent publicity exerted a negative impact on consumers' collective probability of smoking. In contrast, the results support the hypothesis that the response to the 1964 Surgeon General's Report is negative, beginning gradually then accelerating during the post-1964 period. Given that the data upon which the estimates are based runs only through 1975, it is somewhat perilous to project the response to 1980, especially since the projected response continues to accelerate through 1980.[53] If the response to information has moderated by 1980, projecting the participation rate equation to 1980 will overstate the effect of disclosures (and the estimates of the value of life saving). Accepting this potential error, these projections were made. The results suggest that in the absence of health disclosures, the smoking participation rate in 1980 would have been 54.2 percent in 1980, compared to the actual participation rate, 32.5 percent.

The data developed above is summarized in table 1 in the text.

[52]Elsewhere, it has been found that the probability of smoking may be independent of income and price (see Ippolito et al.). This does not imply that smoking intensity levels are independent of price and income.
    [53]The estimate of the coefficient c_3 suggests that the participation response accelerates through approximately 1980 then diminishes (but continues) past that point.

References

Atkinson, Anthony B., 1982, Smoking and the economics of government intervention, in: A.B. Atkinson, ed., Social justice and public policy (M.I.T. Press, Cambridge) 371–382.

Atkinson, Anthony B. and J.L. Skegg, 1973, Anti-smoking publicity and the demand for tobacco in the U.K., The Manchester School 41, 265–282.

Blomquist, Glen, 1979, Value of life saving: Implications of consumption activity, Journal of Political Economy 87, 540–558.

Federal Trade Commission, semi-annual, Report of tar and nicotine content.

Fisher, Lawrence and James H. Lorie, 1977, A half century of returns on stocks and bonds (University of Chicago Press, Chicago).

Hamermesh, Daniel S., 1983, Expectations, life expectancy, and economic behavior, National Bureau of Economic Research working paper no. 835.

Hamilton, James L., 1972, The demand for cigarettes, advertising, the health scare, and the cigarette advertising ban, Review of Economics and Statistics 39, 401–411.

Hammond, E. Cuyler, 1967, World costs of cigarette smoking in disease, disability and death (World Conference on Smoking and Health, New York).

Ippolito, Pauline M., 1981, Information and life cycle consumption of hazardous goods, Economic Inquiry 19, 529–558.

Ippolito, Pauline M. and Richard A. Ippolito, 1982, Measuring the value of life from consumer reactions to new information, Federal Trade Commission working paper no. 67.

Ippolito, Richard A., Dennis Murphy and Donald Sant, 1979, Consumer responses to cigarette health information, Federal Trade Commission Staff Report.

Jones-Lee, M.W., 1976, The value of life: An economic analysis (Martin Robertson, London).

Jones-Lee, M.W., 1982, The value of life and safety (North-Holland, Amsterdam).

Klein, Benjamin, Kevin Murphy and Lynne Schneider, 1981, Government regulation of cigarette health information, Journal of Law and Economics 24, 575–612.

Marin, Alan and George Psacharopoulos, 1982, The reward for risk in the labor market: Evidence from the United Kingdom and a reconciliation with other studies, Journal of Political Economy 90, 827–853.

Maxwell, John P., 1975, Historical trends in the tobacco industry (Maxwell Associates, Richmond, Virginia).

Maxwell, John P., 1981, Historical sales trends in the cigarette industry (Lehman Brothers Kuhn Loeb Research, New York).

Mishan, E.J., 1971, Evaluation of life and limb: A theoretical approach, Journal of Political Economy 79, 687–705.

Thaler, Richard and Sherwin Rosen, 1975, The value of saving a life, in: N.E. Terleckyj, ed., Household production and consumption (National Bureau of Economic Research, New York).

U.S. Department of Agriculture, 1981, Outlook and situation.

U.S. Department of Health, Education and Welfare, annual, The health consequences of smoking.

U.S. Department of Health, Education and Welfare, 1975, Adult use of tobacco.

U.S. Department of Health, Education and Welfare, 1964, Smoking and health: Report of the Advisory Committee to the Surgeon General.

U.S. Department of Health, Education and Welfare, 1956, Tobacco patterns in the U.S., Public Health Monograph No. 45.

[18]

A Test of the Expected Utility Model: Evidence from Earthquake Risks

---

David S. Brookshire

University of Wyoming

Mark A. Thayer

San Diego State University

John Tschirhart

University of Wyoming

William D. Schulze

University of Colorado

The purposes of this paper are twofold. The first is to demonstrate that the expected utility hypothesis is a reasonable description of behavior for consumers who face a low-probability, high-loss natural hazard event, given that they have adequate information. The second is to demonstrate that in California information on earthquake hazards was generated by a 1974 state law that created a market for safe housing that previously did not exist.

I. Introduction

In a recent survey article on expected utility theory, Schoemaker (1982) describes the theory as "the major paradigm in decision mak-

The research reported here was funded by the U.S. Geological Survey. We would like to give special thanks to Richard Bernknopf, Edward Dyl, James Murdoch, Robert Wallace, Carl Wentworth, and an anonymous referee.

[*Journal of Political Economy*, 1985, vol. 93, no. 2]

ing since the Second World War." But Schoemaker indicates that in field studies the theory has not been supported. In particular, people do not behave as if they are maximizing expected utility for low-probability, high-loss events such as natural disasters. This conclusion is drawn from the work by Robertson (1974), Kunreuther (1976), and others. For example, Kunreuther interviewed homeowners in flood plains and earthquake-prone areas and concluded that the expected utility model "provides relatively little insight into the individual choice process regarding the purchase of [flood and earthquake] insurance."

The results in this paper are more encouraging for expected utility theory. An expected utility model of self-insurance that incorporates a hedonic price function is developed and applied to low-probability, high-loss earthquake hazards. Individuals can self-insure by purchasing houses in areas where the expected earthquake damage is relatively low. Our empirical results establish the existence of a hedonic price gradient for safety in the Los Angeles and San Francisco areas; ceteris paribus, individuals pay less for houses located in relatively hazardous areas. Moreover, the magnitude of the price gradient is consistent with our theoretical results when reasonable estimates of earthquake probabilities and potential damages are used, thereby lending support to the expected utility paradigm.[1]

The existence of a safety price gradient implies that individuals in the Los Angeles and San Francisco areas possess information on the relative danger of different locations. Yet Kunreuther found that Californians residing in earthquake-prone areas did not purchase earthquake insurance, in spite of subjective values on probabilities and magnitudes of potential losses that suggest such insurance may have been desirable. Our empirics show that a 1974 law passed by the state of California provided information that has allowed individuals to self-insure. Essentially, the law's passage created a market for safety that affected housing values.

The paper is organized as follows: In Section II, a simple theoretical model of self-insurance that includes a hedonic price function is developed. Empirical results on the existence of a safety price gradient and the source of safety information are presented in Section III. Section IV demonstrates the applicability of the expected utility model. A review of alternative evidence and qualifications to our analysis follows in Section V.

---

[1] Our approach can be likened to that of Gould (1969), who shows that the expected utility hypothesis cannot be rejected as a description of behavior for consumers purchasing auto insurance.

II. Theory

The theoretical model combines previous work on self-insurance in an expected utility framework with hedonic housing value analysis. Ehrlich and Becker (1972) discuss the acquisition of market insurance as a method of redistributing resources toward the less well-endowed states. They indicate that in lieu of market insurance, individuals may choose to perform a similar redistribution through self-insurance. The latter is therefore seen as a substitute for market-obtained insurance. Familiar examples of self-insurance include procuring a burglar alarm to thwart thieves or wearing a helmet while riding a bicycle. For earthquake hazards, self-insuring would entail, inter alia, locating one's residence in an area of relative safety.[2] If enough consumers possess information on where the relatively safer areas are located, one would expect to see higher housing values in these areas ceteris paribus. Location, with regard to safety, is a housing attribute much the same as other attributes including structural, neighborhood, and community characteristics. Thus, consumers choose a level of self-insurance through their locational choices with respect to earthquake safety.

In order to incorporate housing attributes into the self-insurance model, a hedonic price function similar to the type introduced by Rosen (1974) is utilized. Housing value studies using hedonic prices have proved fruitful for valuing public goods such as clean air (Anderson and Crocker 1971; Harrison and Rubinfeld 1978), social infrastructure (Cummings, Schulze, and Mehr 1978), and noise level (Nelson 1979), as well as estimating prices for more traditional attributes such as square footage, fireplaces, and swimming pools. The safety attribute is novel, however, in that it is random; it enters the consumer's utility function differently depending on the state of the world that prevails. It has a mitigating effect on damage if an earthquake occurs, whereas if there is no earthquake, there is no damage.

The existence of a hedonic price gradient for the safety attribute reveals that information about natural hazards is available and that

---

[2] Ehrlich and Becker (1972) distinguish between self-insurance and self-protection. The former reduces the loss in the event (e.g., earthquake) state whereas the latter reduces the probability that the loss will occur. It might be argued that location away from an earthquake hazard area accomplishes either or both of these objectives. However, reducing the loss in the case of an event rather than reducing the probability of the event and the associated loss seems more plausible. Therefore, we view the location decision as equivalent to the purchase of self-insurance. Although market insurance is available in some areas, few consumers purchase it. Only 4 percent of the structures in Los Angeles are covered by earthquake insurance (*Science*, May 1976).

consumers account for this information in their decision making. In our theoretical development, consumers are assumed to be informed about relatively safe and unsafe locations. The information may be attained by visual inspection, word of mouth, or a government program that delineates relatively unsafe housing locations for home buyers. The empirical results in Section III not only support the contention that information is available and considered in home purchase decisions, they shed light on the source of the information.

The consumer's problem is to maximize expected utility over two states of the world: the earthquake state and no earthquake state, which occur with probabilities ρ and $1 - \rho$, respectively. The consumer pays $p(a, s)$ for a house where $a = (a_1, \ldots, a_n)$ is a vector of n attributes and s is the safety attribute. Specifically, s is the monetary loss that the consumer perceives would be sustained during an earthquake. The function $p(a, s)$ is assumed to be twice continuously differentiable in all arguments with first partial derivatives positive for $i = 1, \ldots, n$. This implies that the n attributes are all desirable; if, for instance, neighborhood crime is considered, the attribute is the absence of crime. The partial derivative of the hedonic price equation with respect to the safety attribute is necessarily negative as shown below.

Expected utility is written as

$$V = \rho U[W(a) - p(a, s) - s] + (1 - \rho)U[W(a) - p(a, s)], \quad (1)$$

where U has continuous first and second partial derivatives. The function $W(a)$ is the wealth equivalent of the bundle of attributes the consumer has in the two states and is also assumed to be twice continuously differentiable. The safety attribute (or the amount of self-insurance) appears in both states as a reduction in the price of the house but appears again in the earthquake state as a damage loss.

The optimum choice of attributes is characterized by the following first-order conditions:

$$a_i: \rho U'_e(W_i - p_i) + (1 - \rho)U'(W_i - p_i) = 0, \quad i = 1, \ldots, n; \quad (2)$$

$$s: -\frac{(1 - \rho)p_s}{\rho(1 + p_s)} = \frac{U'_e}{U'}; \quad (3)$$

where subscripts on W and p denote partial derivatives and the e subscript on U denotes evaluation in the earthquake state. Assuming nonsatiation ($U'_e, U' > 0$), condition (2) implies that the ith attribute is chosen where $W_i = p_i$, or its marginal value to the consumer equals its marginal cost in the market. Condition (3) indicates that at the optimum the ratio of marginal utilities in the two states must equal the price ratio of self-insurance where the prices are weighted by the state of the world probabilities.[3] Note also that $-1 < p_s < 0$, or an additional dollar spent on safety must decrease damages by more than a dollar.

Assuming second-order conditions are satisfied, optimum values of a and s solve conditions (2) and (3). Either risk neutrality or risk aversion is compatible with second-order sufficient conditions.[4]

Equation (3) forms the basis for testing the expected utility model. That is, given values for the unknown parameters in equation (3) one can determine whether or not individuals act in accordance with expected utility theory. The empirical analysis presented in the next section is directed at determining both the existence of a price gradient with respect to relative earthquake safety and the magnitude of any price differential (p_s). In addition, the source of this location information is examined. In Section IV the estimated price differential is combined with probability and expected damage estimates to analyze the expected utility model.

III. Empirical Analysis: Hedonic Housing Equations

In the theoretical model it was hypothesized that individuals, acting on hazard information and possessing varying levels of risk aversion, would locate along a hedonic price gradient, with relatively safer homes commanding higher prices, everything else equal. In this section, a methodology that enables this hypothesis to be tested is described. Empirical tests are conducted for both Los Angeles County and the San Francisco Bay Area counties—Alameda, Contra Costa, and San Mateo. Also included is a description of the data base and the test results.

Proximity to earthquake-related hazards is the important variable under study. Relatively hazardous areas have been delineated through research programs conducted by the U.S. Geological Survey and the California Division of Mines and Geology. The outcome of these efforts was the Alquist-Priolo Special Studies Zone Act passed by the California legislature in 1972 and amended in 1974, 1975, and 1976. This act represents an attempt to provide society with information concerning relative earthquake-associated risk.

Special Studies Zones (SSZs) are designated areas of elevated relative risk determined by potentially and recently active earthquake fault traces (surface displacement has occurred in Holocene time, i.e.,

---

[3] See Ehrlich and Becker (1972) for graphical interpretations of a similar result.

[4] One of the sufficient conditions for a maximum is that $V_{ss} = -\rho(U''_a p_s + U'_a p_{ss}) - (1 - \rho)(U'' p_s + U' p_{ss}) < 0$. This is satisfied if the marginal cost of safety is increasing, $p_{ss} > 0$, and if either $U'' = 0$ or $U'' < 0$ for risk neutrality or risk aversion, respectively.

over the last 11,000 years). The evidence of faults may be directly observable (ruptured streets, crooked fences, etc.) or inferred (i.e., geomorphic shapes). The length of an SSZ coincides with the fault length whereas the width is generally one-eighth of a mile on each side of the fault.

Within California, the total number of SSZs designated through January 1979 was 251. There are two important ways in which consumers become aware of these. First, when an SSZ is designated, property owners in the zone are notified. Second, consumers selling property in an SSZ are required to notify prospective buyers that the property is in a zone (Alquist-Priolo Special Studies Zones Act 1974). This latter requirement has been implemented by the Department of Real Estate by having agents disclose the information via an addendum to the purchase contract. The buyer is then granted a period to collect additional information or to cancel the sale.

The potential effects of the Alquist-Priolo Act form the basis of a testable hypothesis. The null hypothesis is that consumers respond to the awareness of hazards associated with SSZs with the alternative being that they do not.

Data Specifics

The study areas are Los Angeles County and the San Francisco Bay Area counties, and observations are confined to single family residences. Thus, we do not consider the impact of hazard location on other structures (multiple family dwellings, mobile homes, commercial, etc.) or other ownership types (rental, leasing, etc.). Therefore, within our sample, this research asks if Los Angeles and San Francisco Bay Area households will pay a premium in the form of higher housing values for homes located outside an SSZ and what is the magnitude of that willingness to pay.

The data base was constructed so that hypotheses concerning the impact of SSZ location differences on housing sale price could be tested. The dependent variable in the entire analysis is the sale price of owner-occupied single family residences.[5] The independent variable set consists of variables that correspond to three levels of aggregation: house, neighborhood, and community. The Appendix describes further the data employed in the study.

The housing characteristic data, obtained from the Market Data Center (a computerized appraisal service centered in Los Angeles),

---

[5] Note that sale price or the discounted present value of the flow of rents rather than actual rent is used as the dependent variable. The two are interchangeable given the appropriate discount rate.

EXPECTED UTILITY MODEL   375

pertain to houses sold in 1978 and contain information on nearly
every important structural and/or quality attribute. The Appendix
provides summary statistics for the housing, neighborhood, and community characteristics used in the hedonic analysis. It should be emphasized that housing data of such quality (e.g., micro level of detail)
are rarely available for studies of this nature. Usually outdated data
that are overly aggregate (for instance, census tract averages) are
employed. These data yield functions relevant for the "census tract"
household but are only marginally relevant at the household (micro)
level.

The Market Data Center provided computer data tapes listing all
houses sold in Los Angeles County and the San Francisco Bay Area
counties during the period specified. The number of entries was un-
manageably large, so the data set was reduced as follows. First, a data
set was constructed that contained houses within SSZs.[6] This was accomplished by first searching the tape for all houses located in census
tracts that were wholly or partly in an SSZ. This list was further
reduced through a random number matching system. The addresses
of the remaining entries were then checked against a detailed map to
select those clearly within an SSZ. The numbers of valid Los Angeles
County and the San Francisco Bay Area SSZ data points were 292 and
745, respectively.

Second, data sets were constructed that included houses not located
in hazard areas. After deletion of incomplete data entries, a random
number matching system was utilized to choose sample sizes of approximately five thousand observations in each study area. The safety
variable is then represented by a dummy variable that takes on the
value one for houses in an SSZ and zero otherwise.

In addition to the immediate characteristics of a home, other variables that could significantly affect its sale price are those that reflect
the condition of the neighborhood and community in which it is
located. That is, school quality, ethnic composition, proximity to employment centers (and in Los Angeles County, distance to the beach),
and measures of the ambient air quality have a substantial effect on
sale price. In order to capture these impacts and to isolate the independent influence of location vis-à-vis the SSZs, these variables were
included in the econometric modeling.

The data base assembled for the housing value study is appropriate
to test the hypotheses outlined above for two reasons. First, the housing characteristic data are extremely detailed at the household level of
aggregation and extensive in that a relatively large number of observations are considered. Second, a variety of neighborhood and com-

---

[6] See Hart (1977) for the location of SSZs.

TABLE 1

ESTIMATED HEDONIC EQUATIONS FOR LOS ANGELES COUNTY AND BAY AREA COUNTIES

Variables	Los Angeles County	Bay Area Counties
Site-specific characteristics:		
Sale date	.002	.008
	(17.92)	(8.17)
Age of home	−.002	.0005
	(−11.37)	(2.37)
Square feet of living area	.0003	.00005
	(36.85)	(14.85)
Number of bathrooms	.098	.260
	(11.58)	(40.12)
Number of fireplaces	.124	.188
	(17.90)	(27.86)
Pool	.093	.067
	(8.66)	(4.83)
View	.143	.128
	(11.56)	(12.68)
SSZ location	−.056	−.033
	(−3.76)	(−3.39)
Community characteristics:		
School quality	.020	.012
	(20.72)	(12.85)
Home density	−.00004	−.00002
	(−7.72)	(−14.15)
Percent black	−.006	−.006
	(−33.55)	(−29.91)
Percent greater than 62 years old	.003	.009
	(6.35)	(18.22)
Air pollution	−.001	−.004
	(−5.01)	(−9.76)
Location characteristics:		
Distance to employment	−2.313	−.401
	(−2.04)	(−.17)
Distance to beach	−.016	N.A.
	(−22.44)	
Alameda County	N.A.*	−.158
		(−15.78)
Contra Costa County	N.A.	−.27
		(−21.20)
Constant	5.003	5.335
	(60.59)	(77.17)
R^2	.79	.69
Residual sum square	281.02	302.570
Number of observations	4,865	5,438

NOTE.—Dependent variable = ln(home sale price in 1978 $100s); *t*-statistics in parentheses.
*N.A. = not applicable.

munity variables that make it possible to isolate the SSZs' location influence on housing values have been included.

Empirical Results

The underlying structure of the hypothesis test is a single-equation empirical model that attempts to explain the variation in sale prices of houses located in Los Angeles County and the San Francisco counties.[7] The estimated coefficients of these hedonic equations specify the effect a change in a particular independent variable has on sale price. In reference to the SSZ location variable, this procedure allows one to focus on its significance while separating out the influence of other extraneous variables. Therefore, this analysis yields two outputs concerning the relationship of hazard location differentials to housing price. First, the relative significance of location variations is determined and, second, the estimated coefficient pertaining to location implicitly measures its monetary value.

The estimated Los Angeles and San Francisco hedonic gradients that provide the best fit of the data are presented in table 1.[8] A number of aspects of the equations are worth noting. First, as measured by R^2, the nonlinear form is a significant improvement over linear specifications. In addition, a comparison of the log of the likelihood values (semilog to the linear) indicated that the semilog form was a significant improvement at the 1 percent level (see Judge et al. 1980). As Rosen (1974) pointed out, this is to be expected since consumers cannot always arbitrage by dividing and repackaging bundles of housing attributes. Thus, on both theoretical and empirical grounds the semilog specification proved to be a better functional form.

Second, in the semilog equations all coefficients have the expected sign and are significantly different from zero at the 1 percent level. The SSZ dichotomous location variable has the a priori expected relationship to home sale price and is significant at the 1 percent level. This result is invariant with respect to various sample sizes, model formulations (various independent variable sets were tested), and estimated functional form.[9] These results indicate that individuals are

---

[7] See Freeman (1979) and Mäler (1977) for a review of estimates of hedonic housing equations.

[8] The main difference between the Los Angeles and Bay Area analyses is the locational variables. In the Bay Area distance to beach (ocean) is unimportant due to the presence of the bay. In addition, the three Bay Area counties were assigned dichotomous variables to account for county differences. San Mateo County is the excluded group and therefore is included in the constant term.

[9] Since the SSZ location variable is a zero-one variable then our choice set over functional forms was essentially restricted to the linear and semilog forms. Thus, possi-

acting on hazard information when making locational choices, and this action is translated into a measurable hedonic gradient.

Regarding the monetary impact on housing sale price, the non-linear specification does not allow straightforward interpretation since the effect of any independent variable depends on the level of all other variables. However, the Los Angeles County (Bay Area) results indicate that if all other variables are assigned their mean values, then living outside of an SSZ causes an increase in home value of approximately $4,650 ($2,490) over an identical home located in an SSZ. In relative terms the magnitude has approximately one-half the impact of a swimming pool or one-third the value of a view.

In the next section, these monetary figures are used to test the expected utility model. But before proceeding to this analysis, we can confirm the source of the hazard information used by home buyers. As indicated above, the Alquist-Priolo Act was enacted in 1974. Therefore, a pre-1974 analysis of the housing market would yield insight concerning the importance of the act in providing consumers relative risk information.

Housing data for the 1972 time period are used in the test of the Alquist-Priolo Act. Successful enhancement of consumers' awareness by the Alquist-Priolo disclosure provisions would require a change in the hedonic rent gradient over time. This change could take one of two forms: (i) an SSZ location would be an insignificant housing characteristic in 1972 yet significant in 1978; or (ii) the location variable would be significant in both years but its relative magnitude would increase over time. The first type of change could be considered a strong test of the impact of the Alquist-Priolo Act since the act would have filled an existing information void. Thus evidence of a direct market effect would be available. The magnitude change of the SSZ variable would imply a weaker response since it would be evident that consumers had hazard location information from some other source and were already acting on it before passage of the Alquist-Priolo Act.

The relative impact of hazard information independent of the Alquist-Priolo Act is also tested using the pre- and postdata sets; that is, if SSZ location remains a stable (no relative magnitude change), significant determinant of housing price, then consumers are acting on some available information although their preferences have not been enhanced or changed by the public disclosure program.

---

ble forms such as quadratic, log, inverse semilog, exponential, semilog exponential, and the Box-Cox transformation of the SSZ location variable are not available since they inevitably reduce to zero-one or cannot be estimated (e.g., log of zero). Further, a Box-Cox transformation of the dependent variable that is not equivalent to linear or semilog yields difficult to interpret results. Finally, the translog transformation is not available because the objective is to determine the separate influence of SSZ locations.

The 1972 time period results are presented in table 2. The semilog functional form provides the best fit of the data, and all coefficients, with the exception of SSZ location, are significant at the 1 percent level and related to home sale price as expected. However, the most noteworthy aspect of the equations is that the SSZ location variable does not demonstrate significance in 1972, even at the 10 percent level. The combined 1972 and 1978 results indicate that the Alquist-Priolo Act *has* caused a structural change in the hedonic gradient over time. This is evidenced both by the significant monetary impact change over time and by the change in significance. Therefore, in the study areas the Alquist-Priolo Act does pass a strong test of effectiveness, suggesting that the act provided information that consumers used in their market decisions.

IV. Empirical Results: Expected Utility Model

If consumers behave as if they maximize expected utility, then first-order condition (3) must necessarily be satisfied. The terms in condition (3) include the probability of an earthquake, marginal utilities of income, marginal damage to a house, and the marginal change in the house price. Our approach is to solve equation (3) for this latter term by substituting in reasonable values of all the former terms for the Los Angeles region. This provides an analytical solution for the price difference between houses in and out of SSZs. This price difference is then compared to the observed difference in housing prices estimated in the previous section. The two differences are shown to be close, thereby supporting the expected utility paradigm.

In the empirical work, houses were described as either in or out of unsafe areas so that the safety attribute was discrete. In equation (3) the attribute is continuous. Therefore, the partial derivative p_s in (3) is approximated as $\Delta p / \Delta s$, where Δp is the total price difference between safe and unsafe houses, and Δs is the total damage in dollars resulting from an earthquake. Equation (3) can then be rewritten as

$$\Delta p \cong \frac{U'_e}{U'} \left\{ \frac{-\rho \Delta s}{1 - \rho[1 - (U'_e/U')]} \right\} < 0. \qquad (4)$$

The hedonic housing equation provides an estimate of Δp of $-\$4,650$ for an average house worth \$83,153. On an annual basis using the prevailing home mortgage interest rate in 1978 (9.5 percent), this implies a home outside of an SSZ would cost \$442 more per year in mortgage payments than one in an SSZ. One possible assumption is that this is the perceived annual cost of living outside of an SSZ to home buyers, which may be plausible given a home turnover rate of once every 3–4 years in 1978. However, if home buyers properly

TABLE 2

<small>Estimated Hedonic Equations for Los Angeles County and Bay Area Counties</small>

Variables	Los Angeles County	Bay Area Counties
Site-specific characteristics:		
Sale date	.004	.004
	(5.20)	(6.96)
Age of home	−.005	−.002
	(−19.52)	(−15.17)
Square feet of living area	.0003	.0002
	(41.71)	(47.42)
Number of bathrooms	.133	.084
	(19.51)	(15.35)
Number of fireplaces	.091	.103
	(18.10)	(20.52)
Pool	.131	.105
	(14.73)	(9.57)
View	.130	.080
	(10.36)	(10.20)
SSZ location	.0002	−.022
	(.0174)	(−1.44)
Community characteristics:		
School quality	.0098	.003
	(12.44)	(7.34)
Home density	−.000017	−.00001
	(−3.88)	(−8.83)
Percent black	−.0029	−.002
	(−22.64)	(−15.147)
Percent greater than 62		
years old	.002	.004
	(4.83)	(13.25)
Air pollution	−.0018	−.004
	(−6.33)	(−13.18)
Location characteristics:		
Distance to employment	−7.64	−8.113
	(−8.40)	(−4.74)
Distance to beach	−.0095	N.A.*
	(−16.74)	
Alameda County	N.A.	1.020
		(−135.04)
Contra Costa County	N.A.	−.233
		(−25.34)
Constant	5.54	6.126
	(82.05)	(170.53)
R^2	.80	.91
Residual sum square	169.44	150.700
Number of observations	4,927	5,460

<small>Note.—Dependent variable = ln(home sale price in 1972 $100s); *t*-statistics in parentheses.
*N.A. = not applicable.</small>

perceive the role of inflation and keep their homes for a longer period, then use of the real rate of interest would be more appropriate in calculating the true cost differential for living outside of an SSZ. From the early 1950s up until 1978 the real rate of interest on home mortgages averaged around 3 percent. If we use this rate of interest, we obtain a real cost differential of $140 per year. These figures provide a range for comparison to Δp from equation (4) after substituting in values for ρ, Δs, and U'_e/U'.

First, consider a range of values for U'_e/U'. As a lower bound, and to be consistent with second-order maximization conditions, we use risk neutrality where $U'_e/U' = 1$. For risk aversion, however, $1 < U'_e/U' < \infty$. To establish an upper bound we appeal to recent work that employs cross-sectional data on household assets to establish properties of household utility functions. In particular, Cohn et al. (1975) found evidence that the coefficient of relative risk aversion is slightly decreasing in wealth. Friend and Blume (1975) found that "if there is any tendency for increasing or decreasing proportional risk aversion, the tendency is so slight that for many purposes the assumption of constant proportional risk aversion is not a bad first approximation" (p. 915). More recently, Morin and Suarez (1983) found the coefficient to be slightly decreasing for wealth levels up to $100,000, after which it becomes approximately constant. Furthermore, Friend and Blume estimated the market price of risk to determine a value for the coefficient, which they argue is greater than one and may be as high as two. Since we are interested in the ratio of marginal utilities and not the coefficient of relative risk aversion, we cannot use these results directly; but we can explore the implications suggested by this work.

To determine an upper bound, one approach is to examine U'_e/U' for various utility functions that exhibit the properties cited above. The largest upper bound is associated with a utility function exhibiting constant relative risk aversion equal to two; thus, we use $U(A) = -A^{-1}$, where A is total wealth. The denominator of U'_e/U' is evaluated at total wealth, while the numerator is evaluated at total wealth minus the dollar value of earthquake damage. Again, to determine the largest upper bound, we assume the maximum expected damage of about $20,000 developed below. To obtain total wealth we note from Friend and Blume's data (table 3, p. 908) that over their entire sample the market value of a house as a percentage of total wealth averaged 16 percent.[10] Since the average market value of houses in

---

[10] The use of 16 percent as the ratio of market value of houses to total wealth may seem small until one realizes that Friend and Blume (1975) define wealth to include human wealth. The authors regard this as the most appropriate definition; consequently, we use it here.

our sample is $83,153, we use as an estimate of total wealth $A =$ $83,153/.16 = \$519,706$. Finally, using $U(A) = -A^{-1}$, we obtain $U'_e/U' = 519,706^2/499,706^2 = 1.08$ for the largest upper bound.

Another approach for estimating U'_e/U' is to use a linear approximation (first-order Taylor series expansion) for describing changes in U'. Thus, we assume $U'(A) \cong U'(A_0) + U''(A_0)(A - A_0)$, where the Taylor series expansion takes place around the level of wealth A_0. Since the coefficient of relative risk aversion is defined as $c = | U''(A_0)A_0/U'(A_0) |$ we can then rewrite our approximation for $U'(A)$ as

$$U'(A) \cong U'(A_0) \cdot \left[1 - c\left(\frac{A - A_0}{A_0}\right)\right].^{11}$$

If we let A_0 equal the level of wealth before the earthquake and let A equal the level of wealth after the earthquake, dividing the expression above by $U'(A_0)$ gives

$$\frac{U'_e}{U'} \cong 1 - c\left(\frac{A - A_0}{A_0}\right)$$

as an approximation of the ratio of marginal utilities in the two states of the world. This expression does not depend on use of a particular utility function, but rather will be a good approximation for utility functions that have small higher order terms for U''' and beyond. Using the highest estimated value for c of 2 and the highest estimate of damages of about $20,000 we obtain

$$\frac{U'_e}{U'} \simeq 1 - 2\left(\frac{499,706 - 519,706}{519,706}\right) = 1.08.$$

This second approach gives an identical estimate to the first developed above and suggests that risk aversion plays a surprisingly small role in our analysis apparently due to the relatively small changes in lifetime wealth involved.

To estimate the odds of an event in the Los Angeles area, we use two sources. First, Kunreuther et al. (1978) report results of a survey question among California residents on the subjective beliefs concerning the odds of an earthquake. The average perceived odds of an event from that survey are about 2 percent per year.[12] To obtain a more objective estimate of the risk of an event we turn to a report

---

[11] Note that $U''A/U'$ will be a negative number for risk-averse individuals. Thus, we replace $U''A/U'$ by $-c$ in developing this formula.

[12] The average of the perceived odds used here was obtained from fig. 5.7 on p. 96 of Kunreuther et al. (1978) by taking the average of the end point risk of each risk category and multiplying by the reported frequency of occurrence.

EXPECTED UTILITY MODEL   383

issued by the Federal Emergency Management Agency (FEMA 1980), which estimated the odds of a large earthquake to be from 2 percent to 5 percent per year for the Los Angeles area. The upper bound of that range, 5 percent, resulted from scientific concerns over the Palmdale bulge, a temporary uplifting of the desert floor north of Los Angeles that occurred in the late 1970s. The lower bound estimate, which was widely publicized prior to the FEMA report, is based on the historical pattern of large earthquakes that have occurred in the Los Angeles area (Sieh 1978). For the relevant time period for our study, 1972–78, and for the Los Angeles area, there exists a remarkable coincidence between subjective and objective measures of risk of an earthquake. The FEMA lower bound estimate, which is appropriate prior to the occurrence of the Palmdale bulge, and the Kunreuther et al. estimate both imply $\rho = .02$ for estimating Δp in equation (4).

Finally, we need to develop an estimate of earthquake losses or damages associated with residing in an SSZ as opposed to residing outside of an SSZ, defined as Δs in equation (4). Again, we can obtain a subjective estimate of about \$20,000 from Kunreuther et al. (1978) for the average total damage people expect to occur to their homes if an earthquake occurs.[13] As an alternative measure, engineering studies suggest that the *average* damage to a single-story frame house should a great earthquake occur near Los Angeles would be about 5 percent of the home's value (NOAA 1973). This implies a level of damage for the average house in our property value sample (worth \$83,153) of \$4,158. However, homes in areas of maximum ground shaking, such as would occur in an SSZ if the local fault ruptured, would suffer damage equal to about 25 percent of the home's value (NOAA 1973). For the average house in our sample, this implies damages of \$20,788 (for a home in an area of maximum ground shaking). These figures obviously span the Kunreuther et al. estimate, with the upper bound figure quite close, suggesting that households answering the Kunreuther survey may have perceived the question to imply that their home would be located in an area of maximum damage. Note, however, that Δs represents the difference in damages an individual would expect from living in versus outside of an SSZ should an earthquake occur. Thus, as an absolute upper bound, we will use a value of Δs of \$20,000 consistent with a subjective assessment that homes outside of an SSZ will suffer no damage. As a lower bound we will take the difference in the objective engineering assess-

---

[13] Again, this average was obtained by weighting expected damage by frequency of occurrence among the survey respondents from fig. 5.6, p. 94, of Kunreuther et al. (1978).

ments ($20,788 minus $4,158) of $16,630. Thus, the lower bound assumes homes in an SSZ will suffer the maximum level of ground shaking and homes outside an SSZ will suffer average levels of ground shaking.

To obtain an upper bound estimate for the annual value of living outside of an SSZ to an expected-utility-maximizing household, we substitute values of $U''_e/U' = 1.08$, $\rho = .02$, and $\Delta s = \$20,000$ into equation (4). These figures are consistent with the highest observed coefficient of relative risk aversion of 2 and the subjective evidence obtained by Kunreuther et al. on earthquake risk and damages. To obtain a lower bound estimate we assume risk neutrality so $U''_e/U' = 1$ and use scientific-engineering evidence for $\rho = .02$ and $\Delta s = \$16,630$. These assumptions yield a range for Δp of from $333 to $431 per year. In contrast, from the estimated property value equation, the perceived annual cost of living outside of an SSZ ranges from $140 to $440 depending on use of real or nominal interest rates. This evidence suggests that the estimated property value equation for Los Angeles is consistent with utility-maximizing behavior with respect to earthquake risks.

V. Conclusion

Schoemaker (1982, p. 552) summarizes the problems of expected utility theory as follows: "As a descriptive model seeking insight into how decisions are made, EU [expected utility] theory fails on at least three counts. First, people do not structure problems as holistically and comprehensively as EU theory suggests. Second they do not process information, especially probabilities, according to the EU rule. Finally, EU theory, as an 'as if' model, poorly predicts choice behavior in laboratory situations. Hence, it is doubtful that the EU theory should or could serve as a general descriptive model." Our analysis provides only indirect evidence with respect to Schoemaker's first point. However, having demonstrated consistency between our property value market results and the expected utility model for Los Angeles, we can strengthen the argument considerably by briefly considering the San Francisco case.

For San Francisco, home sale prices, damage to homes should an earthquake occur, and, presumably, risk preferences are all similar to the Los Angeles case analyzed in the previous section. However, the probability of a damaging earthquake is considerably less according to available scientific evidence. For example, the FEMA report (1980, p. 3) states: "the current estimated probability . . . is smaller [than for Los Angeles] but significant," and later gives annual odds for a great earthquake on the San Andreas fault near San Francisco as 1 percent.

EXPECTED UTILITY MODEL   385

These are half the odds given for a great earthquake in the Los Angeles area in the same report. Thus, from equation (4) of the previous section one would predict, on the basis of expected utility theory, that the property value differential for houses in SSZs in the Bay Area should be about half that observed in Los Angeles. From the two property value studies the differentials are $2,490 and $4,650, respectively. This successful "prediction" suggests both that individual households process probability information in a reasonably rational and accurate way and that, at least in a market situation with a well-defined institutional mechanism, the expected utility model may perform well in predicting behavior. It should be pointed out that through the decade of the 1970s, the media in California carried an average of two stories per week relating to local earthquake events, actual or possible damages, and probabilities (see, e.g., *Los Angeles Times*, April 7, 1975; April 4, 1976; April 22, 1978). Possible earthquake events are a topic of considerable interest within the state, and the level of awareness among state residents is very high (Turner et al. 1979). The scientific evidence summarized in the 1980 FEMA study used in our calculations was widely publicized throughout the 1970s and may well be responsible for the similarity between the Kunreuther et al. (1978) subjective probability estimates of earthquake risk and more objective scientific assessments.

In summary, the property value studies make a strong case for self-insuring behavior consistent with maximization of expected utility. Further support of this result can be found by comparing the property value studies with surveys (Brookshire et al. 1982). In our survey of homeowners located in SSZs in Los Angeles (Brookshire et al. 1980), when asked how much more they would pay to purchase the same home outside of an SSZ, only 26 percent of respondents were willing to pay anything more. However, the average of all responses (including zero bids) was $5,920, very close to the average sale price differential of $4,650 from the Los Angeles property value study.[14]

Efficient prices should convey information to consumers. We have shown that the property value markets for both Los Angeles and San Francisco convey hedonic price differentials to consumers that correspond closely to expected earthquake damages for particular homes located in SSZs. Although the information provided by the SSZ program is by no means perfect, our results suggest that programs to provide consumers with hazard information may well be effective.

[14] Interestingly, when homeowners located outside of an SSZ were asked how much less expensive their house would have to be to get them to relocate in an SSZ, the average response was $28,250 (see Brookshire et al. 1980). This asymmetry between willingness to accept and willingness to pay measures of value has been demonstrated in a number of studies (see, e.g., Hovis, Coursey, and Schulze 1983).

Appendix

TABLE A1
Variables Used in Analysis of Housing Market

Variable	Definition (Expected Effect on Housing Sale Price)	Units	Source
Dependent			
Sale price	Sale price of owner-occupied single family residences	$100	Market data center
Independent—housing:			
Sale date	Month home was sold (positive)	January 1972 = 1 December 1972 = 12 January 1978 = 1 December 1978 = 12	Market data center
Age	Age of home (negative)	Years	Market data center
Bathrooms	Number of bathrooms (positive)	Number	Market data center
Living area	Square feet of living area (positive)	Square feet	Market data center
Pool	1 if pool, 0 if no pool (positive)	0 = no pool 1 = pool	Market data center
Air conditioning	1 if air conditioned, 0 if not (positive)	0 = no air conditioning 1 = air conditioned	Market data center
Fireplaces	Number of fireplaces (positive)	Number	Market data center
Independent—neighborhood:			
Distance to beach	Miles to nearest beach (negative)	Miles	Calculated
Age composition	Percent greater than 62 in census tract (positive)	Percent	1970 census
Ethnic composition	Percent black in census tract	Percent	1970 census
Distance to employment	Weighted distance to 10 employment centers (negative)	Miles	Calculated
SSZ location	1 if in SSZ, 0 if not (negative)	1 = SSZ 0 = not in SSZ	Fault hazard zones in California (E. W. Hart)
Independent—community:			
School quality	Community's twelfth-grade reading score (positive)	Percent	California Assessment Program (1979)
Housing density	Homes per square mile in surrounding community (negative)	Houses/square mile	1970 census, Southern California Association of Governments, Bay Area Association of Governments
Air pollution (TSP)	Total suspended particulates (negative)		California Air Resource Board

386

TABLE A2

MEANS AND STANDARD DEVIATIONS (in Parentheses) FOR THE VARIABLES USED IN THE HEDONIC HOUSING EQUATIONS

VARIABLE	LOS ANGELES COUNTY		BAY AREA COUNTIES	
	1978	1972	1978	1972
Sale price (1978 dollars)	83,153	64,075	75,650	58,959
	(55,938)	(35,213)	(37,581)	(36,881)
Sale date	5.382	6.61	6.33	6.141
	(2.86)	(3.25)	(3.22)	(3.40)
Age of home	27.57	24.43	25.00	20.159
	(17.09)	(12.91)	(17.69)	(15.64)
Square feet of living area	1,442	1,439	1,430.714	1,494.796
	(642.3)	(626.8)	(994.19)	(531.89)
Number of bathrooms	1.690	1.62	1.670	1.724
	(.71)	(.66)	(.62)	(.61)
Number of fireplaces	.663	.63	.825	.897
	(.62)	(.61)	(.52)	(.50)
Pool	.130	.12	.059	.045
	(.33)	(.32)	(.23)	(.20)
View	.095	.05	.126	.098
	(.29)	(.22)	(.33)	(.29)
SSZ location	.060	.049	.137	.022
	(.24)	(.22)	(.34)	(.14)
School quality	60.83	69.67	63.544	69.810
	(3.70)	(3.70)	(4.19)	(6.41)
Home density	2,213.5	2,262	2,476	2,431
	(731.96)	(697.9)	(2,152)	(2,018)
Percent black	5.47	9.91	6.636	4.603
	(18.00)	(24.5)	(16.37)	(13.17)
Percent greater than 62 years old	10.94	11.69	9.802	10.113
	(7.01)	(7.84)	(7.37)	(7.75)
Air pollution	107.7	106.12	52.319	51.585
	(14.16)	(13.93)	(11.91)	(11.92)
Distance to employment	.0183	.0183	.007	.007
	(.004)	(.004)	(.002)	(.002)
Distance to beach	12.41	11.48		
	(7.69)	(7.48)		
Number of observations	4,865	4,927	5,438	5,460

References

Alquist-Priolo Special Studies Zones Act, Sec. 2621.9, California, 1974.

Anderson, Robert J., Jr., and Crocker, Thomas D. "Air Pollution and Residential Property Values." *Urban Studies* 8 (October 1971): 171–80.

Brookshire, David S.; Schulze, William D.; Tschirhart, John; Thayer, Mark A.; Hageman, Rhonda; Pazand, Reza; and Ben-David, Shaul. "Methods Development for Valuing Hazards Information." Technical Report. Washington: U.S. Geological Survey, 1980.

Brookshire, David S.; Thayer, Mark A.; Schulze, William D.; and d'Arge, Ralph C. "Valuing Public Goods: A Comparison of Survey and Hedonic Approaches." *A.E.R.* 72 (March 1982): 165–77.

Cohn, Richard A.; Lewellen, Wilbur G.; Lease, Ronald C.; and Schlarbaum, Gary G. "Individual Investor Risk Aversion and Investment Portfolio Composition." *J. Finance* 30 (May 1975): 605–20.

Cummings, Ronald G.; Schulze, William D.; and Mehr, Arthur F. "Optimal Municipal Investment in Boomtowns: An Empirical Analysis." *J. Environmental Econ. and Management* 5 (September 1978): 252–67.

Ehrlich, Isaac, and Becker, Gary S. "Market Insurance, Self-Insurance, and Self-Protection." *J.P.E.* 80 (July/August 1972): 623–48.

Federal Emergency Management Agency (FEMA). *An Assessment of the Consequences and Preparations for a Catastrophic California Earthquake: Findings and Actions Taken.* Washington, 1980.

Freeman, A. Myrick, III. "Hedonic Prices, Property Values and Measuring Environmental Benefits: A Survey of the Issues." *Scandinavian J. Econ.* 81, no. 2 (1979): 154–73.

Friend, Irwin, and Blume, Marshall E. "The Demand for Risky Assets." *A.E.R.* 65 (December 1975): 900–922.

Gould, John P. "The Expected Utility Hypothesis and the Selection of Optimal Deductibles for a Given Insurance Policy." *J. Bus.* 42 (April 1969): 143–51.

Harrison, David, Jr., and Rubinfeld, Daniel L. "Hedonic Housing Prices and the Demand for Clean Air." *J. Environmental Econ. and Management* 5 (March 1978): 81–102.

Hart, Earl W. *Fault Hazard Zones in California.* Special Publication 42, rev. Sacramento: California Div. Mines and Geol., 1977.

Hovis, John J.; Coursey, Don L.; and Schulze, William D. "A Comparison of Alternative Valuation Mechanisms for Non-Market Commodities." Unpublished manuscript, Univ. Wyoming, 1983.

Judge, George G.; Griffiths, William E.; Hill, R. Carter; and Lee, Tsoung-Chao. *The Theory and Practice of Econometrics.* New York: Wiley, 1980.

Kunruether, Howard. "Limited Knowledge and Insurance Protection." *Public Policy* 24 (Spring 1976): 227–61.

Kunreuther, Howard; Ginsberg, Ralph; Miller, Louis; Sagi, Philip; Slovic, Paul; Borkan, Bradley; and Katz, Norman. *Disaster Insurance Protection: Public Policy Lessons.* New York: Wiley, 1978.

Mäler, Karl-Göran. "A Note on the Use of Property Values in Estimating Marginal Willingness to Pay for Environmental Quality." *J. Environmental Econ. and Management* 4 (December 1977): 355–69.

Morin, Roger-A., and Suarez, A. Fernandez. "Risk Aversion Revisited." *J. Finance* 38 (September 1983): 1201–16.

National Oceanic and Atmospheric Administration (NOAA) and Environmental Research Laboratories. *A Study of Earthquake Losses in the Los Angeles,*

California Area. Report prepared for the Federal Disaster Assistance Administration, Department of Housing and Urban Development. Washington: Government Printing Office, 1973.

Nelson, Jon P. "Airport Noise, Location Rent, and the Market for Residential Amenities." *J. Environmental Econ. and Management* 6 (December 1979): 320–31.

Robertson, L. "Urban Area Safety Belt Use in Automobiles with Starter Interlock Belt Systems." Washington: Insurance Inst. Highway Safety, 1974.

Rosen, Sherwin. "Hedonic Prices and Implicit Markets: Product Differentiation in Pure Competition." *J.P.E.* 82 (January/February 1974): 34–55.

San Fernando, California, Earthquake of February 9, 1971. Vols. 1–4. Washington: Dept. Commerce, National Oceanic and Atmospheric Admin., 1973.

Schoemaker, Paul J. H. "The Expected Utility Model: Its Variants, Purposes, Evidence and Limitations." *J. Econ. Literature* 20 (June 1982): 529–63.

Sieh, Kerry E. "Prehistoric Large Earthquakes Produced by Slip on the San Andreas Fault at Pallett Creek, California." *J. Geophysical Res.* 83 (August 10, 1978): 3907–39.

Turner, Ralph H.; Nigg, Joanne M.; Paz, Denise H.; and Young, Barbara S. *Earthquake Threat: The Human Response in Southern California*. Los Angeles: Inst. Social Sci. Res., Univ. California, 1979.

[19]

The Economic Journal, 95 (*March* 1985), 49–72
Printed in Great Britain

THE VALUE OF SAFETY: RESULTS OF A NATIONAL SAMPLE SURVEY*

M. W. Jones-Lee, M. Hammerton and P. R. Philips

> In the circumstances, economists seriously concerned with coming
> to grips with the magnitudes may have to brave the disdain of their
> colleagues and consider the possibility that data yielded by surveys
> based on the questionnaire method are better than none....
>
> Mishan (1971)

Public sector allocative and legislative decisions typically involve the assessment of a variety of prospective consequences. In some cases, notably in transport, energy and medical care, these consequences may include significant beneficial or harmful effects on individual safety. If such decisions are to be taken in a systematic and consistent manner and if, in particular, scarce resources are to be allocated efficiently and to greatest advantage, then it would seem to be necessary to have a method of associating explicit values with anticipated improvements in safety – and costs with deteriorations – in order that these effects can be weighed in relation to the other desirable and undesirable consequences of the decisions.

The case in favour of the 'willingness-to-pay' approach to the definition of such costs and values has been extensively developed in the literature.[1] This approach is essentially within the tradition of what Sen and Williams (1982) describe as welfarist consequentialism and is also based upon the *ex ante* (or endostochastic) as opposed to the *ex post* (or exostochastic) assessment of uncertain consequences.[2] Briefly, the fundamental premises of the willingness-to-pay approach are (*a*) that social decisions should, so far as possible, reflect the interests, preferences and attitudes to risk of those who are likely to be affected by the decisions and (*b*) that in the case of safety, these interests, preferences and attitudes are most effectively summarised in terms of the amounts that individuals would be willing to pay or would require in compensation for (typically small) changes in the probability of death or injury during a forthcoming period. Consequently, the willingness-to-pay approach tends to be concerned principally with individual marginal rates of substitution of wealth for risk of death or for risk of injury. These marginal rates of substitution are

* The research reported in this paper was conducted under contract to the Department of Transport. While publication is with the Department's permission, it must be stressed that opinions expressed in the paper are solely the responsibility of the authors and do not necessarily reflect the views of the Department of Transport. We are grateful to Ian Russell and Vicki Abbott for their help and suggestions.

[1] See, for example, Drèze (1962), Schelling (1968), Mishan (1971), Jones-Lee (1976) or Bergstrom (1982).

[2] For a discussion of the distinction between the *ex ante* and *ex post* approaches, see Broome (1978, 1982), Hammond (1982), Hahn (1982) and Ulph (1982). It should be noted that the distinction vanishes if social and individual choices satisfy the Harsanyi postulates (see Harsanyi (1955) and Broome (1982)).

usually incorporated in the definition of values of safety improvement (and costs of deterioration) along the lines dictated by the principles of conventional social cost benefit analysis or, at a slightly more general level, in accordance with the conditions for the *ex ante* Pareto-efficient provision of public goods.[1] In either case, it turns out that under a wide range of circumstances the appropriate value to place upon the avoidance of one 'statistical' death (or, more succinctly, the 'value of statistical life')[2] is given by the population mean of the relevant marginal rates of substitution.[3] Similar comments apply to the value of avoidance of statistical injury. In specifying these values it is clearly important to distinguish between different ways of dying and different severities of injury.

While it has to be admitted that the willingness-to-pay approach is not without its critics,[4] it is significant that a number of public sector or related bodies appear to have been persuaded to regard this way of defining costs and values as worthy of serious consideration. For example:

> ... the general principles of cost-benefit analysis ... would suggest that the Department [of Transport] should aim to find the amount that an average individual would be willing to pay (or would require in compensation for) for a reduction (increase) of (correctly perceived) risk of sustaining an accident.
>
> (Leitch Committee Report on Trunk Road Assessment (1977), p. 104)

Practical application of the willingness-to-pay approach clearly has, as its main requirement, empirical estimates of the marginal rates of substitution

---

[1] For an example of the former see Jones-Lee (1976), and of the latter Bergstrom (1982) or Dehez and Drèze (1982).

[2] A safety improvement giving changes δp_i ($i = 1, ..., n$), in the probability of death during a forthcoming period for each of n individuals, such that $\Sigma_i \delta p_i = -1$, is said to involve the avoidance of one 'statistical' death (or the saving of one 'statistical' life). Some writers reserve the term for the case in which the probability changes are independent.

[3] For example, ignoring for the time being people's concern for others' safety, aggregate willingness to pay for small changes δp_i ($i = 1, ..., n$) in the probability of death during a forthcoming period can, with little error, be written as $-\Sigma_i m_i \delta p_i$ where m_i (> 0) denotes the ith individual's marginal rate of substitution of wealth for risk of death. If, in particular ($\forall i$) $\delta p_i = -1/n$, so that all risk reductions are equal and entail the avoidance of one statistical death, then $-\Sigma_i m_i \delta p_i = (1/n) \Sigma_i m_i$. In the more general case in which δp_i varies over i but $\Sigma_i \delta p_i = -1$ (so that we again have the avoidance of one statistical death) then $-\Sigma_i m_i \delta p_i = (1/n) \Sigma_i m_i - n \operatorname{cov}(m_i, \delta p_i)$. Since it seems reasonable to suppose that m_i and δp_i will typically be uncorrelated across individuals, we again have the value of statistical life given by the mean of m_i taken over the affected population. For the derivation of similar results within the more general framework of the Pareto-efficient provision of public goods, see Bergstrom (1982) or Dehez and Drèze (1982). Clearly, if distributional weights are introduced into the analysis then the value of statistical life will be given by the appropriate *weighted* average of m_i. Finally, to the extent that people are willing to pay for others' safety as well as their own, it would seem appropriate to augment the value of statistical life by a sum that reflects this additional willingness to pay, though Bergstrom (1982) provides an interesting counter-argument on this point.

[4] Notably, Broome (1978, 1982) Zeckhauser (1975) and Linnerooth (1982). At this point it is also worth remarking that much of the theoretical literature dealing with the willingness-to-pay approach is based upon subjective expected utility theory, which has itself come in for considerable criticism in the recent literature – see, for example, Kahneman and Tversky (1979) or Loomes and Sugden (1982). However, it must be stressed that the conceptual core of the willingness-to-pay approach is the function relating an individual's willingness to pay on the one hand and probability variations on the other. The existence and properties of these functions are ultimately *empirical* questions and – like demand functions – their status is quite independent of the robustness (or lack of it) of particular theories used in their a priori analysis. Having said this, it is interesting to note that the empirical results reported below do tend to confirm the predictions of subjective expected utility theory in this context.

referred to above. Basically, there are two ways of obtaining these estimates: either from 'revealed preferences' or with the use of questionnaires.[1] In the revealed preference approach one attempts to identify and observe choices in situations in which people actually do trade off income against physical risk (typically in labour markets where riskier occupations can be expected to carry wage premia for risk[2]). By contrast, the questionnaire approach involves asking a sample of people more or less directly how much they would each be willing to pay to effect various reductions in their own or other people's physical risk or would require as compensation for various increases in risk. These two estimation procedures both have particular strengths and weaknesses. For example, the revealed preference approach has the advantage of basing estimates on real choices but is subject to the difficulties presented by the fact that pure wealth/risk tradeoffs are rare so that it is usually necessary to disentangle the effects of other factors. In addition, situations in which wealth/risk tradeoffs are most readily identifiable can be expected to involve somewhat biased samples of individuals – no doubt steeplejacks' and deep sea divers' wages carry clearly identifiable risk premia, but it seems unlikely that such individuals' attitudes to risk will be typical.[3] On the other hand, the questionnaire approach has the great advantage of allowing the researcher to 'tailor' his survey instrument and sampling procedure to provide precisely the kind of information that he requires. In particular, this approach is capable of generating estimates of marginal rates of substitution (together with data concerning factors such as age, income, etc., that are likely to affect the latter) for particular individuals whereas the revealed preference approach provides information only at a far more highly aggregated level – market equilibrium wage premia for risk, for example. The principal disadvantage of the questionnaire approach is, of course, that it deals with hypothetical rather than actual choices.

I. THE SURVEY AND QUESTIONNAIRE

After extensive discussions and correspondence with one of the authors of this paper, the U.K. Department of Transport (D.Tp.) decided that, in view of its flexibility and potential for shedding light on a wide variety of pertinent issues, the questionnaire approach warranted more thorough evaluation and testing than it had received hitherto. Following a one-year feasibility study (see Hammerton *et al.* (1982)) the D.Tp. therefore commissioned a nationally representative sample survey to be conducted by a professional survey organisation using a questionnaire designed and piloted in Newcastle. The survey was put out to tender early in 1982 and N.O.P. Market Research Ltd. was awarded the contract. After detailed modification and piloting of the questionnaire by N.O.P., the main survey was conducted in June and July of 1982 using a two-stage, stratified random sample drawn from 93 consituencies in England, Scotland and Wales which produced 1,103 full and 47 partial interviews (the latter were

[1] Blomquist (1982) provides a lucid discussion of these alternatives.
[2] See, for example, Thaler and Rosen (1976) or Marin and Psacharopoulos (1982).
[3] Though it should be said that Marin and Psacharopoulos (1982) somewhat surprisingly found no evidence of this effect.

terminated before completion for a variety of reasons, the most common of which was that the respondent was very old and simply unable to cope with the questions).[1]

The questionnaire, which took, on average, 45 minutes to complete, contained 37 questions (many multi-part) that fall into three broad categories:

(A) *Valuation questions* – intended to provide estimates of relevant marginal rates of substitution, relative valuation of fatal and non-fatal accidents, etc.

(B) *Perception/consistency questions* – intended to test the quality of individual perceptions of transport risks and ability to handle probability concepts; to examine the veracity and stability of valuation responses; and finally to test conformity with the standard axioms of 'rational' choice under uncertainty in this context.[2]

(C) *Factual and other questions* – concerning vehicle ownership, annual mileage, etc. as well as the usual questions concerning age, income and other personal details.

A follow-up survey was also conducted about a month after the main survey on a subsample of 210 respondents who were asked to answer a selection of questions from the original questionnaire. This exercise was intended to test for the temporal stability of responses.

The questions raised and problems encountered in designing the questionnaire were, needless to say, substantial if only because no exercise of this kind has ever been undertaken before on this sort of scale.[3] For example, the tradeoff between avoidance of ambiguity and avoidance of excessive complexity (and hence unintelligibility) in the wording of questions proved to be a pervasive difficulty. Another problem involved the selection of a method of eliciting valuation responses that would be both effective and free from bias. Experience in the feasibility study indicated that provision of a table of amounts of money for the respondent to tick is effective in generating responses but this device suffers from a notorious bias in that there is a tendency for respondents to pick middle points in the table – see Poulton (1975). Sequential bidding ('would you pay more than £5 or less?' If more, 'would you pay £10 or less?', etc.) is also effective in producing responses but is likely to lead to irritation and

---

[1] Full details of the sampling procedure, response rate, etc., are available on request.

[2] While there is a growing body of evidence suggesting that people can be induced to behave incoherently (i.e. to violate the Von Neumann Morgenstern or Savage axioms) if presented with particular kinds of choice (see, for example, Kahneman and Tversky (1979) or Lichtenstein and Slovic (1971)), we believe that the valuation questions posed to our respondents were not of this type. Thus, while our questions concerned awesome, unwanted events, they also involved 'simpler' choices than those that typically give rise to incoherence and would almost certainly be immune to most of the factors which have been suggested as the primary sources of incoherence. It therefore seemed appropriate to test for coherence in simpler choices in which such effects could be expected to have no significant impact.

[3] While earlier attempts have been made to estimate individual willingness to pay for safety improvement using the questionnaire method, these have typically been based upon very small and/or non-random samples. See, for example Acton (1973), Melinek *et al.* (1973), Jones-Lee (1976), Maclean (1979) and Brown and Green (1981). As far as we are aware, the only large random sample survey to have included questions concerning willingness to pay for safety is reported in Prescott-Clarke (1982). Unfortunately the wording of these questions is such as to make unambiguous inference of marginal rates of subsitution virtually impossible.

boredom on the part of the respondent especially if a number of valuation questions have to be asked. The method actually used is described below in Section II. Selection of the appropriate format in which to present information concerning probabilities also proved to be far from straightforward. Following piloting it was decided to present all probabilities in the form 'x in 100,000'[1] with – at N.O.P.'s suggestion – all probability statements supplemented by a pictorial representation in which the appropriate number of squares had been blacked out on a piece of graph paper containing 100,000 squares.

Quite apart from practical difficulties associated with the wording and presentation of valuation and probability questions, serious doubts were expressed by some members of D.Tp. about the reliability and credibility of valuation responses. In particular it was argued (a) that one would have no way of knowing whether responses to hypothetical valuation questions would give any indication of 'true' willingness to pay and (b) that respondents might have little or no real understanding of the probability numbers presented to them, so that their 'subjective' probabilities for the situations described might bear little or no relation to the 'objective' probabilities quoted in the questions. If this were so then it would not be legitimate to employ these objective probabilities in estimating marginal rates of substitution. It was essentially for these reasons that it was decided, so far as possible, to build 'consistency' and 'perception' tests into the questionnaire to detect the more obvious cases of misrepresentation or random guessing in valuation responses and inability to handle probability concepts. Respondents and interviewers were also asked to give their views concerning the difficulty or ease of dealing with valuation and probability questions. Finally it was decided to test whether the provision of reference information has any significant impact on perception of risk. If respondents had simply been expected to form probability assessments 'cold' (e.g. told only that a particular safety improvement would halve the risk of death in a car accident), then one would have grounds for doubting the quality of the typical respondent's subjective estimate of the implied risk reduction. Instead, respondents were in all cases told the magnitude of the base risk (e.g. that the average car driver faces a risk of death in a road accident of about 10 in 100,000 per annum).

II. ANALYSIS OF THE DATA AND RESULTS

In this section results are given for complete interviews ($n = 1,103$) and do not include the partial results of the 47 interviews terminated before completion. Responses have been weighted (a) to correct for the differential probability of selecting electors and non-electors in the sampling procedure and (b) to ensure that the adjusted sample is representative of the propulation of Great Britain as judged by age, sex, occupational group and region. This gives a weighted sample of 1,057 complete interviews. A detailed commentary on and evaluation of these results is given below in Section III.

---

[1] 10^5 is the smallest denominator which ensures that x is integer-valued for the kind of risks considered in this study.

(A) *Valuation Questions*

A (i) *Death* v. *Injury*. Because the D.Tp.'s definition of serious injury is so broad and includes, for example, all injuries involving an overnight stay in hospital, it was felt to be important to obtain information concerning the types of injury that the public regards as serious. Respondents were therefore given a list of various injuries and asked which they regarded as serious and which not. The results (with types of injury arranged in apparent order of seriousness, rather than the order in which they were presented to respondents) are given in Table 1.[1] Here and throughout we give 95 % confidence intervals that have been adjusted to take account of the fact that N.O.P.'s sample design produces standard errors which are larger than those for a simple random sample of the same size.

Table 1

Seriousness of Different Types of Injury

Type	Not serious (%)	Serious but death worse (%)	As bad as death (%)	Slightly worse than death (%)	Much worse than death (%)	Very much worse than death (%)
Cut and bruised but can leave hospital after a couple of days and recover fully within a month	81·3 (±4)	18·7 (±4)	0·0	0·0	0·0	0·0
Break an arm	63·1 (±5)	36·7 (±5)	0·1 (±0·3)	0·1 (±0·3)	0·0	0·0
In hospital for a year, but recover fully	15·3 (±3)	83·7 (±3)	0·6 (±0·7)	0·4 (±0·6)	0·0	0·0
Lose a leg	3·2 (±2)	86·7 (±3)	6·2 (±2)	2·4 (±1)	1·2 (±1)	0·3 (±0·5)
Lose an eye	3·1 (±2)	89·0 (±3)	5·0 (±2)	1·9 (±1)	0·6 (±0·7)	0·3 (±0·5)
Badly scarred for life and in hospital for a year	3·1 (±2)	84·4 (±3)	7·7 (±3)	3·0 (±2)	1·2 (±1)	0·5 (±0·6)*
Confined to a wheelchair for the rest of your life	0·3 (±0·5)	48·3 (±5)	27·7 (±4)	10·8 (±3)	8·7 (±3)	4·3 (±2)
Permanently bed-ridden	0·2 (±0·4)	36·5 (±5)	33·4 (±4)	11·9 (±3)	11·2 (±3)	6·9 (±2)

Note. Here and in all other tables reporting sample proportions, we give 95 % confidence intervals for the population proportions, adjusted to take account of N.O.P.'s sampling procedure. In some cases, the lower bound of the confidence interval gives a negative value for a strictly non-negative variable. This because the normal approximation to the sampling distribution is strictly inappropriate. In this case a binomial confidence interval should, ideally, have been computed but this would be tedious and would in any case almost certainly have little effect on the upper bound of the interval.

[1] Although they are not directly comparable, these results appear to be broadly consistent with those of a psychometric study reported in Kind *et al.* (1982).

It is fairly easy to show[1] that if an individual is indifferent between an increase, Δp, in the probability of death and an increase, Δq, in the probability of serious injury during a forthcoming period, then $m_D/m_I = \Delta q/\Delta p$, where m_D is the individual's marginal rate of substitution of wealth for risk of death and m_I is his marginal rate of substitution of wealth for risk of serious injury. It follows that if the individual would rather face the increase, Δp, in the probability of death than the increase, Δq, in the probability of serious injury then $m_D/m_I < \Delta q/\Delta p$ and that if he would rather face the increase in the risk of serious injury then $m_D/m_I > \Delta q/\Delta p$.

Question 16 asked: 'If you had to choose between them, which one of these risks would you rather face: a risk of 10 in 100,000 of being killed; or a risk of 1,000 in 100,000 of serious injury?' The responses are given in Table 2. In this question the term 'serious injury' was quite deliberately left undefined – prior to the survey itself we had no clear idea of what kinds of injury were commonly regarded as 'serious'. The responses summarised in Table 2 must therefore be

Table 2

Risk of Death v. Risk of Serious Injury

Prefer 10 in 10^5 chance of being killed (%)	Prefer 1,000 in 10^5 chance of serious injury (%)
63 (± 4)	37 (± 4)

interpreted as indicating that substantially more than 50 % of respondents have marginal rates of substitution of wealth for risk of serious injury (where 'serious' is to be construed in the sense reflected in Table 1) of more than one hundredth the corresponding rate of substitution for risk of death.

A (ii). *Valuation of Safety.* The questionnaire contained five different questions (some multi-part) intended to shed light on individual willingness to pay for reduction in the risk of death or requirement of compensation for increased risk. In order to facilitate interpretation of the results, these questions are reproduced in full below, though in order to economise on space, instructions to interviewers and code boxes have been omitted. The ordering of the various parts of Questions 18 and 20 is that given in Version 1 of the questionnaire, administered to 52 % of the sample. Orderings were permuted in Version 2, administered to the remaining 48 %, to test for the possibility that the ordering has a significant effect on responses.

Q. 14(a)   Each year in England and Wales, motor accidents, heart disease and cancer cause roughly these number of deaths among people under the age of 55:

---

[1] If the individual faces a probability, p, of death and a probability, q, of serious injury during a forthcoming period then expected utility, $E(U)$, is given by $E(U) = (1-p-q) L(w) + pD(w) + qI(w)$, where $L(w)$, $D(w)$ and $I(w)$ denote, respectively, utility of wealth conditional on survival of, death during and serious injury during the forthcoming period. Differentiation with respect to p and q respectively gives expressions for m_D and m_I and substitution from the expected utility equality implied by indifference between the risks, produces the result asserted.

Motor accidents cause 4,000 deaths
Heart disease, 11,000 deaths
and cancer, 16,000 deaths.

Suppose that, for a given amount of money, it were possible to reduce the number of deaths from just one of these causes by *100* next year. Which one cause would you choose to have reduced?

Q. 14(*b*)   If *you* were asked to make a single payment to help raise the money needed to avoid these 100 deaths, what is the most that you personally would be prepared to pay, bearing in mind how much you can afford?

Q. 18   Imagine that you have to make a long coach trip in a foreign country. You have been given £200 for your travelling expenses, and given the name of a coach service which will take you for exactly £200. The risk of being killed on the journey with this coach firm is 8 in 100,000.
You can choose to travel with a safer coach service if you want to, but the fare will be higher, and you will have to pay the extra cost yourself.

(*a*) How much extra, if anything, would you be prepared to pay to use a coach service with a risk of being killed of 4 in 100,000 – that is half the risk of the one at £200?

(*b*) How much extra, if anything, would you be prepared to pay to use a coach service with a risk of being killed of 1 in 100,000 – one eighth the risk of the one at £200?

Instead of paying extra to travel by a safer coach service, you could keep some of the £200 and use a cheaper, but more dangerous coach service.

(*c*) How much of the £200 travelling expenses would you expect to keep if you used a coach service with a risk of being killed of 16 in 100,000 – twice the risk of the service at £200 – or would you not travel on this service?

(*d*) How much of the £200 travelling expenses would you expect to keep if you used a coach service with a risk of being killed of 32 in 100,000 – four times the risk of the service at £200 – or would you not travel on this service?

Q. 20   Suppose that you are buying a particular make of car. You can, if you want, choose to have a new kind of safety feature fitted to the car at extra cost. The next few questions will ask about how much extra you would be prepared to pay for some different types of safety feature. You must bear in mind how much you personally can afford.

(*a*) As we said earlier, the risk of a car driver being killed in an accident is 10 in 100,000. You could choose to have a safety feature fitted to your car which will halve the risk of the *car driver* being killed, down to 5 in 100,000. Taking into account how much you personally can afford, what is the most that you would be prepared to pay to have this safety feature fitted to the car?

(*b*) An alternative safety feature would reduce the risk of *the driver* being killed by 20% – to 8 in 100,000. Taking into account how much you personally can afford, what is the most you would be prepared to pay for that safety feature?

(*c*) I now want to ask you about a safety feature which would reduce the risk of death for not only the *driver*, *but also the passengers* in the car. Bear in mind that the average car journey involves one passenger as well as the driver, and the passenger's risk of being killed is broadly the same as the driver's.

Suppose you could choose a safety feature which would halve the risk of the *driver* and *any passengers* in the car being killed in an accident. Bearing in mind how much you personally can afford, what is the most you would be prepared to pay to have this safety feature fitted to the car?

The following question was put to drivers only:

Q. 21(*b*) Suppose it were proved that changing your tyres when the treads were *2 millimetres* deep, instead of waiting until they reach the legal (1 mm) limit would reduce the risk of a fatal accident by 15%. Would you change your tyres sooner, or not?

If sooner

Q. 21(*c*) At what tread depth would you change your tyres?

	When treads at or above 2 mm deep 1
	When treads less than 2 mm but more than 1 mm
Probe as necessary	deep 2
	When 1 mm deep 3
	When less than 1 mm deep 4
	Don't know 5

Q. 22 A road improvement scheme has been designed for a town of half-a-million people. The improvements will cut by one quarter the risk of death or serious injury on the roads for everyone in the town – including drivers, passengers, riders of motorbikes and bicycles, and pedestrians. It will cut the risk from 12 to 9 in 100,000 (INDICATE ON SHEET). However, the Council do not have enough money to pay for the scheme, and two suggestions have been made for collecting money.

(*a*) It could be raised by a single door-to-door collection. Everyone in the town would be asked to contribute but it would not be compulsory. How much do *you* honestly think your household would be prepared to give to this single *voluntary* collection?

(*b*) On the other hand, the money could be collected by raising the rates or taxes for a year. Some households could afford to pay more than others. Bearing in mind how much your household could afford, what do you think would be a reasonable sum to collect from every household?

In all cases valuation questions were, in the first instance, asked directly and without prompts or tables of amounts of money for the respondent to tick. If the respondent hesitated so that a prompt appeared to be necessary (typically in only about 20–30 % of cases) then the interviewer was instructed to proceed as follows:

If respondent is unable to give a sum, use prompt in box below

---

I'll read out some amounts of money. Please stop me when I get to an amount beyond which you would not be prepared to pay. *Read out figures quickly and steadily.*

Nothing, £1, £2, £5, £10, £20, £50, £100, £200, £500, £1,000

When respondent stops you, ask;

You stopped me at ...... can you tell me how much you would actually be prepared to pay?

If ' Less than . . .', ask:

How much would you be prepared to pay? (*Probe for an estimate.*)

Questions 18, 20 and 21 clearly involve safety effects that are privately rather than publicly provided and were designed to avoid the non-revelation effects that might be expected to influence responses to questions involving public goods. The principal purpose of Question 14 was to give comparative valuations for avoidance of different ways of dying, though it should be noted that this question also involves the avoidance of anonymous rather than statistical death. Finally, Question 22 was intended to test for the impact of the non-revelation effects referred to above and involves safety improvements that are very obviously in the nature of public goods.[1]

The results of Question 14 (*a*) are presented in Table 3.

Table 3

Cause of Death Chosen to be Reduced

Cause of death	Prefer to have reduced (%)
Motor accidents	11 (±3)
Heart disease	13 (±3)
Cancer	76 (±4)

Estimates of marginal rates of substitution of wealth for risk of death computed from the responses to the valuation questions are given in Tables 4–7, the ordering of the various parts of Questions 18 and 20 being that given in Version 1 of the questionnaire. Marginal rates of substitution for self-only risk

---

[1] Unfortunately, last-minute editing of the questionnaire introduced an unintended ambiguity into Question 22, in that it is not made clear to the respondent for how long the safety improvement is to be effective nor whether the door-to-door collection in 22(*a*) would be once and for all or repeated annually. Marginal rates of substitution have been computed on the assumption that respondents interpreted all information in the question as applying to a single year. If, in fact, respondents recognised that the safety improvement might be effective for a number of years *and* treated the payment in 22 (*a*) as once for all, then the marginal rates of substitution implied by the responses to this question will be even lower than those reported in Table 7.

are denoted by m, for self plus (average number of) passengers carried by m^+, for self plus all others by m^* and for one other person only (where the other person is a car passenger – presumably normally a close relative or friend) by $\tilde{m}$. 'Trimmed' means were computed with outliers removed. The principle employed in trimming was to remove any upper-tail responses that displayed a very obvious discontinuity in terms of order of magnitude in relation to other responses, the suspicion being that these were either fanciful responses or (more

Table 4
Estimates of m (self only)

	Mean m	Trimmed mean m	Median m
18 (a)	£3·42 × 10⁶ ($\pm 2\cdot03 \times 10^6$)	£1·60 × 10⁶ ($\pm 210,000$)	£1·24 × 10⁶ (+340,000) (−270,000)
	$n = 988$	$n = 981$	$n = 988$
18 (b)	£2·22 × 10⁶ ($\pm 1\cdot04 \times 10^6$)	£1·39 × 10⁶ ($\pm 200,000$)	£720,000 (+190,000) (−150,000)
	$n = 1{,}005$	$n = 999$	$n = 1{,}005$
18 (c)	For those who would use (19 % of sample) £790,000 ($\pm 120,000$) For those who would not use, $m \geqslant £2.50 \times 10^6$	£790,000 ($\pm 120,000$)	£630,000 (+290,000) (−190,000)
18 (d)	For those who would use (13 % of sample) £290,000 ($\pm 52,000$) For those who would not use, $m \geqslant £830,000$	£290,000 ($\pm 52,000$)	£210,000 (+140,000) (−80,000)
20 (a)	£1·43 × 10⁶ ($\pm 500,000$)	£1·21 × 10⁶ ($\pm 220,000$)	£500,000 (+94,000) (−76,000)
	$n = 952$	$n = 950$	$n = 952$
20 (b)	£2·21 × 10⁶ ($\pm 400,000$)	£2·21 × 10⁶ ($\pm 400,000$)	£770,000 (+161,000) (−130,000)
	$n = 957$	$n = 957$	$n = 957$

probably) instances of coding errors. In particular, one response of £9,990 was removed from Question 14 (b). In connection with the latter it is worth noting that the code for 'Don't know' in this question was 9999. In Question 18 (a) all of the seven responses removed were coded 9998. This was the code for 'would pay over £9,997' and differed in only one digit from the code for 'Don't know' (9999). Similarly, all of the six responses removed from 18 (b), the two removed from 20 (a) and three of those removed from 20 (c) were coded 9998, the code for 'Don't know' being again 9999. In none of the questions in which extreme responses were trimmed was it the case that such responses tended to be given by individuals with high incomes.

Table 5
Estimates of m+ (self and passengers)

	Mean m^+	Trimmed mean m^+	Median m^+
20 (c)	£1·77 × 10⁶	£1·50 × 10⁶	£500,000
	(±540,000)	(±270,000)	(+98,000)
			(−76,000)
	$n = 966$	$n = 962$	$n = 966$
21 (c)		'Change ⩾ 2mm.'(62%)	
		$m^+ ⩾ £330,000$	
		'Change < 2mm.' (38%)	
		$m^+ < £330,000$	

Table 6
Estimates of m̃ (average passenger)

	Mean $\tilde{m}$	Trimmed mean $\tilde{m}$	Median $\tilde{m}$
20 (c) and 20 (a)	£500,000	£500,000	£0.0
	(±200,000)	(±200,000)	
	$n = 945$	$n = 943$	$n = 945$

Table 7
Estimates of m* (self + all others)

	Mean m^*	Trimmed mean m^*	Median m^*
14(b)	£20·34 × 10⁶	£16·84 × 10⁶	£2·86 × 10⁶
All	(±11·52 × 10⁶)	(±6·11 × 10⁶)	(+830,000)
			(−470,000)
	$n = 982$	$n = 981$	$n = 982$
14 (b)	£7·35 × 10⁶	£7·35 × 10⁶	£1·57 × 10⁶
Motor accidents*	(±1·48 × 10⁶)	(±1·48 × 10⁶)	(+1·7 × 10⁶)
			(−680,000)
	$n = 113$	$n = 113$	$n = 113$
14 (b)	£13·23 × 10⁶	£13·23 × 10⁶	£2·88 × 10⁶
Heart disease*	(±11·44 × 10⁶)	(±11·44 × 10⁶)	(+2·19 × 10⁶)
			(−1·28 × 10⁶)
	$n = 120$	$n = 120$	$n = 120$
14 (b)	£23·12 × 10⁶	£18·53 × 10⁶	£2·88 × 10⁶
Cancer*	(±15·06 × 10⁶)	(±8·50 × 10⁶)	(+930,000)
			(−560,000)
	$n = 742$	$n = 741$	$n = 742$
22 (a)	£200,000	£200,000	£30,000
	(±69,000)	(±69,000)	(+6,000)
			(−4,000)
	$n = 986$	$n = 986$	$n = 986$
22 (b)	£280,000	£280,000	£67,000
	(±59,000)	(±59,000)	(+14,000)
			(−12,000)
	$n = 955$	$n = 955$	$n = 955$

* Cause of death chosen to be reduced.

A (iii). *Regression Analysis of Valuation Results.* The results of multiple regression analyses of marginal rates of substitution on those variables that appeared from preliminary breakdowns to have an influence on these rates of substitution are reported in Table 8. The pairwise correlation coefficients between explanatory variables are not reproduced here but are on the whole small, the largest being that between the household car ownership and 'missing mileage' dummies which is equal to -0.514. Estimates of the elasticity, ϵ_Y, of marginal rates of substitution with respect to income for those cases in which income coefficients are significant (or nearly so) at $P = 0.10$ are also given in Table 8. These elasticities have been computed at the mean values of the relevant variables. Figures in parentheses are standard errors. All cases with outlying marginal rates of substitution were removed prior to the regression analysis.[1]

As can be seen, only a relatively small proportion of the coefficients in these regressions are significant, even at $P = 0.10$. Of the coefficients which are significant, that for the quadratic 'age minus mean age' variable is the most consistently so, with income, 'age minus mean age', and social class dummies also having significant coefficients in some, but by no means all of the regressions. In those cases in which income coefficients are significant, the elasticity of the marginal rate of substitution with respect to income is in the region of 0.3, which confirms the qualitative predictions of theory (see, for example, Jones-Lee (1976)) and coincides with the empirical estimate given in Blomquist (1979). As fas as age is concerned, in all parts of Question 20 marginal rates of substitution appear to follow a consistent 'inverted-u' life-cycle, peaking in the region of mean age. In Question 18 (a) the relationship is similar, though the peak occurs at about nine years above mean age. These results coincide broadly with the theoretical predictions of Shepard and Zeckhauser (1982). In Question 22, marginal rates of substitution show a tendency to decline with age and in Questions 14 (b) and 18 (b) there is no significant relationship. Where social class has a significant effect, it appears to do so only in Questions 14 (b) and 22.

The general insignificance of the coefficient of the 'missing mileage' dummy in the regressions for Question 20 suggests that there was no significant difference between the responses of drivers and non-drivers, as such, in this question.[2] In order to confirm this, separate regressions were run for drivers and non-drivers and *F*-tests of structural change were then used to compare these results. These tests rejected the hypothesis of a significant difference in all parts of Question 20.

A (iv). *Output Losses.* In order to determine whether or not they took account of direct economic effects in assessing their willingness to pay for safety improvements,[3] Question 23 asked:

---

[1] Cases removed were the same as those omitted in the computation of trimmed means – see Section A (ii) above.

[2] For the purposes of this study 'non-drivers' are defined as people who had not driven during the twelve months prior to the survey and constituted 42% of the sample of complete interviews. Not surprisingly, the majority of non-drivers did not hold a valid driving licence. Clearly there are potential difficulties in interpreting the responses of non-drivers to parts (a) and (b) of Question 20 which concern risks to drivers only. However, the questionnaire contained an explicit instruction to interviewers to tell non-drivers to answer Question 20 *as if they were car drivers.*

[3] It is clearly appropriate to add in to the value of statistical life a component to reflect the 'direct'

Table 8

Multiple Regression Results

	m (self only)				m+ (self and passengers)	m̄ (average passenger) Q.20(a) and Q.20(c)	m* (self and all others)		
	Q.18(a)	Q.18(b)	Q.20(a)	Q.20(b)	Q.20(c)	Q.20(c)	Q.14(b)	Q.22(a)	Q.22(b)
Constant	1·78 × 10⁶** (0·33 × 10⁶)	1·20 × 10⁶** (0·31 × 10⁶)	871,000* (340,000)	1·62 × 10⁶** (0·62 × 10⁶)	1·27 × 10⁶** (0·41 × 10⁶)	812,000* (307,000)	−7·19 × 10⁶ (9·51 × 10⁶)	153,000† (82,100)	115,000 (91,300)
Household's annual income from all sources before tax (£)	3·49 (25·9)	31·8 (25·0)	54·6* (27·1)	124* (49·1)	53·2 (33·2)	−14·2 (24·5)	1,060 (757)	1·76 (6·58)	9·09 (7·27)
Age minus mean age (years)	12,480* (4,650)	3,610 (4,440)	−3,070 (4,890)	6,860 (8,820)	−4,950 (5,930)	−4,430 (4,400)	−31,800 (135,000)	−1,990† (1,190)	−5,600* (1,320)
(Age minus mean age)²	−660* (264)	−374 (250)	−601* (277)	−928† (500)	−821† (335)	−534* (249)	11,800 (7,580)	18·2 (65·7)	125† (73·7)
Social class dummy (AB = 1)	−242,000 (303,000)	−277,000 (292,000)	202,000 (320,000)	58,900 (579,000)	214,000 (391,000)	−131,000 (289,000)	16·9 × 10⁴† (8·88 × 10⁴)	136,000† (77,500)	259,000* (85,100)
Social class dummy (C1 = 1)	−293,000 (261,000)	−197,000 (252,000)	−30,200 (280,000)	−428,000 (507,000)	−83,000 (341,000)	−109,000 (252,000)	7·93 × 10⁴ (7·67 × 10⁴)	61,700 (66,800)	81,100 (73,400)
Social class dummy (C2 = 1)	−163,000 (248,000)	−58,000 (241,000)	57,500 (264,000)	7,150 (482,000)	−93,400 (322,000)	−305,000 (238,000)	7·21 × 10⁴ (7·30 × 10⁴)	105,000† (63,600)	133,000† (70,300)

Social class dummy (D = 1)	94,100 (252,000)	325,000 (242,000)	222,000 (267,000)	214,000 (484,000)	138,000 (325,000)	−81,600 (241,000)	1.93×10^6 (7.34×10^6)	62,500 (64,100)	52,200 (70,400)
Miles driven last year	−6.03 (9.93)	4.48 (9.66)	11.0 (10.5)	7.92 (19.0)	8.27 (12.9)	−5.91 (9.45)	226 (296)	−3.71 (2.56)	−5.78* (2.77)
Car ownership dummy (household owns = 1)	165,000 (195,000)	77,100 (187,000)	71,000 (205,000)	5,050 (371,000)	137,000 (248,000)	135,000 (185,000)	7.32×10^6 (5.69×10^6)	−788 (49,800)	25,000 (54,500)
Accident experience dummy (Respondent involved in car accident = 1)	−52,700 (189,000)	−96,800 (181,000)	129,000 (198,000)	392,000 (359,000)	270,000 (241,000)	236,000 (179,000)	908,000 (5.50×10^6)	21,400 (48,100)	27,800 (52,800)
Accident experience dummy (Respondent knows someone involved in car acc. = 1)	−45,900 (165,000)	147,000 (159,000)	33,700 (174,000)	425,000 (315,000)	53,600 (212,000)	15,600 (157,000)	251,000 (4.84×10^6)	−63,100 (42,000)	12,100 (45,900)
Missing mileage dummy (No miles driven last year = 1)	96,700 (169,000)	40,200 (162,000)	−216,000 (176,000)	−521,000 (319,000)	−162,000 (215,000)	125,000 (159,000)	−408,000 (4.95×10^6)	3,940 (43,100)	33,700 (47,200)
Missing income dummy (No income given = 1)	141,000 (171,000)	−70,300 (162,000)	−82,300 (183,000)	−142,000 (329,000)	−223,000 (221,000)	−182,000 (165,000)	$−3.43 \times 10^6$ (4.95×10^6)	−33,200 (43,700)	−104,000* (47,800)
R^2	0.017	0.017	0.042	0.037	0.040	0.017	0.021	0.016	0.053
n	980	999	950	957	962	942	980	984	954
ε_r	—	—	0.32	0.40	0.25	—	0.44	—	—

* Significant at $P = 0.05$. † Significant at $P = 0.10$.

'At the earlier questions you were asked to think only about death and injury. However, traffic accidents can have other effects beside death and injury and they are listed on this page. Now although you were *not* asked to, did you in fact take any of these things into account when giving your answer to the earlier questions?'

The results were as follows (Table 9):

Table 9
Direct Economic Effects Considered in Answering Valuation Questions

Effect	Took account (%)	Did not take account (%)
Lost working hours	19 (±4)	81 (±4)
Inconvenience	11 (±3)	89 (±3)
Cost of repairs	14 (±3)	86 (±3)
Police and medical costs	12 (±3)	88 (±3)

A (v). *Anonymous* v. *Statistical Life*. In order to investigate peoples' relative valuation of the saving of anonymous life (avoidance of the death of one as yet unidentified person) and statistical life (eg. independent reductions of $1/n$ in the probability of death during a forthcoming period for each of n people)[1] respondents were asked to suppose that they lived in an area with 100,000 inhabitants. All inhabitants of the area have been given an immunising injection

Table 10
Attitudes to Gritting v. *Injecting*

Would not care (%)	Would care (%)	Prefer re-injecting (%)	Prefer gritting (%)
17 (±4)	83 (±4)	56 (±5)	44 (±5)

but one injection is known to be faulty (though it is not known to whom it was administered) and the recipient will certainly die unless re-injected. The government of the area faces the choice of *either* reinjecting everyone *or* gritting the roads in the winter, which it is estimated, will reduce the risk of road deaths by 1 in 100,000 for each person. Respondents were asked whether they would care which alternative was chosen and if so which they would prefer (Question 24). The responses were as above (Table 10).

---

economic effects of a safety improvement (such as avoided police, damage and medical costs as well as losses of net output) as suggested in Jones-Lee (1976) *only if* individuals have not already taken account of such effects in their responses to valuation questions.

[1] One of the objections to the *ex ante* willingness to pay approach is that it generates values of avoidance of statistical death, whereas in some public sector allocative decisions one knows with a very high degree of probability that in the event a particular project will avoid (or cause) anonymous death. While it is by no means the only consideration pertinent to the problem, it seemed important to try to establish how people tend to view the avoidance of anonymous as opposed to statistical death.

(B) *Perception/Consistency Questions*

In the interests of economy of space, we give only a brief summary of the responses to these questions and reserve detailed discussion of these results for a later paper.

B (i). *Perception of Transport Risks.* Respondents' perception of the *relative* risks of different transport modes were, on the whole, fairly accurate. By contrast, respondents tended to overestimate substantially the absolute numbers of fatalities on various modes, though Version 2 respondents – who were given reference data concerning the actual number of car deaths – on the whole did markedly better than Version 1 respondents who were given no reference data.

B (ii). *Probability Concepts.* In order to investigate people's ability to process simple probability information (as opposed to the relatively complex information contained in conditional probability statements – see Hammerton (1973), Question 17 asked:

'Imagine that you have to face two different risks of being killed:

in one, your risk of death is 2 in 100,000
in the other your risk of death is 20 in 100,000.

You cannot avoid either of these risks but you can choose to have one of them reduced. Which would you prefer:

the risk of 2 in 100,000 reduced to 1 in 100,000
the risk of 20 in 100,000 reduced to 15 in 100,000?'

The responses to this question were rather disappointing in that 47 % of the sample expressed a preference for reduction in the risk of 2 in 100,000 (which is of course prima facie the 'wrong' answer) while 48 % expressed the opposite preference and 5 % gave a 'don't know' response.

B (iii). *Coherence.* In order to investigate the extent of people's conformity with the standard axioms of rational choice under uncertainty in 'simple'[1] decisions, respondents were asked about their preferences in a sequence of three pairwise choices between bets on the weather of Christmas Day, 1982.[2]

The responses to this set of questions were more encouraging in that 75 % of the response patterns were coherent.

B (iv). *Internal Consistency and Temporal Stability of Valuation Responses.* Comparison of a respondent's answers to multipart valuation questions involving different variations in the same base risk gives a direct indication of the consistency and rationality (or otherwise) of these responses. For example, one would not wish to place great reliance upon the responses of a person who indicated increased willingness to pay for a smaller reduction in the same base risk. While only 8 % of respondents displayed such plainly inconsistent response patterns in Questions 18(a)/(18(b) and 11 % in Questions 20(a)/20(b), it is rather more disturbing that 42 % of respondents gave the *same* valuation response

---

[1] See footnote 2 on p. 52.
[2] Specifically, these choices represented direct tests of conformity with Savage's postulate P_2 (the first part of the 'sure thing' principle) and P_4 (a postulate ensuring robustness of subjective probabilities).

for different risk reductions in Questions 18(*a*) and 18(*b*) and 47% in Questions 20(*a*) and 20(*b*).

A further test of the reliability of valuation responses is provided by the fact that the ordering of the multipart valuation Questions 18 and 20 differed between the two versions of the questionnaire. Clearly, if ordering has a significant effect upon responses then one would have cause for concern. In fact, non-parametric tests of the significance of the effect of ordering produce mixed results – some parts of some questions appear to have been significantly affected and others not. It is perhaps reassuring, however, that there was an order of magnitude difference between the trimmed mean responses to a particular question in only one case out of seven.

The temporal stability of valuation responses was tested by asking a subset of 210 respondents from the original sample to re-answer Question 14(*b*) (along with various other non-valuation questions) about a month after the main survey. The encouraging features of these results are (*a*) that the distribution of response differences is relatively symmetrical with its modal cell (containing 59% of observations) centred on zero and (*b*) that a Wilcoxon matched-pairs, signed-ranks test indicates no significant difference between original and recall responses at $P = 0.05$. The less favourable feature of the recall results is the large spread of the distribution of response differences, the standard deviation being almost twice the mean response at first interview.

Finally, respondents' and interviewers' comments on the ease or difficulty of handling probability concepts and providing valuation responses suggest that, while some respondents had indeed experienced considerable difficulty, these people were by no means in a majority.

III. CONCLUDING COMMENTS

Before proceeding to assess the policy implications of the results, it is necessary to form a view on the apparent veracity of the valuation responses and also on the quality of respondents' perception of risk and ability to handle probability concepts. While much can be said on these questions, for the sake of brevity we will simply list what we perceive to be the key results supporting and detracting from the credibility of the estimated marginal rates of substitution and other responses to the questionnaire.

(A) *Results Supporting Credibility*

(*a*) Broadly similar nature of frequency distributions of estimates of *m* from Questions 18(*a*), 18(*b*), 20(*a*) and 20(*b*).

(*b*) Relationship between central tendency measures of estimates of *m* from Questions 18(*a*)/18(*b*) and 20(*a*)/20(*b*) in accord with predictions of theory (willingness-to-pay an increasing, concave function of risk reduction).

(*c*) High proportion of respondents giving 'unwilling to travel' response to Questions 18(*c*) and 18(*d*) lends support to estimates of *m* from 18(*a*) and 18(*b*) on the assumption that required compensation is an increasing convex function of increase in risk.

(*d*) Relationship between *m*, income and age revealed by regression analysis broadly in accord with predictions of theory.

(*e*) Generally accurate qualitative perception of relative risk of different transport modes.

(*f*) Apparent effectiveness of 'reference data' in improving accuracy of respondents' estimates of fatality rates.

(*g*) Possible source of bias in valuation responses is misperception of transport risks. For example, if people who tend to overestimate car risks also over-estimated the risk reductions involved in Question 20, then their valuation responses to this question will have been biased upward. However, regression analysis[1] indicates no significant relationship between individual valuation responses to Questions 18 or 20 and subjective estimates of transport fatalities in Question 13, suggesting that valuation responses were not biased by misperception of transport risks.

(*h*) High proportion of respondents displaying 'coherence' in simple choices under uncertainty.

(*i*) Distribution of differences between original and recall responses to valuation question relatively symmetrical with modal cell centred on zero. Also no significant difference at $P = 0.05$ between original and recall responses on Wilcoxon matched-pairs, signed-ranks test.

(*j*) Respondents' and interviewers' generally favourable comments on understanding of probability concepts and ease or difficulty in providing valuation responses.

(B) *Results Casting Doubt on Credibility*

(*a*) 42 % of respondents giving same valuation response for different risk reductions in Questions 18 (*a*)/18 (*b*) and 47 % in Questions 20 (*a*)/20 (*b*).

(*b*) 8 % of respondents indicating lower willingness to pay for larger risk reductions in Question 18 and 11 % in Question 20.

(*c*) 47 % of respondents giving 'wrong' answer to question involving comparison of probability reductions.

(*d*) High spread of the frequency distribution of differences between original and recall responses to Question 14 (*b*).

(C) *Results Neutral with Respect to Credibility*

(*a*) Mixed results of non-parametric tests of the significance of the effect of ordering of multi-part valuation questions. Order of magnitude difference in only one case out of seven.

(*b*) Valuation responses from respondents requiring prompts significantly lower than from those not requiring prompts. Proportion of respondents requiring prompts between 13 % and 32 %. Some evidence that subjects requiring prompts from lower income, social class or education groups.

Clearly, it would be inappropriate to regard the case in favour of credibility as having been established simply by the fact that the number of 'pro' points

---

[1] Because of space constraints, these regression results – as well as the results of many of the subsidiary analyses conducted in the course of the study – were not reported in the preceding section.

exceeds the number of 'cons'. One must also consider the qualitative importance of the various pieces of evidence and this is ultimately a matter of personal
judgement. Our view is that the balance of arguments and evidence is rather
strongly in favour of regarding the estimates of marginal rates of substitution of
wealth for physical risk as an adequately reliable indication of the order of
magnitude of the 'true' values. Taken as a whole, the valuation results display
an overall pattern and degree of conformity with the predictions of theory and
the dictates of common sense that would be highly improbable if most respondents had been hopelessly muddled about the more basic and elementary
notions of probability or prone to mendacity or mere randomness in their
answers to valuation questions. Certainly the first and third 'con' points listed
above are rather disturbing, but in neither case was it a majority of respondents
that gave implausible or 'wrong' answers. It is also worth noting that the
distributions of valuation responses for these people do not appear to be
markedly different from the responses of the sample as a whole.

So, if our results are indeed a reliable indication of the order of magnitude
of typical marginal rates of substitution, what do they imply about the value of
statistical life for transport risks? Questions $14(b)$, 18, 20 and 22 all provide
estimates of marginal rates of substitution. However, the primary purpose of
Question 22 was to test for the impact of non-revelation effects in the case of
safety improvements that have obvious public goods properties and it was never
intended that values of statistical life estimated from responses to this question
should form the basis for public sector allocative decision making.[1] As far as
Question $14(b)$ is concerned, this is clearly different in kind from the other
valuation questions, in that it involves causes of death other than road accidents
and the saving of anonymous rather than statistical life. The fact that 76 % of
the responses to this question were expressions of willingness to pay to avoid
cancer deaths, coupled with the very large value of m^* implied by these
responses, suggests that people do make significant distinctions between different
ways of dying and would be willing to pay very substantial sums to avoid the
protracted period of physical and psychological pain prior to cancer death.
Given the peculiar features of Questions $14(b)$ and 22, it would therefore
appear that the estimates most directly relevant for our purposes are those given
by Questions 18 and 20. On the assumption that the individual risk reductions
afforded by public sector safety projects are uncorrelated with marginal rates
of substitution then as noted in the introductory remarks, the standard Paretian
efficiency conditions imply that the value of statistical life, taking account of
'own' risks only, is given by the mean marginal rate of substitution for the
affected group of individuals. The trimmed[2] estimates of mean m from Questions
18 and 20 given in Table 4 therefore imply a value of statistical life for transport
risks of about £$1 \cdot 5 \times 10^6$. However it has been suggested to us that there are

---

[1] In fact, comparison of the estimates of marginal rates of substitution from Question 22 with those
obtained from all other questions suggests a very marked tendency for people to under-reveal willingness
to pay for publicly provided safety.

[2] While there is, admittedly, a degree of arbitrariness involved in the process of trimming, we none
the less believe that, as argued in Section II, there are strong grounds for ignoring the few responses for
which there is a strong suspicion of coding errors or fanciful answers.

reasons for supposing that individual risk reductions and rates of substitution may be negatively correlated, particularly in the case of transport projects.[1] We have therefore also computed the value of statistical life that would be appropriate for projects giving risk reductions that are perfectly negatively correlated with rates of substitution on the 'worst case' assumption that the risk reduction goes to zero as we move towards the upper tail of the frequency distribution of rates of substitution.[2] This gives a value of statistical life about 19 % lower than that for the 'uncorrelated' case.

If the value of statistical life is also to take account of people's concern for the safety of others (presumably, mainly the safety of family and friends) then it would seem appropriate to add to the population mean of m a sum that reflects willingness to pay for others' safety.[3] The results summarised in Table 6 indicate that the mean of individual i's marginal rate of substitution of wealth for risk to an 'average' passenger j ($j \neq i$) is £500,000. Since j will typically be a relative or friend of i we can take it that this is indicative of the mean marginal rate of substitution of wealth for risk to relatives and friends. One might be tempted to suppose that the median value of zero reported in Table 6 indicates that 50 % of the sample gave answers to Question 20 (c) that implied a *negative* valuation of other people's safety which, had it been the case, would have cast serious doubt upon the credibility of these responses. However, the frequency distribution of $\tilde{m}$ derived from responses to Question 20 (a) and 20 (c) has $\tilde{m} < 0$ in only 14 % of cases, the median of zero reflecting the fact that 47 % of respondents gave identical answers to Questions 20 (a) and 20 (c) (implying $\tilde{m} = 0$). There would therefore seem to be no more reason for doubting the reliability of the responses to Question 20 (c) than for any of the other valuation questions. Thus, if the estimate of mean $\tilde{m}$ is to be taken as an indicator of people's concern (and hence willingness to pay) for others' safety then it would appear to be necessary to increase the value of statistical life by at least £500,000 to take account of this concern,[4] giving an overall value of about £2 × 10⁶ for the case in which risk reductions and rates of substitution are uncorrelated. In addition, to the extent that a substantial majority of respondents appear not to have taken account of the 'direct' economic effects of

---

[1] This would be so if more cautious people (a) tend to have higher marginal rates of substitution and (b) experience smaller risk reductions as a result of safety improvements because they behave more carefully anyway.

[2] If $-\delta p_i$ and m_i are perfectly negatively correlated then we shall have $\delta p_i = a + b m_i$ with $a < 0$ and $b > 0$ (recall that for a risk reduction, $\delta p_i < 0$). The avoidance of one statistical death entails $\Sigma_{i=1}^{n} \delta p_i = -1$ so that $na + bn\bar{m} = -1$, where $\bar{m}$ is the mean of m_i. If in addition we require that $a + b m_{max} = 0$, where m_{max} is the maximum of m_i over the affected population, then a little algebraic manipulation gives $-\Sigma_{i=1}^{n} m_i \delta p_i = \bar{m} - \text{var } m/(m_{max} - \bar{m})$.

[3] Though, as noted above, Bergstrom (1982) gives conditions under which it would *not* be appropriate to supplement the value of statistical life in this way.

[4] Indeed, to the extent that many people have large numbers of relatives and friends or others whose safety they care about, the appropriate increase in the value of statistical life is probably somewhat greater than this. However, it should be noted that if an individual's marginal rate of substitution of wealth for risk to one relative or friend is $\tilde{m}$, it does not necessarily follow that he would be willing to pay a total of $-n\tilde{m}\,\delta p$ for risk changes of δp for each of n relatives or friends. In a study based on kidney transplant data, Needleman (1976) estimates the increase in the value of statistical life required to take account of concern for all relatives' safety as being about 45%. Given our estimate of £1·5 × 10⁶ for the value of statistical life for 'own' risks, this would imply an overall value of about £2·2 × 10⁶.

safety improvement – such as reductions in police, damage and medical costs as well as losses of net output – in their responses to valuation questions (see Table 9) it would also seem to be appropriate to add a further component to the value of statistical life to reflect these effects. However, the sum involved will probably be somewhat less than £30,000.[1]

While there are clearly many other potentially important policy implications of our results, in view of the constraints on space we will discuss only two further points which we believe to be of particular significance, namely the robustness of our estimate of the value of statistical life with respect to variations in the distribution of income and the relationship between estimates of mean and median marginal rates of substitution.

We have run regression analyses with both linear and quadratic income variables and also with a quadratic income variable only. In neither case did the regression results reject the hypothesis that the marginal rate of substitution of wealth for physical risk increases linearly with income. If this hypothesis is correct, then variations in the distribution of income will have no effect whatsoever on the value of statistical life defined as the population mean of individual marginal rates of substitution. However, for the sake of completeness we have also computed the effect upon the value of statistical life of a redistribution of income to complete equality under the alternative, non-linear hypotheses. Even this very substantial redistribution produced variations in the mean marginal rate of substitution of less than 10 %. It would therefore appear that our estimate of the value of statistical life for transport risks is very robust indeed with respect to distributional variations.[2]

The substantial difference between mean and median values of m (reflecting the highly right-skewed nature of the frequency distributions) has the intriguing implication that if people understood what was meant by a 'value of statistical life' and how such a value would be used in allocative decision making, then a majority would regard the value of statistical life for transport risks given by mean m as *too high*. One simply has to face the fact that setting the value of statistical life at the level implied by mean m would result in a situation in which a minority of individuals with very high marginal rates of substitution would be 'dragging along' an unwilling majority. Furthermore, since it would be virtually impossible to identify individuals with high rates of substitution, there would be no way, even in principle, of arranging for compensating taxes and transfers. This might therefore be a case in which efficiency ought, to a degree, to be sacrificed in the interests of democracy, with the value of statistical life being set at the median value of m. The results reported in Tables 4 and 6 indicate that this approach would yield a value of statistical life of about £800,000.[3] We would not necessarily want to make a case for the use of medians rather than means, but as far as we are aware, this is an issue that has not so far been considered in the literature – largely, we suspect, because there has not

[1] For 1963 Dawson (1967) estimates the direct economic costs of a fatal road accident as £3,430.
[2] Of course, this is not to say that variation in *distributional weights* would have little effect on the value of statistical life.
[3] In this case the results reported in Table 6 (median $\bar{m} = 0$) indicate that it would be inappropriate to add any allowance for concern for others' safety.

hitherto existed such stark evidence of skewness in a distribution of individual marginal valuations.

Finally, it is worth noting that the value of statistical life for transport risks based on our estimates of mean m is very similar to the estimate of the value of statistical life for 'self only' occupational risks ($£1 \cdot 25 \times 10^6$ in 1981 prices) found in the most extensive 'revealed preference' study so far conducted in the United Kingdom, namely Marin and Psacharopoulos (1982), updated in Marin (1983). Certainly, for the reasons adumbrated in the introductory remarks, the results of revealed preference studies based on wage premia for risk must be accepted with caution. However, the inherent biases of such studies will be less marked the wider the range of occupations considered and the Marin/ Psacharopoulos study (in contrast to some other revealed preference exercises) employed data from a very wide class of occupations. The fact that two studies concerned with different types of risk, using radically different methods and completely different samples produce such similar estimates is, we believe, very powerful evidence in favour of the credibility of these estimates, particularly as one would have expected, *a priori*, that the majority of people would tend to be more or less equally averse to the prospect of dying in a transport accident and the prospect of dying in an accident at work.

Department of Economics, Department of Psychology and Health Care Research Unit, University of Newcastle upon Tyne.

Date of receipt of final typescript: June 1984

REFERENCES

Acton, J. P. (1973). *Evaluating Public Programs to Save Lives: The Case of Heart Attacks*. Santa Monica: Rand.

Bergstrom, T. C. (1982). 'When is a man's life worth more than his human capital?' In Jones-Lee (1982), pp. 3–26.

Blomquist, G. (1979). 'Value of life saving: implications of consumption activity.' *Journal of Political Economy*, vol. 87, pp. 540–58.

—— (1982). 'Estimating the value of life and safety: recent developments.' In Jones-Lee (1982), pp. 27–40.

Broome, J. (1978). 'Trying to value a life.' *Journal of Public Economics*, vol. 9, pp. 91–100.

—— (1982). 'Uncertainty in welfare economics and the value of life.' In Jones-Lee (1982), pp. 201–16.

Brown, R. A. and Green, C. H. (1981). 'Threats to health and safety: perceived risk and willingness to pay'. *Social Science and Medicine*, vol. 15, pp. 67–75.

Chase, S. B. (1968) (ed.). *Problems in Public Expenditure Analysis*. Washington: Brookings.

Dawson, R. F. F. (1967). *Cost of Road Accidents in Great Britain*. Road Research Laboratory Report LR79. Crowthorne: Road Research Laboratory.

Dehez, P. and Drèze, J. H. (1982). 'State dependent utility, the demand for insurance and the value of safety'. In Jones-Lee (1982), pp. 41–65.

Drèze, J. H. (1962). 'L'utilité sociale d'une vie humaine.' *Revue Français de Recherche Opérationelle*, vol. 22, pp. 139–55.

Hahn, F. (1982). 'On some difficulties of the Utilitarian economist.' In Sen and Williams (1982), pp. 187–98.

Hammerton, M. (1973). 'A case of radical probability estimation.' *Journal of Experimental Psychology*, vol. 101, pp. 252–4.

——, Jones-Lee, M. W. and Abbott, V. (1982). 'The consistency and coherence of attitudes to physical risk.' *Journal of Transport Economics and Policy*, vol. 16, pp. 181–99.

Hammond, P. J. (1982). 'Utilitarianism, uncertainty and information.' In Sen and Williams (1982), pp. 85–102.

72   THE ECONOMIC JOURNAL   [MARCH 1985]

Harsanyi, J. C. (1955). 'Cardinal welfare, individualistic ethics and interpersonal comparisons of utility.' *Journal of Political Economy*, vol. 83, pp. 309–21.

Jones-Lee, M. W. (1976). *The Value of Life: An Economic Analysis*. London: Martin Robertson; Chicago: University of Chicago Press.

—— (1982) (ed.). *The Value of Life and Safety*. Amsterdam: North Holland.

Kahneman, D. and Tversky, A. (1979). 'Prospect theory: an analysis of decision under risk.' *Econometrica*, vol. 47, pp. 263–91.

Kind, P., Rosser, R. and Williams, A. (1982). 'Valuation of quality of life: some psychometric evidence.' In Jones-Lee (1982), pp. 159–70.

Leitch, G. (1977). *Report of the Advisory Committee on Trunk Road Assessment*. London: H.M.S.O.

Lichtenstein, S. and Slovic, P. (1971). 'Reversal of preferences between bids and choices in gambling decisions.' *Journal of Experimental Psychology*, vol. 89, pp. 46–55.

Linnerooth, J. (1982). 'Murdering statistical lives...?' In Jones-Lee (1982), pp. 229–61.

Loomes, G. and Sugden, R. (1982). 'Regret theory: an alternative theory of rational choice under uncertainty.' ECONOMIC JOURNAL, vol. 92, pp. 805–24.

Maclean, A. D. (1979). *The Value of Public Safety: Results of a Pilot-Scale Survey*. London: Home Office Scientific Advisory Branch.

Marin, A. (1983). 'Your money or your life.' *The Three Banks Review*, vol. 138, pp. 20–37.

—— and Psacharopoulos, G. (1982). 'The reward for risk in the labor market: evidence from the United Kingdom and a reconciliation with other studies.' *Journal of Political Economy*, vol. 90, pp. 827–53.

Melinek, S. J., Woolley, K. D. and Baldwin, R. (1973). *Analysis of a Questionnaire on Attitudes to Risk*, Fire Research Note 962. Borehamwood, Fire Research Station.

Mishan, E. J. (1971). 'Evaluation of life and limb: a theoretical approach.' *Journal of Political Economy*, vol. 79, pp. 687–705.

Needleman, L. (1976). 'Valuing other people's lives.' *Manchester School*, vol. 44, pp. 309–42.

Prescott-Clarke, P. (1982). *Public Attitudes Towards Industrial, Work-Related and Other Risks*. London: SCPR.

Poulton, E. C. (1975). 'Range effects in experiments on people.' *American Journal of Psychology*, vol. 88, pp. 3–32.

Schelling. T. C. (1968). 'The life you save may be your own.' In Chase (1968), pp. 127–76.

Sen, A. and Williams, B. (1982). *Utilitarianism and Beyond*. Cambridge: Cambridge University Press.

Shepard, D. S. and Zeckhauser, R. J. (1982). 'Life-cycle consumption and willingness to pay for increased survival.' In Jones-Lee (1982), pp. 95–141.

Thaler, R. and Rosen, S. (1976). 'The value of saving a life: evidence from the labour market.' In Terleckyj (1976), pp. 265–302.

Terleckyj, N. E. (1976) (ed.) *Household Production and Consumption*. New York: N.B.E.R.

Ulph, A. (1982). 'The role of ex ante and ex post decisions in the valuation of life.' *Journal of Public Economics*, vol. 18, pp. 265–76.

Zeckhauser, R. (1975). 'Procedures for valuing lives.' *Public Policy*, vol. 23, pp. 419–64.

[20]

THE VALUE OF AVOIDING A *LULU*: HAZARDOUS WASTE DISPOSAL SITES

V. Kerry Smith and William H. Desvousges*

Abstract—This paper develops and estimates a demand model to describe a household's demand for distance from a landfill with hazardous wastes. This model provides one basis for gauging the intensity of a household's desire to avoid living near this type of facility. Using the conceptual framework of a hedonic property value model to provide the basis for demand for distance questions, a survey in suburban Boston elicited this information from 609 households. The demand estimates imply that the average household would realize a consumer surplus between $330 to $495 annually for each mile between its residence and a landfill containing hazardous waste.

I. Introduction

NUCLEAR power plants and hazardous waste disposal sites seem to be the least acceptable *Locally Undesirable Land Uses (LULUs)*.[1] This paper proposes an economic framework for estimating a dollar measure of a household's desire to avoid having one such use—land-based disposal sites for hazardous wastes—near its residence. In 1979 the Environmental Protection Agency (EPA) described the siting problem for such facilities as critical, with local opposition threatening the viability of all efforts to regulate hazardous waste disposal. The 1984 amendments to the Resource Conservation and Recovery Act (RCRA) reflect the legislative responses to public concern over these land uses by severely restricting and, in some cases, completely banning land disposal. While the overall intent of the amendments was to eliminate RCRA's loopholes, reducing the economic incentives for land-based disposal of hazardous wastes was also a major concern.

These changes will be costly. The Congressional Budget Office (CBO) (1985) estimates that by 1990 the annual compliance costs (after adjusting for inflation) would be nearly double 1983 levels, with the largest part of this due to prohibitions on land disposal.[2] Consequently, it is likely that decisions on the use of landfills for hazardous waste disposal will come under increased scrutiny. Evaluating the economic efficiency implications of these decisions will require estimates of households' valuations for avoiding these sites together with information on the costs and benefits of the available alternatives.

This paper uses the general framework of a hedonic model to characterize households' residential site selections. Based on this logic a partial equilibrium model is formulated to describe the demand for distance from a disposal site. The model was estimated using responses from homeowners in suburban Boston, which has long-standing experience with hazardous waste problems. Our findings indicate that the average household would realize a consumer surplus of $330 to $495 annually for each mile between its residence and a landfill containing hazardous wastes.

II. The Model

Rosen's (1974) formulation of the hedonic model maintains that a group of heterogeneous commodities can be described using a specific set of characteristics, denoted by a vector Z, which contribute to an individual's utility, as in equation (1):

$$U = U(Z, x) \tag{1}$$

where x = numeraire commodity with price normalized to unity. The market exchanges of these goods are assumed to define an equilibrium locus that specifies the relationship between the relevant commodity's price and its mix of characteristics. Since no individual buyer or seller can influence this equilibrium, the locus can be treated as a constraint to each person's optimal choices. Assuming each consumer purchases only one unit of

Received for publication April 29, 1985. Revision accepted for publication September 5, 1985.

*Vanderbilt University and Research Triangle Institute, respectively.

Thanks are due Ann Fisher and two anonymous reviewers for most constructive comments on an earlier draft. Although the research described in this paper has been funded in part by the United States Environmental Protection Agency through Cooperative Agreement CR-811075 to Vanderbilt University, it has not been subject to the Agency's peer and administrative review and therefore does not necessarily reflect the views of the Agency. No official endorsement should be inferred.

[1] This term was apparently first coined by Frank J. Popper. For general discussion of the issues, see Popper (1983).

[2] CBO (1985) estimates these costs to be $6.1 billion (in 1983 dollars) annually by 1990 without the 1984 RCRA amendments. With these amendments, and in the absence of significant waste reduction, compliance costs are estimated to reach $11.2 billion (in constant dollars).

the differentiated good, with y the available income and $P(Z)$ the hedonic price function, we can write the budget constraint as

$$y = x + P(Z). \tag{2}$$

The model implies that the slope of the price locus with respect to any characteristic will simultaneously equal the household's marginal willingness to pay for that attribute and the supplier's marginal offer price. More formally, for the household, we observe that

$$\partial P(Z)/\partial z = U_z/U_x, \tag{3}$$

where z is one element in Z, and U_i = partial derivative with respect to i.

Unfortunately, the process of using this framework is not as straightforward as early applications of Rosen's suggestions seemed to imply. The equilibrium is not akin to implicit markets with demand and supply functions for each characteristic. Rather, it involves a matching of buyers and sellers who are assumed to have full information on the prices of bundles of characteristics. Moreover, non-linearities (in attributes) in the hedonic price function create modeling and estimation problems when the framework is used to value any changes in a particular attribute (see Bartik and Smith (forthcoming)). While some analysts have dealt with these concerns by adding information in the form of further restrictions to elements of the model, we have taken a different approach by designing survey questions to eliminate the problems.

Our questions rely on a model that assumes housing choices are based on physical characteristics of the home, neighborhood attributes, and other site-specific features of the home's location.[3] The model focuses on a household's decisions about the distance between its residence and an industrial facility with a landfill containing hazardous wastes on its premises. Distance in this case is an attribute reflecting both the disamenities associated with proximity to the types of industrial plants that produce such wastes and the risks of exposure to hazardous wastes. We used a demand function to describe households' preferences for distance from facilities with hazardous waste landfills.

Our survey questions asked each individual to consider a situation in which he could select this distance. Respondents were asked to choose between two homes that had identical physical characteristics, neighborhood features, etc. However, the prices of the homes were described to differ depending on the distance from a facility with a hazardous waste landfill. A home with immediate proximity was specified to have the price corresponding to the average price of homes in the respondent's current neighborhood.[4] The reported values for these prices ranged from \$30,000 to \$300,000 (in 1984 dollars). Distance from the firm with the disposal site raised the purchase price by a specified constant amount per mile. One of four values (\$250, \$600, \$1,000, and \$1,300) for this marginal price was randomly assigned to each respondent.

This question format imposes two important restrictions on the marginal price function (i.e., the left side of equation (3)). First, it maintains that $\partial P(Z)/\partial z$ is constant in z, when z is distance. Second, it holds all other attributes contributing to $P(Z)$ constant. This allows $\partial P(Z)/\partial z$ to be replaced by the constant marginal price on the left side of (3) and also implies the individual's choice of distance need not consider the potential for tradeoffs between distance and other site amenities that might change the marginal rate of substitution on the right side of (3). Since our question explicitly controls all other aspects of the decision process, it simplifies the individual's choice problem. This allows us to interpret the responses as providing a set of points along a partial equilibrium demand function for distance. Tradeoffs among attributes can be ruled out because all non-distance attributes are described as identical. Since the design uses a constant distance–housing cost tradeoff, a Marshallian demand function for distance will exist.[5]

---

[3] There is substantial indirect support for this assumption from recent empirical studies; see, for example, Brookshire et al. (1982) and Palmquist (1984a). For an overview of hedonic models and their findings in relationship to the valuation of amenities, see Bartik and Smith (forthcoming).

[4] Before asking the respondent for his (or her) demand for distance, the individual was asked to estimate the average price of homes in his neighborhood. This response was then used as the basis for the question concerning the distance selected from a disposal site containing hazardous wastes. The text of the two questions is available on request from the authors.

[5] There are two aspects of this conclusion. First, our formulation assumes that the demand for other housing characteristics is insensitive to changes in the marginal price of distance over the range we presented. Second, by holding the marginal price constant, we avoid the concerns with defining a Marshallian demand in the presence of the nonlinear budget constraint that results from a nonconstant marginal price. This problem has been discussed in general terms by Bockstael and McConnell

III. Data and Results

To obtain the data for this demand function along with other information about household attitudes toward hazardous wastes, we employed professional interviewers to conduct a survey of households in suburban Boston in the late spring and summer of 1984. The sample identified two geographic strata — the town of Acton, Massachusetts and the remainder of suburban Boston.[6] Using a stratified, two-stage plan we drew a sample that was designed to be representative of the population in each of these strata. Before implementing the survey, we undertook several measures to improve the communication with respondents. For example, 19 focus group sessions were conducted throughout North Carolina and in suburban Boston. Each session involved discussions with eight to twelve individuals concerning their knowledge and attitudes toward risk in general and hazardous waste risks in particular. We used these sessions for evaluating individuals' responses to alternative question formats. In addition, a detailed pre-test of the questionnaire and intensive interviewer training were part of the survey development (see chapter 8 of Smith, Desvousges, and Freeman (1985) for more details). A total of 609 interviews were completed. This represents 84.6% of the enumerated housing units. Our analysis focuses on the homeowners in this sample.[7]

The first aspect of our results concerns the relative acceptance of living near different types of facilities in relation to hazardous waste landfills. We used a format similar to Mitchell (1980) where, using a national survey, he found that only 10% to 12% of the population would voluntarily live a mile or less from a nuclear power plant, and only about 9% would live that close to a hazardous waste disposal site. Figure 1 reports the results from a similar question given to our sample respondents. This figure provides the cumulative percentage of respondents who report willingness to live at specified distances from each type of facility (as shown on the horizontal axis). The figure displays four of the uses considered by Mitchell along with proximity to a four lane interstate highway.

Clearly, the results confirm nuclear power plants and hazardous waste disposal sites as the most undesirable land uses. However, Mitchell found that the nuclear power plant or hazardous waste site would need to be 100 miles from respondents' residences before 51% would voluntarily accept it. Our results for suburban Boston households indi-

---

We used this model with Heckman's (1979) two-step estimator to evaluate the effect of the selection terms (i.e., the inverse Mills ratio) for the "best" of the demand models. It was not a statistically significant variable. Moreover, none of the parameter estimates fell outside the range considered in our welfare analysis.

(1983) and in relationship to the hedonic framework by Palmquist (1984b).

[6] One hundred census blocks or block clusters were selected for the sample—20 from Acton and 80 from the remainder of suburban Boston. Acton was identified separately to permit individual analysis of these responses. Recent contamination incidents, together with a parallel study of the averting costs resulting from the contamination by Harrison et al. (1983) motivated the design. For a map of the survey area and more details on the design, see chapter 9 of Smith, Desvousges, and Freeman (1985).

[7] The full sample includes 609 households. After accounting for missing values for variables used in our analysis and confining it to homeowners, our sample was reduced to 268 observations. The reason for our reduction in the sample was an assumption that homeowners would be more familiar with these types of choices. Nonetheless, this decision offers the prospect of a selection bias in our estimates. Consequently, we estimated a probit model to evaluate the determinants of homeownership (y) as

$$y = \begin{array}{l} -2.296 \\ (-4.85) \end{array} + \begin{array}{l} 0.038 \; Income \\ (8.280) \end{array} + \begin{array}{l} 0.008 \; Age \\ (1.429) \end{array}$$
$$+ \begin{array}{l} 0.071 \; Years\,at\,Address \\ (7.055) \end{array} + \begin{array}{l} 0.022 \; Education\,. \\ (0.846) \end{array}$$

The numbers in parentheses below the estimated coefficients are the ratios of the estimated parameters to their estimated asymptotic standard errors.

FIGURE 1.—CUMULATIVE PERCENTAGE OF
HOMEOWNERS IN SUBURBAN BOSTON ACCEPTING
PARTICULAR LAND USES

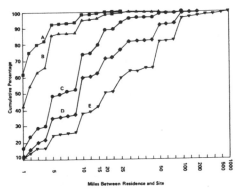

A — 10 story office building
B — 4 lane interstate
C — Coal-fired electric generating plant
D — Landfill containing hazardous waste
E — Nuclear power plant

cate a threshold of about 10 miles for a majority of our respondents to accept a hazardous waste site and about 22 miles for the nuclear plant. This difference may be explained by the set of current land uses in the suburban Boston area which had 11 hazardous waste disposal sites as of 1982.[8] Since individuals in this area live relatively close to these facilities, they may have adjusted their distance responses to reflect their local experiences with them.[9]

Of course, an important limitation to these types of questions is that they do not specify constraints on moving decisions. This makes it difficult to gauge the absolute intensity of individuals' desire to avoid these facilities. The demand for distance approach avoids this problem by specifying the increments to housing cost associated with in-

[8] The specific sites were identified in Harrison and Stock (1984).

[9] Indeed, 90.6% of our sample respondents had read about hazardous waste. Half of the sample had read or heard about it two or more times. The hazardous waste information was most frequently described as relating to the respondent's state.

creased distance and, as a result, leads to a measure of the value of avoiding the facility.[10]

Table 1 reports a selected set of our estimates of the demand for distance from hazardous waste facilities. Two functional specifications are reported—a semi-log with the logarithm of distance as the dependent variable and a double-log form. Our theoretical model suggested that the distance

[10] The presumption of strategic behavior has been the most common criticism of the survey approach for estimating individuals' valuations. Nonetheless, there has been growing evidence that this may not be a serious problem in a large set of cases (see Cummings, Brookshire, and Schulze (1986).) Indeed, Mitchell and Carson's (1984) recent overview of these issues not only summarizes the empirical evidence indicating an absence of strategic behavior, but also identifies a set of theoretical models which would also not be consistent with strategic behavior.

A potentially more serious source of problems relates to the effect of the hypothetical nature of these questions on the responses. While it will never be possible to validate the direct question approach, Cummings, Brookshire, and Schulze (1986) have proposed a criteria of reference accuracy for judging its potential usefulness to policy analysis. Our question format seems to be consistent with these criteria. Moreover, in the focus group, pretest, and actual interviews, we found that respondents had no difficulty with these types of questions.

TABLE 1.—ALTERNATIVE DEMAND FOR DISTANCE MODELS[a]

Independent Variables	Semi-Log Models			Double-Log Models		
	(1)	(2)	(3)	(1)	(2)	(3)
Intercept	2.003	2.054	1.577	1.257	2.486	1.047
	(12.114)	(5.528)	(3.518)	(1.582)	(2.012)	(0.785)
Housing Price[b]	0.003	0.003	0.003	0.381	0.419	0.501
	(2.294)	(2.219)	(2.100)	(2.405)	(2.612)	(3.026)
Marginal Price of Distance	−0.0003	−0.0004	−0.0004	−0.190	−0.225	−0.228
	(−2.815)	(−3.158)	(−2.977)	(−2.323)	(−2.759)	(−2.832)
Income[b]	0.005	0.002	0.003	0.145	0.002	0.006
	(1.924)	(0.648)	(0.979)	(1.661)	(0.023)	(0.059)
Education		0.037	0.054		0.435	0.615
		(1.754)	(2.353)		(1.613)	(2.251)
Age		−0.008	−0.006		−0.475	−0.320
		(−2.334)	(−1.119)		(−2.600)	(−1.298)
Number of Children less than 17 years[c]			0.049			0.037
			(0.953)			(0.722)
Years at Specific Address			−0.0013			−0.027
			(−0.214)			(−0.371)
Acton[c,e]			−0.335			−0.359
			(−2.785)			(−2.966)
Attitude Toward Hazardous Waste[d,e]			0.029			0.028
			(1.688)			(1.658)
R^2	0.089	0.122	0.158	0.082	0.120	0.155
F	9.579	8.078	5.415	7.930	7.172	5.258
S	0.816	0.813	0.814	0.840	0.826	0.815

[a] The numbers in parentheses below the estimated coefficients are t-ratios for the null hypothesis of no association.
[b] These variables are measured in thousands of dollars.
[c] Dummy variable equal to unity if the individual was a resident of Acton, the location of several water supply contamination incidents involving hazardous wastes since 1978.
[d] An index of the individual's rating of degree of harm associated with hazardous waste pollution ranging from 1 = not harmful to 10 = very harmful. This variable was elicited from sample respondents using a scale card in which they were asked to provide a numerical rating of their views on extent of harm. It is used here as an index of the individual's perception of harm and severity of the problem.
[e] Measured in linear form with double-log models.

responses would be determined by the (constant) marginal price of distance posed to each household, the household income, and the other features of the house and neighborhood. In addition, we would expect that several other factors may affect these distance responses. These include: each individual's attitude toward the degree of harm posed by hazardous wastes; the information and experience each respondent had with hazardous wastes; and the number of individuals in the household that might be exposed to the wastes.

To examine the influence of attitude/information factors on the distance responses we consider several variables. For example, a respondent-reported index (ranging from 1 to 10) of the degree of harm associated with hazardous wastes was used to measure attitude toward hazardous waste. Length of residence at the specific address and a dummy variable for residence in Acton (the town experiencing recent contamination incidents) provide measures of the available information about hazardous wastes. Of course, both variables also may reflect other influences. For example, the length of residence might reflect attachment to a neighborhood and residence in Acton might reflect the town's net amenities. The effect of household size was described using the number of children in the household under 17 years of age.

Time limitations in the interview prevented the acquisition of the information necessary to control for all of the features of the house and the neighborhood on the demand for distance. To offset this limitation, we have assumed that the estimated average price of the houses in the respondents' neighborhood, which was the proposed base price in the question, would reflect the effects of all of these factors on the demand for distance.

Based on the explanatory performance and the estimation of statistically significant parameters for the relevant economic variables, the semi-log and double-log specifications clearly dominated linear specifications for all models. A Box-Cox transformation was also applied to the dependent variable, using an iterative search criteria to estimate the Box-Cox parameter (λ) (see Spitzer (1982)). The estimates implied that the curvature of the demand function would be closely approximated with the semi-log model.[11] Given its

slightly smaller standard errors (S) compared to the double-log specifications, the semi-log was selected as our "best" functional form (see Theil (1957)). However, to provide some information on the implications of the form of the demand function, we also report consumer surplus estimates for the double-log model.

Generally, our demand estimates agree with theoretical expectations. The estimated parameters for the marginal price of distance, level of the price of housing, income, and most of the socioeconomic variables are consistent with our a priori expectations. Moreover, both the marginal price and housing price coefficients are statistically significant. While these findings could be interpreted as inconsistent with Nelson's (1981) findings of no effects of proximity to nuclear power plants on property values using actual data, we believe that an alternative interpretation is possible. (This is best illustrated with Nelson's findings, but is also relevant to Gamble and Downing (1982).) For the Three Mile Island incident, Nelson found that proximity to the power plant did not seem to affect property values once the initial accident period was over and the reactors shut down. This should not be surprising since any source of risk is not present once the plant is shut down. Indeed, any negative effects of the accident could be offset by the expectation of federal and state assistance.

Since the influence of the model selection procedures can limit the reliability and potential relevance of our empirical analysis, we have followed recent recommendations (see Leamer (1983), Lovell (1983), and Denton (1984)) and considered the sensitivity of economically relevant estimated parameters to the inclusion or exclusion of variables without direct theoretical relevance. Based on this criterion our findings are quite robust. Table 1 presents a sample of our results with progressive expansion in the specified determinants of the distance responses using both functional forms. This shows that the estimated parameter for the marginal price is quite stable across models. Since

---

[11] The estimated Box-Cox parameter, λ, lies in the interval -0.03 to -0.04 based on iterative least squares estimates over

a 40 point grid as suggested by Spitzer (1982). Given the difficulty with applying inference with the Box-Cox method (see Amemiya and Powell (1981)), the proximity of these estimates to the case of the semi-log form ($\lambda = 0$), and the convenience of this form for benefit estimation, we did not pursue refinement in the Box-Cox model, and interpreted the results as generally supportive of the semi-log form as a reasonable approximation for the demand function.

this coefficient is used in our measures of the consumer surplus associated with avoiding proximity to hazardous waste disposal sites, these estimates can be expected to be quite robust as well.

A convenient summary measure of the consumer surplus per unit demanded can be derived for the case of the semi-log specification. It is the absolute magnitude of the inverse of the estimated parameter for the marginal price.[12] For the double-log models the relationship is somewhat more complex, because the assumed level of the choke price, the base price, and the estimated price elasticity of demand all affect the estimated per unit consumer surplus. Since our price measure is defined in terms of the change in an asset price, it is also necessary to annualize the consumer surplus per mile of distance (CSM) from the disposal site. Assuming an interest rate of 13% and terms of 15 and 30 years, the semi-log demand estimates imply values for CSM from $330 to $495.[13]

Using a maximum price (i.e., as the choke price) that is five times the size of the base price (the approximate differential in our specified marginal prices from $250 to $1300), the same interest rate, and a 15 year time horizon, the double-log estimates imply values for CSM from $124 to $647 over the range of marginal prices.[14] While this is a

wider discrepancy than implied by the semi-log estimates, when the double-log is evaluated at the mean value of the marginal price the results are nearly coincident—$340 with 30 years and $394 with 15 years. Thus, the estimates from both specifications offer a fairly robust and convenient basis for summarizing the intensity of individuals' preferences to avoid hazardous waste disposal sites.

IV. Summary and Implications

This paper has reported some of the results of a survey of suburban Boston households' attitudes toward the risks posed by land-based disposal of hazardous wastes. For the homeowners in our sample, we estimated a demand for distance from disposal sites that implies consumer surplus estimates ranging from $330 to $495 per year per mile from a disposal site.

These estimates have direct policy implications. On the federal level, the Hazardous and Solid Waste Amendments of 1984 seek to limit the land disposal for hazardous wastes. The ultimate regulatory strategy for overall management of hazardous wastes will require tradeoffs between the benefits and costs of the available alternatives —various types of land disposal, incineration, source reduction, etc. If we assume individuals' values for avoiding proximity to these land disposal sites are derived with recognition of the risk of exposure to hazardous wastes at different distances from the sites, then our estimates provide one component of the information that is required for evaluating these legislative mandates within the benefit–cost framework established by Executive Order 12291 for all major regulations. Moreover, the size of our empirical estimates helps to explain the observed resistance of homeowners to the siting of these facilities in or near their neighborhoods. Thus, our results indicate that on the state and local levels, the siting of facilities involved with hazardous wastes is likely to be a major policy issue for some time.

---

[12] The result can be derived from the limiting properties of the consumer surplus integral.

[13] The specific results vary primarily due to assumed terms. They are derived using the conventional annualization factor:

$$AF = r/\left(1 - (1 + r)^{-n}\right)$$

Coefficient for Marginal Price	$n = 15$	$n = 30$
−.0003	$495	$440
−.0004	$371	$330

[14] To derive these estimates let $q = CP^{-\alpha}$, with the postulated maximum price for benefit estimation $P^c = kP$. Consumer surplus per unit (CSM) can then be expressed as:

$$CSM = (P/1 - \alpha)(k^{1-\alpha} - 1).$$

Using $\alpha = 0.22$, the estimated annualized consumer surplus measures for the double-log model with $k = 5$ are:

Marginal Price	15 years	30 years
250	$124	$107
600	$299	$258
1000	$498	$429
1300	$647	$558
791[a]	$394	$340

[a] The sample average.

REFERENCES

Amemiya, Takeshi, and James L. Powell, "A Comparison of the Box-Cox Maximum Likelihood Estimator and the Non-Linear Two Stage Least Squares Estimator," *Journal of Econometrics* 17 (Dec. 1981), 351–382.

Bartik, Timothy J., and V. Kerry Smith, "Urban Amenities and Public Policy," in Edwin S. Mills (ed.), *Handbook on Urban Economics* (Amsterdam: North Holland, forthcoming).

Bockstael, Nancy E., and Kenneth E. McConnell, "Welfare Measurement in the Household Production Framework," *American Economic Review* 73 (Sept. 1983), 806–814.

Brookshire, David S., Mark A. Thayer, William D. Schulze, and Ralph C. d'Arge, "Valuing Public Goods: A Comparison of Survey and Hedonic Approaches," *American Economic Review* 72 (Mar. 1982), 165–177.

Congressional Budget Office, *Hazardous Waste Management: Recent Changes and Policy Alternatives* (Washington, D.C.: U.S. Government Printing Office, May 1985).

Cummings, Ronald G., David S. Brookshire, and William D. Schulze, *Valuing Public Goods: The Contingent Valuation Method* (Totowa, NJ: Rowman & Allanheld Publishers, 1986).

Denton, Frank T., "Data Mining as an Industry," this REVIEW 67 (Feb. 1985), 124–127.

Gamble, Hays B., and Roger H. Downing, "Effects of Nuclear Power Plants on Residential Property Values," *Journal of Regional Sciences* 22 (Dec. 1982), 457–478.

Harrison, David Jr., Lane Krahl, and Mary O'Keefe, "Using the Costs of Averting Actions to Measure the Benefits of Hazardous Waste Disposal Regulations," unpublished paper, Kennedy School, Harvard University, Sept. 1983.

Harrison, David Jr., and James H. Stock, "Hedonic Housing Values, Local Public Goods and the Benefits of Hazardous Waste Cleanup," unpublished paper, Kennedy School, Harvard University, Sept. 1984.

Heckman, James, "Sample Bias as a Specification Error," *Econometrica* 47 (Jan. 1979), 153–162.

Leamer, Edward E., "Let's Take the Con Out of Econometrics," *American Economic Review* 73 (Mar. 1983), 31–43.

Lovell, Michael C., "Data Mining," this REVIEW 65 (Feb. 1983), 1–12.

Mitchell, Robert Cameron, "Patterns and Determinants of Aversion to the Local Siting of Industrial, Energy and Hazardous Waste Dump Facilities by the General Public," unpublished paper, Resources for the Future, May 22, 1980.

Mitchell, Robert Cameron, and Richard T. Carson, "Will Respondents Answer Honestly? Observations on Strategic Bias and Contingent Valuation Survey," unpublished paper, Resources for the Future, 1984.

Nelson, Jon P., "Three Mile Island and Residential Property Values: Empirical Analysis and Policy Implications," *Land Economics* 57 (Aug. 1981), 363–372.

Palmquist, Raymond B., "Estimating the Demand for the Characteristics of Housing," this REVIEW 66 (Aug. 1984a), 394–404.

——, "Welfare Measurement with Nonlinear Budget Constraints," unpublished paper, North Carolina State University, Oct. 1984b.

Popper, Frank J., "LULU's," *Resources* 73 (June 1983), 2–4.

Rosen, Sherwin, "Hedonic Prices and Implicit Markets: Product Differentiation in Pure Competition," *Journal of Political Economy* 82 (1974), 34–55.

Smith, V. Kerry, William H. Desvousges and A. Myrick Freeman III, *Valuing Changes in Hazardous Waste Risks: A Contingent Valuation Analysis*, Vol. I, Draft Interim Report to U.S. Environmental Protection Agency under Cooperative Agreement No. CR-811075, Vanderbilt University, Feb. 1985.

Spitzer, John J., "A Primer on Box-Cox Estimation," this REVIEW 64 (May 1982), 307–313.

Theil, Henri, "Specification Errors and the Estimation of Economic Relationships," *Review of the International Statistical Institute* 25 (1957), 41–51.

U.S. Environmental Protection Agency, *Siting of Hazardous Waste Management Facilities and Public Opposition*, Office of Water and Waste Management, SW809, Nov. 1979.

[21]

NOTES

THE VALUATION OF RISKS TO LIFE: EVIDENCE FROM THE MARKET FOR AUTOMOBILES

Scott E. Atkinson and Robert Halvorsen*

Abstract—Using hedonic regression techniques, estimates of the willingness-to-pay for changes in the risks of dying can be inferred from actual behavior in market situations involving risk-dollar trade-offs. Thaler and Rosen (1975) pioneered this approach, obtaining estimates of the value of a statistical life using labor market data. While subsequent studies have mainly explored labor market data, in this paper we use the hedonic technique to obtain the first estimates of the value of a statistical life from data on the market for automobiles. Our estimated value of a statistical life for the sample as a whole is $3.357 million 1986 dollars.

I. Introduction

Using hedonic regression techniques, estimates of the willingness-to-pay for changes in the risks of dying can be inferred from actual behavior in market situations involving risk-dollar trade-offs.[1] Thaler and Rosen (1975) pioneered this approach, obtaining estimates of the value of a statistical life using labor market data. Although hedonic estimates of the value of a statistical life could also be obtained from market data for consumption activities, subsequent studies have mainly been restricted to further explorations of labor market data. In this paper we use the hedonic technique to obtain the first estimates of the value of a statistical life from data on the market for automobiles.

II. Econometric Model

Automobile purchasers are faced with a wide range of alternative models that vary with respect to price, fuel efficiency, and performance characteristics such as acceleration, comfort, and safety. The performance characteristics enter the utility function directly, while price and fuel efficiency affect the budget constraint. The user cost of an automobile with performance characteristics X, $C(X)$, is defined as the sum of capital costs and fuel costs. Assuming market equilibrium, the implicit valuation (or hedonic price) of the ith automobile characteristic can be estimated by regressing user costs on automobile characteristics and differentiating with respect to X_i.

The performance characteristic of principal interest is the risk of a fatal accident. The best available measure of the fatality risk associated with each automobile model is the actual fatal accident rate, which is calculated as the number of accidents involving occupant fatalities during the first full year of operation divided by the model's total unit sales.[2] However, because differences in accident rates across automobile models may reflect differences in the personal characteristics of the drivers involved in the accidents, as well as differences in the inherent riskiness of the automobiles, it is desirable to control for the effect of driver characteristics on accident rates.

The hedonic equation to be estimated can be written,

$$C = f(R, \tilde{X}), \tag{1}$$

where C is user cost, R is the inherent risk of a fatal accident associated with the automobile model, and $\tilde{X}$ is a vector of its other performance characteristics. The available data are for the model's actual fatal accident rate, F, which is a function of both R and a vector of characteristics, D, of the drivers involved in the fatal accidents, $F = g(R, D)$. Assuming F is monotonic in R, the inherent risk can be implicitly measured by the inverse function, $R = g^{-1}(F, D)$. Substituting for R in equation (1), the hedonic equation to be estimated becomes,

$$C = h(F, D, \tilde{X}). \tag{2}$$

The choice of the driver and performance characteristics to be included in the hedonic equation involves the

Received for publication November 18, 1987. Revision accepted for publication May 3, 1989.

* University of Georgia and University of Washington, respectively.

We are grateful to Martin J. Bailey, Christopher Garbacz, Pauline Ippolito, and two anonymous referees for helpful comments.

[1] Estimates of the willingness-to-pay for changes in risk can also be obtained directly using interview techniques (e.g., Jones-Lee, Hammerton, and Philips, 1985).

[2] The available information on risk at the time of purchase would include safety features incorporated in the automobile's design as well as the historic safety record of it and similar models. We assume that the purchaser's perceptions of risk are consistent with the actual risk, as measured by the ensuing fatal accident rate adjusted for driver characteristics.

[133]

usual trade-off between the possibility of omitted variable bias from including too few characteristics and the possibility of serious multicollinearity problems from including too many. Characteristics for which data are available are described in table 1. The driver characteristics included in the equation are age, alcohol use, gender, and seat belt usage. The included performance characteristics are acceleration, front-seat comfort, and traditional styling.

III. Data and Estimation Procedures

The hedonic equation, (2), is estimated with data for 112 models of new 1978 automobiles. Unit sales by model vary from a minimum of 5,857 to a maximum of 401,392. In order to have the estimated coefficients reflect the actual market importance of each model, each observation is weighted by the model's market share.

The capital cost of automobile ownership is calculated as the purchase price times the sum of the real rate of interest, the rate of depreciation, the effective property tax rate on automobiles, and the cost of insurance expressed as a percentage of the value of the automobile. Depreciation is calculated as the average fraction of total life-cycle miles driven in the first year of ownership.[3] The total effect of the real interest rate, effective property tax rate, and insurance cost on the cost of capital is assumed to be equal to 15% of the purchase price of the automobile.[4] Fuel expenditures are calculated using data for each model's fuel efficiency, the average price per gallon of gasoline in 1978, and average miles driven in the first year of ownership.

The choice of functional form for the hedonic regression is based on the variable transformations suggested by Box and Cox (1964). The hedonic equation is written in general form as

$$C^{(\gamma)} = \Sigma_i \alpha_i V_i^{(\delta)} + e, \qquad (3)$$

where

$$C^{(\gamma)} = \frac{C^\gamma - 1}{\gamma} \quad \gamma \neq 0,$$

$$V_i^{(\delta)} = \frac{V_i^\delta - 1}{\delta} \quad \delta \neq 0.$$

The limit of $C^{(\gamma)}$ as $\gamma \to 0$ is $\ln C$ and the limit of $V_i^{(\delta)}$ as $\delta \to 0$ is $\ln V_i$.

As discussed by Amemiya and Powell (1981), the Box–Cox assumption of normality of the error term, e, cannot hold in general, because the transformation of the dependent variable imposes restrictions on its range. Following Maddala (1983), .we assume that the error term has a truncated normal distribution and correct the likelihood function accordingly. Maximum likelihood estimates of the parameters are then obtained using a weighted least squares procedure, with values of γ and δ varying from zero to 2.0 in increments of 0.01.[5] Following Spitzer (1982), a consistent estimator of the asymptotic standard errors is obtained by computing the covariance matrix using the second-order partial derivatives of the log-likelihood function with respect to the Box–Cox parameters as well as the coefficients of the explanatory variables.

IV. Estimation Results

The maximum likelihood estimates of both γ and δ are equal to zero, implying a double-logarithmic functional form. The estimated coefficients of the explanatory variables are shown in table 2. All of the performance characteristics, including fatality risk, are statistically significant at the 0.01 level, but the coefficients of the driver characteristics are not statistically significant even at the 0.10 level.[6] However, given the importance of controlling for driver characteristics to avoid possible upward biases in the estimates of the value of a statistical life, we have retained these variables in the final form of the model.[7]

---

[3] Data for average miles driven during the first year and over the total life of an automobile are from National Highway Traffic Safety Administration (1977).

[4] Differences between average and model-specific insurance costs and depreciation will introduce measurement errors in the dependent variable but will not result in biased estimates of the coefficients unless the errors are correlated with the explanatory variables. We tested the null hypothesis that the fatality risk variable is independent of the errors using Hausman's (1978) instrumental variables test. The instruments comprised the other characteristics included in the equation as well as comfort of ride, repair record, and previous offenses. The value of the Chi-square test statistic was 0.25, compared to a critical value at the 0.10 level of 14.7.

[5] The definition of the Box–Cox transformation does not permit direct substitution of zero values for γ and δ. Therefore zero values for these parameters were replaced by 0.001 in performing the grid search procedure.

[6] The value of the Chi-square test statistic for the null hypothesis that the coefficients of all four driver characteristics are equal to zero is 2.1. The critical value at the 0.10 level is 7.8.

[7] Failing to control for relevant driver characteristics would result in a negative bias in the (negative) coefficient of the fatality risk variable, and therefore an upward bias in the estimates of the value of a statistical life. The effect of deleting all four of the driver characteristics included here is to increase the estimates by only 26%, suggesting that any remaining bias from omitted driver characteristics is not large.

NOTES   135

TABLE 1.—VARIABLE DEFINITIONS

Variable Name	Definition
Fatal Accident Rate[a]	Number of 1979 accidents involving occupant fatalities per thousand 1978 model automobiles sold.
Age of Driver[a]	Percentage of drivers 18 to 24 years old.
Gender of Driver[a]	Percentage of male drivers.
Alcohol[a]	Percentage of fatal accidents with alcohol involvement.
Seat Belt Usage[a]	Percentage of drivers wearing seat belts.
Previous Offenses[a]	Percentage of drivers with no previous offenses.
Acceleration[b]	Inverse of acceleration time from 0 to 60 miles per hour.
Traditional Styling[b]	Length plus width divided by height.
Front Seat Comfort[b]	*Consumer Reports* rating of comfort for two in front.
Ride Quality[b]	*Consumer Reports* rating of quality of ride.
Repair Record[b]	*Consumer Reports* five-year frequency of repair rating.
Purchase Price[b]	Average of sticker price and dealer cost, adjusted for standard equipment.
Fuel Efficiency[b]	Harmonic weighted average of EPA urban and non-urban mileage ratings, in miles per gallon.

[a] Data on fatal automobile accidents and the characteristics of the drivers involved in the accidents are from the Fatal Accident Reporting System Data Base of the National Highway Traffic Safety Administration. We are grateful to Plina Doyle and Grace Hazard of the NHTSA for their help in obtaining the data for these variables.
[b] For further discussion of the data on automobile characteristics see Boyd and Mellman (1980). We are grateful to Hayden Boyd for providing us with the data for these variables.

The estimated marginal willingness to pay to reduce the risk of a fatal accident is derived as

$$-\frac{\partial C}{\partial F} = -\frac{bC}{F}, \tag{4}$$

where b is the estimated coefficient of the fatality risk variable. While this estimate of the willingness to pay to reduce risk would be of direct interest in many policy contexts involving automobile safety,[8] it is not equal to the value of a statistical life, because an accident may involve more than one occupant fatality. Therefore we divide by the average number of occupant fatalities per fatal accident, 1.15, in calculating estimates of the value of a statistical life.[9]

The estimated value of a statistical life is inversely related to the level of risk. Calculating the estimated value of a statistical life for the level of risk and user cost for each model of automobile in our sample, and weighting by each model's market share, the weighted average estimate of the value of a statistical life for the sample as a whole is $3.357 million. The weighted average estimate of the value of a statistical life is $6.598 million for the lowest risk quartile and $0.764 million for the highest risk quartile.

Leamer's (1978) specification search procedure is used to examine the sensitivity of the estimates of the value of a statistical life to the choice of variables to be included in the hedonic equation. Two automobile performance characteristics, ride quality and repair record,

[8] For example, benefit–cost analyses of the 55 mile-per-hour speed limit use data on the number of fatal accidents avoided.
[9] Data on the average number of fatalities per accident are from the Fatal Accident Reporting System Data Base; see footnote a in table 1.

TABLE 2.—PARAMETER ESTIMATES

Variable[a]	Estimated Coefficient	Standard Error
Constant	7.7026	6.1100
Acceleration	0.7843[b]	0.1363
Traditional Styling	0.5822[b]	0.1875
Front Seat Comfort	0.2814[b]	0.0944
Fatal Accident Rate	−0.1565[b]	0.0336
Age of Driver	0.0424	0.0843
Gender of Driver	0.0155	0.0169
Alcohol	0.0069	0.0072
Seat Belt Usage	−0.0056	0.0047
R^2	0.6578	

[a] All variables are in logarithmic form.
[b] Significant at the 0.01 level.

and one driver characteristic, previous offenses, are treated as "doubtful variables." The extreme lower and upper bounds for the estimated coefficient of fatality risk were found to be −0.1598 and −0.1360, respectively. The implied extreme lower and upper bounds of the weighted average estimate of the value of a statistical life for the sample as a whole are $2.916 and $3.428 million, respectively.

It is interesting to compare the estimates of the value of a statistical life obtained here with estimates obtained using labor market data. In order to control for the effects of differences in the levels of risk in the two markets, the comparison is based on the results of three studies using semilogarithmic wage equations that included a quadratic term in risk to allow the estimated value of a statistical life to vary (linearly) with the level of risk (Leigh and Folsom, 1984; Olson 1981; Viscusi, 1981).

The three labor market studies obtained similar estimates of the value of a statistical life. For example, at the average mean risk level in the samples used in these studies, 0.117 per thousand employees, the estimated values of a statistical life in the Leigh and Folsom, Olson, and Viscusi studies are $6.996, $7.742, and $6.988 million 1986 dollars, respectively.[10] Evaluated at the same level of risk, using the weighted-average user cost, the estimated value of a statistical life implied by the automobile market results is substantially lower, $4.438 million. However, because equation (4) is non-linear in risk, the relative magnitudes of the labor market estimates and the estimates obtained using automobile market data vary with the level of risk.

Evaluated at the median level of risk in Viscusi's labor market data, 0.054, the automobile market estimate of the value of a statistical life, $9.616 million, is 19% larger than the average of the labor market estimates, $8.073 million. Evaluated at the median level of risk in the automobile market data, 0.212, the automobile market estimate, $2.449 million, is 59% smaller than the average of the labor market estimates, $5.989 million.

The results of the three labor market studies cannot be reliably extrapolated much beyond the levels of risk encountered in their samples.[11] The average estimate of the value of a statistical life becomes negative at a risk level of 0.666, and attains a value of −$4.211 million at the highest level of risk in the automobile data, 0.985. The automobile market estimates evaluated at these risk levels are $0.780 million and $0.527 million, respectively.

V. Concluding Comments

In this paper we obtain the first estimates of the value of a statistical life using data on automobile purchase decisions. The estimated value of a statistical life varies inversely with the level of risk. In evaluating policies affecting automotive fatality risks facing the general public, an appropriate estimate of the value of a statistical life would be the weighted average estimate for the sample as a whole, $3.357 million 1986 dollars.

REFERENCES

Amemiya, Takeshi, and James L. Powell, "A Comparison of the Box–Cox Maximum Likelihood Estimator and the Non-Linear Two-Stage Least Squares Estimator," *Journal of Econometrics* 17, 3 (Dec. 1981), 351–381.

Box, G. E. P., and D. R. Cox, "An Analysis of Transformations," *Journal of the Royal Statistical Society*, Series B, 26, No. 2 (1964), 211–252.

Boyd, Hayden J., and Robert E. Mellman, "The Effect of Fuel Economy Standards on the U.S. Automotive Market: An Hedonic Demand Analysis," *Transportation Research* 14A (Oct. 1980), 367–378.

Hausman, Jerry A., "Specification Tests in Econometrics," *Econometrica* 46 (Nov. 1978), 1251–1271.

Jones-Lee, Michael W., M. Hammerton, and P. R. Philips, "The Value of Safety: Results of a National Sample Survey," *Economic Journal* 95 (Mar. 1985), 49–72.

Leamer, Edward E., *Specification Searches: Ad Hoc Inference with Nonexperimental Data* (New York: John Wiley, 1978).

Leigh, J. Paul, and Roger N. Folsom, "Estimates of the Value of Accident Avoidance at the Job Depend on the Concavity of the Equalizing Difference Curve," *Quarterly Review of Economics and Business* 24 (Spring 1984), 55–66.

Maddala, G. S., *Limited-Dependent and Qualitative Variables in Econometrics* (New York: Cambridge University Press, 1983).

National Highway Traffic Safety Administration, U.S. Department of Transportation, *Data and Analysis for 1981–84 Passenger Automobile Fuel Economy Standards* (1977).

Olson, Craig A., "An Analysis of Wage Differentials Received by Workers on Dangerous Jobs," *Journal of Human Resources* 16 (Spring 1981), 167–185.

Spitzer, John J., "A Primer on Box–Cox Estimation," this REVIEW 64 (May 1982), 645–652.

Thaler, Richard, and Sherwin Rosen, "The Value of Saving a Life: Evidence from the Labor Market," in Nestor E. Terleckyj (ed.), *Household Production and Consumption* (New York: National Bureau of Economic Research, 1975), 265–298.

Viscusi, W. Kip, "Occupational Safety and Health Regulation: Its Impact and Policy Alternatives," in John P. Cecine (ed.), *Research in Public Policy Analysis and Management* (Greenwich, Conn.: JAI Press, 1981), 281–299.

[10] Leigh and Folsom reported results obtained with two sets of data and Olson (1981) reported results for two measures of wages. In both cases, the alternative results are very similar.

[11] The highest level of risk in Viscusi's (1981) data is 0.618.

Risk Analysis, Vol. 10, No. 4, 1990

The Effect of Risk Beliefs on Property Values: A Case Study of a Hazardous Waste Site[1]

Gary H. McClelland,[2] William D. Schulze,[3] and Brian Hurd[4]

Received April 4, 1989; revised May 16, 1990

Health risk beliefs of homeowners near a landfill site were assessed in a survey and compared to expert judgments of the health risks of living near the site. A bimodal distribution of health risk beliefs suggested sharp disagreement between the experts and at least some of the residents. Correlates of high risk beliefs included perception of odor from the site, exposure to media coverage of the problem, having children living at home, age (younger respondents more concerned), and gender (females more concerned). An aggregated neighborhood health risk belief predicted reductions in home prices even after controlling for home physical characteristics, such as size and other disamenities such as proximity to a freeway. In the 4100 homes near the site, the estimated depression in property values was estimated to total about $40.2 million before the site was closed and to be about $19.7 million after closure. Implications of these results for community conflict and for benefit–cost analysis of hazard site remediation are discussed.

KEY WORDS: Health risk; toxic wastes; benefit–cost analysis; perceived risk; property values.

1. THE POLICY DILEMMA OF HAZARDOUS WASTE SITES

For people who live near a hazardous waste site, fears of cancer or other health problems often loom large. In contrast, experts sometimes judge the risks from particular hazardous waste sites to be very small, or at least significantly smaller than they are in the judgment of the residents. The discrepancy between the large subjective risk that the public believes is at issue and the small risk

experts believe is scientifically founded creates a policy dilemma for institutions concerned with risk management.

Should large sums of money be spent cleaning up hazardous waste sites when experts judge the risk imposed by the waste site to be small? Is the harm to residents near such sites real even if health is not actually affected adversely? If a hazardous waste site is not cleaned up because the expert assessments of risk indicate only a small risk and the local population still believes the site to be harmful, has a disservice been done?

The study summarized herein explores these questions in the context of a particular hazardous landfill site located near a large number of homes. Expert estimates of the risks associated with this site were low, but nearby residents were quite concerned about the effects of the landfill on their health. We modeled housing prices to determine whether the residents' concerns were measurable in terms of economic damages, and we surveyed residents to identify the sources of these economic and psychological damages.

---

[1] This paper summarizes a study entitled *A Case Study of A Hazardous Waste Site: Perspectives from Economics and Psychology*, which was supported by the Economic Research Program of the Office of Policy, Planning and Evaluation of the U.S. Environmental Protection Agency (USEPA) under Cooperative Agreement CR812054-02-1.
[2] Department of Psychology, University of Colorado, Boulder, Colorado 80309.
[3] Department of Economics, University of Colorado, Boulder, Colorado 80309.
[4] Department of Agricultural Economics, University of California, Davis, California 95616.

2. THE SITE

As background for our survey and study of property values, we briefly describe the site and its history. The Operating Industries Inc. (OII) Landfill is located between the communities of Montebello and Monterey Park in the Los Angeles, California metropolitan area. OII opened in 1948 as a municipal landfill and began accepting hazardous wastes in 1976. OII stopped accepting hazardous materials in January 1983; in October 1984 the landfill reached its capacity and was closed. At that time the OII Landfill was proposed for inclusion on the National Priorities List for "Superfund" monies. The landfill covers 190 acres and contains approximately 30 million cubic yards of refuse, which at the time of our study was generating sufficient landfill gas (methane) to be commercially extractable.

Several land use and policy changes have affected the site and the surrounding area. During the 1970s, the city of Montebello approved development plans for residential housing along the southern edge of the landfill. Original plans were to reclaim the landfill area and to build a golf course and park. The housing development coincided with several other land use changes in the area, including the construction of the Pomona Freeway, which bisects the OII landfill. Construction of the freeway restricted activities at the landfill to the area of the site south of the freeway. As compensation for this loss of area, the height restrictions at the landfill were relaxed. This increase in the height limitation caused increased erosion, including slope failure and mud slides, which exposed decaying refuse.

Soon after residents occupied the newly constructed homes in the mid 1970s, they began to complain of odors to the offices of the South Coast Air Quality Management District. Complaints of rodents and leachate pooling off-site accompanied the odor problems. Additional wells for collection of landfill gas and better leachate control systems have been installed since 1983 to mitigate odors and reduce risks. In early 1985, the U.S. Environmental Protection Agency began feasibility studies of further remedial measures.

In 1979, some residents in neighborhoods near OII formed a group called Homeowners to Eliminate Landfill Problems (HELP) to organize their efforts to eliminate odor and health and safety problems attributable to the OII Landfill. HELP had a membership of approximately 460 dues-paying families at the time of the study. Issues on the HELP agenda included possible health problems associated with the site, leachate disposition, migrating gas, landfill use after closure, and property devaluation.

Media attention at the site has been intense for many years. Television, radio, and regional newspaper coverage has accompanied local coverage from newspapers, community meetings, and an EPA newsletter, *The OII Update*. The nomination of the OII Landfill for the National Priorities List was also a significant catalyst for media attention. In December 1988, 60 companies that had placed wastes in the landfill agreed to a $66 million settlement to clean up the site.

3. EXPERT JUDGMENTS OF THE HEALTH RISK

It is not our purpose either to defend or to criticize the scientific studies of the OII Landfill or the expert judgment of its risk to health. In this section we simply want to document what that judgment is so that we can compare it to the judgments of the residents living near the OII site.

The scientific studies and expert judgment have sought to answer two questions about the health risks of OII: Are there any known hazardous chemicals emanating from the site that can be detected in the surrounding neighborhoods? Are there any demonstrable ways in which the health of current residents differs from the health of people living in nearby control communities? We consider each question in turn.

The Regional Water Quality Control Board has monitored the groundwater supply continually since 1976 and has found no evidence of contamination. In April 1983 the off-site level of vinyl chloride, a carcinogen, was measured at 19 ppb, which exceeds the California regulatory level of 10 ppb. However, workers experiencing long-term exposures many times these levels have not experienced health problems,[1] and more recent random samples of air within homes showed no detectable levels of vinyl chloride gas (above 2 ppb). No other hazardous chemicals have been detected in appreciable quantities in off-site air monitoring. Thus, Satin *et al.*,[2] in a study conducted by the California Department of Health concluded that "the recent environmental monitoring of the area indicates that with the levels of chemicals found, long-term [health] problems would not be expected to occur."

The second approach to assess the health risk has been to compare the health status of residents living near OII to others living in the Los Angeles metropolitan area. A study conducted by Los Angeles County Department of Health Services in 1983 concluded that no consistent pattern of absences from school had occurred around the landfill. Nearby residents had not suffered excess mortality, nor had they experienced more adverse outcomes of conception than had residents in other parts of Los Angeles County. Of course, current epidemiological studies may not indicate serious health effects that may arise in the future because of, for example, the long latency periods for many types of cancer.

The California Department of Health conducted a survey of residents living near the OII Landfill and residents of comparable control communities approximately 10 miles away. There were no statistically significant differences between the OII area and the control communities in terms of mortality or increased incidences of adverse pregnancy outcomes, cancer, and liver disease. There was a statistically significant difference in self-reports of headache, sore throats, sleeping problems, eye and skin irritation, and feeling tired.[3] These reported health problems were greater in those neighborhoods near OII where odor was more frequently a problem. However, toothaches were also more frequently reported in neighborhoods located near OII. Because there is no known biological mechanism for toothache involving any of the possible toxic chemicals at the landfill site, this finding suggests that residents may have (a) simply monitored their health more carefully, (b) remembered these minor health problems better because they were aware of the possible association with OII, or (c) been more sensitive to aches and pains due to an increased stress level caused by concern about the site.

In summary, although the OII Landfill is not a pleasant place, the experts believe there is no indication that it has caused serious health problems, and, based on water and air monitoring, that major health problems in the future are unlikely. The possibility does remain that there is some as yet undetected toxic chemical that may cause a future health risk presently unanticipated by the experts or that there is some direct or indirect adverse consequence from long-term exposure to the odor.

4. RESIDENTS' JUDGMENTS OF THE HEALTH RISK

In the fall of 1985, we conducted a mail survey to assess judgments of health risk for people living near the OII site. There are approximately 4100 homes in the relevant area. From maps, reverse telephone books provided by Pacific Bell, and records of real estate transactions, we constructed a sample address list of 1912 residences near OII. Surveys were mailed to all 1912 addresses. Using standard follow-up reminders,[4] we obtained responses from 768 residents, which, after adjustment for bad addresses, represent 45% of the original

sample. In interpreting the survey results reported below, it is necessary to consider the possiblity that those most concerned about OII were more likely to return the survey.

The survey questionnaire assessed residents' beliefs about health and safety risks, odor problems, sources of information about the site, and attitudes towards local, state, and federal officials, the news media, and landfill operators. The questionnaire also included standard sociodemographic questions.

On a "risk ladder" (see Fig. 1) respondents matched their beliefs about the health risks they faced from the OII Landfill to specific levels of risk defined in terms of the probability of death. Respondents reported retrospectively their belief about risk before site closure, as well as their current belief about risk after site closure.

Figure 2 shows on log scales the frequency distributions of subjective health risk both before and after closure of the OII Landfill. There are two striking features of the frequency distribution of subjective health risk before closure of the site. First, there is a wide diversity of opinion; every category on the risk ladder received responses. Second, the distribution is bimodal with a sizable proportion of the respondents estimating the risk to be about 10^{-2}, approximately the risk of smoking at least one pack of cigarettes per day, and another segment of the sample clustering around estimates of the risk about 10^{-5}, approximately the risk from the average consumption of saccharin. In other words, some residents believed the risk to be very large, whereas others judged the risk to be very small.

Schulze et al.[5] obtained a similar bimodal distribution of responses in a laboratory study of risky decision-making with low probability risks. The distribution from the laboratory experiment was very similar to the distribution in Figure 2a. Other researchers have also observed a similar bimodality. In a national telephone survey about the proposed high-level nuclear waste repository at Yucca Mountain, Nevada,[6] the two most frequent responses on a 10-point seriousness-of-risk scale were "1, not at all serious" (16%) and "10, very serious" (21%). The third most frequent response was "5" (12%), giving a trimodal distribution. As Slovic et al.[7] have noted, "people often attempt to reduce the anxiety generated in the face of uncertainty by denying the uncertainty, thus making the risk seem so small it can safely be ignored or so large that it clearly should be avoided." It therefore appears that bimodality of risk judgments characterizes responses to low probability risks: some people dismiss the risk while others may exaggerate its importance.

Figure 2b shows the frequency distribution of be-

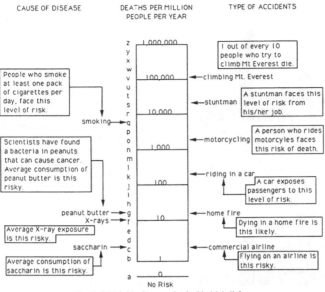

Fig. 1. Risk ladder for assessing health risk beliefs.

liefs about risk after closure of the site. The bimodality, although present, is much less pronounced than for judgments before closure, and the judgments of risk are in general lower.

5. COMPARISON OF EXPERT AND RESIDENT HEALTH RISK BELIEFS

The epidemiological studies undertaken around the OII landfill have found virtually no health risk. From that perspective most respondents believe the health risk to be higher than the expert estimate. Monitoring at the site has also not been able to detect levels of toxic chemicals that are believed to be hazardous even in long-term exposures. The bimodality also implies that whatever the true risk approximately half the respondents seriously misestimate that risk. Either those at or near the high mode are greatly overestimating the true risk or those at or near the low mode are greatly underestimating the true risk. For all these reasons it is reasonable to conclude that the subjective health risk beliefs for many respondents differ substantially from the true risk, whatever it may be.

A comparison in Fig. 2 of the frequency distributions of beliefs of risk before and after closure of the site also suggests another way in which the beliefs of residents are inaccurate. There was a substantial believed reduction in health risk as a function of site closure. More precisely, 51% of the respondents believed the health risk was one or more steps lower after closure of the site than before, 43% judged the risk to be the same before and after closure, while less than 6% reported a higher risk belief after closure than before. However, at the time of closure OII had already stopped accepting hazardous materials and whatever toxic chemicals may have emanated from the site before closure would be just as likely or even more likely to emanate from the site after closure. Thus, the reported reductions in subjective judgments of the health risk are unlikely to be accurate.

6. A MODEL OF SUBJECTIVE BELIEFS ABOUT RISK

The great variation in estimates of subjective health risk suggests that those judgments might be influenced by psychological and sociological factors, as well as by

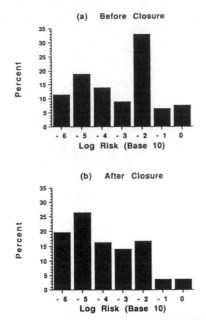

Fig. 2. Frequency distributions of subjective health risk beliefs before (a) and after (b) closure.

judgments of the true health risk. We therefore model subjective health risk judgments using psychological and sociodemographic variables assessed in the survey. We use the numerical step on the risk ladder as the dependent variable; this is roughly a logarithmic scale. Given that we have two health belief judgments for each respondent, we can address two questions: (a) which variables predict the magnitude of concern about the health risks of living near the landfill site and (b) which variables predict the reported change in health risk beliefs attributable to the closure. Having two health risk beliefs from each respondent creates a statistical problem of nonindependence in a single data analysis. We solve this problem by conducting separate analyses of total health risk belief (the sum of the before-closure estimate and the after-closure estimate) and the change in health risk beliefs (the difference between the before-closure and after-closure estimates).[5] Potential variables for inclu-

---

[5] Separate analyses of the sum and difference of two nonindependent observations are statistically equivalent to conducting what psychologists refer to as "within-subjects" or "repeated measures" analysis-of-variance.[8]

sion in each model are described below in two conceptual groups.

6.1. Experiential Variables

The more experience has made one aware of the potential health problems from the landfill, the higher one's estimate of the health risk is likely to be and the more one's estimate could change as a function of closure. Thus, the model includes variables that assess awareness of the potential problem through several sources. In particular, the model includes respondent awareness of media attention to the problem and perception of odor[6] from the site as experiential variables. Respondents made before-closure and after-closure judgments of the odor, so the sum and difference of the two odor responses are used, respectively, to model the sum and difference of the health belief judgments. Also included is geographic distance to the site as a proxy variable for other experiential effects. Presumably, those respondents who live near the landfill will have had more perceptual reminders (e.g., waste truck traffic) of the potential health hazards.

6.2. Sociodemographic Variables

Judgments of health risk may vary as a function of various sociodemographic variables. For example, older respondents will have necessarily survived many hazards and may therefore place the present landfill risk in a different context than a younger respondent who is raising children. Previous surveys have sometimes found women to have higher estimates or greater concern about environmental health risks.[9,10] Risk judgments might reasonably vary with education and income. We therefore include the demographic variables age, children living at home, gender, education, and income as possible components in the two models of health risk judgments.

6.3. Model of Health Risk Judgments

The mean total risk judgment is 19.6 (SD = 12.4). Table I presents an analysis of the variation in total risk judgments. In particular, Table I reports, for each pre-

---

[6] The odor variable was constructed by multiplying a frequency index by an intensity index. The resulting scale ranged from 0, corresponding to "never bothered," to 50, corresponding to "very frequently bothered by an extremely strong odor." Actual responses ranged from 0 to 39 before closure and from 0 to 19.5 after closure.

Table I. Model Analysis for Total Risk Judgments

Variable	Mean	SD	r	b_j	t	PRE	p
Constant				18.41	5.09	0.05	<0.001
Frequency of hearing or reading about OII	4.04	1.06	0.12[b]	1.01	2.11	0.01	0.036
Perceived odor sum (before + after)	31.50	23.50	0.46	0.21	9.74	0.16	<0.001
Distance from site (blocks)	3.68	1.51	−0.16	−0.45	−1.38	—[a]	0.17
Children at home (1 = yes, 0 = no)	0.47	0.50	0.16	1.23	1.10	—	0.27
Age	49.63	13.45	−0.23	−0.14	−3.26	0.02	0.001
Income (15 categories)	5.01	2.28	0.11	0.12	0.53	—	0.60
Gender (1 = male, (0 = female)	0.77	0.42	0.20	−4.37	−3.77	0.03	<0.001
Education (1–9 scale)	6.10	1.92	0.14	0.22	0.79	—	0.43

$N = 508$; $R^2 = 0.28$.
[a]Indicates PRE <0.005.
[b]All reported correlations are statistically significant, $p < 0.02$.

dictor variable, descriptive statistics, the simple correlation with the total risk judgment, the partial regression coefficients, the associated *t*-statistic testing whether the partial regression coefficient reliably differs from zero, and PRE (proportional reduction in error achieved by adding that predictor variable last to the model, also known as the coefficient of partial determination; see Judd and McClelland[8]). The reported *t*-statistics are tests for partial regression coefficients; they ask whether the given variable reliably explains a portion of the variation in health risk after controlling for all the other variables included in the model. With covariation among the predictor variables this can produce conservative conclusions about the importance of a variable.

All of the predictor variables have statistically significant ($p < 0.02$) simple relationships with total risk judgments. Hearing or reading about OII, perceiving odor, living close to the site, having children living at home, being younger, having higher income, being female, and having more education are all individually associated with greater levels of total concern about the health risks associated with the landfill site.

A regression model using all the predictors simultaneously produces $R^2 = 0.28$ but, due to the pattern of intercorrelations, the partial regression coefficients for only four variables—frequency of hearing or reading about OII, perceived odor, age, and gender—are reliably different from zero. The regression model indicates the considerable importance of perceptions of the odor. Over half of the explained variation ($0.16/0.28 = 57\%$) is

due uniquely to perceptions of the odor. Across the range of the odor variable (from 0 to about 60), the estimated regression coefficient predicts a difference of ($60 \times 0.21)/2 = 6.3$ steps[7] on the risk ladder, about one and one-half orders of magnitude. Note also that odor captures most of the effect of distance: distance to the site is a significant predictor by itself (PRE $= r^2 = 0.025$, $p < 0.001$) but when included in a model with odor the effect of distance disappears (PRE $= 0.003$, $p = 0.17$).

The other three reliable predictors that emerged in the model have small unique contributions to the total explained variation due to the pattern of intercorrelations among the demographic variables. However, the predicted effects controlling for the other variables are substantial for both age and gender. The model predicts that the risk judgments of residents differing in age by 40 years would differ, all else being equal, by ($40 \times 0.14)/2 = 2.8$, about one half an order of magnitude on the log scale of the risk ladder, with the younger person's predicted judgment being higher. Similarly, the model predicts that women, all else being equal, judge the health risk of the landfill to be about $4.37/2 = 2.2$ steps higher than do men; this is also about one half an order of magnitude. This gender difference is consistent with, for example, surveys on nuclear energy,[9] industrial hazards,[10] and nuclear-waste repositories[6] that

---

[7] Dividing by 2 corrects for the summation and returns to the step-size on the risk ladder.

have found women to be more uncertain and more concerned than men about technological risks. For example, in the last study, 50% of the women in a national sample, compared with only 29% of the men, rated the risks of the repository in the highest three categories of a 10-point rating scale.

The mean reported difference in before- and after-risk judgments was a decrease after closure of 3.6 (SD = 5.5) steps on the risk ladder. Table II reports the analysis of the difference (reported change) in risk judgments from before closure of the site to after. Both the simple correlations and the regression model indicate that reported change in odor perception is the only reliable predictor of reported changes in risk judgments from before closure to after. Only 9% of the variation in reported risk changes is explainable by the set of predictor variables and almost all of that ($0.08/0.09 = 89\%$) is due to perceived odor changes. None of the demographic variables related to total risk judgments is reliably related to the difference in risk judgments.

It is important to recognize that a cross-sectional survey, such as this, must necessarily suffer from causal ambiguity. For example, we have included frequency of exposure to media attention as a predictor of health risk judgments. However, it might be the case that someone who becomes concerned about the health risks will pay more attention to and seek out media reports about the problem. Similarly, someone who is concerned about the health risk may be more alert for the odor problem

or be more troubled by the odor and hence report having experienced it a greater number of times.

In both models, the importance of the perceptual odor variable above and beyond the other variables is striking. It is reasonable to speculate that without vivid, perceptual cues from the site, risk judgments would be greatly reduced. A perceptual cue, such as odor, may serve as a *signal* of potentially more ominous events.[11,12] Easterling and Leventhal[13] have shown that situational cues make people more likely to interpret neutral symptoms as being related to cancer. Thus, even if people living near a landfill site did not have an increased frequency of headaches, stomach aches, and rashes, they would still be more likely to attribute those to the landfill and to worry more about cancer.

In summary, there is great variability in judgments of health risks. That variation in health risk judgments is not random but can be related to systematic differences between respondents. In particular, respondent reports of their perceptions of the landfill situation are associated with concern about the associated health risks.

7. THE REAL ESTATE MARKET AROUND OII

In this section we use the Hedonic Price Method[15] to value the environmental disamenity represented by the OII Landfill. That is, we assess the economic damages of the neighborhood hazardous waste problem by mea-

Table II. Model Analysis for Difference in Risk Judgments (Before – After)

Variable	Mean	SD	r	b_j	t	PRE	p
Constant				2.79	1.55	—[a]	0.12
Frequency of hearing or reading about OII	4.04	1.06	0.04	−0.01	−0.06	—	0.95
Change in perceived odor (Before – After)	12.13	11.24	0.28[b]	0.14	6.50	0.08	<0.001
Distance from site (blocks)	3.68	1.51	−0.01	0.16	1.00	—	0.32
Children at home (1 = yes, 0 = no)	0.47	0.50	0.03	0.15	0.28	—	0.78
Age	49.63	13.45	−0.04	−0.01	−0.60	—	0.55
Income (15 categories)	5.01	2.28	−0.04	−0.18	−1.57	—	0.11
Gender (1 = male, 0 = female)	0.77	0.42	0.06	−0.25	−0.43	—	0.67
Education (1 – 9 scale)	6.10	1.92	0.00	0.04	0.27	—	0.79

N = 508; R^2 = 0.09.
[a]Indicates PRE < 0.005.
[b]p < 0.001; all other simple correlations are not significant, $p > 0.15$.

suring changes in the real estate market near the site. Several previous studies have examined the property value effects of hazardous waste sites (see, for example, Smith and Desvousges[15]) but all explicitly or implicitly use distance as a proxy for risk beliefs. In our analysis we additionally determine whether health risk beliefs (described in the previous section) have an effect, independent of distance, on property values. In overview, the analysis strategy is to determine whether the prices of homes sold, after controlling for standard objective characteristics, are related to the level of health risk beliefs in the neighborhoods in which the homes were located.

We obtained, through a real estate information network, property value data for 181 home sales in the communities adjacent to the OII Landfill site. These data included sales prices and property characteristics (e.g., floor area, pool, fireplace, number of rooms) for the period from August 1983 through November 1985, which spans the closing of the OII Landfill late in 1984. Three properties were dropped from the sample because they had unusually early construction dates (e.g., before 1910) or unusually low prices (e.g., below $30,000). These were either data recording errors or they represented original farm structures; in either case it would be inappropriate to include them in an analysis of the other data. Hence, the effective sample size is 178 home sales.

Prices almost surely depend on physical characteristics of the homes. The question to be asked in the analysis is whether they also depend on the seller's and buyer's risk beliefs and other subjective judgments. However, there are two technical problems in combining objective property characteristics and subjective variables in the same model. First, those residents who sold their homes before the date of the risk belief survey obviously had no chance to participate and some residents who sold their homes after the survey did not return completed questionnaires. Thus, subjective responses from the survey cannot be linked to the objective characteristics of specific properties in many instances. Our solution, discussed more fully below, is to construct "neighborhood" variables. Second, we have two sets of subjective responses: risk and odor assessed for both before and after closure of the site. Obviously, we want to use the set of subjective responses that corresponds to when the house was sold; however, there is undoubtedly a lag before the after-closure subjective responses apply. That issue is also discussed more fully below.

7.1. Neighborhood Variables

As noted above, individual subjective risk judgments could not be attached to individual properties

in many instances. Instead, we develop an aggregate estimate of the collective neighborhood risk judgment. This collective judgment is in fact the more appropriate variable theoretically. In selling one's house, it makes no difference what the seller thinks the house is worth or whether the individual seller thinks the local health risks are high or low if one's neighbor down the street is selling a comparable house for $5000 less because of concerns about the health risks. One may not even be selling a house but may be applying for a home equity loan. The loan applicant's estimate of the health risk will clearly have no impact on an appraiser who uses neighborhood selling prices to estimate a value for the home. But of course the aggregate neighborhood risk estimate will have an impact on those sale prices and thus through the appraiser will have an impact on appraised values. On the other hand, although residents may well be willing to sell at a price adjusted downward by their willingness to sell to avoid any subjective risk associated with proximity to the OII Landfill, they are likely to list homes, after consulting a realtor, at the current market rate. If others in the neighborhood are not as concerned about the health risk as the seller, then the seller may well be able to obtain a price higher than his or her actual willingness to sell. The observed price for homes in a particular neighborhood will fall as more homeowners in the neighborhood feel threatened by the site. Thus, the neighborhood's collective risk judgment is the appropriate predictor of price rather than the risk judgment of the individual seller.

We unfortunately have no information on the subjective risk beliefs held by potential purchasers except that 62% of recent purchasers were not aware of the site when they bought their homes, despite local requirements for information disclosure to new buyers. Those that were aware may, of course, have lowered their offered bids, causing a further decline in observed prices. Without data on the subjective risks for prospective purchasers, we must assume that residents' subjective risk measured for each neighborhood around the OII Landfill can provide a proxy for purchasers' subjective risks. Again, we must develop an aggregate risk estimate for the neighborhood.

We plotted households responding to the survey on an aerial photograph of the area surrounding OII. From the photographs, we divided the area into "neighborhoods" with about 10 to 15 survey respondents in each neighborhood. Then we calculated for each of these neighborhoods the proportion of responses that fell into the high risk group of the bimodal distribution of risk judgments before closure and after closure.[8] The dividing line between the two groups is the letter "L" on the risk ladder in Fig. 1, approximately 5×10^{-4} per year. Approximately 51% of the sample was in the high health risk group before closure. The proportion in the high risk group varies across neighborhoods between 0 and 0.86 with a mean of 0.47 before closure and between 0 and 0.6 with a mean of 0.23 after closure. In the subsequent analysis we attached the neighborhood's health risk proportion, either the before-closure proportion or the after-closure proportion as appropriate, to the property characteristics data for each house sold in a given neighborhood. A similar aggregation strategy was followed for constructing neighborhood odor variables for before and after closure as the mean of the individual odor judgments in a neighborhood.

7.2. Market Lag

Determining the proper lag for the switch from before-closure neighborhood health risk and odor variables to after-closure neighborhood values is important. Using too short a lag will cause a regression model to underestimate the effect of those variables on house prices and too long a lag will leave too few cases to estimate after-closure effects. We used an empirical approach for selecting an appropriate lag. We simply repeated the analysis in the following section with different lags to determine the sensitivity of the results to those lags. There was a clear break for a lag of about 4 months. Lags shorter than that produced essentially the same results and lags of 4 months, 5 months, 6 months, and longer produced the same result as each other until the lag was so long there were inadequate cases for analysis. We therefore use a lag of 4 months in the reported analyses.

7.3. A Model of Housing Prices

The mean selling price of homes in the neighborhoods around the OII Landfill was $135,733 (SD = 35,310). In order to determine if risk beliefs had an effect on those selling prices, it is first necessary to control for the physical characteristics of the houses (e.g., square feet, number of rooms, and amenities such as pools) and their physical proximity to other disamenities (e.g., the Pomona Freeway). So our analysis strategy was first to develop the best model of housing prices without the neighborhood risk and odor variables and then determine whether these variables added any predictability to the best property value model. Table III reports the resulting best model.[9] This model is *best* in several senses. First, no other variable in the dataset could be added with a coefficient reliably different from zero. Second, Mallow's $C(p)$ criterion identifies this as the best model in a search of all possible models and it is the best model in terms of R^2 or PRE for a model with this number of variables. Third, removing any of these variables would significantly reduce R^2.

The property characterisitcs included in the best model are not surprising. Despite a moderate amount of colinearity, the estimated coefficients for the property characteristics make sense in terms of both direction and magnitude. Not surprisingly, square footage is an important predictor of sale price. The presence of the square of square footage in the model indicates a nonlinear relationship between square footage and sale price; in effect, there is a premium for larger houses. Other indicators of property size, such as number of rooms, number of bathrooms, number of stories, etc., were not reliable predictors after controlling for square footage.

Newer houses, controlling for size and other factors, sold for $973 more per year. Controlling for size and age, houses with a pool sold for about $12,613 more and houses near the freeway that bisect the study area sold for about $13,273 less. Other amenities, such as fireplaces, were not reliable predictors of sale price. Houses increased in value due to inflation and a regional upward price trend; over the time period of the study this increase averaged about $373 per month.[10]

The most important aspect of the model in Table III for our purposes is that after controlling for property size, amenities and disamenities, age, and sale date, there was a reliable effect of the neighborhood risk variable on sale price. For each increase of 10% in the proportion of neighborhood respondents in the high risk group, house

---

[8] A referee has suggested that more statistical power might have been obtained had we not dichotomized this predictor variable. While it is true that reducing the number of categories of normally distributed predictor variables sacrifices statistical power, that is not necessarily the case for predictor variables which have nonnormal distributions (for an example in the risk context see Weinstein *et al.*[16]). In this case, however, the issue of adequate statistical power is moot because as shown in the subsequent section, the dichotomized variable is a statistically significant predictor.

[9] A detailed examination of the residuals revealed four potential outliers as identified by levers and Studentized deleted residuals. Removing these outliers did not appreciably affect the parameter estimates but did increase the values of the test statistics slightly. We present in Table III the more conservative model that does include the potential outliers.

[10] Using logarithms to test other theoretically more appropriate model forms for inflation revealed that this simple additive representation did just as well.

Table III. Model Analysis of Home Sale Prices

Variable	Mean	SD	r	b_j	t	PRE	p
Constant				2963	0.34		
Square feet	1602	476	0.86[a]	44.4	10.86	0.41	<0.001
(Square feet mean)²/1000	225	263	0.48	22.4	4.37	0.10	<0.001
Year built (last two digits)	59.1	9.1	0.75	973	4.58	0.11	<0.001
Sale date (1 = Aug. 1983, 28 = Dec. 1985)	15.1	7.8	0.12	373	2.04	0.02	0.043
Pool (1 = pool; 0 = none)	0.17	0.38	0.23	12,614	4.02	0.09	<0.001
Freeway (1 = near freeway, (0 = otherwise)	0.06	0.24	-0.09	-13,273	-2.64	0.04	0.009
Neighborhood risk	0.38	0.20	0.15	-20,839	-2.73	0.04	0.007

N = 178; R^2 = 0.81.

[a]All correlations greater in absolute value than 0.145 are statistically significant, $p < 0.05$.

prices in that neighborhood decreased on average by about $2084. The mean neighborhood risk proportion in the high group before closure was 47% and after closure it was 23%. Thus, closing the landfill increased the average house value by approximately $(0.47-0.23) \times$ $20,839 = $5001. If we venture an extrapolation to the limits of the range of the data, even after closing the site, the house prices are approximately $0.23 \times $20,839 = $4793 lower than they would be if there were no health risk beliefs. Multiplying these values times the 4100 homes in the study area reveals very rough estimates of the total subjective property value damages to the community as a whole. Before closure the subjective damages are roughly ($5001 + $4793) × 4100 = $40.2 million. After-closure subjective damages reduce to roughly $4793 × 4100 = $19.7 million, for a savings of about $20.5 million attributable to closing the landfill site. If somehow health risk beliefs could be reduced to zero — either by cleaning up the site or convincing residents that there was no real risk — then the model predicts an additional savings of $19.7 million.[11] Regardless of whether the health risks are veridical, they appear to have a real and sizeable impact on the behavior of the people who hold those beliefs and, as a consequence, are associated with real economic losses. Remember also that the neighborhood health risk variable is a rough indicator that contains lots of error. The true effect of health risk beliefs on sale prices is likely even stronger than indicated in Table III due to the attenuation induced by measurement error. Furthermore, if buyers

[11] Note that these estimates do not represent willingness-to-pay because we have not employed the second stage of the Rosen[14] procedure.

were to become more aware of the landfill and its problems, then the likely losses in property values would be even larger.

It is interesting to consider which variables are *not* included in the model of property values. In particular, it would seem that both the subjective neighborhood odor variable and the objective distance to the site would represent disamenities that ought to be captured in the property value model. However, neither odor (at any lag) nor distance (with or without any transformation such as the inverse) is even close to being a reliable predictor ($|t| <$ 1 in all cases) in the context of the property value model of Table III. The reason is that both odor and distance are partially redundant with other predictors that were included in the model — not so redundant as to pose a serious colinearity estimation problem, but sufficient to preclude their inclusion in the model. Both odor and distance are important predictors of a respondent's health risk beliefs (see Tables I and II). It therefore appears that odor and distance do not have impacts on property values over and above their contributions to the health risk variable. A further problem for the distance variable is that it is partially redundant with year built and square feet — the largest homes were built near the site more recently when it was still believed that the landfill site would be reclaimed as a park and golf course. For predicting distance from year built, square feet, and square feet squared, the R^2 = 0.40. Thus, inclusion of year built and square feet in the model makes it difficult to find an independent contribution of distance from the site to property values. In any case, distance did not have an effect on sale price when controlling for year built and square footage.

Some similar studies have found, as we have, that

property value losses are associated with levels of risk concern; others have not. Brookshire *et al.*[17]provide a consistent example in their study of the effect of designating earthquake hazard zones in California; they found that the magnitude of property value losses were consistent with the subjective risks. However, Nelson[18] was unable to find a significant decrease in residential property values as a result of the accident at Three Mile Island (TMI) nuclear power plant. Nelson suggests that real estate prices cannot adjust to changes in perception of risk as rapidly as the perceptions themselves change. However, in our study the effect of reduced risk judgments, associated with the closure of the site, were reflected in improved property values within several months. There must therefore be other important differences in these two case studies to explain why one study found a property value effect and the other did not. One possibility is that the landfill problem with its perceptual cues and signals — the odor and the high volume of truck traffic before closure — was viewed as a more chronic problem. Indeed, Nelson suggests that the effects of the TMI accident were perceived as short-term or acute. However, one then wonders why the visible cooling towers and other such perceptual cues did not continue to provide similar reminders of the potential hazard of the nuclear power plant.

8. CONCLUSIONS

The analyses of the health risk beliefs and the home sale prices reveal several important conclusions:

1. The bimodal distribution of health risks indicates that a sizeable proportion of the residents have inaccurate beliefs about the actual risks posed by living in the vicinity of the OII Landfill.
2. If one accepts existing toxicological and epidemiological studies, it appears as if those residents in the high risk group have substantially overestimated the actual health risk of living near this landfill site.
3. Perceptual cues that provide people with continual reminders about the hazard appear to lead to higher health risk judgments.
4. A change in perception of the odor after closure is associated with a large reduction in health risk beliefs.
5. This large reduction in health risk beliefs after closure of the site is not likely to be veridical; whatever toxic hazards might have been there before closure are still there after closure.

6. These health risks beliefs, even though they may be seriously overestimated and even though their marked decline after closure is not likely to be veridical, have a substantial negative correlation with property values.

In this section we discuss the implications of these results for community conflict, the use of benefit-cost analysis to decide on remediation, and the larger policy issues raised by deleterious effects of overestimation of risks.

The existence of bimodal distributions or even just a wide variation of health risk beliefs has obvious implications for conflict within a community. For many environmental hazards facing communities, one group of residents believes that there is very little risk and another large group believes that there is a serious health risk posed by the environmental hazard. In this study, one group believed there was virtually no risk and the other group believed the risk was equivalent to smoking a pack of cigarettes per day. The former group is mad at the latter because they believe that the exaggerated concerns have or will lower property values. At the OII site, that indeed appears to be the case. On the other hand, the concerned group is mad at the unconcerned group because they won't help put pressure on the proper authorities to implement appropriate remediation measures. It is easy to imagine one of these people at a public hearing complaining that the unconcerned people are more worried about their property values than the health of the community's children.

If bimodal distributions are common for low probability, high consequences risks—and based on this study and laboratory studies we believe they are common— then community conflict will almost certainly be high. And at least one of the two groups will necessarily be wrong, although it may often be difficult or impossible to determine absolutely which group is wrong. More likely, both groups are wrong. The unconcerned group ought to be more worried than they are and the concerned group probably has an unrealistically exaggerated concern about the risk.

Benefit–cost analyses, either formal or informal, are frequently used to decide how many resources, if any, will be allocated to mitigating a particular environmental hazard. If toxicological, epidemiological, and other scientific studies cannot demonstrate any appreciable risk, then officials often presume that there would be no benefit of cleaning up the site and that remediation resources would best be allocated elsewhere. The results of this study suggest that another important component that is too often left out of such benefit–cost analyses is the effect of subjective risk beliefs on property values. The losses in reduced property values are real even if the risk beliefs that may be causing those losses are not veridical. Including those losses in the analysis may yield a very different conclusion about the usefulness of remedial actions.

In the present study, community-wide property value losses attributable to health risk beliefs were roughly $40.2 million. Even after the site stopped accepting new waste shipments, losses attributable to health risk beliefs were still about $19.7 million. If either of those amounts were entered into a benefit–cost analysis as approximate measures of willingness-to-pay, it would justify considerable efforts to reduce resident concern about the health risks. One obvious method for reducing resident concern would be to rehabilitate the site to a level that would meet resident approval. That is, it might be cost effective to conduct a full-scale cleanup of the site even though there were no demonstrable health risks.

Cleaning up a site with no demonstrable health risks might be politically, legally, or practically impossible. For example, how would one specify and monitor a contract to clean up particular chemicals when none where known to need removal? An alternative to full-scale cleanup would be to fund risk communication projects that would attempt to reconcile resident concerns with expert judgments. Simple risk communication strategies such as media campaigns and public meetings are unlikely to be successful. This is especially true if the risk communication is funded and organized by the U.S. Environmental Protection Agency, which other questions in our survey revealed to have very little credibility in this community.

Our model of health risk beliefs suggests another alternative. Perceptual cues, such as odor, and other physical reminders of the site are strongly related to health risk beliefs. We cannot infer causal direction from the cross-sectional data and therefore cannot conclude that reducing those cues would substantially reduce health risk beliefs. However, it is reasonable to consider the hypothesis that conducting cleanup operations to eliminate the odor and that building berms or planting trees to make the site less visible would reduce judged health risks and that, in turn, property value losses would not be so extreme. It might also reassure residents if permanent monitoring equipment were installed to detect toxic chemicals that might subsequently emanate from the site. A potential recovery of $19.7 million for this community would certainly justify a considerable expenditure, whether for clean-up operations or for reductions in perceptual cues that might in the long run be the most effective means of risk communication.

The more general policy issue raised by this study is this: what should be the policy response to situations in which people perhaps overestimate risks? The opposite policy question of what to do when people underestimate risks has been frequently considered. For example, Pauly *et al.*[19] consider the policy problems caused by citizen underestimates of the probability of flood and of the benefits of passive restraints in automobile accidents. However, the policy issues of what to do when citizens perhaps overestimate a risk are much less studied. The results of this research demonstrate that the economic consequences of overestimating a risk are just as real as those of underestimating risk. Losing $5000 of the value of one's house because of the neighborhood's risk beliefs is just as damaging as suffering an uninsured $5000 property loss in a flood. By providing subsidized insurance (e.g., flood), by making disaster relief loans (e.g., hurricanes and earthquakes), by funding risk communication efforts (e.g., radon), and by promulgating regulations (e.g., automobile safety standards), the government appears to have an important policy role in ameliorating the losses caused by citizen underestimation of risks. Should government have a similar role in mitigating the losses caused by citizen overestimation of risks? Just as society has agreed to share the risk of people who underestimate the risks of buying property in floodplains and along coastlines, ought not society to share the risks of people who overestimate the risks of owning property near landfill sites that have the appearance but not the reality of being hazardous? Or should landfill operators and waste generators perhaps bear legal liability to remedy harmful subjective risks when no actual risk can be identified? These are policy questions that our study raises but cannot answer.

ACKNOWLEDGMENT

We wish to thank Frederick Allen, Alan Carlin, Ann Fisher, and Mark Thayer of the USEPA and Doug Easterling, Howard Kunreuther, Lou McClelland, and Paul Slovic for their comments and suggestions. Thanks also go to Sandra Carroll, Ann Fenn, Daphne Gemmill, Patricia Post, and Cheryl Swanson of the USEPA Community Relations Programs in Washington D.C. and Region IX as well as to Ric Notini and Ken Satin of the California Department of Health Services, to Mark Strassburg of the Los Angeles County Department of Health Services, and to Earl Roberts of the South Coast Air Quality Management District for their assistance and comments on this study. We are also indebted to Rebecca Boyce, Glenn Russell, and Joy Smith for their research assistance, to Janet Grassia for editorial advice, and to Melinda Berg for secretarial assistance. However, all opinions expressed herein are the sole responsibility of the authors.

REFERENCES

1. United States Environmental Protection Agency, Carcinogen Assessment Group, "Air Toxics Problem in the United States: An Analysis of Cancer Risks for Selected Pollutants," USEPA Office of Policy, Planning and Evaluation (EPA 450/1-85-001), Washington, DC, 1985.
2. K. P. Satin, S. Huie and L. Croen, "Operating Industries, Inc. Health Effects Study," Technical Report, California Department of Health, October (1986).
3. California Department of Health Services, *Operating Industries Inc. Site: DHS Announces Health Study Results,* Press release by Epidemiological Studies Section of the [California] State Department of Health Services, November (1986).
4. D. Dillman, *Mail and Telephone Surveys: The Total Design Method* John Wiley & Sons, (New York 1978).
5. W. D. Schulze, G. H. McClelland and D. L. Coursey, "Valuing Risk: A Comparison of Expected Utility with Models from Cognitive Psychology," Technical Report, Laboratory for Economics and Psychology, University of Colordao, Boulder, Colorado (1986).
6. H. Kunreuther, W. H. Desvousges, and P. Slovic, "Nevada's Predicament: Public Perceptions of Risk from the Proposed Nuclear Waste Repository," *Environment* 30(8), 16–20, 30–33 (1988).
7. P. Slovic, B. Fischhoff, and S. Lichtenstein, "Informing the Pub-

lic About the Risks from Ionizing Radiation," *Health Physics* 41, 589–598 (1981).
8. C. M. Judd and G. H. McClelland, *Data Analysis: A Model Comparison Approach* Harcourt, Brace Jovanovich, (San Diego, 1989).
9. R. Kasperson, G. Berk, D. Pijawka, A. Sharaf, and J. Wood, "Public Opposition to Nuclear Energy: Retrospects and Prospects," *Science, Technology and Human Values* 5, 11–23 (1980).
10. P. J. M. Stallen and A. Tomas, "Public Concern About Industrial Hazards," *Risk Analysis* 8, 237–245 (1988).
11. P. Slovic, S. Lichtenstein, and B. Fischhoff, "Modeling the Societal Impact of Fatal Accidents," *Management Science* 30, 464–474 (1984).
12. P. Slovic, "Perception of Risk," *Science* 236, 280–285 (1987).
13. D. V. Easterling, and H. Leventhal, "Contribution of Concrete Cognition to Emotion: Neutral Symptoms as Elicitors of Worry About Cancer," *Journal of Applied Psychology* 74, 787–796 (1989).
14. S. Rosen, "Hedonic Prices and Implicit Markets: Product Differentiation in Pure Competition," *Journal of Political Economy* 82, 34–55 (1974).
15. V. K. Smith and W. H. Desvousges, "The Value of Avoiding a LULU: Hazardous Waste Disposal Sites," *The Review of Economics and Statistics* 68, 293–299 (1986).
16. N. D. Weinstein, M. L. Klotz, and P. M. Sandman, "Promoting Remedial Response to the Risk of Radon: Are Information Campaigns Enough?" *Science, Technology, & Human Values* 14, 360–379 (1989).
17. D. S. Brookshire, M. A. Thayer, J. Tschirhart, and W. D. Schulze, "A Test of the Expected Utility Model: Evidence from Earthquake Risks," *Journal of Political Economy* 93, 369–389 (1985).
18. J. P. Nelson, "Three Mile Island and Residential Property Values: Empirical Analysis and Policy Implications," *Land Economics* 57, 363–372 (1981).
19. M. Pauly, H. Kunreuther, and J. Vaupel, "Public Protection Against Misperceived Risks: Insights from Positive Political Economy," *Public Choice* 43, 45–64 (1984).

[23]

RATES OF TIME PREFERENCE AND CONSUMER VALUATIONS OF AUTOMOBILE SAFETY AND FUEL EFFICIENCY*

MARK K. DREYFUS and W. KIP VISCUSI

National Economic Research Associates and Duke University

ABSTRACT

This article estimates hedonic price models for automobiles using a data set on almost 3,000 households from the U.S. Department of Energy Residential Transportation Energy Consumption Survey. The standard hedonic models are generalized to recognize the role of discounting of fuel efficiency and safety, yielding an estimated rate of time preference ranging from 11 to 17 percent. This range includes the prevailing rate of interest for car loans in 1988 and is consequently consistent with market rates. Purchasers exhibit an implicit value of life ranging from $2.6 to $3.7 million, which is within the range found in the labor market as well as other market contexts. The model also estimates a significant price effect for auto injury risks and fuel efficiency.

I. INTRODUCTION

AUTOMOBILES are among the most regulated consumer products. Two of the chief forms of regulation affecting cars are safety and fuel economy regulations. In the case of safety, the regulatory structure consists of government-mandated design standards for various safety features ranging from seat belts to air bags. Government interventions affecting fuel economy are more diverse, as they include fuel economy standards for corporate fleets (CAFE standards), a gas guzzler tax for low-mileage cars, and gasoline taxes intended to promote energy conservation.

If market forces were fully effective, these interventions would not be necessary to correct for inadequacies in consumer decisions. There would, of course, be a need to address broader societal externalities. Advocates of government intervention note the presence of externalities and also frequently assume that automobile owners may not appropriately value the safety features and fuel economy of their cars. The nature

* This research was supported in large part by the Environmental Protection Agency Cooperative Agreement with Duke University CR-817478-02, which was directed by Dr. Alan Carlin. Tonja Lindsey of the National Highway Traffic Safety Administration compiled automotive fatality data. Patricia Born provided computer assistance, and an anonymous referee provided helpful comments.

[*Journal of Law and Economics*, vol. XXXVIII (April 1995)]

of individual choices in the market affects not only the rationale for government intervention but also the degree to which market-based interventions, such as various tax mechanisms, can be used to promote safety and fuel economy. For example, do gasoline excise taxes simply lower the welfare of automobile purchasers, or do they also promote the purchase of more fuel-efficient cars and reduce the total number of miles traveled?

In the case of business vehicles, such as company-owned cars, the effect of regulations such as the CAFE standards should reflect sound economic decisions. Companies presumably do not face the same degree of capital constraints that might influence consumer behavior. Moreover, businesses should be relatively sophisticated vehicle purchasers and will weight the long-term fuel efficiency and safety characteristics of vehicles appropriately.

This article examines the valuations of safety and fuel economy by a possibly less sophisticated purchasing group, private automobile owners. First, what is the implicit value of life and the injury-price trade-off that consumers exhibit in the market? Do these values indicate a trade-off rate similar to that found in other market contexts? The marginal trade-offs may differ, in part because of government-mandated safety equipment, which consumers may not value as highly as safety attributes purchased voluntarily. In addition, trade-offs will vary depending on the preferences of the affected group. Automobile purchasers and workers need not have the same risk-money trade-off.

Second, to what extent do individuals value the differences in fuel economy across cars? Do they internalize the incentives created by higher financial costs, such as gasoline taxes and the gas guzzler tax, or must the government utilize command-and-control regulations, such as CAFE standards?

Third, what is the implicit interest rate that individuals exhibit when valuing the long-run safety and fuel economy attributes of their automobiles? Do they weight these long-run effects in a manner that is consistent with their discounting behavior in financial contexts, or do they exhibit temporal myopia? The nature of this temporal weighting is of consequence, not only in diagnosing the extent to which there is market failure, but also in indicating whether policy interventions that affect the initial vehicle price, such as a gas guzzler tax, will have a greater effect on automobile choice than higher gasoline taxes that create a financial operating cost over time.

Thus, in each of these areas of inquiry, our concern will be twofold. First, what is the nature of the market trade-offs and is there any clear-cut evidence of market failure? Second, to what extent can we rely on mar-

CONSUMER VALUATIONS OF AUTO SAFETY   **81**

ket-based policy interventions to promote government objectives with respect to automobile use?

This research utilizes the general econometric approach developed in the hedonic price literature. For over a half century, there has been concern with obtaining quality-adjusted prices of automobiles, as exhibited in the work of A. T. Court,[1] Jack E. Triplett,[2] Zvi Griliches,[3] Makoto Ohta and Griliches,[4] and Keith Cowling and John S. Cubbin.[5] The most recent literature in this vein has exhibited a concern for fuel economy, as in the studies by Allen C. Goodman,[6] Thomas F. Hogarty,[7] Scott E. Atkinson and Robert Halvorsen,[8] and Ohta and Griliches,[9] although the estimated fuel economy signs are opposite of the predicted direction in many instances. In addition, one study, that of Atkinson and Halvorsen,[10] examined the price-vehicle safety trade-off but not the fuel economy–price relationship.

Although the implicit price literature for automobiles is well established, this article offers several advances over previous studies. This will be the first study to provide estimates of the implicit rates of interest used by individuals in assessing the long-run effects of automobiles, both with respect to safety and fuel economy. Automobiles are a consumption good that is durable in nature. Although used cars can be sold or possibly even rented, in each case the long-term attributes of the car, such as its

---

[1] A. T. Court, Hedonic Price Indexes with Automotive Examples, in The Dynamics of Automobile Demand (1939).

[2] Jack E. Triplett, Automobiles and Hedonic Quality Measurement, 77 J. Pol. Econ. 408 (1969); and Jack E. Triplett, The Economic Interpretation of Hedonic Methods, 66 Surv. Current Bus. 36 (1986).

[3] 3. Zvi Griliches, Hedonic Price Indexes for Automobiles: An Econometric Analysis of Quality Change, in Technology, Education and Productivity (1988); Price Indexes and Quality Change (Zvi Griliches ed. 1971).

[4] Makoto Ohta & Zvi Griliches, Automobile Prices Revisited: Extensions of the Hedonic Hypothesis, in Household Production and Consumption (Nestor E. Terleckyj ed. 1976).

[5] Keith Cowling & John S. Cubbin, Hedonic Price Indexes for United Kingdom Cars, 82 Econ. J. 963 (1972).

[6] Allen C. Goodman, Willingness to Pay for Car Efficiency: A Hedonic Price Approach, 17 J. Transport. Econ. & Pol'y 247 (1983).

[7] Thomas F. Hogarty, Price-Quality Relations for Automobiles: A New Approach, 7 Applied Econ. 41 (1975).

[8] Scott E. Atkinson & Robert Halvorsen, A New Hedonic Technique for Estimating Attribute Demand: An Application to the Demand for Automobile Fuel Efficiency, 66 Rev. Econ. & Stat. 417 (1984).

[9] Makoto Ohta & Zvi Griliches, Automobile Prices and Quality: Did the Gasoline Price Increases Change Consumer Tastes in the U.S.? 4 J. Bus. & Econ. Stat. 187 (1986).

[10] Scott E. Atkinson & Robert Halvorsen, The Valuation of Risks to Life: Evidence from the Market for Automobiles, 72 Rev. Econ. & Stat. 133 (1990).

expected longevity, will influence its value. Since an automobile is a capital asset, an important question to ask is, what is the extent to which the implicit rates of time preference for key attributes of the product are consistent with prevailing market rates of interest?

The second innovation of this article is that, instead of relying on average published prices for lines of cars, as in previous studies, we utilize individual household automobile holdings data. With this information, it will be possible to match cars with the household characteristics of those who own them. We have further refined our econometric analysis by including estimates of the fuel economy–price trade-off as well as the value of the life-price trade-off. Moreover, the value-of-life estimates will be generated by a price equation that also includes a variable categorizing the nonfatal injury risks associated with automobiles, so that the value-of-life estimates will not be capturing the omitted influence of nonfatal risk attributes of cars.

Section II of the article introduces the hedonic model, which extends the existing frameworks in the literature by incorporating the various discounting considerations. After discussing the sample characteristics and the variables in Section III, Section IV reports on the price equation estimates, including the role of discounting. The estimated real rate of interest is between 11 and 17 percent. As indicated in the conclusion in Section V, these estimates are consistent with prevailing interest rates for automobile purchases. The value-of-life estimates are on the order of $2.6–$3.7 million in 1988 prices.

II. THE HEDONIC MODEL

A. The Hedonic Framework

The basic elements of the econometric approach are based on Sherwin Rosen's paper on hedonic pricing,[11] which we will extend to consider intertemporal dimensions of automobile holdings. Automobiles embody a bundle of characteristics, designated below by A_k, where

$$\text{auto} = (A_1, A_2, A_3, \ldots, A_n). \tag{1}$$

In a competitive equilibrium, the price of the good is a function of the implicit prices of the bundle of its attributes:

$$P_{\text{auto}} = P(A_1, A_2, A_3, \ldots, A_n). \tag{2}$$

---

[11] Sherwin Rosen, Hedonic Prices and Implicit Markets: Product Differentiation in Pure Competition, 82 J. Pol. Econ. 34 (1974).

This relationship, P(auto), defines the hedonic price function, the equilibrium locus of vehicle prices resulting from the market interactions of producers and consumers for different bundles of vehicle characteristics.

Each implicit marginal price, $p(A_k)$, is the partial derivative of the equilibrium hedonic price locus with respect to the attribute of interest, A_k, or

$$p(A_k) = \frac{\partial P_{(auto)}}{\partial A_k} = P_{A_k}(A_1, A_2, A_3, \ldots, A_n). \tag{3}$$

This value simultaneously reflects consumers' marginal willingness to pay for an additional unit of that attribute and the firm's marginal cost of providing another unit of the attribute.

We use data drawn from household vehicle holdings to estimate vehicle price as a function of a set of individual automobile i's attributes, A_{ik}, and owner characteristics, X_{iz}, that is linked to automobile accident rates (for the zth characteristic of the owner of vehicle i). The reduced-form estimation equation is

$$P_{(auto)i} = \sum_k \beta_k A_{ik} + \sum_z \delta_z X_{iz} + e_i, \tag{4}$$

where the price of auto i is a function of vehicle and owner attributes and other unmeasured attributes represented by a random error term e_i.

B. Discounting and Hedonic Prices

Because of the durable nature of automobiles, the specification of the price equation ideally should be extended to account for the long-run nature of this consumer product. In particular, consumer discount rates enter as an important variable of concern in valuing the long-run cost and safety of the product.

The recent literature has included a variety of attempts to ascertain the implicit rates of time preference associated with consumer decisions, although none of the product market studies has used a hedonic price approach. In his examination of household purchases of home room air conditioners, using a simultaneous model of air conditioner purchase and utilization rate for 46 households, Jerry A. Hausman found that future energy expenditures were discounted at a mean rate of 26.4 percent, with a range of 5.1–89 percent, depending on the household's income level.[12]

---

[12] Jerry A. Hausman, Individual Discount Rates and the Purchase and Utilization of Energy-Using Durables, 10 Bell J. Econ. 33 (1979).

Dermot Gately employed a similar model to analyze consumer choices of household refrigerators, for which he found that discount rates could be as high as 300 percent, with the lowest calculated discount rate equaling 45 percent.[13] Jeffrey A. Dubin examined explicit rates of discount affecting the type of heating for households, where he found discount rates at a similar range, such as 44 percent for fuel expenditures associated with water heaters.[14] Finally, Douglas A. Houston examined hypothetical energy choices in a contingent-valuation study, for which he ascertained a discount rate of 22.5 percent, although once again there was a considerable range of values.[15]

The approach adopted here will be somewhat different in that we will derive the implicit rates of discount from a hedonic price equation. In that respect, this analysis most closely parallels the labor market hedonic wage studies by Michael J. Moore and W. Kip Viscusi[16] and Viscusi and Moore.[17] In particular, they examined how the discounted expected life years lost due to job risks affected wage rates. However, their approach dealt with a continuous job activity, not a capital good, so the structure of the models differs. Our approach will analyze how consumers' discount rates for operating costs and remaining life years of the vehicle owner affect the automobile price. Thus, the task is to structure the fuel-efficiency and the risk components of equation (4) to incorporate these intertemporal aspects of the automobile purchase decision.

Using data on the age distribution of the vehicle fleet, we determined each vehicle's expected remaining useful life, T_i. The present discounted value of operating costs (PDVOC) is the discounted sum of operating

---

[13] Dermot Gately, Individual Discount Rates and the Purchase and Utilization of Energy-Using Durables: Comment, 11 Bell J. Econ. 373 (1980).

[14] Jeffrey A. Dubin, Will Mandatory Conservation Promote Energy Efficiency in the Selection of Household Appliance Stocks? 7 Energy J. 99 (1986). Some authors have not estimated discount rates explicitly but instead have determined the payback period for appliance types and the discount rates implicit in the estimated payback period. Henry Ruderman, Mark D. Levine, & James E. McMahon, The Behavior of the Market for Energy Efficiency in Residential Appliances Including Heating and Cooling Equipment, 8 Energy J. 101 (1987), found discount rates ranging from 20 percent for room and central air conditioners to as high as 800 percent for electric water heaters.

[15] Douglas A. Houston, Implicit Discount Rates and the Purchase of Untried, Energy-Saving Durable Goods, 10 J. Consumer Res. 236 (1983).

[16] Michael J. Moore & W. Kip Viscusi, The Quantity-Adjusted Value of Life, 26 Econ. Inquiry 369 (1988); Michael J. Moore & W. Kip Viscusi, Discounting Environmental Health Risks: New Evidence and Policy Implications, 18 J. Envtl. Econ. S51 (1990); Michael J. Moore & W. Kip Viscusi, Models for Estimating Discount Rates for Long-Term Health Risks Using Labor Market Data, 3 J. Risk & Uncertainty 381 (1990).

[17] W. Kip Viscusi & Michael J. Moore, Rates of Time Preference and Valuations of the Duration of Life, 38 J. Pub. Econ. 297 (1989).

costs in each year of the vehicle's remaining life,

$$\text{PDVOC}_i = (1 + e^{-r} + e^{-2r} + \ldots + e^{-(T_i - 1)r})\text{OPERATING COST}_i, \quad (5)$$

which can be solved to yield

$$\text{PDVOC}_i = \frac{1 - e^{-rT_i}}{r}\text{OPERATING COST}_i, \quad (6)$$

where r is the implicit discount rate. The implicit discount rate of any individual will reflect the individual's rate of time preference and any premia for liquidity, risk, and uncertainty. The econometric analysis will estimate the average value of r for the sample, not for each individual.

A variable pertaining to the discounted operating cost per unit weight will also be included to capture the importance of operating cost characteristics in relation to the size of the vehicle. The relationship between fuel economy and weight is a result of the fundamental principle that additional mechanical energy is required to overcome additional inertia or weight. Holding all other design and performance factors equal, a heavier car will be less fuel efficient. But if weight could be held constant, other design factors would explain variations in fuel economy. To capture this connection, operating costs are included in the model as a stand-alone variable to reflect variability in fuel economy related to vehicle weight and other factors. Operating costs also enter through operating cost per unit weight, which should reflect the influence of variability in fuel economy across cars, adjusting for variations in weight.

Similarly, individual j's discounted remaining life years are calculated as

$$\text{discounted remaining life years}_j = \frac{1 - e^{-L_j r}}{r}, \quad (7)$$

where L_j is the expected remaining life of the jth individual and r is the discount rate over additional life years. Although the discount rate on operating costs and the discount rate over remaining life years theoretically may differ, these values could not be distinguished empirically. The discounted expected life years lost from accidents involving one's specific automobile holdings is calculated based on the discounted expected life years lost from fatality risks in each year the car is owned, multiplied by the discounted number of years the car is owned,[18] or

---

[18] This formulation is an approximation, as it abstracts from the change in the value of life expectancy over the course of the vehicle life. This approach was more feasible to estimate than even more complex nonlinear functions.

$$\text{discounted expected life years lost}_{ij} =$$

$$\left[\frac{1 - e^{-rT_i}}{r}\right] \quad \times \quad \left[\frac{1 - e^{-rL_j}}{r}\right] \quad \times \quad \text{pr[mortality]}_i. \qquad (8)$$

$$\underset{\substack{\text{discounted life} \\ \text{of vehicle}}}{} \times \underset{\substack{\text{discounted life} \\ \text{of owner at risk}}}{} \times \underset{\substack{\text{annual mortality} \\ \text{risk}}}{}$$

This expression captures the expected discounted years of life that the individual will lose during the discounted expected life of the vehicle. The potential life of the vehicle, T_i, will be less than the individual's life, L_j, but it is assumed that the consumer uses the same rate of time preference r in each of the two component discounting terms. The discounted expected life years lost term in equation (8) extends the Moore and Viscusi measure of quantity-adjusted life years[19] to situations involving capital goods in which the exposure to the risk and the individual life have a temporal aspect that must be taken into account.

Injury rates for autos also affect their long-term attractiveness and enter the model in discounted form. As in the case of vehicle operating costs, the relevant time frame for discounting the injury rating is over the life of the vehicle, not the life of the individual. An injury is by definition nonfatal, and the probability of an injury changes as an individual changes the vehicle driven. The injury risk term and the operating cost terms are defined analogously, where the difference in the annual injury rating for vehicle i replaces the operating cost for vehicle i in equation (6). The discounted expected operating costs and injury rating over the remaining vehicle life and the expected life years lost are substituted into the hedonic formulation for the operating cost and safety attributes.

The dependent variable in the model will be the natural logarithm of the price, and to permit flexibility in the functional form for the independent variables, we use a Box-Cox transformation with a coefficient λ to be estimated.[20] Given the recognition of life-cycle concerns in the operating cost and safety variables, including the discounted expected life years lost term from equation (8), the equilibrium hedonic price locus can now be specified as

---

[19] Moore & Viscusi, The Quantity-Adjusted Value of Life, *supra* note 16.

[20] Preliminary empirical analysis varying the functional form of the dependent variable suggested that the logarithm of price was a more pertinent formulation than the linear form. The logarithmic formulation is also standard in most labor market hedonic wage studies as well.

$$\ln[P_{(auto)i}] = \beta_0 + \beta_1 \left[\frac{1 - e^{-rL_j}}{r} \frac{1 - e^{-rT_i}}{r} \text{ MORTALITY RISK}_i \right]^\lambda$$

$$+ \beta_2 \left[\frac{1 - e^{-rT_i}}{r} \text{ INJURY}_i \right]^\lambda$$

$$+ \beta_3 \left[\frac{1 - e^{-rT_i}}{r} \text{ OPERATING COST}_i \right]^\lambda \qquad (9)$$

$$+ \beta_4 \left[\frac{1 - e^{-rT_i}}{r} \frac{\text{OPERATING COST}}{\text{WEIGHT}}_i \right]^\lambda$$

$$+ \sum_k \beta_k A_{ki}^\lambda + \sum_z \delta_z X_{iz} + e_i,$$

where λ is the Box-Cox transformation coefficient, which is interpreted as follows:

$$A_{ki}^\lambda = \frac{A_{ki}^\lambda - 1}{\lambda} \quad \text{for } \lambda \neq 0. \qquad (10)$$

If the transformation coefficient equals one, the model is linear, but as λ approaches zero, the right-hand side takes a logarithmic form:

$$\lim_{\lambda \to 0} A_{ki}^\lambda = \ln A_{ki}.$$

III. SAMPLE CHARACTERISTICS AND VARIABLES

The data used to obtain the empirical estimates differ from those used in earlier studies in the literature in that these data reflect actual consumer automobile holdings. In particular, we utilize the 1988 Residential Transportation Energy Consumption Survey (RTECS) conducted by the U.S. Department of Energy (DOE).[21] In 1988, DOE collected transportation-related energy data from a cross section of 2,986 sampled households. The survey included questions on vehicle holdings, usage, selected vehicle characteristics, and socioeconomic characteristics of the respondents. Additional vehicle attribute data have been collected from industry

---

[21] For a description of the survey, see U.S. Department of Energy, Household Vehicles Energy Consumption 1988 (1990).

TABLE 1

MEANS, STANDARD DEVIATIONS, AND ANTICIPATED SIGNS OF SELECTED VARIABLES WITH
RESPECT TO PRICE

Variable	Mean*	Standard Deviation	Anticipated Sign
PRICE	6,622.81	4,109.10	N.A.
MORTALITY RATE (× 1,000)	.1962	.0957	−
INJURY RATING	100.93	23.61	−
OPERATING COST	563.65	144.08	−
POWER	.04	.01	+
CARGO CAPACITY	15.18	5.57	+
WEIGHT	2,724.65	568.20	−
MAINTENANCE RATING	.91	.28	+
LUXURY-SPORT	.18	.39	+
AUTOMATIC TRANSMISSION	.76	.43	+
TWO-SEAT	.02	.14	?
WAGON	.03	.16	?
CONVERTIBLE	.01	.06	?
DIESEL	.01	.10	?
RESALE VALUE RETAINED†	57.59	16.77	+

NOTE.—N.A. = not applicable.
* Means weighted by Residential Transportation Energy Consumption Survey population sampling statistics.
† Excluding 1988 model year new cars.

sources to supplement the RTECS data. The variables used are summarized below, and Table 1 provides selected summary statistics.

PRICE = Vehicle price as of end-of-year 1988. New price for model year 1988 vehicles, used car market prices for older cars.

MORTALITY RATE = Number of fatalities occurring in that make/model/year vehicle divided by number of vehicles on the road.

INJURY RATING = Vehicle injury rating measured relative to the rating for the median vehicle. Median rating equals 100, and lower values are safer cars.

OPERATING COST = Vehicle operating costs measured in dollars of fuel expenditure per year. Calculated as gas price

	divided by miles per gallon times average miles traveled.
OPERATING COST: WEIGHT =	Vehicle operating cost per unit of vehicle weight.
POWER =	The horsepower-to-weight ratio as a measure of vehicle power/acceleration.
CARGO CAPACITY =	Vehicle cargo space in cubic feet.
MAINTENANCE RATING =	A discrete variable coded as one if the *Consumer Reports* maintenance rating is two or higher and coded as zero if the maintenance rating is below two.
LUXURY-SPORT =	A discrete variable coded as one if the vehicle is classified as a luxury or sport vehicle.
AUTOMATIC TRANSMISSION =	A discrete variable coded as one if the vehicle has an automatic transmission.
TWO-SEAT =	A discrete variable coded as one if the vehicle is a two-seat model.
CONVERTIBLE =	A discrete variable coded as one for convertibles.
WAGON =	A discrete variable coded as one for station wagons.
DIESEL =	A discrete variable coded as one for diesel models.
AMC, FORD, GM, CHRYSLER, GERMANY, JAPAN, OTHER ORIGIN =	Discrete variables coded as one for the manufacturer of domestic vehicles and for foreign vehicles, coded as one for the nation of origin if that designation is pertinent and zero otherwise.
YEARXX =	Discrete variables coded as one for the vehicle model year.
SIZEX =	Discrete variables coded as one for the appropriate size category. Four size categories are included, from SIZE1, smallest, to SIZE4, largest.

RESALE VALUE RETAINED = The percentage of original sales
                                             value retained, as of end-of-year
                                             1988.

Because the data set contains information on the actual holdings of
households, each vehicle represents the actual trade-offs among attributes made by some consumer in the marketplace. A wide selection of
alternative vehicle models is included in this data set because many models are available equipped with a variety of optional engine types; hence,
a named model may appear repeatedly with different attributes. Most
previous studies included only one observation for a standardized version
of each vehicle model.

Another unique aspect of this study is that the data reflect actual automobile holdings at a specific point in time—a snapshot of consumer behavior. Each vehicle's market price reflects the opportunity cost of owning that specific vehicle. The implicit attribute values derived from a
household's vehicle holdings will provide insight into the trade-offs in
their vehicle stock.

Based on a review of the economics literature related to vehicle choice
and the available marketing information, we selected safety, fuel economy, power, reliability, and durability as the most important attribute
variables. Other important variables include physical characteristics, vehicle size, manufacturer/nation of origin, and vehicle age. In most prior
studies, a measure of vehicle safety has been an important missing element. Only Atkinson and Halvorsen include a measure of vehicle safety,[22]
but fuel economy is not included in their model, precluding an examination of the trade-offs between fuel economy and safety. Some studies
incorporated vehicle weight as a proxy for safety, but this attribute affects
other aspects of vehicle performance as well.

Several vehicle attributes are closely related, such as different vehicle
size parameters. Economists have recognized the difficulties posed by
the relationship of vehicle weight to other attributes of interest for over
half a century.[23] Including all possible variables of interest will create
multicollinearity problems, as several authors have reported coefficient
instability. While there are inherent problems of collinearity among motor
vehicle attributes such as fuel economy and size in all such data sets, we
attempted to reduce these problems by carefully choosing our measures

---

[22] Atkinson & Halvorsen, *supra* note 10.

[23] In his 1939 study, *supra* note 1, at 113, Court recognized that "car weight per se is
undesirable and in a complete analysis would have a negative net regression." This statement presumably means that the weight coefficient should be negative.

of vehicle characteristics. For example, as a measure of vehicle power/ acceleration, we chose the horsepower-to-weight ratio (as have several other authors), in part because of the lower collinearity than was created by measures such as zero-to-sixty acceleration.

Vehicle weight is an important design characteristic because of its physical contribution to several different aspects of vehicle performance. Holding all else equal, heavier cars are typically safer and have higher operating costs per mile traveled.[24] Following the lessons of prior studies, weight is not included as a stand-alone attribute but is entered as an interaction term where appropriate.

Several other variables which embody elements of vehicle styling are included, such as dummy variables for luxury and sport vehicles and vehicle size categories.[25]

A. Vehicle Transactions Prices

Because the hedonic price locus represents equilibrium transactions prices of different attribute bundles, an empirical analysis should ideally incorporate actual automobile marketplace transactions prices. Our analysis focuses on existing vehicle holdings. Average market prices for most vehicles, based on actual transactions, are widely available. Hence, the estimated vehicle prices should mirror retail market transactions prices.[26] These prices average $6,623 for our sample of vehicles.

---

[24] Triplett, Automobiles, *supra* note 2, paid particular attention to vehicle weight because of the correlation between weight and other attributes and because weight served as a proxy for other variables in his model. In the truncated model, he speculated that weight could have represented a number of desirable vehicle characteristics, such as the size or capacity of the vehicle, its durability, or its insulation against sound or vibration.

Griliches, Hedonic Price Indexes, *supra* note 3, raised another difficulty associated with these models, especially those including weight as an explanatory variable. He noted that the correlation coefficients between several of his right-hand-side variables, including weight, length, and horsepower, fell in the range between 0.73 and 0.92. Such highly correlated explanatory variables led to coefficient instability across several different model specifications.

[25] George E. Hoffer & Robert J. Reilly, Automobile Styling as a Shift Variable: An Investigation by Firm and by Industry, 16 Applied Econ. 291 (1984), found that styling and styling changes were important factors underlying automobile demand. Another variable commonly included in similar models but not incorporated here is vehicle handling. The only available measure of handling, the turning radius, proved to be too highly correlated with other characteristics to merit inclusion. Other attributes that have been used in hedonic automobile studies include slalom time as a measure of vehicle handling, noise and vibration insulation, leg room, ease of entry and exit, interior space, number of passengers seated comfortably, braking distance, and a variety of measures of vehicle size.

[26] Price data are for year-end 1988 from the Automobile Red Book: Official Used Car Valuations.

92   THE JOURNAL OF LAW AND ECONOMICS

B. Vehicle Safety Measures

Vehicle safety is incorporated into the model with two separate measures. The first is the vehicle mortality rate, measured by the ratio of the number of fatalities occurring in each make/model/year vehicle to the number of those vehicles on the road. Vehicle mortality rates were calculated based on information from the U.S. Department of Transportation's *Fatal Accident Reporting System* (FARS) for calendar year 1989.[27] For each make/model/year vehicle, the mortality rate was calculated as follows:

MORTALITY RATE =

$$\frac{\text{TOTAL FATALITIES FOR 1989}}{\text{NUMBER MANUFACTURED} \times \text{ON-ROAD FACTOR}}, \quad (11)$$

where the on-road factor accounts for the difference in the total number of that make/model/year vehicle manufactured and the estimated number on the road in calendar year 1989.

The second safety measure is an index of the relative number of personal injury claims filed for each vehicle model normalized by the total insurance exposure written by insurance firms for that model.[28] Since nonfatal accidents are much more frequent than fatal ones, this variable equals a nonfatal risk measure, or the likelihood of injury resulting from a given accident in a specific vehicle. The sign on the coefficients of the two risk variables should be negative since less safe cars (higher value of the variables in each case) are expected to have a lower price when holding all other attributes constant.

Vehicle accident rates also depend upon how safely the vehicle is driven. Measures of mortality risk are consequently a composite of vehicle and driver characteristics.[29] An ideal risk measure would relate fatalities strictly to the structural characteristics of each vehicle, exclusive of driver characteristics. Of course, no such comprehensive measure exists. To account partially for the joint determination of mortality risk due to

---

[27] Atkinson & Halvorsen, *supra* note 10, similarly relied on the FARS data for their fatality measure.

[28] These data are published annually by the Highway Loss Data Institute, an affiliate of the Insurance Institute for Highway Safety.

[29] Vehicle and driver characteristics may not be independent because certain vehicles are more likely to be owned by those with particular demographic characteristics (for example, households with children may own safer vehicles) and because, as Peltzman recognized, driving behavior may respond to vehicle safety characteristics. See Sam Peltzman, The Effects of Automobile Safety Regulation, 83 J. Pol. Econ. 677 (1975).

both automobile and driver characteristics in the FARS data set, a number of variables are included in the model which account for non-vehicle-specific determinants of mortality risk. This approach is similar to that of Atkinson and Halvorsen, who also used mortality data derived from the FARS database.[30] These variables measure the proportion of fatalities in each make/model/year vehicle for which the specific characteristic applies.

The variables used to categorize driver behavior as it affects auto risks are listed below. They include the proportion of young drivers and that of older drivers, the proportion of accidents occurring late at night, the proportion of one-car accidents, the proportion of alcohol-related accidents, the proportion of drivers wearing seat belts, and the proportion of male drivers. These variables encompass many of the important risk factors for vehicle accidents and key measures of risk-related behavior, such as whether drivers wear seat belts.

YOUNG DRIVER = Proportion of fatalities in this make/model/year vehicle in which the driver was younger than 25 years.

OLDER DRIVER = Proportion of fatalities in this make/model/year vehicle in which the driver was 45 or older.

LATE NIGHT = Proportion of fatalities in this make/model/year vehicle which occurred between the hours of midnight and six in the morning.

ONE-CAR ACCIDENT = Proportion of fatalities in this make/model/year vehicle in which only one vehicle was involved.

SEAT BELT = Proportion of fatalities in this make/model/year vehicle in which the driver was wearing a seat belt.

ALCOHOL INVOLVEMENT = Proportion of fatalities in this make/model/year vehicle in which the on-scene police officer reported alcohol involvement.

MALE DRIVER = Proportion of fatalities in this make/model/year vehicle in which the driver was male.

---

[30] Atkinson & Halvorsen, *supra* note 10.

C. Vehicle Operating Cost

The fuel efficiency of each vehicle is measured by annual vehicle op-erating cost, which is determined by the gallon cost of gasoline divided by the miles per gallon of fuel times average annual vehicle miles,

$$\text{OPERATING COST} = \left(\frac{\$}{\text{gallon}}\right) \Big/ \left(\frac{\text{miles}}{\text{gallon}}\right)$$

$$\times \text{ average miles driven} = \frac{\$}{\text{year}}. \tag{12}$$

The price of gasoline is determined by the household's regional location and the fuel type reported for that vehicle. Vehicle miles per gallon is an estimate of actual in-use fuel efficiency.[31] Average vehicle miles are calculated from the subset of RTECS respondents with valid responses to the mileage survey.[32] In the empirical analysis, vehicle operating cost is reformulated as a discounted value over the vehicle life cycle.

If consumers behave rationally in their automobile holdings, the dis-counted operating cost coefficient should be negative. Indeed, if the mar-ket efficiently capitalizes life-cycle costs into vehicle prices, the increase in price should exactly compensate for the discounted value of the fuel savings over the anticipated vehicle life.

In several previous hedonic studies of automobiles, unanticipated signs on fuel economy resulted, as reported in Goodman,[33] Cowling and Cub-bin,[34] and Hogarty.[35] These and subsequent authors[36] have speculated that the unexpected sign on fuel economy resulted from multicollinearity

---

[31] This estimate is based on a U.S. Department of Energy adjustment algorithm described in an appendix available from the authors.

[32] Valid mileage estimates were much more likely to be missing from the RTECS data than for other variables because valid beginning and end-of-year contacts are required to generate a number. Respondents also must check the odometer reading, which requires more effort than recalling, for example, the number of seats in the car. Fewer than 65 percent of RTECS respondents supplied valid mileage values. Mileage estimates for the remaining households were imputed for RTECS reporting using a multiple regression proce-dure. Comparing the reported mileage values with the imputed mileage values shows that the imputation consistently underestimated vehicle miles. No differences in demographic characteristics between the reporting households and the imputed households could be demonstrated by the authors to account for the differences. The valid mileage results were used to calculate the average mileage for new 1988 model year vehicles and for pre-1988 vehicles in the household stock.

[33] Goodman, *supra* note 6.

[34] Cowling & Cubbin, *supra* note 5.

[35] Hogarty, *supra* note 7.

[36] For example, Atkinson & Halvorsen, *supra* note 8.

among automobile attributes used as explanatory variables for vehicle price.[37]

D. *Vehicle Power/Acceleration*

The power of each vehicle is measured by the horsepower-to-weight ratio. The horsepower-to-weight ratio should most accurately reflect vehicle acceleration because raw horsepower is adjusted for the amount of weight which must be overcome.[38]

E. *Vehicle Maintenance/Reliability*

A vehicle reliability measure is drawn from *Consumer Reports*. The raw data collected for reliability provide an ordinal measure of reliability rather than a cardinal measure. Therefore, reliability is incorporated in the regressions as a dummy variable with a value of one for vehicles with a 5-year average reliability rating of two and above and a value of zero for a rating of less than two.

F. *Cargo Capacity*

Vehicle cargo capacity is included as a measure of vehicle size. Consumers may choose between specific vehicles based on the convenience provided by cargo space.

G. *Durability and Vehicle Life*

Vehicle durability will be incorporated by a proxy variable measuring the proportion of the original sale value of the vehicle retained as of the end of 1988. No true measure of vehicle durability that would vary from one vehicle make/model/year to another was available. Though resale value retained is also an imperfect proxy for durability, it is presumed that vehicles with high retained resale values will have a longer life than vehicles with a lower proportion of original value retained.

The key components that determine the various terms of the model

---

[37] The potentially most troublesome remaining source of multicollinearity in this data set is that between operating cost and safety as measured by personal injury claims, with a correlation coefficient of -0.5. The simple correlation between operating cost and weight equals 0.73, while that between the safety measure and weight is -0.71.

[38] Alternative measures of power that have been used in prior studies include zero-to-sixty acceleration, horsepower, and this ratio. A measure of vehicle acceleration would have been desirable as acceleration is most readily interpretable by consumers, but comprehensive acceleration data were not available. An added advantage associated with this measure is that the ratio is uncorrelated with other explanatory variables.

involving discounting pertain to the expected useful life of the vehicle
and the lifetime of the driver. The expected remaining life of the vehicle
is determined from historic data on the age distribution of the vehicle fleet. The expected vehicle life is based on the age at which 50 percent
of the vehicles for a particular model year are expected to be scrapped.
These values are computed from historical reports of the number of vehicles in use in each calendar year for each vehicle model year cohort.[39]
Based on this trend data, 50 percent of 1987 model year vehicles will
remain in use for 13 years. This measure is intended to represent a consumer's expectation of the vehicle's useful life at the time of purchase.
Although data are not available to differentiate expected vehicle life by
manufacturer or vehicle type, the durability measure based on the retained resale value of each vehicle is included to capture some of the
variability in expected vehicle life within each model year.[40]

The average automobile owner expects to hold a particular vehicle
about 5 years, but because the vehicle is in turn purchased by a new
owner—at a price approximating the present value of the vehicle, given
its expected operating costs—the expected life of the vehicle, not its
expected length of ownership, is the appropriate discounting time frame.

Similarly, the life expectancy data were derived from life expectancy
tables that recognize the dependence of life expectancy on age, gender,
and race of vehicle owners. The expected remaining life of each vehicle
owner is determined as of the end of 1988.[41]

IV. Estimation Results: Discounting Long-Term Risks and Operating Costs

The estimation of equation (9) utilized 1,775 observations for the model
years 1981–87. Cars older than the 1981 model year are not included
because of limited safety data availability, nor are trucks, vans, and mini-
vans held in household vehicle stocks.

Nonlinear least squares estimates of the model appear in Table 2 for
three separate models, each of which was convergent. Three equations
are estimated. The first equation includes the quantity-adjusted life years,
the discounted injury rating, the two discounted operating cost variables,

---

[39] Motor Vehicle Manufacturers Association, MVMA Motor Vehicles Facts & Figures
(1992 and other years).

[40] This approach ignores any bequested value of the vehicle, which even in the preacci-
dent condition should be several orders of magnitude smaller than the implicit value of life,
a term that is being estimated.

[41] U.S. Department of Health and Human Services, Vital Statistics of the United States
1988, Vol. 2, Mortality, Pt. A (1991).

TABLE 2
Nonlinear Least Squares Results

Variable	Model (1)	Model (2)	Model (3)
CONSTANT	4.529	4.124	3.655
	(1.824)	(1.318)	(1.321)
QUANTITY-ADJUSTED LIFE YEARS	−1.092	−.479	−.499
	(.590)	(.213)	(.213)
DISCOUNTED INJURY RATING	−.015	· · ·	· · ·
	(.007)		
DISCOUNTED DURATION OF ANNUAL OPERAT-ING COSTS	.017	.048	.069
	(.010)	(.029)	(.029)
DISCOUNTED DURATION OF ANNUAL OPERAT-ING COSTS: VEHICLE WEIGHT	−.905	−.935	−.979
	(.101)	(.070)	(.070)
POWER	.305	.286	.273
	(.129)	(.100)	(.101)
CARGO CAPACITY	−.054	−.046	−.040
	(.011)	(.011)	(.010)
RESALE VALUE RETAINED	.070	.115	.121
	(.021)	(.035)	(.035)
MAINTENANCE RATING	.030	.029	.034
	(.013)	(.013)	(.013)
LUXURY-SPORT	.208	.207	.213
	(.012)	(.013)	(.013)
AUTOMATIC TRANSMISSION	.026	.027	.026
	(.010)	(.011)	(.011)
TWO-SEAT	−.207	−.111	−.072
	(.070)	(.074)	(.073)
STATION WAGON	.147	.084	.053
	(.036)	(.032)	(.032)
CONVERTIBLE	.330	.349	.348
	(.055)	(.057)	(.057)
DIESEL	−.003	.005	−.004
	(.034)	(.035)	(.035)
SIZE2	−.008	.005	.018
	(.013)	(.014)	(.014)
SIZE3	.036	.059	.072
	(.020)	(.021)	(.021)
SIZE4	.040	.083	.096
	(.031)	(.031)	(.032)
AMERICAN MOTORS	−.116	−.072	−.124
	(.084)	(.086)	(.087)
GENERAL MOTORS	.006	.018	.022
	(.010)	(.010)	(.010)
CHRYSLER	.039	.044	.055
	(.013)	(.014)	(.014)
GERMANY	.283	.370	.400
	(.028)	(.028)	(.028)
JAPAN	.184	.222	.241
	(.014)	(.014)	(.014)

TABLE 2 (*Continued*)

Variable	Model (1)	Model (2)	Model (3)
OTHER ORIGIN	.140	.173	.180
	(.028)	(.028)	(.028)
YEAR82	.231	.211	.221
	(.017)	(.016)	(.016)
YEAR83	.386	.347	.368
	(.021)	(.020)	(.020)
YEAR84	.555	.491	.528
	(.027)	(.025)	(.024)
YEAR85	.692	.620	.670
	(.034)	(.031)	(.029)
YEAR86	.838	.759	.818
	(.041)	(.036)	(.034)
YEAR87	.961	.865	.933
	(.047)	(.040)	(.038)
YOUNG DRIVER	−.063	−.089	. . .
	(.025)	(.026)	
OLDER DRIVER	−.048	−.017	. . .
	(.021)	(.022)	
LATE NIGHT	.019	.017	. . .
	(.024)	(.025)	
ONE-CAR ACCIDENT	.021	.009	. . .
	(.053)	(.031)	
SEAT BELT	.097	.144	. . .
	(.028)	(.029)	
ALCOHOL INVOLVEMENT	.049	.038	. . .
	(.023)	(.023)	
MALE DRIVER	.004	.027	. . .
	(.028)	(.028)	
DISCOUNT RATE	.174	.107	.125
	(.024)	(.025)	(.031)
λ	.500	.370	.330
	(.075)	(.076)	(.076)

NOTE.—Asymptotic standard errors are in parentheses.

vehicle characteristic variables, and driver characteristic variables. The second equation omits the discounted injury rating variable since this variable is correlated with fatality risks and may be capturing to some extent the influence of the fatality variable.[42] Finally, the third equation omits the set of driver characteristic variables since these measures of the attributes of drivers in fatal accidents for particular vehicle types may

---

[42] In a survey of the literature on compensating wage differentials for job risks, W. Kip Viscusi, Fatal Tradeoffs: Public and Private Responsibilities for Risk (1992), found that a minority of these studies included measures of fatal and nonfatal risks and only a few of these 25 studies reviewed successfully estimated significant injury and fatality coefficients.

capture to some extent omitted attributes of the car related to safety. Ideally, the driver characteristic variables included in equations (1) and (2) should pertain to the particular vehicle, but since these data are not available, averages across the vehicle type are included, thus introducing a possible source of measurement error.

The principal coefficients of interest are consistently significant (95 percent confidence level, one-tailed test). The quantity-adjusted life years variable is significant in all equations, and the injury variable is significant in the first equation, the only one in which it is included. Both of the operating cost variables are statistically significant in all three specifications.

A. Discount Rate Estimates

The estimates of the discount rate presented in the bottom row of Table 2 are 17 percent (eq. [1]), 11 percent (eq. [2]), and 13 percent (eq. [3]). The highest discount rate is for the equation including injury and mortality risks. The 95 percent confidence intervals for the discount rate are [.13, .22] for equation (1), [.06, .16] for equation (2), and [.06, .19] for equation (3). Even at the lower bound of the confidence limits, a discount rate of zero is excluded.

There are a number of interest rate reference points that could be used to assess the nominal appropriateness of the discount rate. The first benchmark that one might use is the riskless societal rate of interest. The prevailing real rate of return in the U.S. economy in the sample year 1988 is typically estimated in the 2–5 percent range.[43] These values are outside the estimated confidence limits for the discount rate.

Adding the actual 1988 inflation rate of 4.1 percent to the mean estimated real discount rate in Table 2 implies nominal discount rate estimates of 21 percent, 15 percent, and 17 percent. These rates of time preference are in line with rates found in many other studies of consumer discounting discussed above and in fact are below most of these estimated rates, which typically are real rates of time preference.

Moreover, these high nominal rates of interest may not reflect temporal myopia since the riskless rates of return may not reflect consumer access to capital markets. Several different financing options are available to car buyers including commercial banks, savings and loans, credit unions,

---

[43] The lower bound is measured as 90-day Treasury-bill rate minus annual change in gross national product implicit price deflator (both for 1988). The upper bound is measured as AAA bond rate minus price deflator. See Council of Economic Advisors, *Economic Report of the President* (1993).

100   THE JOURNAL OF LAW AND ECONOMICS

finance companies, and manufacturer-provided financing.[44] Financing may be more difficult to arrange for used car purchases as the average nominal interest rate for new car financing in 1988 was 12.6 percent, but for the used cars considered in our survey it averaged 15.1 percent.[45] This value lies within the 95 percent confidence interval for all three estimates of the discount rate. The estimated discount rates are consequently quite consistent with prevailing rates of interest facing members of the sample.

B.   Value of Life Estimates

Discounted remaining life years are calculated based on the characteristics of the household head as reported in the DOE RTECS survey data. If the household head is not the purchaser/holder of a vehicle reported for the household, then an error may be introduced. The statistical value of life estimated in the life-cycle context is given by

$$\frac{\partial \text{PRICE}}{\partial \text{MORTALITY RATE}} = \beta_1 \times \frac{\partial \text{ELYL}^\lambda}{\partial \text{MORTALITY RATE}} \times \text{PRICE}, \quad (13)$$

where ELYL stands for the discounted expected lost years of life, and the final multiplication by price is necessary because the model was estimated on the natural log of price.

The estimates of the implicit value of life are $2.6 million for equation (1), $3.1 million for equation (2), and $3.7 million for equation (3). In column 2 of Table 2, results are presented for the model excluding the injury variable. The mean statistical value of life in this case is $3.1 million, 19 percent higher, indicating that excluding a separate measurement for nonfatal injuries causes the fatality valuation to reflect the value of nonfatal injuries.[46] By way of comparison, the Atkinson and Halvorsen estimate of automobile purchasers value of life was $3.6 million (in 1988 dollars)[47]—an estimate very close to those obtained here.

Because we also estimate the implicit rate of discount for life years lost, we can also calculate the value per discounted marginal life year. This amount is $476,000 for equation (1), $367,000 for equation (2), and

---

[44] In 1990, 62 percent of new car purchases were financed. Of those financed, 32 percent were financed through manufacturers. See Motor Vehicle Manufacturers Association, *supra* note 39.

[45] *Id.* at 52.

[46] An analogous result was first demonstrated in the labor market by W. Kip Viscusi, Employment Hazards: An Investigation of Market Performance (1979).

[47] Atkinson & Halvorsen, *supra* note 10.

$496,000 for equation (3). These discounted values per life year estimates are over twice as high as the estimated discounted value per year of life lost of $170,000 (in 1986 prices) implied by workers' choice of hazardous jobs by Moore and Viscusi.[48]

C. *Other Parameter Estimates*

The first two regression results in Table 2 include controls for the driver characteristics in fatal accidents. The mortality risk measure used in the model does not represent a pure measure of automobile-specific risk because driver characteristics are not excised from the rates. Therefore, selected characteristics of drivers in fatal accidents are included in the model as control variables. These variables measure the proportion of fatal accidents occurring in each make/model/year vehicle that reflect the characteristic in question. The first column in Table 2 indicates that the proportion of drivers who are young, who are older, who are wearing seat belts, and who have alcohol involvement were all statistically significant at the 0.05 level.

Another key market performance test is the extent to which fuel efficiency cost differences are fully capitalized into the price. The dollar value of consumers' marginal willingness to pay for changes in the annual cost of driving can be calculated from the transformation coefficients of the annual operating cost variable and the variable interacting annual operating cost with vehicle weight. Because PDVOC is a present value, the effect of PDVOC on price, based on both of the PDVOC terms in equation (9), is the capitalization rate of operating expenses. The capitalization rate refers to the rate at which the marketplace incorporates life-cycle fuel costs into market prices of vehicles. If markets function perfectly, there is full capitalization, that is a one-to-one correspondence between changes in the discounted value of life-cycle operating costs and vehicle price, and the capitalization rate is one. If, however, there is no relationship between life-cycle fuel expenditures and vehicle price, the capitalization rate would be zero.

The capitalization rate for discounted life-cycle operating costs is estimated at -0.35, implying that a $1 increase in life-cycle operating costs lowers vehicle price by $0.35. Several factors could account for this re-

---

[48] Moore & Viscusi, Quantity-Adjusted Value of Life, *supra* note 16. Our overall value of life estimates are, however, more reasonable than those obtained in their labor market discounting study.

sult. Consumers may, for example, not believe the time before the vehicle is scrapped is as great as we have assumed.[49]

V. Conclusion

If automobile markets functioned perfectly, consumers would fully value the safety and fuel efficiency of their vehicles, and the government could restrict regulatory intervention to broader societal externalities. Additional problems arise if consumers are myopic and neglect their future selves and the future ramifications of car purchases with respect to safety and fuel efficiency. This type of market failure also limits the efficacy of regulatory interventions that exploit consumers' responsiveness to prices. If, for example, consumers ignore the fuel efficiency attributes of their autos, then higher gasoline taxes that raise the operating costs of vehicles would not affect their vehicle purchase decisions.

Our findings suggest that these extreme consumer responses are not evident. The implicit value of life estimates for automobile owners were in the range of approximately $2.6–$3.7 million, where these estimates accounted for the injury risk of the autos and were obtained within the context of a nonlinear model that discounted the expected life years at risk. This estimated value-of-life range is the same range as previous estimates in the literature, including previous evidence on the value of life for automobile purchasers.[50] These findings provide no basis for concluding that consumers undervalue automobile safety. The safety of automobiles is highly regulated and mandated through government regula-

---

[49] Both the low capitalization rate and the high discount rate could be the result of the application of the estimation model. It is assumed in these estimates that a vehicle lasts 13 years and then has no scrap value. This assumption is based on the median time to scrap for all vehicles on the road. The median time that car buyers expect to keep their new cars is only 5.5 years. Motor Vehicle Manufacturers Association, *supra* note 39. After this period, well over 90 percent of vehicles are still on the road. Upwardly biased rates could occur if a consumer bases a vehicle ownership decision on a short time frame, but the discount rate is calculated for a longer time frame. The computed discount rate may appear higher than the rate underlying the ownership decision.

Two sources of measurement error may have been introduced by data on the expected lives of vehicles and vehicle owners. The 13-year expected vehicle life ignores variability among different makes and models. However, other variables, such as manufacturer and durability, may act as controls for variability across vehicles, minimizing any errors associated with measurement of expected vehicle life.

[50] Viscusi, *supra* note 42, reviews the literature on the estimates of the value of life and health. Although most of the estimates in the literature are clustered in the $3 million–$7 million range, estimates in the $2 million–$3 million range, such as that yielded in one of our specifications, are not unprecedented. For example, eight of the labor market studies he reviews and six of the value of life studies outside of the labor market have estimated values of life at or below this level.

CONSUMER VALUATIONS OF AUTO SAFETY 103

tions. If these safety regulations provide more safety than is optimal from the standpoint of a fully informed consumer, one would expect to observe a lower estimated marginal value of life for automobiles than for other areas of choice in which the safety level provided is freely chosen.

The focal point of the analysis was on the role of discounting as it relates to consumers' valuation of the fuel economy attributes of cars and the life and health effects of automobiles. The estimated rates of time preference range from 11 to 17 percent. Although these rates of time preference exceed the riskless rates of return in the economy, they are quite consistent with the prevailing rates of interest for automobile purchases. Moreover, these estimated rates are at the low end of the estimated implicit rate of interest found in a variety of other contexts in the literature. Consumer discounting for automobiles appears to be consistent with prevailing market rates and in a much more reasonable range than many estimated discount rates for energy efficiency for home appliances and similar choices.

Although these results are not sufficiently precise to imply that there is pinpoint accuracy in the discounting behavior of consumers, the results do suggest that there is sufficient consumer orientation toward the present value of decisions that market interventions can be utilized that affect the stream of payoffs associated with choices. These interventions need not be restricted to those with an immediate effect. Consumers do have a long-term perspective with respect to safety and fuel efficiency, and government officials can potentially influence the choices consumers make by affecting the perceived time stream of payoffs along these dimensions. Whether there is a legitimate rationale for such intervention hinges on concerns outside the scope of this paper.

Safety and fuel efficiency are two of the most prominent concerns of transportation regulation policymakers. These attributes of automobiles are salient for consumers as well. The principal application of our findings is that policymakers contemplating intervention in this market context should be cognizant of the extent to which there are already market forces in operation. Moreover, if we do choose to intervene, we should attempt to design the interventions to work in concert with the powerful market forces that exist in this market rather than to be independent of them.

BIBLIOGRAPHY

Atkinson, Scott E., and Halvorsen, Robert. "A New Hedonic Technique for Estimating Attribute Demand: An Application to the Demand for Automobile Fuel Efficiency." *Review of Economics and Statistics* 66, No. 3 (1984): 417–26.
Atkinson, Scott E., and Halvorsen, Robert. "The Valuation of Risks to Life:

Evidence from the Market for Automobiles." *Review of Economics and Statistics* 72, No. 1 (1990): 133–36.

Automobile Red Book: Official Used Car Valuations. Vol. 78, No. 7. Chicago: McClean Hunter Market Reports, 1988.

Council of Economic Advisors. *Economic Report of the President.* Washington: U.S. Government Printing Office, 1993.

Court, A. T. "Hedonic Price Indexes with Automotive Examples." In *The Dynamics of Automobile Demand.* New York: General Motors Corporation, 1939.

Cowling, Keith, and Cubbin, John S. "Hedonic Price Indexes for United Kingdom Cars." *Economic Journal* 82 (1972): 963–78.

Dubin, Jeffrey A. "Will Mandatory Conservation Promote Energy Efficiency in the Selection of Household Appliance Stocks?" *Energy Journal* 7, No. 1 (1986): 99–118.

Gately, Dermot. "Individual Discount Rates and the Purchase and Utilization of Energy–Using Durables: Comment." *Bell Journal of Economics* 11 (1980): 373–74.

Goodman, Allen C. "Willingness to Pay for Car Efficiency: A Hedonic Price Approach." *Journal of Transport Economics and Policy* 17 (1983): 247–66.

Griliches, Zvi. "Hedonic Price Indexes for Automobiles: An Econometric Analysis of Quality Change." In *Technology, Education and Productivity.* New York: Basil Blackwell, Inc., 1988. Originally published in 1961.

Griliches, Zvi, ed. *Price Indexes and Quality Change.* Cambridge, Mass.: Harvard University Press, 1971.

Hausman, Jerry A. "Individual Discount Rates and the Purchase and Utilization of Energy-Using Durables." *Bell Journal of Economics* 10, No. 1 (1979): 33–54.

Hoffer, George E., and Reilly, Robert J. "Automobile Styling as a Shift Variable: An Investigation by Firm and by Industry." *Applied Economics* 16 (1984): 291–97.

Hogarty, Thomas F. "Price-Quality Relations for Automobiles: A New Approach." *Applied Economics* 7 (1975): 41–51.

Houston, Douglas A. "Implicit Discount Rates and the Purchase of Untried, Energy-Saving Durable Goods." *Journal of Consumer Research* 10 (1983): 236–46.

Moore, Michael J., and Viscusi, W. Kip. "The Quantity-Adjusted Value of Life." *Economic Inquiry* 26, No. 3 (1988): 369–88.

Moore, Michael J., and Viscusi, W. Kip. "Discounting Environmental Health Risks: New Evidence and Policy Implications." *Journal of Environmental Economics and Management* 18 (1990): S51–S62.

Moore, Michael J., and Viscusi, W. Kip. "Models for Estimating Discount Rates for Long-Term Health Risks Using Labor Market Data." *Journal of Risk and Uncertainty* 3 (1990): 381–401.

Motor Vehicle Manufacturers Association. *MVMA Motor Vehicles Facts and Figures.* Detroit: Motor Vehicle Manufacturers Association, various years.

Ohta, Makoto, and Griliches, Zvi. "Automobile Prices Revisited: Extensions of the Hedonic Hypothesis." In *Household Production and Consumption,* edited by Nestor E. Terleckyj. New York: National Bureau of Economic Research, 1976.

Ohta, Makoto, and Griliches, Zvi. "Automobile Prices and Quality: Did the Gasoline Price Increases Change Consumer Tastes in the U.S.?" *Journal of Business and Economic Statistics* 4, No. 2 (1986): 187–98.

Peltzman, Sam. "The Effects of Automobile Safety Regulation." *Journal of Political Economy* 83, No. 4 (1975): 677–725.

Rosen, Sherwin. "Hedonic Prices and Implicit Markets: Product Differentiation in Pure Competition." *Journal of Political Economy* 82 (1974): 34–55.

Ruderman, Henry; Levine, Mark D.; and McMahon, James E. "The Behavior of the Market for Energy Efficiency in Residential Appliances Including Heating and Cooling Equipment." *Energy Journal* 8, No. 1 (1987): 101–24.

Triplett, Jack E. "Automobiles and Hedonic Quality Measurement." *Journal of Political Economy* 77 (1969): 408–17.

Triplett, Jack E. "The Economic Interpretation of Hedonic Methods." *Survey of Current Business* 66 (1986): 36–40.

U.S. Department of Energy. Energy Information Administration. *Household Vehicles Energy Consumption 1988.* Washington, D.C.: U.S. Government Printing Office, 1990.

U.S. Department of Health and Human Services. Public Health Services. Center for Disease Control. National Center for Health Statistics. *Vital Statistics of the United States 1988.* Vol. 2, *Mortality, Pt. A.* Hyattsville, Md.: U.S. Department of Health and Human Services, 1991.

Viscusi, W. Kip. *Employment Hazards: An Investigation of Market Performance.* Cambridge, Mass.: Harvard University Press, 1979.

Viscusi, W. Kip. *Fatal Tradeoffs: Public and Private Responsibilities for Risk.* New York: Oxford University Press, 1992.

Viscusi, W. Kip, and Moore, Michael J. "Rates of Time Preference and Valuations of the Duration of Life." *Journal of Public Economics* 38 (1989): 297–317.

[24]

PRIVATE VALUES OF RISK TRADEOFFS AT SUPERFUND SITES: HOUSING MARKET EVIDENCE ON LEARNING ABOUT RISK

Ted Gayer, James T. Hamilton, and W. Kip Viscusi*

Abstract—This paper incorporates a Bayesian learning model into a hedonic framework to estimate the value that residents place on avoiding cancer risks from hazardous-waste sites. We show that residents are willing to pay to avoid cancer risks from Superfund sites before the U.S. Environmental Protection Agency (EPA) releases its assessment (known as the Remedial Investigation) of the site. Residents' willingness to pay to avoid risks actually decreases after the release of the Remedial Investigation, suggesting that the information lowers the perceived levels of risk. This estimated willingness to pay implies a statistical value of cancer similar to the value-of-life estimates in labor market studies.

I. Introduction

WHEN asked to evaluate the severity of environmental hazards, people often rank hazardous-waste sites as a top environmental threat. In answering a similar question, an Environmental Protection Agency (EPA) expert panel characterized hazardous-waste sites as only a low-to-medium threat to the public.[1] The same disparity in risk rankings is evident in the McClelland, Schulze, and Hurd (1990) survey of health-risk beliefs of residents near a landfill, which finds that the residents' assessments of the risk were much higher than the assessments of experts.

These studies suggest that the public overestimates cancer risks from hazardous-waste sites, which would be consistent with evidence that people overestimate low-probability events. This overreaction to risk may generate pressure on the EPA to undertake expensive site remediations through its Superfund program. In addition, residents surrounding Superfund sites may prefer more ambitious and, consequently, more costly remediations, because costs are spread across taxpayers and consumers. Viscusi and Hamilton (1996) find that the median cleanup cost per case of cancer prevented by the Superfund program exceeds one billion dollars per expected cancer case avoided, which places it among the most expensive government programs for reducing risk.

To assess properly the benefits of cleaning up Superfund toxic-waste sites, one must distinguish between the private values that residents place on risk reduction and the values of risk reduction expressed publicly in surveys or implied in regulatory decisions. For this article, we have constructed a large risk and housing price data set for a local market using the choices people make in the greater Grand Rapids, Michigan, housing market. These data enable us to assess the value residents place on hazardous-waste risk reduction in their private decisions. By relying on market data instead of survey data, our results control for the incentive that

Received for publication May 2, 1997. Revision accepted for publication July 7, 1999.

* Georgetown University and University of California at Berkeley, Duke University, and Harvard University, respectively.

[1] See the U.S. EPA Report (1987) for a summary of the survey (conducted by the Roper Organization) and for the expert panel rankings.

residents have to press for stringent cleanups when others' money is being spent on risk remediation. Political pressures do appear to be consequential in driving cleanup decisions, as Viscusi and Hamilton (1999) find that the level of the EPA's remediation efforts is responsive to measures of the political participation of the surrounding community.

The greater Grand Rapids area contains seven Superfund toxic-waste sites. We formulate residents' assessments of cancer risk from these sites as a Bayesian process of updating prior assessments with information obtained from the EPA's assessment of site risks (contained in the site Remedial Investigation report) and from the local media. Using a composite measure of risk from the Superfund sites, we estimate the implicit value people place on risk reduction through the effect of risk on housing values. Our hypothesis is that residents demonstrate a willingness to pay for risk reduction even before the EPA releases its site Remedial Investigation. We also hypothesize that the EPA's release of the Remedial Investigation alters households' risk beliefs, resulting in a change in the effect of risk on housing values.

Estimation of the marginal effect of cancer risk on housing prices can generate an implied value of averting a statistical cancer. Portney (1981) was the first researcher to publish estimates of the value of life using a hedonic property model. He coupled the estimate of the price gradient with respect to total dustfall (obtained from a study on Allegheny County, Pennsylvania) with a separate EPA study that related total particulate concentration to mortality rates. By linking these studies, he demonstrated that the ratio of these two estimates is a measure of the statistical value of life, which he found to be $300,000 (1996 dollars).

We find that, before residents receive the risk information provided by the EPA's Remedial Investigation, their estimated value of a statistical cancer case is much higher than the value-of-life estimates found in job market studies. This result is consistent with broader evidence on risk-perception biases, which demonstrates that people tend to overestimate low-probability risks (Lichtenstein et al., 1978; Tversky & Kahneman, 1982). This overreaction can lead to a higher willingness to pay for risk reduction.

After the release of the EPA's Remedial Investigation, residents update their risk perceptions. The postinformation estimated value of a statistical cancer case is similar to the value-of-life estimates found in previous labor market studies. Once residents are properly informed of the risks, their choices made in the greater Grand Rapids housing market indicate a value of hazardous-waste risk similar to the values of risk faced in other settings. This similarity between the risk–money tradeoff for avoiding hazardous-waste risks and the tradeoffs for job risks suggests that there is no evidence that consumers are overreacting to the

The Review of Economics and Statistics, August 2000, 82(3): 439–451

hazardous-waste risks in their private decisions after the release of the EPA's Remedial Investigation.[2] Additionally, even before the release of the EPA's Remedial Investigation, residents' implied risk–money tradeoff is several orders of magnitude lower than regulatory expenditures per cancer case averted in the Superfund program. Thus, although surveys demonstrate that people express a high willingness to spend public funds on Superfund risk reduction, our results demonstrate that residents are much less willing to spend their own funds on risk reduction.

In section II, we model residents' perceptions of hazardous-waste site risks as a Bayesian learning process and link this model to a hedonic framework, which is tested by using the data described in section III. In section IV, we describe the results of different empirical specifications, which are used in section V to analyze reactions to site risks. In section VI, we offer conclusions about current assessments of individuals' reactions to Superfund site risks.

II. Theoretical Model

A. The Hedonic Model

We formulate individuals' subjective perceptions of the risk of cancer (π) arising from hazardous-waste risks as a Bayesian learning process. People are assumed to update their prior probability assessment of site risks based on information provided by the EPA's Remedial Investigation and by local publicity. Our learning model uses a beta distribution to characterize this Bayesian process.[3] This distribution is quite flexible and can assume a wide variety of skewed and symmetric shapes.

Individuals have a prior cancer risk assessment of p, which has associated informational content, φ_0. The information weight, φ_0, measures the precision of the prior risk assessment. It is equivalent to observing φ_0 draws from a Bernoulli urn in which a fraction, p, is occurrences of cancer. Our conjecture is that this prior probability is a function of the actual risks from the Superfund sites. People form their priors based in part on the observable characteristics of the site, past EPA involvement with the site, and local knowledge and perceptions of site hazards. People update their risk perceptions taking into account the probability, q, which is implied by information provided by the EPA's Remedial Investigation. The information provided by the EPA may serve as good news or as bad news; thus, q may be less than or greater than p. People also update their risk perceptions taking into account the probability, r, which is implied by information provided by the news media. Note that residents need not read the Remedial Investigation individually or consume each media article to be influenced by these information sources. The diffusion of information from

these sources within the local real estate market can influence perceptions even among those who have not read site documents or specific media coverage. The risk implied by the Remedial Investigation has the informational content denoted as ξ_0, and the risk implied by the news media has the informational content denoted as κ_0. For simplicity, we treat φ_0, ξ_0, and κ_0 as given parameters and focus only on the risk levels p, q, and r.[4]

The cancer risk-perception function takes the form

$$\pi(p, q, r) = \frac{\varphi_0 p + \xi_0 q + \kappa_0 r}{\varphi_0 + \xi_0 + \kappa_0}. \tag{1}$$

By denoting the fraction of the total informational content associated with each information source as

$$\varphi = \frac{\varphi_0}{\varphi_0 + \xi_0 + \kappa_0}, \qquad \xi = \frac{\xi_0}{\varphi_0 + \xi_0 + \kappa_0},$$

$$\text{and} \quad \kappa = \frac{\kappa_0}{\varphi_0 + \xi_0 + \kappa_0},$$

the risk-perception function is rewritten as

$$\pi(p, q, r) = \varphi p + \xi q + \kappa r. \tag{2}$$

While the underlying hypothesis is that of a rational Bayesian learning model, other learning models may also be consistent with this linearly weighted average formulation. Our use of the Bayesian approach gives us a concrete economic interpretation of the coefficients, but it does not test explicitly whether people are Bayesians, as opposed to adhering to other learning frameworks in which a variety of sources of risk information may alter risk judgments.

Individuals maximize expected utility over two states of the world, with U_1 representing utility in the sick (cancer) state and U_2 representing utility in the healthy (non-cancer) state. We assume for any given level of income that people prefer being healthy ($U_2 > U_1$), that utility functions within states are risk-neutral or risk-averse, and that the marginal utility of income is greater when healthy. Utility in each state is a function of a vector of characteristics of the house, z, a composite good, x, and the visual disamenities of the site, s.[5] The consumer purchases one house at price h, which is a function of housing characteristics, risk perceptions, and the Superfund visual disamenities. The consumer's income is y.

Accounting for the separate health and visual aesthetic effects of Superfund sites yields a model in which consum-

---

[2] Note that the comparison is between values placed on mortality risk and values placed on cancer risk, in which type of cancer, latency period, and probability of death are considerations.

[3] Viscusi (1979) introduced this particular reparameterization of the Bayesian learning model with a beta distribution.

[4] We assume that the probabilities p, q, and r reflect the risks that are implied by a series of independent draws from the same Bernoulli urn, which reflects the risks from hazardous waste. Although these are independent sources of information, the risks implied will be related, as they all reflect the dangers of the same waste site. The overlapping information case can also yield an additive linear form, but the interpretation of the weights differs (Zeckhauser, 1971).

[5] We assume that only the closest site contributes visual disamenities.

ers maximize expected utility as follows:

$$\text{Max } V = \pi(p, q, r)U_1(x, z, s)$$
$$+ [1 - \pi(p, q, r)]U_2(x, z, s) \tag{3}$$

subject to

$$y = x + h(z, \pi(p, q, r), s). \tag{4}$$

By construction, consumer risk perceptions, $\pi(p, q, r)$, will be an increasing function of p and q (that is, $\xi_0/(\varphi_0 + \xi_0 + \kappa_0) > 0$, $\varphi_0/(\varphi_0 + \xi_0 + \kappa_0) > 0$). Therefore, the equilibrium conditions for the effect of higher informational risk values, p and q, on housing prices, and the expected signs are

$$\frac{\partial h}{\partial q} = \frac{(U_1 - U_2)\dfrac{\partial \pi}{\partial q}}{\pi \dfrac{\partial U_1}{\partial x} + (1 - \pi)\dfrac{\partial U_2}{\partial x}} < 0, \quad \text{and}$$

$$\frac{\partial h}{\partial p} = \frac{(U_1 - U_2)\dfrac{\partial \pi}{\partial p}}{\pi \dfrac{\partial U_1}{\partial x} + (1 - \pi)\dfrac{\partial U_2}{\partial x}} < 0, \tag{5}$$

which, because $\partial h/\partial q = (\partial h/\partial \pi)(\partial \pi/\partial q)$ and $\partial h/\partial p = (\partial h/\partial \pi)(\partial \pi/\partial p)$, reduces to

$$\frac{\partial h}{\partial \pi} = \frac{(U_1 - U_2)}{\pi \dfrac{\partial U_1}{\partial x} + (1 - \pi)\dfrac{\partial U_2}{\partial x}} < 0. \tag{6}$$

As first presented by Rosen (1974), the hedonic price function reflects the locus of tangencies between the offer and bid curves. The marginal price is equivalent to the marginal willingness to pay for an incremental decrease in objective risk. Therefore, one can compute the welfare effects of a marginal change in objective risk from the price gradient.

To estimate the welfare effects of a nonmarginal change in a characteristic, we would need to know the willingness-to-pay function. The endogeneity of marginal prices and quantities limits the use of instrumental variables in a two-stage estimation of willingness-to-pay. Bartik (1987) suggested using data from multiple markets in order to estimate the structural equations.[6] However, Epple (1987) showed that—even using multiple markets—very strong

orthogonality conditions must be met to identify the equations. Bartik (1988) and Palmquist (1992) demonstrated that, for local disamenities (such as Superfund sites), the slope of the hedonic price function is an approximate measure of the willingness to pay for a nonmarginal change.

The impact of the release of the Remedial Investigation on perceptions enters the hedonic price analysis by a comparison of the price gradients before ($\partial h/\partial p$) and after ($\partial h/\partial \pi$) the EPA releases the Remedial Investigation. The Bayesian model suggests that people will demonstrate possibly different willingness to pay for risk reduction before and after the release of the Remedial Investigation. A comparison of these gradients indicates whether the willingness to pay for risk reduction increases or decreases given the information provided by the EPA's Remedial Investigation. If the information in the Remedial Investigation raises residents' perceptions of risk, then we would expect an increase in willingness to pay for risk reduction. If the Remedial Investigation information indicates that the site is not as hazardous as previously perceived, then we would expect a decrease in willingness to pay for risk reduction.

B. The Empirical Specification

We estimate the hedonic price function using the conventional practice of postulating the independent variable, the log of housing price adjusted for inflation (ln *Price*), as a function of a vector of structural variables (*Structural*) and a vector of neighborhood variables (*Neighborhood*).[7] These structural and neighborhood variables measure the characteristics of the house, which were denoted as z in the theoretical model. The empirical model also includes measures of the overall level of the environmental condition of the neighborhood. These measures are the number of other environmental disamenities within 0.25 mile from the house (*Sites₁*), between 0.25 and 0.5 mile from the house (*Sites₂*), between 0.5 and 0.75 mile from the house (*Sites₃*), and between 0.75 and 1.0 mile from the house (*Sites₄*). Prices are also a function of the Superfund aesthetic disamenities (*Visual*), which were denoted as s in the theoretical model. The empirical model also controls for fixed time effects and city effects by using dummy variables indicating the year of the sale (denoted with a subscript $t = 1, \dots, 5$) and the city location of the house (denoted with a subscript $i = 1, \dots, 4$).[8] A further enhancement, as outlined in the theoretical model, is that the model includes the role of risk from Superfund sites. The semilogarithmic form of the hedonic price function is expressed as

$$\ln \textit{Price} = \alpha + \beta \textit{Structural} + \gamma \textit{Neighborhood}$$
$$+ \rho_i \textit{City}_i + \tau_t \textit{Year}_t + \zeta_1 \textit{Sites}_1 + \cdots \tag{7}$$
$$+ \zeta_4 \textit{Sites}_4 + \eta \textit{Visual} + \delta \pi(p, q, r) + u.$$

---

[6] This approach results in identified structural equations only if consumer preferences are assumed to be the same across markets, while the price function is assumed to differ due to differences in the matching process (Kahn & Lang, 1988). It is difficult to assume that preferences are homogeneous across housing markets.

[7] See Bartik and Smith (1987) for a review.
[8] The omitted city dummy variable is for Grand Rapids, and the omitted annual dummy variable is for 1988.

If we expand the risk-learning model and recognize the components of risk beliefs π from equation (2), we can rewrite the hedonic price function as

$$\ln Price = \alpha + \beta Structural$$
$$+ \gamma Neighborhood + \rho_i City_i + \tau_t Year_t$$
$$+ \zeta_1 Sites_1 + \cdots + \zeta_4 Sites + \eta Visual \quad (8)$$
$$+ \delta_1 p + \delta_2 q + \delta_3 r + u,$$

where $\delta_1 = \delta\varphi$, $\delta_2 = \delta\xi$, and $\delta_3 = \delta\kappa$. As mentioned in the previous subsection, the prior and updated probabilities have a negative effect on housing values. The relative impact of the prior probability compared to the updated probability is $\delta_1/\delta_2 = \varphi/\xi = \varphi_0/\xi_0$. Thus, the regression estimates indicate the effect of risk on housing prices and the change in the magnitude of this effect after the release of the Remedial Investigation.

We operationalize the values of p, q, and r in the following manner. In the case of perceived cancer risk arising from Superfund sites, the prior probability, p, is characterized by the information known to the residents before the EPA's release of their Remedial Investigation.[9] In capturing the prior probability, p, we follow two approaches. In one approach, we set this value in the pre-Remedial Investigation release period equal to the objective risk level subsequently revealed in the EPA study. This approach assumes that people use observable information on risk to form accurate risk judgments in much the same manner that hedonic wage studies assume that workers are aware of Bureau of Labor Statistics objective risk measures. In a second approach, we examine the explicit influence of the observable risk factors that could potentially affect people's prior beliefs. Although it will not be possible to construct a pre-Remedial Investigation implicit value of cancer in this instance, it will be possible to assess whether the influence of these prior observable risk factors are in the expected direction and whether the post-Remedial Investigation tradeoffs reflect plausible values per expected cancer case.

The prior information available to residents includes the area of the closest Superfund site, the ranking of the closest site on the EPA's National Priorities List (which, for all sites, occurred before the housing sales examined in this study), the elapsed time since the closest Superfund site was placed on the National Priorities List, and the type of site (such as, landfill versus industrial chemical plant). A site receives a National Priorities List ranking according to its score on the Hazardous Ranking System (HRS), which is a preliminary

risk assessment applied to sites to determine if the site should be designated a Superfund site. We first examine the effects of these variables on housing prices, and then we examine the effect of the actual risk on housing prices before and after the release of the Remedial Investigation. For the latter analysis, we assume that people use the observable risk factors available prior to the Remedial Investigation in order to form accurate risk judgments. We then test whether the Remedial Investigation provides new information, resulting in people updating their perceptions. This allows us to estimate the statistical value of cancer before and after the release of the Remedial Investigation.

In order to justify using the objective risk as a proxy for the prior perceptions, we test whether the prior risk indicators serve as reasonable predictors of the objective risk. We regress the objective risk level against the area of the closest site, the ranking of the closest site on the National Priorities List, the elapsed time since the closest site was placed on the National Priorities List, and the type of site. For robustness, we run an alternative functional form that includes a variable that interacts the distance measure and the NPL ranking, and another variable that interacts the distance measure and the type of site. The results suggest that the objective risk is a reasonable approximation of households' prior risk perceptions.[10]

Because the objective risk level is a reasonable approximation of prior probability, we can estimate the dollar value that people place on a reduction in Superfund risk before the release of the Remedial Investigation. We then test whether the value of the risk reduction changes after the release of the information provided in the Remedial Investigation. Our conjecture is that people tend to overestimate the prior risk before the release of the EPA's Remedial Investigation. People then update their risk perceptions after the release of

---

[9] Sites placed on the National Priorities List (NPL) qualify for federal remediation funds. NPL sites undergo a site characterization process known as the Remedial Investigation and Feasibility Study (RI/FS). The RI/FS contains a baseline risk assessment and provides regional EPA decision-makers with a quantitative assessment of human health risk at a site, a description of remedial action objectives, and an analysis of the alternatives proposed to reach these objectives. After evaluating an RI/FS, the EPA selects a remedial action and then documents the reasons for its selection in the Record of Decision.

[10] The equation results are as follows (with t-statistics in parentheses):

1) $\ln \hat{Risk} = -7.424 - 0.012 \, Area \, of \, Site - 0.006 NPLRanking$
        (116.1)   (18.1)   (50.4)

    $- 0.013 Months \, Since \, NPL - 1.711 Distance - 0.031 Type \, of \, Site,$
        (27.5)   (133.5)   (0.7)

    $Adj.R^2 = 0.6062$, $F \, Statistic = 5213.168$.

2) $\ln \hat{Risk} = -8.174 - 0.013 Area \, of \, Site - 0.004 NPL \, Ranking$
        (68.4)   (19.0)   (19.3)

    $- 0.013 Months \, Since \, NPL - 1.294 Distance - 0.516 Type \, of \, Site$
        (27.8)   (25.3)   (7.9)

    $- 0.001(Distance*NPL \, Ranking) + 0.274(Distance*Type \, of \, Site),$
        (10.9)   (10.2)

    $Adj.R^2 = 0.6121$, $F \, Statistic = 3816.704$.

For both equations, all the coefficient estimates are significantly different from zero at the 1% level, except for the coefficient estimate on the type of site in the first equation, which is not significantly different from zero. As expected, $Risk$ decreases with the time since a site's placement on the NPL, the distance to the closest site, and the NPL ranking. $Risk$ also decreases for larger sites, which suggests that houses surrounding these sites may be farther from sources of contamination at the sites.

the Remedial Investigation. An additional updating of risk perceptions occurs after receiving the newspaper publicity about all the Superfund sites in the greater Grand Rapids area.[11]

We use the distance to the closest Superfund site as a proxy for the visual disamenities of the site.[12] We incorporate into the hedonic price function the variables that serve as indicators of the actual risk before the release of the EPA information. We also include a variable measuring the publicity surrounding the sites, along with a dummy variable indicating if the house was sold after the release of the EPA's Remedial Investigation. Additionally, we include a measure of the actual risk for those houses sold after the release of the Remedial Investigation (that is, we interact the actual risk with a dummy variable indicating if the house was sold after the Remedial Investigation). The first hedonic price function to be estimated is

$$
\begin{aligned}
\ln Price = &\ \alpha + \beta Structural + \gamma Neighborhood \\
&+ \rho_i City_i + \tau_t Year_t + \zeta_1 Sites_1 + \cdots \\
&+ \zeta_4 Sites_4 + \eta Distance + \omega_1 Area \\
&+ \omega_2 NPL + \omega_3 Type + \omega_4 NPLTime \\
&+ \gamma_2 News + \theta_1 After + \theta_2 (After \times Risk) \\
&+ u,
\end{aligned}
\tag{9}
$$

where *Distance* is the distance from the house to the closest Superfund site,

Area is the area of the closest Superfund site,

NPL is the National Priorities List ranking of the closest Superfund site,

Type describes what type of operations occurred at the closest Superfund site,

NPLTime is the number of months since the closest Superfund site was placed on the NPL,

News is the number of words printed in the *Grand Rapids Press* about all the Superfund sites in the year previous to the sale of the house,

[11] Other studies have considered the effect that information has on the hedonic gradient, although not in a Bayesian framework. Kohlhase (1991) found that a positive relationship between distance to the closest site and the price of the house occurred only after the site was placed on the EPA's National Priorities List. Michaels and Smith (1990) found that, for certain submarkets, the price-distance gradient changes slope depending on whether the house was sold within six months of the discovery of hazardous waste at the closest site. Kiel and McClain (1995) found no price–distance relationship before the construction of an incinerator, despite rumors of its imminent construction. However, they found a positive price–distance relationship during the construction phase, and also throughout the duration of the operation of the incinerator.

[12] Most previous hedonic studies have used distance (from the house to the disamenity) as a proxy for both the (non-risky) aesthetic and (risky) health effects of the disamenity. Where more than one disamenity is present, studies have typically used the distance to the closest site as a proxy. Michaels and Smith (1990) and Harrison and Stock (1984) examined alternative measures of distance. Note that, even though we control for cancer risks generated at a site, the difficulty of indexing non-cancer health risks means that the distance variable may also reflect, in part, reactions to those health effects.

After is a dummy variable indicating if the house was sold after the release of the EPA's Remedial Investigation,

After $\times$ *Risk* is an interaction variable that measures the objective lifetime excess cancer risk (described in the next section) from all the sites to those individuals in a house purchased after the release of the Remedial Investigation, and the other variables are as defined earlier.

The interaction variable tests whether housing prices react to the objective level of risk for houses sold after the release of the Remedial Investigation.

Our conjecture is that, before the release of the Remedial Investigation, *Area*, *NPL*, *Type*, and *NPLTime* serve as indicators to the residents of the actual risks from the sites. Because this information is correlated with the actual risk from the sites (see footnote 10), the housing prices should react to the level of the actual risk before the release of the Remedial Investigation. We therefore estimate another hedonic equation that replaces the risk indicators with a measure of the actual risk from the Superfund sites. This allows us to test the stability of the post-Remedial Investigation *Risk* coefficient, as well as to obtain an estimate of the dollar value of a risk reduction before the release of the Remedial Investigation. This specification also includes an interaction term of *After* and *Risk* to test whether the effect of the actual risk on housing prices changes after the release of the Remedial Investigation. This second hedonic price function is

$$
\begin{aligned}
\ln Price = &\ \alpha + \beta Structural + \gamma Neighborhood \\
&+ \rho_i City_i + \tau_t Year_t + \zeta_1 Sites_1 + \cdots \\
&+ \zeta_4 Sites_4 + \eta Distance + \gamma_1 Risk \\
&+ \gamma_2 News + \theta_1 After \\
&+ \theta_2 (After \times Risk) + u.
\end{aligned}
\tag{10}
$$

Among other things, *Distance* serves as a proxy for the visual disamenities associated with the Superfund sites. *News* measures the publicity about the Superfund sites and is thus a measure of the updating information, *r*. The effect of this publicity on housing prices is equivalent to the joint effect of news information on perceptions and perceptions on prices. (Comparing equations (8) and (10) shows that γ_2 is a measure of δ_3, or the informational weight on media coverage.) The effect of risk on housing prices before the release of the Remedial Investigation is equal to the joint effect of prior risk information on perceptions and perceptions on prices. (Comparing equations (8) and (10) shows that γ_1 is a measure of δ_1, or the weight on prior risk beliefs if these beliefs equal the value of *Risk*.) The effect of *Risk* on housing prices after the release of the Remedial Investigation is equal to the joint effect of updating risk information on perceptions and perceptions on prices. (Comparing equations (8) and (10) shows that $\gamma_1 + \theta_2$ is a measure of δ_2.)

Household risk perceptions are positively related to the risk levels associated with prior beliefs and new informa-

444   THE REVIEW OF ECONOMICS AND STATISTICS

tion, because $\partial\pi/\partial p = \varphi$, $\delta\pi/\delta q = \xi$, $\partial\pi/\partial r = \kappa$, and $0 < \varphi$, ξ, $\kappa < 1$. As indicated in equation (5), the model predicts these risk levels will have a negative impact on housing prices. The effect of risk on housing prices before the release of the Remedial Investigation (as measured by γ_1) and the effect of risk on housing prices after the release of the Remedial Investigation (as measured by $\gamma_1 + \theta_2$) are both expected to be negative. However, θ_2 can either be positive or negative depending on whether the risk analysis indicates a hazard higher or lower than prior beliefs.

We estimate a separate hedonic equation to determine whether publicity serves to communicate the risks of the Superfund sites. If newspaper publicity were correlated with *Risk*, the coefficient estimate for *Risk* would be biased. Therefore, we estimate a separate equation without the *News* variable to check whether this changes the price-risk relationship. The third hedonic price function estimated is

$$\ln Price = \alpha + \beta Structural + \gamma Neighborhood$$
$$+ \rho_i City_i + \tau_t Year_t + \zeta_1 Sites_1 + \cdots$$
$$+ \zeta_4 Sites_4 + \eta Distance + \gamma_1 Risk \quad (11)$$
$$+ \theta_1 After + \theta_2 (After \times Risk) + u.$$

In addition to measuring public valuations of Superfund risk, the model also tests whether willingness to pay for risk reduction is affected by the release of the EPA's Remedial Investigation. The coefficient on the interaction term estimates the influence that the Remedial Investigation has on the valuation of the risks of the sites. For equations (10) and (11), a negative value for θ_2 would indicate that household perceptions of cancer risk increased after the release of the Remedial Investigation, and therefore drove down housing prices. A positive value for θ_2 would indicate that residents perceived the risks as smaller after the release of the Remedial Investigation, resulting in an increase in housing prices.

III. Data Description

For our analysis, we constructed a sample of housing prices for 16,928 houses sold in the greater Grand Rapids area between January 1, 1988, and December 31, 1993. (The greater Grand Rapids area consists of the cities of Grand Rapids, Walker, Wyoming, Kentwood, and Grandville.) The area is ideal for a hedonic analysis of Superfund risk because it is a local market that contains seven Superfund sites, only one of which does not have quantitative EPA risk data.[13] A local housing market with numerous Superfund sites enhances the analysis because of a heterogeneity of risk among the households, yet there are few extraneous sites that can contaminate the analysis by contributing unmeasured risk to the households. The housing-price offer curves will also be

[13] The Spartan site contains only a qualitative analysis, which does not contain pathway risk estimates.

TABLE 1.—DESCRIPTIVE STATISTICS (N = 16,928 HOUSES)

Variable	Mean	Standard Deviation
Price (in 1996 dollars)	74,176	17,600
Bedrooms (number)	3.01	0.73
Bathrooms (number)	1.53	0.60
Fireplaces (number)	0.38	0.66
Basement (0/1)	0.79	0.41
Lot size (square feet)	10,826	20,856
Garage (0/1)	0.91	0.29
Household income (median in census tract)	37,914	5,247
Race (proportion black in census tract)	0.08	0.13
High school education (proportion in census tract)	0.80	0.08
Tax (property tax rate)	5.75	0.44
Distance to central business district (in miles)	3.83	1.74
School quality (% 7th graders in district in top category)	20.19	20.90
Under 19 (proportion in census tract)	0.28	0.04
Crime rate (per capita for city in previous year)	0.08	0.02
Grand Rapids (0/1)	0.57	0.50
Grandville (0/1)	0.03	0.17
Kentwood (0/1)	0.11	0.31
Walker (0/1)	0.04	0.21
Wyoming (0/1)	0.25	0.43
Year88 (0/1)	0.16	0.37
Year89 (0/1)	0.17	0.38
Year90 (0/1)	0.16	0.37
Year91 (0/1)	0.16	0.36
Year92 (0/1)	0.17	0.37
Year93 (0/1)	0.18	0.38
Distance (miles to the closest Superfund site)	1.90	0.93
Sites$_1$ (# of Non-NPL, RCRA, and PCS sites within 0.25 mile)	0.07	0.34
Sites$_2$ (... between 0.25 and 0.5 mile)	0.39	0.83
Sites$_3$ (... between 0.5 and 0.75 mile)	0.76	1.25
Sites$_4$ (... between 0.75 and 1.0 mile)	1.19	1.60
Area of the closest Superfund site (in acres)	22.52	38.01
National Priorities Listing rank of the closest Superfund site	519.61	138.40
Time since closest site was placed on NPL (in months)	57.06	30.91
Type of site (1 = landfill, 0 = chemical plant or battery repository)	0.32	0.47
Risk (lifetime excess cancer risk from Superfund sites)	1.81E-06	2.16E-05
After (0/1 if house sold after the release of the Remedial Investigation)	0.38	0.49
News (# words of Superfund newspaper coverage in last year)	4,192	1,621

more similar within a local market than if a national data set were used.

The price and structural data come from the Multiple Listing Service of the Grand Rapids Society of Realtors. Additionally, a Geographic Information System (GIS) analysis determined the longitude and latitude coordinates of the houses and computed the distances of each house to the neighborhood Superfund sites. Using GIS technology, we also linked each house to the demographic data of its census tract, city, and school district. Table 1 presents the descriptive statistics for the variables used in the analysis.

The mean housing sale prices for each year was $60,196 for 1988, $64,436 for 1989, $68,082 for 1990, $68,983 for 1991, $70,507 for 1992, and $72,812 for 1993. The mean housing price in 1996 dollars for the entire sample is $74,176. Of the sample of 16,957 housing transactions,

16.3% occurred in 1988, 17.2% occurred in 1989, 16.5% occurred in 1990, 15.7% occurred in 1991, 16.8% occurred in 1992, and 17.4% occurred in 1993. The structural variables include the number of bedrooms, the number of bathrooms, the number of fireplaces, whether there is a basement, the size of the lot in square feet, and whether there is a garage. The neighborhood variables include the median household income in the census tract, the proportion of blacks in the census tract, the proportion of people with a high school education in the census tract, the property tax rate, the distance to the central business district, the percentage of seventh-graders in the school district who scored in the highest category for the Michigan reading assessment test, the proportion of people in the census tract under the age of nineteen, and the per capita crime rate for the city in the previous year. The estimation utilizes a fixed-effects model, including annual dummy variables as well as city dummy variables.

The environmental variables include the measure of the distance to the closest Superfund site. Although distance of the house to the closest site is also correlated with health risks from the site, we assume it is a proxy for the Superfund aesthetic disamenities. Additionally, four variables ($Sites_1$, $Sites_2$, $Sites_3$, and $Sites_4$) serve as proxies for the overall quality of the environment within the vicinity of the house. These variables measure the sum of the non-NPL CERCLA sites (sites that are not on the NPL but fall under the Comprehensive, Environmental Response, Compensation, and Liability Act of 1980), RCRA sites (sites that fall under the Resource Conservation and Recovery Act), and PCS water-pollution sites (sites monitored by the EPA's Permit Compliance System) within quarter-mile rings around the house.[14] These quarter-mile rings are from 0 to 0.25 mile, 0.25 to 0.5 mile, 0.5 to 0.75 mile, and 0.75 to 1 mile from the house.

We also include variables that serve as prior indicators for the risks from the Superfund sites. These variables measure the area (in square acres) of the closest site, the NPL ranking of the closest site, the number of months since the placing of the closest site on the NPL, and a dummy variable that is 1 if the closest site were a landfill and 0 if it were an industrial chemical plant or battery repository.

The risk variables measure both the objective excess cancer risks to the household and the timing of the release of this information with respect to the sale of the house.[15] We measure the objective cancer risk by aggregating the soil and groundwater pathway risk estimates and coupling them with

dilution estimates. We standardize the pathway definitions used in the EPA's risk assessments of the Superfund sites. Additionally, we use the mean exposure and chemical concentration levels in order to determine the cancer risk at each site.[16]

To compute the cancer risk to each household in the greater Grand Rapids area, we couple the site risk assessments with dilution estimates for soil and groundwater exposure. Soil dilution estimates come from EPA guidelines and are a function of the distances to the sites. To estimate groundwater dilution, we use maps of plumes to estimate the probability that a house is located above a contaminated plume. For each block group, we use data from the U.S. Bureau of the Census to determine the proportion of households that draw their water from groundwater.[17] Multiplying the probability of being above a contaminated plume by the probability that the house receives its drinking water from a well results in an estimate for groundwater exposure dilution. The household cancer risk from each site is the product of the soil cancer risk and the soil dilution estimate, plus the product of the groundwater cancer risk and the groundwater dilution estimate. Summing the cancer risk from each of the Superfund sites results in the total lifetime excess cancer risk to the household. The mean cancer risk to an individual in a household is 1.81E-06.[18]

We do not assume that individuals living near a site can state with precision the numbers calculated in our objective risk measure. The risk measure is meant to reflect a consistently developed point estimate of cancer risks based on risk-assessment assumptions consistent with EPA practices. To the extent that residents' assessments of site risks are related to the underlying magnitude of hazards as measured in cancer-risk assessments, we expect housing prices to react negatively to the risk measure.

A dummy variable measures the timing of the risk information. This variable has a value of 1 if the house was sold after the EPA released its Remedial Investigation and Feasibility Study (RI/FS) for the closest site, and 0 if it was sold before this release. We use press coverage in the *Grand Rapids Press,* which serves the entire greater Grand Rapids area, as the publicity measure. The publicity variable is the total number of printed words in articles about the local Superfund sites within the year before the sale of the house.

IV. Empirical Results

Table 2 presents the ordinary least-squares estimates of the hedonic price function, and the three equations correspond to equations (9), (10), and (11). Along with the structural and neighborhood variables, the specifications include measures of the environmental quality in the vicinity

---

[14] CERCLA and RCRA data are maintained by the EPA's Office of Solid Waste and Emergency Response. PCS tracks the National Pollutant Discharge Elimination System program under the Clean Water Act.

[15] We examine only cancer risk. For noncarcinogenic risk, the EPA's assessment entails computing the ratio of a chemical's calculated exposure intake to its reference dose, the level of exposure thought to be without appreciable risk of non-cancer effects. A ratio above 1 for a chemical triggers greater scrutiny. Because non-cancer risk varies in its severity (such as, from skin rashes to reproductive damage), there is no way to summarize accurately the aggregate non-cancer risk arising from multiple chemicals at a given site.

[16] Hamilton and Viscusi (1999) uses a similar methodology.

[17] Each block group in our data set has approximately 300 houses.

[18] The cancer-risk estimate is for an individual residing in the house. EPA guidance indicates that a site risk greater than 1.0E-04 generally warrants action and that a site risk between 1.0E-04 and 1.0E-06 is allowed discretion in the remediation consideration. The household risk used in this paper couples the site risk estimates with dilution estimates.

TABLE 2.—REGRESSION RESULTS FOR THE SEMI-LOG HEDONIC PRICE FUNCTION

	Equation (1)		Equation (2)		Equation (3)	
Variables	Coefficient	t-stat	Coefficient	t-stat	Coefficient	t-stat
Intercept	10.256[a]	(56.14)	10.300[a]	(56.15)	10.303[a]	(56.15)
Bedrooms	0.048[a]	(22.57)	0.050[a]	(23.69)	0.050[a]	(23.70)
Bathrooms	0.168[a]	(60.11)	0.172[a]	(61.10)	0.172[a]	(61.05)
Fireplaces	0.087[a]	(36.84)	0.087[a]	(36.77)	0.087[a]	(36.78)
Basement	0.017[a]	(4.74)	0.013[a]	(3.75)	0.013[a]	(3.73)
Lot Size	1.49E-06[a]	(21.43)	1.48E-06[a]	(21.15)	1.49E-06[a]	(21.14)
Garage	0.103[a]	(20.95)	0.102[a]	(20.59)	0.102[a]	(20.57)
Household income	8.82E-06[a]	(16.14)	9.85E-06[a]	(18.45)	9.85E-06[a]	(18.45)
Race	−0.093[a]	(5.84)	−0.125[a]	(7.92)	−0.125[a]	(7.91)
High school education	0.435[a]	(12.65)	0.414[a]	(12.59)	0.414[a]	(12.58)
Tax	−0.082[a]	(2.93)	−0.094[a]	(3.34)	−0.095[a]	(3.38)
Distance to CBD	0.051[a]	(23.33)	0.049[a]	(25.08)	0.049[a]	(25.11)
School quality	1.10E-04	(0.38)	1.86E-05	(0.07)	2.90E-05	(0.10)
Under 19	−1.030[a]	(22.77)	−1.090[a]	(23.83)	−1.089[a]	(23.81)
Crime rate	−0.560	(1.22)	−0.800[c]	(1.72)	−0.819[c]	(1.76)
Grandville	−0.020	(0.64)	−0.076[b]	(2.37)	−0.078[b]	(2.43)
Kentwood	−0.148[a]	(4.20)	−0.149[a]	(4.18)	−0.151[a]	(4.23)
Walker	−0.145[a]	(2.81)	−0.139[a]	(2.69)	−0.141[a]	(2.74)
Wyoming	−0.096[a]	(3.92)	−0.109[a]	(4.45)	−0.110[a]	(4.50)
Year89	0.032[a]	(4.10)	0.047[a]	(6.02)	0.045[a]	(5.82)
Year90	0.044[a]	(3.81)	0.074[a]	(6.63)	0.073[a]	(6.50)
Year91	0.024	(1.11)	0.076[a]	(3.54)	0.072[a]	(3.38)
Year92	−0.005	(0.21)	0.063[a]	(2.69)	0.060[b]	(2.56)
Year93	−0.043[b]	(2.01)	0.037[c]	(1.86)	0.035[c]	(1.74)
Sites₁	−0.021[a]	(4.83)	−0.020[a]	(4.60)	−0.020[a]	(4.60)
Sites₂	−0.011[a]	(5.29)	−0.009[a]	(4.55)	−0.009[a]	(4.55)
Sites₃	0.001	(0.96)	0.003[c]	(1.85)	0.003[c]	(1.84)
Sites₄	0.004[a]	(3.70)	0.006[a]	(4.96)	0.006[a]	(4.95)
Distance	0.014[a]	(7.70)	0.012[a]	(5.93)	0.012[a]	(5.91)
After	−0.006	(1.12)	−0.012[b]	(2.26)	−0.013[b]	(2.52)
Risk			−1771.214[b]	(2.27)	−1779.076[b]	(2.28)
After × risk	−139.135[b]	(2.13)	1635.245[b]	(2.09)	1644.076[b]	(2.10)
Area of site	−0.001[a]	(11.62)				
Type of site	0.095[a]	(15.03)				
NPL ranking	−1.62E-04[a]	(7.08)				
Months since NPL	0.001[a]	(9.27)				
News	−2.51E-06[b]	(2.46)	−2.31E-06[b]	(2.25)		
	Adj. R^2 = 0.6703		Adj. R^2 = 0.6649		Adj. R^2 = 0.6648	
	N = 16,928		N = 16,928		N = 16,928	

[a] Significant at the 1% level, two-sided test.
[b] Significant at the 5% level, two-sided test.
[c] Significant at the 10% level, two-sided test.

of the house. The first equation incorporates an objective risk measure only for houses sold after the release of the Remedial Investigation. This equation also includes variables that serve as indicators for the actual risks of the sites. Equations (2) and (3) each incorporate an objective risk measure, along with the term interacting the objective risk and the dummy variable indicating if the house was sold after the release of the EPA's Remedial Investigation. Equations (1) and (2) include a publicity measure to test if the probability assessment that is implied by this updating information affects housing prices. Equation (3) omits the *News* variable from the hedonic equation. The risk coefficient in this model thus captures the direct effect of risk on prices as well as the effect through newspaper coverage. If newspaper coverage of the sites communicates the level of risk, one would expect that dropping the *News* variable would result in an increase in the magnitude of the effect of the *Risk* coefficient.

A. *Estimates of the Hedonic Model*

Table 2 reports the results of the hedonic price function of equations (9), (10), and (11). As discussed previously, the hedonic price gradient with respect to a good (such as a structural or neighborhood attribute) is equal to the marginal value of the good. A priori expectations are that coefficients for the structural house variables are positive, and the regression results of the three equations are consistent with these expectations: an increase in a structural attribute of a house increases the price of the house. All the estimates for the neighborhood variables also have the expected sign (positive for goods, negative for bads). However, the parameter estimates for school quality and for the crime rate in equation (1) are not significantly different from zero. There are no a priori expectations for the signs of the coefficients of the city and annual dummy variables. The estimated coefficient for the distance to the closest Superfund site is positive and significant for each equation, suggesting that people are willing to pay to live farther away from the visual disamenities that are associated with Superfund sites.

One of the concerns about the distance proxy used in previous studies is that it also measures the distance to other neighborhood characteristics. Multiple environmental disamenities could exist at the same distance to the house as the closest Superfund site. These other disamenities would then be reflected in the estimate of the distance gradient. The ring variables $Sites_1$, $Sites_2$, $Sites_3$, and $Sites_4$ address this concern by controlling for other neighborhood environmental disamenities. The coefficient estimates of these disamenity variables indicate a negative and significant price effect of the number of such sites at 0.25 and 0.5 mile from the house.

Equation (1) tests whether certain variables act as indicators for the risks associated with the Superfund sites. The findings suggest that people do incorporate this prior information in the expected manner. Specifically, the size of the closest Superfund site and the NPL ranking of the closest Superfund site have negative effects on housing prices. The more time that has elapsed since the placing of the site on the NPL results in higher housing price, as these sites that merit lower priority may pose smaller risks. Another possibility is that alarmist responses to a site being placed on the NPL moderate over time. And homes near industrial chemical plants or the battery repository have lower prices then homes near the landfills.

As outlined in section II, we test the potential impacts that information from the EPA's Remedial Investigation and local newspaper coverage has on perceptions and, consequently, on equilibrium housing prices. The hedonic price gradient with respect to total cancer risk gives the marginal valuation of cancer risk (the value of avoiding cancer risks) for households. As was described in section II.B, the expected sign for this gradient is negative both before and after the release of the Remedial Investigation. Similarly, if publicity increases perceptions of risk, then we expect a negative sign for the price gradient with respect to publicity.

Equation (1) estimates the effect of *Risk* only after the release of the Remedial Investigation. The negative coefficient estimate suggests that people are willing to pay less for houses for which there is a Superfund cancer risk. For equations (2) and (3), we rely on the evidence presented in section II.B to claim that perceptions of the prior risk are correlated with the actual risk. Using these results, it is possible to estimate the dollar value that people place on risk reduction both before and after the Remedial Investigation. The negative coefficient estimates for *Risk* indicate that, before the Remedial Investigation, the public is willing to pay more for houses exposed to lower levels of Superfund cancer risk.

The interaction variable is the product of *Risk* and the dummy variable that indicates if the house was sold after the release of the EPA's Remedial Investigation. Using this interaction term gives the following marginal effect of *Risk* on housing prices:

$$\frac{\partial Price}{\partial Risk} = (\hat{\gamma}_1 + \hat{\theta}_2 After)Price. \tag{12}$$

The term $\hat{\gamma}_1$ represents the estimated *Risk* coefficient, and $\hat{\theta}_2$ represents the interaction term's estimated coefficient. The positive sign of the interaction term's estimated coefficient indicates that the negative effect of risk on housing prices was smaller after the EPA released their Remedial Investigation. Our conjecture is that the release of the EPA's Remedial Investigation provided risk information that lowered perceptions of the risk, which were initially alarmist, resulting in a decrease in magnitude of the price-risk gradient. It is also noteworthy that the post-Remedial Investigation price effect of *Risk* is comparable for all of the equations. The net effects on the ln *Price* variable range from -135 to -139, or a price drop that is approximately \$220 less (for a change in *Risk* by the mean level) than the effect of risk beliefs before the completion of the EPA risk analysis.

The results also indicate that, controlling for the risk level, newspaper publicity about the local Superfund sites has a negative effect on housing prices. Previous studies have suggested that substantial newspaper coverage leads to overestimation of mortality risks (Combs & Slovic, 1979). However, this bias cannot be inferred from the gradient here because the effect of publicity on perceptions cannot be separated from the effect of perceptions on housing prices.

Equation (3) in table 2 presents estimates of the hedonic equation without the *News* variable. The signs, magnitudes, and significance of the estimates are virtually identical to those reported in equation (2). Dropping *News* from the regression does not significantly alter the gradients before and after the release of the Remedial Investigation. Apparently, although newspaper publicity during the time of the Remedial Investigation has a negative effect on housing prices, it does not seem to communicate new information about the Superfund cancer risks to the residents.

B. Estimates of the Box-Cox Model

To further explore the nature of the risk-dollar relationship, we use a Box-Cox transformation of the dependent variable to estimate the hedonic price function.[19] The transformation of the dependent variable, *Price*, yields the regression model

$$Price^{(\lambda)} = \alpha + \sum \beta_k X_k + \epsilon, \tag{13}$$

where $Price^{(\lambda)} = (Price^\lambda - 1)/\lambda$ and X_k are the independent variables as expressed in equation (10). The transformation

[19] Cropper, Deck, and McConnell (1988) found that a linear Box-Cox model performs well in a housing market when all attributes are observed and also in the presence of specification error.

TABLE 3.—REGRESSION RESULTS FOR THE BOX-COX TRANSFORMATION*

Variables of Interest	Coefficient	t-stat
Risk	-18.789^b	(2.21)
After	$-1.07E\text{-}04^c$	(1.86)
After $\times$ risk	17.048^b	(2.01)
News	$2.30E\text{-}08^b$	(2.06)
	Adj. $R^2 = 0.6588$	
	$N = 16,928$	
	$\lambda = -0.42$	

^{b} Significant at the 5% level, two-sided test.
^{c} Significant at the 10% level, two-sided test.
* Other variables included in the equation are the same as in table 2.

parameter, λ, is taken to be an unknown parameter, and we scan a range of values to determine the least-squares values of λ, α, and the β_k's.

Table 3 presents the results of the Box-Cox model. The least-squares estimate for the transforming parameter, λ, is -0.42. The marginal effect of risk on housing price is

$$\frac{\partial Price}{\partial Risk} = (\hat{\beta}_1 + \hat{\beta}_2 After) Price^{(1-\lambda)}. \tag{14}$$

The negative value of $\hat{\beta}_1$ indicates that people are willing to pay for a reduction of cancer risk. The positive value of $\hat{\beta}_2$ indicates that the price-risk tradeoff is greater before the release of the EPA's Remedial Investigation.

V. Estimation of Welfare Effects

A. The Benefits of Risk Reduction and the Value of a Statistical Cancer Case

Remediation of Superfund sites addresses, among other objectives, the targeted reduction of cancer risks. Previous hedonic property-value studies computed cleanup benefits by equating remediation with movement of the houses to a certain distance in which the gradient levels out. (See, for example, Kohlhase (1991) and Kiel and McClain (1995).) This approach captures the distance-risk relationship imperfectly, because it assumes that remediation will alleviate both the (risky) health and (non-risky) aesthetic attributes of the site. The distance gradient is also incapable of estimating the benefits of a partial reduction in the risk, which is usually the EPA's goal.

By incorporating objective cancer-risk measures in the hedonic property model, we can estimate the change in housing prices given any level of risk reduction. To compare these implied benefits with the cost of remediation, we compute the change in prices before the release of the Remedial Investigation. For example, using the coefficient estimates of equation (2) in table 2, we find that a reduction of individual cancer risk by 1.81E-06 (the mean level of Superfund site risk to an individual in a household) before the release of the Remedial Investigation results in a price increase of $238 per household (in 1996 dollars). With 42,598 households within the relevant census tracts, the total

price change (an upper-bound measure of welfare benefits) is $10.1 million for reducing cancer risks at the six sites. Using the Box-Cox coefficient estimates, a reduction of household cancer risk by the mean level before the release of the Remedial Investigation results in a price increase of $232 per household, and a total price change of $9.9 million.

These estimates of the value of risk reduction are much smaller than the EPA's estimated costs of remediating the sites. The total present value cost of the EPA's remediation plans for the six greater Grand Rapids Superfund sites is $56.8 million. By contrast, the total present value cost of only institutional controls (such as fencing and deed restrictions) would have been $5.4 million had they been implemented at the six sites.[20] Using residents' valuations of cancer-risk reductions, permanent remedies would not pass this test of cost versus implicit willingness to pay, although the use of institutional controls to restrict access to sites would.

By evaluating the price gradient with respect to cancer risk, we can estimate the value of a statistical cancer case. The methodology is similar to value-of-life studies, in which a wage hedonic is used to determine the gradient with respect to job risk (Viscusi, 1992). In the job risk literature, the wage compensation for an incremental change in job fatality risk is divided by the risk increment, resulting in the value of a statistical life. Viscusi (1981) demonstrated that value-of-life estimates are heterogeneous over different risk levels. Different members of the population attach different values to risk. People who are most tolerant of risk are drawn to the riskier jobs, and higher wages must be paid to lure additional workers into risky jobs. Such heterogeneity of risk preferences illustrates the complexity that is inherent in policy applications. Value-of-life estimates obtained from a certain population of workers may not be appropriate for another population. While hedonic wage studies have been quite successful in estimating compensation to workers for job risk, values may be quite different for populations including non-workers, white-collar workers, or children.

Previous attempts have been made to obtain risk-dollar tradeoffs in market transactions other than the job market. Unlike the labor market studies, many of these attempts rely on imputing values for at least one component of the tradeoff. For example, studies attempting to evaluate the risk-dollar tradeoff associated with aspects of auto safety (Ghosh, Lees, & Seal, 1975; Blomquist, 1979) assume that

---

[20] For each of the sites, the costs (converted to 1996 dollars) of the proposed remediation plans are as follows: Butterworth, $19.4 million; Chem-Central, $2.6 million; Folkertsma, $1.9 million; H. Brown, $18.8 million; Kentwood, $7.1 million; Organic Chemical, $7.4. The costs of the institutional controls had they been implemented are as follows: Butterworth, $2.3 million; Chem-Central, $0.6 million; Folkertsma, $0.7 million; H. Brown, $0.6 million; Kentwood, $0.7 million; Organic Chemical, $0.6 million. One reason for the high cleanup costs could be the EPA's preference for more-permanent remediation actions, even though the benefits of permanence are still uncertain. Gupta, Van Houtven, and Cropper (1996) show that the premium that the EPA places on onsite incineration of waste (over and above the cost of capping it) is $12 million at small sites and up to $40 million at large sites (1987 dollars).

PRIVATE VALUES OF RISK TRADEOFFS AT SUPERFUND SITES   449

TABLE 4.—ESTIMATES OF THE VALUE OF AVOIDING A STATISTICAL CANCER
CASE (IN MILLIONS OF DOLLARS, 1996)

Equation Estimates	Value of Cancer before RI	Value of Cancer after RI
Equation (1)	NA	$4.1
Equation (2)	$51.1	$3.9
Equation (3)	$51.3	$3.9
Box-Cox	$49.9	$4.6

the wage rate equals the opportunity cost of time associated with driving fast or using seat belts.

The objective risk measures used in this study pertain to the cancer risk to an individual living in the household. To determine the value of a statistical cancer to an individual, the average household size must be divided into the risk coefficient. According to the 1990 Census, the average number of members per household in the pertinent census tracts (computed by matching block group data to the sample) was 2.573.

Table 4 lists the estimates for the statistical value of cancer given different specifications.[21] Equation (1) considers the effect of objective risk on housing prices only after the Remedial Investigation. Using this parameter estimate, the value-of-cancer estimate after the Remedial Investigation is $4.1 million. Using the estimates of equation (2) in table 2 and dividing by the number of people per household results in a value-of-cancer estimate of $51.1 million before the release of the Remedial Investigation and $3.9 million after the release of the Remedial Investigation. To test whether the publicity picks up some of the effect of risk on housing prices, equation (3) in table 2 drops the *News* variable from the regression. The value-of-cancer estimate before the Remedial Investigation increases by only approximately $200,000 dollars, and there is no change in the value-of-cancer estimate after the Remedial Investigation. Using the coefficient estimates in the Box-Cox model, the value-of-cancer estimate before the Remedial Investigation is $49.9 million. After the Remedial Investigation, the value-of-cancer estimate is $4.6 million.

The value-of-cancer estimates before the release of the Remedial Investigation are roughly an order of magnitude larger than the value-of-life estimates found in job market studies. This finding suggests that risk biases could affect individual reactions to Superfund risks before the EPA releases its Remedial Investigation.[22] Residents update their risk perceptions after the release of the Remedial Investigation, and the resulting value-of-cancer estimates of $3.9 million to $4.6 million are very similar to the value-of-life estimates found in job market studies.[23] Once the EPA

[21] Estimates are computed at the mean housing price.
[22] Slovic, Fischhoff, and Lichtenstein (1982) and Tversky and Kahneman (1982) offer explanations of the cognitive heuristics that can lead to risk-perception biases.
[23] For example, Viscusi (1981) estimated value of life at $7.8 million, Garen (1988) at $16.1 million, Moore and Viscusi (1988) at $8.7 million (all estimates converted to 1996 dollars). See Viscusi (1992) for a complete survey.

TABLE 5.—MEAN WILLINGNESS TO PAY
FOR SUPERFUND-RELATED ATTRIBUTES

Sources of Estimates	Additional Mile from Closest Site	Removal of Industrial Site within 0.25 Mile Ring	House Sold Before Release of Remedial Investigation	One Fewer Word of Publicity in Previous Year
Equation (1)	$1,085	$1,588	$ 450	$ 0.19
	(145)	(323)	(409)	(0.08)
Equation (2)	$ 859	$1,486	$ 661	$ 0.17
	(145)	(323)	(404)	(0.08)
Equation (3)	$ 857	$1,486	$ 756	NA
	(145)	(323)	(402)	NA
Box-Cox	$ 627	$1,982	$ 520	$ 0.16
	(175)	(390)	(488)	(0.08)

Note: Standard errors in parentheses.

releases the Remedial Investigation, the value people place on avoiding Superfund risks is similar to the value they place on job market risk.

B. The Marginal Willingness to Pay for Housing Attributes

The coefficient estimates of equations (1), (2), and (3), as well as the coefficient estimates of the Box-Cox equation, can determine the mean marginal willingness to pay for various attributes. The hedonic price function reflects the tangency of the consumer offer curves with the price function; thus, the marginal price of an attribute is equivalent to the marginal willingness to pay. Table 5 presents the results for multiple attributes.[24]

Using the coefficient estimates from equation (1) of table 2, we find that the marginal willingness to pay for an additional mile from the closest site is $1,085. The marginal willingness to pay for one fewer non-NPL CERCLA site, RCRA site, or PCS site within 0.25 mile of the house is $1,588. An additional printed word about any of the Superfund sites decreases a house's price by $0.19.

Replacing the variables that measure the risk indicators with the actual risk does not result in markedly different estimates for the willingness to pay for the Superfund-related attributes. The estimates from equation (2) of table 2 indicate that the marginal willingness to pay for an additional mile from the closest site is $859. The marginal willingness to pay for one fewer non-NPL CERCLA site, RCRA site, or PCS site within 0.25 mile of the house is $1,486. An additional printed word about any of the Superfund sites decreases a house's price by $0.17. With the average newspaper article on the local Superfund sites being 550 words in length, the price decrease is $94 per article.

The results indicate that a house sold before the release of the EPA risk information on the closest site sold for $661 more than one sold after the information was made public. Thus, while the impact of risk on housing prices diminishes after the release of the Remedial Investigation, housing

[24] The marginal prices are evaluated at the mean housing price. All figures are in 1996 dollars.

prices nonetheless decrease after the release of the Remedial Investigation.[25]

The coefficient estimates from equation (3) of table 2 yield very similar estimates of marginal willingness to pay for the various attributes. The marginal willingness to pay for an additional mile from the closest site is $857. A house sold before the release of the Remedial Investigation for the closest site sold for $756 more than one sold after the Remedial Investigation was made public.

The marginal willingness to pay for a unit reduction of a non-NPL CERCLA site, RCRA site, or PCS site within 0.25 mile of the house is $1,486. This estimate for the value of a removal of one non-NPL CERCLA site, RCRA site, or PCS site within 0.25 mile of the house is equivalent to a cancer-risk reduction of 1.7E-05.[26] Of the 850 RCRA sites studied in a Regulatory Impact Analysis, 640 of the sites had risk estimates between 1.0E-06 and 1.0E-04. Housing-price reactions to RCRA sites imply resident assessments of risk similar to those estimates in the RCRA Regulatory Impact Analysis. For comparison, the mean level of risk from a greater Grand Rapids Superfund site within 0.25 mile is 1.16E-04.

The Box-Cox coefficient estimates yield slightly different estimates of the marginal willingness to pay for attributes. The marginal willingness to pay for an additional mile from the closest site is $627. The marginal willingness to pay for one fewer non-NPL CERCLA site, RCRA site, or PCS site within 0.25 mile of the house is $1,982. An additional printed word about any of the sites decreases the price by $0.16. A house sold before the release of the EPA's Remedial Investigation for the closest site sold for $520 more than one sold after the Remedial Investigation was made public.

Our estimates indicate that removing a hazardous-waste site that is not a Superfund site yields a benefit between $1,486 and $1,982 for a household within 0.25 mile of the site. Using the other estimated coefficients for the *Sites* variables, we find that the average benefit of removing a site (to a resident within one mile of the site) ranges from $385 to $714. These estimates are similar to those found in Stock (1991), who estimated the benefit to an average household in suburban Boston from removing the Nyanza hazardous-waste site (located in Ashland, MA). His unrestricted OLS model found a benefit ranging from $487 to $885, and his nonparametric model found a benefit ranging from $155 to $161. (All estimates are converted to 1996 dollars.)[27]

---

[25] The marginal value of a house sold after the release of the Remedial Investigation is computed as the change in price with respect to a change in the dummy variable, and is evaluated at the mean level of risk. This net impact of the dummy variable differs from the analysis of the change in the impact of risk on prices after the release of the Remedial Investigation, which is represented by the interaction term.

[26] This estimate was determined by taking the mean willingness to pay for removal of a non-NPL CERCLA, RCRA, or PCS site and calculating the Superfund cancer risk that yields the same mean willingness to pay.

[27] Stock (1991) estimated that the total value of a cleanup of the Ashland site ranged from $7 million to $42 million (in 1996 dollars).

VI. Conclusion

Assessing the cost effectiveness of the EPA's Superfund program requires comparing the costs of the program with the benefits accrued from the reduction in the health risk. Previous studies have suggested that people overreact to the threats from hazardous wastes, resulting in an inefficient outcome in which the EPA spends too much on remediation. Pressures for public spending or safety, however, may be quite different from private willingness to pay amounts. Our results suggest that residents have heightened perceptions of the risks from Superfund sites before they receive the information provided in the Remedial Investigation. When the residents are informed of the risks through the EPA's Remedial Investigation, and when they must spend their own funds to avoid the Superfund risks, their willingness to pay is similar to tradeoffs made in other encounters with risk, such as those made in labor market decisions.

Before the EPA releases the Remedial Investigation, the estimated willingness to pay for a risk reduction implies an upper-bound benefit of cleaning up the six sites ranging between $9.1 million and $10.1 million for a reduction of the mean level of cancer risk. For comparison, the total present value cost of the EPA's remediation plans for the six neighborhood Superfund sites is $56.8 million. Had the EPA undertaken only institutional controls for the remediation, the total present value cost would be $5.4 million, a figure more consistent with values implied by residents' willingness to pay to avoid Superfund risk.

The housing choices in the greater Grand Rapids housing market provide evidence on private valuation of Superfund risk reduction. The findings indicate that, after the EPA releases its Remedial Investigation, the tradeoff between cancer risk and housing prices is similar in magnitude to the tradeoff between mortality risk and wages found in previous labor market studies. This similarity suggests that there appears to be no evidence that people substantially overestimate the risk of cancer when making informed decisions for which they must pay for greater safety.

REFERENCES

Bartik, Timothy J., "The Estimation of Demand Parameters with Single Market Data: The Problems Caused by Unobserved Tastes," *Journal of Political Economy* 95 (1987), 81–88.
—— "Measuring the Benefits of Amenity Improvements in Hedonic Price Models," *Land Economics* 64(2) (1988), 172–183.
Bartik, Timothy J., and V. Kerry Smith, "Urban Amenities and Public Policy," in Edwin S. Mills (Ed.), *Handbook on Urban Economics* (Amsterdam: North-Holland, 1987).
Blomquist, Glenn C., "Value of Life Saving Implications of Consumption Activity," *Journal of Political Economy* 96 (1979), 675–700.
Combs, Barbara, and Paul Slovic, "Causes of Death: Biased Newspaper Coverage and Biased Judgments," *Journalism Quarterly* 56 (1979), 837–843.
Cropper, Maureen L., Leland B. Deck, and Kenneth E. McConnell, "On the Choice of Functional Form for Hedonic Price Functions," this REVIEW 70(4) (1988), 668–675.
Epple, Dennis, "Hedonic Prices and Implicit Markets: Estimating Demand and Supply Functions for Differentiated Products," *Journal of Political Economy* 95 (1987), 59–80.

PRIVATE VALUES OF RISK TRADEOFFS AT SUPERFUND SITES   451

Garen, John, "Compensating Wage Differentials and the Endogeneity of Job Riskiness," this REVIEW 70(1) (1988), 9–16.

Ghosh, Debapriya, Dennis Lees, and William Seal, "Optimal Motorway Speed and Some Valuations of Time and Life," *Manchester School of Economics and Social Studies* 43 (1975), 134–143.

Gupta, Shreekant, George Van Houtven, and Maureen Cropper, "Paying for Permanence: An Economic Analysis of EPA's Cleanup Decisions at Superfund Sites," *RAND Journal of Economics* 27(3) (1996), 563–582.

Hamilton, James T., and W. Kip Viscusi, "How Costly is 'Clean'? An Analysis of the Benefits and Costs of Superfund Site Remediations," *Journal of Policy Analysis and Management* 18(1) (1999), 2–27.

Harrison, David, and James H. Stock, "Hedonic Housing Value, Local Public Goods, and the Benefits of Hazardous Waste Cleanup," *Energy and Environmental Policy Center,* John F. Kennedy School of Government, Harvard University (1984).

Kahn, Shulamit, and Kevin Lang, "Efficient Estimation of Structural Hedonic Systems," *International Economic Review* 29(1) (1988), 157–166.

Kiel, Katherine, and Katherine T. McClain, "House Prices during Siting Decision Stages: The Case of an Incinerator from Rumor through Operation," *Journal of Environmental Economics and Management* 28 (1995), 241–255.

Kohlhase, Janet E., "The Impact of Toxic Waste Sites on Housing Values," *Journal of Urban Economics* 30 (1991), 1–26.

Lichtenstein, Sara, Paul Slovic, Baruch Fischhoff, Ulaark Layman, and Barbara Combs, "Judged Frequency of Lethal Events," *Journal of Experimental Psychology: Human Learning and Memory* 4 (1978), 551–578.

McClelland, Gary H., William D. Schulze, and Brian Hurd, "The Effect of Risk Beliefs on Property Values: A Case Study of a Hazardous Waste Site," *Risk Analysis* 10(4) (1990), 485–497.

Michaels, R. Gregory, and V. Kerry Smith, "Market Segmentation and Valuing Amenities with Hedonic Models: The Case of Hazardous Waste Sites," *Journal of Urban Economics* 28 (1990), 223–242.

Moore, Michael, and W. Kip Viscusi, "The Quantity-Adjusted Value of Life," *Economic Inquiry* 26(3) (1988), 369–388.

Palmquist, Raymond B., "Valuing Localized Externalities," *Journal of Urban Economics* 31 (1992), 59–68.

Portney, Paul R., "Housing Prices, Health Effects, and Valuing Reductions in Risk of Death," *Journal of Environmental Economics and Management* 8 (1981), 72–78.

Rosen, Sherwin, "Hedonic Prices and Implicit Markets: Product Differentiation in Pure Competition," *Journal of Political Economy* 82 (1974), 34–55.

Slovic, Paul, Baruch Fischhoff, and Sara Lichtenstein, "Facts Versus Fears: Understanding Perceived Risks," in Daniel Kahneman, Paul Slovic, and Amos Tversky (Eds.), *Judgment Under Uncertainty: Heuristics and Biases* (Cambridge, UK: Cambridge University Press, 1982).

Stock, James H., "Nonparametric Policy Analysis: An Application to Estimating Hazardous Waste Cleanup Benefits," in William A. Bennett, James Powell, and George E. Tauchen (Eds.), *Nonparametric and Semiparametric Methods in Econometrics and Statistics: Proceedings of the Fifth International Symposium in Economic Theory and Econometrics, Cambridge* (New York: Cambridge University Press, 1991).

Tversky, Amos, and Daniel Kahneman, "Judgment Under Uncertainty: Heuristics and Biases," in Daniel Kahneman, Paul Slovic, and Amos Tversky (Eds.), *Judgment Under Uncertainty: Heuristics and Biases* (Cambridge, UK: Cambridge University Press, 1982).

U.S. Environmental Protection Agency, *Unfinished Business: A Comparative Assessment of Environmental Problems* (1987).

Viscusi, W. Kip, *Employment Hazards: An Investigation of Market Performance* (Cambridge, MA: Harvard University Press, 1979).

——— "Occupational Safety and Health Regulation: Its Impact and Policy Alternatives," in John P. Crecine (Ed.), *Research in Public Policy Analysis and Management* (Greenwich, CT: JAI Press, 1981).

——— (1992). *Fatal Tradeoffs: Public and Private Responsibilities for Risk* (New York: Oxford University Press, 1992).

Viscusi, W. Kip and James T. Hamilton, "Cleaning Up Superfund," *The Public Interest* 124 (Summer) (1996), 52–60.

——— "Are Risk Regulators Rational? Evidence from Hazardous Waste Cleanup Decisions," *American Economic Review* 89(4) (1999), 1010–1027.

Zeckhauser, Richard, "Combining Overlapping Information," *Journal of the American Statistical Association* 66 (1971), 91–92.

Part IV
Discounting and the Quantity of Life

[25]

THE QUANTITY-ADJUSTED VALUE OF LIFE

MICHAEL J. MOORE and W. KIP VISCUSI*

The traditional compensating differential analysis is extended to reflect the effects on wages of the duration of life at risk and of insurance benefits to the surviving spouse and dependents. The implicit discount rate that workers use in making their life-cycle employment decisions is also estimated. The revealed discount rate ranges from 10 to 12 percent, and the implicit value per year of life is $175,000. There is also evidence of significant wage reductions resulting from higher workers' compensation benefits for fatal and nonfatal injuries, suggesting an important trade-off between ex ante and ex post compensation for risk.

I. INTRODUCTION

In the past decade, labor economists have devoted substantial effort to analyzing Adam Smith's proposition in *The Wealth of Nations* that workers will demand compensating differentials for health and safety risks and for other unattractive job characteristics.[1] Although this theoretical proposition is not controversial, attempts to estimate these differentials have yielded mixed results, with various measures of the riskiness of the job yielding the strongest findings.

Two simplifying assumptions are typically made in the empirical death-risk and injury-risk studies. First, the measure of risk used—the probability of a fatal or nonfatal accident—abstracts altogether from life-cycle issues such as variation across individuals in the potential losses resulting from death or injury.[2] Some losses, such as immediate pain and suffering and medical expenses, are likely to be similar across individuals for similar accidents. In the case of nonfatal accidents, it is probably not too great a simplification to assume that these losses are similar for different persons, since the duration of a given injury type is not highly variable. There may be greater differences, however, in the financial losses and the associated reduction in utility that result from

* Assistant Professor, Duke University and George G. Allen Professor of Economics, Duke University. This research was supported in part by the Business Associates Fund at the Fuqua School of Business, and by the University of Chicago Center for the Study of the Economy and the State through a grant from the John M. Olin Foundation. Preliminary versions of this paper were presented at the University of Chicago, Duke University, the University of Illinois, the U.S. Environmental Protection Agency, Northwestern University, and the 1986 Summer Meetings of the Labor Studies Program of the National Bureau of Economic Research. The editor and an anonymous referee provided helpful comments.

1. The result that compensating differentials must exist to lead workers to accept hazardous jobs is shown for a wide variety of contexts in Viscusi [1979]. Also see Adam Smith [1776], Thaler and Rosen [1976], Smith [1976, 1979], and Viscusi [1983, 1986], among others, for contributions to this literature.

2. Theoretical analyses of life-cycle job risk models have appeared in the literature. See, for example, Conley [1976], Viscusi [1979], and Arthur [1981].

369

a permanent change in health status, particularly with respect to the extreme loss of welfare that results from death.

In the case of fatalities, a young person loses a much greater amount of lifetime utility than does an older person, a source of variation in risk that has not been reflected in past empirical studies of the value of life. In this paper, this variation is incorporated by weighting the standard death risk measure by the remaining life of each sample member. More specifically, the information used includes expected lifetimes, the worker's current age, a discount rate that is computed as part of the estimation process, and measures of death risk. This information makes it possible to calculate the worker's expected remaining life at risk, reflecting the fact that the worker's principal concern is not simply the probability of a fatal accident, but the discounted duration of life and the associated lifetime utility at risk on the job. This discounted duration of life at risk is referred to below as the quantity-adjusted death risk and is used in calculating the quantity-adjusted value of life. The quantity-adjusted value of life differs from conventional estimates of the value of life in that the trade-off is not between wages and death risk probabilities, but between wages and death risks that have been weighted by the discounted number of potential years of life lost.

Obtaining a quantity-adjusted measure of the value of life also has potentially important policy implications. Analysts have long noted that the appropriate value of life for policy analysis cannot be divorced from the duration of life involved since lives are extended, not permanently saved.[3] The task of actually developing a measure of the value of life that incorporates changes in expected lifetime utility has never been undertaken, however, in large part because there was no sound empirical basis for doing so. The results reported here will take into account quite explicitly the influence of the duration of life.

A related issue arises in obtaining these quantity-adjusted measures. That is, what discount rate do people use in valuing their future utilities? Estimates of discount rates have appeared elsewhere in the literature, as in the studies by Fuchs [1982], Hausman [1979], Lang and Rudd [1986], and Weiss [1972], but none of these studies addressed the job risk problem. The closest of these studies to the health risk issues considered here is that of Fuchs. His analysis obtained rates of time preference from survey questions relating to financial opportunities at different dates, which he then related to health concerns such as cigarette smoking.

Estimated discount rates that diverge substantially from the financial market rates faced by workers are of interest in their own right to the extent that these diversions provide evidence pertaining to irrationality in the valuation of future health losses. It has long been suggested that people are myopic in

3. Zeckhauser and Shepard [1976] provide an extensive policy discussion of their concept of quality-adjusted life years. Arthur [1981], Shepard and Zeckhauser [1984], Rosen [1988], and Cropper and Sussman [1986] have developed elaborate life-cycle models. Arthur and Rosen explicitly treat the quantity of life effects that are the principal focus here.

their risk-taking decisions. This issue is addressed quite explicitly in this paper by comparing estimated discount rates to financial market interest rates for the period. These estimated rates are also of interest in that they suggest the appropriate rate of time preference to use in discounting future effects of health and safety policy.

A second simplification that until recently has been applied universally in wage-risk studies is the omission of expected ex post compensation for accidents in the form of accident insurance benefits available to workers.[4] Practically every state now provides workers' compensation insurance, so that approximately 90 percent of the work force is covered by some form of accident insurance. From a conceptual standpoint, increases in ex post compensation for accidents should reduce ex ante compensation and should, if possible, be incorporated explicitly in any analysis of the relationship between wages and job risks. Ex post compensation is taken into account by including in the estimating equation a death benefit variable that reflects the worker's marital status, spouse's remainaing life, number of dependents, and characteristics of the state workers' compensation system covering each worker. These benefits are also discounted at a rate that is calculated in the process of estimation.

In section II, the data used in the analysis, from the 1977 University of Michigan Quality of Employment Survey, are described. These survey data are coupled with risk and insurance variables that are collected from external sources and matched to workers in the sample. In section III, estimates of compensating differential equations are presented; they include both the quantity-adjusted risks to life and the present value of death benefits to the surviving spouse as regressors. Estimates are also reported that condition the industry risk measures on individual assessments of working conditions, thus controlling partially for the measurement error that has impeded many previous attempts to match industry data to workers in micro data sets.

In all of the cases considered, there is strong support of the hypothesized rationality of employment decisions. Workers receive wage premiums for exposure to risk that reflect the remaining lifetime at risk. They trade ex post for ex ante compensation for exposure to risks, and they discount future utilities and the utilities of their heirs at rates consistent with observed explicit interest rates.

II. DESCRIPTION OF THE SAMPLE AND THE VARIABLES

The empirical analysis utilizes the 1977 Quality of Employment Survey. This survey, which pertains to workers' employment experience in 1976, represents the third in a series of such surveys beginning with the 1969–70 Survey of Working Conditions and the 1972–73 Quality of Employment Survey. The 1977 data set shares with its predecessors a detailed set of job characteristic questions, making it possible to disentangle premiums for job risks from other

---

4. The following studies include measures of workers' compensation benefits for nonfatal injuries: Arnould and Nichols [1983], Viscusi and Moore [1987a, 1987b], Moore and Viscusi [forthcoming], Butler [1983], and Dorsey and Walzer [1983].

job attributes correlated with riskiness. Past studies of these data sets in a similar vein include Duncan's [1976] and Viscusi's [1979] analyses of the Survey of Working Conditions and Viscusi and Moore's [1987b] paper on nonfatal risks using the 1977 Quality of Employment Survey.

The 1977 data offer two major advantages over their predecessors. First, the survey ascertains the worker's hourly wage so that one need not use annual earnings as the dependent variable. Second, the timing of the survey makes it possible to match more reliable industry risk measures to workers in the sample. Mandatory industry reporting of injuries to the U.S. Bureau of Labor Statistics did not begin until the 1970s, with the first publicly released figures issued in 1972. Because of confusion over reporting requirements, early reports on nonfatal injuries are unreliable. The survey year 1976 thus permits sufficient time for these reporting practices for nonfatal risks to become stabilized, and it offers several years of retrospective data on death risks.

In many compensating differential studies it is necessary to restrict the sample to male or blue collar workers to estimate wage premiums successfully. Such restrictions were not required for the 1977 Quality of Employment Survey because the detailed job characteristic questions made it possible to disentangle the role of job risks in influencing workers' wages. The sample was restricted to nonfarm household heads who were not self-employed and who worked more than twenty hours per week. Workers in industries for which the Bureau of Labor Statistics does not gather death statistics were also excluded. Thus, for example, government employees were not included in the sample.

Table I defines the key variables, and Table II summarizes many of the principal characteristics of the sample of 317 workers. The sample has an average age of thirty-eight, 6 percent black workers, and 8 percent female workers. About one-fifth of the workers have not completed high school, one-fourth have some college education, less than one-fifth have a college degree plus additional training, and the remaining two-fifths have a high school diploma. The average firm size for workers is 783 employees. Almost two-thirds of the workers hold blue-collar jobs, and 39 percent are union members.

The dependent variable in the analysis is the worker's after-tax hourly wage rate. Since workers' compensation benefits are included in the equation in their after-tax form (benefits are tax exempt), for comparability the wage variable is the worker's after-tax hourly wage in 1976 dollars. These taxes include both state and Federal income taxes and are calculated using infor-mation on the worker's wage rate and family structure.[5] We assume that each worker took the standard deduction. This tax adjustment of wages, which appears to be the first such correction in the literature on compensating dif-ferentials for job hazards, is clearly preferable theoretically and had an influ-ence on some of the tests of statistical significance of the coefficients.

Three job risk variables are used in the analysis. The first and most important is the worker's death risk. The approach used matches the workers in the

_____

5. Tax rates for 1976 are from Commerce Clearing House, Inc. [1977a, 1977b].

sample to a death risk variable based on death risk statistics for the worker's two-digit industry.[6] Since death risks involve a low probability of death (on the order of 5/100,000 per worker in this sample), even at this level of aggregation death risks may vary substantially across years, particularly if there is a major catastrophe that results in multiple deaths. To eliminate the distorting influence of such random fluctuations, we use as our death risk measure the average probability of death over the 1973–76 period. Unlike the nonfatal accident statistics, death rate data were not subject to the classification problems that were present in the early 1970s under the new reporting requirements. Use of shorter term average measures yielded little change in our results.

The main focus of this paper is on the quantity of life adjustment of the standard death risk measure. Information on the worker's age, race, sex, and remaining life data from life expectancy tables are used to calculate the remaining life of worker i, R_i.[7] Discounted remaining life years are then

$$\text{Discounted Remaining Life}_i = (1/r)[1 - \exp(-rR_i)],$$

where r is the worker's rate of time preference. Weighting the discounted remaining life by the probability of a fatality yields the expected discounted life years lost variable,

$$\text{Expected Life Years Lost}_i = \text{Death Risk}_i \times \text{Discounted Remaining Life}_i.$$

The variable representing expected life years lost is inserted as a regressor in a compensating differential equation to estimate the impact of changes in expected remaining lifetime on wages. Since this particular risk variable is a nonlinear function of the discount rate parameter, it is necessary to estimate the model using nonlinear regression techniques.

It is useful to interpret the effect of expected life years lost on wages in the context of Arthur's [1981] theoretical paper on the value of extensions to life. In a general equilibrium intertemporal consumption-loans model, Arthur shows that the welfare gains associated with a reduction in age-specific risks consist of three forces affecting consumption—the increase due to lengthened life, and the increased productivity that is due to both increased work years and increased births over the extended life span. These gains are offset to an unknown degree by the fact that the increased consumption during later years must be financed by someone's decreased consumption. This last term is shown by Arthur to depend upon the consumption elasticity of utility, a parameter that has been estimated elsewhere by Viscusi and Moore [1987a] and by Rosen [1988]. If this elasticity has a value close to zero, financing considerations can effectively be ignored, since extended life affects utility independently of the changes in consumption that it entails. In Viscusi and Moore [1987a] this

---

6. This level of detail in terms of industry aggregation is greater than is available from published sources. Death risk measures were obtained by copying death statistics manually from the death statistic files at the Bureau of Labor Statistics office in Washington.

7. Life expectancies are taken from U.S. Department of Health and Human Services [1980].

TABLE I
Variable Definitions

Variable	Definition
Age	Age in years.
Race	Race dummy variable (d.v.): 1 if worker is black, 0 otherwise.
Sex	Sex d.v.: 1 if worker is female, 0 otherwise.
Poor health status	Severity of health limitation d.v.: 1 if limiting physical or nervous condition has created either sizable or great problems in working on or in getting jobs, 0 otherwise.
Less than high school education	Education d.v.: 1 if worker did not finish high school, 0 otherwise.
High school education	Education d.v.: 1 if worker finished high school, 0 otherwise.
Some college education	Education d.v.: 1 if worker has some college education, 0 otherwise.
College degree	Education d.v.: 1 if worker has at least a college degree, 0 otherwise.
Experience	Experience variable: years worked for pay since age 16.
Firm size	Firm size: midpoints assigned to intervals.
Blue-collar occupation	Collar color d.v.: 1 if the worker is in a blue collar occupation, 0 otherwise.
Union status	Union status d.v.: 1 if worker belongs to a union or employee's association, 0 otherwise.
Wage	Computed hourly after-tax wage measure.
Fast work pace	Work pace d.v.: 1 if job requires worker to work very fast a lot, 0 otherwise.
Job security	Job security d.v.: 1 if it is very true that the worker's job security is good, 0 otherwise.
Supervisory status	Supervisory status d.v.: 1 if worker supervises anyone as part of his job, 0 otherwise.
Overtime work requirements	Overtime work d.v.: 1 if worker works overtime often, 0 otherwise.
Availability of training	Training program d.v.: 1 if employer makes available a training program to improve worker skills, 0 otherwise.
Fatal accident rate	BLS industry hazard variable: average annual fatality rate by 2-digit SIC code, averaged over 1973–76 period.
Lost workday accident rate	BLS industry hazard variable: annual incidence rate of lost workday cases by 3-digit SIC code.
Hazard perceptions	Hazardous working conditions d.v.: 1 if worker cited at least one dangerous or unhealthy working condition, 0 otherwise.
Replacement rate	Workers' compensation replacement rate: benefit level/wage.
r	Discount rate.
Residence in an urban area	Urban area d.v.: 1 if worker lives in a major SMSA, 0 otherwise.
Marginal tax rate	Marginal federal and state income tax rate.

TABLE I
Continued

Variable	Definition
R	Expected remaining life of worker, based on reported age, race, and sex. Remaining life reported in Census life tables.
S	Spouse's expected remaining life.
Residence in the northeast region	Northeast region d.v.: 1 if worker lives in northeastern United States, 0 otherwise.
Residence in the southern region	Southeastern region d.v.: 1 if worker lives in southeastern U.S., 0 otherwise.
Residence in the north central region	North Central region d.v.: 1 if worker lives in north central U.S., 0 otherwise.
Residence in the western region	Western region d.v.: 1 if worker lives in western U.S., 0 otherwise.

parameter is estimated to be less than .10, while in Rosen [1988] it equals approximately .25, suggesting that the financing considerations associated with life extension are not of major consequence.

The remaining influences will be reflected in the wage equation if decreasing death risks increases productivity as well as utility. Otherwise, firms will not compensate workers for placing their life years, productivity, and fertility at risk, and workers will sort themselves into more risky jobs, the less important these considerations are. In principle, empirical separation of these influences is possible. In addition to the information on life years at risk, estimation of these effects would require data on both fertility and labor force participation over the life cycle. These factors could then be incorporated into the model to hold constant the fertility and productivity effects, allowing estimation of the "pure" value of extended life. Since these effects are not incorporated here, the gross estimates of the quantity adjusted value of life are overstated if expected life years lost are correlated with expected labor force participation and fertility gains effects, and if these factors increase wages.[8]

The second job risk measure included was the nonfatal lost workday accident rate for the worker's three-digit industry. This measure pertains to the incidence rate of nonfatal accidents that entail at least one lost day of work. Workers in the sample have an average annual probability of a lost workday injury of 1/20. This accident measure is a more reliable index of injuries than the total injury and illness rate, since the definition of what consitutes an accident is clearcut. Inclusion of this measure prevents the fatality risk variable from capturing the omitted influence of nonfatal risks.

The final accident measure is the worker's subjective assessment of whether

---

8. Of the two, it seems likely that increased participation will be compensated, while increased fertility will not. Based upon the results in Arthur, however, the participation effect is small relative to the life year effect (about 10 percent), so failure to include participation should not bias the results significantly.

TABLE II
Selected Sample Characteristics

Variable	Mean (Standard Deviation)
Age	38.09 (12.22)
Race	0.06 (0.24)
Sex	0.08 (0.27)
Less than high school education	0.22 (0.41)
Some college education	0.25 (0.44)
College degree	0.13 (0.33)
Experience	21.30 (12.49)
Firm size	783.82 (1110.54)
Blue collar occupation	0.63 (0.48)
Union status	0.39 (0.49)
Wage (after taxes)	5.49 (1.88)
Fatal accident rate (per 100,000 workers)	5.89 (8.98)
Lost workday accident rate (per 100 workers)	4.68 (2.38)
Hazard perceptions	0.85 (0.36)
Replacement rate	0.79 (0.35)
Sample size	317

the job exposes him to dangerous or unhealthy conditions. This binary variable assumes a value of one if the worker cites one or more hazards of his job. Unlike the more directive danger perception question in the Survey of Working Conditions data analyzed in Viscusi [1979], the 1977 Quality of Employment Survey does not ascertain explicitly whether a worker's' job poses any hazards but instead inquires whether he can cite specific risks. This change in wording contributed to a higher rate of danger perception than in previous surveys, as 85 percent of the sample viewed their job as exposing them to some health or safety risk.

A well-known problem with the use of industry data to measure individual level risks is that workers in the same industry face different risks in different occupations. Some of these job-specific variations can be taken into account by utilizing the question in the Quality of Employment Survey for which the worker reports his own perception of the presence or absence of hazards. That is, the industry level risk data can be conditioned by the presence of a perceived hazard, as in Viscusi [1979]. Multiplication of the binary hazard perception variable by the fatal and nonfatal industry injury rates yields a risk measure that equals zero if a worker perceives no risk on his job, and equals the industry risk level if the worker reports his job as hazardous.

The interpretation of expected life years lost is as a measure of lifetime exposure to job risk. The implication of this use of the measure is that, for given characteristics of the job and the worker, the lifetime utility at risk is greater for a younger person than for an older one. An alternative interpretation is that the quantity adjustment serves as a proxy for "tastes for risks," i.e., that younger workers have a lower aversion to risk and, therefore, choose a higher value of expected life years lost. If this were so, expected life years lost would not be a valid measure of risk, since it would be subject to the sorting problems inherent in the compensating differential model. In the case of pure taste-sorting, there would be no evidence of a risk premium for any given point on firms' offer curves. It is more likely, however, that younger workers (who typically work on more dangerous jobs) do so because they are more productive in those jobs than are older workers, and that firms are willing to compensate workers with greater exposure for their greater productivity.

Besides ex ante wage compensation for risk, workers also receive ex post compensation through the state workers' compensation programs. Higher workers' compensation levels should reduce the wage rates for workers in hazardous jobs. As shown in Viscusi and Moore [1987b], the theoretically appropriate measure of compensation for nonfatal injuries is the expected benefit amount, which equals the probability of an injury multiplied by the benefit level.

As a measure of insurance for nonfatal injuries, we use the expected earnings replacement rate, following a procedure discussed in Viscusi and Moore [1987b]. The variable involves an interaction of the probability of collecting benefits, which is given by the lost workday accident rate, and the wage replacement rate under workers' compensation. The workers' compensation replacement rate for nonfatal accidents is defined by b_i/w_i, where b_i is the benefit amount and w_i is the after-tax wage rate.

The benefits variable b_i is governed by complex formulas that vary by state. The measure adopted here uses the benefit amounts for permanent total disabilities, which account for the majority of all claims.[9] This measure takes into

---

9. Detailed actuarial measures of other benefit categories are not feasible. Viscusi and Moore [1987b] document the plausibility of this measure and its positive correlation with other benefit categories.

account state minimum and maximum benefit amounts, the relation of the benefit to the worker's wage rate, and the benefits' favorable tax status.[10] Although this variable only approximates actual expected benefits from all injury categories, it is the most detailed and pertinent workers' compensation measure included in a wage equation to date.[11] To prevent problems of endogeneity, the wage variable w_i in the denominator has been replaced by its predicted value from a first-stage regression.

The final benefit measure is the discounted expected annuity for survivors. Estimation of the wage equation using a wage replacement rate for death insurance produced results consistent with those reported below. However, since death benefits are a measure of lifetime compensation, the discounted lifetime annuity captures the nature of the benefit better than a current period replacement rate, and its effects are therefore reported below.

Based on the state death benefit formulas and the worker's wage rate, family structure, and state of residence, one can calculate the annual annuity amount, $A(b_i)$. The value of these benefits to the family of the deceased worker also depends on their duration. Using information on the spouse's age, race, and sex, and life expectancy tables, one can calculate the spouse's expected remaining lifetime S_i. The discounted value of the annuity is consequently

$$\text{Discounted Annuity}_i = (1/r)A(b_i)[1 - \exp(-rS_i)].$$

When there are no heirs, the annuity is assigned a value of zero.

For the purpose of the empirical analysis, the appropriate variable is the worker's expected annuity, where

$$\text{Expected Annuity}_i = \text{Death Risk}_i \times \text{Discounted Annuity}_i.$$

Estimates of the parameter r in the regressions using nonlinear techniques are reported below.

In principle, the discount rates applied to a worker's future utility and to the utilities of his heirs need not be equal. This restriction was tested as a preliminary step in the analysis; the hypothesis that workers weight the utilities of other family members equally could not be rejected. It should be noted, however, that estimation of two separate discount rates increases the demands placed upon the data substantially. The unconstrained estimates were therefore less precise than the single estimate reported below, and this imprecision is partially responsible for the failure to reject the restriction. In the unrestricted estimation, the worker's own discount rate has a statistically significant effect, as in the restricted estimates reported below.

Finally, each question includes a detailed set of other variables pertaining to the worker and his job. These variables include work experience (years

---

10. See U.S. Chamber of Commerce [1976].

11. In addition, as noted above, the expected replacement rate variable offers several additional refinements over those appearing in the literature, including recognition of their favorable tax status, the appropriateness of the interaction with the lost workday accident rate, and detailed calculation of the worker-specific benefit levels. See Viscusi and Moore [1987b] for detailed comparisons with other benefits approaches.

worked since age sixteen), and dummy variables indicating health status, speed of work, job security, whether the worker is a supervisor, overtime work requirements, training program availability, and residence in an urban area, the south, the west, or the north central United States. Of particular importance in the estimation are the job characteristic variables. These detailed job variables are not available in the larger data sets often used to estimate compensating differentials for working conditions, and in their absence industry dummy variables are necessary as a proxy for capturing differences in jobs correlated with the worker's industry. Inclusion of such industry dummy variables makes it difficult to estimate the effects of an industry-based job risk measure that is constructed using the industry information. Since the equations include several job-specific measures of job attributes, industry dummy variables are not necessary to control for industry differences in job characteristics.

III. EMPIRICAL RESULTS

The empirical analysis focuses on a series of wage equations. Both the after-tax wage and its natural logarithm are used as dependent variables to control for sensitivity of the results to this aspect of model specification. For each equation, two versions are estimated; one conditions the death risk variables by the dummy hazard perceptions variable, and one is an unconditional estimate.

The basic form of the model is given by the equation

$$
\begin{aligned}
\text{Wage}_i = {} & \alpha_0 + \alpha_1 \text{Expected Life Years Lost}_i + \alpha_2 \text{Expected Annuity}_i \\
& + \alpha_3 \text{Lost Workday Accident Rate}_i \\
& + \alpha_4 \text{Lost Workday Accident Rate}_i \times \text{Replacement Rate}_i \\
& + \Sigma_m \beta_m x_{im} + \epsilon_i,
\end{aligned}
\tag{1}
$$

and its semi-logarithmic counterpart, where the x_{im} are the aforementioned variables pertaining to the worker and his job.

This equation is in the same general spirit as the conventional compensating differential equation, with four important differences. First, the dependent variable is the after-tax hourly wage rate. An after-tax measure is especially appropriate to put wages and workers' compensation benefits on a comparable basis. Further, since it is the after-tax wage that is relevant to worker decisions, use of the pre-tax wages will introduce error into the dependent measure. Second, this is the first such equation to include the discounted expected value of the annuity in the estimating equation. Third, whereas some studies have included a workers' compensation variable analogous to the expected replacement rate, no such analysis has also included a fatality risk measure in the wage equation.[12] Finally, and most importantly, the death risk measure (expected life years lost) takes into consideration the discounted duration of remaining life that is at risk on the job. Expected life years lost is the worker's

---

12. Arnould and Nichols[1983] include the fatality rate as the risk measure and average workers' compensation replacement rates for injuries as the benefit measure.

discounted remaining life multiplied by the death risk, or discounted expected life years lost. This adjustment of the standard death risk variable reflects the fact that what is at stake is not death per se, but loss of years of life, that the amount of life lost is of consequence, and that individuals discount the utility attached to future years of life. The discount rate used in adjusting remaining life is computed in the estimation process. The procedure does not constrain the discount rate to be nonzero, so that the possibility that workers do not discount is not ruled out a priori.

Finally, both weighted and unweighted estimates are reported; they are derived using the two-stage technique proposed by Amemiya [1977]. Heteroskedasticity, which is common in cross section data, is usually ignored in compensating differential studies. However, given the nonlinear nature of this model, controlling for heteroskedasticity is crucial, since bias in estimates of standard errors carries over to estimates of the coefficients in this case. As shown below, weighting produced important changes in some significance levels.

In constructing the weights, it was assumed that the variances of the individual error terms, ϵ_i, were approximately a linear function of the vector z. This vector z included worker experience in both linear and squared forms, nonfatal and fatal risks, and annuity terms. These variables were chosen based on residual plots from unweighted estimates, and entered as regressors in an equation with e_i^2 as the dependent variable, where e_i is the nonlinear least squares residual. This procedure was iterated twice, yielding estimates of weights that have been shown by Amemiya [1977] to be asymptotically normal and consistent.

Table III reports weighted and unweighted nonlinear least squares estimates of equation (1). A nonlinear least squares technique was required to estimate the worker's implicit discount rate. The control variables (x_{im}) generally perform as expected. Education increases wages, as does residence in an urban area, and black and female workers earn significantly lower wages.[13] The race variable is not statistically significant, no doubt because there were only nineteen black workers in the sample. In the unweighted results, a year of experience increases wages by three-tenths of a percent. Poor health causes a reduction in wages of 14 percent that is in the expected direction but is not significantly different from zero.

The job-related variables perform in a manner similar to studies that used the earlier surveys—the 1970 Survey of Working Conditions and the 1973 Quality of Employment Survey.[14] Union members receive a wage premium of 14 percent, and workers in large firms have higher wages, consistent with previous research. Workers in blue-collar occupations earn, on average, 13 percent less than those in white-collar jobs. Of those job characteristic variables

---

13. For purposes of estimation, the categorical variables indicating a high school degree and residence in the northeast are excluded.

14. The most extensive analyses of the Survey of Working Conditions are Viscusi [1979] and Duncan [1976]. Moore [1984] utilizes the 1973 survey.

TABLE III
Ln(Wage) Equation Estimates of Unconditional Risk Model* Coefficients
and Standard Errors

Independent Variable	Unweighted Estimates	Weighted Estimates
Race	−0.028	−0.085
	(0.071)	(0.073)
Sex	−0.255	−0.273
	(0.066)	(0.068)
Poor health status	−0.139	−0.124
	(0.096)	(0.100)
Less than high school education	−0.095	−0.071
	(0.046)	(0.047)
Some college education	−0.034	−0.023
	(0.043)	(0.045)
College degree	0.096	0.123
	(0.046)	(0.062)
Experience	0.003	0.002
	(0.001)	(0.002)
Firm size	$5.2E - 5$	$4.9E - 5$
	$(1.7E - 5)$	$(1.9E - 5)$
Blue-collar occupation	−0.128	−0.148
	(0.042)	(0.043)
Union status	0.141	0.145
	(0.041)	(0.042)
Fast work pace	−0.069	−0.072
	(0.045)	(0.048)
Job security	0.051	0.060
	(0.034)	(0.035)
Supervisory status	0.065	0.043
	(0.038)	(0.039)
Overtime work requirements	−0.043	−0.041
	(0.036)	(0.038)
Availability of training	0.044	0.035
	(0.037)	(0.039)
Lost workday accident rate	0.049	0.058
	(0.013)	(0.014)
Lost workday accident rate × replacement rate	−0.048	−0.055
	(0.013)	(0.013)
Expected life years lost	11.945	17.732
	(6.861)	(5.880)
Expected annuity	$-1.4E - 3$	$-2.4E - 3$
	$(0.7E - 3)$	$(0.8E - 3)$
r (discount rate)	0.096	0.122
	(0.063)	(0.043)
$\bar{R}^2$	0.387	0.390

* Each equation also included dummy variables pertaining to the worker's residence in an urban area, and the south, the west, or the north central United States.

measuring nonpecuniary attributes, only the supervisory status dummy variable has a statistically significant effect among the subsidiary working condition variables, and its sign is in the expected direction. In most other cases, the signs approach significance at the .05 level, so the variables are included to separate their effects from those of the risk variables.

The results of primary interest are the estimated effects of the injury rate variables, the insurance variables, and the estimate of r—the worker's implicit discount rate. In the unweighted estimates, each effect has the expected sign. Furthermore, all of the injury and insurance variables are statistically significant at the .05 confidence level (one-tailed test).

The importance of weighting is seen by comparing estimates of the discount rate. In the unweighted regressions, the estimated real discount rate of 9.6 percent is not statistically significant at the 5 percent level, with a t-ratio of 1.52. The two-stage weighting, however, causes an increase in significance for many variables, including the accident and insurance variables. Most pertinent here is that it also causes an increase in the estimated discount rate to 12.2 percent and a decrease in the standard error to .043, rendering the estimate significant at the .01 level. Based on this estimate, one can reject both extreme alternative hypotheses that workers exhibit a zero discount rate or an infinite discount rate when making their job choices.

To compare the estimate of the discount rate to observed explicit rates for the year 1976, it is necessary to convert it to a nominal rate. Using the increase in the GNP deflator of 6 percent in 1976 as a measure of the expected rate of inflation yields a nominal discount rate of 18 percent for the weighted regressions. This discount rate is above the 9 percent nominal rate for new home mortgages in 1976 but equal to the 18 percent rate of interest charged in most states by credit card companies.[15] Our estimated rate of time preference is thus consistent with a hypothesis of rationality of workers' intertemporal trade-offs.

This estimate is also among the most reasonable estimates of implicit discount rates in the literature. The estimated rate of time preference for life years is in a more plausible range than consumers' implicit rates of discount for appliance energy efficiency, which Hausman [1979] found to be around 20 percent or more and Gately [1980] found to be between 45 and 300 percent. Similarly, Fuchs [1982] generated survey data on consumers' rates of time preference that implied a mean implicit rate of time preference of 30 percent. During the recent low inflation period, corporate executives have also been found to use nominal rates of discount on the order of 15 percent or more,[16] so that the estimated nominal rates of 18 percent for this equation should not be viewed as unreasonably large.

15. The home mortgage interest rate is the Federal Home Loan Bank Board rate on new-home mortgage yields, from U.S. Council of Economic Advisers [1980, 278].

16. The results from a poll by Lawrence Summers suggest that the rate of interest companies use to discount investments is on the order of 15 percent or more for a majority of firms. See *Washington Post*, National Weekly Edition, July 16, 1986, 22.

Similar estimates are obtained with other specifications as well. Table IV summarizes the key parameters in a weighted estimation of the unconditional equations in which the job risk variables appear in their conventional form. In addition, Table 4 includes conditional equations in which the risk variable represents the interaction of the objective risk measure and the subjective hazard perception dummy variable. Workers will not demand wage premiums for jobs that they do not perceive as dangerous, and the subjective risk perception variable is incorporated in the risk measure to capture this effect. It is important to note that the conditional estimates eliminate some of the measurement error involved in the matching of average industry risks to workers. As expected, coefficients on the conditional estimates are uniformly larger than their unconditional counterparts for the death risk variables. However, the opposite holds for the injury risk coefficients.

Although the worker's subjective risk perception is the theoretically appropriate variable, the hazard perception variable may not represent the ideal adjustment for these subjective factors. The wording of the hazard perception question, which requires that the worker cite specific hazards, may not elicit perceptions of very small risks. In particular, how large must the risk be before it passes the worker's threshold for categorization as dangerous or unhealthy? Since the conditional risk measure is not necessarily more meaningful than the unconditional, both sets of findings are presented to explore the robustness of the results. The estimates reported in Table IV for the conditional and unconditional measures are very similar.

The rates of discount individuals use to discount years of life are significantly different from zero at the 5 percent level in all cases and range in magnitude from 10 to 12 percent. One can thus reject the hypothesis that workers have a zero rate of time preference. Similarly, one can reject the other extreme hypothesis that workers are myopic and, in effect, have infinite rates of discount. The 95 percent confidence interval for rates of discount is restricted to generally plausible values.

The findings in Table IV also offer striking support for the theoretical predictions regarding risks and the compensation mix. Both risk measures are consistently positive and statistically significant at the 5 percent level. The implicit values per additional expected year of life are in the $170,000–$200,000 range, which is remarkably consistent across the four equations given the wide range of life values reported previously in the literature. If the discounted number of life years is used as the denominator in this calculation, the average value of a year of life rises to almost $725,000.

These values represent the average willingness to pay for an additional year of life in present value terms. More important for policy purposes is the marginal value of a life year. If a worker expects to live thirty-five more years, then a one-year life extension is worth only $11,000 now. However, an older worker who expects to live only five years will value an additional year of life at approximately $400,000.

The value of life extension also depends on the discount rate. If the real

384　　　　　　　　　　　　ECONOMIC INQUIRY

TABLE IV

Summary of Selected Statistics for Wage Equations with Discounted Expected Life Years Lost* Coefficients and Standard Errors

Independent Variable	Unconditional Risk Measure		Conditional Risk Measure	
	Wage	ln(Wage)	Wage	ln(Wage)
Expected life years lost	7.8E + 1	1.8E + 1	1.0E + 2	1.9E + 1
	(3.7E + 1)	(0.6E + 1)	(0.5E + 2)	(0.5E + 1)
Expected annuity	−8.6E − 3	−2.4E − 3	−1.3E − 2	−2.5E − 3
	(4.2E − 3)	(0.8E − 3)	(0.7E − 2)	(0.8E − 4)
Lost workday accident rate	0.235	0.058	0.184	0.047
	(0.071)	(0.014)	(0.071)	(0.014)
Lost workday accident rate × replacement rate	−0.255	−0.055	−0.247	−0.053
	(0.075)	(0.013)	(0.080)	(0.014)
Discount rate (r)	0.096	0.122	0.122	0.122
	(0.052)	(0.043)	(0.056)	(0.034)
Implicit value of life** (1986 dollars)	$6.8E + 6	$6.2E + 6	$6.0E + 6	$6.2E + 6
Implicit value per life year***	$194,285	$177,143	$171,429	$177,143

* Each equation also included the variables pertaining to the worker's race, sex, experience, union status, blue-collar occupation, firm size, health status, education, speed of work, job security, supervisory status, overtime work, training, and residence in an urban area, the south, the west, or the north central United States.

** Calculated as the product $\partial w/\partial p \times 2000$ hours $\times 1.891$, where 1.891 is the price inflator and p is the probability of a fatal accident.

*** Calculated as the implicit value of life/remaining life.

rate of time preference is lower, additional life years increase in value. The worker described above with thirty-five years of life remaining who values an extra year at $11,000 when the discount rate is 12 percent will value his marginal year of life at over $125,000 if the discount rate is 5 percent. Likewise, the older worker with five years of life remaining will pay $570,000 for an additional year when his discount rate is 5 percent.

As the figures at the bottom of Table IV indicate, the value of life estimates on the order of $6.0 million (1986 prices) are similar to those obtained in many traditional estimates, but larger in magnitude than estimates for high risk samples such as Thaler and Rosen [1976]. Thaler and Rosen calculate the implicit value of life at about $600,000 in 1986 prices using occupational risk data. Viscusi [1981], on the other hand, generates value of life estimates of $5.3 million, again in 1986 prices, using industry risk data. It should be noted also that the annual death risk level for the sample used here of 5/100,000 is below the 1/1000 value in Thaler and Rosen [1976] and the 1/10,000 value in Viscusi [1979]. The discounted value of life estimates are larger than the average value of life for these two studies. Given the self-selection of workers with lower values of life into higher risk jobs, these results are quite consistent with the literature.

Similar calculations of the willingness to pay to avoid a nonfatal injury indicate that individuals value this element of job safety at between $15,000 and $30,000 per accident. Although not as stable as the value of life estimates, these values are also consistent with those found elsewhere in the literature that have controlled for the role of accident insurance and with those of Viscusi [1979], whose estimated values in current dollars range from fourteen to twenty-five thousand dollars. Since the value of the nonfatal accident wage replacement rate is .80, these values represent the implicit costs of pain and suffering and the uninsured wage losses.

The annuity and workers' compensation variables have the expected signs and in every instance they pass a test for statistical significance at the 5 percent (one-tailed) level. An additional dollar of weekly workers' compensation benefits for disabilities leads to a weekly wage reduction of 18 cents. As shown in Viscusi and Moore [1987b], this is higher than the optimal rate of trade-off between wages and benefits (-6.00 cents) that would exist if there were perfect insurance markets. Likewise, the rate of trade-off between wages and the discounted annuity, which equals -0.80 cents in these estimates, is much larger than the ideal rate of -0.06 cents. Abstracting from the problems of moral hazard, which may be considerable, these estimated rates of trade-off imply that benefit levels were too low in 1976. Estimates from a more recent data set reported in Moore and Viscusi [forthcoming] indicate that the dramatic increase in benefit levels since 1976 has lowered the rate of trade-off so that benefit levels are no longer suboptimal. The principal implication of these results is that there is an important trade-off between ex ante wage compensation and ex post insurance compensation for job risks.

386   ECONOMIC INQUIRY

IV. CONCLUSION

Consideration of the implications of fatality risks for workers' future life-times enables one to assess the roles of the duration of life lost and workers' implicit rates of time preference with respect to future life years. The most notable result was that workers discount future life years at real rates of 9.6–12 percent. Since these values converted to nominal rates are bounded from below by the prevailing home mortgage interest rate and bounded from above by credit card interest rates, there is little evidence of intertemporal irrationality.

Consideration of the duration of life lost also makes it possible to consider the value of each year of life lost. This value, which averaged more than $170,000 in 1986 prices, was associated with an implicit value of one's future life of about $6.0 million. The valuation level greatly exceeds workers' annual earnings, which is not necessarily inconsistent since it represents the rate of risk-dollar trade-off for very small risks, not the amount that workers would pay for certain life extension. Compared with other studies this estimated value of life is toward the higher end of the spectrum, but it is generally consistent with past estimates for workers with jobs of similar riskiness.

The ex post compensation for fatalities and nonfatal injuries played a more prominent role in this study than in previous analyses in the literature. Both forms of ex post compensation led to a reduction in ex ante compensation through wage reductions. Rewards for exposure to job risk thus involve two components of compensation: ex ante wage compensation and ex post insurance compensation.

In all of the aspects of this analysis, recognition of the role of the temporal dimension of job risks bolsters the support for an economic model of rational job choice. Although temporal misallocations may exist, the magnitude of any departure from rationality appears small.

REFERENCES

Amemiya, Takeshi. "A Note on a Heteroskedastic Model." *Journal of Econometrics*, November 1977, 365–70.

Arnould, Richard J. and Len M. Nichols. "Wage-Risk Premiums and Workers' Compensation: A Refinement of Estimates of Compensating Wage Differential." *Journal of Political Economy*, April 1983, 332–40.

Arthur, W. B. "The Economics of Risks to Life." *American Economic Review*, March 1981, 54–64.

Butler, Richard J. "Wage and Injury Rate Response to Shifting Levels of Workers' Compensation," in *Safety and the Work Force: Incentives and Disincentives in Workers' Compensation*, edited by John D. Worrall. Ithaca: Industrial and Labor Relations Press, 1983.

Commerce Clearing House, Inc. *1977 U.S. Master Tax Guide*. New York: Commerce Clearing House, 1977a.

——. *1977 State Tax Handbook*. New York: Commerce Clearing House, 1977b.

Conley, Bryan C. "The Value of Human Life and the Demand for Safety." *American Economic Review*, March 1976, 45–55.

Cropper, M. L. and F. G. Sussman. "Valuing Future Risks to Life." University of Maryland Bureau of Business and Economics Research working paper, 1986.

Dorsey, Stuart and Norman Walzer. "Workers' Compensation, Job Hazards, and Wages." *Industrial and Labor Relations Review*, July 1983, 642–54.

Duncan, Greg J. "Earnings Functions and Nonpecuniary Benefits." *The Journal of Human Resources*, Fall 1976, 462–83.

Fuchs, Victor R. "Time Preference and Health: An Exploratory Study," in *Economic Aspects of Health*, edited by Victor Fuchs. Chicago: University of Chicago Press, 1982.

Gately, Dermot. "Individual Discount Rates and the Purchase and Utilization of Energy-Using Durables: Comment." *Bell Journal of Economics*, Spring 1980, 373–76.

Hausman, Jerry. "Individual Discount Rates and the Purchase and Utilization of Energy-Using Durables." *Bell Journal of Economics*, Spring 1979, 33–54.

Lang, Kevin and Paul A. Rudd. "Returns to Schooling, Implicit Discount Rates, and Black-White Wage Differentials." *The Review of Economics and Statistics*, November 1986, 41–47.

Moore, Michael J. "Three Essays in Labor Economics." Ph.D. dissertation, University of Michigan, 1984.

Moore, Michael J. and W. Kip Viscusi. "Have Increases in Workers' Compensation Benefits Paid for Themselves?" *Proceedings of the Sixth Annual Conference on Economic Issues in Workers' Compensation*, edited by David Appel, forthcoming.

Rosen, Sherwin. "The Value of Changes in Life Expectancy." *Journal of Risk and Uncertainty*, 1988, forthcoming.

Shepard, Donald and Richard Zeckhauser. "Survival Versus Consumption." *Management Science*, April 1984, 423–39.

Smith, Adam. *The Wealth of Nations*. New York: Modern Library, 1776, reprinted edition 1937.

Smith, Robert S. "Compensating Differentials and Public Policy: A Review." *Industrial and Labor Relations Review*, April 1979, 339–52.

———. *The Occupational Safety and Health Act: Its Goals and Achievements*. Washington, DC: American Enterprise Institute, 1976.

Thaler, Richard and Sherwin Rosen. "The Value of Saving a Life: Evidence from the Labor Market," in *Household Production and Consumption*, edited by N. Terleckyj. New York: Columbia University Press, 1976.

U.S. Chamber of Commerce. *Analysis of Workers' Compensation Laws, 1976 edition*. Washington, DC: U.S. Chamber of Commerce, 1976.

U.S. Council of Economic Advisers. *Economic Report of the President, 1980*. Washington, DC: U.S. Government Printing Office, 1980.

U.S. Department of Health and Human Services, Public Health Service, National Center for Health Statistics. *Vital Statistics of the United States*. 1978, Vol. II, Section 5—Life Tables, DHHS Publication No. (PHS) 81-1104. Hyattsville, MD, 1980.

Viscusi, W. Kip. *Employment Hazards: An Investigation of Market Performance*. Cambridge: Harvard University Press, 1979.

———. "Occupational Safety and Health Regulation: Its Impact and Policy Alternatives," in *Research in Public Policy Analysis and Management*, Vol. 2, edited by J. Crecine. Greenwich, CT: JAI Press, 1981.

———. *Risk by Choice: Regulating Health and Safety in the Workplace*. Cambridge: Harvard University Press, 1983.

———. "The Valuation of Risks to Life and Health: Guidelines for Policy Analysis," in Proceedings of 1984 NSF Conference, *Benefits Assessment: The State of the Art*, edited by J. D. Bentkover, V. T. Covello, and J. Mumpower. Dordrecht, Holland: D. Reidel Publishing Co., 1986.

——— and Michael J. Moore. "Rates of Time Preference and Valuations of the Duration of Life." Center for the Study of Business Regulation working paper 86-18, Duke University, 1987a.

——— and ———. "Workers' Compensation: Wage Effects, Benefit Inadequacies, and the Value of Health Losses." *The Review of Economics and Statistics*, May 1987b, 249–61.

Weiss, Yoram. "The Risk Element in Occupational and Educational Choices." *Journal of Political Economy,* December 1972, 1203–13.

Zeckhauser, Richard and Donald Shepard. "Where Now for Saving Lives?" *Law and Contemporary Problems,* Autumn 1976, 5–45.

[26]

Journal of Risk and Uncertainty, 1: 285–304 (1988)
© 1988 Kluwer Academic Publishers

The Value of Changes in Life Expectancy

SHERWIN ROSEN
The University of Chicago

Key words: value of life, cost–benefit analysis, mortality risks, life expectancy

Abstract

Valuation formulas for age-specific mortality risks are derived from life-cycle allocation theory under uncertainty and related to empirical estimates of the value of life. A change in an age-specific mortality risk affects all subsequent survivor functions and reallocates consumption and labor supply over the entire life cycle. The value of eliminating a risk to life at a specific age is the expected present value of consumer surplus from that age forward. Approximate numerical extrapolations from cross-section estimates imply that values decrease rapidly in current age and in the distance between current age and age at risk.

Professional interest in cost–benefit analysis of safety, illness, and death probabilities had its origins in the environmental concerns and the growth of the medical sector of the 1960's as a practical matter, and in the pioneering work of Schelling (1968) and Mishan (1971) as an intellectual one. Subsequent work has followed two distinct lines. One, beginning with Usher (1973), has analyzed intertemporal risks affecting life expectancy (Conley, 1976; Cropper, 1977; Ehrlich and Chuma, 1984; Arthur, 1981; Shepard and Zeckhauser, 1984; Moore and Viscusi, 1988), where risks are implicitly evaluated at various points in the life cycle. The other uses simpler, atemporal models to guide empirical work (Jones-Lee, 1976; Thaler and Rosen, 1975; Viscusi, 1978). The relationship between the two is developed below.

Section 1 briefly reviews the single-period model, and explores some unusual consequences of state-dependent preferences. The net difference in utility between life and death states is an essential aspect of preferences for life-risk valuation. Paradoxically, risk-averse people can actually prefer more life-risk gambles to less in order to convexify preferences in certain cases. The consumption elasticity of net utility is established as a key determinant of the value of life.

Section 2 examines a deterministic life cycle model and establishes two points. First, intertemporal substitution possibilities in life cycle preferences determine

I am indebted to Al Harberger, Ken Judd, Kevin M. Murphy, and Kip Viscusi for helpful discussions. This research was supported by the Environmental Protection Agency and the National Science Foundation, but neither agency is responsible for the contents of this paper.

the value of life extensions: greater substitution reduces the willingness to pay for life extensions because *quantity* (life-years) and *quality* (consumption per year) of life are better substitutes. Second, the marginal value of life extensions increase with age, a phenomenon that can lead to regret in old age from having voluntarily exposed oneself to irreversible risks when young. However, this is neither inter-temporally inconsistent nor irrational.

Section 3 addresses the stochastic life cycle problem and derives valuation formulas for perturbations in age-specific death (hazard) rates. The value of eliminating a risk to life at a specific age is the expected present value of the additional consumer surplus it gives rise to. Using the fact that the value of a current (age-independent) risk is estimated by equalizing wage differences on risky jobs, section 4 imputes middle-of-life-cycle valuations of death hazards based on an approximation of the valuation formula developed in section 3. Valuations of current risks decrease with age in this range of approximation. They also decrease with the future age of risk exposure. These calculations illustrate how to value risk exposures, such at to carcinogenic substances, that involve delays between initial exposure and subsequent risk. Suggestions for future research appear in the concluding section.

1. Some consequences of normalization

Valuing risks to life requires some unusual normalizations of preferences because utility is inherently state-dependent in this problem. The basic issues have not been thoroughly treated in the literature and are best illustrated in a one-period model (e.g., Bailey, 1980; Rosen, 1981).

Consider a person without heirs or altruism toward others. There are two states: If an accident doesn't occur, the risk-averse person survives and enjoys utility $\bar{u}(c)$, where c is consumption. The person dies if an accident occurs, so it is meaningless to think of consumption. Instead, assign a constant M to utility in this state (with $M \gtrless 0$). Expected utility is

$$E\tilde{U} = p\bar{u}(c) + (1 - p)M, \tag{1}$$

where p is the probability of survival.

In expected utility theory, preferences are independent of states and the utility function is defined only up to an increasing linear transformation. When preferences are state-dependent, any increasing linear transformation is acceptable so long as the *same* transformation is consistently applied to the utility function of each state. In the case at hand, subtracting M from utility in each state normalizes the utility of nonsurvival to zero:

$$EU = p[\bar{u}(c) - M] + (1 - p)[M - M] = pu(c), \tag{2}$$

where

THE VALUE OF CHANGES IN LIFE EXPECTANCY   287

$$u(c) = \bar{u}(c) - M \tag{3}$$

is the differences in utility between life and death. Only the difference matters, because (1) and (2) order life-and-death gambles in exactly the same way.

The value of life is defined as the willingness to pay for a small increment dp in the survival rate. Budget opportunities obviously enter into this calculation. The person is endowed with nonhuman wealth W. What happens to ownership of these assests if the person dies? Assume the atemporal equivalent of an actuarially fair annuity, a tontine in which all survivors share equally in the unintended bequests of decendents. In a large group of equally endowed persons, a proportion $(1 - p)$ die and their wealth is distributed to p survivors. A survivor's consumption equals initial endowment W plus the tontine share $(1 - p)W/p$, or W/p in all, so the budget constraint is

$$W = pc. \tag{4}$$

Totally differentiate (2) and (4) and eliminate dc:

$$d(\text{EU}) = \frac{\partial \text{EU}}{\partial p} dp + \frac{\partial \text{EU}}{\partial W} dW = \left[u - \left(\frac{W}{p} \right) u' \right] dp + u' dW. \tag{5}$$

The value of life is the marginal rate of substitution between W and p:

$$v = -\frac{dW}{dp} = \frac{u}{u'} - \frac{W}{p} = \left[\frac{u/(W/p)}{u'} - 1 \right] \frac{W}{p} = \frac{1 - \varepsilon}{\varepsilon} \frac{W}{p}, \tag{6}$$

where $\varepsilon = d \log u / d \log c$ is the ratio of marginal to average utility evaluated at $c = W/p$. Equation (6) shows that a person will pay to reduce death risk if and only if $\varepsilon < 1$. The person will pay to increase risk if $\varepsilon > 1$. The following argument proves that $0 < \varepsilon < 1$ covers all economically interesting cases (for persons without earnings). Two possible configurations of $u(c) = \bar{u}(c) - M$ must be considered to show this.

(i) Suppose $u(c) > 0$ for $c > 0$; that is, $u(c)$ has a nonnegative intercept (figure 1). Since $u(c)/c$ is the slope of a line from the origin to a point on $u(c)$, it follows from the figure that $u'(c) < u(c)/c$ and $\varepsilon < 1$ for all c. Furthermore, $\varepsilon > 0$ because u is positive—the utility of survival is at least as large as the utility of death for all c. This, however, need not be true. The second case is more interesting.

(ii) Suppose $u(c) \lessgtr 0$ as $c \lessgtr \bar{c}$: $u(c)$ has a negative intercept (figure 2) and $\bar{c} > 0$ is *minimum survival* consumption. Since the utility of death has been normalized to zero, death is the preferred state if $c < \bar{c}$ because $M > \bar{u}(c)$ in that range. Nevertheless, for $\bar{c} < c < c^*$, $\bar{u}(c) > M$ and the slope of the cord linking the origin with $u(c)$ is less than $u'(c)$. Therefore $\varepsilon > 1$, so equation (6) implies that the person would pay to reduce survival chances even though survival is preferred to nonsurvival. Survival seems to be a bad, not a good, in this range.

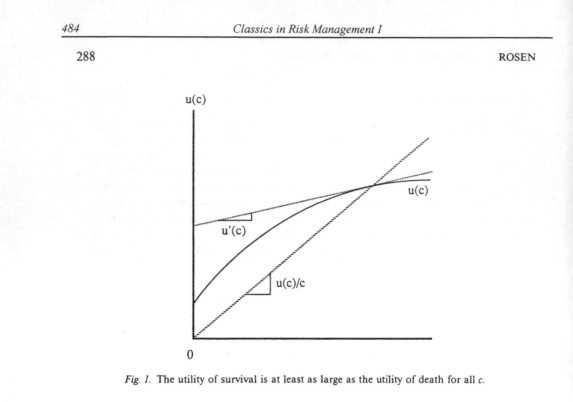

Fig. 1. The utility of survival is at least as large as the utility of death for all *c*.

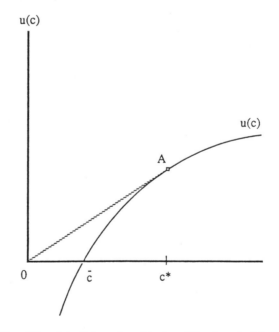

Fig. 2. The utility of death is preferred to the utility of survival for $c < \bar{c}$.

THE VALUE OF CHANGES IN LIFE EXPECTANCY   289

It is incorrect to apply equation (6) in case (ii) because of a nonconvexity in the utility function. The effective utility function in figure 2 is the abscissa for c in the range $[0,\bar{c}]$ connecting to $u(c)$ for $c \geqslant \bar{c}$. It exhibits an increasing return because the outcome is indivisibile—one either lives or dies. However, the indivisibility is smoothed (or *convexified*) by randomizing between death (zero utility) and life utility at consumption c^* if one survives. From figure 2, if W/p falls in the interval $(0,c^*)$ there exists $p^* = W/c^*$, with $0 < p^* < p < 1$ such that survivors enjoy $u(c^*) = u(W/p^*)$ and nonsurvivors receive zero utility. Ex ante expected utility is on the cord connecting 0 and $u(c^*)$ and is larger than the sure thing for $0 < c < c^*$. The smoothed utility function is the envelope 0A for $0 < c < c^*$ and the original function AB thereafter. $\varepsilon = 1.0$ on the straight line segment and $\varepsilon < 1.0$ for $c > c^*$.

Put differently, calculations leading to (6) imply $\partial EU/\partial p = \lambda[(1 - \varepsilon)/\varepsilon]W/p$, where λ is the marginal utility of money. If $c < c^*$ then $(1 - \varepsilon) < 0$ and $\partial EU/\partial p < 0$. Think of a choice problem in which p^* is chosen to maximize EU in (2) subject to (4) and to the constraint $p^* \leqslant p$. The solution $p^* = W/c^*$ is the optimum value of p^* when $\varepsilon > 1$ in the utility function $u(c)$. $p = p^*$ is chosen when $\varepsilon \leqslant 1$.

Convexification is achieved by adopting modes of behavior that increase the risk sufficiently to enable survivors to attain consumption standard c^*. Applying equation (6) to the convexified utility function shows that the person will not pay anything to extend life chances in the straight line section of figure 2 because excess risks are already being taken to smooth out preferences before the experiment is presented to the person.[1] Whatever risk is offered will be undone by randomization.[2]

For a working person, specify utility in the first state as $u(c,l)$, where l is leisure, and the budget equation as

$$c = w(1 - l) + \frac{W}{P},\tag{7}$$

where w is the wage rate, and earnings (but not assets) are assumed to be at risk. If expected utility maximization implies that the person does not work, the analysis remains as above. If some labor is supplied to the market, the envelope theorem yields

$$v = \frac{\partial EU}{\partial p} \Big/ \frac{\partial EU}{\partial W} = -\frac{dW}{dp} = \frac{1 - \varepsilon}{\varepsilon}c + w(1 - l),\tag{8}$$

where c and l in (8) are their optimal values and $\varepsilon = cu_c/u$ is evaluated at those values. Foregone earnings are now included in v.

In this case, the derivative $\partial EU/\partial p$ is proportional to the right-hand side of (8). There is no scope for randomization to increase expected utility if that sum is positive. In particular, $\varepsilon > 1$ is consistent with utility maximization and no randomization for a working person so long as $w(1 - l) > (1 - \varepsilon)c/\varepsilon$. Consequently, the value of life can either exceed or fall short of earnings according as $\varepsilon \gtrless 1$, and no theoretical bounds connecting the two can be established a priori. The early human capital estimates of Weisbrod (1971) and Rice (1966) remain unjustified from utility theory, unless other evidence suggests that $\varepsilon \approx 1$. If ε is so large that $v < 0$ in (8) then randomization reduces v to zero, whatever earnings and consumption happen to be.

2. Deterministic life-cycle model

Consider the following problem. A person with time-separable preferences and access to a perfect capital market lives for certain until age T. How much wealth will the person give up to extend life years by a small increment dT? The concept of risk aversion in the one-period problem is replaced with the concept of intertemporal substitution in a life-cycle problem. Furthermore, discounting of future risks implies that the value of life extension systematically changes with age.

2.1 The decision problem

Preferences remain state-dependent in this problem. Assume the person enjoys a flow of utility $\tilde{u}(c(t))$ at age t. Assigning a constant M to instantaneous "utility" beyond the age of death T,

$$\tilde{U} = \int_0^T (\tilde{u}(c(t)))e^{-\rho t}dt + \int_T^\infty Me^{-\rho t}dt$$

$$= \int_0^T (\tilde{u}(c(t)) - M)e^{-\rho t}dt + M/\rho, \tag{9}$$

where ρ is the rate of time preference. However, the constant M/ρ may be dropped because any monotone transformation of $\tilde{U}$ preserves orderings, resulting in

$$U = \int_0^T (\tilde{u}(c(t)) - M)e^{-\rho t}dt = \int_0^T u(c)e^{-\rho t}dt, \tag{10}$$

where $u(c)$ has exactly the same form as equation (3).

A person endowed with wealth W confronts a pure-consumption-loans market at interest rate r and cannot die in debt. Then all capital is consumed in the lifetime, so the choice of consumption path $c(t)$ is constrained by

$$W = \int_0^T c(t)e^{-rt}dt. \tag{11}$$

The Lagrangian expression for this problem is

THE VALUE OF CHANGES IN LIFE EXPECTANCY   291

$$\int_0^T u(c(t))e^{-\rho t}dt + \lambda\left[W - \int_0^T c(t)^{-rt}dt\right],\qquad(12)$$

and the marginal condition is familiar:

$$u'(c(t))e^{-\rho t} = \lambda e^{-rt}\qquad\text{for } 0 \leqslant t \leqslant T.\qquad(13)$$

2.2. Valuation of longevity

Indirect utility is a function of W and T (and r and ρ),

$$U(W,T;r,\rho) = \max_{c(t)}\int_0^T u(c(t))e^{-\rho t}dt \quad\text{s.t. (11)},\qquad(14)$$

and defines (W,T) indifference curves from which the marginal rate of substitution $-dW/dT = v$ follows. Applying the envelope theorem to (12),

$$U_W = \lambda,$$
$$U_T = u(c(T))e^{-\rho T} - \lambda c(T)e^{-rt} = [u(c(T)) - c(T)u'(c(T))]e^{-\rho T},\qquad(15)$$

after exploiting (13). The marginal utility of life-years has two components. Extending life has a direct effect which adds a term $u(c(T))$ to the lifetime sum of utilities on the one hand, but it also requires reallocating consumption away from other points in the life cycle, given W, on the other. These indirect increments are valued at *marginal cost* $u'(c(T))$. The term in square brackets in (15) is the utility surplus at $t = T$, and is discounted by the rate of time preference, ρ, since it occurs T years in the future.

Collecting results,

$$v = -\frac{dW}{dT} = \frac{\partial U/\partial T}{\partial U/\partial W} = u(c(T))e^{-\rho t}/\lambda - c(T)e^{-rT}$$
$$= \left[\frac{u(c(T))}{u'(c(T))} - c(T)\right]e^{-rT} = \frac{1 - \varepsilon(T)}{\varepsilon(T)}c(T)e^{-rT}.\qquad(16)$$

2.3. Discussion

v is decreasing in ε in both the one-period and intertemporal problems, but now ε is related to the concept of intertemporal substitution in preferences. This is illustrated by examining some extreme cases.

For $|M|$ sufficiently small, $u(c)$ approaches a linear function of c as ε goes to unity, and from (10), U is essentially summable in $c(t)$. How that total is distributed over time hardly matters, because consumption at any one time is a very good substitute for consumption at any other time. Equation (16) shows that v goes to zero in this case. A person won't pay for an increment dT because the increased horizon is completely offset by lower per-period consumption. This is the sense in which large intertemporal substitution implies large substitution between the *quantity* (T) and the *quality* (c) of life.

If M is small but ε goes to zero, the indifference curves between $c(t)$ and $c(t')$ increasingly resemble those of fixed proportions, and v grows very large. A person with such preferences is willing to pay a great deal for dT because each year of life becomes essential, and quantity and quality of life are poor substitutes. Intertemporal substitution plays a similar role in life-cycle theory as risk aversion does in atemporal models.[3]

The presence of the discount factor in (16) implies that v systematically increases with age. It is known that consumption plans are intertemporally consistent when preferences are time-separable. No matter what the person's age, planned consumption at T, $c(T)$, remains unchanged and so does $\varepsilon(T)$. Nonetheless, v changes because the horizon is shortened. If $v(t)$ is the value at age t and $v(t')$ is the value at some later age t', equation (16) implies

$$v(t') = v(t)e^{r(t'-t)}. \tag{17}$$

A person close to the end is willing to pay more to extend life than a person whose horizon is longer. One implication is that risky personal actions that have long latency periods have smaller value to younger people than to older people. The young may appear reckless on this account, but such recklessness may pass a personal cost–benefit test. Moreover, there is a natural tendency for participation in the risky activity to fall as the person ages.

There is nothing irrational about this. Suppose a person trades $v(t)$ dollars for a reversible decrement $-dT$ at age t. Investing the money makes it grow to $v(t') = v(t)e^{r(t'-t)}$ at age t'. At that point, the person would be willing and able to pay $v(t')$ to re-extend life by dT. However, if the earlier action is irreversible, the willingness to pay $v(t') - v(r)$ at t' in excess of compensation at t suggests a sense in which earlier actions are regretted later, even when regrets are fully foreseen (if information is perfect) when the initial action is taken. Regret is not irrational. It is similar to a gambler regretting having played a game ex post even though the prospect of losing was fully weighed in the decision to gamble in the first place.

Extending the analysis to include labor supply is straightforward. Earnings at T discounted back to the present are added to (16). Again $v = 0$ if randomization is optimal.

3. Valuation of risks over the life cycle

The more general problem of a stochastic horizon is analyzed in this section.

3.1. Tastes, opportunities, and optimization

A person who lives exactly t years enjoys utility (as in (10)) of

$$U(t) = \int_0^t u(c(\tau), l(\tau)) e^{-\rho \tau} d\tau. \tag{18}$$

Let $f(t)$ be the probability density of living for t years, and let $F(t)$ be the *cdf*, the probability of dying on or before age t. Then expected utility is

$$EU = \int_0^\infty f(t) U(t) dt = \int_0^\infty \int_0^t f(t) u(c(\tau), l(\tau)) e^{-\rho \tau} d\tau dt$$

$$= \int_0^\infty (1 - F(t)) u(c(t), l(t)) e^{-\rho t} dt, \tag{19}$$

where the third equality follows from changing the order of integration. $(1 - F(t))$ is the survivor function (from birth), hereafter written $S(t)$, and is itself a function of the pattern of age-specific death rates:

$$S(t) = (1 - F(t)) = e^{-\int_0^t h(\tau) d\tau} \tag{20}$$

where $h(t) = f(t)/(1 - F(t))$ is the death rate at age t. Substituting (20) in (19) shows that the force of mortality increases the effective rate of time preference. The future is discounted more heavily because a person may not live to see it.

Analysis is confined to the stochastic equivalent of a perfect capital market in which actuarially fair life-assured annuities (Yaari, 1965) are available.[4] In effect a person assigns all current and future claims to income to an insurance company in exchange for a contract that guarantees consumption $c(t)$ until death. The consumption risk of death is insured because those who die earlier than the average leave enough wealth behind to finance the consumption claims of those who live longer than the average.

A person who lives for exactly t years imposes a capital liability on the insurance company of

$$\int_0^t [c(\tau) - w(\tau)(1 - l(\tau))] e^{-r\tau} d\tau,$$

where $w(1 - l)$ is earned income. Budget balance requires that the expected liability over all claimants equals endowed wealth, or

$$W = \int_0^\infty \int_0^t f(t) [c - w(1 - l)] e^{-r\tau} d\tau dt$$

$$= \int_0^\infty S(t) [c(t) - w(t)(1 - l(t)) e^{-rt} dt \tag{21}$$

after changing the order of integration. Mortality increases the net interest rate because net credits are earned on those who die early.

Optimal choices of $c(t)$ and $l(t)$ maximize EU subject to constraint (21). The marginal conditions

$$u_c(c(t),l(t))e^{-pt} = \lambda e^{-rt},$$

$$u_l(c(t),l(t))e^{-pt} = w(t)\lambda e^{-rt}, \tag{22}$$

are identical to a deterministic problem because financial uncertainty is fully insured by annuities.

3.2. Valuation of life risks

Valuation formulas follow, as usual, from the indirect utility function. However, there are two technical complications. First, expected utility in the optimal program varies with attained age because the probability of surviving to any given age depends on age itself. The conditional probability of attaining some future age must be continually renormalized as the person ages. If $S(t)$ in (20) is the survival probability at birth, the conditional probability of surviving until age t given that one has survived until age a is

$$S_a(t) = S(t)/S(a) = e^{-\int_a^t h(\tau)d\tau}. \tag{23}$$

Writing EU_a for discounted expected utility given that the person has survived until age a, (19) becomes

$$\text{EU}_a = \int_a^\infty S_a(t)u(c(t),l(t))e^{-p(t-a)}dt. \tag{24}$$

Second, expected utility at a depends on the *entire function* $S_a(t)$, and calculating marginal rates of substitution requires extending the concept of differentiation to a perturbation or variation in the function $S(t)$. This is technically a Frechet derivative, as pointed out by Arthur (1981). Willingness to pay for any pattern of (small) changes in death probabilities can be calculated by examining how variations in $h(t)$ affects $S_a(t)$.

Using notation δ to indicate this kind of differentiation, from (24),

$$\frac{\delta \text{EU}_a}{\delta S_a} = \int_a^\infty \left(u + S_a u_c \frac{\delta c}{\delta S_a} + S_a u_l \frac{\delta l}{\delta S_a} \right)(\delta S_a)e^{-p(t-a)}dt,$$

where δS_a is the variation is $S_a(t)$ and δc and δl are the equilibrium variations in $c(t)$ and $l(t)$ that are caused by it. Exploiting the time-consistent nature of the solution, reconditioning and differentiation of constraint (21) yields

$$\int_a^\infty S_a\left(\frac{\delta c}{\delta S_a} + w\frac{\delta l}{\delta S_a}\right)(\delta S_a)e^{-r(t-a)}dt = -\int_a^\infty (c - w(1-l))(\delta S_a)e^{-r(t-a)}dt.$$

These two expressions and the marginal conditions give the envelope result

$$\frac{\delta EU_a}{\delta S_a} = \int_a^\infty [u - u_c \cdot (c - w(1-l))](\delta S_a)e^{-\rho(t-a)}dt. \tag{25}$$

Similarly, $\delta EU_a/\delta W^a = \partial EU_a/\partial W^a = u_c e^{(r-\rho)(t-a)}$, where W^a is wealth remaining at age a, so the appropriate marginal rate of substitution reduces to

$$-\frac{\delta W^a}{\delta S_a} = \int_a^\infty \left[\left(\frac{1-\varepsilon}{\varepsilon}\right)c + w(1-l)\right](\delta S_a)e^{-rt}dt, \tag{26}$$

which generalizes equation (16) above.[5] The value of a perturbation in $S_a(t)$ is the change in expected discounted consumer surplus it gives rise to along the optimum (c,l) path. Further calculations reveal that $\delta EU_a/\delta w = \lambda\int_0^\infty (1 - l(t))e^{-rt}dt$, implying that

$$\frac{\delta w}{\delta S_a} = \frac{\delta W^a}{\delta S_a} \Big/ \int_0^\infty (1 - l(t))e^{-rt}dt \tag{27}$$

is the intertemporal version of Slutsky compensation for a change in the intertemporal pattern of wage rates.

3.3. The value of saving a life

$S_a(t)$ is related to $h(t)$ through (23). Taking logs and differentiating,

$$\delta S_a = -S_a(t)\int_a^t \delta h(\tau)d\tau. \tag{28}$$

Substituting (28) into (26) gives the valuation formula for changes in death rates, the natural primitives of the problem.

Consider the canonical experiment where δh is the Dirac-delta function taking a point-mass jump of size Δ at age α and otherwise remaining unchanged. Then the perturbation δS in (26) is zero for $t < \alpha$, because $\delta h = 0$ for $t < \alpha$, and also for a $> \alpha$ because the person has survived the risk. However, for $a < \alpha$ and $t > \alpha$ there is a persistent effect of $S_a(t)$ because $-\log S_a(t)$ is the sum of all previous hazard rates, from (23).

$$\begin{aligned}
\delta S_a &= 0 && \text{for } a > \alpha, \\
\delta S_a &= 0 && \text{for } t < \alpha \text{ and } a < \alpha, \\
\delta S_a &= -\Delta[S(t)/S(a)] = -\Delta \cdot S_a(t) && t \geq \alpha \text{ and } a < \alpha.
\end{aligned} \tag{29}$$

The money value of an excess risk incurred at age α from the prespective of a person currently of age $a < \alpha$ is, from (26) and (29),

$$v(a,\alpha) = \int_\alpha^\infty Z(t)S_a(t)e^{-r(t-a)}dt, \tag{30}$$

where

$$Z(t) = \frac{1-\varepsilon}{\varepsilon}c + w(1-l) \tag{31}$$

is consumer surplus at t. Of course, the value is zero for a person older than α. Define $V(\alpha) = v(\alpha,\alpha)$ as the value of eliminating a current risk. Then

$$V(\alpha) = \int_\alpha^\infty Z(t)S_\alpha(t)e^{-r(t-\alpha)}dt, \tag{32}$$

and after simple manipulations,

$$v(a,\alpha) = \frac{S(\alpha)}{S(a)}e^{-r(\alpha-a)}V(\alpha). \tag{33}$$

$V(\alpha)$ in (32) is the value of saving a current life. It is the expected present value of consumer surplus at age α. Since $h(\alpha)$ is a probability, the jump Δ lies in the unit interval. For example, suppose $\Delta = 1/1000$. Then $\Delta \cdot V(\alpha)$ in (32) is the amount of money an age α person would pay to eliminate the extra risk, and $1/\Delta = 1000$ such people would collectively pay $(V \cdot \Delta)/\Delta = V$ to eliminate a risk that on average takes one life among them. The value of a prospective risk in (30) or (33) is smaller than the value of a current risk for two reasons. First, $Z(t)$ is discounted by $e^{-r(a-a)}$ because it occurs in the future, as in the deterministic model; and second, not all people of age a will survive until age α to enjoy the benefit. The term $S(\alpha)/S(a)$ in (33) reflects this latter fact. In that sense $v(a,\alpha)$ is the *fractional value of a life* with fraction $S(\alpha)/S(a)$. It is a *whole life* value when $a = \alpha$. Prospective risks have smaller value than current risks at a given age because they are discounted by interviewing mortality as well as by the rate of interest.

Since $V(\alpha)$ is the value of eliminating exposure to a current risk, its derivative indicates whether older people would pay more or less than younger people to eliminate age-independent risks. We have

$$\frac{dV(\alpha)}{d\alpha} = -Z(\alpha) + (r + h(\alpha))V(\alpha). \tag{34}$$

$$= \int_0^\infty [Z'(\tau + \alpha) - (h(\tau + \alpha) - h(\alpha))Z(\tau + \alpha)]S_\alpha(\tau + \alpha)e^{-r\tau}d\tau.$$

The first form of (34) follows the usual relationship between flow and stock values, taking care to gross-up the interest rate by the current mortality rate. Value is rising with age if current surplus is small relative to discounted future surpluses. The second form of (34) shows that $Z(t)$ must be increasing for $V(a)$ to be increasing, which is likely to be true in the interval between youth and middle age. [6] Surplus $Z(t)$ would be constant in the case where $r = \rho$ and $w(t)$ is constant. Then V falls with age because $h(t)$ is strictly increasing. The latter fact must make V fall in very old age in any case, because there is little surplus left to discount. This point would be reinforced if age-dependence had been specified in utility to reflect deteriorating health and quality of life with age as well as greater mortality per se.

Older persons may nonetheless put greater value on some risks than younger people because the risk is more immediate, as in the difference between (32) and (33). As longevity increases, it is natural to expect more resources to be devoted to curing specific diseases of older age, such as cancer and Alzeimer's disease, because in earlier eras people did not live long enough to be exposed to them. However, $V(a)$ declining for a large a is paradoxical for the incidence of voluntary exposure to immediate risks. To account for why such risks are most often borne by younger people requires an auxilary physiological hypothesis that younger people produce less real risk per unit of exposure than older people do.

4. Estimates

Applying (30) − (33) requires estimates of surplus Z and the elasticity ε. It is important to understand that ε cannot be inferred from consumption or labor supply behavior because marginal conditions (22) do not involve the parameter M or other aspects of mortality, and ε depends on M, the curvature of $\bar{u}$, and on c and l. In principle ε could be identified by repeated observations on risky choices over the life cycle. The estimate below is based on cross-section wage premiums observed on risky jobs. Since panel data are not available, only average values of Z and ε can be estimated.

The idea of the method is to interpret observed wage–risk premiums as an estimate of $v(a,a) = V(a)$ in (30) or (32). Then assume a factorization of (32) into its Z and discount components and use data on consumption and earnings to infer average value of ε and Z.

The risks that are priced in labor market studies generally refer to immediate risks to life from fatal accidents at the work site. This is not strictly true in all cases, but is a reasonable assumption for most of the risky occupations used by Thaler and Rosen (1975; T–R hereafter), in which case that study estimates $V(a)$ in (32). Now $\int S_a(t)dt$ is remaining life expectancy for a person who has attained a years of age; and if the interest rate were zero, $V(a)$ in (32) is approximately the remaining average annual surplus times average remaining life-years. Discounting requires a simple actuarial adjustment because $\int_a^\infty S_a(t)e^{-r(t-a)}dt = A(a,r)$ is the present value of a unit annuity at age a when the interest rate is r, tabulated (as a_x) in actuarial tables.

To proceed, assume a factorization of (32):

$$V(a) = Z \cdot A(a,r). \tag{35}$$

Then average surplus Z is approximately $V(a)/A(a,r)$. Finally, use consumption and earnings data to infer ε from (31) interpreted as a relationship about averages.

This procedure is *exact* if $\rho = r$ and w does not change over the remaining horizon (though the implied estimate of ε is valid only in the neighborhood of the constant equilibrium values of c and l). If $\rho \neq r$ and w changes with age, the approximation may be less useful. Still, the average worker in the T–R sample is observed in the middle of work life, when relative age-earnings growth has mostly disappeared and subsequent living standards are largely set. Insofar as earnings and consumption growth are correlated over time due to the common factor of economic growth, the growth rate is netted out of the real interest rate r in discounting. When all is said and done, however, the quality of the approximations is unknown. A warning of *caveat emptor* hardly seems necessary, but a crude estimate may be better than none at all.

Using (27) to transform the risk-earnings estimate of T–R to a wealth estimate (with annual hours worked at the sample mean in the denominator because the estimate refers to one year each of risk and wage rates) implies a value for $V(a)$ of $630,000$, converted to dollars of 1986 purchasing power.[7] The mean age of workers in that sample is 41.8, so $a = 42$. Table 1 reports $A(42,r)$ based on mortality experience of white males. The third column reports corresponding values of Z in 1986 dollars, dividing $A(42,r)$ into $V(a) = 630,000$ from (35). The estimate of Z is sensitive to the rate of interest, rising by about 6000 for each percentage point in r for small r and by $11,000$ for large values of r.

Table 1. Estimated elasticities and average consumer surplus, 42-year-old white males, by interest rate

$r(\%)$	$A(42,r)$	Z (1986\$)	ε
0	32.1	\$19,660	1.06
2	24.4	25,820	.81
4	16.9	37,280	.56
6	13.2	47,730	.44
8	10.8	58,330	.36
10	9.0	70,000	.30
12	7.7	81,820	.25

Notes: $A(42,r)$ from U.S. Social Security Administration. Office of the Actuary, "Actuarial Tables Based on U.S. Life Tables, 1979–81." Actuarial Study No. 96, August 1986. Z in 1986 dollars based on $v(42,42) = 630,000$, from T–R. Elasticity calculated assuming $c = w(1 - l) = 20,800$ in 1986 dollars, from T–R.

The estimate of ε in column 4 is based on mean earnings of \$20,800 (1986 dollars) in the sample. This was a relatively low-income population whose full-time earnings averaged 25% below the mean of all full-time wage and salary earners, so their consumption expenditure must have been well approximated by earnings. The estimate in column 4 assumes $c = w(1 - l) = 20,800$, implying $\varepsilon = w(1 - l)/Z$ from (31). The sensitivity of Z to r in the third column carries over to ε, with the estimate declining geometrically at about 10% per percentage point increase in r. The estimate also is sensitive to the estimate of $V(a)$, which had a sampling error alone of 25% of the estimated level value.[8]

There are several additional possible sources of bias in these numbers.

i) Savings. Assume that $c = \beta w(1 - l)$ with $\beta < 1$. If β is .9, the implied saving rate is 10% and the estimates in column 4 fall by less than 5%. A 10% savings rate surely is an upper bound for this population.

ii) Costs of Mortality. If medical and other costs of mortality are fixed at D, then incorporating them into the model (assuming full insurance) involves setting up a sinking fund and charging interest rD against consumer surplus in (31). Approximately 10% of all medical expenses are accounted for by people in their last year of life, or \$22,000 in 1986 dollars. Adding a generous allowance for other expenses increases the estimate of ε in table 1 by 3% and decreases the estimate of Z by 5% at $r = .10$. The adjustments are less at lower interest rates.

iii) Taxes. The survey data underlying T–R's study probably refer to before-tax earnings, so $V(a)$ should be multiplied by $(1 - \gamma)$ where γ is the marginal tax rate. For this population γ lies within [.15,.20], (see Steuerle and Hartzmark, 1981) and the values of Z and $V(\alpha)$ in tables 1 and 2 should be multiplied by .80 or .85. The estimate of ε is hardly affected by marginal taxes of this size.

iv) Cross-Section Life Table. Though the T–R data are from 1968, the 1979–1981 life table is used for $A(42.r)$ in table 1. Falling mortality rates causes cohort bias in cross-section life tables. Substantial increases in longevity during the 1970s made the 1979–1981 life table more accurate for this population. However, using the 1969–1971 life table gives estimates of ε that are only 3–6% smaller than those reported.

v) Retirement. Since earnings fall to zero during retirement and consumption changes as well, average Z in (31) is itself a weighted average of pre- and postretirement years. However, the weight on retirement years is smaller than the weight on working years for 42-year-olds, and it decreases with the rate of interest. Assuming retirement at age 65, 29% of A falls in the retirement years when $r = .01$, but only 9% of it does when $r = .08$. If $u(c,l)$ is strongly separable and $\rho = r$, ε in table 1 is underestimated by 7% at $r = .01$, by 3.5% at $r = .04$ and by 1% at $r = .08$. If $u(c,l)$ is not separable, things are more complicated. However, at respectable interest rates, the calculation above suggests small bias from this source unless ε falls dramatically during retirement.

Taken in total, all of these refinements would affect the estimates of Z and ε in table 1 by relatively little compared to their sensitivity to r. There is little professional consensus on the appropriate size of r. It ranges from the 0–1% long-run

average after-tax rate of return found on individual portfolio items relevant to annuities to the 15% gross rate of return on capital implicit in aggregate production
studies. A value of 8% is chosen here as middle ground, since the applicable rate
for individuals should be as large as the after-tax rate on corporate capital on risk-
premium considerations alone. Futhermore, Moore and Viscusi (1988) estimate
only a slightly larger value in their recent study of the nonlinear interactions between wage–risk premiums and age.

Extrapolations of table 1 to $v(a,a)$ in (33) must be confined to persons near the
same age and income levels, since ε and Z may change markedly outside that
neighborhood. Maintaining $c \approx w(1 - l)$, equation (31) implies $Z \approx w(1 - l)/\varepsilon =$
$2.8w(1 - l)$ for $r = .08$ and (30) implies $V(42) \approx Z \cdot A(42,.08) = 30w(1 - l)$. For each
dollar increase in earnings near $20,800, consumer surplus rises by $2.8 and the
current value of life rises by $30. These are lower bounds because, on selection
grounds, individuals with larger-than-average values of ε would find risky jobs
more attractive, and also because the T–R estimates are smaller than other
estimates.

Equation (33) is extrapolated in an age range six years on either side of age 42 in
table 2, assuming constant income in this range (a good approximation after net-
ting out time-series growth effects from r), and Z is held fixed at $58,330 as es-
timated for $r = .08$ in table 1.[9] Column 1 shows that the value of a current risk
declines with age, following the pattern of $A(a,.08)$, because Z is assumed constant
in this age range. Other columns evaluate willingness to pay now by a person a
years old to eliminate a prospective risk that occurs x years from now, for $x = 1, 2$.
3, and 4. These numbers decline markedly with x. A risk that is only four years in
the future has $190,000 less value (about 70%) than an immediate risk. A risk that is
ten years away would have less than half the value of an immediate risk. However.
estimates of ε and Z at other incomes and ages are necessary to evaluate risks for
younger and older persons.[10] Again, the numbers in table 2 are on the conservative
side for the same reason as mentioned above.

Table 2. Value of Current and Future Risks, by Age (in 1986 Dollars)

a	$v(a,a)$	$v(a + 1,a)$	$v(a + 2,a)$	$v(a + 3,a)$	$v(a + 4,a)$
36	658,000	604,100	554,300	508,300	465,800
38	649,200	595,300	545,600	499,600	458,400
40	639,300	585,400	537,200	489,800	447,400
42	630,000	574,400	524,600	478,900	436,600
44	616,100	562,300	512,600	467,000	424,900
46	602,800	548,900	499,400		
48	588,400				

Notes: $v(a,a) = V(a) = Z \cdot A(a,.08)$, for $Z = 58,330$ from Table 1. $v(a + x,a) = (S(a + x))/(S(a)) \cdot v(a +$
$x,a + x)/(1 + r)^x$ for $r = .08$, from equation (33).

The benefit side of a project affecting age-specific mortality always respects the current values of the population. For the case at hand, total benefits are the sum $\int v(a,a)\phi(a)da$, where $\phi(a)$ is the current age distribution function. Project evaluation can change as the age distribution changes. A project affecting mortality of the elderly receives a low score in a population that has relatively large numbers of young people, but the score may increase over time as the large cohort ages and the risks become more immediate.

5. Conclusions

This paper has spelled out the close connection between cross-section estimates of willingness to pay to reduce mortality risk and the valuation of changes in intertemporal survivor functions obtained from expected utility theory. It goes without saying that the most urgent needs in this area are better empirical estimates of the valuation of risks, and reconciliation of the differences in existing estimates based on different data sources.

Much work remains to be done on refining the conceptual apparatus as well. First, most models generally recognize only the two states of life and death, and do not consider illness states. This might be repaired by using a semi-Markov transition process among states, with death being the absorbing state. Since long-term disability and other serious health problems are correlated with mortality rates, risk estimates are some amalgam of the two. A more complete theory would show how to evaluate the incidence of morbidity risks. Another problem in extrapolating from table 1 to the longer-term risks in table 2 is that the manner of death may be different between immediate hazards and long-term hazards associated with lengthy periods of illness and suffering prior to death. The numbers in table 2 may be biased downward for this reason.

Second, bequests have been ignored in this study because of a belief that existing treatments are flawed. The prevailing method introduces a bequest function $B(\bar{c})$ in place of M, where $\bar{c}$ is descendants' consumption. Such a specification necessarily reduces the value of risks to life, because by leaving a large bequest, the decendent lives on through descendants. A complete analysis must incorporate the utility the person receives from dependents when alive. Surely family members are worse off when the head dies in the prime of life. A more refined treatment of altruism and preference dependencies is necessary to do justice to these issues. Since resource transfers among family members are important ways in which people cope with imperfect insurance and loan markets, such an analysis would go a long way in treating capital market imperfections as well as bequests.

Finally, the valuation formulas in (30) and (33) deal with known risks. Statistics on instantaneous exposure and risk are quite accurate in many cases, but there is much more uncertainty about the connections between exposure and changes in subsequent age-specific death rates when exposure has delayed and cumulative effects. In only a few cases, such as cigarette smoking and asbestos exposure, are the data extensive enough to determine these effects with precision. The relation between exposure and timing cannot be quantified even for such potent carcinogens as aflatoxin and vinyl chloride. Expected utility theory replaces the *pdf* $f(t)$ in (19) with a subjective *pdf* in these cases. However, the constraint (21) is affected in a different way. Uncertainty about hazards has the effect of introducing nontrivial load factors on consumption–annuity premiums because such risks are not diversifiable. The insurance company runs large risks of ruin and must charge large loads to create the necessary contingency reserves. Insurance is incomplete and may break down altogether (as it has in the case of asbestos exposure). Personal exposure to uncertain risks therefore must involve a significant degree of self-insurance, and this leads to larger valuations compared to known risks. Whether they are large enough on these grounds alone to account for the extreme social caution and prohibitions often observed among some risks remains to be shown, notwithstanding Peltzman's (1973) emphasis on the optimal production of risk information and the balancing of type I and type II errors.

Notes

1. The value of lotteries for dealing with indivisibilities and nonconvexities has been increasingly recognized in the past few years. Bergstrom (1974) was the first economist to notice the possible optimality of lotteries for mortality risks. Marshall (1984) emphasized preferences for life-risk lotteries in the context of bequests. Bergstrom (1986) gives a superb account of the case for a draft lottery over a voluntary army. Townsend (1986) presents the most complete general equilibrium theory yet available. Viscusi (1979) showed value for uncertainty in the present problem based on incomplete information and option value, which is a different basis for risk-preferring behavior. Notice that there is possible moral hazard in a randomization scheme. It is in the interests of a person to agree to the scheme ex ante and then to defect from it ex post, given that everyone else follows through with it. If everyone defects then it is the case that $v < 0$. As usual, some form of commitment is required to eliminate this problem.

2. It is easy to show that the indifference curves between W and p are convex so that v is decreasing in p: the greater the hazard rate, the more a person is willing to pay to reduce it. This must be qualified in case (ii), where the convexified indifference curve has a zero slope at high values of p and willingness to pay is zero there. Finally, differentiate (6) with respect to W to obtain $\partial v/\partial W = s/\varepsilon p > 0$, where $s = -u'' \cdot c/u'$ is the coefficient of relative risk aversion: safety is a normal good.

3. The statement is loose because the connection between ε and the intertemporal elasticity of substitution is lost if $|M|$ is large.

4. Shephard and Zeckhauser (1984) consider a lending but no borrowing constraint and simulate valuations that are very close to the full annuities case. Other possible ways of specifying such constraints may give much different results.

5. The marginal conditions for constraints $h^*(t) < h(t)$ where $h^*(t)$ is chosen to convexify preferences are

$$\lambda \int_t^\infty \left\{ \frac{1-\varepsilon}{\varepsilon} c(\tau) + w(\tau)(1 - l(\tau)) \right\} S(\tau) e^{-r(\tau-t)} d\tau \geq 0, \text{ all } t.$$

The intergral enters because a change in $h(t)$ has a permanent effect on future values of S (see below). The *discounted* expected surplus at every age must be nonnegative or else randomization is desirable. Notice that this condition allows instantaneois surplus (in curly braces) to take on some negative values, so long as the sum is positive or zero. Since this condition places a lower bound of zero on the value of life as before, it is ignored hereafter.

6. If $\rho = r$, then (22) implies that $Z'(t+a) = w'(t + a)(1 - l(t + a))$ and $Z(t)$ varies with the wage rate. If $\rho \neq r$, the expression for Z' is much more complicated and not very helpful.

7. The regression coefficient of the weekly wage on excess death risk is about $4 per .001 risk increment in 1968 dollars. The average person in the sample worked 50 weeks per year, for an increment of $200 per year per .001 unit of excess risk. Dividing by .001 and multiplying the result by 3.15 to convert to 1986 dollars yields $V = $630,000$.

8. Estimates of V based on industry rather than on occupation risks are as much as five times (!) larger than those in T–R. The implied estimates of Z are five times larger and the estimates of ε are one-fourth the size of those in table 1. Interested readers are invited to adjust the estimates in table 2 correspondingly.

9. The numbers in table 2 refer to the steady state. The transitional problem of recontracting annuities among existing cohorts after the risk has been eliminated is ignored here.

10. Suppose exposure changes the flow death rate by $\Delta(t)$ from age a onward. Here $\delta S_a(t) = 0$ for $t < a$ as before, but $\Delta(t)$ now has cumulative effects on subsequent survival rates from (28), so $\delta S(t) = S_a(t) \int_a^t \Delta(\tau) d\tau$ for $t > a$. Substituting into (26) gives a valuation formula for any age-risk pattern. In distinction to the stock experiment in (29), where the weight on future survival rates is reduced by discounting, approximation errors are greater for these flow changes because the cumulation of effects in $\delta S_a(t)$ for $t > a$ offsets the discount factor, and expected surplus at much older ages gets much greater weight. More precise knowledge of Z and ε are required to implement these more elaborate experiments.

References

Arthur, W. Brian. The Economics of Risks to Life. *American Economic Review* (Vol. 71, 1981), pp 54-64.

Bailey, Martin J. *Reducing Risks to Life: Measurement of the Benefits.* Washington, D.C.: American Enterprise Institue Study, No. 243, 1980.

Bergstrom, Theodore C. Preference and Choice in Matters of Life and Death. In: Jack Hirshleifer, Theordore C. Bergstrom, and Edward Rappaport, eds., *Applying Cost–Benefit Concepts to Projects Which Alter Human Mentality.* Research Report, UCLA School of Engineering, 1974.

Bergstrom, Theodore C. Soldiers of Fortune. In: W.P. Heller, R.M. Starr, and D.A. Starret, eds., *Social Choice and Public Decision-Making: Essays in Honor of Kenneth Arrow*, Vol. 1. Cambridge: Cambridge University Press, 1986.

Conley, Brian C. The Value of Human Life in the Demand for Safety. *American Economic Review* (Vol. 66, 1976), pp 45-55.

Cropper, Maureen L. Health, Investment in Health and Occupational Choice. *Journal of Political Economy* (Vol.85,1977), pp 1273-1294.

Ehrlich, Isaac & Chuma, H. The Demand for Life: An Economic Analysis. University of Buffalo, 1984.

Jones-Lee, M.W. *The Value of Life: An Economic Analysis.* Chicago: University of Chicago Press, 1976.

Marshall, John M. Gambles and the Shadow Price of Death. *American Economic Review* (Vol. 74, 1984) pp 73-86.

Mishan, Ezra J. The Evaluation of Life and Limb. *Journal of Political Economy* (Vol. 79, 1971) pp 687-705.

Moore, Michael J. & Viscusi, Kip W. The Quantity Adjusted Value of Life. *Economic Inquiry*, 1988 forthcoming.

Peltzman, Sam. An Evaluation of Consumer Drug Protection Information: The 1962 Drug Amendments. *Journal of Political Economy* (Vol. 81, 1973), pp 1049-1091.

Rice, Dorothy P. *Estimating the Costs of Illness*, Health Economics Series, No. 6 Washington, D.C.; U.S. Public Health Service, 1966.

Rosen, Sherwin. Valuing Health Risk. *American Economic Review* (Vol. 71, 1981) pp 241-245.

Schelling, Thomas G. The Life You Save My Be Your Own. In: S.B. Chase, eds., *Problems in Public Expenditure Analysis*, Washington, D.C.: Brookings Institution, 1986.

Shepard, Donald S. & Zeckhauser, Richard J. Survival Versus Consumption. *Management Science* (Vol. 30, 1984), pp 423-439.

Steuerle, Eugene & Hartzmark, Michael. Individual Income Taxation, 1949-79. *National Tax Journal* (Vol. 34, 1981), pp 145-166.

Thaler, Richard & Rosen, Sherwin. The Value of Saving A Life: Evidence from the Labor Market. In: N. Terleckyj, ed. *Household Production and Consumption*. New York: National Bureau of Economic Research, 1975.

Townsend, Robert. Arrow–Debreu Programs as Microfoundations for Macroeconomics. Discussion paper 86-7, Program In Quantitive Economic Analysis, National Opinion Research Center, 1986.

Usher, Daniel. An Imputation to the Measure of Economic Growth for Changes in Life Expectancy. In: M. Moss, ed., *The Measurement of Economic and Social Performance*. New York: National Bureau of Economic Reasearch, 1973.

Viscusi, W. Kip. Wealth Effects and Earnings Premiums for Job Hazards. *Review of Economics and Statistics* (Vol. 60, 1978), p 408-416.

Viscusi, W. Kip. Insurance and Individual Incentives in Adaptive Contexts. *Econometrica* (Vol. 47, 1978), pp 117-140.

Weisbrod, Burton A. Costs and Benefits of Medical Research: A Case Study of Poliomyelitis. *Journal of Political Economy* (Vol. 79, 1971), pp 523-544.

Yaari, Menachem E. Uncertain Lifetime, Life Insurance and the Theory of the Consumer. *Review of Economic Studies* (Vol. 32, 1965), pp 137-150.

[27]

Journal of Public Economics 38 (1989) 297–317. North-Holland

RATES OF TIME PREFERENCE AND VALUATIONS OF THE DURATION OF LIFE

W. Kip VISCUSI and Michael J. MOORE*

Duke University, Durham, NC 27706, USA

Received November 1987, revised version received December 1988

This paper develops a multi-period Markov model of the lifetime choice of occupational fatality risks. The empirical model analyzes the wage effects of job risks using the 1982 University of Michigan Panel Study of Income Dynamics in conjunction with death statistics from the U.S. National Traumatic Occupational Fatality Survey. Evidence regarding workers' intertemporal choices with respect to risks with long-term implications is broadly consistent with rational behavior. Workers' implicit real rate of time preference with respect to future life years equals approximately 11 percent. This rate of time preference decreases with education.

1. Introduction

Perhaps the most severe test of economic rationality comes in markets that combine elements of intertemporal choice and uncertainty. Intertemporal rationality has long been a concern among economists. Indeed, Pigou (1932, pp. 24–25) viewed market situations involving intertemporal choice as posing the greatest exception to efficient market performance, concluding that 'people distribute their resources between the present, the near future and the remote future on the basis of a wholly irrational preference'. Uncertainty poses an additional set of problems for individual decision, as a now substantial literature documents a variety of difficulties arising with respect to risky decisions.[1]

These open issues regarding the performance of intertemporal markets are particularly acute with respect to intertemporal allocations involving individual health. Although money is readily transferable across time, health status

*Preliminary versions of this paper were presented at the University of Chicago, Duke University, the University of Illinois, the U.S. Environmental Protection Agency, Northwestern University, and the Summer Meetings of the Labor Studies program of the National Bureau of Economic Research. Gregory M. Duncan, Robert Winkler, Gary Zarkin and two anonymous referees provided helpful comments. This research was supported in part by the endowment of the George G. Allen professorship and by the Fuqua School of Business.
[1]See, for example, the reviews by Machina (1987) and Tversky and Kahneman (1986).

is not. As a result, the ambiguities usually associated with the selection of an appropriate rate of discount for policy evaluation are exacerbated in the case of health effects. As Lave (1981, p. 44) has observed: 'The set of virtually unanswerable questions includes the discount rate used for future health status.'

The rate of time preference used in weighting the utility of future periods of life has assumed substantial policy importance in recent years. Some observers, such as Fuchs and Zeckhauser (1987), are unwilling to make any distinctions with respect to discount rates for health outcomes. However, U.S. government agencies confronted with the task of discounting deferred health impacts of regulatory policies are becoming increasingly reluctant to use interest rates from financial markets in these calculations. No explicit intertemporal market in human health exists, and some economists express doubts as to whether capital market rates accurately reflect the tradeoffs individuals make with respect to health status in different years. Moreover, if there is a discrepancy, its direction is not clear.

Our objective in this paper is to explore the empirical properties of individuals' discount rates for intertemporal choices involving health status. In particular, we assess the discount rates that individuals themselves place on intertemporal health risks. These private values in turn provide guidance in selecting the appropriate social rates of discount for policies that affect health status over time. Although our estimates of the rate of time preference do not completely resolve the potentially difficult policy issue of selecting the appropriate discount rate for the health effects of policy interventions, they do provide objective market estimates of the discount rates applied by the individuals themselves.

The manner in which labor markets deal with death risks provides a promising empirical context for exploring the implications of coupling risks with intertemporal choice. This form of risk involves not only an obvious probabilistic element but also an intertemporal component: How much should the worker require in present compensation to offset the loss in utility due to the risks to his future welfare? The rather substantial compensating wage differential literature for the most part abstracts from this intertemporal component, as death risks have been viewed using the empirical simplification of a single-period model.

We refine the standard approach in order to isolate the intertemporal aspects of worker decisions and to explore several related aspects of the worker's multi-period choice problem. In the most important modification of the usual approach, we alter the death risk measure to take into account the loss in the duration of life. We base our empirical framework on an equation that explicitly recognizes the loss in discounted lifetime utility from a job fatality. Using these results, we generate estimates of the real discount rate applied to future health status.

The importance of taking into account the duration of life lost has been stressed by a number of authors, including Zeckhauser and Shepard (1976), Viscusi (1979, 1983), Rosen (1988), and Fuchs and Zeckhauser (1987). In recent years, economists such as Arthur (1981), Shepard and Zeckhauser (1984), and Rosen (1988) have developed elaborate life-cycle risk models in an effort to explicitly incorporate duration-of-life effects.

These theoretical concerns have not been reflected to the same degree in the empirical literature, in large part because the theoretical models are not empirically tractable. Indeed, empirical models generally ignore the duration-of-life issue. In the most common formulation, authors abstract altogether from the duration issue by using the simple death risk variable as the risk measure. Although there have been attempts to recognize the influence of life duration in unstructured models through age–death risk interactions, as in Thaler and Rosen (1976) and Viscusi (1979), these formulations abstract from the role of discounting and changes in life expectancy with age. The discounting issue can be addressed within the content of a standard hedonic wage model, as in Moore and Viscusi (1988a), who utilize as their death risk variable the discounted life years lost. The model we develop here makes the duration issue a fundamental concern, so that the focus of the empirical analysis is on the individual's implicit rate of time preference with respect to years of life.

The potentially pivotal role of rates of time preference with respect to health investments has been a major concern in the health economics literature. In particular, estimation of discount rates for future health status is the focal point of the work by Fuchs (1986), who conducted an extensive interview study of a variety of health risks to assess the intertemporal rationality of health-related decisions. The implicit rate of discount used by workers is similarly of substantial economic consequence since it provides an index of the degree to which individuals take into account future welfare losses when making risky job choices. If individuals are myopic, then labor market outcomes for risks with long-term implications are more prone to market failure than outcomes for short-term risks such as temporary work disability.

Perhaps most fundamentally: How much do individuals value the length of their life? One advantage of greater longevity is that one's lifetime wealth rises as a result of additional years in the labor force. For any given level of lifetime wealth, however, the duration of life is also a matter of concern if an individual cannot consume his lifetime wealth in a single period without suffering any diminishing marginal utility of consumption. Our results suggest that the duration of life is a substantial matter of concern, as one might expect.

In section 2 we develop the theoretical structure of our empirical model, which consists of a Markov model of the multi-period job risk problem. We estimate our model using a large individual data set – the 1982 University of Michigan Panel Study of Income Dynamics (PSID). This survey information has been coupled with U.S. job risk measures from the National Traumatic Occupational Fatality Survey. These data and the variables used are discussed in section 3. In section 4 we report estimates of the multi-period job choice model. Estimates of a more traditional formulation are reported in our companion paper, Moore and Viscusi (1988a). The results, which are quite consistent across the two models, lend strong support to the hypothesized rationality of employment decisions.

2. A multi-period model of job risks

2.1. The worker choice problem

Adam Smith's insight that risky jobs command compensating differentials is quite robust with respect to the economic context in which the issue arises. Most analyses to date have focused on the single-period case in which the worker faces some lottery on health status and must receive a wage premium to compensate him for the extra risk. In the case of non-fatal health risks, this simplification has considerable appeal in that one can view the job choice as a sequence of independent lotteries.

For the death risk situation, however, the worker's problem is more complex. Acceptance of a risky job in period t generates some increase in the probability p that the worker will not survive to period $t+1$ so that the expected value of all future rewards is affected. Although the death risk situation has been considered theoretically within multi-period contexts, these analyses were not concerned with developing a formulation that could be estimated empirically.[2]

In this section we develop a simple job choice model involving death risks. We then use the model to develop the two-equation empirical model estimated in subsequent sections of the paper. Our approach is unique in that it is the only empirical analysis of death risks that incorporates the theoretical structure of the multi-period death risk problem. Rather than estimate a simple ad hoc wage equation to which a death risk variable has been added, we derive a functional form of the worker's indifference curve from the theory that enables us to consider a wide variety of conceptual issues. Then, treating the market-determined wage–risk locus as a constraint from which individuals choose their wage–risk combinations, we estimate the structural parameters of the model. The empirical approach utilizes the

---

[2]See, for example, Conley (1976) and Viscusi (1979). Zeckhauser and Shepard's (1976) concern for quality-adjusted life years is in a similar vein, though not directly related to labor market risks. Arthur (1981), Rosen (1988), and Shepard and Zeckhauser (1984) also develop elaborate life-cycle models.

maintained assumption that the worker's indifference curve is tangent to the wage–risk locus in equilibrium in order to identify and estimate the key parameters of the model. The most novel feature of our empirical results is the estimation of the discount rate that individuals use in valuing future years of life.

Development of functional forms for the model requires that we impose some structure on the worker's multi-period job choice problem. The assumed structure that we impose on the job choice problem so as to obtain an estimable functional form is much less restrictive than the implicit assumptions one makes in the standard approach by including only a death risk term in the wage equation. Moreover, it also allows structural interpretations of the terms related to death risk. The standard approach abstracts altogether from length of life issues and implicitly imposes far more severe assumptions. Use of an age–risk interaction term is a common empirical remedy for the duration-of-life problem, but this approach ignores the role of discounting, differences in life expectancy, and changes in life expectancy with age.

Our model's assumptions are far more modest. As a check on the plausibility of our assumptions, we test the second-order conditions implied by the market equilibrium model. These conditions relate to the curvature of workers' indifference curves at the point of tangency with the market opportunity locus.

Consider the following situation. Assume that the time horizon for both living and working is infinite. In each period the worker faces a lottery on life and death, where p is the probability of death, which we assume constant for simplicity, and $1-p$ is the probability of survival.[3] The total risk of death, p, is the sum of the job risk, p_j, and other risks to life, p_o. For each year that the individual is alive, he reaps consumption x equal to his income in that period. The worker's utility function $U(x)$ satisfies the usual assumptions for a risk-averse worker ($U_x > 0$ and $U_{xx} < 0$). The role played by the shape of the utility function is discussed further below. The consumption level is determined by the wage rate $w(p_j)$, where the worker picks his optimal wage–job risk combination from a schedule of available wage–risk combinations. It can be shown that $\partial w/\partial p_j$, the rate of tradeoff between wages and risks on the point of the wage offer curves selected by the worker, must be positive for the worker to accept the risky job.[4]

In effect, we are assuming that the individual worker equates consumption and earned income in each period. This assumption is borne out in more

---

[3]Learning about risk over time and changes in the riskiness of the job can be handled theoretically, but not in a form that can easily be estimated. On the other hand, given the relative importance of lifetime jobs and the stability of death risks over time, this assumption may not be overly restrictive.

[4]See Viscusi (1979).

complete models if labor market earnings are the only income source and workers have access to perfect capital markets. We take as the individual's objective the desire to maximize discounted expected lifetime utility.

In terms of its general structure, this model recognizes the multi-period aspects of job risks and the impact of death risks on the worker's time horizon. A variety of complicating influences are not considered. These include the role of bequests, changes in earnings capacity over the life cycle, savings, changes in risk levels over time, and imperfections in capital and insurance markets. Some of these concerns have been addressed in previous conceptual analyses, most notably by Rosen (1988), but are much too complex to be incorporated into an empirical framework. In particular, in some cases these factors preclude a closed-form solution of the worker's choice problem.

The worker's objective of maximizing discounted expected utility from the wage schedule $w(p_j)$ takes the form of a time-invariant Markov decision problem:

$$\max_{p_j} V = (1-p)U(w(p_j)) + \beta(1-p)^2 U(w(p_j)) + \cdots$$

$$+ \beta^{t-1}(1-p)^t U(w(p_j)) + \cdots. \tag{1}$$

The utility of survival in any period t is weighted by the probability of surviving at least t periods, $(1-p)^t$, and the discount factor, β^{t-1}. Utility in the death state is normalized to equal zero, which involves no loss of generality provided that the bequest equals some constant.

In effect, we assume the worker picks a lifetime risk p initially that remains constant over time. In an infinite time horizon model, this approach is the optimal solution provided that the rewards and risks are time invariant. With a finite time horizon, the optimal p does not vary greatly until one nears the final periods of the problem. At that point the worker may be reluctant to switch jobs because of the high transactions costs of job changing or the poor job prospects for workers near retirement age. This simplification ignores the role of learning and changes in the choice of the optimal job risk over time [see Viscusi (1979)]. In the theoretical model, we abstract from such issues for reasons of simplicity.

Upon collecting terms, one can express eq. (1) as:

$$\max_{p_j} V = U(w(p_j))(1-p) \sum_{t=1}^{\infty} [\beta(1-p)]^{t-1}. \tag{2}$$

To simplify the notation, define a new term $G(p)$, where

$$G(p) = \sum_{t=1}^{\infty} [\beta(1-p)]^{t-1} = 1/[1-\beta(1-p)], \tag{3}$$

so that the worker selects p_j to

$$\max_{p_j} V = U(w(p_j))(1-p)/[1-\beta(1-p)]. \tag{4}$$

The optimal value of p_j satisfies:

$$V_{p_j} = 0 = U'(w(p_j))(1-p)(\partial w/\partial p_j)G(p) + U(w(p_j))(1-p)G'(p)$$

$$- U(w(p_j))G(p). \tag{5}$$

Solving eq. (5) for $\partial w/\partial p_j$ yields:

$$\frac{\partial w}{\partial p_j} = \frac{U}{U'}\left[\frac{1}{(1-p)} - \frac{G'}{G}\right]. \tag{6}$$

The numerator of the second term in the bracketed expression is $G'(p)$, which, upon differentiating eq. (3), is:

$$G'(p) = -\beta/[1-\beta(1-p)]^2. \tag{7}$$

Combining eqs. (3) and (7) yields:

$$G'/G = -\beta/[1-\beta(1-p)],$$

and eq. (6) becomes:

$$\frac{\partial w}{\partial p_j} = \frac{U}{U'}\left[\frac{1}{1-p} + \frac{\beta}{1-\beta(1-p)}\right]. \tag{8}$$

The object of this analysis is the derivation of a wage equation suitable for estimation. We could solve the first-order differential equation (8) by integration if we made the additional assumption that U/U' is constant. In the analysis below we adopt a different approach to avoid imposing this restriction.

2.2. The empirical model

Our empirical estimation strategy utilizes a structural approach to the estimation of hedonic labor market equilibrium models. The model consists of two equations. Eq. (8) describes the worker's marginal rate of substitution between wages and job risks, $\partial w/\partial p_j$, which constitutes the implicit price of risk. The second equation in the model, the market opportunities locus for risky jobs, $w(p_j)$, acts as the constraint for the worker. Our estimation strategy assumes a tractable functional form for the utility function in eq. (8). This yields an expression for the marginal rate of substitution equation that involves only observable data, the unknown constant, β, a risk aversion parameter, c, and the implicit prices. The implicit prices are estimated from the market opportunities locus in a first-stage regression. We then use the estimated implicit prices of job risks as regressors in estimating the parameters of eq. (8).

The wage equation is of the form $w = w(p_j; y_1, \varepsilon_1)$, where y_1 is the vector of observed variables that shift the constraint and ε_1 represents the effects of unobservable wage determinants. Similarly, eq. (8) could be rewritten to include a vector of observed variables that capture individual differences in tastes, y_2, and unobservable 'taste-shifters', ε_2, so that

$$\partial w/\partial p_j = \partial w/\partial p_j(p_j; y_2, \varepsilon_2).$$

To estimate the model empirically requires functional forms for the wage function and the implicit price of safety function. Consider first the worker's implicit price equation. Eq. (8) describes the worker's marginal rate of substitution and contains unspecified forms of the state-dependent utility function, U, and the marginal utility function, U'. The constant relative risk-aversion utility function represents a specification of U with desirable properties that yields an estimable version of eq. (8).[5] This function in general equals:

$$U = a + bw^c,$$

where a and b are arbitrary constants, ($b > 0$), and $c \in (0, 1)$. The constant c

[5]See Keeney and Raiffa (1976, p. 173).

provides an index of the individual's aversion to risk. With no loss of generality, let $a = (-1/c)$ and $b = (1/c)$. The utility function then equals:

$$U = \frac{w^c - 1}{c}.$$

Important special cases of this utility function include the extreme values of c, since U approaches $\ln w$ as c approaches 0 and $U = w - 1$ when $c = 1$. Thus, the parameter c determines the curvature of U, and in the limiting cases yields the popular logarithmic and linear (risk-neutral) utility functions.

In general, the constant relative risk aversion utility function yields an estimable relationship between a function of the implicit price of risk and a function of the wage. Given the definition

$$U = \frac{w^c - 1}{c},$$

marginal utility, U', equals w^{c-1}, and

$$\frac{U}{U'} = \frac{1}{c}(w - w^{1-c}).$$

Upon substitution for U/U', eq. (8) now becomes:

$$\frac{\partial w_i}{\partial p_j} = \frac{1}{c}(w_i - w_i^{1-c})\left[\frac{1}{1-p_i} + \frac{\beta}{1-\beta(1-p_i)}\right] \tag{9}$$

where the i subscript captures the individual-specific nature of the utility function. Multiplying through eq. (9) by the term cw^{c-1} and dividing by the term in brackets, yields:

$$\left[\frac{1}{1-p_i} + \frac{\beta}{1-\beta(1-p_i)}\right]^{-1} cw_i^{c-1}\frac{\partial w_i}{\partial p_j} = w_i^c - 1.$$

Using the fact that $\partial w^c = cw^{c-1}\partial w$ and simplifying the bracketed term then yields the expression:

$$w_i^c = 1 + [(1-p_i) - \beta(1-p_i)^2]\frac{\partial w_i^c}{\partial p_j}. \tag{10}$$

Two special cases of eq. (10) are of particular interest. In the first of these, evaluating eq. (10) as c approaches 0 yields the specification corresponding to the logarithmic utility function:

$$\ln w_i = 1 + [(1-p_i) - \beta(1-p_i)^2] \frac{\partial \ln w_i}{\partial p_j}.$$

Similarly, for the risk-neutral case where $c=1$, eq. (10) becomes:

$$w_i = 1 + [(1-p_i) - \beta(1-p_i)^2] \frac{\partial w_i}{\partial p_j}.$$

Adding the variables in the vector y_2 and the unobservables ε_2, eq. (10) becomes:

$$w_i^c = 1 + [(1-p_i) - \beta(1-p_i)^2] \frac{\partial w_i^c}{\partial p_j} + \sum_k \alpha_k y_{2ki} + \varepsilon_{2i}.$$

In the empirical analysis, we evaluate the sensitivity of our estimates of β to the value of c. We also find the maximum likelihood estimate of c, which provides an estimate of the degree of risk aversion exhibited by the workers in our sample. For purposes of illustration, however, let us focus on the logarithmic specification:

$$\ln w_i = [(1-p_i) - \beta(1-p_i)^2] \frac{\partial \ln w_i}{\partial p_j} + \sum_k \alpha_k y_{2ki} + \varepsilon_{2i}. \tag{11}$$

In principle, if we had measures of p, $\partial \ln w/\partial p_j$, and y_2 we could estimate the parameter β and the α_k's. The first problem in doing so arises because, as a practical matter, the extremely small magnitudes of the overall mortality risk p leave the variables $(1-p)$ and $(1-p)^2$ virtually indistinguishable. To circumvent this problem, we treat them as approximately equal, and estimate the parameter β in the model:

$$\ln w_i = (1-\beta)(1-p_i) \frac{\partial \ln w_i}{\partial p_j} + \sum_k \alpha_k y_{2ki} + \varepsilon_{2i}. \tag{12}$$

The second problem in estimating eq. (11) arises from the unobservability of the variable $\partial \ln w/\partial p_j$. This variable, which represents the implicit price of risk, equals the slope of the wage–risk equilibrium locus and can be computed from a first-stage regression of wages on job risks and other control variables. As noted by Biddle and Zarkin (1988), structural equations such as eq. (12) are only identified if the market wage equation contains variables that are excluded from the structural equation. Shifts in the wage equation then trace out the individuals' indifference curves. Logical candidates for instrumental variables to achieve this identification include variables indicating geographically distinct markets, such as regional dummy variables. Furthermore, Kahn and Lang (1988) show that the interactions of the region dummy variables with the exogenous variables in the indifference curve equation (the y_2's) are also valid instruments.

Eq. (12), as written, imposes the assumption that all workers have the same rate of time preference. To relax this assumption, let the discount rate term $1 - \beta$, which equals $r/1 + r$, vary due to differences in education S_i, and unobserved individual effects ε_{3i}:

$$1 - \beta = (1 - \beta)_0 + \beta_s S_i + \varepsilon_{3i}.$$

Substitution of this expression into eq. (12) yields:

$$\ln w_i = (1 - \beta_0)(1 - p_i)\frac{\partial \ln w}{\partial p_j} + \beta_s S_i (1 - p_i)\frac{\partial \ln w_i}{\partial p_j} + \sum \alpha_k y_{2ki} + \varepsilon_i^*. \qquad (13)$$

Allowing for individual variability in discount rates introduces heteroskedasticity into the model, since

$$\varepsilon_i^* = \varepsilon_{2i} + \varepsilon_{3i}(1 - p_i)\frac{\partial \ln w_i}{\partial p_j},$$

and therefore

$$\mathrm{Var}\,(\varepsilon_i^* = \mathrm{E}(\varepsilon_i^{*2}) = \sigma_2^2 + \sigma_3^2\left[(1 - p_i)\frac{\partial \ln w_i}{\partial p_j}\right]^2 + 2\sigma_{23}(1 - p_i)\frac{\partial \ln w_i}{\partial p_j}.$$

We control for heteroskedasticity of this form in the estimation of eq. (13).

The wage equation used to compute the implicit prices is

$$\ln w = \sum_{k=1}^{4} (\phi_k R_k p_j + 0.5\delta_k R_k p_j^2) + \sum_m \gamma_m y_{1m} + \varepsilon_1, \qquad (14)$$

where the i subscripts have been dropped for notational convenience. The R_k variables are region dummy variables indicating residence in either the Northeast, North Central, Southeast, or West. The remaining variables, y_1, are other determinants of the position of the wage–risk constraint, such as experience, job tenure, and education. The implicit prices equal the derivatives of eq. (14) with respect to job risk:

$$\frac{\partial \ln w}{\partial p_j} = \sum_{k=1}^{4} (\phi_k R_k + \delta_k R_k p_j). \tag{15}$$

The implicit price of risk varies according to both region and risk level. Variation in $\partial \ln w/\partial p_j$ by region represents shifts in the market opportunities locus, while variation by risk level represents movements along the locus. Thus, the regional variables (and their interactions with the y_2 variables) identify the indifference curve parameters in eq. (13). We estimate eqs. (13) and (14) using non-linear two-stage least squares.

The preceding analysis also yields a test of the plausibility of the assumptions of the model. The second-order condition for a maximum of eq. (2) requires that the derivative of eq. (5) with respect to p_j be negative. This implies the testable restriction, based on eq. (10):

$$\frac{\partial^2 w^c}{\partial p_j^2} < \frac{\partial w^c}{\partial p_j}\left[\frac{1}{1-p} + \frac{\beta}{1-\beta(1-p)}\right] + w^c\left[\frac{1}{(1-p)^2} - \frac{\beta^2}{(1-\beta(1-p))^2}\right]. \tag{16}$$

Given estimates of β and c, this expression can be evaluated for each worker in the sample using information on overall mortality risk p, wages, and the values of $\partial w^c/\partial p_j$ and $\partial^2 w^c/\partial p_j^2$, computed from eq. (14) conditional on some chosen value of c.

In summary, the empirical model consists of two equations – a market wage equation [eq. (14)] and an expression describing the worker's rate of substitution between wages and job risks [eq. (13)]. The estimation strategy consists of estimating the parameters of eq. (14), computing the implicit prices from these estimates, and using these computed prices as regressors in estimating eq. (13). Since the implicit prices and the term $1-p$ are endogenous, eq. (13) must be estimated using two-stage least squares. Regional dummy variables and their interactions with the other variables in eq. (13) are used as instrumental variables. The estimate of β_0 is derived from the coefficient on the variable $(1-p_i)\partial \ln w_i/\partial p_j$ in eq. (12). The maximum likelihood estimates of the risk-aversion parameter, c, and of the other coefficients, are found by searching over values of c between 0 and 1.

3. Description of the sample and the variables

The empirical analysis utilizes the 1982 wave of the University of Michigan Panel Study of Income Dynamics (PSID). The PSID, a national survey of demographic characteristics and economic data of workers in the United States, is the primary data set used in our analysis. The PSID data are matched to data on mortality risk and job fatality risk to form the final data set.

As our measure of the job fatality risk, we use the recently published National Traumatic Occupational Fatality (NTOF) death risk data collected by the U.S. National Institute for Occupational Safety and Health. These data, which are described more fully below and in Moore and Viscusi (1988b, forthcoming), cover the years 1980–84. The 1982 wave of the PSID is the first panel year covered by the death risk data that has three-digit measures for the worker's industry, so we use this particular year of the PSID for our empirical analysis. In constructing our data set, we include only the randomly selected observations in the PSID, thus excluding the poverty subsample. Farmers, farm managers, miners, and cases with missing observations are excluded. All of these exclusions are standard in the literature. Our remaining sample contains 1,463 observations.

In many compensating differential studies it is necessary to restrict the sample to male or blue-collar workers to estimate wage premiums success-fully. Such restrictions were not required for the 1982 PSID. The only sample restrictions imposed were that we focused on non-farm household heads who were not self-employed and who worked more than 20 hours per week. The availability of death risk statistics for the worker's industry also limited the sample size. For example, death statistics are not reported by the NTOF Survey for government employees.

Table 1 defines the variables used in the empirical analysis, and table 2 summarizes many of the principal characteristics of the PSID sample. The average sample member has an hourly after-tax wage of $7, one dependent child, and 13 years of education. Eight percent of the workers are black, and 17 percent are female. Job tenure and experience are approximately 5 and 12 years, on average. Thirty percent of the workers are covered by a collective bargaining agreement and approximately one-half of the workers hold blue-collar jobs.

The dependent variable in the analysis is the worker's after-tax annual wage rate, assuming 2,000 annual hours worked. The annual wage is used to correspond with the time frame of the death risk. Sample members in the PSID report their marginal tax rate directly. This tax adjustment of wages, which is not typical in the literature on compensating differentials for job hazards, is clearly preferable theoretically and had an influence on some of the tests of statistical significance of the coefficients.

The job risk variable used in the analysis is the worker's annual death risk. The approach taken matches the workers in the sample to a death risk variable based on newly released death risk statistics for the worker's state and industry. These data represent a substantial improvement over pre-

Table 1
Variable definitions.

Variable	Definition
Wage	Hourly after-tax wage.
Implicit price	Estimated wage–risk tradeoff from market wage locus.
Number of dependents	Number of dependent children.
Education	Years of schooling.
Black	Race dummy variable (d.v.): 1 if worker is black, 0 otherwise.
Female	Sex d.v.: 1 if worker is female, 0 otherwise.
Job tenure	Years worked on the current job.
Experience	Years worked since age 16.
Union status	Collective bargaining d.v.: 1 if workers's job is covered by a collective bargaining agreement, 0 otherwise.
Job risk	Annual job fatality rate: Number of deaths per 100,000 workers.
Mortality risk	Annual mortality rate: Number of deaths per 100,000 of population.
Northeast region	Region d.v.: 1 if worker lives in the Northeastern U.S., 0 otherwise.
Southeast region	Region d.v.: 1 if worker lives in the Southeastern U.S., 0 otherwise.
North Central region	Region d.v.: 1 if worker lives in the North Central U.S., 0 otherwise.
West region	Region d.v.: 1 if worker lives in the Western U.S., 0 otherwise.

viously used measures. The NTOF data are based on a census of occupations rather than the survey method used by the U.S. Bureau of Labor Statistics (BLS), so that sampling error is not present in the NTOF data. Furthermore, the NTOF data are available for over 400 state–industry combinations, giving a much less aggregated measure of risk than the BLS data, which measure death risks at the national two-digit industry level only.

Since job risks involve a low probability of death, on the order of 8/100,000 per worker, even at this level of aggregation risks may vary substantially across years, particularly if there is a major catastrophe that results in multiple deaths. The distorting influence of such random fluctuations is not present in the NTOF data, however, since they represent the average probability of death over the 1980–84 period. Furthermore, unlike the non-fatal accident statistics, death rate data were not subject to the

Table 2
Descriptive statistics; means and standard deviations.

Variable	Mean (standard deviation)
Wage	6.92 (2.42)
Implicit price ($\partial \ln w / \partial p_j$)	8.7E-3 (4.4E-3)
Number of dependents	1.01 (1.16)
Education	12.90 (2.51)
Black	0.08 (0.27)
Female	0.17 (0.38)
Job tenure	5.07 (6.27)
Experience	11.96 (10.56)
Union status	0.29 (0.46)
Job risk (per 100,000)	7.83 (9.66)
Mortality risk (per 100,000)	2,271.6 (2,687.6)
Northeast region	0.21 (0.41)
Southeast region	0.31 (0.46)
North Central region	0.29 (0.45)
West region	0.19 (0.39)
Sample size	1,463

classification problems that were present in the early 1970s under the new U.S. Bureau of Labor Statistics (BLS) reporting requirements.

Computation of the discounted remaining life risk terms in eq. (6), G and G', requires information on the probability of death by any means, p. The value of p is calculated using information on the worker's age, race, and sex, and life expectancy tables.[6] Estimates of the parameters β_0 and β_s, the

---

[6]See the *Statistical Abstract of the United States*, 1985 edition, p. 69.

remaining unknown terms in G and G', are derived in the estimation of eq. (13).

Also included in the equations estimated are variables that control the position of the wage–risk locus and the indifference curve. These variables include work experience, job tenure, and their squares, regional dummy variables, occupation dummy variables, and the worker characteristics des-cribed above.

4. Estimates of the wage equation

Consider first the estimates of the market wage equation [eq. (14)]. These estimates define the market opportunities locus, which in turn determines the available opportunity set for the worker's optimization problem. Table 3 presents the wage equation estimates. Of primary interest are the region–job risk interaction variables, since these are used in computing the implicit prices. In terms of total effects, these variables perform quite well. Significant compensation for job risks is found in all four regions, where a 1/100,000 increase in the annual fatality risk on the job results in percent wage increases of approximately 0.01. In each of the regions, the linear risk effect is positive and statistically significant. The region–death risk squared inter-actions indicate that the wage–risk locus is concave, as they are negative in all four cases and significant in three. Furthermore, the linear and squared risk terms are jointly significant in each region. This suggests in particular that the lack of significance on the squared risk term in the Southeast is likely due to collinearity.

The remaining estimated coefficients in the wage equation perform as expected. Workers with more dependents earn higher wages, as do more educated workers. The estimated rate of return to education of approxi-mately 4 percent per year is quite consistent with the human capital literature. Job tenure and experience increase wages at decreasing rates, and coverage by a collective bargaining agreement increases wages by about 17 percent. Black and female workers earn lower wages.

5. Discount rates and the value of remaining life

The second segment of the empirical model deals with the worker's choice from the available wage locus and, in particular, defines the marginal rate of substitution between wages and risk as a function of the implicit price of risk, mortality risk, rate of time preference, and other variables. The coefficients on the region–risk interaction variables are used to compute the implicit prices using eq. (15). The implicit price variable is then interacted with one minus the mortality variable, p, and used as a regressor in estimating eq. (13). To estimate the effect of education on the rate of time preference, we include the interaction of the years of education variable, S,

Table 3
Market wage equation estimates.

Variable[a]	Coefficients and standard errors
Northeast × job risk	0.025** (0.008)
Northeast × job risk^2	−9.4E-4* (4.7E-4)
North Central × job risk	0.023** (0.005)
North Central × job risk^2	−7.6E-4** (1.9E-4)
Southeast × job risk	0.004* (0.002)
Southeast × job risk^2	−0.2E-4 (0.5E-4)
West × job risk	0.021** (0.006)
West × job risk^2	−5.4E-4** (1.6E-4)
Number of dependents	0.033** (0.007)
Education	0.039** (0.004)
Black	−0.049* (0.029)
Female	−0.191** (0.023)
Job tenure	0.007** (0.003)
Job tenure^2	−0.8E-5 (1.1E-5)
Experience	0.023** (0.003)
Experience^2	−4.7E-4** (0.8E-4)
Union status	0.172** (0.018)
Adjusted R-squared	0.403

[a]Also included as regressors are six occupation dummy variables.
*Statistically significant at the 0.05 confidence level, one-tailed test.
**Statistically significant at the 0.01 confidence level, one-tailed test.

Table 4

Implicit price equation estimates; coefficients and standard errors.[a]

Variable (coefficient)	Unweighted	Weighted
Implicit price $\times (1-p)(1-\beta)_0$	0.278**	0.279**
	(0.097)	(0.096)
Implicit price $\times (1-p) \times$ education (β_s)	−0.014*	−0.014*
	(0.007)	(0.007)
Implied discount rate (r)[b]	10.7	10.7
Education	0.033**	0.033**
	(0.007)	(0.007)
Black	−0.006	−0.008
	(0.033)	(0.032)
Female	−0.266**	−0.268**
	(0.025)	(0.025)

[a]Occupational dummies were also included as regressors.
[b]Evaluated at the sample mean value of the education variable (12.90).
*Statistically significant at the 0.05 confidence level, one-tailed test.
**Statistically significant at the 0.01 confidence level, one-tailed test.

with the variable $(1-p)\, \partial w^c/\partial p_j$. This interaction will capture the education-specific variation in the rate of time preference. Also included as regressors in eq. (13) are proxies for differences in tastes that control for other determinants of the worker's marginal rate of substitution between wages and risk. These variables include measures of the worker's education, race, sex, and occupation.

Table 4 presents estimates of eq. (12) for the logarithmic versions of the utility function. The coefficients on the implicit price variables provide an estimate of $(1-\beta)$ equal to 0.28–0.014S, which yields an estimate of the implied discount rate, r, equal to 11 percent for a person with 12.9 years of education. The estimated discount rate parameters are highly significant, as the t-ratios on both implicit price variables exceed the level necessary at the 0.05 confidence level. The two implicit price variables are also jointly significant.

The 11 percent discount rate measures the average worker's real discount rate. By comparison, nominal long-term financial market interest rates for 1981 (the year covered by the 1982 PSID), such as the corporate Aaa bond rate (Moody's), were approximately 12 percent. To convert these measures to a real interest rate, we take the 8.8 percent rate of inflation (GNP deflator) from the prior year (1980) as a rough measure of inflationary expectations, yielding a real interest rate of approximately 3.2 percent.

Estimated rates of time preference depend systematically upon the level of education in the expected manner. Workers with eight years of schooling, for instance, reveal implicit rates of about 15 percent, while college-educated workers discount rates equal 5.5 percent. This relationship, which has been documented in another context by Fuchs (1986), reflects either differences in underlying preferences that also determine investment in education, or differential access to capital markets. The close correspondence between the college–age discount rate and market rate for the period is supportive of the latter explanation. In either case, the negative education–discount rate relationship provides one explanation for the observed negative relationship between education and injury rates documented by Viscusi (1979). That is, individuals with low discount rates show a systematic preference for the deferred benefits of investments in health and in education.

These estimates assume that the value of the parameter c, which measures aversion to risk, approaches zero. Two other important values of c include the risk-neutral case, in which c equals 1, and the maximum likelihood estimate of c. In this particular sample, c equal to 0.3 maximizes the value of the likelihood function. This estimate is significantly different from 0 ($\chi_1^2 = 27$) and from 1 ($\chi_1^2 = 54$), rejecting both the logarithmic and linear utility models as special cases of the model. When the risk-aversion parameter equals 0.3, the estimated values of $(1-\beta)_0$ and β_s equal 0.486 and -0.024, with asymptotic t-ratios of 2.68 and -1.76. These estimates provide unconstrained maximum likelihood estimates of the discount rate, which equals approximately 19 percent for a worker with a high school degree, 10 percent for a college-educated worker, and an average of 17 percent for the sample. Thus, the maximum likelihood estimates do not indicate access to perfect capital markets for highly educated workers.

As a final reference point, the parameter estimates under the risk-neutrality assumption are $(1-\beta)_0 = 0.201$ and $\beta_s = -0.009$, with asymptotic t-ratios equal to 2.11 and -1.22. The implied discount rate for the average worker in this case equals 54 percent, which is quite high.

The asymptotic 95 percent confidence interval for the maximum likelihood estimate of the discount rate equals $r \in (0.09, 0.26)$ at the mean value of S. This interval includes the estimate from the logarithmic utility function. Thus, although rejected as a specific functional form, the popular logarithmic utility function yields an estimated discount rate consistent with the unconstrained estimate. The estimated discount rate from the risk-neutral model of 0.54 lies well outside the 95 percent confidence interval.

Checks on the robustness of our estimates are found in Moore and Viscusi (1988a, 1989). Estimations based on more conventional wage equations, including two measures of risk using both the 1976 Quality of Employment Survey and the 1982 PSID, result in implied real discount rates ranging between 2 and 12 percent. Perhaps most importantly, both sets of real discount rate estimates are broadly consistent with observed nominal interest rates and rates of inflation for the periods covered by the data.

The rate of time preference for life years is in a more reasonable range than consumers' implicit rates of discount for appliance energy efficiency, which Hausman (1979) found to be around 20 percent or more, and those estimated by Gately (1980) for refrigerator purchases of between 45 and 300 percent. Furthermore, Fuchs (1986) found individual rates of time preference for health to be on the order of 30 percent, and corporate executives have been found to use nominal rates of discount on the order of 15 percent or more.[7]

Despite the fact that the data and the models' assumptions are not sufficiently refined to enable one to make precise judgments regarding intertemporal misallocations, at a very broad level it does appear that the implied rates of time preference are in a reasonable range. There is no clearcut evidence of severe temporal myopia or undue emphasis on future rewards, although some misallocations may exist for less educated workers. One's assessment of the direction of the bias depends upon the explicit market rate that is used for comparison.

The theoretical model also yields one empirical test of the validity of the model, given in eq. (16). This restriction, which tests the second-order condition of the model, will hold if the worker's indifference curve is more convex than the market locus. Evaluating eq. (16) for each worker in the sample, the restriction is never rejected for all values of c between 0 and 1, inclusive. The plausibility of the model is further strengthened by the fact that each worker's indifference curve is upward sloping, as required by the theory.

6. Conclusion

Consideration of the implications of fatality risks for workers' future lifetimes enables one to assess the role of the workers' implicit rate of time preference with respect to future life years. The most notable result was that workers discount future life years at a real rate of 11 percent. The discount rate estimate for more educated workers is consistent with prevailing real rates as reflected in the difference between nominal rates of interest and rates of expected inflation for the period. However, there is a divergence for workers with at most a high school education, suggesting perhaps that unequal access to capital leads to suboptimal behavior on the part of these workers.

In all of the aspects of our analysis, application of the model of utility maximization to the choice of a potentially hazardous job yields results that strengthen our understanding of how workers make decisions. Although temporal misallocations may exist, the magnitude of any departure from rationality does not appear substantial.

The similarity between individual and market rates of time preference for

---

[7]The results from a poll by Lawrence Summers suggest that the rate of interest companies use to discount investments is on the order of 15 percent or more for a majority of firms. See *Washington Post*, National Weekly Edition, 16 July, p. 22.

highly educated workers suggests that social rates of time preference should not be different from market rates when evaluating the policy implications of health-related efforts aimed at this particular group. The substantial difficulties in selecting a social rate of time preference appear to apply more to low-education groups.

References

Arthur, W.B., 1981, The economics of risks to life, American Economic Review 71, no. 1, 54–64.
Biddle, Jeff and Gary Zarkin, 1988, Worker preferences and market compensation for job risk, Review of Economics and Statistics 70, no. 4, 660–667.
Conley, Bryan C., 1976, The value of human life and the demand for safety, American Economic Review 66, no. 1, 45–55.
Fuchs, Victor, 1986, The health economy (Harvard University Presss, Cambridge, MA).
Fuchs, Victor and Richard Zeckhauser, 1987, Valuing health – A priceless commodity, American Economic Review Papers and Proceedings 77, no. 2, 263–268.
Gately, Dermot, 1980, Individual discount rates and the purchase and utilization of energy-using durables: Comment, Bell Journal of Economics 11, 373–376.
Hausman, Jerry, 1979, Individual discount rates and the purchase and utilization of energy-using durables, Bell Journal of Economics 10, no. 1, 33–54.
Kahn, Shulamit and Kevin Lang, 1988, Efficient estimation of structural hedonic systems, International Economic Review 29, no. 1, 157–166.
Keeney, Ralph L. and Howard Raiffa, 1976, Decisions with multiple objectives: Preferences and value tradeoffs (John Wiley and Sons, New York).
Lave, Lester, 1981, The strategy of social regulation (Brookings Institution, Washington, DC).
Machina, Mark, 1987, Choice under uncertainty: Problems solved and unsolved, Journal of Economic Perspectives 1, no. 1, 121–154.
Moore, Michael J. and W. Kip Viscusi, 1988a, The quantity adjusted value of life, Economic Inquiry 26, no. 3, 369–388.
Moore, Michael J. and W. Kip Viscusi, 1988b, Doubling the estimated value of life: Results using new occupational fatality data, Journal of Policy Analysis and Management 7, no. 3, 476–490.
Moore, Michael J. and W. Kip Viscusi, 1989, Discounting environmental health risks: New empirical evidence and policy implications, Journal of Policy Analysis and Management, forthcoming.
Moore, Michael J. and W. Kip Viscusi, forthcoming, Compensation mechanisms for job risks: Wages, workers' compensation, and product liability (Princeton University Press, Princeton, MA).
Pigou, A.C., 1932, The economics of welfare, 7th edition (Macmillan, New York).
Rosen, Sherwin, 1988, The value of life expectancy, The Journal of Risk and Uncertainty 1, no. 3, 285–304.
Shepard, Donald and Richard Zeckhauser, 1984, Survival versus consumption, Management Science 30, no. 4, 423–439.
Thaler, Richard and Sherwin Rosen, 1976, The value of saving a life: Evidence from the labor market, in: N. Terleckyz, ed., Household production and consumption, NBER Studies in Income and Wealth 40 (Columbia University Press, New York), 265–298.
Tversky, Amos and Daniel Kahneman, 1986, Rational choice and the framing of decisions, Journal of Business 59, no. 4, Part 2, 251–278.
U.S. Department of Commerce, U.S. Bureau of the Census, 1985, Statistical Abstract of the United States 1986 (U.S. Government Printing Office, Washington, DC).
Viscusi, W. Kip, 1979, Employment hazards: An investigation of market performance (Harvard University Press, Cambridge, MA).
Viscusi, W. Kip, 1983, Risk by choice: Regulating health and safety in the workplace (Harvard University Press, Cambridge, MA).
Zeckhauser, Richard and Donald Shepard, 1976, Where now for saving lives? Law and Contemporary Problems 40, 5–45.

[28]

Journal of Risk and Uncertainty, 3:369–379 (1990)
© 1990 Kluwer Academic Publishers

Discounting and the Evaluation of Lifesaving Programs

MAUREEN L. CROPPER
Department of Economics, University of Maryland; Resources for the Future, Washington, D.C. 20036

PAUL R. PORTNEY*
Resources for the Future, Washington, D.C. 20036

Key words: discounting, latency, risk valuation

Abstract

The evaluation of lifesaving programs whose benefits extend into the future involves two discounting issues. The intragenerational discounting problem is how to express, in age-j dollars, reductions in an individual's conditional probability of dying at some future age k. Having discounted future lifesaving benefits to the beginning of each individual's life, one is faced with the problem of discounting these benefits to the present—the intergenerational discounting problem. We discuss both problems from the perspectives of cost-benefit and cost-effectiveness analyses. These principles are then applied to lifesaving programs that involve a latency period.

In evaluating a proposed regulation or making a public investment decision, it is standard practice to compare the discounted present value of costs and benefits of the project, i.e., to apply a benefit–cost criterion. Application of this criterion, however, often meets with resistance when benefits or costs take the form of lives saved. This is especially true when lives are saved or lost in the future, thus raising the question of whether these lives, or the monetary value of the corresponding risk reductions, should be discounted.

The problem of discounting human lives arises frequently in the context of environmental policy. Perhaps the most striking example is nuclear waste disposal, which may impose risks on generations thousands of years into the future. The time pattern of risks to human life is, however, important even in the context of shorter planning horizons. Many environmental programs—for example, those concerned with asbestos—reduce exposure to carcinogens with long latency periods. This implies that, while the costs of reduced exposure may largely be borne today, the benefits do not occur until the end of the latency period. Compared with a program that reduces an individual's risk of death today, a program that reduces that same person's risk of death at the end of a 20-year latency period saves fewer expected life-years. This fact has often been ignored in valuing the benefits of environmental regulations.

*The authors are, respectively, Associate Professor of Economics, University of Maryland and Senior Fellow, Resources for the Future; and Senior Fellow and Vice President, Resources for the Future. We thank the National Science Foundation for their support under grant DIR-8711083.

The purpose of this article is to clarify some of the discounting issues that arise in valuing health and safety programs. We identify two discounting problems that are frequently encountered in making environmental policy: 1) how to discount lifesaving benefits that accrue at some future point in a person's life; and 2) how to discount lifesaving benefits to members of future generations. The first problem, which we term the intragenerational discounting problem, arises in regulating substances that involve a latency period, such as pesticides, asbestos or radon. Reducing a person's exposure at age 20 to a carcinogen with a 20-year latency period does not begin to reduce the individual's conditional probability of death until the end of the latency period.[1] Lifesaving benefits that do not occur for 20 years must be discounted to the present so that they may be compared with the costs of reducing exposure in the current year.

The intergenerational discounting problem arises whenever substances are regulated that have long residence times in the environment. Nuclear waste is probably the most famous example of such a substance, but chlorofluorocarbons (CFCs) and greenhouse gases also come to mind.

We illustrate the distinction between intragenerational and intergenerational with a simple diagram (figure 1) that shows the time pattern of benefits resulting from a capital expenditure, for example, the construction of a safer nuclear waste disposal facility, that confers benefits to members of generations currently alive and to generations as yet unborn.[2] To simplify the problem, suppose that members of each generation live at most two periods and that these periods are 20 years long. Persons are 20 years old at the beginning of the first period of their lives and 40 at the beginning of the second period.[3]

For all persons near the facility, building a stronger depository reduces the conditional probability of dying at the beginning of period 1 and at the beginning of each subsequent period. At the beginning of period 1, the safer facility reduces the conditional probability of dying at age 40 for members of generation 1 (D_{40}) and the conditional probability of dying at age 20 for members of generation 2 (D_{20}). At the beginning of period 2, it reduces the conditional probability of dying at age 40 for members of generation 2 and the conditional probability of dying at age 20 for members of generation 3.

Assuming, for simplicity, that all costs of the facility are incurred at the beginning of period 1, the project will pass a benefit–cost test if the present value of the benefits of the risk reductions to all future generations exceeds the cost of constructing the facility. The

REDUCTIONS IN RISK OF DEATH DUE TO SAFER NUCLEAR WASTE DISPOSAL

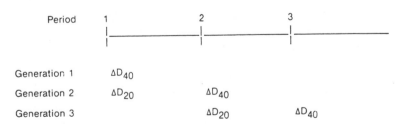

Figure 1. Changes in the conditional probability of death at age $t(D_t)$ due to safer nuclear waste disposal.

intragenerational discounting problem is to discount future lifesaving benefits for members of a single generation to the time of their birth.[4] In figure 1 this corresponds to discounting ΔD_{40} for members of generation 2 to the beginning of period 1. The rate at which members of each generation should be willing to discount their own future lifesaving benefits may be obtained from a life-cycle consumption–saving model, as we discuss in section 1 below. The intergenerational discounting problem is to discount the value of benefits to future generations to the present. In figure 1, having discounted the benefits to members of generation 3 to the beginning of period 2 (the intragenerational problem), one is then faced with the problem of discounting this amount to the beginning of period 1. This problem, which is clearly the more controversial of the two, is discussed in section 2.

As noted in section 2, it is difficult to avoid the conclusion that benefits to future generations should be discounted to the present, so long as three conditions hold: 1) individuals can be made indifferent to increases (decreases) in mortality risk if they are given (made to surrender) money payments; 2) there are alternative uses for lifesaving resources; and 3) capital investment yields a positive rate of return.

Many people, however, are uncomfortable with the notion that future lifesaving benefits should be discounted at a positive rate of interest, or even with the idea of monetizing lifesaving benefits. If the funds to be spent on lifesaving programs are fixed, so that the decision maker's problem is simply to allocate them among alternative programs,[5] then no monetization of benefits is required. The decision maker must, however, have a function that weights lives saved at different points in time. Assuming all costs are incurred today, the rate at which future lives saved are discounted is the rate implicit in this weighting function. We discuss the discounting implications of the cost-effectiveness approach to regulatory analysis in section 3.

We conclude the article by examining a class of environmental problems, namely, the regulation of environmental carcinogens, that raises intragenerational discounting questions because these carcinogens involve a latency period. How this latency period should be treated was the subject of a heated debate between the U.S. Environmental Protection Agency (EPA) and the Office of Management and Budget (OMB) in the case of asbestos regulation (U.S. House of Representatives, 1985). We argue that the positions of both the EPA and the OMB on the benefits of asbestos regulation were incorrect, and examine the implications of section 1 for the correct treatment of latency periods.

1. Intragenerational discounting issues

The question we address in this section is how lifesaving benefits that occur at different ages, to members of the same generation, can be expressed in a single year's dollars.[6] Equivalently, how much is an individual in the generation willing to pay at age j for a change in his conditional probability of dying at some future age k?

A natural framework in which to answer this question is a life-cycle consumption model with uncertain lifetime.[7] In the life-cycle model, expected utility at age j, V_j, is the present discounted value of utility of consumption, $U(c_t)$, from $t = j$ to some maximum age T, weighted by the probability that the individual survives to age t, given that he is alive at age j, $q_{j,t}$,

$$V_j = \sum_{t=j}^{T} (1 + \rho)^{j-t} q_{j,t} U(c_t), \tag{1}$$

where ρ is the subjective rate of time preference.

The level of utility achieved depends on the individual's budget constraint. Suppose that the individual has wealth of W_j at his current age, j, and earns y_t at age $t, t = j, \ldots, T$, provided he is alive. If the individual can lend at the riskless rate r, but can never be a net borrower, he faces the budget constraints

$$W_j + \sum_{k=j}^{t} (y_k - c_k)(1 + r)^{j-k} \geq 0, \qquad\qquad j < t \leq ,T, \tag{2}$$

which force him always to have nonnegative wealth. Other capital market assumptions, such as the availability of actuarially fair annuities, do not change the discounting results below (Cropper and Sussman, 1990).

A program to build a safer nuclear waste containment facility affects survival probabilities in the following way. Given that an individual is alive at age j, the probability that he is alive at age k is the product of the probabilities that he does not die at ages j through $k - 1$,

$$q_{j,k} = (1 - D_j)(1 - D_{j+1}) \ldots (1 - D_{k-1}), \tag{3}$$

where D_k is the conditional probability of dying at age k, i.e., the probability that the individual dies at age k given that he has survived to that age.

A health or safety program affects survival probabilities by altering the value of the D_k's. A program to clamp down on drunken driving or to strictly enforce speed limits in a single year reduces D_k for that year alone. A program that reduces an individual's exposure at age 30 to a carcinogen with a 20-year latency period reduces the conditional probability of dying at all ages after 50 ($D_{50}, D_{51}, D_{52}, \ldots$), while a program to increase the safety of a nuclear containment facility reduces D_k beginning in the year the facility is built and at all subsequent ages. It should be emphasized that when the conditional probability of death is altered at age k, it affects the probability of surviving to ages $k + 1$ and beyond, $q_{j,k+1}, q_{j,k+2}, \ldots, q_{j,T}$, by virtue of equation (3).

The monetary value to an individual of a change in D_k, termed his willingness to pay (WTP), is the amount of money that can be taken away from him when D_k is reduced that will keep his expected utility constant. WTP at age j for a marginal change in D_k, $\text{WTP}_{j,k}$, is given by

$$\text{WTP}_{j,k} = -\frac{dV_j/dD_k}{dV_j/dW_j} dD_k. \tag{4}$$

The first term on the right-hand side of equation (4), the rate at which the individual is willing to substitute wealth for risk, is typically termed the value of life. Applying the Envelope Theorem to the Lagrangian function that corresponds to equations (1) and (2), $\text{WTP}_{j,k}$ can be written

DISCOUNTING AND THE EVALUATION OF LIFESAVING PROGRAMS   373

$$\text{WTP}_{j,k} = \left[(1 - D_k)^{-1}[U'(c_j)]^{-1} \sum_{t=k+1}^{T} (1 + \rho)^{j-t} q_{j,t} U(c_t)\right] dD_k. \tag{5}$$[8]

Equation (5) states that the value to a person at age j of reducing his conditional probability of death at age k is the expected utility he would lose if he died at age k, divided by
the marginal utility of consumption at age j.

    The main insight that the life-cycle model yields for intragenerational discounting is
that the individual's willingness to pay at age 20 for a change in his conditional probability of death at age 40 ($\text{WTP}_{20,40}$) is what he would pay at age 40 for a change in his
current probability of death, $\text{WTP}_{40,40}$, discounted to age 20 at the consumption rate of
interest. This can be seen by combining equation (5), evaluated at ages j and $j + 1$, with
the first-order conditions for utility maximization, to yield

$$\frac{\text{WTP}_{j+1,k}}{\text{WTP}_{j,k}} = \frac{U'(c_j)}{U'(c_{j+1})}(1 - D_j)^{-1}(1 + \rho) = 1 + \delta_j, \tag{6}$$

where δ_j is the consumption rate of interest at age j. If it is the case that the wealth
constraint is not binding, then the consumption rate of interest equals the market rate of
interest ($\delta_j = r$); otherwise δ_j may exceed the market rate of interest.[9]

    Repeated use of equation (6) implies that the discount factor $\Gamma_{j,k}$ applied to $\text{WTP}_{k,k}$ to
yield $\text{WTP}_{j,k}$ is the product of the annual discount factors $1/(1 + \delta_t), t = j, \ldots, k - 1$,

$$\text{WTP}_{j,k} = \Gamma_{j,k} \text{WTP}_{k,k},$$
$$\Gamma_{j,k} = \prod_{t=j}^{k-1} (1 + \delta_t)^{-1}. \tag{7}$$

The empirical significance of equation (7) is that, if one can extrapolate estimates of
WTP for a change in conditional probability of death in the future ($\text{WTP}_{k,k}$) from labor
market or contingent valuation studies, then these estimates can be discounted using
equation (7) to estimate WTP today for the future risk change ($\text{WTP}_{j,k}$). For this to be
successful, however, estimates of WTP for a change in current conditional probability of
death must be age dependent and must reflect differences in income streams between
cohorts. Returning to figure 1 for illustration, a contingent valuation study conducted in
the year the waste disposal facility is built would estimate the value of a change in D_{40} to
members of generation 1 ($\text{WTP}_{40,40}$). Before this can be discounted to estimate the value
at the beginning of period 1 of a change in D_{40} to persons in generation 2 ($\text{WTP}_{20,40}$), one
must adjust $\text{WTP}_{40,40}$ for differences in lifetime earnings between generations 1 and 2.

2. Intergenerational discounting issues

Equation (7) indicates that, in the context of a life-cycle consumption model, rational individuals within each generation would discount future lifesaving benefits at the consumption

rate of interest. This does not, however, solve the problem of how, in figure 1, a policy maker should discount the benefits to generation 3 from period 2 to period 1.

Suppose the planner combines the life-cycle utilities of members of each generation in a social welfare function. Let P_t denote the population of generation t and α the utility rate of discount. Assume social welfare is given by

$$S = \sum_{t=0}^{N} (1 + \alpha)^{-t} P_t V_{jt}(W_{jt}),$$

(8)

where V_{jt} is, as in equation (1), evaluated for persons in generation t. If the planner's problem is to determine the initial wealth to be given to each generation W_{jt}, and the amount to be spent on lifesaving programs, it is hard to escape the fact that he will discount lifesaving benefits to future generations at the rate of return on capital. This is true even if $\alpha = 0$, i.e., even if there is no utility discounting. The reason is that resources not devoted to lifesaving programs for future generations can be invested at a positive interest rate so as to increase W_{jt} for members of these generations.[10]

We hasten to add that the discounting of the dollar benefits of lifesaving does not imply that the planner is unconcerned about the welfare of future generations. If $\alpha = 0$, the utility of future generations will be higher than the utility of current generations, assuming that increasing consumption over time is technologically feasible. As long as consumption and survival probabilities are substitutes in the utility function, future generations can always be compensated for changes in their risk of death.

One problem, of course, is that the institutions necessary to guarantee that this compensation occurs may not exist. In an overlapping generations context, altruism might be sufficient to guarantee that compensating wealth transfers take place from one generation to another; however, there is evidence that people behave differently in a private context than they believe society should behave (Svenson and Karlsson, 1989). This implies that government programs may be required to enforce such compensation.

3. Cost-effectiveness analysis versus cost–benefit analysis

If a policymaker has a fixed budget to be spent on lifesaving programs, and if there are no alternative uses for the funds, then it is possible both to avoid monetizing the benefits of lifesaving programs (a necessity if there are alternative uses for lifesaving resources) and to avoid discounting future lives saved.

Suppose that a decision maker must choose among alternative lifesaving programs and that all program costs are incurred today. The benefits of such programs are evaluated by a function that ranks the expected number of persons alive at each age in the current and in future generations. This function might take the form

$$S' = \sum_{t=0}^{N} (1 + \alpha)^{-t} P_t \left[\sum_{m=j}^{T} (1 + \rho)^{-m} q_{j,m}^t \right].$$

(9)

The term in brackets is the discounted life expectancy at age j, for a person in generation t. It is the intragenerational objective function (1) with consumption omitted. Discounted life expectancy is weighted by the number of persons in generation t, P_t. α is the discount rate applied to life-years saved in future generations.

It is easily verified that the optimal allocation of funds among lifesaving programs calls for equalizing the present value of future benefits per dollar spent. Formally,

$$\frac{(1 + \alpha)^{-t}P_t \sum_{m=k+1}^{T} q_{j,m}^t}{\partial C/\partial D_k^t} = \frac{(1 + \alpha)^{-t-1}P_{t+1} \sum_{m=k+1}^{T} q_{j,m}^{t+1}}{\partial C/\partial D_k^{t+1}} \tag{10}$$

where $\partial C/\partial D_k^t$ is the marginal cost of a change in the age-k mortality rate for members of generation t, and the numerator of each expression represents the number of discounted expected life-years saved by each risk change. (To simplify the expression, we have set $\rho = 0$.) Equation (10) implies that, if $\alpha = 0$, future lives count equally with present lives, holding constant expected life-years saved.

An interesting question is whether, in their role as social decision makers, people believe that future and present lives saved should count equally, holding constant expected life-years saved. In other words, what value do they attach to α? It is also of interest to know what value people attach to ρ, the rate at which future life-years are discounted within a generation.

Two recent studies shed light on these questions. Svenson and Karlsson (1989) asked students at the University of Stockholm to assign a number between 0 and 10 to the seriousness of a leakage of spent nuclear fuel in the years 3100, 4100, 10,000, 100,000, 1,000,000, and 2,000,000, assuming that the seriousness of such a leakage in the year 2100 equals 10. Approximately 30% of the 108 respondents did not discount the seriousness of future waste leakages at all. Among those who did, the mean value attached to an accident in the year 10,000 was 5, implying a value of $\alpha = 8.66 \times 10^{-5}$.

Over shorter periods, however, people may have higher values of α. Horowitz and Carson (1990) report mean discount rates between 4.5% and 12.8% when respondents were asked to compare lives saved now versus lives saved 3 to 5 years into the future. It is not, however, clear to what extent respondents viewed these risks as applying to themselves or to others.

4. Regulations involving a latency period

We now apply the insights of the preceding sections to the regulation of environmental carcinogens—substances that are characterized by a lag (latency period) between exposure and effect. Since, by definition, cancerous cells do not appear until the end of the latency period, exposure to a carcinogen does not increase one's risk of dying of cancer until the end of this period. The latency period for asbestos is thought to be between 20 and 40 years, while for arsenic it is 30 to 50 years.

Figure 2 illustrates the effect of a 20-year latency period on the stream of benefits from reducing exposure to asbestos at the beginning of period 1. Assuming that this is accomplished by removing asbestos-containing materials from buildings, all persons who would have been exposed to asbestos will benefit, beginning at the end of their respective latency periods.[11] An important difference between the asbestos and nuclear waste examples is that there are no benefits from asbestos removal early in life to members of any generation ($\Delta D_{20} = 0$ in figure 2). Assuming equal ΔD_{40}'s in both figures, fewer expected life-years are saved by removing asbestos than by building a safer nuclear waste disposal facility.

This fact, however, is often ignored in risk–benefit analyses, where the focus is on deaths avoided, regardless of their timing. An example of insensitivity to the approach recommended here is the EPA's original analysis of the benefits of prohibiting the manufacture of certain asbestos-containing products under the Toxic Substances Control Act (TSCA). In calculating benefits, the EPA assumed that the reduction in risk began on the date of exposure rather than at the end of the latency period. Assuming that 40 is the average age of exposure, this is equivalent to valuing lives saved using $WTP_{40,40}$. If, however, asbestos does not result in cancer until 20 years after exposure, then the program should be valued by discounting $WTP_{60,60}$ back to the present rather than using $WTP_{40,40}$.[12]

It should be emphasized that the difference between $WTP_{60,60}$, discounted to the present (the correct benefit measure), and $WTP_{40,40}$ is the result of two factors:

1. *Fewer life-years saved.* $WTP_{60,60}$ reflects the fact that only life-years beginning at age 60 are saved by asbestos removal; the years between ages 40 and 60 are not at risk.
2. *Discounting.* The life-years saved by asbestos removal do not start until age 60; hence they must be discounted to the present.

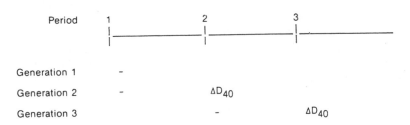

Figure 2. Changes in the conditional probability of death at age $t(D_t)$ due to asbestos removal, assuming a 20-year latency period.

Cropper and Sussman (1990) illustrate possible magnitudes for these effects. They calculate that, for a white male with an isoelastic utility function $[U(c) = c^{0.2}]$ and $r = \rho = .05$, $WTP_{60,60}$ is 70% of $WTP_{40,40}$. The fact that fewer life-years are saved thus reduces WTP by 30%. Discounting $WTP_{60,60}$ to the present implies that the correct benefit measure ($WTP_{40,60}$) is 26% of $WTP_{40,40}$.

One further observation about the control of environmental carcinogens should be made. We have illustrated this class of problems with the decision to remove asbestos from buildings, a case in which we assume all regulatory expenditures are made up front. For pesticide regulation, the cost of not using a pesticide (e.g., reduced crop yields) is incurred at the beginning of each time period. Here the correct decision rule is to compare the present value of benefits from not exposing people in period t, discounted to the beginning of period t, with period t costs. Because the only people to benefit from pesticide regulation in period t are people who are alive at that time, pesticide regulation is not really an intergenerational issue.[13] It does, however, involve *intra*generational discounting because of the latency period involved.

5. Conclusions

Regulatory decisions involving lifesaving will always be controversial; however, this controversy can be lessened if decision makers understand clearly the nature of the benefits that programs provide and use appropriate valuation techniques. We have emphasized the distinctions between 1) programs that reduce risk of premature mortality immediately; 2) those that reduce such risks but only after a latency period; and 3) those that provide risk reductions to individuals not yet born. While some programs might provide all three types of benefits, each is valued differently.

Even if the valuation techniques are correctly understood at the conceptual level, there remains the problem of empirical implementation. This will require at least two types of approaches. Programs to reduce risk of death immediately can be valued by hedonic wage techniques—by estimating a compensating wage differential received by workers in risky occupations. However, because compensating wage differentials reflect the preferences of persons who accept employment in risky jobs, they may not accurately value risk reductions for a randomly chosen person in the population. Contingent valuation studies (Jones-Lee, Hammerton, and Philips, 1985) may be needed to provide benefit estimates for a broader spectrum of the population.

Programs that reduce risk of death after a latency period can be valued by contingent valuation methods (Mitchell and Carson, 1986; Smith and Desvousges, 1987), i.e., by asking respondents about their willingness to pay today for a reduction in their conditional probability of dying 30 years hence. Alternatively, one can discount estimates of willingness to pay for a reduction in risk of death at the end of the latency period ($WTP_{k,k}$) to the present at the consumption rate of discount.

What policymakers need to know when making policies that affect future generations is the marginal rate of substitution between lives saved now and lives saved in the future.

378   MAUREEN L. CROPPER/PAUL R. PORTNEY

This could be elicited via a contingent valuation survey in which respondents choose between future- and present-oriented lifesaving programs. Such a survey would provide information that could be used directly in a cost-effectiveness context, and is a necessary input into a benefit–cost analysis.

Notes

1. The conditional probability of dying at age t is the probability that the individual dies between his tth and $t + $ 1st birthdays, assuming he is alive on his tth birthday.
2. Our assumption is that this new facility reduces the risk of a sudden and massive release of radioactivity that would result in acute fatalities.
3. This admittedly stylized approach enables us to avoid discussing the willingness to pay for risk reductions on the part of a two-year-old, for instance.
4. In the case of generations currently alive, benefits are discounted to the present.
5. This is probably not a bad description of the problem faced by the officials at a regulatory agency. While there is theoretically no limit on the amount of society's resources that the agency can commit to lifesaving in a given year, the agency's operating budget surely constrains the rulemaking it can do. This may have the effect of forcing the agency to adopt a cost-effectiveness approach.
6. To focus on the discounting issue, we assume that all persons in a single generation are identical. They are born in the same year, inherit the same wealth, face the same income stream and same probability distribution over the date of their death, and have the same tastes.
7. This model, originally developed by Yaari (1965), has been used to value changes in current risk of death over the life cycle by Arthur (1981) and by Shepard and Zeckhauser (1982, 1984). The discounting results presented here were obtained by Cropper and Sussman (1990).
8. See Cropper and Sussman (1990).
9. Viscusi and Moore (1989) estimate that individuals discount future lifesaving benefits at about 12%, a finding consistent with the fact that consumption is income-constrained.
10. For a discussion of discounting in a social planning context, see Dasgupta (1982). Cropper and Sussman (1990) obtain a similar result in the context of an overlapping generations model with altruism.
11. Unlike the nuclear waste example, benefits from removing asbestos do not extend to generations in the distant future if buildings containing asbestos would eventually have been torn down and replaced and if, upon demolition, the asbestos were captured and safely disposed of.
12. The OMB's solution to this problem also appears to have been incorrect. To take account of the latency period, the OMB also used $1 million as the value of statistical life. It then treated this sum, which corresponds to $WTP_{40,40}$, as occurring 20 years into the future and discounted it (rather than $WTP_{60,60}$) back to the present.
13. We are assuming that the effects of pesticide exposure are primarily carcinogenic, not teratogenic, and also that pesticide use will play no role in long-lived ecological damage.

References

Arthur, W. Brian. (1981). "The Economics of Risks to Life," *American Economic Review* 71, 54–64.

Cropper, Maureen L. and Frances G. Sussman. (1990). "Valuing Future Risks to Life," *Journal of Environmental Economics and Management* 19, 160–174.

DISCOUNTING AND THE EVALUATION OF LIFESAVING PROGRAMS   379

Dasgupta, Partha. (1982). "Resource Depletion, Research and Development, and the Social Rate of Discount." In Robert C. Lind (ed.), *Discounting for Time and Risk in Energy Policy*. Washington, DC: Resources for the Future.

Fuchs, Victor R. and Richard J. Zeckhauser. (1987). "Valuing Health—A 'Priceless' Commodity," *American Economic Review* 77, 263–268.

Horowitz, John and Richard T. Carson. (1990). "Discounting Statistical Lives," *Journal of Risk and Uncertainty*, this issue.

Jones-Lee, M. W., M. Hammerton, and P. R. Philips. (1985). "The Value of Safety: Results of a National Sample Survey," *Economic Journal* 95, 49–72.

Mitchell, Robert C. and Richard T. Carson. (1986). "Valuing Drinking Water Risk Reductions Using the Contingent Valuation Method: A Methodological Study of Risks from THM and Giardia." Paper prepared for Resources for the Future. Washington, DC: Resources for the Future.

Shepard, Donald S. and Richard J. Zeckhauser. (1982). "Life Cycle Consumption and Willingness to Pay for Increased Survival." In Michael W. Jones-Less (ed.), *The Value of Life and Safety*. Amsterdam, North-Holland.

Shepard, Donald S. and Richard J. Zeckhauser. (1984). "Survival Versus Consumption," *Management Science* 30, 423–439.

Smith, V. Kerry and William H. Desvousges. (1987). "An Empirical Analysis of the Economic Value of Risk Changes," *Journal of Political Economy* 95, 89–114.

Svenson, Ola and Gunnar Karlsson. (1989). "Decision-Making, Time Horizons, and Risk in the Very Long-Term Perspective," *Risk Analysis* 9, 385–399.

U. S. House of Representatives. (1985). *EPA's Asbestos Regulations. Hearing Before the Committee on Energy and Commerce, 99th Congress*. Washington, DC: U.S. Government Printing Office.

Viscusi, W. Kip and Michael J. Moore. (1989). "Rates of Time Preference and Valuations of the Duration of Life," *Journal of Public Economics* 38, 297–317.

Yaari, Menahem E. (1965). "Uncertain Lifetime, Life Insurance, and the Theory of the Consumer," *Review of Economic Studies* 32, 137–150.

[29]

Journal of Risk and Uncertainty, 3: 403–413(1990)
© 1990 Kluwer Academic Publishers

Discounting Statistical Lives

JOHN K. HOROWITZ
Department of Agriculture and Resource Economics, University of Maryland, College Park, Maryland 20742

RICHARD T. CARSON*
Department of Economics, D-008, University of California, San Diego, LaJolla, CA 92093

Key words: discount rate, statistical life, discrete choice

Abstract

Benefit–cost analysis of government projects that reduce health risks over an extended period of time requires an estimate of the *value of a future life*. This in turn requires a discount rate. We suggest and carry out a method to estimate the discount rate using observations on discrete choices between projects with different time horizons. This method is implemented in a survey context. For our primary example, the estimated median discount rate is close to the market rate. A substantial proportion of the sample is estimated to have quite low discount rates. We provide some evidence that discount rates may differ for different types of risks.

Economists have come to accept the idea that placing a dollar value on life is unavoidable in choosing among projects that reduce mortality risks. A related and possibly more controversial question, however, has now surfaced: What is the present value of a risk reduction that occurs in the future? If the value of future risk reductions is to be discounted, what discount rate should be used?

This question arises, for instance, in decisions about when to undertake the cleanup of a toxic waste site, how quickly to phase out the use of a dangerous pesticide, or what kind of sewage treatment plant to build.[1] Environmental and consumer groups have argued that a zero discount rate should be used for public policies that reduce risk. Proponents of this vew are concerned about issues like environmental quality, market failure, and the welfare of future generations. They often believe that programs that reduce long-term health risks address these issues. Thus, they favor a low discount rate for statistical lives since this promotes government action to reduce long-term health risks. The Office of Management and Budget, on the other hand, has adopted the position that a market rate

*This research was supported in part by the U.S. Environmental Protection Agency under Cooperative Agreement in Environmental Economics Research CR-813557-01-0. The opinions expressed do not necessarily reflect the views of the U.S. Environmental Protection Agency. We would like to thank Paul Portney for bringing the importance of discounting statistical lives to our attention, and John Conlisk, Maureen Cropper, Mark Machina, Robert Mitchell, Peter Navarro, and Walter Oi for helpful comments.

is appropriate.[2] Proponents of this view point out that project funds could be invested at a market rate of interest and the future revenue used to buy $(1 + r)$ amounts of risk reduction in the following period. The practical implication of this viewpoint is that less emphasis is placed on reducing long-term health risks in favor of a greater emphasis on programs that can achieve very quick reductions in health risks, even if those programs may save fewer statistical lives in the long run than an alternative program that produces less immediate results. A third viewpoint is that the characteristics of the risks are important and a different discount rate should be used for evaluating each risk. To look at public attitudes toward health risks and to distinguish between these competing views about the appropriate discount rate requires a method that estimates individuals' discount rates and allows for the possibility that their discount rates for different types of risks are different.

In this article, we demonstrate a method to elicit individuals' discount rates for a particular risk. The intuition behind our approach can be seen in the following example. Consider program A, which reduces a particular risk and saves ten lives in the year 1990, and program B, which saves 16 statistical lives from the same risk in the year 1995. Both programs cost the same and must be initiated in 1990. If an agent prefers program A to program B, then his discount rate must be greater than 10%. If program B is preferred, then the agent's discount rate must be less than 10%.

Our method, which can be based either on surveys or on observations of actual behavior, uses agents' choices between policies that differ in the timing and/or number of the statistical lives that are saved. Agents are not required either to put a dollar value on risk reduction or to formulate a discount rate explicitly, both of which can be fairly difficult tasks. Furthermore, the interval in which the agent's discount rate is estimated can be narrowed by changing either the times when lives are saved by the programs or the number of lives that are saved by the programs and then observing choices between the new set of policies. Alternatively, if the set of possible programs varies randomly across subjects, with changes in either the timing or the number of lives saved, then the distribution of discount rates in the population can be estimated without asking an agent to make more than one binary discrete choice.

Because our method estimates discount rates by observing choices between programs that reduce the same type of risk, we do not rely on differences in risks to define the discount rate. This allows the distribution of the public's discount rates to be different for different risks. Treating risks separately is consistent with previous work by Slovic, Fischhoff, and Lichtenstein (1985), which suggests that people view a particular risk as a bundle of characteristics, such as how voluntary or how dreaded it is. In this light, the public's discount rate for a risk might be seen as one more of its characteristics, but one with fairly large implications for public policy decisions. A hypothesis as to whether the median discount is the same for all risks is then testable. In the same vein, other testable hypotheses are whether the median discount rate for a particular risk is equal to zero, whether it is equal to the market rate, and whether a significant fraction of the population holds discount rates that are consistent with being zero or the market rate.

We implement this method using a sample of students and look at three different types of risk. For our sample, we show that the median discount rate for each of the three types of risks can be robustly estimated. Our very limited work suggests that for some risks the median discount rate may be close to the real market discount rate, while for other risks it may not, and that we can reject the hypothesis that the discount rates for all risks are equal.

1. The value of a statistical life

There is a large literature beginning with Schelling (1968) and Mishan (1971) that examines the value of a statistical life and the willingness to pay for decreases in risk.[3] These works led to utility-based theories of the value of life that included both atemporal models (Jones-Lee, 1976) and intertemporal, life-cycle models in which the timing of risks could be considered (Arthur, 1981; Ehrlich and Chuma, 1987). Only recently has the life-cycle utility model been used to derive a theoretical expression for an individual's discount rate for risks (see Rosen, 1988; Horowitz, 1989).

Virtually all the empirical work on the value of risk reductions has considered risks that occur entirely in the present, e.g., accidents (Jones-Lee, Hammerton, and Phillips, 1985), or has used the atemporal model. The few empirical studies that have measured willingness to pay to avoid (only) future risks, using exposure to carcinogens with a long latency period as the source of risk, have not varied the timing dimension and thus cannot be used to estimate a discount rate directly (Mitchell and Carson, 1986; Smith and Desvousges, 1987).[4]

Empirical estimates of the discount rate for risk reductions, like empirical estimates of values of other nonmarketed goods, can be obtained either by inferring them from market transactions or by eliciting them directly through the use of experiments and surveys (Hausman, 1979; Fuchs, 1982). The indirect market approach was recently adopted by Moore and Viscusi (1988; Viscusi and Moore, 1989) using wages and risks from different occupations.

An experiment or survey for estimating discount rates has a number of strengths and weaknesses relative to inference from actual market transactions. Our survey method's strengths are that it can be used to elicit discount rates for different types of risks, not just those for which close market substitutes exist, and it can also explicitly specify the size of the risks, thereby giving all individuals (and the researcher) a common set of information. The potential weakness of survey methods is, of course, that they are based on responses to hypothetical situations. The method itself, however, is not tied only to an experimental or survey context, but could in principle be used with actual observed choices in a market or voting context.

2. A method for estimating discount rates

In this section, we introduce some mathematical notation and show how estimates of the discount rate for the reduction in statistical lives lost to a particular hazard can be estimated. This is done by showing how simple binary discrete choices between programs that save statistical lives over different time horizons reveal information about the population's underlying distribution of discount rates.

2.1. The relationship between discount rates and discrete choice

The value to an individual of a project that saves statistical lives over a period of time can be expressed as

$$\sum_{t=0}^{T} L(t)V_i(t),$$
(1)

where $L(t)$ is the number of statistical lives saved in year t, T is the duration of the project, and $V_i(t)$ is individual i's present value of a statistical life saved in year t.[5] Estimates of the value of a statistical life in the current period, $V_0 = V(0)$, are given by Jones-Lee (1976), Thaler and Rosen (1976), and many others (see Fisher, Chestnut, and Violette, 1989, for a summary). The assumption of exponential discounting yields $V_i(t) = V_0/(1 + \delta_i)^t$, where δ_i is the individual's (constant) discount rate.[6]

To estimate an individual's discount rate, and to estimate the distribution of discount rates in the population, we introduce a discrete choice problem. Consider two projects that save statistical lives. One project saves L_1 lives per year for every year from the present year T, until the project expires. The second project saves L_2 lives per year and has the same horizon T, but does not take effect until year $j > 0$. For individual i under the specification $V_i(t) = V_0/(1 + \delta_i)^t$, the values of the two projects are

$$\text{Value of present project} = \sum_{t=0}^{T} L_1 \frac{V_0}{(1+\delta_i)^t}$$
(2a)

and

$$\text{Value of future project} = \sum_{t=j>0}^{T} L_2 \frac{V_0}{(1+\delta_i)^t}.$$
(2b)

For these two projects we can define an implicit *rate of return* or *equilibrating discount rate* as the discount rate an individual must have if he is indifferent between the two projects. We denote this equilibrating discount rate as δ^*. It is the level of δ such that the value of the present policy is equal to the value of the future policy,

$$\sum_{t=0}^{T} L_1 \frac{V_0}{(1+\delta^*)^t} = \sum_{t=j}^{T} L_2 \frac{V_0}{(1+\delta^*)^t}.$$
(3)

In our experiment each participant is asked which of the two projects he prefers, given L_1, L_2, j, and T. A participant who prefers the present policy must have a discount rate δ_1 greater than δ^*, since $\delta_1 > \delta^*$ is equivalent to $\sum_{t=0} L_1/(1 + \delta_1)^t > \sum_{t=j} L_2/(1 + \delta_1)^t$. A participant who prefers the future policy must have a δ_1 smaller than δ^*. Note that under our specification V_0 can be canceled from the equation. Preference depends only on the relationship between δ^* and δ_1. This allows us to separate discounting behavior from questions about the value of a statistical life.

The parameter δ^* provides either an upper or a lower bound on the individual's discount rate, given his or her choice of a rate greater than or less than δ^*. We exploit this feature in the experiment's design by giving each participant a different pair of projects to choose between—namely, each person's future project used a different value of L_2. Because one-to-one mapping exists between each L_2 and δ^* (given L_1, j, and T), this random assignment of L_2 is equivalent to assigning a different δ^* (say δ_i^*) to each participant. We observe which of the two projects is preferred for the given value of L_2 and thus for the given δ^*. We then estimate a relationship between δ^* and the proportion of the individuals assigned that δ^* who were in favor of the future project.[7] This relationship is an estimate of the cumulative distribution function for discount rates in the population.

2.2. Estimating the relationship between choice and δ_i

Suppose that individual discount rates are distributed in the population according to $g(\delta_i) = \mu + h(X_i, \gamma) + \epsilon_i$, where the function $g(\cdot)$ is increasing; the function $h(\cdot)$ is centered around zero with arguments X_i, a vector of individual taste variables, and γ, a vector of parameters; ϵ is a zero-mean disturbance term with variance σ^2; and μ is a location parameter, such as the mean or median, of the distribution of discount rates.

Following the argument presented in the preceding section, we assume that an individual chooses the future policy if his δ_i is less than his assigned δ_i^* or, equivalently, if $g(\delta_i)$ is less than $g(\delta_i^*)$. The probability that a randomly selected individual who faces a choice at δ_i^* chooses the future policy $(CHOICE_i = 1)$ is

$$PROB(CHOICE_i = 1|\delta_i^*) = PROB(g(\delta_i^*) > g(\delta_i)) = PROB(g(\delta_i^*) - \mu$$
$$- h(X_i, \gamma) > \epsilon_i). \quad (4)$$

This probability P can be estimated in a straightforward manner once we make an assumption about the distribution of ϵ (the subscript i will be suppressed from here on whenever no possibility for confusion arises). For example, if ϵ is distributed normally with standard deviation $\sigma = 1/\beta$, then this probability is

$$P = PROB(CHOICE) = 1|\delta^*) = \int_{-\infty}^{\beta[g(\delta^*) - \mu - h(X,\gamma)]} \frac{1}{(2\pi)^{1/2}} EXP\left[-\frac{t^2}{2}\right] dt$$

$$= F[\beta g(\delta^*) - \beta\mu - \beta h(X,\gamma)]. \quad (5)$$

where $F(\cdot)$ is the standard normal cumulative distribution function.

We can estimate the parameters in (5) through maximum likelihood methods. This leads to a standard probit regression. A typical feature of probit models is that only the product $\beta\mu$ (i.e., μ/σ) can be estimated, and not the individual parameters β and μ. In the formulation of our model, though, separate estimates of both β and μ are possible as can be seen by examining the likelihood function. Because the treatment variable $g(\delta^*)$ enters linearly with respect to μ, we can estimate β as the coefficient on $g(\delta^*)$ and can estimate μ separately by dividing $\beta\mu$ by β (Cameron and James, 1987). We also note that random assignment of the δ_i^* implies that functions of δ_i^* are independent of $h(X_i,\gamma)$. This means that β and μ can be estimated from either the conditional distribution ($h(\cdot)$ included) or the unconditional distribution ($h(\cdot)$ excluded).

We estimated the parameters of interest under the specification $g(\delta_i) = \delta_i$, which implies that the unconditional distribution of discount rates in the population is $\delta_i = \delta_m + \nu_i$, where δ_m is the unconditional mean (and median) discount rate and $\nu_i = \epsilon_i + h(X_i,\gamma)$. In Horowitz and Carson (1988), we also estimate δ_m using the specification $g(\delta_i) = \ln(\delta_i)$.[8]

3. Experimental design

To estimate individuals' discount rates for statistical lives, we conducted an experiment using the discrete choice setup described above. Seventy-five undergraduates who were enrolled in an upper-division environmental economics class at the University of California, San Diego took part.

The experiment portrayed scenarios for three types of risk. In each scenario there was a choice between two policies, one that saved a given number of lives starting immediately and an alternative policy that saved a possibly different number of lives but that started later. Only one scenario will be detailed here. The policies described in this scenario were improvements in the design of airplanes or airports that reduced the risk of fatal airplane collisions.[9]

The air travel scenario question is as follows:

> Airplane accidents result in a number of deaths each year, mostly from landings and takeoffs. One option to reduce the number of deaths is to require that a safety feature be placed on the existing fleet of airplanes. This feature will save an expected 20 lives per year over the next 15 years (the life of the safety feature). However, the government could instead require that a new radar system be installed at the airport. Construction of the radar system would take about 5 years and would be financed by the airlines. The radar will save about (L_2) lives per year over the next 10 years (year 5 to year 15).
>
> The costs of these two alternatives are the same. But because these costs are large, the government will not require both actions to be taken and it must make a choice about which one to use. Which action should the government require?
>
> _____ Airlines should be required to install safety equipment immediately.
>
> _____ Airlines should be required to construct the radar system, to be ready in 5 years.

The first policy presented in this question involves the immediate installation of a safety feature on airplanes that is expected to prevent $L_1 = 20$ deaths per year for the next $T = 15$ years, beginning immediately, $j = 0$. The second, "future" policy involves the construction of a radar system that will be completed $j = 5$ years from the present and will last for $T - j = 10$ years. This policy is predicated to prevent L_2 deaths per year, with the value for L_2 randomly assigned to each participant. Between one and seven participants were assigned each value of L_2. L_2 ranged from 29 to 54. Because of the unique relationship between L_2 and δ^*, we can refer to each possible L_2 value by its δ^*. The equilibrating discount rate when $L_2 = 32$, for example, is $\delta^* = 0.036$, or 3.6%. The equilibrating discount rates that we randomly assigned in the air travel scenario ranged from -1% to 20% with a mean of 6.6% and a median of 7.5%.[10]

4. Results

Our data for the airplane safety experiment consist of each respondent's choice ($CHOICE_i\epsilon\{0,1\}$) and the δ^* assigned (through L_2). They also include the total number of participants who were assigned each value of δ^* and the proportion, p, of those that favored each policy.

Values of p are plotted against δ^* in figure 1. Results from the probit estimation are reported in (6) with the asymptotic t-statistics given in parentheses:

$$\Phi(\hat{p}) = -0.458 + 10.082\ \delta^*.$$
$$(-1.71) \quad (2.97) \tag{6}$$

Here $\Phi(\cdot)$ is the inverse of the standard normal cumulative probability function. Predicted probabilities from (6) are graphed in figure 1.

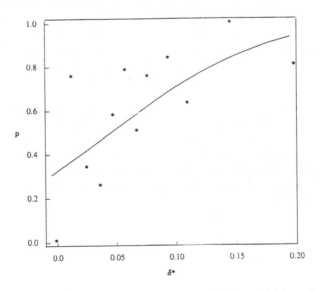

Figure 1. Proportion of individuals choosing the future project as a function of δ^* (air travel scenario). Each point represents the proportion of choices in favor of the future policy of the individuals who were assigned that value of δ^*. The solid line is derived from the relationship estimated in (6): $\Phi(\hat{p}) = -0.458 + 10.982\ \delta^*$.

With δ^* as the independent variable, the estimated median (and by the symmetry of the normal distribution, the estimated mean) discount rate is 4.54% [δ_m = 0.0454(2.91);$\hat{\sigma}_v$ = 0.099(2.46)]. Our null hypothesis was δ_m = 0, which implies that the median individual does not discount future reductions in risk; in other words, future lives are equal in value to present lives. We reject this hypothesis in favor of the alternative that the median discount rate is not equal to zero with t = 2.91. A positive median discount rate, however, does not imply positive individual discount rates for all individuals. Under the assumption that the errors are normally distributed, approximately 32% of the population does implicitly espouse a discount rate of zero or less.

The next hypothesis we test is that the discount rate is equal to the market rate, r. A simple measure of the real rate of return is the difference between the nominal rate of return on 25-year treasury bonds and the rate of inflation in the consumer price index at the time of the experiment. This gives a value for r of 5.16%. Using this value, the t-statistic for the hypothesis δ_m = r is 0.40, and thus we do not reject the hypothesis that the discount rate is equal to the market rate. Although other definitions of the real rate could be used for this test, it is clear that we would not reject the null for a wide range of plausible values for r since the 95% confidence interval for the median (and mean) discount rate in the air travel scenario includes rates from 1.42% to 7.66%.

Looking at the scenarios for the other two types of risks (see Horowitz and Carson, 1988, for details), we uncovered median discount rates of 4.66% for worker safety improvements and 12.8% for traffic safety improvements. These discount rates are significantly greater than zero (t = 2.44 and t = 5.09), and the second is significantly different from the market interest rate when r = 5.16% (t = 3.04). These results suggest that different discount rates may be appropriate for different risks since we can also statistically reject that the traffic risk has the same discount as the other two risks. The different rates could also have arisen because different combinations of L_2, j, and T were used in each scenario if individuals are not exponential discounters. We were not able to test this hypothesis using only our three scenarios. We also have not examined whether our estimates of the discount rates are sensitive to the particular way in which the questions were framed. The estimation of individual discount rates (as opposed to population median rates) from our data can be achieved by parameterizing the $h(X_i, \gamma)$ function in (4). In contrast to estimating the median discount rate, which can be done nonparametrically and without reference to an individual's characteristics, this generally requires one to make the fairly strong functional form and distributional assumptions typical of the labor market studies of risk. Some empirical results are provided in Horowitz and Carson (1988).

5. Conclusions

This article has proposed an approach for examining the question: What discount rate should be used for future reductions in mortality risks? The distribution of individuals' discount rates was estimated. The approach we used is based on a relationship between an individual's discrete choice between two policies that save statistical lives and the discount rate at which the individual would be indifferent between the two policies. This relationship can be used under fairly general assumptions to estimate median discount rates and, under stronger assumptions, to estimate individual discount rates as well.

Our experimental method is versatile and simple and appears to work well. Our sample of students is probably adequate for making the claim that the median discount rate for risks is greater than zero, but it is less likely to be so for making claims about what discount rate policymakers should use in any particular situation. The next step in addressing this question is to apply the method using a large random sample of the national population. Our method allows this to be accomplished at a fairly low cost.

The experimental method proposed is especially useful because it does not require estimating the value of a statistical life. There are at least two situations in which the discount rate is likely to be a more important factor in policy evaluation than the value of statistical life. First, in many cases, the timing dimension is one of the key aspects of regulation over which government agencies have jurisdiction. This situation arises, for instance, when a specific level of risk reduction has been mandated by legislation but the actual mechanisms to be used to meet this target are not specified. What often remains for the regulatory agency to decide is what technological changes should be required (a decision that simultaneously determines how quickly the technologies will be installed, since some technologies require a longer time to be put in operation or to become commercially available) or at what time a given technology should be adopted. Such decisions involve questions of *when* rather than *whether* to undertake a particular risk-reducing project.

The second situation arises when several risks compete for the regulator's attention and those risks have quite different time profiles. The choice is then which risk to reduce first. One good example is in the regulation of drinking water quality. The U.S. Environmental Protection Agency may be forced to choose between mandating reduced risks of contamination from active biological agents, which poses a risk of immediate illness and mortality, and reduced trihalomethane contamination, which pose a risk of future mortality from cancer. The limited financial resources of the municipalities involved generally prevent the adoption of both projects, even when both appear warranted. This tradeoff too can be seen as a tradeoff in the timing of the risks, rather than a tradeoff of risk for money.

Notes

1. To make this example more concrete, consider, for example, a coastal city that has been undertaking primary treatment of its sewage and that is considering constructing a secondary sewage treatment facility. Secondary sewage treatment would reduce the morbidity and mortality risks to swimmers and consumers of seafood. The city could build one particular type of secondary sewage treatment plant that would begin operation almost immediately, or it could build another type of plant that would be more effective in treating sewage and reducing risks but that would require a much longer time to construct. Whether the construction delay is warranted by the greater risk reduction depends in part on the discount rate for mortality risks. This scenario describes in part the situation faced by the city of Los Angeles in the late 1970s with respect to sewage emptied into Santa Monica Bay.

2. Conflict between these two claims was highlighted during the 1987 nomination of Douglas Ginsburg to the U.S. Supreme Court.

3. Changes in the probability of mortality multiplied by the number of individuals affected gives the number of statistical lives saved by a given project. Statistical lives are a common measure of policy effectiveness in reducing risk when small risks are borne by a large group of people rather than large risks by a few specific individuals (Bailey, 1980).

4. Studies using future risks (Mitchell and Carson, 1986) as well as studies that have used actuarial risks, which combine both present and future risks (Thaler and Rosen, 1976), have tended to estimate lower values for a statistical life than studies in which only immediate risks are considered. This relationship suggests that future risks are discounted.

5. This expression can be derived from a life-cycle model of preferences over personal risks. See Horowitz and Carson (1988).

6. When L is constant over time, the discount rate is, for an individual of a given age, one minus the marginal rate of substitution between risk reductions at times t and $t + 1$, i.e., $V(t)/V(t + 1) - 1$. This definition is different from Moore and Viscusi's (1988) discount rate definition, which is based on how the value of a current risk reduction changes with age.

7. This procedure is analogous to the dose–response procedure used in bioassays (Finney, 1978). In our model, δ^* is the stimulus and the choice between the projects is the response.

8. Note that while the assumptions that ϵ is normally distributed and that $g(\cdot)$ is either linear or logarithmic are convenient for estimation, they are not necessary. Assuming $g(\cdot)$ is known, estimates of the median (and the other central quantiles of the distribution of δ_i) will be relatively robust against reasonable alternative distributions for ϵ. On the other hand, if we assume the distribution of the error terms is known, then it is possible to estimate $g(\cdot)$ and $h(\cdot)$ in (4) semi-parametrically using, for instance, smoothing splines or generalized additive models (Hastie and Tibshirani, 1986). If one wants to avoid making assumptions about the functional forms of $g(\cdot)$ and $h(\cdot)$ and the distribution of ϵ, then a completely nonparametric approach such as the ACE algorithm proposed by Breiman and Friedman (1985) can be used to estimate the entire cumulative conditional or unconditional distribution function for δ_i.

9. The air travel risk scenario was loosely modeled after a well-known midair collision over San Diego between a Pacific Southwest Airlines plane and a small private plane. The other two scenarios described traffic and worker safety policies. The traffic risk scenario involved the choice between putting up a traffic signal or completely remodeling the traffic intersection. This scenario was loosely modeled after a controversy over a major intersection near campus which had taken place several years earlier. The worker safety scenario involved vapors from toxic spills and involved the choice between installing technology that was currently available or waiting for a much improved technology that would be available at a later date. This scenario was intended to reflect the type of choice which often faces EPA and OSHA in this area.

10. A negative equilibrating discount rate can be assigned by making $L_1(T) > L_2(T - j)$.

References

Arthur, W. B. (1981). "The Economics of Risks to Life," *American Economic Review* 71, 54–64.

Bailey, Martin J. (1980). *Reducing Risks to Life: Measurement of the Benefits*. Washington, DC: American Enterprise Institute.

Breiman, Leo and Jerome Friedman. (1985). "Estimating Optimal Transformations for Multiple Regression and Correlation," *Journal of the American Statistical Association* 80, 580–598.

Cameron, Trudy A. and Michelle D. James. (1987). "An Efficient Method for Closed-Ended Contingent Valuation Surveys," *Review of Economics and Statistics* 64, 269–276.

Ehrlich, Isaac and Hiroyuki Chuma. (1987). "The Demand for Life: Theory and Applications." In G. Radnitzky and P. Bernholz (eds.), *Economic Imperialism*. New York: Paragon House.

Finney, David. (1978). *Statistical Methods in Biological Assay*, 3rd edition. New York: McMillan.

Fisher, Ann, Lauraine Chestnut, and Daniel Violette. (1989). "The Value of Reducing Risks of Death: A Note on New Evidence," *Journal of Policy Analysis and Management* 8, 80–100.

Fuchs, Victor. (1982). "Time Preference and Health: An Exploratory Study." In Victor Fuchs (ed.), *Economic Aspects of Health*. Chicago: University of Chicago Press.

Hastie, Trevor and Robert Tibshirani. (1986). "Generalized Additive Models," *Statistical Science* I, 297–309.

Hausman, Jerry A. (1979). "Individual Discount Rates and the Purchase and Utilization of Energy-Using Durables," *The Bell Journal of Economics* 10, 33–54.

Horowitz, John and Richard T. Carson. (1988). "Discounting Statistical Lives," Discussion Paper 88-16, Department of Economics, University of California, San Diego.

Horowitz, John. (1989). "An Economic Theory of Latency," Working Paper 89-29, University of Maryland.

Jones-Lee, M. W. (1976). *The Value of Life*. Chicago: University of Chicago Press.

Jones-Lee, M. W., M. Hammerton, and P. Phillips. (1985). "The Value of Safety: Results of a National Sample Survey," *The Economic Journal* 95, 49–73.

Mishan, Ezra J. (1971). "Evaluation of Life and Limb: A Theoretical Approach," *Journal of Political Economy* 79, 687–705.

Mitchell, Robert Cameron and Richard T. Carson. (1986). "Valuing Drinking Water Risk Reductions Using the Contingent Valuation Method: A Methodological Study of Risks from THMs and *Giardia*." Report to the U.S. Environmental Protection Agency.

Moore, Michael J. and W. Kip Viscusi. (1988). "The Quantity-Adjusted Value of Life," *Economic Inquiry* 26, 369–388.

Rosen, Sherwin. (1988). "The Value of Changes in Life Expectancy," *Journal of Risk and Uncertainty* 1, 285–304.

Schelling, Thomas C. (1968). "The Life You Save May Be Your Own." In Samuel B. Chase (ed.), *Problems in Public Expenditure Analysis*. Washington, DC: Brookings Institution.

Smith, V. Kerry and William H. Desvousges. (1987). "An Empirical Analysis of the Economic Value of Risk Changes," *Journal of Political Economy* 95, 89–118.

Slovic, P., B. Fischhoff, and S. Lichtenstein. (1985). "Characterizing Perceived Risk." In C. Hohenemser, R.W. Kates, and J. Kasperson (eds.), *Perilous Progress: Managing the Hazards of Technology*. London: Westview Press.

Thaler, Richard and Sherwin Rosen. (1976). "The Value of Saving a Life: Evidence from the Labor Market." In N. Terleckyj (ed.), *Household Production and Consumption*. New York: Columbia University Press.

Viscusi, W. Kip and Michael J. Moore. (1989). "Rates of Time Preference and Valuations of the Duration of Life," *Journal of Public Economics* 38, 297–317.

Name Index